Register of William Degroot's FAMILY

WILLIAM DEGROOT WAS BORN June 7th 1751.

ANN LATOURRETTE WAS BORN Jan 26th 1751.

They Join'd and in holy Matrimony December 30th 1780.

THEIR PROGENEY

NAMES	Births	Marriages	Deaths
ALTIE O. Degroot	October 15th 1782		March 26th 1803
HENRY L. Degroot	February 8th 1784		April 28th 1787
SUSAN P. Degroot	February 8th 1784		
SARAH L. Degroot	November 5th 1785	April 25th 1804	June 27 1830
WILLm O. Degroot	October 25th 1787		
HENRY Degroot	May 25th 1789		Feb: 21st 1835
ANN Degroot	August 7th 1791	August 13th 1835	
ELIZh Degroot	March 12th 1793	November 15th 1814	
IOHN Degroot	March 27th 1797		

Guide to GENEALOGICAL RESEARCH IN THE NATIONAL ARCHIVES

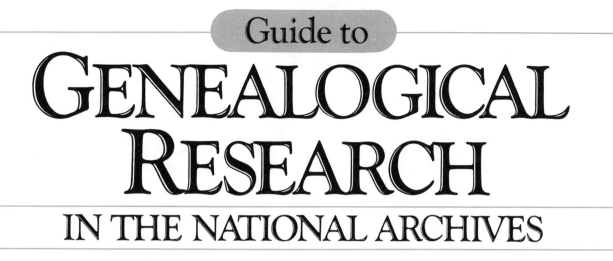

Guide to GENEALOGICAL RESEARCH IN THE NATIONAL ARCHIVES

NATIONAL ARCHIVES AND RECORDS SERVICE
WASHINGTON, D.C.
1982

PUBLISHED FOR
THE NATIONAL ARCHIVES AND RECORDS SERVICE
BY THE
NATIONAL ARCHIVES TRUST FUND BOARD

Frontispiece: The family register of William and Ann Latourrette Degroot. Artist Unknown. About 1804. From the file of William Degroot, New Jersey, W-417, Revolutionary War Pension Records, Record Group 15.

Library of Congress Cataloging in Publication Data

United States. National Archives and Records Service.
Guide to genealogical research in the National Archives.

Includes bibliographies and index.
1. United States—Genealogy—Bibliography—Catalogs. 2. Registers of births, etc.—United States—Bibliography—Catalogs. 3. United States. National Archives and Records Service—Catalogs. I. Title.
Z5313.U5U54 1983 [CS68] 016.929'1'072073 82-21040

Hardcover ISBN 0-911333-00-2
Paperback ISBN 0-911333-01-0

Table of Contents

List of Illustrations

List of Tables

Preface

The National Archives of the United States document American history from the time of the First Continental Congress and hold the permanently valuable records of the three branches of the federal government. The archives are preserved and made available because of their continuing practical use in the necessary processes of government, for the protection of public and private rights, and for the uses that can be made of the information contained in them by scholars, students, and the general public.

The records amount to more than 1 million cubic feet. They are in the custody of the National Archives and Records Service and are housed in the National Archives building in Washington, D.C., in the archives branches in the Washington National Records Center in Suitland, Md., and in eleven regional archives branches located in Federal Archives and Records Centers around the country. They are described in the comprehensive *Guide to the National Archives of the United States* (Washington: National Archives and Records Service, 1974). In each of the National Archives repositories, additional finding aids are available. These include inventories, preliminary inventories, special lists, indexes, and supplemental guides on specific subjects.

The present work supersedes the 1964 *Guide to Genealogical Records in the National Archives*, compiled by Meredith B. Colket, Jr. and Frank E. Bridgers. A complete revision and enlargement, the new guide includes records not described in the earlier edition, particularly records of genealogical value in the regional archives branches. It also contains illustrations and photographs, citations to microfilm publications, and expanded and clarified descriptions of the records.

Many archivists contributed to the work of this revised guide, evaluating and verifying descriptions of records and compiling new information. Special thanks are due to Bruce Ashkenas, Joel Baker, Joel Buckwald, Peter Bunce, Kent Carter, Kenneth Hall, Robert M. Kvasnicka, Phillip E. Lothyan, Robert Matchette, Henry Mayer, James K. Owens, James Paulaskas, Gayle Peters, Geraldine Phillips, Robert Plowman, Dorothy Provine, Kenneth F. Rossman, Ronald Swerczek, Ferris Stovel, Thomas Trudeau, Howard Wehmann, R. Reed Whitaker, and Jo Ann Williamson.

Incidental help was graciously given by George Chalou, Mary Jane Dowd, Janet L. Hargett, Michael P. Musick, and Richard Smith.

Major contributions of time, talent, and good will were made by Jan S. Danis, Robert H. Gruber, James Harwood, Edward E. Hill, Bill R. Linder, Maida Loescher, Teresa Matchette, Gary L. Morgan, Susan P. Viola, and James D. Walker.

The cooperative work of these people makes the present guide an important resource that explains the research potential of genealogical materials in the National Archives of the United States and assists family historians in their use.

Robert M. Warner
Archivist of the United States

Introduction

I.1 Value and Limitations of Federal Records

Today, more and more Americans are discovering the rewards of genealogy—the study of the history of families and the documentation of lines of ancestry and descent. The National Archives and Records Service (NARS), the keeper of the historically valuable records of the federal government, can aid genealogical research in many ways.

Some of the records in NARS help to establish lines of ancestry. In the records, the relationships between generations of a family are often given or implied. Genealogists often use census records and pension applications for this purpose. Other federal records give information about individuals—physical descriptions in some cases, places of birth and residence, and activities and occupations—and thereby expand the researcher's picture of the life of an ancestor. The records that document military service, immigration, and the settlement of public domain lands are perhaps those most widely used to trace ancestry, but many other groups of records are full of information useful to genealogists. In fact, every record contains, even if indirectly, some information about some person.

Three important limitations, however, face genealogists doing research in these archives. First, NARS keeps only federal records. Birth, marriage, and death—the milestones of life and the backbone of genealogy—have never been the first concern of the federal government, and the best evidence of these events will be found, if it exists, in family, local, and state records.

Second, the colonial period of American history is not documented in the National Archives; very few records predate the Revolutionary War. Most of the records described in this guide pertain to the nineteenth century, a time when government did not touch the lives of most Americans to the extent that it does today. Wartime was one big exception, of course, and consequently, military records are useful to many genealogists.

The third limitation arises from the nature of archives: records are arranged to reflect their original purposes, usually just as they were kept by the agency that created them. They cannot be arranged in ways that might seem most helpful to genealogists, partly because family history is only one of many present-day uses of archives. Names are not listed alphabetically in census records, for example; the records are arranged geographically because the primary reason for taking the census was to determine a state's representation in the U.S. House of Representatives.

Because of these limitations, a researcher should never ask an archivist for information about an ancestor about whom only the name is known. The researcher should come to the archives with information about when and how and, if possible, where an ancestor came into contact with the federal government; sometimes the exact date and place and circumstances of contact are necessary.

Indeed, the more detailed searchers' knowledge of American history and geography, the more effective will be their use of the National Archives. A general understanding of patterns of immigration, migration, and settlement and of law, government, and economics, and specific information or ideas of how the lives of ancestors fit into these patterns are helpful, especially to avoid being overwhelmed by the sheer volume of documentation about the past. If this sounds discouraging, it should be noted that a broader knowledge of American history is a natural consequence of doing genealogy well—and one of its chief rewards.

This introduction contains only a few suggestions about getting started in genealogical research, followed by remarks about the organization of records in general, finding aids, microfilm, and research facilities and special programs at the National Archives Building and the Federal Archives and Records Centers (FARCs). The chapters contain specific information about particular groups of records—why they were created, how they are arranged, how they can be used, and what one can expect to find. Additional facts about the availability of microfilm, finding aids, and help with research are included where applicable. The descriptions of records are grouped in chapters according to broad subject areas. Each genealogist will find some chapters to be more interesting and pertinent to his or her research than others, and the order of the chapters is not significant.

I.2 Research Methods and Aids

Every researcher should start with himself or herself, the first twig on the family tree, and work backwards toward the unknown, finding all the vital information available about parents, grandparents, and great-grandparents. The place to begin is at home, with family Bibles, newspaper clippings, military certificates, birth and death certificates, marriage licenses, diaries, letters, scrapbooks, labels on the backs of pictures, baby books, and so forth. From these many and varied documents, four key items can be obtained: names, dates, places, and relationships. These are tools of the family historian. People can be identified in records by their names, the dates of events in their lives (birth, marriage, death), the places they lived, and their relationships to others.

Older relatives may have information. More often than not, data on a particular family may have already been gathered; even distant relatives may have performed research. Advertisement in local genealogical bulletins of a city, county, or state where ancestors lived may result in valuable contacts. The most widely circulated genealogical magazine (which also specializes in getting together people who are working on the same families) is the *Genealogical Helper*, Everton Publishers, Inc., P.O. Box 368, Logan, UT 84321.

Some states began to keep records of birth and death earlier than others, but in most of the United States, birth and death registration became a governmental requirement beginning between 1890 and 1915. Before that time, evidence of births and deaths were usually maintained in county records, some dated as early as the establishment of the county. Some churches have records of important events in the lives of members. Researchers should investigate the possibility of finding genealogical data in the records of the churches to which their ancestors belonged. Records of property acquisition and disposition are often good sources of genealogical information. Deeds, wills, and other such records are normally found in county courthouses. Often the earliest county records, or copies of them, are also available in state archives.

Before turning to the National Archives, researchers should investigate their regional and local institutions thoroughly. Libraries, historical and genealogical societies, and state and local archival depositories are all good sources for genealogical and family history data. The staffs of such institutions are often experienced in assisting genealogical researchers, and local collections of secondary works relating to genealogy are often extensive. The works listed in table 1 may be helpful.

TABLE 1

Selected Genealogical Research Aids: General Reference

Doane, Gilbert H. *Searching for Your Ancestors*. 4th ed. Minneapolis: University of Minnesota, 1973.

Genealogical Research: Methods and Sources. Volume 1 edited by Milton Rubincam. Washington: American Society of Genealogists, 1960. Volume 2 edited by Kenn Stryker-Rodda. Washington, 1971.

Greenwood, Val D. *The Researcher's Guide to American Genealogy*. Baltimore: Genealogical Publishing Co., 1973.

Linder, Bill R. *How to Trace Your Family History: A Basic Guide to Genealogy*. New York: Everest House, 1980.

I.3 Records at the National Archives

The records of genealogical value described in this guide were created to satisfy legal requirements or to meet the administrative or other needs of the originating federal agencies. Every document in the National Archives has been assigned to a numbered **record group** on the basis of its origin. A record group commonly consists of the records of a bureau (e.g., Records of the U.S. Customs Service, Record Group 36), but some record groups may include the records of an entire agency, and a few include records collected from several sources. Record groups are sometimes very large, measured in cubic feet. There are more than 450 record groups for the 1,369,000 cubic feet of records in the National Archives. The holdings of the archives include billions of pages; millions of photographs, motion pictures, aerial photographs, maps, and charts; thousands of sound recordings, video recordings, architectural and engineering drawings; and more than 1,000 machine-readable tapes.

In this guide, the unit of description is usually the **series** a smaller body of records filed together because they relate to the same subject, function, or activity, or because of some other relationship arising from their origin and use. Within most series, records are kept in the order that best served the needs of the creating agency. The arrangement of records in a series sometimes makes finding specific facts difficult and determines what previous information a researcher must have to frame a research question that can be answered. For example, if a series is not arranged alphabetically and there are no indexes, the researcher will need identifying information in addition to the name of a person to search the series adequately for other information about that person. The nature of the additional information varies from series to series; it will be discussed in this guide along with the description of the records.

Many of the records that the genealogist will be seeking are in the general correspondence series of various agencies, so a few minutes taken to learn the arrangement of a nineteenth century government office file will stand the searcher in good stead. Throughout most of the nineteenth century, government agencies usually filed correspondence in two series: "letters sent," for outgoing communications, and "letters received," for incoming communications. Often the letters were folded in thirds, and an endorsement was written across one of the three sections. The endorsement usually consisted of the date of the letter, name of correspondent, subject, and sometimes a list of enclosures and the action taken. The letters were then filed so that the endorsements could be examined without taking the letters out of the file. In other cases, letters received or copies of letters sent may have been bound into a volume that might or might not have an index. It was also customary to make an entry for each letter sent or received in a **register**. Letters could be assigned an identifying symbol, perhaps an alphanumerical expression consisting of the first letter of the surname of the correspondent and a number assigned serially in order of dispatch or receipt. If the letters were filed chronologically, the entry in the register might be made in alphabetical sections according to the symbol assigned. Registers contain varying information, consisting of some or all of the following: name of correspondent, date of communication, abstracts of contents and reply or other note of action taken, and possibly a cross reference to other letters on the same subject or to the symbol of the reply or incoming letter in the corresponding series. Registers therefore serve as finding aids to the correspondence series.

I.4 NARS Finding Aids

The National Archives and Records Service publishes several different kinds of finding aids to assist researchers in using its vast holdings. Some record groups are described in inventories or preliminary inventories (PI). Such finding aids contain a history of the organization and functions of the agency that created the records and descriptions of the series in the record group. Inventories are cited in this guide if one has been prepared for the record group being discussed. A typical citation is, Carmen R. Delle Donne, comp., *Preliminary Inventory of the Records of the Children's Bureau*, PI 102 (1976). This guide describes series most valuable for genealogy, but researchers may wish to consult inventories of other record groups to find documents related to their research.

Other types of finding aids include guides, reference

information papers, and special lists relating to particular subjects. Such finding aids may cover many record groups—as guides do—or focus on a specific type of document within one record group—as some special lists do. The finding aids especially valuable for genealogical research are cited in this guide at appropriate points in the text.

All finding aids are listed in General Information Leaflet 3, *Select List of Publications of the National Archives and Records Service* (Washington: National Archives and Records Service, 1982). Except for guides, all NARS finding aids in print are available free of charge from the Publications Sales Branch (NEPS), General Services Administration, Washington, DC 20408. Finding aids published before 1968 have been microfilmed as National Archives Microfilm Publication M248, 24 rolls.

I.5 NARS Microfilm Publications

Many series of records that have high research value have been microfilmed by the National Archives and Records Service. Generally, if a series has been filmed, the film is used for research rather than the original. This extensive microfilm program, underway since the 1940s, has resulted in two notable achievements: preservation and enhanced access. Priceless, fragile, and awkwardly bound documents can be removed from reference circulation where they would have been exposed to damage and deterioration from ordinary use. Also, microfilm makes valuable records available to researchers in many parts of the country. All National Archives microfilm publications are available for use in the National Archives building. Many of the important microfilm publications—including microfilm of federal census schedules, 1790–1910—are available in the archives branches at Federal Archives and Records Centers in 11 metropolitan regions. The addresses of the branches are listed in table 2.

In addition, many state and local archives, historical and genealogical societies, libraries, and research institutions have purchased copies of National Archives microfilm and make it available to their patrons. Individuals can buy rolls to use on a microfilm reading machine at home or with permission at a local library. Because microfilmed records are widely distributed, researchers should explore their own community resources completely before planning research trips to Washington, D.C.

Series that have been microfilmed are cited in this guide by title and number. A typical citation is, *Index to Compiled Service Records of Volunteer Soldiers Who Served From 1784 to 1811*, M694, 9 rolls. Many microfilm publications numbers begin with "M." Most of these are accompanied by descriptive pamphlets that contain thorough explanations of the origin, content, and arrangement of the records. Other microfilm numbers begin with "T." These publications do not include explanatory introductions or notes. Both "M" and "T" publications are available for use in the Microfilm Research Room in the National Archives building.

In the *Catalog of National Archives Microfilm Publications* (Washington: National Archives and Records Service, 1974), the title, "M" or "T" number, and the number of rolls for each publication are listed by record group according to the hierarchical organization of the government. The catalog is indexed. The latest edition includes a supplement that lists titles of microfilm publications 1974–1982. Also available are *Federal Population Censuses, 1790–1890* (Washington: National Archives and Records Service, 1977), *1900 Federal Population Census: A Catalog of Microfilm Copies of the Schedules* (Washington: National Archives Trust Fund Board, 1978); and *1910 Federal Population Census: A Catalog of Microfilm Copies of the Schedules* (Washington: National Archives Trust Fund Board, 1982). They can be obtained by writing to the Publication Sales Branch (NEPS), General Services Administration, Washington, DC 20408.

I.6 Government Publications

Many federal records have been published as government documents which are available in many libraries all over the United States. Series of records are discussed in this guide, and information is provided about where the researcher can find a printed copy of the records or an index to the records. The researcher should use these printed materials as much as possible; the expense of a trip to Washington or to one of the regional archives branches can be saved if the same information is available in printed from in a nearby library. In some cases, the citation of a published document in this guide will be followed by a "SuDocs No." (Superintendent of Documents Number), such as "Z4.14/1: HD4", or a serial number, such as "Ser. 4535." These are numbers assigned by the Government Printing Office to documents printed for an agency, or in the case of the serial, for one of the houses of Congress. These numbers are helpful to librarians who are asked to locate one of these publications for a researcher.

I.7 Research Facilities at the National Archives

The research entrance to the National Archives building is at Pennsylvania Avenue and Eighth Street, N.W. The officer at the desk in the lobby will direct researchers to the orientation area, where they will be asked to complete a brief application, including name, address, the purpose of research, and other information that will enable the staff to provide quick and effective service. The orientation staff will issue identification cards that are valid for two years and are renewable. The staff will also discuss the regulations governing the use of public records and rules established for the protection of the documents. A reference consultant will, if necessary, arrange interviews with other archivists, and order records from the stacks.

Microfilm copies of census records, indexes to military service records and pension applications, and all other microfilm publications of the National Archives are located in the Microfilm Research Room and the adjacent stack area. Researchers must sign the register near the door each day and may consult the many finding aids provided in the room. The research room attendants will help locate appropriate microfilm rolls and give instructions in operating the reading machines if necessary. Rolls should be returned to the staff or placed on the cabinet tops; researchers should not refile the rolls.

TABLE 2

National Archives and Records Service Regional Archives Branches

Addresses

Boston
380 Trapelo Road
Waltham, MA 02154

Serves Connecticut, Maine, Massachusetts, New Hampshire, Rhode Island, and Vermont.

New York
Building 22—MOT Bayonne
Bayonne, NJ 07002

Serves New Jersey, New York, Puerto Rico, and the Virgin Islands.

Philadelphia
5000 Wissahickon Avenue
Philadelphia, PA 19144

Serves Delaware, Pennsylvania, Maryland, Virginia, and West Virginia.

Atlanta
1557 St. Joseph Avenue
East Point, GA 30344

Serves Alabama, Georgia, Florida, Kentucky, Mississippi, North Carolina, South Carolina, and Tennessee.

Chicago
7358 South Pulaski Road
Chicago, IL 60629

Serves Illinois, Indiana, Michigan, Minnesota, Ohio, and Wisconsin.

Kansas City
2306 East Bannister Road
Kansas City, MO 64131

Serves Iowa, Kansas, Missouri, and Nebraska.

Records that have not been microfilmed can be used in the Central Research Room. The consultants, archivists, or attendants at the main desk will assist in the ordering of records. Typewriters are available here; cameras without flash attachments and tape recorders may also be used if they do not disturb other researchers. The research room attendants have information about the procedures for using such equipment.

Photocopies of most records can be obtained, and paper copies can be made from microfilm. The costs are moderate, but there are limits on the number of documents that can be copied for immediate use. Large orders must be arranged through a research consultant or an archivist.

Current information about the hours of service is in General Information Leaflet 25, *A Researcher's Guide to the National Archives* (Washington: National Archives and Records Service, 1977.

I.8 Research at Regional Archives Branches

Eleven of the Federal Archives and Records Centers include archives branches. As a rule, each regional archives branch accessions records created by field offices of federal agencies in that area. Many field activities of the federal government are performed in all regions, so many of the records accessioned by the branches are similar. Some records, however, are unique to a single branch, and archival holdings do vary from region to region. Records in the archives branches valuable for genealogy are discussed by subject in this guide.

In addition to making original records available for research, the archives branches have acquired, and will continue to receive over a period of years, copies of many National Archives microfilm publications. Included are records of U.S. diplomatic missions, large bodies of material relating to the Revolutionary and Civil Wars, German records captured at the end of World War II, territorial papers, and census returns. *Prologue: Journal of the National Archives* periodically lists the microfilm publications deposited in the branches. Addresses of the archives branches are listed in table 2. Direct inquiries to the Chief, Archives Branch, Federal Archives and Records Center. For more general information about the regional branches of the National Archives, order General Information Leaflet 22, *Regional Branches of the National Archives* (free) from the Publications Sales Branch (NEPS), General Services Administration, Washington, DC 20408.

Records of field offices of U.S. government agencies in the District of Columbia are in the Civil Archives Division at the Washington National Records Center, Suitland, Md.

I.9 Genealogical Services at the National Archives

The National Archives makes records freely available to researchers at all of its facilities, but does not perform research for patrons. The National Archives does not trace family lineage or attempt genealogical conclusions, nor does it maintain files or publications about specific families. The

Fort Worth
4900 Hemphill Street (building address)
P.O. Box 6216 (mailing address)
Fort Worth, TX 76115

Serves Arkansas, Louisiana, New Mexico, Oklahoma, and Texas.

Denver
Building 48, Denver Federal Center
Denver, CO 80225

Serves Colorado, Montana, North Dakota, South Dakota, Utah, and Wyoming.

Los Angeles
24000 Avila Road
Laguna Niguel, CA 92677

Serves Arizona; the southern California counties of Imperial, Inyo, Kern, Los Angeles, Orange, Riverside, San Bernadino, San Diego, San Luis Obispo, Santa Barbara, and Ventura; and Clark County, Nevada.

San Francisco
1000 Commodore Drive
San Bruno, CA 94066

Serves Hawaii, Nevada (except Clark County), California (except the counties served by the Los Angeles Branch), and American Samoa.

Seattle
6125 Sand Point Way NE.
Seattle, WA 98115

Serves Alaska, Idaho, Oregon, and Washington.

I.8 Research at Regional Archives Branches

I.9 Genealogical Services at the National Archives

National Archives does not maintain a list of persons who do genealogical research for a fee, but researchers may obtain the names of professional genealogists from the Board for Certification of Genealogists, P.O. Box 19165, Washington, DC 20036. Genealogists also advertise their services in the *Genealogical Helper*.

At one time the National Archives made minimal searches in the census schedules in response to mail requests. This research service has been discontinued, however, because copies of the census records are now available at the regional archives branches and at other institutions.

Special service by mail is, however, still available. When exact identifying information is given, the National Archives can furnish photocopies of records for a fee. Copies of compiled service records, bounty land warrant application files, pension application files, passenger arrival records, and census pages are examples of the records that may be photocopied as the result of exact identifying information in a mail request. Details about the exact information required, and whether special order forms can be used, will be found in the guide in the chapters relating to particular kinds of records.

CHAPTER

I

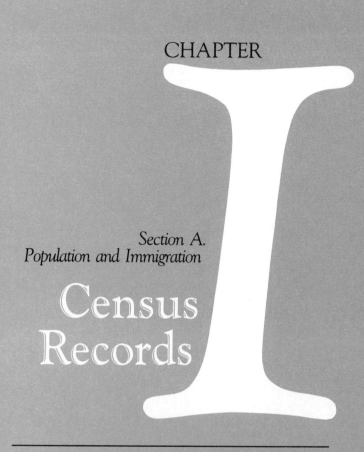

Section A.
Population and Immigration

Census Records

1.1 The Federal Schedules

1.1.1 Population Schedules

A census has been taken in the United States every ten years, beginning in 1790, for the purpose of enumerating the population for apportioning representatives to the lower house of Congress. Information about households and individuals was collected by house-to-house canvass and entered on large sheets. These filled-in forms constitute the **population schedules** for each decennial census. The records of these enumerations in the custody of the National Archives include the original 1790–1870 schedules, a microfilm copy of the 1880 schedules, the surviving fragments of the 1890 schedules, and microfilm copies of the 1900 and 1910 schedules. To protect the privacy of the American people whose names appear in each schedule, population schedules are restricted for 72 years after the census is taken, and are not available to researchers during that time. Accordingly, the release date for the 1910 census schedules was 1982; for 1920 it is 1992; and so on.

TABLE 3

Checklist of National Archives Publications Relating to Census Records

Federal Population Censuses, 1790–1890: A Catalog of Microfilm Copies of the Schedules (1977).

1900 Federal Population Census: A Catalog of Microfilm Copies of the Schedules (1978).

1910 Federal Population Census: A Catalog of Microfilm Copies of the Schedules (1982).

Population Schedules, 1800–1870: Volume Index to Counties and Major Cities. Special List 8 (1951).

Federal Population and Mortality Census Schedules, 1790–1910, in the National Archives and the States: Outline of a Lecture on Their Availability, Content and Use. Special List 24 (1982).

Newman, Debra L., comp. *List of Free Black Heads of Families in the First Federal Census, 1790.* Special List 34 (rev. 1974).

Delle Donne, Carmen R., *Federal Census Schedules, 1850–80: Primary Sources for Historical Research.* Reference Information Paper 67 (1973).

Fishbein, Meyer H., *The Censuses of Manufactures, 1810–1890.* Reference Information Paper 50 (1973).

Davidson, Katherine H., and Ashby, Charlotte M., comps. *Records of the Bureau of the Census.* Preliminary Inventory 161 (1964).

Rhoads, James B., and Ashby, Charlotte M., comps. *Cartographic Records of the Bureau of the Census.* Preliminary Inventory 103 (1958).

The census records for many states are incomplete. Table 6 on page 38 shows by census year the states for which there are schedules. Before 1830, often only the numbers of persons were forwarded to Washington. Because different information was recorded about the American population in every census year, the nature and contents of the schedules for each decennial census are discussed below in chronological order by census year, and shown briefly in table 5 on page 32. The last part of this chapter is devoted to a section featuring the states in alphabetical order with information about special federal and territorial censuses or state censuses for each.

The schedules are part of the Records of the Bureau of the Census, Record Group 29, which is described in *Records of the Bureau of the Census*, Preliminary Inventory 16, compiled by Katherine H. Davidson and Charlotte M. Ashby (Washington: National Archives and Records Service, 1964). Other NARS publications may be even more helpful for research in census records; all are mentioned at appropriate points in this chapter and listed in table 3.

1.1.2 Nonpopulation Census Schedules: Mortality Schedules

The first two federal decennial censuses, 1790 and 1800, were population counts. Beginning with the 1810 census, enumerators gathered additional information, such as statistics of manufacturing, industry, and agriculture, and other social and economic data. In some years, records of persons who had died during the previous year, **mortality schedules**, were also collected. These various schedules are called **nonpopulation schedules**. The particular information gathered during each census is noted in the section of this chapter that deals with censuses by year on pages 33–39.

Except for the mortality schedules, few of the nonpopulation schedules contain names of individuals. The mortality schedules, however, can be useful if the subject of research died within one year preceding 1 June of 1850, 1860, 1870, or 1880, because an entry often records the cause of death.

The original schedules of the mortality censuses were distributed to non-federal repositories in 1918 and 1919, long before the establishment of the National Archives. Whenever possible, the National Archives acquires microfilm or published copies of these schedules. Those that are available on National Archives microfilm are listed by state in table 4 on page 26. Schedules in the holdings of other repositories are noted by state in the latter part of this chapter. Further information about their availability appears in "The Mortality Schedules," *National Genealogical Quarterly* 31 (June 1943): 45–49; in *Federal Population and Mortality Census Schedules, 1700–1910*; and in *Federal Census Schedules, 1850–80*. See table 3 for full information. A shelf list of schedules is also maintained in the Microfilm Research Room in the National Archives building.

1.1.3 Other Information

Location of Federal Schedules

The National Archives and its regional archives branches are not the only depositories of population census schedules. The law often required the prepartion of more than one set of schedules. The duplicate sets for the 1800, 1810,

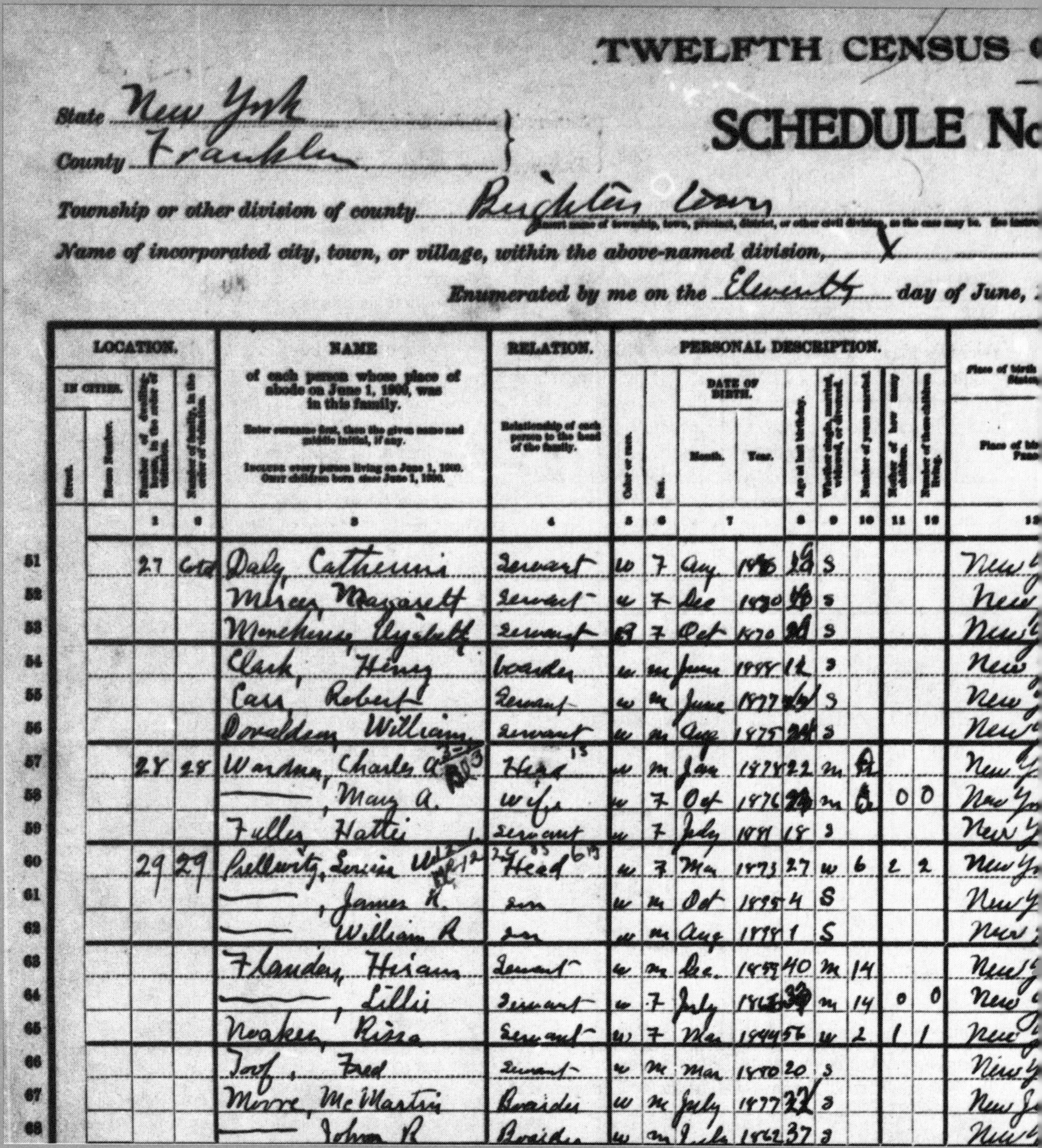
TWELFTH CENSUS

SCHEDULE No

State New York

County Franklin

Township or other division of county Brighton town

Name of incorporated city, town, or village, within the above-named division, X

Enumerated by me on the Eleventh day of June,

Line	House number	Dwelling	Family	Name	Relation	Color	Sex	Month	Year	Age	Marital	Yrs married	Mother of	Living	Place of birth
51		27		Daly, Catherine	Servant	W	F	Aug			S				New
52				Mc ..., Margaret	Servant	W	F	Dec	1880		S				New
53				..., ...	Servant		F	Oct	1870		S				New
54				Clark, Henry	Boarder	W	M	June	1888	12	S				New
55				Carr, Robert	Servant	W	M	June	1877		S				New
56				..., William	Servant	W	M	Aug	1875		S				New
57		28	28	..., Charles A.	Head	W	M	Jan	1878	22	M				New
58				———, Mary A.	Wife	W	F	Oct	1876		M		0	0	New
59				Fuller, Hattie	Servant	W	F	July	1881	18	S				New
60		29	29	..., Louise W.	Head	W	F	Mar	1873	27	W	6	2	2	New
61				———, James R.	Son	W	M	Oct	1895	4	S				New
62				———, William R.	Son	W	M	Aug	1898	1	S				New
63				Flanders, Hiram	Servant	W	M	Dec.	1859	40	M	14			New
64				———, Lillie	Servant	W	F	July			M	14	0	0	New
65				Noakes, Rissa	Servant	W	F	Mar	1844	56	W	2	1	1	New
66				..., Fred	Servant	W	M	Mar	1880	20	S				New
67				Moore, McMartin	Boarder	W	M	July	1877		S				New
68				———, John R.	Boarder	W	M		1862	37	S				New

Upper part of a page from the 1900 Census Population Schedules. Records of the Bureau of the Census, Record Group 29. National Archives Microfilm Publication T623.

THE UNITED STATES. B

—POPULATION.

Supervisor's District No. 5
Enumeration District No. 65
Sheet No. 2

Name of Institution, x

Ward of city, x

Arthur C Davis, *Enumerator.*

61

NATIVITY.		CITIZENSHIP.			OCCUPATION, TRADE, OR PROFESSION of each person TEN YEARS of age and over.		EDUCATION.				OWNERSHIP OF HOME.				
…and parents of each person enumerated. If born in the United …Territory; if of foreign birth, give the Country only.															
Place of birth of Father of this person.	Place of birth of Mother of this person.	Year of immigration to the United States.	Number of years in the United States.	Naturalization.	Occupation.	Months not employed.	Attended school (in months).	Can read.	Can write.	Can speak English.	Owned or rented.	Owned free or mortgaged.	Farm or house.	Number of farm schedule.	
14	15	16	17	18	19	20	21	22	23	24	25	26	27	28	
Ireland	Ireland				Kitchen Girl	4		yes	yes	yes					51
Ireland	Ireland				Table waiter	4		yes	yes	yes					52
New York	New York				Laundress			yes	yes	yes					53
New York	New York				At School		10	yes	yes	yes					54
New York	New York				Farm Laborer			yes	yes	yes					55
New York	New York				Farm Laborer			yes	yes	yes					56
New York	New York				Boarding House Keeper			yes	yes	yes	O	M	H	-	57
New York	New York							yes	yes	yes					58
Vermont	Vermont				Domestic			yes	yes	yes					59
New York	New York				Boarding House Keeper			yes	yes	yes	O	M	F	21	60
New York	New York														61
New York	New York														62
New York	New York				Farm Laborer	4		yes	yes	yes					63
New York	New York				Chambermaid	.		yes	yes	yes					64
Vermont	New York				Nurse			yes	yes	yes					65
New York	New York				Chore boy	6		yes	yes	yes					66
Vermont	Virginia	Home in Elizabeth N.J. Has been here one year						yes	yes	yes					67
New York	New York	Home at [illegible] mechanic [illegible] Has been here since July 1898.						yes	yes	yes					68

TABLE 4

Mortality Census Schedule Microfilm

Arizona

T655

1870	Mohave County—Yuma County	Roll 1
1880	Apache County—Yuma County	Roll 2

Colorado

T655

1870	Arapahoe County—Weld County	Roll 3
1880	Arapahoe County—Weld County	Roll 4

District of Columbia

T655

1850	Indexes and Schedules	Roll 5
1860	Indexes and Schedules	Roll 5
1870	Indexes and Schedules	Roll 5
1880	Indexes and Schedules	Roll 6

Georgia

T655

1850	Appling County—Wilkinson County	Roll 7
1860	Appling County—Worth County	Roll 8
1870	Appling County—Worth County (Rolls 7–9 include both Indexes and Schedules)	Roll 9
1880	Appling County—Franklin County	Roll 10
1880	Fulton County—Pulaski County	Roll 11
1880	Putnam County—Worth County (Rolls 10–12 contain Schedules only)	Roll 12

Illinois

T1133

1850	Adams County—Woodford County	Roll 58
1860	Adams County—Kendall County	Roll 58
1860	Knox County—Woodford County	Roll 59
1870	Adams County—Ogle County	Roll 59
1870	Ogle County—Woodford County	Roll 60
1880	Adams County—Clinton County	Roll 60
1880	Coles County—Cook County	Roll 61
1880	Crawford County—Livingston County	Roll 62
1880	Livingston County—Sangamon County	Roll 63
1880	Sangamon County—Woodford County	Roll 64

Iowa

T1156

1850	Appanoose County—Washington County	Roll 54
1860	Adair County—Wright County	Roll 55
1870	Adair County—Hancock County	Roll 56
1870	Hardin County—Shelby County	Roll 57
1870	Sioux County—Wright County	Roll 58
1880	Adair County—Des Moines County	Roll 59
1880	Dickinson County—Linn County	Roll 60
1880	Louisa County—Van Buren County	Roll 61
1880	Wapello County—Wright County	Roll 62

Kansas

T1130

1860	Allen County—Wyandotte County	Roll 1
1870	Allen County—Wyandotte County	Roll 3
1880	Allen County—Lyons County	Roll 6
1880	Marion County—Wyandotte County	Roll 7

Kentucky

T655

1850	Pendleton County—Woodford County	Roll 13
1860	Adair County—Woodford County	Roll 14
1870	Adair County—Woodford County (Rolls 13–15 include Indexes and Schedules)	Roll 15
1880	A—Mere	Roll 16
1880	Meri—Z (Rolls 16 & 17 contain Indexes and Abstracts for 1880)	Roll 17
1880	Adair County—Jackson County	Roll 18
1880	Jefferson County—Mason County	Roll 19
1880	Meade County—Woodford County (Rolls 18–20 contain Schedules)	Roll 20

Louisiana

T655

1850	Ascension Parish—Vermilion Parish	Roll 21
1860	Ascension Parish—Winn Parish	Roll 22
1870	Ascension Parish—Winn Parish (Rolls 21–23 contain Indexes and Schedules)	Roll 23
1880	Ascension Parish—Natchitoches Parish	Roll 24
1880	Orleans Parish—Winn Parish (Rolls 24 & 25 contain Schedules)	Roll 25

Massachusetts

T1204

1850	Barnstable County—Plymouth County	Roll 9
1850	Suffolk County—Worcester County	Roll 10
1860	Barnstable County—Worcester County	Roll 17
1870	Barnstable County—Middlesex County	Roll 22
1870	Nantucket County—Worcester County	Roll 23
1880	Barnstable County—Newburyport, Essex County	Roll 37

1880	Salem, Essex County—Hampshire County	Roll 38
1880	Middlesex County—Norfolk County	Roll 39
1880	Plymouth County—Worcester County	Roll 40

Michigan

T1163

1850	Allegan County—Wayne County	Roll 1

T1164

1860	Allegan County—Wayne County	Roll 15
1870	Alcona County—Livingston County	Roll 26
1870	Mackinac County—Wexford County	Roll 27
1880	Alcona County—Gratiot County	Roll 74
1880	Hillsdale County—Lenawee County	Roll 75
1880	Livingston County—Roscommon County	Roll 76
1880	Saginaw County—Wexford County	Roll 77

Montana

GR6

1870	Bears Head—Missoula	Roll 1
1880	Missoula—Jefferson County	Roll 1

Nebraska

T1128

1860	Burt County—Shorter County	Roll 2
1870	Buffalo County—York County	Roll 3
1880	Adams County—Saunders County	Roll 14
1880	Seward County—Unorganized Territory	Roll 15

New Jersey

GR21

1850	Atlantic County—Warren County	Roll 1
1860	Atlantic County—Warren County	Roll 1
1870	Atlantic County—Middlesex County	Roll 1
1870	Middlesex County—Warren County	Roll 2
1880	Hunterdon County—Union County	Roll 2
1880	Union County—Warren County	Roll 3
1880	Atlantic County—Hudson County	Roll 3
1880	Hudson County, Cont.	Roll 4

North Carolina

GR1

1850	Alamance County—Yancey County	Roll 1
1860	Alamance County—Yancey County	Roll 2
1870	Alamance County—Yancey County	Roll 3
1880	Alamance County—Pitt County	Roll 4
1880	Polk County—Yancey County	Roll 5

Ohio

T1159

1850	Hamilton County—Marion County	Roll 14
1850	Medina County—Wyandot County	Roll 15
1860	Adams County—Huron County	Roll 29
1860	Jackson County—Wyandot County	Roll 30
1880	Adams County—Clinton County	Roll 102
1880	Columbia County—Darke County	Roll 103
	Defiance County—Geauga County	Roll 104

Pennsylvania

T956

1850	Adams County, Berwick Township—Philadelphia County, 6th Ward, Kensington	Roll 14
1850	Philadelphia County, 7th Ward, Kensington—York County, Shrewsbury Township	Roll 15
1860	Adams County, Araban Township—Potter County, West Branch Township	Roll 16
1860	Schuykill County, Ashland Township—York County, North Codens Township	Roll 17
1870	Adams County—Erie County, 4th Ward	Roll 18
1870	Erie County—Philadelphia, 89th District	Roll 19
1870	Philadelphia—York County	Roll 20
1880	Adams County, Franklin Township—Centre County, Boggs Township	Roll 21
1880	Centre County, Union Township—Lancaster County, West Lampeter Township	Roll 22
1880	Lancaster County, Lancaster Township—Philadelphia	Roll 23
1880	Philadelphia—York County, Rock Belton Township	Roll 24

South Carolina

GR22

1850	Abbeville County—Williamsburg County	Roll 1
1860	Abbeville County—York County	Roll 1
1870	Abbeville County—York County	Roll 2
1880	Abbeville County—York County	Roll 3

(table continued on following page)

TABLE 4 (CONTINUED)

Mortality Census Schedule Microfilm

Tennessee
T655

1850	Anderson County—Wilson County	Roll 26
1860	Anderson County—Wilson County (Rolls 26 & 27 include Indexes and Schedules)	Roll 27
1880	Anderson County—Greene County	Roll 28
1880	Grundy County—Moore County	Roll 29
1880	Morgan County—Wilson County (Rolls 28–30 contain Schedules only)	Roll 30

Texas
T1134

1850	Anderson County—Camal County (Roll 53 also contains the 1880 Schedule for Defective, Dependent, and Delinquent Classes, 1880)	Roll 53
1850	Camal County—Wharton County	Roll 54
1860	Anderson County—Titus County	Roll 54
1860	Titus County—Zapata County	Roll 55
1870	Anderson County—Menard County	Roll 55
1870	Menard County—Zavala County, Texas	Roll 56
1870	Beaver County—Iron County, Utah	Roll 56
1880	Anderson County—Cherokee County	Roll 56
1880	Cherokee County—Grayson County	Roll 57
1880	Grayson County—McLennan County	Roll 58
1880	Upshur County—Zavala County	Roll 59
1880	McLennan County—Upshur County	Roll 60

Utah
GR7

1870	Beaver County—Weber County	Roll 1

Utah
T1134

1870	Beaver County—Iron County	Roll 56

Vermont
GR7

1870	Addison County—Windsor County	Roll 1

Virginia
T1132

1850	Accomack County—York County	Roll 1
1860	Accomack County—York County	Roll 5
1870	Accomack County—York County	Roll 10
1880	Accomack County—Henrico County	Roll 18
1880	Henrico County—York County	Roll 19

Washington
T1154

1860	Clark County—Wallla Walla County	Roll 3
1870	Chehalis (Grays Harbor)—Yakima County	Roll 3
1880	Chehalis (Grays Harbor)—Yakima County	Roll 3

1820, 1830, and 1840 censuses were filed with the federal district or superior courts. The duplicate sets for 1850, 1860, and 1870 were filed with county courts. Many schedules filed with county courts have been deposited in state libraries or state archives. The original 1880 schedules were so fragile that they were transferred to various nonfederal depositories in 1956 after they were microfilmed.

As mentioned above, mortality schedules and some of the other nonpopulation schedules—agriculture, industry, and social statistics—were also transferred to nonfederal depositories. These depositories are identified in the discussions of the schedules by state.

Many state and local libraries have sets of the published 1790 schedules and microfilm copies of some of the population and mortality schedules. Some of these institutions are identified in Special List 24, *Federal Population and Mortality Census Schedules, 1790–1910* (Washington: National Archives and Records Service, 1982).

Microfilm Copies of Census Schedules

The National Archives has reproduced as microfilm publications all of the available federal population census schedules. They can be used in the Microfilm Research Room in the National Archives building and in the research rooms of the regional archives branches in the Federal Archives and Records Centers. The microfilm publication numbers are cited in this chapter as the schedules are discussed by census year. Researchers are required to use the microfilm for their research, although they may be permitted to use the original schedules (or photostats) in bound volumes if the microfilm copy is illegible.

Positive microfilm copies of the schedules are also available for sale from the National Archives. Information about the cost and contents of each roll of the various microfilm publications is given in each of the three federal census microfilm catalogs listed in table 3 above. Buying the microfilm, however does not guarantee that the researcher will find the entries he or she is seeking.

Research Method for Census Records

The schedules are arranged by census year; thereunder, they are arranged alphabetically by name of state; then, with a few exceptions, alphabetically by name of county. Researchers must know in which county the subject of their

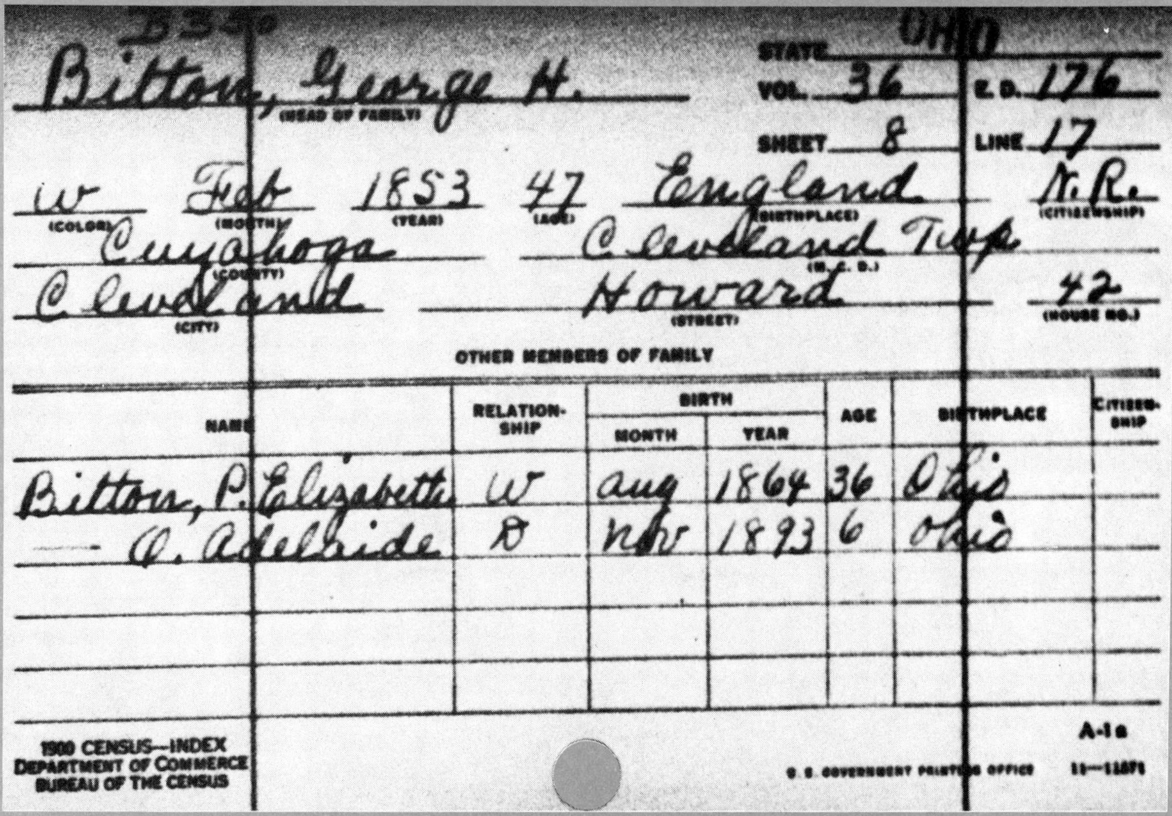

STATE OHIO

Bitton, George H. (HEAD OF FAMILY)

VOL. 36 E.D. 176

SHEET 8 LINE 17

W (COLOR) Feb (MONTH) 1853 (YEAR) 47 (AGE) England (BIRTHPLACE) N.R. (CITIZENSHIP)

Cuyahoga (COUNTY) Cleveland Twp (M.C.D.)

Cleveland (CITY) Howard (STREET) 42 (HOUSE NO.)

OTHER MEMBERS OF FAMILY

NAME	RELATIONSHIP	BIRTH		AGE	BIRTHPLACE	CITIZENSHIP
		MONTH	YEAR			
Bitton, P. Elizabeth	W	Aug	1864	36	Ohio	
— O. Adelaide	D	Nov	1893	6	Ohio	

1900 CENSUS—INDEX
DEPARTMENT OF COMMERCE
BUREAU OF THE CENSUS

A-1a

U.S. GOVERNMENT PRINTING OFFICE

Typical soundex card from the index to the 1900 Census Population Schedules for Ohio. Records of the Bureau of the Census, Record Group 29. National Archives Microfilm Publication T1065.

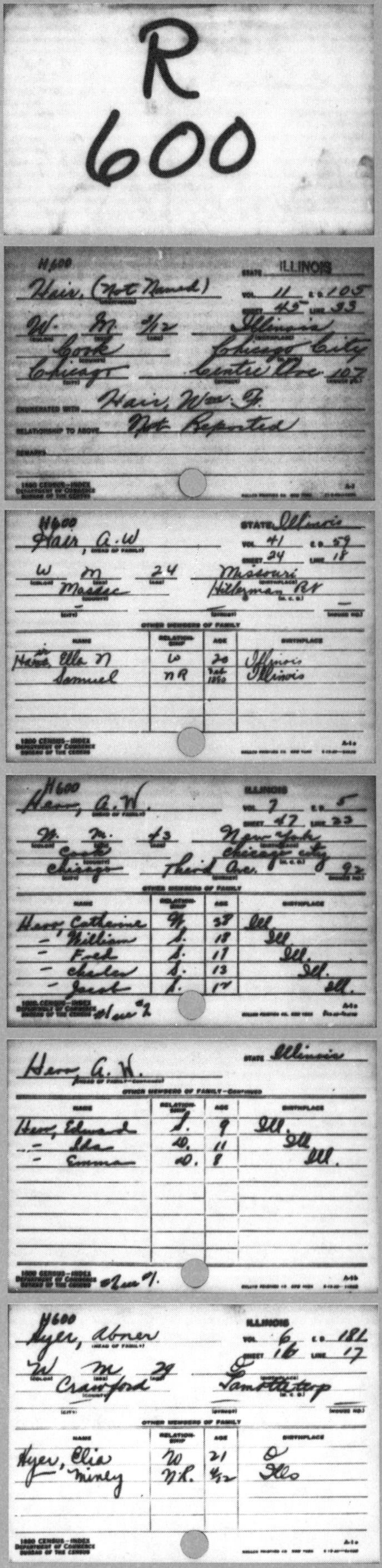
R
600

H600
Hair, (Not Named) — ILLINOIS — Vol. 11, E.D. 105, Sheet 45, Line 33
W. M. 2/12 Illinois
Cook — Chicago City
Chicago — Centre Ave 107
Enumerated with: Hair, Wm. J.
Relationship to above: Not Reported

H600
Hair, A.W — State Illinois — Vol. 41, E.D. 59, Sheet 24, Line 18
W M 24 Missouri

Name	Relationship	Age	Birthplace
Hair, Ella M	W	20	Illinois
Samuel	NR		Illinois

H600
Harr, A.W. — ILLINOIS — Vol. 7, E.D. 5, Sheet 47, Line 23
W. M. 43 New York
Cook — Chicago city
Chicago — Third Ave. 92

Name	Relationship	Age	Birthplace
Harr, Catherine	W.	38	Ill.
– William	S.	18	Ill.
– Fred	S.	17	Ill.
– Charles	S.	13	Ill.
– Jacob	S.	14	Ill.

#1 see #2

Harr, A.W. — State Illinois

Name	Relationship	Age	Birthplace
Harr, Edward	S.	9	Ill.
– Ida	D.	11	Ill.
– Emma	D.	8	Ill.

#2 see #1

H600
Hyer, Abner — ILLINOIS — Vol. 6, E.D. 181, Sheet 16, Line 17
W M 29 O
Crawford

Name	Relationship	Age	Birthplace
Hyer, Elia	W	21	O
– Minley	N.R.	4/12	Ills

Series of soundex cards from the index to
the 1900 Census Population Schedules for Illinois, showing
several names bearing the same soundex code.
Records of the Bureau of the Census, Record Group 29.
National Archives Microfilm Publication T1043.

research lived during the census year, and may need to know an exact address.

Usually a microfilm roll contains all the schedules for one county or several small counties. The arrangment of surnames on a page of the schedules is usually in the order in which the enumerator visited the households. To search for a particular name in the schedules—once the year, the state, and the county have been established—necessitates scanning each page from top to bottom. This process is tedious, but the method is simple.

Indexes

The existing schedules for the 1790 census were published by the federal government in the early 1900s, with the schedules for each state in a separate indexed volume. They have since been privately reprinted. The government has not published other schedules or indexes, but many privately published abstracts and indexes are available. Although these private publications vary considerably in format, geographic scope, and accuracy, they frequently save researchers from fruitless searches and facilitate the location of specific entries in the schedules. Some of these publications are available in the research rooms at the National Archives building and the regional archives branches.

The National Archives also has microfilm copies of card indexes that can be useful for the 1880, 1890, 1900, and 1910 censuses. The 1890 index is a simple alphabetical name index; those for 1880 and 1900 were prepared according to the soundex system. The soundex filing system, alphabetic for the first letter of surname and numeric thereunder as indicated by divider cards, keeps together names of the same and similar sounds but of variant spellings.

To search for a particular name, the researcher must first work out the code number for the surname of the individual. No number is assigned to the first letter of the surname. If the name is Kuhne, for example, the index card will be in the "K" segment of the index. The code number for Kuhne, worked out according to the system below, is 500.

Soundex Coding Guide

Code	**Key Letters and Equivalents**
1	b, p, f, v
2	c, s, k, g, j, q, x, z
3	d, t
4	l
5	m, n
6	r

The first letter of a surname is *not* coded. The letters a, e, i, o, u, y, w, and h are *not* coded. Every soundex number must be a 3-digit number. A name yielding no code numbers, as Lee, would thus be L 000; one yielding only one code number would have two zeros added, as Kuhne, coded as K 500; and one yielding two code numbers would have one zero added, as Ebell, coded as E 140. Not more than three digits are used, so Ebelson would be coded as E 142, not E 1425.

When two key letters or equivalents appear together, or one key letter immediately follows or precedes an equivalent, the two are coded as one letter, by a single number, as follows: *Kelly*, coded as K400; *Buerck*, coded as B620; *Lloyd*, coded as L300.

If several surnames have the same code, the cards for them are arranged alphabetically by given name. There are divider cards showing most code numbers, but not all. For instance, one divider may be numbered 350 and the next one 400. Between the two divider cards there may be names coded 353, 350, 360, 364, 365, and 355, but instead of being in numerical order they are interfiled alphabetically by given name.

Such prefixes to surnames as "van," "Von," "de," "le," "Di," "D'," "dela," or "du" are sometimes disregarded in alphabetizing and in coding.

The following names are examples of soundex coding and are given only as illustrations.

Name	**Letters Coded**	**Code No.**
Allricht	l, r, c	A 462
Eberhard	b, r, r	E 166
Engebrethson	n, g, b	E9xfr 521
Heimbach	m, b, c	H 512
Hanselmann	n, s, l	H 524
Henzelmann	n, z, l	H 524
Hildebrand	l, d, b	H 431
Kavanagh	v, n, g	K 152
Lind, Van	n, d	L 530
Lukaschowsky	k, s, s	L 222
McDonnell	c, d, n	M 235
McGee	c	M 200
O'Brien	b, r, n	O 165
Opnian	p, n, n	O 155
Oppenheimer	p, n, m	O 155
Riedemanas	d, m, n	R 355
Zita	t	Z 300
Zitzmeinn	t, z, m	Z 325

Indexes to the 1910 census cover the schedules for only twenty-one states. There are soundmaster (similar to soundex) indexes for Alabama, Georgia, Louisiana, Mississippi, South Carolina, Tennessee, and Texas. Another index, which is constructed on much the same principle as soundex but is called "miracode" has been prepared for each of the following states: Arkansas, California, Florida, Illinois, Kansas, Kentucky, Michigan, Missouri, North Carolina, Ohio, Oklahoma, Pennsylvania, Virginia, and West Virginia.

Helpful Maps

County boundaries of the areas in which the 1790 census was taken and the same areas in 1900 are shown on maps on pages 61–70 of *A Century of Population Growth, From the First Census of the United States to the Twelfth* (Washington: Bureau of the Census, 1909). The volume has been reprinted by the Genealogical Publishing Co., Baltimore, 1967, and the maps have been reprinted on a smaller scale in *Research in American Genealogy*, by E. Kay Kirkham (Salt Lake City, 1956).

The National Archives has outline maps prepared by the Department of Agriculture that show the names and locations of each county in the United States for each decennial year, 1840–1910. Also available in the Microfilm Research Room are photocopies of many city ward maps.

Census enumeration district maps and enumeration subdivision and district descriptions are discussed generally in chapter 20.2. The maps are listed in *Cartographic Records of the Bureau of the Census*, Preliminary Inventory 103, compiled by James B. Rhoads and Charlotte M. Ashby (Washington: National Archives and Records Service, 1958).

In a useful publication of the Bureau of the Census, *Twenty Censuses Population and Housing Questions, 1790–1980* (Washington: Government Printing Office, 1979), the headings of the enumeration form and instructions to enumerators for each federal decennial census are reproduced. The booklet is for sale by the Superintendent of Documents, U.S. Government Printing Office, Washington, DC 20402, Stock No. 003-024-01874-8.

Ordering Copies of Census Records by Mail

At one time, the National Archives made minimal searches in the census schedules in response to mail requests. Because copies of the census records are now available at the regional archives branches, however, this research service formerly provided by mail has been discontinued. The National Archives will furnish photocopies of census pages only when the researcher can cite the state, county, enumeration district for 1880, 1900 and 1910, volume number, and exact page on which a family is enumerated. The pages of schedules were numbered by the census taker; when the schedules were arranged later, they were often renumbered. It is possible, therefore, for some volumes to have two or more series of page numbers. A hand stamp was used for numbering the pages in many of the volumes. This number, if it is present, should be used when ordering photocopies. No special form is necessary; the information should be clearly stated in a letter addressed to the Reference Services Branch (NNIR), General Services Administration, Washington, DC 20408.

A Note About American Indians

Census enumerators did not count Indians not taxed, that is, Indians who lived on reservations or who roamed as nomads over unsettled tracts of land. Whether or not they were of mixed blood, Indians who lived among the white population or on the outskirts of towns were counted as part of the ordinary population.

The records of the Bureau of Indian Affairs include many tribal census rolls. These rolls are completely unrelated to the decennial census schedules. They are described in chapter 11 of this guide. Researchers trying to trace Indians may find these rolls more useful than the decennial census schedules.

1.1.4 Descriptions of Federal Schedules by Year

As noted above, each year the federal census was taken, more information was gathered. For no two censuses were exactly the same questions asked at each household. The following pages present a brief description of the information recorded in each census to help the researcher decide whether finding a household in a particular census will provide the information needed about persons in that household. Reference Information Paper 67, *Federal Census Schedules, 1850–80: Primary Sources for Historical Research*, contains very detailed descriptions of mid-to-late nineteenth-century census schedules. (See table 3.)

1790 Census

Population schedules. Although there were only 13 states in the Union in 1790, the census was taken in an area constituting 17 present-day states. Schedules survive for two-thirds of those states. The National Archives microfilm publication of the extant original schedules is M637, 12 rolls. In the early 1900s, the Bureau of the Census published these schedules in a single indexed volume for each state;

TABLE 5

Contents of Census Schedules, 1790–1840 and 1850–1910

1790–1840

	1790	**1800**	**1810**	**1820**	**1830**	**1840**
Name of head of family and number of free white males (within specified age groups) and free white females (age groups unspecified in each household)	Yes	Yes	Yes	Yes	Yes	Yes
Number of free white females, within specified age groups, in each household	No	Yes	Yes	Yes	Yes	Yes
Name of slaveowner and number of slaves owned by each owner	Yes	Yes	Yes	Yes	Yes	Yes
Number of male and female slaves, within specified age groups, owned by each owner	No	No	No	Yes	Yes	Yes
Number of foreigners, in each household, not naturalized	No	No	No	Yes	Yes	No
Number of deaf, dumb, and blind persons, within specified categories, in each household	No	No	No	No	Yes	Yes
Name and age of each person receiving a federal military pension	No	No	No	No	No	Yes
Number of persons in each household attending specified classes at school	No	No	No	No	No	Yes

CHAPTER I

Census Records

1.1 The Federal Schedules

1850–1910 (free inhabitants of each household)

	1850	1860	1870	1880	1885*	1890	1900	1910
Name and age	Yes	Yes	Yes	Yes	Yes	Yes	Yes	Yes
Name of street and number of house	No	No	No	Yes	Yes	Yes	Yes	Yes
Relationship to head of family	No	No	No	Yes	Yes	Yes	Yes	Yes
Month of birth, if born within the year	No	No	Yes	Yes	Yes	No	Yes	No
Sex, color, birthplace, and occupation	Yes	Yes	Yes	Yes	Yes	Yes	Yes	Yes
Whether naturalized or whether naturalization papers had been taken out	No	No	No	No	No	Yes	Yes	Yes
Number of years in the United States	No	No	No	No	No	Yes	Yes	Yes
Value of personal estate	No	Yes	Yes	No	No	No	No	No
Value of real estate	Yes	Yes	Yes	No	No	No	No	No
Whether home and farm free of mortgage	No	No	No	No	No	Yes	Yes	Yes
Marital status	No	No	No	Yes	Yes	Yes	Yes	Yes
Whether married within the year	Yes	Yes	Yes	Yes	Yes	Yes	No	No
Month of marriage, if married within the year	No	No	Yes	No	No	No	No	No
Whether temporarily or permanently disabled	No	No	No	Yes	Yes	No	No	No
Whether suffering from acute or chronic disease	No	No	No	No	No	Yes	No	No
Whether crippled, maimed, or deformed	No	No	No	Yes	Yes	Yes	No	No
Time unemployed during the census year	No	No	No	Yes	Yes	Yes	Yes	Yes
Whether deaf, dumb, blind, or insane	Yes	Yes	Yes	Yes	Yes	Yes	No	Yes
Whether a pauper	Yes	Yes	No	No	No	Yes	No	No
Whether a prisoner or homeless child	No	No	No	No	No	Yes	No	No
Whether a convict	Yes	Yes	No	No	No	Yes	No	No
Whether able to speak English	No	No	No	No	No	Yes	Yes	Yes
Whether able to read and write and whether attended school within the year	Yes	Yes	Yes	Yes	Yes	Yes	Yes	Yes
Birthplaces of father and mother	No	No	No	Yes	Yes	Yes	Yes	Yes
Whether father or mother of foreign birth	No	No	Yes	Yes	Yes	Yes	Yes	Yes
Number of living children, if a mother	No	No	No	No	No	Yes	Yes	Yes
Whether soldier, sailor, or marine during the Civil War (U.S. or Conf.), or widow of such person	No	No	No	No	No	Yes	Yes	Yes
Number of years in present marriage	No	No	No	No	No	No	Yes	Yes
Number of children born	No	No	No	No	No	No	Yes	Yes
Mother tongue	No	No	No	No	No	No	No	Yes

*Five states and territories (Colorado, Florida, Nebraska, New Mexico, and Dakota Territory) chose to take an 1885 census with federal assistance.

they have since been privately reprinted. The published 1790 schedules were also microfilmed by the National Archives, on T498, 3 rolls.

There are microfilmed schedules (original and printed) for 1790 for Connecticut, Maine, Maryland, Massachusetts, New Hampshire, New York, North Carolina, Pennsylvania, Rhode Island, South Carolina, and Vermont. The schedules for Delaware, Georgia, Kentucky, New Jersey, Tennessee, and Virginia were burned during the War of 1812. The 1790 schedules for Virginia that appear on T498 were reconstructed from state enumerations.

The schedules for each state, both the originals and those in the printed volumes, are arranged by county and in some cases by minor subdivisions of counties. The minor subdivisions of the counties for many of the states are given in the Census Office publication *Return of the Whole Number of Persons Within the Several Districts of the United States . . .* (Philadelphia: Childs and Swaine, 1791). Other editions were published under the same title, including one of 1802 that has been reprinted by Arno Press, New York, 1976.

An entry in the 1790 schedules shows the name of a head of household, number of free white males under the age of 16 in the household, number of free white males ages 16 and older, number of free white females, number of all other free persons, and number of slaves.

1800 Census

Population schedules. Extant schedules for fourteen states are microfilmed on M32, 52 rolls. The schedules for 1800 are arranged alphabetically by state or territory, thereunder by county, and thereunder in some cases by minor subdivision.

In most instances a subdivision is a town or village. The minor subdivisions of the counties for many states are given in *Return of the Whole Number of Persons Within the Several Districts of the United States . . .* (Washington: 2d Census, 1801). The copy at the National Archives is a bound photocopy. An 1802 edition of the volume has been reprinted by Arno Press, New York, 1976. Entries are usually arranged in the order of enumeration; in rare cases they are arranged in rough alphabetical order by initial letter of surname.

Each entry shows the name of the head of household; number of free white males and free white females in these age categories: under 10, 10 and under 16, 16 and under 26, 26 and under 45, and 45 and older; number of all other free persons, except Indians not taxed; and number of slaves.

1810 Census

Population schedules. Extant schedules for sixteen states and territories are microfilmed on M252, 71 rolls. The schedules are arranged by state or territory, thereunder by county, and thereunder by minor subdivision, usually a town or village. For identification of the minor subdivisions of the counties, see *Aggregate Amount of Each Description of Persons Within the United States . . . 1810* (Washington: 3d Census, 1811). This volume has been reprinted by Arno Press, New York, 1976. Entries are usually arranged in order of enumeration.

Each entry shows the name of the head of household; number of free white males in the following age categories: under 10, 10 and under 16, 16 and under 26, 26 and under 45, 45 and older; number of free white females in the same age categories; number of all other free persons, except Indians not taxed; and number of slaves.

Indexes. *Index to the 1810 Population Census Schedules for Virginia*, T1019, 35 rolls, reproduces a card index for Virginia only.

Census of manufactures. In 1810, manufacturing schedules were prepared, and the results were published in *A Statement of the Arts and Manufactures of the United States of America . . .*, prepared by Tench Coxe (Washington: P. Cornman, Jr., 1814), reprinted in *American State Papers, Finance* (Washington: Gales and Seaton, 1832), 2:425–439, also reprinted by Maxwell Reprint Co., Elmsford, N.Y., 1971. The schedules are not extant, except for fragments among the population schedules. Those that do exist contain for each manufacturing establishment the name of the owner, the kind of establishment, the quantity and estimated value of the goods manufactured, and, in some cases, the quantity of raw materials used. The available schedules are listed in Appendix IX of Preliminary Inventory 161, *Records of the Bureau of the Census*.

1820 Census

Population schedules. The 1820 schedules for twenty-two states and territories are microfilmed on M33, 142 rolls. The schedules are arranged by state or territory, thereunder by county, and thereunder by minor subdivision, generally a town or village. For minor subdivisions of the counties, see *Census for 1820 . . .* (Washington: 4th Census, 1821). The volume has been reprinted by Arno Press, New York, 1976.

In addition to the data recorded in previous censuses, the 1820 schedules include information about aliens and occupations. Entries are usually arranged in order of enumeration.

Each entry shows the name of the head of a household; number of free white males in the following age categories: under 10, 10 and under 16, between 16 and 18, 16 and under 26, 26 and under 45, 45 and older; number of free white females in the same age categories, except 16 to 18; number of foreigners not naturalized; number of free colored males in the following age categories: under 14, 14 and under 26, 26 and under 45, and 45 and older; number of free colored females in the same age categories; number of male and female slaves in the same age categories; and number of all other persons, except Indians not taxed.

Census of manufactures. The 1820 enumerations include fourteen items relating to the nature and names of articles manufactured, including market value of articles annually manufactured; kind, quantity, and cost of raw materials annually consumed; number of men, women, boys, and girls employed; quantity and kind of machinery; amount of capital invested; amount paid annually in wages; amount of contingent expenses; and general observations. The extant schedules are on microfilm as *Records of the 1820 Census of Manufactures*, M279, 27 rolls. There is an index on each roll.

1830 Census

Population schedules. The 1830 schedules for twenty-eight states and territories are microfilmed on M19, 201 rolls. The schedules are arranged by state or territory, thereunder by county, and thereunder by minor subdivision in some cases. For minor subdivisions of the counties, see *Fifth Census; or, Enumeration of the Inhabitants of the United States . . .* (Washington: 5th Census, 1832). This publication is available as item 8 on roll 4 of *Publications of the Bureau of the Census*, T825, 42 rolls.

The 1830 schedules are printed forms of uniform size. Each entry spans two facing pages; the left-hand page contains chiefly family data, and the right-hand page contains slave data. Information collected in the 1830 census that was not found on previous schedules includes the number of persons, white and slave, who were blind or deaf-mute.

Each entry shows the name of the head of a household; number of free white males in the household in the following age categories: under 5, 5 and under 10, 10 and under 15, 15 and under 20, 20 and under 30, 30 and under 40, 40 and under 50, 50 and under 60, 60 and under 70, 70 and under 80, 80 and under 90, 90 and under 100, 100 and older; number of free white females in each of the same age categories; number of free colored males in the following age categories: under 10, 10 and under 24, 24 and under 36, 36 and under 55, 55 and under 100, and 100 and older; number of free colored females in the same age categories; number of slave males and number of slave females in the same age categories; number of white blind persons and number of blind slaves and colored persons; number of white deaf-mutes and number of deaf-mute slaves in each of three age categories; and number of white aliens.

1840 Census

Population schedules. The 1840 schedules for thirty states and territories are microfilmed on M704, 580 rolls. The schedules are arranged by state or territory, thereunder by county, and thereunder by minor subdivision in most cases. A subdivision may be a city, ward, town, township, parish, precinct, hundred, or district. The minor subdivisions of the counties are given in *Sixth Census; or, Enumeration of the Inhabitants of the United States . . . 1840* (Washington: 6th Census, 1841).

The population schedules are on printed forms of uniform size. Each entry spans two facing pages. The left-hand page contains chiefly family data; the right-hand page, contains slave, employment, and pension data. The entries were expanded in 1840 to include information about military pensioners, schooling, and literacy. The entries are usually arranged in order of enumeration.

Each entry shows the name of the head of a household; number of free white males in the household in the following age categories: under 5, 5 and under 10, 10 and under 15, 15 and under 20, 20 and under 30, 30 and under 40, 40 and under 50, 50 and under 60, 60 and under 70, 70 and under 80, 80 and under 90, 90 and under 100, 100 and older; number of free white females in each of the same age categories; number of free colored males in the following age categories: under 10, 10 and under 24, 24 and under 36, 36 and under 55, 55 and under 100, 100 and older; number of free colored females in the same age categories; number of male and female slaves in the same age categories; number of persons in each family engaged in the following occupations: mining, agriculture, commerce, manufactures and trade, navigation of the oceans, navigation of canals, lakes, and rivers, and learned professions and engineering; names and ages of military pensioners; number of both white and colored deaf, mute, and blind persons; number of students; number of scholars at public charge; and number of free white persons older than 20 who could not read and write.

The names and ages of the military pensioners listed in the 1840 schedules were printed in *A Census of Pensioners for Revolutionary or Military Services; With Their Names, Ages, Places of Residence . . .* (Washington: Department of State, 1841). This publication has been microfilmed at the end of roll 3 of T498, and has been reprinted by the Southern Book Co., Baltimore, 1954, and by the Genealogical Publishing Co., Baltimore, 1967. Also available is *A General Index to a Census of Pensioners . . . 1840*, compiled by the Genealogical Society (Baltimore: Genealogical Publishing Co., 1965).

1850 Census

Population schedules. Often called "the first modern census," the 1850 schedules for free inhabitants were separated from slave schedules for states where slavery was still protected by law. The schedules are microfilmed on M432, 1,009 rolls. Schedules are arranged by state or territory, thereunder by status (slave or free), thereunder by county, and thereunder by minor subdivision. For a printed list of minor subdivisions see "Population by Subdivision of Counties," *The Seventh Census . . .* (Washington: 7th Census, 1853).

Beginning in 1850, more comprehensive census information was gathered. Before 1850, only the name of the head of the household was recorded. In the 1850 schedules, for the first time, the name of each free person in a household is given. In addition, an entry for each free person shows name; age; sex; color (white, black, or mulatto); occupation for males over 15; value of real estate owned; the state, territory, or country of birth; whether the person attended school or was married within the year; whether the person could read and write if over 20; and whether the person was deaf-mute, blind, insane, an idiot, a pauper, or a convict.

On separate slave schedules, the name of each slaveowner appears with number of slaves owned, and number of slaves manumitted. Under the slaveholder's name, a line for each slave shows age, color, sex, whether or not deaf-mute, blind, insane, or idiotic; and whether or not a fugitive from the state. Names of slaves were not entered.

Mortality schedules. The mortality schedules give the following information for each person who died during the year ending 1 June 1850: name; age; sex; color (white, black, or mulatto); whether married or widowed; place of birth; occupation; month of death; cause of death; number of days ill.

Agriculture schedules. Every farm with an annual produce worth $100 or more for the year ending 1 June 1850 was enumerated, giving the name of the owner, agent, or tenant and the kind and value of acreage, machinery, livestock, and produce.

Industrial schedules. For the year ending 1 June 1850, the enumerators recorded information about manufacturing, mining, fisheries, and every mercantile, commercial, and trading business with an annual gross product of $500 or more. The schedules show the name of the company or owner; kind of business; amount of capital invested; and quantity and value of materials, labor, machinery, and products.

1860 Census

Population schedules. For 1860, there are schedules for free inhabitants and, for certain states, separate schedules for slave inhabitants. The schedules are microfilmed on M653, 1,438 rolls. They are arranged by state, thereunder by status (slave or free), thereunder by county, and thereunder by minor subdivision. The names of the cities, towns, and other minor subdivisions of the counties in 1860 are listed under the name of each state and territory in *Population of the United States in 1860* (Washington: 8th Census, 1864).

For each free person in a household an entry shows the name; age; sex; color (white, black, or mulatto); occupation of persons over 15; value of real estate; value of personal estate; name of state, territory, or country of birth; whether the person was married during the year; and whether the person was deaf-mute, blind, insane, an idiot, a pauper, or a convict.

The information in the schedules of slave inhabitants is the same as that in the slave schedules of the 1850 Census.

Mortality schedules. The mortality schedules give the following information about each person who died during the year ending 1 June 1860: name; age; sex; color (black, white, or mulatto); whether slave or free; whether married or widowed; place of birth; occupation; month of death; cause of death; and number of days ill.

Agriculture schedules. For the year ending 1 June 1860, the schedules show the name of the owner, agent, or tenant of farms with an annual produce worth $100 or more. The enumerators also recorded information about the kind and value of acreage, machinery, livestock, and produce.

Industrial schedules. For the year ending 1 June 1860, the enumerators recorded information about manufacturing, mining, fisheries, and all kinds of mercantile, commercial, and trading businesses, if the annual gross product amounted to $500. The schedules show the name of the company or owner; kind of business; capital investment; and quantity and value of materials, labor, machinery, and products.

1870 Census

Population schedules. The 1870 schedules are microfilmed on M593, 1,748 rolls, and (Minnesota census schedules only) T132, 13 rolls. The schedules are arranged alphabetically by state or territory, thereunder by county, and thereunder by minor subdivision. For information about minor subdivisions in 1870, see "Population of Civil Divisions Less Than Counties" in *The Statistics of the Population . . . , 1870* (Washington: 9th Census, 1872).

The forms for recording the 1870 schedules contained 20 columns with the following headings (punctuation and capitalization as in the original):

1. Dwelling houses numbered in the order of visitation.
2. Families numbered in the order of visitation.
3. The name of every person whose place of abode on the first day of June, 1870, was in this family.

Description

4. Age at last birthday. If under 1 year, give months in fractions, thus 3/12.
5. Sex.—Males (M.), Females (F.).
6. Color.—White (W.), Black (B.), Mulatto (M.), Chinese (C.), Indian (I.).
7. Profession, Occupation, or Trade of each person, male or female.

Real Estate Owned

8. Value of Real Estate.
9. Personal Property.
10. Place of Birth, State or Territory of U.S., Country if foreign born.

Parentage

11. Father of foreign birth.
12. Mother of foreign birth.
13. If born within the year, state month (Jan., Feb., & c.).
14. If married within the year, state month (Jan., Feb., & c.).
15. Attended school within the year.

Education

16. Cannot read.
17. Cannot write.
18. Whether deaf and dumb, blind, insane or idiotic.

Constitutional Relations

19. Male Citizen of the U.S. of 21 years of age and upwards.
20. Male Citizen of U.S. 21 years of age and upwards whose right to vote is denied or abridged on other grounds than rebellion or other crime.

Mortality schedules. The schedules show the following information about each person who died within the year ending 1 June 1870: name; age; sex; whether white, black, mulatto, Chinese, or Indian; whether married or widowed; place of birth; whether father and mother foreign-born; occupation; month of death; and cause of death.

Agriculture schedules. For the year ending 1 June 1870, the schedules show the name of the owner, agent, or tenant of farms of three acres or more or with an annual produce worth $500. The enumerators also recorded information about the kind and value of acreage, machinery, livestock, and produce.

Industrial schedules. The enumerators recorded information about manufacturing, mining, and fisheries if the annual gross product amounted to $500 for the year ending 1 June 1870. The schedules show the name of the company or owner, kind of business, amount of capital invested, and information about the quantity and value of materials, labor, machinery, and products.

1880 Census

Population schedules. The 1880 schedules are microfilmed on T9, 1,454 rolls. The schedules are arranged by state or territory, thereunder by county, and thereunder by minor subdivision. The subdivisions were smaller than those of previous censuses. The states were divided into supervisors' districts and thereunder into enumeration districts. The boundaries of the enumeration districts for many states and territories are described on printed forms bound in four volumes entitled "Tenth Census 1880 Description of Enumeration Districts" and in a typed transcript of such forms in a seven-volume set. The two sets show some variation in coverage. For information about minor subdivisions in 1880, including a comparison with those of 1870, see "Population of Civil Divisions Less Than Counties," *Statistics of the Population of the United States at the Tenth Census* (Washington: 10th Census, 1883).

Each census page lists the post office of entries on that page. For each urban household, an entry shows the name of the street and the house number. For each person in a household, an entry shows name; whether white, black, mulatto, Indian, or Chinese; sex; age; month of birth if born within the year; relationship to the head of the household; whether single, married, widowed, or divorced; whether married within the year; occupation and months unemployed; name of state, territory, or country of birth; father's birthplace and mother's birthplace; school attendance within the year; inability to read if aged 10 or older; inability to write if aged 10 or older; and whether sick or temporarily disabled on the day of enumeration and the reason therefor. Those who were blind, deaf-mute, idiotic, insane, or permanently disabled were recorded in the population schedules, with further information about their condition on supplemental schedules of dependent classes, which are extant for some states among the nonpopulation schedules.

Indexes. The National Archives has a microfilm copy of a card index to those entries on the 1880 schedules that relate to households containing a child aged 10 or under. The cards show the name, age, and birthplace of each member of such households, and there is a separate cross-reference card for each child aged 10 or under whose surname is different from that of the head of the household in which he or she is listed.

The cards are arranged by state or territory; they are filmed on 2,367 rolls of 47 different microfilm publications, one for each state or territory and the District of Columbia. North and South Dakota were combined in Dakota Territory, and no census was taken in Indian Territory (later Oklahoma). The publication numbers and corresponding roll numbers are listed in *Federal Population Censuses, 1790–1890*.

For each state, the cards are arranged according to the soundex system. Its use is explained on page 31.

Mortality schedules. The schedules give the following information about each person who died during the year ending 1 June 1880: name; age; sex; color; marital status; occupation; place of birth; length of residence in the United States; place of birth of father and mother; month of death; cause of death; place cause of death was contracted; and name of attending physician. In Massachusetts, New Jersey, the District of Columbia and nineteen large cities, this information was compiled from official registrations of deaths, and the regular mortality schedules were not used.

Agriculture schedules. The schedules pertain to the year ending 1 June 1880 and show the name of the owner, agent, or tenant of farms of three acres or more or with an annual produce worth $500. The enumerators also recorded information about the quantity and value of acreage, machinery, livestock, and produce.

Industrial schedules. Special agents, rather than the regular enumerators, recorded information for certain large industries and in cities of more than 8,000 inhabitants. These schedules are not extant. The regular enumerators did continue to collect information on general industry schedules and special schedules for twelve industries. The schedules show the name of the company or owner and much specific information about the kind, quantity, and value of materials, labor, machinery, and products.

1890 Census

Population schedules. The original 1890 population schedules were destroyed or badly damaged by a fire in Washington in 1921. Less than 1 percent of the schedules are extant. They are microfilmed on M407, 3 rolls. The surviving fragments are reproduced as follows:

Roll 1. ALABAMA, Perry County (Perryville Beat No. 11 and Severe Beat No. 8).

Roll 2. DISTRICT OF COLUMBIA, Q, 13th, 14th, R, Corcoran, 15th, S, R, and Riggs Streets, and Johnson Avenue.

Roll 3. GEORGIA, Muscogee County (Columbus); ILLINOIS, McDonough County (Mound Twp.); MINNESOTA, Wright County (Rockford); NEW JERSEY, Hudson County (Jersey City); NEW YORK, Westchester County, (Eastchester); and Suffolk County (Brookhaven Twp.); NORTH CAROLINA, Gaston County (South Point Twp. and River Bend Twp.) and Cleveland County (Twp. No. 2); OHIO, Hamilton County (Cincinnati) and Clinton County (Wayne Twp.); SOUTH DAKOTA, Union County (Jefferson Twp.); TEXAS, Ellis County (J.P. No. 6, Mountain Peak, and Ovilla Precinct), Hood County (Precinct No. 5), Rusk County (No. 6 and J. P. No. 7), Trinity County (Trinity Town and Precinct No. 2) and Kaufman County (Kaufman).

Indexes. A card index to the 6,160 names on the surviving 1890 schedules is filmed on *Index to the Eleventh Census of the United States, 1890*, M496, 2 rolls.

Veterans' schedules. The National Archives has some schedules of a special census of Union veterans and widows of veterans in 1890. They are microfilmed on M123, 118 rolls. The schedules are those for Washington, D.C., about half of Kentucky, and Louisiana, Maine, Maryland, Massachusetts, Michigan, Minnesota, Mississippi, Missouri, Montana, Nebraska, Nevada, New Hampshire, New Jersey, New Mexico, New York, North Carolina, North Dakota, Ohio, Oklahoma, and Indian Territories, Oregon, Pennsylvania, Rhode Island, South Carolina, South Dakota, Tennessee, Texas, Utah, U.S. ships and navy yards, Vermont, Virginia, Washington, West Virginia, Wisconsin, and Wyoming. Schedules for other states were destroyed in the same 1921 fire that destroyed the population schedules.

The schedules are arranged by state or territory, thereunder by county, and thereunder by minor subdivision.

Each entry shows the name of a Union veteran of the Civil War; name of his widow, if appropriate; veteran's rank, company, regiment, or vessel; dates of enlistment and discharge and length of service in years, months, and days; post office address; nature of any disability; and remarks.

Unlike the other census records described in this chapter, these schedules are part of the Records of the Veterans Administration, Record Group 15. They are discussed in Evangeline Thurber's "The 1890 Census Records of the Veterans of the Union Army," *National Genealogical Society Quarterly* 34 (Mar. 1946): 7–9.

1900 Census

Population schedules. The 1900 schedules are microfilmed on T623, 1,854 rolls. The schedules are arranged by state or territory, thereunder by county, and thereunder by minor subdivision. States were divided into supervisors' districts and enumeration districts.

TABLE 6

Availability of Population Schedules

State	**1790**	**1800**	**1810**	**1820**	**1830**	**1840**	**1850**	**1860**	**1870**	**1880**	**1890**	**1900**	**1910**
Alabama	–	–	–	No	Yes	Yes	Yes	Yes	Yes	Yes	F	Yes	Yes
Alaska	–	–	–	–	–	–	–	–	–	–	No	Yes	Yes
Arizona	–	–	–	–	–	–	Yes	Yes	Yes	Yes	No	Yes	Yes
Arkansas	–	–	–	No	Yes	Yes	Yes	Yes	Yes	Yes	No	Yes	Yes
California	–	–	–	–	–	–	Yes	Yes	Yes	Yes	No	Yes	Yes
Colorado	–	–	–	–	–	–	–	Yes	Yes	Yes	No	Yes	Yes
Connecticut	Yes	Yes	Yes	Yes	Yes	Yes	Yes	Yes	Yes	Yes	Yes	Yes	Yes
Delaware	No	Yes	Yes	Yes	Yes	Yes	Yes	Yes	Yes	Yes	No	Yes	Yes
District of Columbia	Yes	Yes	No	Yes	Yes	Yes	Yes	Yes	Yes	Yes	FV	Yes	Yes
Florida	–	–	–	–	Yes	Yes	Yes	Yes	Yes	Yes	No	Yes	Yes
Georgia	No	No	No	Yes	Yes	Yes	Yes	Yes	Yes	Yes	F	Yes	Yes
Hawaii	–	–	–	–	–	–	–	–	–	–	–	Yes	Yes
Idaho	–	–	–	–	–	–	–	–	Yes	Yes	No	Yes	Yes
Illinois	–	–	Yes	Yes	Yes	Yes	Yes	Yes	Yes	Yes	F	Yes	Yes
Indiana	–	No	No	Yes	Yes	Yes	Yes	Yes	Yes	Yes	No	Yes	Yes
Iowa	–	–	–	–	–	Yes	Yes	Yes	Yes	Yes	No	Yes	Yes
Kansas	–	–	–	–	–	–	–	Yes	Yes	Yes	No	Yes	Yes
Kentucky	No	No	Yes	Yes	Yes	Yes	Yes	Yes	Yes	Yes	V	Yes	Yes
Louisiana	–	–	Yes	Yes	Yes	Yes	Yes	Yes	Yes	Yes	V	Yes	Yes
Maine	Yes	Yes	Yes	Yes	Yes	Yes	Yes	Yes	Yes	Yes	V	Yes	Yes
Maryland	Yes	Yes	Yes	Yes	Yes	Yes	Yes	Yes	Yes	Yes	V	Yes	Yes
Massachusetts	Yes	Yes	Yes	Yes	Yes	Yes	Yes	Yes	Yes	Yes	V	Yes	Yes
Michigan	–	–	No	Yes	Yes	Yes	Yes	Yes	Yes	Yes	V	Yes	Yes
Minnesota	–	–	–	–	–	–	Yes	Yes	Yes	Yes	FV	Yes	Yes
Mississippi	–	No	No	Yes	Yes	Yes	Yes	Yes	Yes	Yes	V	Yes	Yes
Missouri	–	–	No	No	Yes	Yes	Yes	Yes	Yes	Yes	V	Yes	Yes
Montana	–	–	–	–	–	–	–	Yes	Yes	Yes	V	Yes	Yes
Nebraska	–	–	–	–	–	–	–	Yes	Yes	Yes	V	Yes	Yes
Nevada	–	–	–	–	–	–	–	Yes	Yes	Yes	V	Yes	Yes
New Hampshire	Yes	Yes	Yes	Yes	Yes	Yes	Yes	Yes	Yes	Yes	V	Yes	Yes

For each household, an entry shows the name of the township, city and ward, if any, and the street and house number (if in an urban area). For each person, an entry shows the name; the relationship to the head of the household; color and sex; month and year of birth and age at last birthday; whether single, married, widowed, or divorced; number of years married; for married women, number of children borne and the number of these children living; names of the state, territory, or country of birth, father's birth, and mother's birth; for an alien or naturalized citizen, year of immigration to the United States, number of years in the United States, and whether still an alien, having applied for citizenship, or naturalized; occupation of each person 10 and older and number of months not employed; information about school attendance, literacy, and ability to speak English; whether residence was a farm; and whether the occupant was a homeowner.

There are separate military schedules for military personnel including those at U.S. bases overseas and on naval vessels. They are on rolls 1838–1842 of T623, with a soundex index on T1081, 32 rolls.

Indexes. The National Archives has a microfilm copy of a card index to all heads of households in the 1900 schedules, with cross-reference cards for persons in the household whose surname is different from that of the head of the household. The cards show the name, age, and birthplace of each member of the household. The cards are arranged by state or territory and thereunder by the soundex system, which is described on page 31. The 1900 soundex is filmed on nearly 8,000 rolls of microfilm publications, a different one for each state. In the research rooms at the National Archives building and the regional archives branches are lists of the microfilm rolls of the 1900 census schedules and the microfilm publication numbers of the accompanying soundex. The information is also available in *1900 Federal Population Census: A Catalog of Microfilm Copies of the Schedules.*

There are separate military schedules for army personnel overseas and all navy personnel. Army personnel stationed in the United States were enumerated in the geographical area where they were stationed. There is no index for the military schedules.

	1790	1800	1810	1820	1830	1840	1850	1860	1870	1880	1890	1900	1910
New Jersey	No	No	No	No	Yes	Yes	Yes	Yes	Yes	Yes	FV	Yes	Yes
New Mexico	–	–	–	–	–	–	Yes	Yes	Yes	Yes	V	Yes	Yes
New York	Yes	Yes	Yes	Yes	Yes	Yes	Yes	Yes	Yes	Yes	FV	Yes	Yes
North Carolina	Yes	Yes	Yes	Yes	Yes	Yes	Yes	Yes	Yes	Yes	FV	Yes	Yes
North Dakota	–	–	–	–	–	–	–	–	–	–	V	Yes	Yes
Ohio	–	No	No	Yes	Yes	Yes	Yes	Yes	Yes	Yes	FV	Yes	Yes
Oklahoma	–	–	–	–	–	–	–	Yes	No	I	V	Yes	Yes
Oregon	–	–	–	–	–	–	Yes	Yes	Yes	Yes	V	Yes	Yes
Pennsylvania	Yes	Yes	Yes	Yes	Yes	Yes	Yes	Yes	Yes	Yes	V	Yes	Yes
Puerto Rico	–	–	–	–	–	–	–	–	–	–	–	–	Yes
Rhode Island	Yes	Yes	Yes	Yes	Yes	Yes	Yes	Yes	Yes	Yes	V	Yes	Yes
South Carolina	Yes	Yes	Yes	Yes	Yes	Yes	Yes	Yes	Yes	Yes	FV	Yes	Yes
South Dakota	–	–	–	–	–	–	–	–	–	–	V	Yes	Yes
Tennessee	No	No	F	Yes	Yes	Yes	Yes	Yes	Yes	Yes	V	Yes	Yes
Texas	–	–	–	–	–	–	Yes	Yes	Yes	Yes	FV	Yes	Yes
Utah	–	–	–	–	–	–	Yes	Yes	Yes	Yes	V	Yes	Yes
Vermont	Yes	Yes	Yes	Yes	Yes	Yes	Yes	Yes	Yes	Yes	V	Yes	Yes
Virginia	No	No	Yes	Yes	Yes	Yes	Yes	Yes	Yes	Yes	V	Yes	Yes
Washington	–	–	–	–	–	–	–	Yes	Yes	Yes	V	Yes	Yes
West Virginia	–	–	–	–	–	–	–	–	Yes	Yes	V	Yes	Yes
Wisconsin	–	–	–	Yes	Yes	Yes	Yes	Yes	Yes	Yes	V	Yes	Yes
Wyoming	–	–	–	–	–	–	–	Yes	Yes	Yes	V	Yes	Yes

– State or territory did not exist, or census was not taken.
No Census was taken, but schedules were destroyed.
Yes Schedules available for all, or nearly all, counties.
F Fragments of general schedules only.
V Special schedules for Union veterans and their widows are available.
I Special schedules for Indian reservations only.

*Adapted from Bureau of the Census, *Twenty Censuses: Population and Housing Questions* (Washington: 1978).

1910 Census

Population schedules. The 1910 schedules are microfilmed on T624, 1,784 rolls. A listing of the rolls can be found in *1910 Federal Population Census: A Catalog of Microfilm Copies of the Schedules* (Washington: National Archives Trust Fund Board, 1982). They are arranged alphabetically by state or territory, thereunder by county, and thereunder by minor subdivision. States were divided into enumeration districts.

Each household is entered on a sheet showing the name of the township and city ward, if any. For households in urban areas, the street and number are supplied. For each person enumerated, the entry shows: name; relation to head of household; sex; color or race; age at last birthday; marital status; number of years of present marriage; number of children born (to the wife, widow, or divorcee); number of those children living; birthplace, and, if foreign-born, mother tongue; birthplaces of parents; year of immigration; whether naturalized or alien (foreign born males 21 years of age and over only); whether able to speak English; occupation; employed in what industry; whether out of work on April 15, 1910; number of weeks out of work during 1909; whether able to read (any language) and to write; whether attended school any time since September 1, 1909; whether house is owned or rented, a farm or a house, and whether it is mortgage-free; whether a survivor of Union or Confederate Army or Navy; and whether blind or deaf and dumb.

Indexes. There are soundex indexes for the following states: Alabama, Georgia, Louisiana, Mississippi, South Carolina, Tennessee, and Texas. There are miracode indexes for the following states: Arkansas, California, Florida, Illinois, Kansas, Kentucky, Michigan, Missouri, North Carolina, Ohio, Oklahoma, Pennsylvania, Virginia, and West Virginia. There are no indexes for the remaining twenty-nine states and territories.

Although the format of soundex and miracode indexes is different, the method for using them is basically the same.

1.2 Other Censuses

The organic act establishing a territory or state usually contained provision for taking an enumeration of the inhabitants. The records of these enumerations are especially helpful if there are gaps in the decennial federal census for a state at or near the year of a territorial or state census. For the locations of the schedules of such censuses taken as a result of state legislation, see *State Censuses: An Annotated Bibliography of Censuses of Population Taken After the Year 1790 by States and Territories of the United States* compiled by Henry J. Dubester (Washington: Library of Congress, Census Library Project, 1948). This volume has been reprinted by Burt Franklin, New York, 1969.

1.3 Special Schedules and Problems by State

The next section of this chapter provides information about census records arranged alphabetically by state. Table 6 shows which states' population schedules are available for each census year, and the pages that follow note special conditions peculiar to each state.

Alabama

Population schedules:

1830:	M19	Rolls 1–4
1840:	M704	Rolls 1–16
1850:	M432	Rolls 1–24
1860:	M653	Rolls 1–36
1870:	M593	Rolls 1–45
1880:	T9	Rolls 1–35; soundex index, T734, 74 rolls
1890:	M407	Roll 1 (fragments only)
1900:	T623	Rolls 1044; soundex index, T1030, 180 rolls
1910:	T624	Rolls 1–37; soundex index, T1259, 140 rolls

Remarks:

1820: The extant part of the Alabama territorial census for 1820 is in the Alabama Department of Archives and History, Montgomery. The National Archives has a copy as it was printed in the *Alabama Historical Quarterly* 6 (Fall 1944): 333–515.

1880: The original schedules (23 vols.) were transferred to the Alabama Department of Archives and History, Montgomery, AL 36130.

Alaska

Population schedules:

1900:	T623	Rolls 1828–32; soundex index, T1031, 15 rolls
1910:	T624	Rolls 1748–50; no index

Remarks:

The only available census before 1900 is the Special Census of Sitka, Alaska, taken by the War Department, printed in 1871 as 42nd Cong., 1st sess. H. Ex. Doc. 5, pp. 13–26.

Arizona

Population schedules:

1860:	M653	Roll 712
1870:	M593	Roll 46
1880:	T9	Rolls 36–37; soundex index, T735, 2 rolls
1900:	T623	Rolls 45–48; soundex index, T1032, 22 rolls
1910:	T624	Rolls 38–42; no index

Remarks:

1850, 1860. The schedules for 1850 and 1860 that relate to the present state of Arizona are included among the schedules for New Mexico. *Federal Census—Territory of New Mexico and Territory of Arizona* (89th Cong., 1st sess., S. Doc. 13, serial 12668-1) includes the 1860 census.

1864. The National Archives has photostats in two volumes and typed and mimeographed copies of the Arizona schedules of 1864. The schedules are arranged by judicial district and thereunder by minor subdivision. For each person in a household, an entry shows name, age, sex, and marital status; number of years and months of residence in Arizona; brief naturalization data if appropriate; place of residence of the family; occupation; and value of real and personal estate. *Federal Census—Territory of New Mexico and Territory of Arizona* (cited above) contains the 1864 special territorial census.

1866, 1867, 1869. Photostats of Arizona schedules of 1866, 1867, and 1869 are available in one volume. The schedules are arranged by county. For each person in a household, an entry shows name; place of residence; whether head of family; and whether under 10, 10 but under 21, or over 21. The following list identifies by census year the names of the counties for which schedules are available.

1866. Pahute, Mohave, Pima, Yuma, and Yavapai
1867. Mohave, Pima, and Yuma
1869. Yavapai

1870. *Federal Census—Territory of New Mexico and Territory of Arizona* (cited above) contains the 1870 census.

1880. Original schedules (1 vol.) were transferred to the National Society, Daughters of the American Revolution, Washington, DC 20006.

Arkansas

Population schedules:

1830:	M19	Roll 5
1840:	M704	Rolls 17–20
1850:	M432	Rolls 25–32
1860:	M653:	Rolls 37–54
1870:	M593	Rolls 47–67
1880:	T9	Rolls 38–60; soundex index, T736, 48 rolls
1900:	T623	Rolls 49–80; soundex index, T1033, 132 rolls
1910:	T624	Rolls 43–68; miracode index, T1260, 139 rolls

Remarks:

1860. The 1860 schedules for Little River County are missing.

1880. Original schedules (15 vols.) were transferred to the Arkansas History Commission, Little Rock, AR 72201.

California

Population schedules:

1850:	M432	Rolls 33–36
1860:	M653	Rolls 55–72
1870:	M593	Rolls 68–93
1880:	T9	Rolls 61–86; soundex index, T737,

		34 rolls
1900:	T623	Rolls 81–116; soundex index, T1034, 198 rolls
1910:	T624	Rolls 69–111; miracode index, T1261, 272 rolls

Remarks:

1850. The 1850 schedules for Contra Costa, San Francisco, and Santa Clara Counties are missing from the schedules at the National Archives.

1880. Original schedules (18 vols.) were transferred to the California State Archives, Sacramento, CA 95814.

Colorado

Population schedules:

1870:	M593	Rolls 94–95
1880:	T9	Rolls 87–93; soundex index, T738, 7 rolls
1900:	T623	Rolls 117–130; soundex index, T1035, 68 rolls
1910:	T624	Rolls 112–126; no index

Remarks:

1860. The 1860 schedules relating to the present state of Colorado are included in the 1860 schedules for Kansas.

1880. Original schedules (4 vols.) were transferred to the Colorado Division of State Archives and Public Records, Denver, CO 80203.

1885. Colorado was one of five states and territories to elect to take an 1885 census with federal assistance pursuant to an act of 1879 (20 Stat. 480). The unbound population and mortality schedules are in the National Archives and have been microfilmed on M158, 8 rolls. The schedules show the same type of information as the 1880 schedules, but in many cases, the initial letters of the given names of enumerated persons appear instead of the names.

Connecticut

Population schedules:

1790:	M637	Roll 1
1800:	M32	Rolls 1–3
1810:	M252	Rolls 1–3
1820:	M33	Rolls 1–3
1830:	M19	Rolls 6–11
1840:	M704	Rolls 21–32
1850:	M432	Rolls 37–51
1860:	M653	Rolls 73–93
1870:	M593	Rolls 96–117
1880:	T9	Rolls 94–110; soundex index, T739, 25 rolls
1900:	T623	Rolls 131–152; soundex index, T1036, 107 rolls
1910:	T624	Rolls 127–144; no index

Remarks:

1880. Original schedules (10 vols.) were transferred to the National Society, Daughters of the American Revolution, Washington, DC 20006.

Delaware

Population Schedules:

1800:	M32	Roll 4
1810:	M252	Roll 4
1820:	M33	Roll 4
1830:	M19	Rolls 12–13
1840:	M704	Rolls 33–34
1850:	M432	Rolls 52–55
1860:	M653	Rolls 95–100
1870:	M593	Rolls 119–122
1880:	T9	Rolls 116–120; soundex index, T741, 9 rolls
1900:	T623	Rolls 153–157; soundex index, T1037, 21 rolls
1910:	T624	Rolls 145–148; no index

Remarks:

1790. The missing 1790 census has been reconstructed from local real estate tax lists and published as *Reconstructed 1790 Census of Delaware*, NGS Genealogical Publication 10, by Leon de Valinger, Jr. (Washington: National Genealogical Society, 1954). Entries for each hundred of each county are arranged alphabetically.

1880. Original schedules (3 vols.) were transferred to the Bureau of Archives and Records, Hall of Records, Dover, DE 19901.

District of Columbia

Population schedules:

1800:	M32	Roll 5
1820:	M33	Roll 5
1830:	M19	Roll 14
1840:	M704	Roll 35
1850:	M432	Rolls 56–57
1860:	M653	Rolls 101–105
1870:	M593	Rolls 123–127
1880:	T9	Rolls 121–124; soundex index, T742, 9 rolls
1890:	M407	Roll 2
	M123	Roll 118, special census of veterans
1900:	T623	Rolls 158–164; soundex index, T1038, 42 rolls
1910:	T624	Rolls 149–155; no index

Remarks:

1790. Schedules that relate to the parts of Montgomery and Prince Georges Counties that now form the present District of Columbia are among the schedules of Maryland for 1790. Schedules for that part of Virginia that was formerly a part of the District of Columbia were enumerated as part of the schedules of Virginia; however, the 1790 census schedules for Virginia are not extant (but see page 37 for a substitute).

1800. Entries for the extant 1800 schedules have been alphabetized and printed in Artemas C. Harmon's, "U.S. Census of the District of Columbia in Maryland for the Year 1800," in *The National Genealogical Society Quarterly* 38 (Dec. 1950): 105–110, and 39 (March 1951): 16–19, and (June 1951): 56–59. They cover only the present District of Columbia, which is on the Maryland side of the Potomac River.

1820, 1830, and 1840. Schedules include Alexandria County, the part of the District of Columbia that was retroceded to Virginia in 1846. For the location of the ward boundaries of Washington City and Gerogetown for each of the decennial years 1820–70, see Laurence F. Schmeckebier's "Ward Boundaries of Washington and Georgetown," in *Records of the Columbia Historical Society*, (1955): 51–52 and 66–77, with maps. The National Archives has large-scale copies of these maps.

1880. Original schedules (16 vols.) were transferred to the Columbia Historical Society, 1307 New Hampshire Avenue, N.W., Washington, DC 20036.

Florida

Population schedules:

1830:	M19	Roll 15
1840:	M704	Roll 36
1850:	M432	Rolls 58–60
1860:	M653	Rolls 106–110
1870:	M593	Rolls 128–133
1880:	T9	Rolls 125–132; soundex index, T743, 16 rolls
1900:	T623	Rolls 165–177; soundex index, T1039, 59 rolls
1910:	T624	Rolls 156–169; miracode index, T1262, 84 rolls

Remarks:

1825. The National Archives has photostatic copies of two pages of the territorial census for Leon County, 1825. The originals are in the Florida State Library, Tallahassee.

1880. Original schedules (5 vols.) were transferred to the Florida State University Library, Tallahassee FL 32306.

1885. Florida was one of five states and territories to elect to take an 1885 census with federal assistance pursuant to an act of 1879 (20 Stat. 480). The unbound population and mortality schedules are in the National Archives and have been microfilmed on M845, 13 rolls. The schedules show the same type of information as the 1880 schedules, but in many cases, the initial letters of the given names of enumerated persons appear instead of the names.

Georgia

Population schedules:

1820:	M33	Rolls 6–10
1830:	M19	Rolls 16–21
1840:	M704	Rolls 37–53
1850:	M432	Rolls 61–96
1860:	M653	Rolls 111–153
1870:	M593	Rolls 134–184
1880:	T9	Rolls 133–172; soundex index, T744, 86 rolls
1900:	T623	Rolls 178–230; soundex index, T1040, 214 rolls
1910:	T624	Rolls 170–220; soundex index, T1263, 174 rolls

Remarks:

1790–1820. Tax lists for various years for a few of the counties have been published in *Some Early Tax Digests of Georgia*, edited by Ruth Blair, 2 vols. (Atlanta: Georgia Department of Archives and History, 1926). This publication is used as a substitute for missing 1790, 1800, 1810, and 1820 schedules. Also available is *Substitute for Georgia's Lost 1790 Census* (Albany, Ga: Delwyn Associates, 1975). Wills, deeds, tax digests, court minutes, voter lists, and newspapers were searched to compile this list.

1800. The only schedules known to exist are for Oglethorpe County. These have been published in *1800 Census of Oglethorpe County, Georgia* by Mary B. Warren (Athens, Ga., 1965).

1820. The 1820 schedules for Franklin, Rabun, and Twiggs Counties are missing.

1880. Original schedules (26 vols.) were transferred to the Georgia Department of Archives and History, Atlanta, GA 30334.

Hawaii

Population schedules:

1900:	T623	Rolls 1833–1837; soundex index, T1041, 30 rolls
1910:	T624	Rolls 1751–1755; no index

Remarks:

1900. In this first census taken in Hawaii, schedules for some of the enumeration districts on Hawaii and Kauai islands are missing.

Idaho

Population schedules:

1870:	M593	Roll 185
1880:	T9	Roll 173; soundex index, T745, 2 rolls
1900:	T623	Rolls 231–234; soundex index, T1042, 19 rolls
1910:	T624	Rolls 221–228; no index

Remarks:

1880. The National Archives has photostats of the two pages of the 1880 schedules for the Seventh or Lava District of Alturas County that were not sent to Washington and were therefore not included on the microfilm made by the Bureau of the Census. All the original 1880 schedules for Idaho (1 vol.) are at the Idaho State Historical Society, Boise, ID 83706.

Illinois

Population schedules:

1820:	M33	Rolls 11–12
1830:	M19	Rolls 22–25
1840:	M704	Rolls 54–73
1850:	M432	Rolls 97–134
1860:	M653	Rolls 154–241
1870:	M593	Rolls 186–295
1880:	T9	Rolls 174–262; soundex index, T746, 143 rolls
1890:	M407	Roll 3
1900:	T623	Rolls 235–356; soundex index, T1043, 479 rolls
1910:	T624	Rolls 229–337; miracode index, T1264, 491 rolls

Remarks:

1810. Some of the 1810 schedules together with 1818 schedules for Illinois territory, were transcribed and published in *Illinois Census Returns, 1810, 1818, Collections of the Illinois State Historical Library*, vol. 24, edited by Margaret Cross Norton (Springfield, Ill. 1935). This volume has been reprinted by the Genealogical Publishing Co., Baltimore, 1969.

1820. The 1820 state schedules, which differ slightly from the 1820 federal schedules, have been published in *Illinois Census Returns, 1820, Collections of the Illinois State History Library*, vol. 26, edited by Margaret Cross Norton

(Springfield, Ill., 1934). This volume has been reprinted by the Genealogical Publishing Co., Baltimore, 1969.

1850. The 1850 schedules for Edgar County show the county of birth of each person enumerated. See O. Kenneth Baker's "Virginia (and West Virginia) Origins of Settlers in Edgar Co., Illinois, as Revealed by the 1850 Census," *National Genealogical Society Quarterly* 36 (Sept. 1948): 73–76, and his "Migration From Virginia to Edgar County, Illinois, as Revealed by the 1850 Census Schedules for 200 Families," *National Genealogical Society Quarterly* 38 (Mar. 1950): 1–5, (June 1950): 41–46.

1880. The original schedules (59 vols.) were transferred to the Illinios State Archives, Springfield, IL 62756.

Indiana

Population schedules:

1820:	M33	Rolls 13–15
1830:	M19	Rolls 26–32
1840:	M704	Rolls 74–100
1850:	M432	Rolls 135–181
1860:	M653	Rolls 242–309
1870:	M593	Rolls 296–373
1880:	T9	Rolls 263–324; soundex index, T747, 98 rolls
1900:	T623	Rolls 357–414; soundex index, T1044, 252 rolls
1910:	T624	Rolls 338–389; no index

Remarks:

1880. The original schedules (38 vols.) were transferred to the Indiana State Library, Indianapolis, IN 46204.

Iowa

Population schedules:

1840:	M704	Rolls 101–102
1850:	M432	Rolls 182–189
1860:	M653	Rolls 310–345
1870:	M593	Rolls 374–427
1880:	T9	Rolls 325–371; soundex index, T748, 78 rolls
1900:	T623	Rolls 415–468; soundex index, T1045, 215 rolls
1910:	T624	Rolls 390–430; no index

Remarks:

1836. The National Archives has an index published as *Iowa 1836 Territorial Census*, by Ronald V. Jackson (Provo: Accelerated Indexing Systems, 1973).

1844, 1846. The National Archives has an electrostatic copy of the Iowa Territorial Census for Keokuk County, 1844 and for Louisa, Polk, and Wapello Counties, 1846 (all bound in one volume).

1850–80. The Archives Branch, FARC Kansas City, has nonpopulation schedules on microfilm A1156, 61 rolls. Original 1880 schedules (33 vols.) were transferred to the National Society, Daughters of the American Revolution, Washington, DC 20006.

Kansas

Population schedules:

1860:	M653	Rolls 346–352
1870:	M593	Rolls 428–443
1880:	T9	Rolls 372–400; soundex index, T749, 51 rolls
1900:	T623	Rolls 469–505; soundex index, T1046, 148 rolls
1910:	T624	Rolls 431–461; miracode index, T1265, 145 rolls

Remarks:

1855, 1856, 1857, 1858, 1859. Schedules of these Kansas territorial censuses are in the Kansas State Historical Society, Topeka. The National Archives has microfilm copies on GR28, 3 rolls, and the Archives Branch, FARC Kansas City, has microfilm copies on XC-1, XC-2, and XC-3, 1 roll each.

1860. The Archives Branch, FARC Kansas City, has a microfilm copy of the schedules of the 1860 Kansas territorial census on XC-4, 5 rolls.

1865. The Archives Branch, FARC Kansas City, has a microfilm copy of the 1865 Kansas state census on XC-5, 8 rolls.

1875. The Archives Branch, FARC Kansas City, has a microfilm copy of the 1875 Kansas state census on XC-6, 20 rolls.

1880. Original schedules (21 vols.) were transferred to the Kansas Genealogical Society, Dodge City, KA 67801.

Kentucky

Population schedules:

1810:	M252	Rolls 5–9
1820:	M33	Rolls 16–29
1830:	M19	Rolls 33–42
1840:	M704	Rolls 103–126
1850:	M432	Rolls 190–228
1860	M653	Rolls 353–406
1870:	M593	Rolls 444–504
1880:	T9	Rolls 401–446; soundex index, T750, 83 rolls
1890:	M123	Rolls 1–3, special census of veterans
1900:	T623	Rolls 506–555; soundex index, T1047, 200 rolls
1910:	T624	Rolls 462–506; miracode index, T1266, 194 rolls

Remarks:

1790, 1800. Schedules for 1790 and 1800 have been reconstructed from local tax returns. Entries have been alphabetized and printed in two separate volumes: *"First Census" of Kentucky, 1790*, by Charles Brunk Heinemann and Gaius Marcus Brumbaugh (Washington: G. M. Brumbaugh, 1940), and *"Second Census" of Kentucky, 1800*, compiled by Garrett Glenn Clift (Frankfort, 1954). Both volumes have been reprinted by the Genealogical Publishing Co. of Baltimore, the first in 1965, and the second in 1966.

1880. Original schedules (30 vols.) were transferred to the Kentucky Department of Library and Archives, Frankfort, KY 40601.

Louisiana

Population schedules:

1810:	M252	Roll 10
1820:	M33	Rolls 30–32
1830:	M19	Rolls 43–45
1840:	M704	Rolls 127–135

1850: M432 Rolls 229–247
1860: M653 Rolls 407–431
1870: M593 Rolls 505–535
1880: T9 Rolls 447–474; soundex index, T751, 55 rolls
1890: M123 Rolls 4–5, special census of veterans
1900: T623 Rolls 556–586; soundex index, T1048, 146 rolls
1910: T624 Rolls 507–535; soundex index, T1267, 132 rolls

Remarks:

1880. Original population schedules (17 vols.) were transferred to Louisiana State University, Baton Rouge, LA 70803.

Maine

Population schedules:

1790: M637 Roll 2
1800: M32 Rolls 6–8
1810: M252 Rolls 11–12
1820: M33 Rolls 33–39
1830: M19 Rolls 46–52
1840: M704 Rolls 136–155
1850: M432 Rolls 248–276
1860: M653 Rolls 432–455
1870: M593 Rolls 536–565
1880: T9 Rolls 475–492; soundex index, T752, 29 rolls
1890: M123 Rolls 6–7, special census of veterans
1900: T623 Rolls 587–603; soundex index, T1049, 80 rolls
1910: T624 Rolls 536–548; no index

Remarks:

1800. Some of the 1800 schedules for York County are missing.

1880. Original population schedules (13 vols.) were transferred to the Division of Vital Statistics, Augusta, ME 04333.

Maryland

Population schedules:

1790: M637 Roll 3
1800: M32 Rolls 9–12
1810: M252 Rolls 13–16
1820: M33 Rolls 40–46
1830: M19 Rolls 53–58
1840: M704 Rolls 156–172
1850: M432 Rolls 277–302
1860: M653 Rolls 456–485
1870: M593 Rolls 566–599
1880: T9 Rolls 493–518; soundex index, T753, 47 rolls
1890: M123 Rolls 8–10, special census of veterans
1900: T623 Rolls 604–630; soundex index, T1050, 127 rolls
1910: T624 Rolls 549–570; no index

Remarks:

1830. The 1830 schedules for Montgomery, Prince Georges, St. Marys, Queen Anne's, and Somerset Counties are missing.

1880. Original schedules (19 vols.) were transferred to the Maryland State Law Library, Annapolis, MD 21402.

Massachusetts

Population schedules:

1790: M637 Roll 4
1800: M32 Rolls 13–19
1810: M252 Rolls 17–22
1820: M33 Rolls 47–55
1830: M19 Rolls 59–68
1840: M704 Rolls 173–202
1850: M432 Rolls 303–345
1860: M653 Rolls 486–534
1870: M593 Rolls 600–659
1880: T9 Rolls 519–568; soundex index, T754, 70 rolls
1890: M123 Rolls 11–16, special census of veterans
1900: T623 Rolls 631–697; soundex index, T1051, 314 rolls
1910: T624 Rolls 571–633; no index

Remarks:

1880. Original population schedules were transferred to the Archives of the Commonwealth, State House, Boston, MA 02133.

Michigan

Population schedules:

1820: M33 Roll 56
1830: M19 Roll 69
1840: M704 Rolls 203–212
1850: M432 Rolls 346–366
1860: M653 Rolls 535–566
1870: M593 Rolls 660–715
1880: T9 Rolls 569–614; soundex index, T755, 73 rolls
1890: M123 Rolls 17–21, special census of veterans
1900: T623 Rolls 698–755; soundex index, T1052, 257 rolls
1910: T624 Rolls 634–688, miracode index, T1268, 253 rolls

Remarks:

1880. Original population schedules (31 vols.) were transferred to the Michigan Historical Division, Michigan Department of State, Lansing, MI 48918.

Minnesota

Population schedules:

1850: M432 Roll 367
1860: M653 Rolls 567–576
1870: M593 Rolls 717–719
T132 Rolls 1–13
1880: T9 Rolls 615–638; soundex index, T756, 37 rolls
1890: M407 Roll 3
M123 Rolls 22–25, special census of veterans
1900: T623 Rolls 756–798; soundex index, T1053, 180 rolls
1910: T624 Rolls 689–730; no index

Remarks:

1849. The National Archives has a copy of the 1849 census of the Territory of Minnesota, published as Appendix

D of the *Journal of the House of Representatives, First Session of the Legislative Assembly of the Territory of Minnesota* (St. Paul, 1850).

1857. The 1857 schedules for Minnesota Territory were created pursuant to Section 4 of an act of 1857 (11 Stat. 167) to enable Minnesota Territory to become a state. The schedules are on printed forms in five volumes. They are arranged alphabetically by county, and thereunder by minor subdivision. The enumeration was taken as of 21 September 1857. For each inhabitant of a household, an entry shows name; age; sex; color; state, territory, or country of birth; if a voter, whether native or naturalized; and occupation.

1870. A large part of the 1870 schedules formerly in the possession of the Bureau of the Census was destroyed by fire in 1921; others that were damaged were destroyed by authorization of Congress in 1933. The destroyed schedules pertain to the counties with names running alphabetically from Aitkin to Sibley. National Archives Microfilm Publication T132, 13 rolls, is a copy of the duplicate set of the 1870 schedules in the custody of the Minnesota Historical Society, St. Paul.

1880. Original schedules were transferred to the Minnesota Historical Society, St. Paul, MN 55101.

Mississippi

Population schedules:

1820:	M33	Rolls 57–58
1830:	M19	Rolls 70–71
1840:	M704	Rolls 213–219
1850:	M432	Rolls 368–390
1860:	M653	Rolls 577–604
1870:	M593	Rolls 720–754
1880:	T9	Rolls 639–670; soundex index, T757, 69 rolls
1890:	M123	Roll 26, special census of veterans
1900:	T623	Rolls 799–835; soundex index, T1054, 155 rolls
1910:	T624	Rolls 731–765; soundex index, T1269, 118 rolls

Remarks:

1816. The Mississippi Department of Archives and History, Jackson, has the territorial schedules for 1816 and some other years. The National Archives has a copy of the 1816 schedules as published in *Early Inhabitants of the Natchez District*, by Norman E. Gillis (Baton Rouge, 1963). Persons residing outside the Natchez District in 1816 are listed in an appendix.

1830. The 1830 schedules for Pike County are missing.

1860. The 1860 schedules for free and slave inhabitants for Hancock and Washington Counties and the 1860 schedules for free inhabitants for Tallahatchie County are missing.

1880. Original schedules (23 vols.) were transferred to the National Society, Daughters of the American Revolution, Washington, DC 20006.

Missouri

Population schedules:

1830:	M19	Rolls 72–73
1840:	M704	Rolls 220–223
1850:	M432	Rolls 391–424
1860:	M653	Rolls 605–664
1870:	M593	Rolls 755–826
1880:	T9	Rolls 671–741; soundex index, T758, 114 rolls
1890:	M123	Rolls 27–34, special census of veterans
1900:	T623	Rolls 836–908; soundex index, T1055, 300 rolls
1910:	T624	Rolls 766–828; miracode index, T1270, 285 rolls

Remarks:

1880. Original population schedules (45 vols.) were transferred to the National Society, Daughters of the American Revolution, Washington, DC 20006.

Montana

Population schedules:

1870:	M593	Roll 827
1880:	T9	Roll 742; soundex index, T759, 2 rolls
1890:	M123	Roll 35, special census of veterans
1900:	T623	Rolls 909–915; soundex index, T1056, 40 rolls
1910:	T624	Rolls 829–837; no index

Remarks:

1860. The 1860 schedules that relate to the eastern part of the present state of Montana are included in the volume for the unorganized part of Nebraska Territory; those for the western part are included in the schedules of Washington Territory.

1880. Original schedules (1 vol.) were transferred to the Montana Historical Society, Helena, MT 59601.

Nebraska

Population schedules:

1860:	M653	Roll 665
1870:	M593	rolls 828–833
1880:	T9	Rolls 743–757; soundex index, T760, 22 rolls
1890:	M123	Rolls 36–38, special census of veterans
1900:	T623	Rolls 916–942; soundex index, T1057, 107 rolls
1910:	T624	Rolls 838–857; no index

Remarks:

1854, 1855, 1856. These territorial censuses were published as *1854–1856 Nebraska State Census*, by Evelyn M. Cox (Ellensburg, Wash., 1973).

1880. Original schedules (10 vols.) were transferred to the National Society, Daughters of the American Revolution, Washington, DC 20006. The Archives Branch, FARC Kansas City, has microfilm copies of the 1880 nonpopulation schedules for Nebraska on RA-1, 16 rolls.

1885. Nebraska was one of five states and territories to elect to take an 1885 census with federal assitance pursuant to an act of 1879 (20 Stat. 480). The unbound population and mortality schedules are in the National Archives and have been microfilmed on M352, 56 rolls. The schedules show the same type of information as the 1880 schedules, but in many cases, the initial letters of the given names of enumerated persons appear instead of the names.

Nevada

Population schedules:

1870:	M593	Rolls 834–835
1880:	T9	Rolls 758–759; soundex index, T761, 3 rolls
1890:	M123	Roll 39, special census of veterans
1900:	T623	Roll 943; soundex index, T1058, 7 rolls
1910:	T624	Rolls 858–859; no index

Remarks:

1860. The 1860 schedules that relate to the present state of Nevada are included among the schedules for Utah.

1880. Original schedules (2 vols.) were transferred to the Nevada State Museum, Carson City, NV 89702.

New Hampshire

Population schedules:

1790:	M637	Roll 5
1800:	M32	Roll 20
1810:	M252	Rolls 23–25
1820:	M33	Rolls 59–61
1830:	M19	Rolls 74–78
1840:	M704	Rolls 234–246
1850:	M432	Rolls 425–441
1860:	M653	Rolls 666–681
1870:	M593	Rolls 836–850
1880:	T9	Rolls 760–769; soundex index, T762, 13 rolls
1890:	M123	Roll 40, special census of veterans
1900:	T623	Rolls 944–952; soundex index, T1059, 52 rolls
1910:	T624	Rolls 860–866; no index

Remarks:

1800. Some of the 1800 schedules for Rockingham and Strafford Counties are missing.

1820. The 1820 schedules for Grafton County are missing.

1880. Original schedules (3 vols.) were transferred to the National Society, Daughters of the American Revolution, Washington, DC 20006.

New Jersey

Population schedules:

1830:	M19	Rolls 79–83
1840:	M704	Rolls 247–262
1850:	M432	Rolls 442–466
1860:	M653	Rolls 682–711
1870:	M593	Rolls 851–892
1880:	T9	Rolls 770–801; soundex index, T763, 49 rolls
1890:	M123	Rolls 41–43, special census of veterans
1900:	T623	Rolls 953–998; soundex index, T1060, 203 Rolls
1910:	T624	Rolls 867–912; no index

Remarks:

1790. Substitutes for the missing 1790 census of New Jersey are: *New Jersey in 1793: An Abstract and Index to the 1793 Militia Census of the State of New Jersey*, By James S. Norton (Salt Lake City; Institute of Family Research, 1973), and *Revolutionary Census of New Jersey*, by Kenn Stryker-Rodda (New Orleans: Polyanthos, 1972), which covers 1773–84.

1800–1820. No population schedules for New Jersey in these years have survived.

1880. Original schedules (22 vols.) were transferred to the Library, Rutgers University, New Brunswick, NJ 08901.

New Mexico

Population schedules:

1850:	M432	Rolls 467–470
1860:	M653	Rolls 712–716
1870:	M593	Rolls 893–897
1880:	T9	Rolls 802–804; soundex index, T764, 6 rolls
1890:	M123	Roll 44, special census of veterans
1900:	T623	Rolls 999–1003; soundex index, T1061, 23 rolls
1910:	T624	Rolls 913–919; no index

Remarks:

1790, 1823, 1845. *Spanish and Mexican Colonial Censuses of New Mexico, 1790, 1823, 1845,* by Virginia L. Olmsted (Albuquerque, 1975) is the best record of New Mexico's early censuses.

1880. Original schedules (3 vols.) were transferred to the National Society, Daughters of the American Revolution, Washington, DC 20006.

1885. New Mexico was one of five states and territories to elect to take an 1885 census with federal assistance pursuant to an act of 1879 (20 Stat. 480). The unbound population and mortality schedules are in the National Archives and have been microfilmed on M846, 6 rolls. The schedules show the same type of information as the 1880 schedules, but in many cases, the initial letters of the given names of enumerated persons appear instead of the names.

New York

Population schedules:

1790:	M637	Roll 6
1800:	M32	Rolls 21–28
1810:	M252	Rolls 26–37
1820:	M33	Rolls 62–79
1830:	M19	Rolls 84–117
1840:	M704	Rolls 263–353
1850:	M432	Rolls 471–518
1860:	M653	Rolls 717–885
1870:	M593	Rolls 898–1120
1880:	T9	Rolls 805–949; soundex index, T765, 187 rolls
1890:	M123	Rolls 45–57, special census of veterans
1900:	T623	Rolls 1004–1179; soundex index, T1062, 768 rolls
1910:	T624	Rolls 920–1094; no index

Remarks:

Information about state schedules, 1825–1925, for New York is available as *An Inventory of New York State and Federal Census Records*, revised edition, compiled by Edna L. Jacobson (Albany: New York State Library, 1956).

1870. Two separate enumerations were taken for New York City in 1870. Both have been filmed on M593, the first enumeration on rolls 975–1013 and the second enumeration on rolls 1014–1053.

1880. Original schedules (105 vols.) were transferred to the New York State Library, Albany, NY 12234.

North Carolina

Population schedules:

1790:	M637	Roll 7
1800:	M32	Rolls 29–34
1810:	M252	Rolls 38–43
1820:	M33	Rolls 80–85
1830:	M19	Rolls 118–125
1840:	M704	Rolls 354–374
1850:	M432	Rolls 619–656
1860:	M653	Rolls 886–927
1870:	M593	Rolls 1121–1166
1880:	T9	Rolls 950–988; soundex index, T766, 79 rolls
1890:	M407	Roll 3
	M123	Roll 58, special census of veterans
1900:	T623	Rolls 1180–1225; soundex index, T1063, 168 rolls
1910:	T624	Rolls 1095–1137; miracode index, T1271, 178 rolls

Remarks:

1790. The 1790 schedules for Caswell, Granville, and Orange Counties are not extant. As a substitute in the published 1790 index, local tax records were used.

1810. The 1810 schedules for Craven, Greene, New Hanover, and Wake Counties are missing.

1820. The 1820 schedules for Currituck, Franklin, Martin, Montgomery, Randolph, and Wake Counties are missing.

1880. Original schedules (25 vols.) were transferred to the North Carolina State Archives, Raleigh, NC 27611.

North Dakota

Population schedules:

1860:	M653	Roll 94
1870:	M593	Roll 118
1880:	T9	Rolls 111–115; soundex index, T740, 6 rolls
1890:	M123	Roll 59, special census of veterans
1900:	T623	Rolls 1226–1234; soundex index, T1064, 36 rolls
1910:	T624	Rolls 1138–1149; no index

Remarks:

1880. Some original schedules were transferred to the State Historical Society of North Dakota, Bismarck, ND 58501.

1885. Dakota was one of five states and territories to elect to take an 1885 census with federal assistance pursuant to an act of 1879 (20 Stat. 480). The schedules show the same type of information as the 1880 schedules, but in many cases, the initial letters of the given names of enumerated persons appear instead of the names, The schedules are in depositories in North and South Dakota. Those for the present state of North Dakota have been reproduced in *Collections of the State Historical Society of North Dakota* 4 (1913): 338–448; the names of enumerated persons are in a general index to the volume. There are special veterans' schedules for North and South Dakota which have been microfilmed on GR27, roll 5.

1900. Schedules for the first time were designated "North Dakota" and "South Dakota," rather than "Dakota."

Ohio

Population schedules:

1820:	M33	Rolls 86–95
1830:	M19	Rolls 126–142
1840:	M704	Rolls 375–434
1850:	M432	Rolls 657–741
1860:	M653	Rolls 928–1054
1870:	M593	Rolls 1167–1284
1880:	T9	Rolls 989–1079; soundex index, T1065, T767, 143 rolls
1890:	M407	Roll 3
	M123	Rolls 60–75, special census of veterans
1900:	T623	Rolls 1235–1334; soundex index, T1065, 397 rolls
1910:	T624	Rolls 1150–1241; miracode index, T1272, 418 rolls

Remarks:

1800. The National Archives has a microfilm copy of the 1800 and 1803 censuses for Washington County on GR4, 1 roll.

1810. The National Archives has a microfilm copy of the 1810 census for Washington County on GR3, 1 roll.

1880. Original schedules (68 vols.) were transferred to the Ohio State Museum, Columbus, OH 43211.

Oklahoma

Population schedules:

1890:	M123	Roll 76, special census of veterans
1900:	T623	Rolls 1335–1344; soundex index, T1066, 42 rolls
1910:	T624	Rolls 1242–1277; miracode index, T1273, 143 rolls

Remarks:

1860. The 1860 schedules that relate to the present state of Oklahoma are included with schedules for Arkansas. They appear on roll 52 of M653. The persons enumerated were living on Indian lands.

1890. The National Archives has a microfilm copy of the 1890 territorial census schedules for Logan, Oklahoma, Cleveland, Canadian, Kingfisher, Payne, and Beaver Counties on GR24, 1 roll.

1900. The 1900 schedules are the first to list Oklahoma.

1907. For Seminole County, special agents were employed to take a census as of 1 July 1907. The schedules contain name, age, sex, color, and relationship to head of the family for each person enumerated.

Oregon

Population schedules:

1850:	M432	Roll 742
1860:	M653	Rolls 1055–1056
1870:	M593	Rolls 1285–1288
1880:	T9	Rolls 1080–1084; soundex index, T768, 8 rolls
1890	M123	Roll 77, special census of veterans
1900:	T623	Rolls 1345–1353; soundex index, T1067, 54 rolls
1910:	T624	Rolls 1278–1291; no index

Remarks:

1880. Original population schedules (4 vols.) were transferred to the Oregon State Library, Salem, OR 97310.

Pennsylvania

Population schedules:

1790:	M637	Rolls 8–9
1800:	M32	Rolls 35–44
1810:	M252	Rolls 44–57
1820:	M33	Rolls 96–114
1830:	M19	Rolls 143–166
1840:	M704	Rolls 435–503
1850:	M432	Rolls 743–840
1860:	M653	Rolls 1057–1201
1870:	M593	Rolls 1289–1470
1880:	T9	Rolls 1085–1208; soundex index T769, 168 rolls
1890:	M123	Rolls 78–91, special census of veterans
1900:	T623	Rolls 1354–1503; soundex index, T1068, 612 rolls
1910:	T624	Rolls 1292–1435; miracode index, T1274, 688 rolls

Remarks:

1880. Original population schedules (92 vols.) are in the National Archives.

Puerto Rico

Population schedules:

1910	T624	Rolls 1756–1783; no index

Remarks:

1899. A census was taken in this year, but the schedules were destroyed.

Rhode Island

Population schedules:

1790:	M637	Roll 10
1800:	M32	Rolls 45–46
1810:	M252	Rolls 58–59
1820:	M33	Rolls 115–117
1830:	M19	Rolls 167–168
1840:	M704	Rolls 504–506
1850:	M432	Rolls 841–847
1860:	M653	Rolls 1202–1211
1870:	M593	Rolls 1471–1480
1880:	T9	Rolls 1209–1216; soundex index, T770, 11 rolls
1890	M123	Roll 92, special census of veterans
1900:	T623	Rolls 1504–1513; soundex index, T1069, 49 rolls
1910:	T624	Rolls 1436–1445; no index

Remarks:

1880. Original schedules (6 vols.) were transferred to the National Society, Daughters of the American Revolution, Washington, DC 20006. The Rhode Island Historical Society, 52 Power Street, Providence, RI 12903, has a duplicate manuscript copy.

South Carolina

Population schedules:

1790:	M637	Roll 11
1800:	M32	Rolls 47–50
1810:	M252	Rolls 60–62
1820:	M33	Rolls 118–121
1830:	M19	Rolls 169–173
1840:	M704	Rolls 507–516
1850:	M432	Rolls 848–868
1860:	M653	Rolls 1212–1238
1870:	M593	Rolls 1481–1512
1880:	T9	Rolls 1217–1243; soundex index, T771, 56 rolls
1890:	M123	Roll 93, special census of veterans
1900:	T623	Rolls 1514–1545; soundex index, T1070, 124 rolls
1910:	T624	Rolls 1446–1474; soundex index, T1275, 93 rolls

Remarks:

1820–50. The schedules for Clarendon County for 1820, 1830, 1840, and 1850 are missing.

1880. Original schedules (23 vols.) were transferred to the South Carolina Department of Archives and History, Columbia, SC 29211.

South Dakota

Population schedules:

1860:	M653	Roll 94
1870:	M593	Roll 118
1880:	T9	Rolls 111–115; soundex index, T740, 6 rolls
1890:	M407	Roll 3
	M123	Roll 94, special census of veterans
1900:	T623	Rolls 1546–1556; soundex index, T1071, 44 rolls
1910:	T624	Rolls 1475–1489; no index

Remarks:

1880. Original schedules were transferred to the South Dakota Historical Society, Pierre, SD 57501.

1885. Dakota was one of five states and territories to elect to take an 1885 census with federal assistance pursuant to an act of 1879 (20 Stat. 480). The schedules show the same type of information as the 1880 schedules, but in many cases, the initial letters of the given names of enumerated persons appear instead of the names. The schedules are in depositories in North and South Dakota, although the National Archives has microfilm copies of schedules for present-day South Dakota on GR27, rolls 1–3. Also on GR27 are special veterans' schedules for North and South Dakota, roll 5.

1895. Some schedules of an 1895 census are microfilmed on rolls 4 and 5 of GR27, obtained from the South Dakota State Historical Society. Included are age, sex, and nationality.

Tennessee

Population schedules:

1810:	M252	Roll 63
1820:	M33	Rolls 122–125
1830:	M19	Rolls 174–182
1840:	M704	Rolls 517–537
1850:	M432	Rolls 869–907
1860:	M653	Rolls 1239–1286

1870:	M593	Rolls 1513–1572
1880:	T9	Rolls 1244–1287; soundex index, T772, 86 rolls
1890	M123	Rolls 95–98, special census of veterans
1900:	T623	Rolls 1557–1606; soundex index, T1072, 188 rolls
1910:	T624	Rolls 1490–1526; soundex index, T1276, 142 rolls

Remarks:

1800. Some of the 1800 schedules have been reconstructed from local tax records. See *Early East Tennessee Tax Payers*, compiled by Pollyanna Creekmore (Easley, S.C.: Southern Historical Press, 1980), which is a reprint of material originally published by the East Tennessee Historical Society.

1810. The National Archives has the 1810 schedules for Rutherford County. The 1810 schedules for Grainger County have been transcribed and published in *Grainger County, Tennessee Federal Census of 1810, Population Schedule (Third Census) and County Tax Lists for 1810*, edited by Pollyanna Creekmore (Knoxville: Lawson McGhee, 1956).

1820. The National Archives has the 1820 schedules for twenty-six of the forty-eight counties.

1880. Original schedules (35 vols.) were transferred to the Tennessee State Library and Archives, Nashville, TN 37219.

Texas

Population Schedules:

1850:	M432	Rolls 908–918
1860:	M653	Rolls 1287–1312
1870:	M593	Rolls 1573–1609
1880:	T9	Rolls 1288–1334; soundex index, T773, 77 rolls
1890:	M407	Roll 3
	M123	Rolls 99–102, special census of veterans
1900:	T623	Rolls 1607–1681; soundex index, T1073, 286 rolls
1910:	T624	Rolls 1527–1601; soundex index, T1277, 262 rolls

Remarks:

1829–36. The Texas State Archives, Austin, has extant Texas census schedules, 1829–36. These were published as *The First Census of Texas, 1829–1836*, NGS Special Publication 22, by Marion Day Mullins (Washington: National Genealogical Society, 1976).

1880. Original schedules (34 vols.) were transferred to the Texas State Library, Austin, TX 78711.

Utah

Population schedules:

1850:	M432	Roll 919
1860:	M653	Rolls 1313–1314
1870:	M593	Rolls 1610–1613
1880:	T9	Rolls 1336–1339; soundex index, T774, 7 rolls
1890	M123	Roll 103, special census of veterans
1900:	T623	Rolls 1682–1688; soundex index, T1074, 29 rolls
1910:	T624	Rolls 1602–1611; no index

Remarks:

1880. Original schedules (3 vols.) were transferred to the Utah State Archives, Salt Lake City, UT 84114.

Vermont

Population schedules:

1790:	M637	Roll 12
1800:	M32	Rolls 51–52
1810:	M252	Rolls 64–65
1820:	M33	Rolls 126–128
1830:	M19	Rolls 183–188
1840:	M704	Rolls 538–548
1850:	M432	Rolls 920–931
1860:	M653	Rolls 1315–1329
1870:	M593	Rolls 1614–1629
1880:	T9	Rolls 1340–1350; soundex index, T775, 15 rolls
1890	M123	Roll 105, special census of veterans
1900:	T623	Rolls 1689–1696; soundex index, T1075, 41 rolls
1910:	T624	Rolls 1612–1618; no index

Remarks:

1800. The 1800 schedules have been printed and indexed in *Heads of Families at the Second Census of the United States Taken in the Year 1800: Vermont* (Montpelier: Vermont Historical Society, 1938). The volume has been reprinted by the Genealogical Publishing Co., Baltimore, 1972.

1880. Original schedules are held by the Law and Documents Unit of the Vermont Department of Libraries, Montpelier, VT 05602.

Virginia

Population schedules

1810:	M252	Rolls 66–71
1820:	M33	Rolls 129–142
1830:	M19	Rolls 189–201
1840:	M704	Rolls 549–579
1850:	M432	Rolls 932–993
1860:	M653	Rolls 1330–1397
1870:	M593	Rolls 1630–1682
1880:	T9	Rolls 1351–1395; soundex index, T776, 82 rolls
1890	M1231	Rolls 106–107, special census of veterans
1900:	T623	Rolls 1697–1740; soundex index, T1076, 174 rolls
1910:	T624	Rolls 1619–1652; miracode index, T1278, 183 rolls

Remarks:

1790. The 1790 schedules have been reconstructed and published in two volumes that supplement each other: *Heads of Families at the First Census of the United States Taken in the Year 1790: Records of the State Enumerations, 1782 to 1785, Virginia* (Washington: Bureau of the Census, 1908), and Augusta B. Fothergill and John Mark Naugle, *Virginia Tax Payers, 1782–87, Other Than Those Published by the United States Census Bureau* (Richmond, 1940). The first volume has been reprinted by the Reprint Co., Spartanburg, S.C., 1961 and by The Genealogical Publishing Co., Baltimore, 1966 and 1970. The Fothergill and Naugle volume was reprinted by the Genealogical Publishing Co., in 1966.

1810. The 1810 schedules for the following counties are missing: Grayson, Greenbrier, Halifax, Hardy, Henry, James City, King William, Louisa, Mecklenburg, Nansemond, Northampton, Orange, Patrick, Pittsylvania, Russell, and Tazewell. T1019 reproduces a card index for 1810 census schedules for Virginia.

1820, 1830, 1840. Schedules for Alexandria County are included with schedules for the District of Columbia.

1880. Original schedules (32 vols.) were transferred to the Virginia State Library, Richmond, VA 23219.

Washington

Population schedules:

1860:	M653	Roll 1398
1870:	M593	Roll 1683
1880:	T9	Rolls 1396–1398; soundex index, T777, 4 rolls
1890	M123	Roll 108, special census of veterans
1900:	T623	Rolls 1741–1754; soundex index, T1077, 69 rolls
1910:	T624	Rolls 1653–1675; no index

Remarks:

1860. The 1860 schedules for Benton, Columbia, San Juan, and Snohomish Counties are missing.

1870. The 1870 schedules for Benton and Columbia Counties are missing.

1880. Original schedules (2 vols.) were transferred to the Washington State Library, Olympia, WA 98501.

West Virginia

Population schedules:

1870:	M593	Rolls 1684–1702
1880:	T9	Rolls 1399–1416; soundex index, T778, 32 rolls
1890	M123	Rolls 109–110, special census of veterans
1900:	T623	Rolls 1755–1776; soundex index, T1078, 92 rolls
1910:	T624	Rolls 1676–1699; miracode index, T1279, 108 rolls

Remarks:

1880. Original schedules (14 vols.) were transferred to the West Virginia Historical Society, Charleston, WV 25301.

Wisconsin

Population schedules:

1840:	M704	Roll 580
1850:	M432	Rolls 994–1009
1860:	M653	Rolls 1399–1438
1870:	M593	Rolls 1703–1747
1880:	T9	Rolls 1417–1453; soundex index, T779, 51 rolls
1890	M123	Rolls 111–116, special census of veterans
1900:	T623	Rolls 1777–1825; soundex index, T1079, 188 rolls
1910:	T624	Rolls 1700–1744; no index

Remarks:

1820, 1830. The schedules for 1820 and 1830 are included in the schedules for Michigan.

1836–42, 1846, 1847. The National Archives has a microfilm copy of these Wisconsin territorial censuses on GR20, 3 rolls. Original schedules are in the State Historical Society of Wisconsin, Madison, WI 53706.

1880. Original schedules (32 vols.) were transferred to the State Historical Society of Wisconsin, Madison, WI 53706.

Wyoming

Population schedules:

1870:	M593	Roll 1748
1880:	T9	Roll 1454; soundex index, T780, 1 roll
1890	M123	Roll 117, special census of veterans
1900:	T623	Rolls 1826–1827; soundex index, T1080, 15 rolls
1910:	T624	Rolls 1745–1747; no index

Remarks:

1860. The 1860 schedules for present-day Wyoming are among the schedules for Nebraska.

1880. Original schedules (1 vol.) were transferred to the Wyoming State Archives, Museums, and Historical Department, Cheyenne, WY 82001.

TABLE 7

Authorizing Acts for Federal Censuses

Census Year	Authorizing Act of Congress	Census Taken As Of
1790	1 Mar. 1790 (1 Stat. 101)	First Monday in August 1790
1800	28 Feb. 1800 (2 Stat. 11)	First Monday in August 1800
1810	26 Mar. 1810 (2 Stat. 564)	First Monday in August 1810
1820	14 Mar. 1820 (3 Stat. 548)	First Monday in August 1820
1830	23 Mar. 1830 (4 Stat. 383)	1 June 1830
1840	3 Mar. 1839 (5 Stat. 331)	1 June 1840
1850	23 May 1850 (9 Stat. 428)	1 June 1850
1860	23 May 1850 (9 Stat. 428)	1 June 1860
1870	23 May 1850 (9 Stat. 428)	1 June 1870
1880	3 Mar. 1879 (20 Stat. 473)	1 June 1880
1890	1 Mar. 1889 (25 Stat. 760)	First Monday in June 1890
1900	3 Mar. 1899 (30 Stat. 1014–21)	1 June 1900
1910	2 July 1909 (36 Stat. 1–11)	15 April 1910

For a history of the development of the federal census through 1890, see *The History and Growth of the United States Census*, by Carroll D. Wright and William C. Hunt (56th Cong., 1st sess., S. Doc. 194, serial 385b).

CHAPTER

Passenger Arrival Lists 2

2.1 Introduction

The records of arrivals of passengers at American ports are a rich, widely used source of genealogical information. The passenger arrival records available at the National Archives consist of customs passenger lists, transcripts and abstracts of customs passenger lists, immigration passenger lists, and indexes to some of these lists. The records were created by captains or masters of vessels, collectors of customs, and immigration officials at the ports of entry to comply with federal laws. They are an important genealogical resource because they document a high percentage of the immigration during the century between 1815 and 1914—the period during which the majority of immigrants came to the United States.

Most of the records are in Records of the U.S. Customs Service, Record Group 36. Nearly all of the lists and indexes are available as National Archives Microfilm Publications. Table 8, beginning on page 60, shows the ports for which there are extant lists and indexes, and the publication numbers for those that have been microfilmed. The researcher should be aware that there are problems regarding their coverage and use.

2.1.1 Limitations of Passenger Lists

Most passenger arrival records document the period between 1820 and 1945. There are no records at the National Archives relating to immigration during the colonial period. The earliest lists are dated 1798, but the lists before 1819 are primarily baggage lists or cargo manifests that also show the names of passengers. Such manifests are very fragmentary, but some have been included in the microfilm publications to make the coverage for a particular port as complete as possible. For only a very few ports do the records span the entire 1820–1945 period; for most ports, the records cover only parts of the period. In table 8, gaps of more than a year in the records of a particular port are indicated in the dates given, but the lists are not necessarily complete for the years shown.

The National Archives does not have passenger lists for every place an immigrant might have arrived. During the nineteenth century, no law required passenger arrival records to be kept for persons entering the United States by land from Canada or Mexico. Nearly all of the extant records pertain to ports on the Atlantic Ocean or the Gulf of Mexico. Lists for Pacific coast ports, if they exist, have not been transferred to the National Archives. There are a few passenger lists for the port of San Francisco, for 1920 only, at the archives branch, FARC San Francisco; other San Francisco lists were destroyed by fires in 1851 and 1940. Information concerning some passenger arrivals at San Francisco is in *Ship N' Rail*, a multivolume series by Louis Rasmussen, published by San Francisco Historical Records, 1204 Nimitz Drive; Colma, CA 94015. Immigration and emigration records of American Samoa are described on page 250, in chapter 19, "Miscellaneous Records."

Contributing to the difficulty of using the records of passenger arrivals are their physical characteristics. They were written by many different hands over many years, and the conditions of their preservation before they were placed in the National Archives were not ideal. For this reason, researchers must use microfilm copies of the lists if they have been microfilmed. In addition, many of the original lists are no longer in the National Archives, but have been transferred to Temple University, Philadelphia, PA 19122.

Finally, the records of passenger arrivals are voluminous. For some parts, there are hundreds of lists for each year, many of which contain hundreds of names. A general search—especially in the records of New York or Philadelphia, for example—would be prohibitively time-consuming. The record of a particular immigrant can be found more easily if the port of entry, the name of the vessel, and the exact or approximate date of arrival are known.

2.1.2 Indexes and Research Aids

Many of the records are indexed. Alphabetical card indexes to customs passenger lists were compiled in the mid-1930s for the Immigration and Naturalization Service by the Work Projects Administration (WPA) and the National Youth Administration. There are WPA indexes to lists for Baltimore, 1820–97; Boston, 1848–91; New York, 1820–46; and Philadelphia, 1800–1906. They are available as microfilm publications, the numbers of which are noted in table 8. In addition, *A Supplemental Index to Passenger Lists of Vessels Arriving at Atlantic and Gulf Coast Ports (Excluding New York), 1820–1874*, M334, 188 rolls, is also available. Although this index is incomplete, it is a good resource if an immigrant's port of arrival is not known.

In general, the indexes consist of cards that show for each passenger name, age, sex, marital status, occupation, nationality, last permanent residence, destination, port of entry, name of vessel, and date of arrival. The indexes may contain all the information sought about the arrival of a passenger, but they are neither complete nor infallible. Some lists are not covered in the indexes, particularly those for New York; an index card may not be complete, or the indexer may have made errors in transcribing the information from the lists. When possible, the information should be verified by examination of the passenger list itself or a microfilm copy of it.

If the name of the port of entry and the approximate arrival date are known, it may be possible to determine the exact date and the name of the vessel from records of vessel entrances maintained at the ports. These records, which are in Record Group 36, show the name of each vessel, its captain, the port of embarkation, and the date of arrival. For some ports there are two series, one with entries arranged alphabetically by name of vessel, and the other with entries arranged chronologically. If, in addition to the port of entry and approximate date of arrival, the port of embarkation is known, the search for the name of the vessel and the exact date may be facilitated. For example, if a passenger embarked from Stockholm for New York in a year in which 500 passenger vessels arrived in New York, the search could be narrowed to the relatively few passenger lists for vessels sailing from Stockholm. For some voyagers, however, the port of embarkation was the last port at which the vessel called, not necessarily the port at which the immigrant boarded.

Family records and traditions will facilitate research in passenger arrival records. Naturalization records (see chapter 3) may aid in locating the appropriate passenger list for an

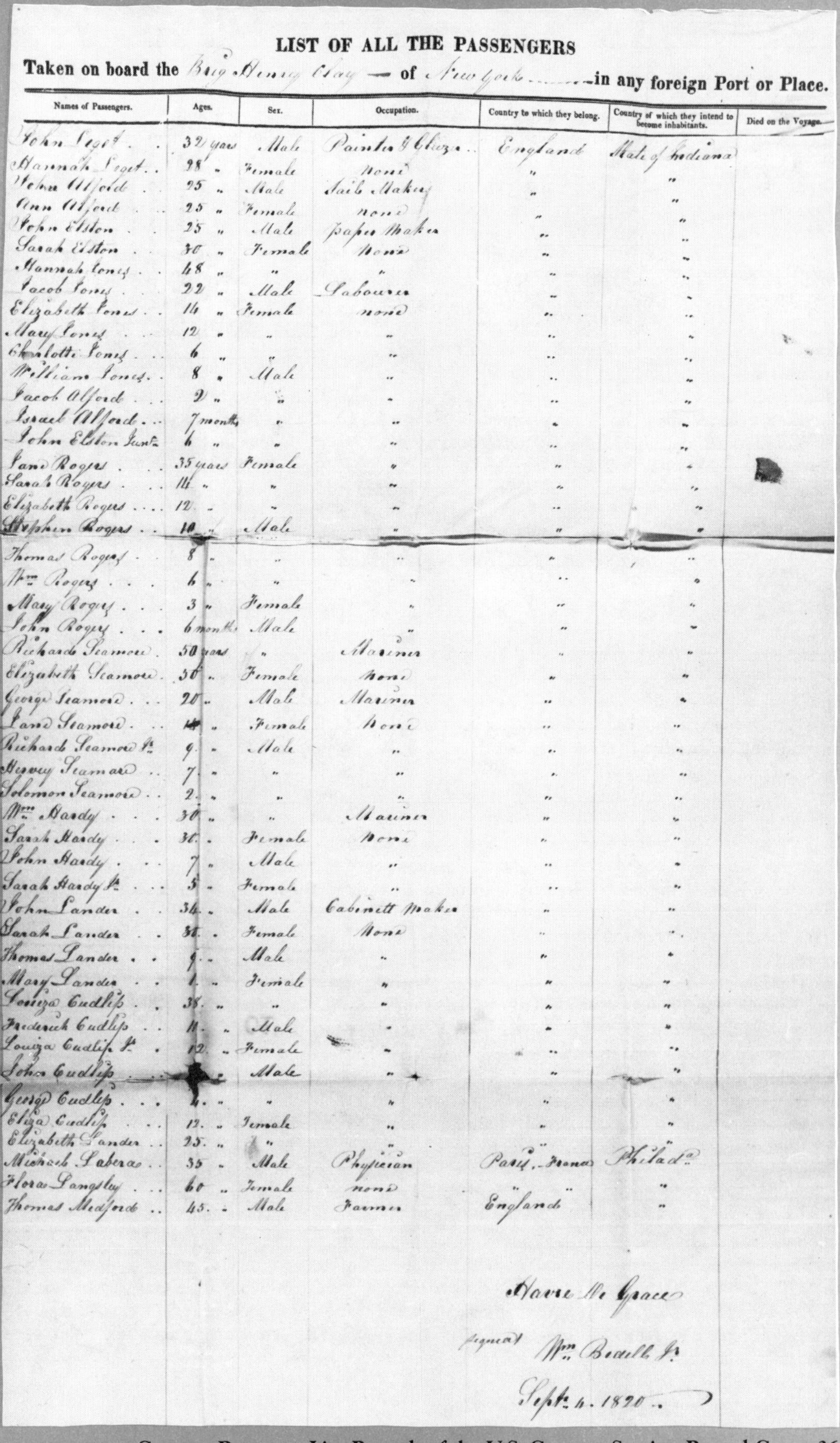

LIST OF ALL THE PASSENGERS

Taken on board the Brig Henry Clay — of New York ....in any foreign Port or Place.

Names of Passengers.	Ages.	Sex.	Occupation.	Country to which they belong.	Country of which they intend to become inhabitants.	Died on the Voyage.
John Legot	32 years	Male	Painter & Glazier	England	State of Indiana	
Hannah Legot	28 "	Female	none	"	"	
John Alford	25 "	Male	Sail Maker	"	"	
Ann Alford	25 "	Female	none	"	"	
John Elston	25 "	Male	Paper Maker	"	"	
Sarah Elston	30 "	Female	None	"	"	
Hannah Jones	48 "	"	"	"	"	
Jacob Jones	22 "	Male	Labourer	"	"	
Elizabeth Jones	14 "	Female	none	"	"	
Mary Jones	12 "	"	"	"	"	
Charlotte Jones	6 "	"	"	"	"	
William Jones	8 "	Male	"	"	"	
Jacob Alford	2 "	"	"	"	"	
Israel Alford	7 months	"	"	"	"	
John Elston Junr.	6 "	"	"	"	"	
Jane Rogers	35 years	Female	"	"	"	
Sarah Rogers	14 "	"	"	"	"	
Elizabeth Rogers	12 "	"	"	"	"	
Stephen Rogers	10 "	Male	"	"	"	
Thomas Rogers	8 "	"	"	"	"	
Wm. Rogers	6 "	"	"	"	"	
Mary Rogers	3 "	Female	"	"	"	
John Rogers	6 months	Male	"	"	"	
Richard Seamore	50 years	"	Mariner	"	"	
Elizabeth Seamore	30 "	Female	None	"	"	
George Seamore	20 "	Male	Mariner	"	"	
Jane Seamore	14 "	Female	None	"	"	
Richard Seamore Jr.	9 "	Male	"	"	"	
Henry Seamore	7 "	"	"	"	"	
Solomon Seamore	2 "	"	"	"	"	
Wm. Hardy	30 "	"	Mariner	"	"	
Sarah Hardy	30 "	Female	none	"	"	
John Hardy	7 "	Male	"	"	"	
Sarah Hardy Jr.	5 "	Female	"	"	"	
John Lander	34 "	Male	Cabinett Maker	"	"	
Sarah Lander	30 "	Female	None	"	"	
Thomas Lander	9 "	Male	"	"	"	
Mary Lander	1 "	Female	"	"	"	
Louiza Cudlips	38 "	"	"	"	"	
Frederick Cudlips	11 "	Male	"	"	"	
Louiza Cudlips Jr.	12 "	Female	"	"	"	
John Cudlips	[illegible]	Male	"	"	"	
George Cudlips	4 "	"	"	"	"	
Eliza Cudlips	12 "	Female	"	"	"	
Elizabeth Lander	25 "	"	"	"	"	
Michael Sabera	35 "	Male	Physician	Paris, France	Philada.	
Flora Langsley	60 "	Female	none	"	"	
Thomas Medford	45 "	Male	Farmer	England	"	

Havre de Grace

signed Wm. Beedle Jr.

Sept. 4. 1820.

Customs Passenger List. Records of the U.S. Customs Service, Record Group 36.
National Archives Microfilm Publication M575.

immigrant who later petitioned for naturalization. Some naturalization records show for each petitioner the full name, the date, and the port of arrival in the United States.

The *Morton Allan Directory of European Passenger Steamship Arrivals* (New York: Immigrant Information Bureau, Inc., 1931) contains information concerning vessels arriving at the ports of New York, 1890–1930, and at Baltimore, Boston, and Philadelphia, 1904–26. It lists by year the name of the steamship company and by exact date the names of the vessels arriving at these ports. This publication has been reprinted by Shenandoah House, Strasburg, Va., 1971.

For information about publications concerning early passenger lists, see *Passenger Lists Bibliography* edited by P. William Filby (Detroit: Gale Research Co., 1981), which is a revision and enlargement of *A Bibliography of Ship Passenger Lists* by Harold Lancour, 3d ed. (New York: New York Public Library, 1963). Another useful work is *Passenger and Immigration Lists Index*, 3 vols. (Detroit: Gale Research Co., 1982) also edited by Filby with Mary K. Meyer.

Excellent studies using the passenger arrival records have been made, such as Nils William Olsson's *Swedish Passenger Arrivals in New York, 1820–1850* (Chicago: Swedish Pioneer Historical Society, 1967), which lists more than 4,000 Swedish immigrants. For a bibliography of such works, see Olga K. Miller's *Migration, Emigration, Immigration* (Logan, Utah: Everton, 1974).

Ordering copies of passenger arrival records by mail. If the specific date of arrival or the name of the ship is known, copies of passenger arrival records can be ordered by mail by using NATF Form 40 (12-79), Order and Billing for Copies of Passenger Arrival Records. Copies of NATF Form 40 (12-79) are free from the Reference Services Branch (NNIR), General Services Administration, Washington, DC 20408.

2.2 Types of Passenger Lists

2.2.1 Customs Passenger Lists

An act of 1819 (3 Stat. 489) and later acts required the master of a ship entering an American port from a foreign port to file a list of passengers with the district collector of customs. The records, known as customs passenger lists, may be in the form of original lists and copies, abstracts, or transcripts of lists. They are in Records of the U.S. Customs Service, Record Group 36.

Original lists exist only for a few ports. The general date span for original lists is 1820–1902, but New Orleans is the only port for which every year of the entire period is covered. An original list was prepared on board ship, sworn to by the master of the vessel, and filed with the collector of customs when the ship arrived at the port. It usually contains the following information: name of vessel, name of master, name of port of embarkation, date of arrival, name of port of arrival, and for each passenger, name, age, sex, occupation, name of country of origin and country of intended settlement, and date and circumstances of death en route, if applicable. The information about passengers was recorded for immigrants, tourists, and U.S. citizens returning from abroad.

Copies and abstracts of original customs passenger lists were made in the offices of the collectors of customs and were usually sent once each quarter to the Secretary of State in accordance with the 1819 act that generated the original lists. Some collectors prepared copies of the individual lists, and other prepared abstracts, which are consolidated lists of names of all passengers who arrived at a given port during the quarter. The practice at a port varied from time to time.

Copies and abstracts exist for many more ports than do original lists. The general date span for copies and abstracts is 1820–1905, but for no port do records exist for every year of that period.

The copies of the customs passenger lists usually contain the name of the vessel, name of port of embarkation, name of port of arrival, and sometimes name of master and date of arrival. The abstracts ususally contain the name of the district or port, quarter-year of arrival, and sometimes name of port of embarkation. Copies and abstracts contain for each passenger the same information that is found in the original lists, but some information may be abbreviated. For example, some copies and abstracts show only the initials of the given names of passengers.

State Department Transcripts of lists, 1819–32, (8 vols.) were apparently prepared at the Department of State from copies or abstracts sent to the Secretary of State by the collectors of customs. Entries in the volumes are arranged by quarter-year of arrival, thereunder by district or port, thereunder by name of vessel, and thereunder by name of passenger.

The entries for some quarters begin in one volume and end in the next. For example, entries for the quarter ending 30 June 1823 begin in volume 3 and continue in volume 4. An entry for a passenger arriving between 1 April 1823 and 30 June 1823 might be in either volume.

A typical entry shows name of vessel, quarter-year of arrival, name of master, name of district or port of arrival, and, for each passenger, name, age, sex, occupation, name of country of emigration, and country of intended settlement, and information about death en route, if applicable.

At one time there were nine volumes of State Department transcripts, but volume 2 is now missing. All entries in volume 1 and some entries from the missing volume 2 were printed in *Letter from the Secretary of State with a Transcript of the List of Passengers Who Arrived in the United States from the 1st October, 1819, to the 30th September, 1820* (16th Cong., 2d sess., S. Doc. 118, serial 45). There is a typescript index to this publication in the National Archives Library; the publication was reprinted with an index by the Genealogical Publishing Co., Baltimore, 1971.

Entries in volumes 5, 8, and 9 were indexed as part of *A Supplemental Index to Passenger Lists of Vessels Arriving at Atlantic and Gulf Coast Ports (Excluding New York), 1820–1874*, M334, and a manuscript index to volume 1 is available. Volumes 3, 4, 6 and 7, however, are not indexed; these four volumes contain 835 pages with approximately 50 names per page, or approximately 41,000 names.

The State Department transcripts are not available as a microfilm publication, and they are not entirely free from errors. They are, however, especially useful when they include information from lists not otherwise extant. For example, the information about New York arrivals during the

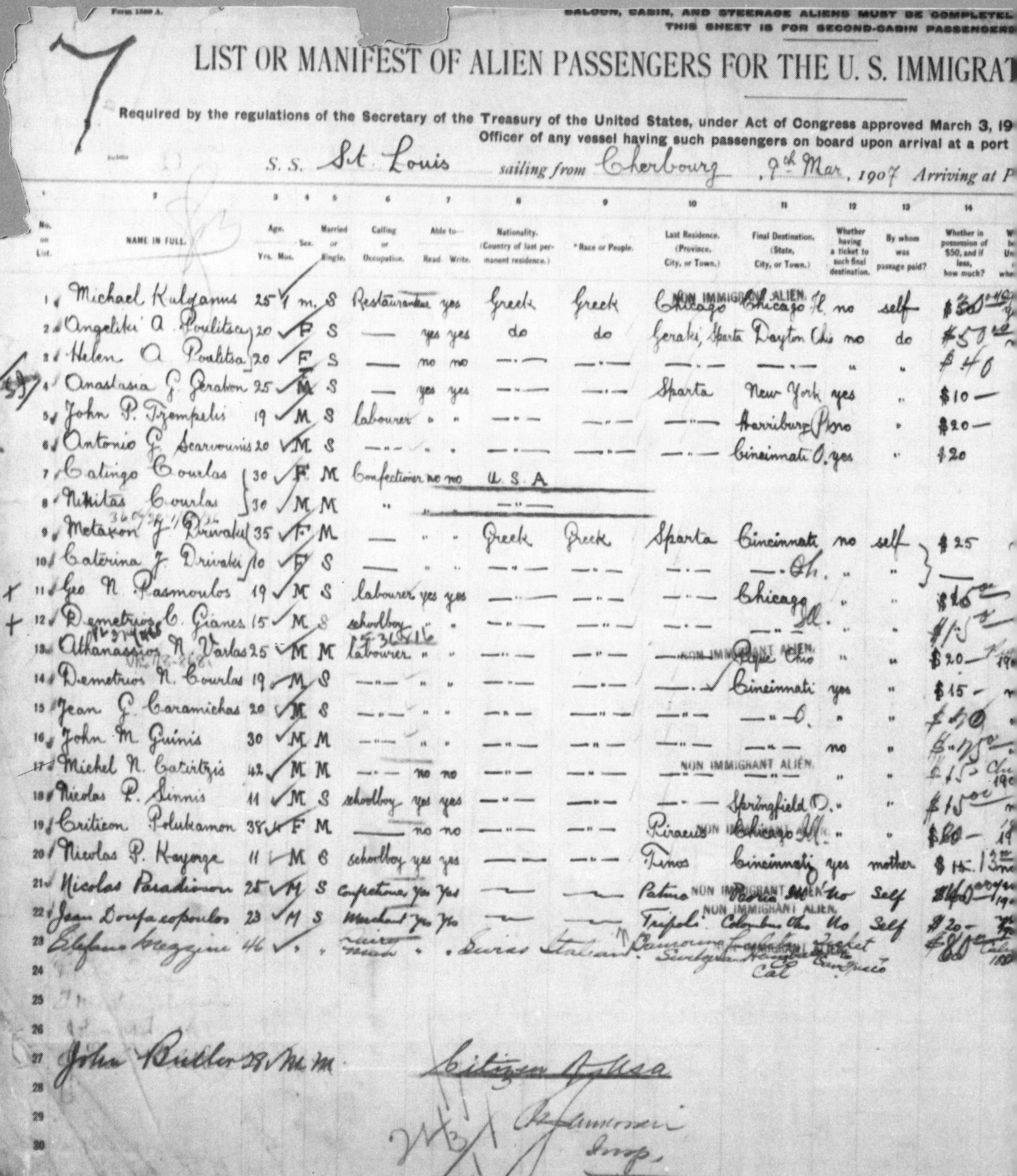

Form 1500 A.

SALOON, CABIN, AND STEERAGE ALIENS MUST BE COMPLETEL

THIS SHEET IS FOR SECOND-CABIN PASSENGERS

LIST OR MANIFEST OF ALIEN PASSENGERS FOR THE U. S. IMMIGRAT

Required by the regulations of the Secretary of the Treasury of the United States, under Act of Congress approved March 3, 19

Officer of any vessel having such passengers on board upon arrival at a port

S. S. St Louis sailing from Cherbourg, 9th Mar, 1907 Arriving at P

No. on List	NAME IN FULL	Age Yrs.	Sex	Married or Single	Calling or Occupation	Able to— Read	Write	Nationality (Country of last permanent residence.)	*Race or People	Last Residence (Province, City, or Town.)	Final Destination (State, City, or Town.)	Whether having a ticket to such final destination	By whom was passage paid?	Whether in possession of $50, and if less, how much?
1	Michael Kulgams	25	m.	S	Restaurantur	yes		Greek	Greek	Chicago	Chicago Il.	no	self	$30
2	Angeliki A. Poulitsa	20	F	S	—	yes	yes	do	do	Geraki, Sparta	Dayton Ohio	no	do	$50
3	Helen A. Poulitsa	20	F	S	—	no	no	—	—	—	—	"	"	$40
4	Anastasia G. Geraton	25	M	S	—	yes	yes	—	—	Sparta	New York	yes	"	$10 —
5	John P. Tzompelis	19	M	S	labourer	"	"	—	—	—	Harrisburg Penn		"	$20 —
6	Antonio G. Scarvounis	20	M	S	—	"	"	—	—	—	Cincinnati O.	yes	"	$20
7	Catingo Courlas	30	F	M	Confectioner	no	no	U. S. A						
8	Nikitas Courlas	30	M	M	"			—						
9	Metaxon J. Drivaki	35	F	M	—	"	"	Greek	Greek	Sparta	Cincinnati	no	self	$25
10	Caterina J. Drivaki	10	F	S	—	"	"	—	—	—	— Oh.	"	"	—
11	Geo N. Pasmoulos	19	M	S	labourer	yes	yes	—	—	—	Chicago	"	"	$15
12	Demetrios C. Gianes	15	M	S	schoolboy	"	"	—	—	—	— Ill.	"	"	$15
13	Athanassios N. Varlas	25	M	M	labourer	"	"	—	—	NON IMMIGRANT ALIEN.		"	"	$20
14	Demetrios N. Courlas	19	M	S	—	"	"	—	—	—	Cincinnati	yes	"	$15 —
15	Jean G. Caramichas	20	M	S	—	"	"	—	—	—	— O.	"	"	$40
16	John M. Guinis	30	M	M	—	"	"	—	—	—	—	no	"	$175
17	Michel N. Gatzitzis	42	M	M	—	no	no	—	—	NON IMMIGRANT ALIEN.				$15
18	Nicolas P. Sinnis	11	M	S	schoolboy	yes	yes	—	—	—	Springfield O.	"	"	$15
19	Criticon Polukamon	38	F	M	—	no	no	—	—	Piraeus	Chicago Ill.	"	"	$60 —
20	Nicolas P. Kayorge	11	M	S	schoolboy	yes	yes	—	—	Tinos	Cincinnati	yes	mother	$15.
21	Nicolas Paradisinon	25	M	S	Confectioner	yes	yes	—	—	Patras	NON IMMIGRANT ALIEN	no	Self	$40
22	Jean Doupacopoulos	23	M	S	Merchant	yes	yes	—	—	Tripoli	NON IMMIGRANT ALIEN. Columbus Ohio	no	Self	$20 —
23	Stefano Guzzini	46						Swiss	Italian					$80
24														
25														
26														
27	John Buttler	28	M	M				Citizen U.S.A						
28														
29														
30														

Insp.

* "Race or People" is to be determined by the stock from which they sprang and the language they speak. List of races will be fo

Immigration Passenger List, Passenger and Crew Lists of Vessels Arriving at New York, 1897–1919.
Records of the Immigration and Naturalization Service, Record Group 85.
National Archives Microfilm Publication T715.

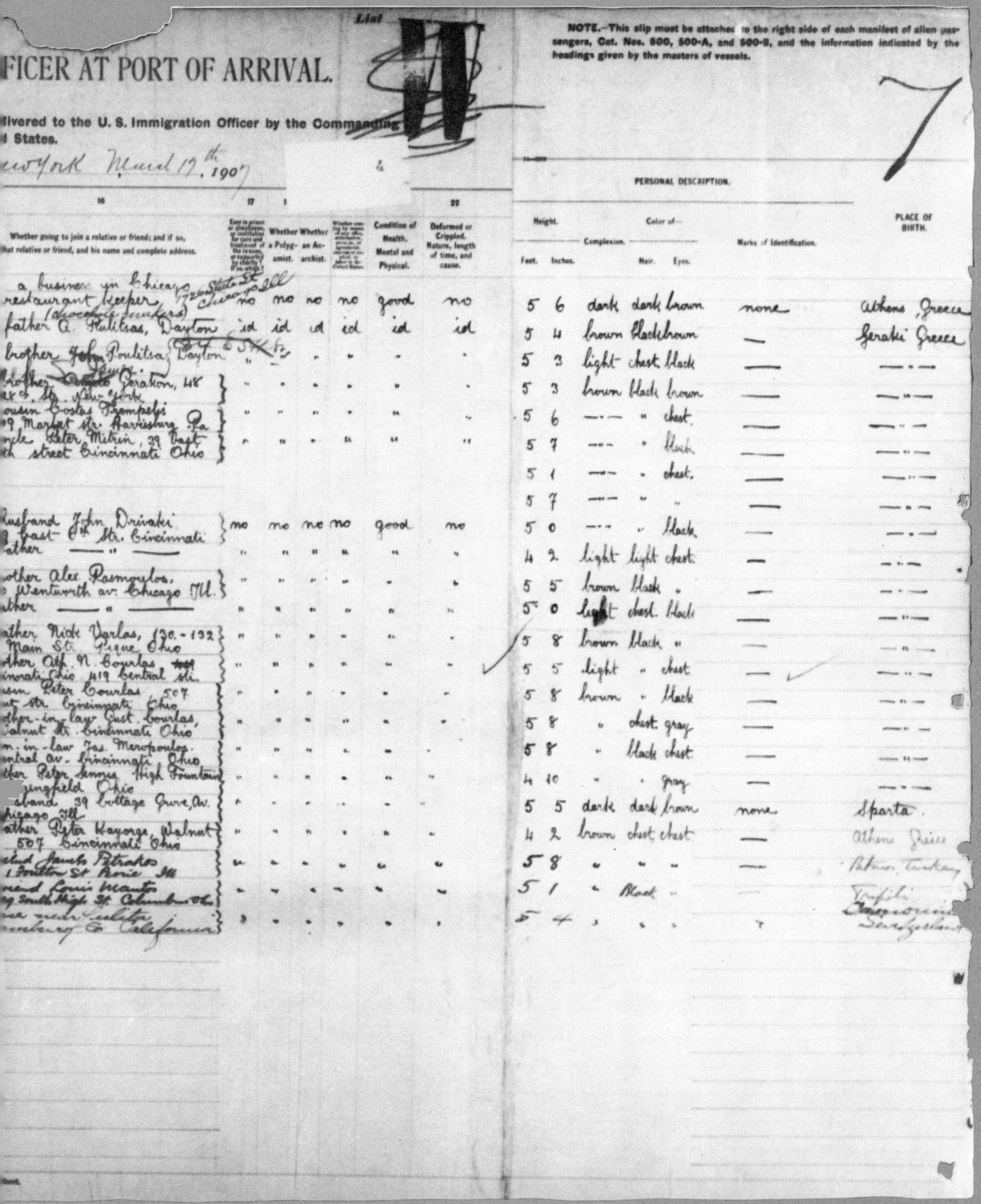

List

...FICER AT PORT OF ARRIVAL.

...livered to the U. S. Immigration Officer by the Commanding ... States.

...ew York March 17th, 1907

NOTE.—This slip must be attached to the right side of each manifest of alien passengers, Cat. Nos. 500, 500-A, and 500-B, and the information indicated by the headings given by the masters of vessels.

7

16 Whether going to join a relative or friend; and if so, what relative or friend, and his name and complete address.	17 Ever in prison or almshouse or institution for care and treatment of the insane, or supported by charity.	Whether a Polygamist.	Whether an Anarchist.	Whether coming by reason of any offer, solicitation, promise or agreement, express or implied, to labor in the United States.	Condition of Health, Mental and Physical.	22 Deformed or Crippled. Nature, length of time, and cause.	Height Feet	Height Inches	Complexion	Color of— Hair	Color of— Eyes	Marks of Identification.	Place of Birth.
a business in Chicago restaurant keeper, 72 State St. Chicago Ill (chocolate makers)	no	no	no	no	good	no	5	6	dark	dark	brown	none	Athens, Greece
father G. Politsas, Dayton	id	id	id	id	id	id	5	4	brown	black	brown	—	Geraki Greece
brother John Poulitsa, Dayton	"	"	"	"	"	"	5	3	light	chest.	black	—	" "
brother ... Geraton, 48 ... St. New York	"	"	"	"	"	"	5	3	brown	black	brown	—	" "
cousin Costas Thompelis ...9 Market St. Harrisburg Pa	"	"	"	"	"	"	5	6	"	"	chest.	—	" "
uncle Peter Mitrin, 39 East ...th street Cincinnati Ohio	"	"	"	"	"	"	5	7	"	"	black	—	" "
							5	1	"	"	chest.	—	" "
							5	7	"	"	"	—	" "
husband John Drivaki ... East 8th Str. Cincinnati	no	no	no	no	good	no	5	0	"	"	black	—	" "
father — " —	"	"	"	"	"	"	4	2	light	light	chest.	—	" "
brother Alex Raimoulos, ... Wentworth av. Chicago Ill.	"	"	"	"	"	"	5	5	brown	black	"	—	" "
father — " —	"	"	"	"	"	"	5	0	light	chest.	black	—	" "
brother Nick Vorlas, 130-132 ... Main St. Piqua Ohio	"	"	"	"	"	"	5	8	brown	black	"	—	" "
brother Ath. N. Courlas ... Cincinnati Ohio 419 Central St.	"	"	"	"	"	"	5	5	light	"	chest.	—	" "
cousin Peter Courlas, 507 ...ut Str. Cincinnati Ohio	"	"	"	"	"	"	5	8	brown	"	black	—	" "
brother-in-law Gust. Courlas, ... Walnut St. Cincinnati Ohio	"	"	"	"	"	"	5	8	"	chest.	gray	—	" "
...n-in-law Jas. Meropoulos ... Central Av. Cincinnati Ohio	"	"	"	"	"	"	5	8	"	black	chest.	—	" "
...ther Peter Ennis High Fountain ... Springfield Ohio	"	"	"	"	"	"	4	10	"	"	gray	—	" "
husband 39 Cottage Grove Av. Chicago Ill	"	"	"	"	"	"	5	5	dark	dark	brown	none	Sparta
father Peter Kayorge, Walnut 507 Cincinnati Ohio	"	"	"	"	"	"	4	2	brown	chest.	chest.	—	Athens Greece
...cle Jacob Petrakos ... Poulton St Peoria Ill	"	"	"	"	"	"	5	8	"	"	"	—	Patras, Turkey
husband Louis Manto... South High St. Columbus Ohio	"	"	"	"	"	"	5	1	"	black	"		[illegible]
... California	"	"	"	"	"	"	5	4	"	"	"	"	[illegible]

Three photographs of immigrants arriving at Ellis Island. Photographs No. 90-G-125-17, 90-G-125-3, and 90-G-125-42. Records of the Public Health Service, Record Group 90.

second quarter of 1820 is not otherwise available; nor are there any original lists or copies for 1819. The law providing for the creation of customs passenger lists did not go into effect until 1 January 1820, but a few collectors apparently reported to the State Department arrivals beginning on 1 October 1819.

In 1821, the Department of State issued a **Register of Passengers arriving in the United States, from the 1st Oct. 1819 to 30th Sept. 1820**. The register lists the names of more than 9,000 passengers, their age, sex, occupation, place of origin, destination, and the ship they arrived on and its commander. After 1820, only statistical abstracts on immigration were published. (Serial 45–118).

2.2.2 Immigration Passenger Lists

An act of 1882 (22 Stat. 214) established procedures for immigrants arriving in the United States. The records maintained by federal immigration officials were often called **immigration passenger lists** or **manifests**. The National Archives has microfilm copies of these lists, dated generally 1883–1945. The lists are part of Records of the Immigration and Naturalization Service, Record Group 85.

The microfilm copies of the immigration passenger lists vary in informational content. For the earliest ones, which are for Philadelphia in 1883, immigration officials used Pennsylvania State forms. They contain the following information: name of master, name of vessel, names of ports of arrival and embarkation, date of arrival, and, for each passenger, name, place of birth, last legal residence, age, occupation, sex, and remarks. Forms prescribed by federal law soon came into use, and by 1893 an immigration passenger list included name of master, name of vessel, names of ports of arrival and embarkation, date of arrival, and the following information for each passenger: full name; age; sex; marital status; occupation; nationality; last residence; final destination; whether in the United States before, and if so, when, and where; and whether going to join a relative and if so, the relative's name, address, and relationship to the passenger. The format of the immigration passenger list was revised in 1903 to include race, in 1906 to include a personal description and birthplace, and in 1907 to include the name and address of the nearest relative in the immigrant's home country.

Immigration passenger lists include the names not only of immigrants but also of visitors and U.S. citizens returning from abroad. For some ports, there are separate lists for aliens and for citizens; such a distinction is shown in table 8 if appropriate. For the most part, lists of aliens include the same information as that discussed above. Lists of citizens show, for each passenger, name, age, sex, and marital status; date and place of birth if born in the United States; date of naturalization and name and location of court if applicable; and current address.

Immigration passenger lists are arranged by port and thereunder chronologically. To find information about a particular individual in these voluminous records, the researcher must know the port, exact date of arrival, and name of vessel.

To some extent, the immigration passenger lists are covered by microfilmed card indexes. With the exception of *Index to Passenger Lists of Vessels arriving at Miscellaneous Ports in Alabama, Florida, Georgia, and South Carolina, 1890–1924*, T517, 26 rolls, the availability of such indexes and dates of coverage is noted in table 8 with appropriate microfilm publication numbers. T517 is not included in table 8 because it is arranged alphabetically by name of passenger rather than by port.

For the ports of Boston, New York, Philadelphia, Portland (Me.), and Providence (R.I.), there are microfilmed book indexes. Entries in them are arranged by date of arrival; they are useful to the researcher who seeks information about an immigrant, but knows only the approximate date of arrival. A researcher who knows the exact date of arrival should go directly to the list itself. The book indexes are described more specifically in the special notes below.

2.3 Special Notes by Port of Entry

Alexandria, Va. There are cargo manifests for Alexandria that contain some passengers' names. These records have not been microfilmed.

Baltimore. In addition to passenger lists required by federal law, an 1835 Maryland State law required masters of vessels to submit to the mayor of Baltimore lists of passengers arriving in that port. The "city lists" were borrowed by the National Archives when *Passenger Lists of Vessels Arriving in Baltimore, 1820–1891*, M255, 50 rolls, was microfilmed, to fill gaps in the federal records for the years 1833–66. Although M255 contains both the federal records and the borrowed city lists, the two parts are indexed separately. *Index to Passenger Lists of Vessels Arriving at Baltimore, 1820–1897 (Federal Passenger Lists)*, M327, 171 rolls, is the index to the lists made in compliance with federal law. It covers mainly the period 1832–97. *Index to Passenger Lists of Vessels Arriving at Baltimore, 1833–1866 (City Passenger Lists)*, M326, 22 rolls, covers the "city lists" only. Both indexes are arranged by the soundex system, which is explained on each roll of microfilm and also on page 31 of this guide. M334, the index for Atlantic and Gulf Coast ports, also serves as an index to some of the Baltimore customs passenger lists.

Boston. *Index to Passenger Lists of Vessels Arriving at Boston, 1848–1891*, M265, 282 rolls, is an alphabetical card index to passenger lists. It was made in compliance with an 1848 Massachusetts State law, but is serves as an index to the federal customs lists for the period. Some Boston passenger lists are also indexed on M334.

T790 is the book index for immigration passenger lists at Boston, 1889–1940. Entries are arranged chronologically by date of vessel arrival, thereunder by class of passenger, and thereunder for the most part in rough alphabetical order by initial letter of passenger's surname. T521 is an alphabetical card index for the years 1902–06.

Jacksonville. Immigration passenger lists for Mayport, Fla., include a list for Jacksonville, 24 February 1916.

New Bedford. There is a card index to customs passenger lists for New Bedford for the period 1875–99. This index has not been microfilmed. M334 serves as an index to earlier lists for New Bedford.

New Orleans. M334 serves as an index to the original lists for New Orleans to about 1850. In addition to micro-

TABLE 8

Available Passenger Arrival Records

	Customs Passenger Lists	
Port or District	**Original Lists**	**Copies or Abstracts**
Alabama		
Mobile	1820–79 (gaps) M575	1832, 1849–52 (gaps)
Connecticut		
Bridgeport		1870 M575
Fairfield		1804–12 (gaps) 1820–21 M575
Hartford		1832 M575
Middletown	1822–33	
New Haven		1820–73 (gaps) M575 1874–91
New London		1820–47 (gaps) M575
Saybrook		1820 M575
Delaware		
Delaware		
Wilmington		1820, 1830–31, 1833, 1840–49 M575
District of Columbia		
Georgetown		1820–21 M575
Florida		
Apalachicola		
Boca Grande		
Carrabelle		
Fernandina		
Jacksonville		
Key West		1837–52, 1857–68 M575
Knights Key		
Mayport		
Miami		
Millville		
Panama City		

Immigration Passenger Lists

State Department Transcripts	Pertinent Indexes	Lists	Pertinent Indexes
1820–23	1820–74 M334	3 Apr 1904 - 24 Dec 1945 *citizen* 4 Aug 1916 - 24 Dec 1945	
	M334		
1820	M334		
	M334	Sep 1929 - Dec 1943	
1822–31	M334		
1820, 1823–27, 1829, 1831	M334		
	M334		
1820			
1820	M334		
1820	M334		
		alien 4 Sept 1918	
		alien 28 Oct 1912 - 16 Aug 1935	
		alien 7 Nov 1915	
		alien 29 Aug 1904 - 7 Aug 1932	
		18 Jan 1904 - 17 Dec 1945 *citizen* 19 May 1922–22 Dec 1945	
	M334	Nov 1898 - Dec 1945 T940 *citizen* 1 Feb 1907-2 Oct 1945	
		7 Feb 1908 - 20 Jan 1912 *citizen* 6 Feb 1908 - 23 Jan 1911	
		alien 16 Nov 1907 - 13 Apr 1916	
		5 Oct 1899 - 29 Dec 1945 *citizen* 16 Jan 1904 - 29 Dec 1945	
		alien 4 July 1916	
		alien 10 Nov 1927 - 12 Dec 1939 *citizen* 10 Sept 1933 - 12 Dec 1939	

(table continued on following page)

TABLE 8 (CONTINUED)

Available Passenger Arrival Records

Port or District	Customs Passenger Lists: Original Lists	Customs Passenger Lists: Copies or Abstracts
Pensacacola		
Port Everglades		
Port Inglis		
Port St. Joe		
St. Andrews		
St. Augustine		1821–22, 1824, 1827, 1870 M575
St. Johns		1865 M575
St. Petersburg		
Tampa		
West Palm Beach		
Georgia		
Brunswick		
Darien		1823, 1825 M575
Savannah	1820–26 M575	1820–22, 1824–26, 1831, 1847–51, 1865–67 M575
Louisiana		
New Orleans	1820–1903 M259	1820–75 M272 1819–90, 1874–92, 1897–98
Maine		
Bangor		1848 M575
Bath	Apr 1806	1825, 1827, 1832, 1867 M575
Belfast		1820–31, 1851 M575
Frenchman's Bay		1821, 1826–27 (gaps) M575
Kennebunk		1820–72, 1842 M575
Passamaquoddy		1820–59 M575
Penobscot		1851 M575
Portland and Falmouth		1820–24, 1826–53, 1856–68 (gaps) M575

Immigration Passenger Lists

State Department Transcripts	Pertinent Indexes	Lists	Pertinent Indexes
		12 May 1900 - 16 Jul 1945	
		citizen 21 Jun 1924 - 15 Dec 1945	
		15 Feb 1932 - 10 Dec 1945	
		citizen 29 Jan 1940 - 5 Dec. 1945	
		alien 29 Mar 1912 - 2 Jan 1913	
		alien 12 Jan 1923 - 13 Oct 1939	
		alien 2 Jan 1916 - 13 May 1926	
1822–24, 1827	*M334*		
	M334		
		15 Dec 1926 - 1 Mar 1941	
		2 Nov 1898 - 30 Dec 1945	
		citizen 13 Feb 1907 - 31 Dec 1945	
		8 Sept 1920 - 21 Nov 1945	
		citizen 27 Mar 1923 - 15 Dec 1945	
		alien 22 Nov 1904 - 27 Nov 1939	
		citizen 15 Sept 1923 - 27 Nov 1939	
	M334		
1820–23, 1825–26, 1831	*M334*	5 Jun 1906 - 6 Dec 1945 *T943*	
		citizen Feb 1943 - 6 Dec 1945	
1820–1827	1820–50 *M334* 1853–99 *T527*	Jan 1903 - Dec 1945 *T905*	1900–52 *T618*
	M334		
	M334		
1820, 1822–24, 1827, 1829 1831	*M334*		
1822, 1825–27	*M334*		
1820, 1822–25, 1827	*M334*		
1822–26, 1831	*M334*		
	M334		
1820–32	*M334*	29 Nov 1893 - Mar 1943 *A1151*	29 Nov 1893 - Mar 1943 *T524* 1907–1930 *T793*

(table continued on following page)

TABLE 8 (CONTINUED)

Available Passenger Arrival Records

Port or District	Customs Passenger Lists: Original Lists	Copies or Abstracts
Waldoboro		1820–21, 1833 M575
Wiscasset		
Yarmouth		1820 M575
Maryland		
Annapolis		1849 M575
Baltimore	1820–91 (gaps) M255	1820–69 (gaps) M596
Havre de Grace		1820 M575
Massachusetts		
Barnstable		1820–26 M575
Beverly (see Salem)		
Boston	1 Jan 1883 - 29 July 1891 M277 1891–1899, 1912	22 Sept 1820 - 31 Mar 1874(gaps) M277
Dighton		1820–36 (gaps) M575
Edgartown		1820–70 M575
Fall River	Jun, Aug, Sep 1865	1837–65 (gaps)
Gloucester	Dec 1905	1820, 1832–39, 1867–68, 1870 M575
Hingham		1852 M575
Marblehead		1820–36, 1849 M575
Nantucket		1820–51, 1857–62 M575
New Bedford	1823–99	1826–52 (gaps) M575
Newburyport		1821–39 (gaps) M575
Plymouth		1821–36, 1843 M575
Provincetown	1887–89, 1893, 1895–96	
Salem and Beverly	1798, 1800	1865–66 M575
Mississippi		
Gulfport		
Pascagoula		
New Hampshire		
Portsmouth		1820–22, 1824, 1826–33, 1835–37, 1842–52, 1857–61 M575
New Jersey		
Bridgetown		1828 M575
Cape May		1828 M575
Little Egg Harbor		1831 M575
Newark		1836 M575
Perth Amboy	1801–37 (gaps)	1820, 1829–32 M575

Immigration Passenger Lists

State Department Transcripts	Pertinent Indexes	Lists	Pertinent Indexes
1820–21	*M334*		
1819, 1829	*M334*		
	M334		
	M334		
1820, 1822–27, 1829	1820–70 *M334* 1820–97 *M327* 1833–66 *M326*	12 Dec 1891 - 30 Nov 1909 *T844*	1897 - July 1952 *T520*
	M334		
1820–26	*M334*		
1820–27	1820–74 *M334* 1848–91 *M265*	1 Aug 1891 - Dec 1943 *T843*	1899–1940 *T790* 1902–6 *T521* 1 Jul 1906 - 31 Dec 1920 *T617*
1819, 1823, 1826, 1828	*M334*		
1820–28, 1831–32	*M334*		
	M334		
	M334	Oct 1906 - Jun 1923, 1 Feb 1930 - Dec 1943	
	M334		
1821-23, 1825–27	*M334*		
1820, 1822–25, 1829, 1831	*M334*		
1822, 1825–27, 1830–31	*M334*	1 Jul 1902 - Jul 1942 *T944*	1 Jul 1902 - 18 Nov 1954 *T522*
1821–31	*M334*		
1822, 1824, 1826–27, 1829–30	*M334*		
1823	*M334*		
			27 Aug 1904 - 28 Aug 1954 *T523*
			15 July 1903 - 21 May 1935 *T523*
	M334		
	M334		
	M334		
	M334		
	M334		
1829	*M334*		

(table continued on following page)

TABLE 8 (CONTINUED)

Available Passenger Arrival Records

	Customs Passenger Lists	
Port or District	**Original Lists**	**Copies or Abstracts**
New York		
New York	1820–17 Jun 1897 M237 1840–74 1875–97 (gaps)	1820–74
Oswegatchie		1821–23 M575
Rochester		1866 M575
Sag Harbor		1829, 1832, 1834 M575
North Carolina		
Beaufort		1865 M575
Edenton		1820 M575
New Bern		1820–45, 1865 M575
Plymouth		1820, 1825, 1840 M575
Washington		1828–31, 1836–37, 1848 M575
Ohio		
Sandusky		1820 M575
Pennsylvania		
Philadelphia	1 Jan 1800 -Dec 1882 M425 1820–54 1883–99	1820–54 Aug 1898 1900–1905
Rhode Island		
Bristol and Warren		1820–26, 1828, 1843–71 M575
Newport	1820–75 (gaps)	1820–52, 1857 M575
Providence	1820, 1822–31	1820–32, 1834–35, 1837, 1839, 1841–52, 1857–62, 1864–1867 M575
Warren (see Bristol)		
South Carolina		
Charleston		1820–28 M575
Georgetown		
Port Royal		1865 M575
Texas		
Galveston		1846–71 M575
Virgnia		
Alexandria		1820–65
East River		1830 M575
Hampton		1821 M575

Immigration Passenger Lists

State Department Transcripts	Pertinent Indexes	Lists	Pertinent Indexes
1820–27	1820–46 *M261*	16 Jun 1897 - 1918 *T715*	16 Jun 1897 - 30 Jun 1902 *T519* 1906–42 *T612* 1 July 1902 - 31 Dec 1943 *T621*
1821–23	M334		
	M334		
1829	M334		
	M334		
1820	M334		
1820–30	M334		
1820, 1823	M334		
1828–29, 1831	M334		
	M334		
1820–22 1824–27 1829	1800–1906 *M360* 1820–74 *M334*	Jan 1883 - 22 Oct 1945 *T840*	1 Jan 1883 - 28 Jun 1948 *T526* 1906–26 *T791*
1820–28	M334		
1820–28, 1830–31	M334		
	M334	17 Jun 1911 - Jun 1943 *A1188*	18 Jun 1911 - 5 Oct 1954 *T518* 13 Dec 1911 - 26 Jun 1934 *T792*
1820–29	M334	9 Apr 1906 - 1945 *citizen* 11 Nov 1919 - 28 Dec 1945 *alien* 17 Jun 1923–24 - Oct 1939	
	M334		
	M334		
1820–31	M334		
1830	M334		
	M334		
1820–32	M334		

(table continued on following page)

TABLE 8 (CONTINUED)

Available Passenger Arrival Records

Port or District	Customs Passenger Lists: Original Lists	Copies or Abstracts
Norfolk and Portsmouth		1820–50 M575
Petersburg		1820–21 M575
Portsmouth (see Norfolk)		
Richmond		1820–24, 1826–30, 1832, 1836–37, 1844 M575

filmed card indexes to passenger arrivals for the periods 1853–99 (T527) and 1900–52 (T618), there is a card index to passengers arriving at New Orleans, 1900–January 1903, that has not been microfilmed.

The National Archives has typewritten volumes prepared by the Work Projects Administration of Louisiana entitled, "Passenger Lists Taken From Manifests of the Customs Service, Port of New Orleans." These volumes, numbered 1, 2, 3, 4, and 6, contain lists for the years 1813–67 and appear to have been copied from cargo manifests and passenger lists now in the National Archives. The alphabetical index in each volume serves as an index, although incomplete, to original passenger lists and abstracts in the National Archives. These volumes have not been microfilmed.

New York. Most nineteenth-century immigrants came through the port of New York. *Index to Passenger Lists of Vessels Arriving at New York, 1820–1846*, M261, 103 rolls, serves the customs passenger lists for that period, and *Index to Passenger Lists of Vessels Arriving at New York, 1897–1902*, T519, 115 rolls, serves the immigration passenger lists of the later period through 30 June 1902. Unfortunately, there is no index for New York arrivals for the period 1847–96.

In *Book Indexes, New York Passenger Lists, 1906–42*, T612, 307 rolls, entries are arranged chronologically by year, thereunder by vessel line or group of vessel lines, thereunder chronologically by date of vessel arrival, and thereunder in rough alphabetical order by initial letter of passenger's surname. An alphabetical index of immigrant passenger lists for 1902–1943 has been microfilmed on T621.

Philadelphia. The earliest original customs lists for Philadelphia are those for 1820. Cargo manifests for 1800–19, and a few later ones that contain names of passengers that do not appear on the customs passenger lists, were filmed with the custom lists on *Passenger Lists of Vessels Arriving in Philadelphia, 1800–1882*, M425, 108 rolls, to make the coverage as complete as possible. The *Index to Passenger Lists of Vessels Arriving at Philadelphia, 1800–1906*, M360, 151 rolls, contains names from cargo manifests, 1800–19; names from passenger lists, 1820–82; and names from some passenger lists, 1883–1906. M334 also serves as an index to some of the original lists for Philadelphia.

In *Book Indexes, Philadelphia Passenger Lists, 1906–26*, T791, 23 rolls, entries are arranged by vessel line, thereunder chronologically by date of vessel arrival, thereunder in part by class of passenger, and thereunder in rough alphabetical order by initial letter of passenger's surname.

Portland, Me. In *Book Indexes, Portland, Maine, Passenger Lists, 1907–1930*, T793, 10 rolls, entries are arranged chronologically by date of vessel arrival and thereunder in rough alphabetical order by initial letter of passenger's surname.

Providence, R.I. In *Book Indexes, Providence Passenger Lists, 1911–34*, T792, 15 rolls, entries are arranged chronologically by date of vessel arrival and thereunder in rough alphabetical order by initial letter of passenger's surname.

Salem and Beverly, Mass. The National Archives has a small group of customs lists of aliens for the ports of Salem and Beverly, Mass., 1798 and 1800. They were made in accordance with an act of 1796, requiring masters of ships coming into U.S. ports to file lists of aliens aboard with the collector of customs. Lists for any other ports are not among the records in the National Archives. Although the act provided that copies of the lists should be submitted to the Department of State, no copies are known to exist.

The lists are arranged alphabetically by name of vessel. There are lists for about ten ships, and they are part of Record Group 36.

Lists of aliens contain some or all of the following information: name of vessel, name of master, date of arrival, names of ports of embarkation and arrival, and, for each alien, name, age, birthplace, name of country of emigration, name of country of allegiance, occupation, and personal description.

The Salem and Beverly lists were transcribed and printed in the *New England Historical and Genealogical Register* 106 (July 1952): 203–209.

Immigration Passenger Lists

State Department Transcripts	Pertinent Indexes	Lists	Pertinent Indexes
1819–20, 1822	M334		
1820–24, 1828, 1830	M334		

Photograph No. 90-G-125-16.

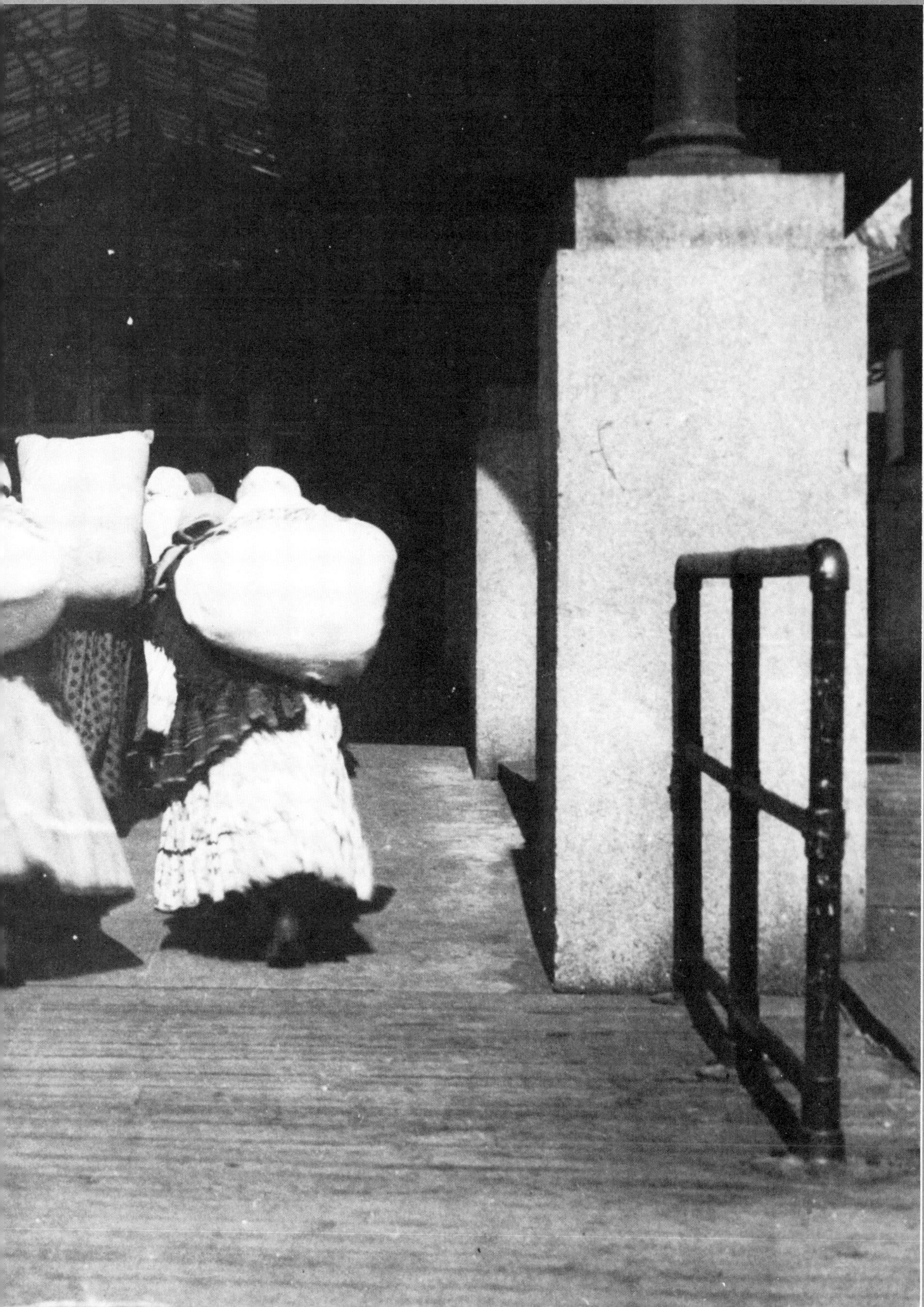

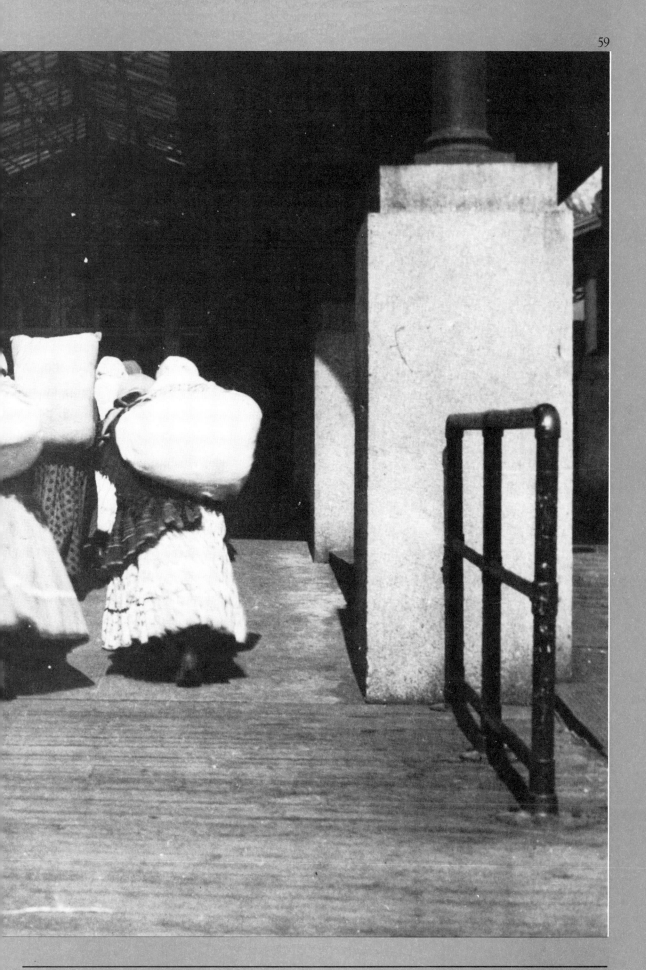

CHAPTER 3

Naturalization Records

CHAPTER 3

Naturalization Records

3.1 Federal Court Records

3.1 Federal Court Records

The first naturalization act, passed in 1790 (1 Stat. 103), provided that an alien who desired to become a citizen of the United States should apply to "any common law court of record, in any one of the states wherein he shall have resided for the term of one year at least." Under this and later laws, and under varying requirements, aliens were naturalized in federal, state, and local courts.

Records of naturalization proceedings in federal courts are usually among the records of the district court for the district in which proceedings took place. These records may still be in the custody of the court, they may have been transferred to an FARC or its regional archives branch, or they may have been transferred to the National Archives. They are all part of the Records of District Courts of the United States, Record Group 21.

A federal naturalization record usually consists of a declaration of intention, petitions, depositions, and a record of naturalization. The nature of the information in these common series is discussed first in this chapter, and the naturalization holdings of court records are identified by state in alphabetical order. There are some indexes, but the researcher should know where and when the subject of research became a citizen before beginning to look for documentation of naturalization.

3.1.1 Common Series of Naturalization Records

Declarations of intention are instruments by which applicants for U.S. citizenship renounced allegiance to foreign sovereignties and declared their intention to become U.S. citizens. Early declarations of intention usually show for each applicant name, country of birth or allegiance, date of the application, and signature. Some show date and port of arrival in the United States.

After 1906, a longer and more detailed form was used, including such information as applicant's name, age, occupation, and personal description; date and place of birth; citizenship; present address and last foreign address; vessel and port of embarkation for the United States; U.S. port and date of arrival in United States; and date of application and signature.

A declaration of intention normally preceded proof of residence or a petition to become a citizen by two or more years, but the declaration was sometimes not required if the citizen had an honorable discharge from certain military service or had entered the country when a minor.

Naturalization petitions are instruments by which those who had declared their intention to become U.S. citizens and who had met the residence requirements made formal application for U.S. citizenship. Information on the petitions includes name, residence, occupation, date and place of birth, citizenship, and personal description of applicant; date of emigration; ports of embarkation and arrival; marital status; names, dates, places of birth, and residence of applicant's children; date at which U.S. residence commenced; time of residence in state; name changes; and signature. Copies of declarations of intention, certificates of arrival, and certificates of completion of citizenship classes are often interfiled with petitions. After 1930, petitions often include photographs of the applicant.

Naturalization depositions are formal statements in support of an applicant's petition by witnesses designated by the applicant. The records indicate the period of applicant's residence in a certain locale and other information, including witnesses' appraisals of the applicant's character.

Records of naturalization and **oaths of allegiance** document the granting of U.S. citizenship to petitioners. The early orders of admission to citizenship are often available only in the minute books of the court. In fact, entries for administration of oaths of allegiance have been found in unlikely places, such as a criminal minute book that happened to be on a clerk's desk at the time. Daily minutes are recorded chronologically, and most minute books have alphabetical indexes showing names of individuals appearing in the minutes. Later records of naturalization are in the form of certificates, often unnumbered, but chronologically arranged in bound volumes with indexes to surnames.

In some cases, all records for one person have been gathered together in a **petition and record**, which usually included the petition for naturalization, affidavits of the petitioner and witnesses, the oath of allegiance, and the order of the court admitting the petitioner to citizenship.

3.1.2 Naturalization Records by State

Alabama

The archives branch, FARC Atlanta, has records of the U.S. District Court for the Southern District of Alabama (Mobile). Records relating to naturalization include petition and record documents, 1906–1929, and declarations of intention, 1855–1929.

Alaska

The archives branch, FARC Seattle, has records of the first and fourth judicial districts of the court for the Territory of Alaska. Records relating to naturalization include, for Juneau, indexed declarations of intention, 1900–29, special court orders, 1914–32, and Schedule C and a miscellaneous cashbook, 1954–60; for Skagway, declarations of intention, 1901–17; for Fairbanks, petition case files, 1910–14; for Iditarod, petition case files, 1910–20; and for Ruby, petition case files, 1910–20.

Arizona

The Archives branch, FARC Los Angeles, has records of the first through fifth judicial districts of the court for the Territory of Arizona. The records relating to naturalization include petitions, certificates, and declarations, 1882–1912; declarations of intention, 1864–1912; certificates of naturalization, 1907–12; an index for Pima County, 1864–1911; an index for Yavapai County, 1865–1906; and clerks' files, 1903–11.

Records relating to naturalization from the U.S. District Court for the District of Arizona include declarations of intention, 1915–66; petitions for naturalization, 1915–65; naturalization petitions of military personnel, 1918 and 1942–46; petitions transferred, 1953–56; naturalization orders granted and denied, 1929–55; naturalization certificates, 1915–23; clerks' files, 1912–14; and petitions for naturalization from the superior court of Pima County, 1912–14.

California

The archives branch, FARC San Francisco, has the records of the U.S. District Court for the Northern District of California (San Francisco). Records relating to naturalization include delarations of intention and petitions for citizenship, 1923–38; depositions, 1906–57; and an index to naturalizations, 1853–67.

The San Francisco archives branch also has records of the U.S. District Court for the Eastern District of California (Sacramento). Records relating to naturalization include declarations of intention, 1917–56; naturalization petitions of military personnel, 1944; petitions for citizenship, 1928–56; naturalization petitions recommended to be granted, 1928–58; duplicate naturalization petitions of military personnel, 1944–45.

The archives branch, FARC Los Angeles, has the records of the U.S. District Court for the Central District of California (Los Angeles). Records relating to naturalizations include an index, 1887–1931; declarations of intention, 1887–1951; petitions for naturalization, 1887–1942; naturalization petitions of military personnel, 1918, 1942–46; petitions for repatriation, 1936–52; petitions for repatriation of military personnel, 1922–46; naturalization petitions of overseas military personnel, 1942–54; a court order book, 1926–31; and a civil order book, 1938–54. The records of the U.S. Circuit Court for the Central District of California include an index to declarations of intention and petitions for naturalization, 1887–1911, located in district court records.

The Los Angeles archives branch also has naturalization records accessioned from the Superior Court of San Diego County that include indexes to declarations and naturalized citizens, 1853–1958; certificates and records of naturalization (including petitions), 1883–1906; petitions for naturalization, 1906–56; naturalization petitions for military personnel, 1918–19; declarations of intention, 1941–55; petitions granted and denied, 1929–48; transferred petitions, 1953–55; and petitions for repatriation, 1936–55. They are now a part of the records of the U.S. District Court for the Southern District of California (San Diego).

Colorado

The archives branch, FARC Denver, has naturalization case files, declarations of intention, petitions, and naturalization records, 1876–1949, for the U.S. Circuit Courts for the District of Colorado at Denver, Pueblo, Del Norte, and Montrose.

Connecticut

The archives branch, FARC Boston, has records of the U.S. District Court for the District of Connecticut. Records relating to naturalization include declarations of intention for New Haven County, 1911–52; declarations of intention for Hartford County, 1911–55; and records of naturalization, 1842–1902. Naturalization records of the U.S. Circuit Court for the district include declarations of intention for New Haven County, 1906–11; declarations of intention for Hartford County, 1906–11; and records of naturalization, 1896–1906.

There are also naturalization records from local courts in Connecticut. These records came into the custody of the federal district court and are therefore now part of Record Group 21. The records consist of declarations of intention (with index cards), 1907–23, and records of naturalization (with index cards), 1906–24, from the City Court of New Haven; records of naturalization, 1875–92, from the City Court of Hartford; declarations of intention, 1928–39, and records of naturalization, 1907–39, from the City Court of Meriden; declarations of intention, 1900–6, and records of naturalization, 1893–1906, from the City Court of Ansonia; and declarations of intention, 1898–1910, from the Court of Common Pleas, New Haven County.

Delaware

The archives branch, FARC Philadelphia, has petitions for naturalization, 1845–1910, from the U.S. District Court for the District of Delaware and petitions for naturalization, 1845–1902, from the U.S. Circuit Court for the District of Delaware.

District of Columbia

Naturalization records from U.S. courts for the District of Columbia include unbound declarations of intention and such related records as proofs of residence, arranged chronologically, 1802–1903; a bound volume of abstracts (and, for 1818, transcripts) of declarations of intention, 1818–65; bound volumes of declarations of intention, 1866–1906; bound volumes labeled "naturalization records," consisting in part of orders of admission, 1824–1906; and a one-volume index to most series of naturalization records, 1802–1909.

The bound naturalization records show, for each petitioner, 1824–39, basically the same information as that contained in the declaration of intention, the date of admission to citizenship, and proof of age; for 1839–65, the name of each person and the term and year of admission, arranged by initial letter of surname; for 1866–1906, the name, place of birth, age, date of declaration of intention, statement of honorable military discharge, or statement of arrival as a minor (at first, before the age of 18, and later 21), and from 1903, the date of arrival.

Florida

The archives branch, FARC Atlanta, has the records of the U.S. District Court for the Southern District of Florida (Key West). Records relating to naturalization include petition and record documents, 1875–1948; declarations of intention, 1867–1948; and military petitions, 1943–48.

Naturalization records of the U.S. District Court for the Southern District of Florida (Miami) include petition and record documents, 1913–48; declarations of intention, 1913–48; naturalization hearings, 1941–48; and naturalization certificate stubs, 1907–26.

Georgia

The archives branch, FARC Atlanta, has records of the U.S. District Court for the Northern District of Georgia (Atlanta). Records relating to naturalization include petition and record documents, 1906–48; declarations of intention, 1913–48; and military petitions, 1918–24. Records of the U.S. Circuit Court for the district include naturalization minutes, 1903–6.

Hawaii

The archives branch, FARC San Francisco, has records of the U.S. District Court for the District of Hawaii. Records relating to naturalization include declarations of intention, 1900–26; naturalization petitions from military personnel, 1918–21; petitions for naturalization, 1902–59; certificates of naturalization, 1907–61; and naturalization docket books, 1901–43.

Illinois

The archives branch, FARC Chicago, has records of the U.S. District Court for the Northern District of Illinois (Chicago). Records of the court before 1871 were destroyed in the 1871 Chicago fire. Extant naturalization records include declarations of intention, 1872–1903 and 1906–64; an index to declarations of intention, 1921–56; orders, 1873–1903 and 1925–54; petitions, 1906–61; an index to petitions, 1940–54; and petitions based on military service, 1918–26. Naturalization records of the U.S. Circuit Court for the district include declarations of intention, 1906–11 and petitions, 1906–11.

The records of the U.S. District Court for the Southern District of Illinois (Springfield) include declarations of intention, 1903–50; naturalization record volumes, 1856–1903; and petition and record documents, 1906–43. Naturalization records for the U.S. Circuit Court for the district include declarations of intention, 1856–1902 and naturalization record volumes, 1862–1903.

Naturalization records of the U.S. District Court for the Southern District of Illinois (Peoria) include declarations of intention, 1907–51; an undated index to declarations of intention and petitions; stubs from certificates of naturalization, 1919–26; petition and record documents, 1908–54; a naturalization order book, 1929–57; overseas naturalizations, 1943–55; and a naturalization record volume, 1887.

Indiana

The archives branch, FARC Chicago, has records of the U.S. District Court for the Southern District of Indiana (Indianapolis). Records relating to naturalization include certificates of naturalization, 1918–25, not inclusive; declarations of intention, 1906–48; petitions, 1908–45; and petitions based on military service, 1918.

Naturalization records of the U.S. District Court for the Northern District of Indiana (Hammond) include declarations of intention, 1906–21.

Iowa

The Archives branch, FARC Kansas City, has declarations of intention, 1853–74 and a naturalization roll, 1857–65, from the U.S. District Court for the Southern District of Iowa (Des Moines).

Kansas

The archives branch, FARC Kansas City, has records of the U.S. District Court for the District of Kansas. Records relating to naturalization include naturalization certificates, 1916–29; declarations of intention, 1915–64; petitions for naturalization, 1915–67; and naturalization record volumes, 1937–66.

Louisiana

The archives branch, FARC Fort Worth, has records of the U.S. District Court for the Western District of Louisiana. For the Alexandria Division, records relating to naturalizations include the declarations of intention, 1919–20; petitions, 1922–64; lists of petitions to be granted, continued, denied, 1930–59; and naturalization certificate record, 1918–28. For the Opelousas Division, records relating to naturalizations include court orders for naturalization petitions, 1930–55; naturalization petitions, 1930–55; and declarations of intention, 1918–56. For the Shreveport Division, records relating to naturalizations include declarations of intention, 1906–42; naturalization service petitions and records, 1902–67; recommendations to grant naturalization petitions, 1929–56.

The archives branch, FARC Fort Worth, has records of the U.S. District Court for the Eastern District of Louisiana. Records relating to naturalizations include petitions and applications, 1898–1903; oaths of applicants, 1876–98; certificates of naturalization, 1837–40; questionnaires for declaration of intention, 1906–28; depositions of witnesses, 1908–27; declarations of intention, 1906–10; questionnaires for petitions, 1911–19; questionnaires for preliminary hearings, 1926–29.

The archives branch, FARC Fort Worth, also has records of the U.S. Circuit Court, Baton Rouge. Records relating to naturalizations include petitions, 1838–61; oaths of applicants, 1863–98; declarations of intention, 1906–11; questionnaires for declarations of intention, 1909–11; questionnaires for petitions, 1906–11.

Maine

The archives branch, FARC Boston, has declarations of intention, 1832–1911, and naturalization records, 1790–1906, from the U.S. District Court for the District of Maine.

Maryland

The archives branch, FARC Philadelphia, has declarations of intention, 1903–52, and naturalization records, 1792–1944, from the U.S. District Court for the District of Maryland. A general index to these records is still in the custody of the district court. Among the records of the U.S. Circuit Court for the District of Maryland are declarations of intention and naturalization records, 1796–1906, with an index, 1797–1853. Also available is *Minutes of the U.S. Circuit Court for the District of Maryland, 1790–1911*, M931, 7 rolls.

Massachusetts

The archives branch, FARC Boston, has records of the U.S. District Court for the District of Massachusetts. Records relating to naturalization include declarations of intention, 1798–1945; records of naturalization, 1790–1945, with an index, 1790–1911; and military naturalization records, 1919. Naturalization records of the U.S. Circuit Court for the district include declarations of intention, 1845–1911, and records of naturalization, 1845–1911, with an index, 1845–1906.

Michigan

The archives branch, FARC Chicago, has records of the

U.S. District Court for the Eastern District of Michigan (Detroit). Records relating to naturalization include declarations of intention, 1856–1906; naturalization depositions, 1911–18; and naturalization petitions, 1837–1941. Naturalization records of the U.S. Circuit Court for the district include declarations of intention, 1874–1906, and naturalization petitions, 1837–1906.

Naturalization records of the U.S. District Court for the Western District of Michigan (Marquette) include declarations of intention and petitions, 1887–1909, and an index, 1887–1909.

From the U.S. District Court for the Western District of Michigan (Grand Rapids) are naturalization record volumes, 1915–29, and declarations of intention, 1907–28.

Minnesota

The archives branch, FARC Kansas City, has records of the U.S. District Court for the District of Minnesota. Records relating to naturalization include naturalization certificates, 1909–18; declarations of intention, 1859–1962; naturalization orders, 1929–60; petitions for naturalization, 1875–1961; military petitions, 1918 and 1945; and overseas petitions, 1947–54.

Mississippi

The archives branch, FARC Atlanta, has records of the U.S. District Court for the Southern District of Mississippi, including naturalization records, 1906–43.

Missouri

The archives branch, FARC Kansas City, has naturalization certificates, 1907–29, and petitions for naturalization, 1907–41, from the U.S. District Court for the Eastern District of Missouri (St. Louis). The records of the U.S. District Court for the Western District of Missouri (Jefferson City) include naturalization certificates, 1906–26, and petitions and declarations of intention, 1916–24.

Montana

The archives branch, FARC Seattle, has records of the court for the Territory of Montana. Records relating to naturalization include for the first judicial district, journal of proceedings, 1868–89; for the second district, journal of proceedings, 1871–89; for the third district, journal of proceedings, 1868–88, and for the fourth district, journal of proceedings, 1886–87.

Records relating to naturalization from the U.S. District Court for the District of Montana (Butte) include declarations of intention, 1894–1902; an index to declarations of intention, 1894–1902; records of citizenship, 1894–1903; an index to records of citizenship, 1894–1903; and petition and record documents, 1910–29.

Naturalization records from the U.S. District Court for the District of Montana (Great Falls) include declarations of intention, 1924, and petition and record documents, 1926.

Naturalization records from the U.S. District Court for the District of Montana (Helena) include declarations of intention, 1892–1929; naturalization records, 1894–1906; an index to naturalization records, 1894–1906; naturalization petitions, 1907–27; certificate stub books, 1900–27; and final records in equity, 1898–1917.

Naturalization records from the U.S. Circuit Court for the District of Montana include declarations of intention, 1891–93; an index of naturalizations, 1891–98; and records of citizenship, 1891–98.

Nevada

The archives branch, FARC San Francisco, has petitions for naturalization, 1908–56, and declarations of intention, 1877–1951, from the U.S. District Court for the District of Nevada (Fallon), and declarations of intention, 1853–1944; petitions for naturalization, 1907–49; and final naturalization papers, 1877–1906, from the U.S. District Court for the District of Nevada (Reno).

New Hampshire

The archives branch, FARC Boston, has records of the U.S. District and Circuit Courts for the District of New Hampshire. Records relating to naturalization include declarations of intention and records of naturalization, 1849–98; an index to declarations, 1841–72; and a list of persons filing declarations, 1870–94. There are also scattered records of naturalizations from 1790 until 1850 among the term papers of the courts.

New Jersey

Naturalization records, 1838–1906, of the U.S. District Court for the District of New Jersey (Trenton) are at the archives branch, FARC New York. An index to these records is in the custody of the court; the New York archives branch does not have a copy.

New Mexico

The archives branch, FARC Denver, has records of the first through seventh judicial districts of the court for the Territory of New Mexico (Santa Fe, Fernandez de Taos and Albuquerque, Albuquerque and Las Cruces, Las Vegas, Roswell, Alamogordo, and Socorro). The records relating to naturalization include certificates of naturalization, 1907–11; declarations of intention, 1882–1917; and petitions for naturalization, 1906–17.

New York

The archives branch, FARC New York, has naturalization record volumes, 1824–1906, and declarations of intention, 1824–1940, from the U.S. District Court for the Southern District of New York (New York City); minutes of this court, 1789–1841, are microfilmed on M886, rolls 1–8 and part of roll 9. For the U.S. Circuit Court for the Southern District of New York, there are declarations of intention, 1845–1911 and minutes, 1790–1841 (microfilmed on M854, 3 rolls). Naturalization records from the U.S. District Court for the Eastern District of New York (Brooklyn) consist of declarations of intention, 1865–1929, and naturalization record volumes, 1865–1929.

There are also WPA photocopies and an index to naturalization records, 1792–1906, from federal, state, and local courts in New York City. These records are described on page 80.

North Carolina
The archives branch, FARC Atlanta, has records of the U.S. District Court for the Eastern District of North Carolina. Records relating to naturalization include petition and record documents, 1926–48, and declarations of intention, 1939–47.

North Dakota
The archives branch, FARC Kansas City, has records of the U.S. District Court for the Southwestern District of North Dakota. The records relating to naturalizations consist of declaration record books, 1892–1906.

Ohio
The archives branch, FARC Chicago, has records of the U.S. District Court for the Northern District of Ohio (Cleveland). Records relating to naturalization include certificates of naturalization, 1907–18; declarations of intention, 1855–91 and 1906–43; an index, 1855–1903; petitions, 1855–1903; and naturalization record volumes, 1856–80.

Naturalization records of the U.S. District Court for the Northern District of Ohio (Toledo) consist of declarations of intention, 1875–1929.

Naturalization records of the U.S. District Court for the Southern District of Ohio (Cincinnati and Columbus) include naturalization certificates, 1907–26; depositions, 1918–35; petition books, 1906–29; declarations of intention, 1906–56; final papers, 1868–97; and naturalization record volumes, 1852–1905. There is also an index to these naturalization records and those of the U.S. Circuit Court for the district, 1852–1905.

Oklahoma
The archives branch, FARC Fort Worth, has records of the U.S. District Court for the Western District of Oklahoma. The records relating to naturalizations consist of correspondence and notices, 1909–60, including lists of persons applying for naturalization.

Oregon
The archives branch, FARC Seattle, has records of the U.S. District Court for the District of Oregon. Records relating to naturalization include declarations of intention, 1859–1962; naturalization petitions, 1868–1970; an index to declarations of intention, 1859–1906; an index to petitions for naturalization, 1868–1906; an index to declarations and petitions for naturalization, 1906–56; military petitions, 1918; and certificates of naturalization, 1907–26.

Naturalization records from the U.S. Circuit Court for the District of Oregon include declarations of intention, 1906–11; an index to declaration of intention, 1870–1907; naturalization petitions, 1877–1912; and an index to petitions for naturalization, 1877–1912.

Pennsylvania
The archives branch, FARC Philadelphia, has records of the U.S. District Court for the Eastern District of Pennsylvania (Philadelphia). Records relating to naturalization include an index to petitions for naturalization, 1795–1951; petitions for naturalization, 1795–1951; an index to declarations of intention, 1795–1840 and 1915–51; and declarations of intention, 1795–1951. Records of the U.S. Circuit Court for the district include an index to declarations of intention and petitions for naturalization, 1790–1840; petitions for naturalization, 1790–1911; and declarations of intention, 1815–1911. The naturalization clerk for the Eastern District of Pennsylvania has custody of an alphabetical index for the petitions, 1790–1951, in the district and circuit courts. Some of the minutes of the district court are microfilmed on M987, and minutes of the circuit court, 1790–1844, are microfilmed on M932.

Naturalization records of the U.S. District Court for the Middle District of Pennsylvania (Scranton) consist of declarations of intention, 1910–27.

Naturalization records of the U.S. District Court for the Western District of Pennsylvania (Pittsburgh) include petitions for naturalization, 1820–1915, and declarations of intention, 1845–1935. Records of the U.S Circuit Court for the Western District of Pennsylvania, 1801–2, are microfilmed on M987.

Rhode Island
The archives branch, FARC Boston, has records of the U.S. District Court for the District of Rhode Island. Records relating to naturalization include declarations of intention, 1901–21; records of naturalization, 1842–44 and 1888–1906; and naturalization certificate stubs, 1907–45. Records of the U.S. Circuit Court for the District of Rhode Island include records of naturalization, 1846–84, 1893–1901, 1904, and 1906.

South Carolina
The archives branch, FARC Atlanta, has records of the U.S. District Court for the Eastern District of South Carolina (Charleston). Records relating to naturalization include petition and record documents, 1906–17 and 1919–29; an index to petitions, 1906–11; declarations of intention, 1906–12 and 1921–22; military petitions, 1918–24; and an index to military petitions, 1918–24. There are also four separate volumes of alphabetical indexes, 1790–1906, to minute books of the court, which show name of naturalized individual, age, country of origin, occuption, date and place of arrival, and date of oath of allegiance. Each entry gives the person's name and the date of administration of oath of allegiance.

Naturalization records of the U.S. District Court for the Eastern District of South Carolina (Columbia) consist of declarations of intention, 1910.

Vermont
The archives branch, FARC Boston, has records of the U.S. District Court for the District of Vermont. Records relating to naturalization consist of declarations of intention, 1859–1917.

Virginia
Among the records of the U.S. District Court for the Eastern District of Virginia are a few declarations, petitions, and certificates of naturalization for the years 1855 and 1864–96. Among the records of the U.S. District Court for the Western District of Virginia (Abingdon) are a few petitions for naturalization, 1907–17, and a few petitions

to set aside certificates of naturalization, 1909. These records are located at the archives branch, FARC Philadelphia.

Washington

The archives branch, FARC Seattle, has records of the U.S. District Court for the Eastern District of Washington (Spokane). Naturalization records consist of deposition case files, 1908–57.

Naturalization records of the U.S. District Court for the Western District of Washington (Seattle) include naturalization indexes, 1890–1950; declarations of intention, 1890–1950; naturalization petitions, 1906–50; naturalization records of adults, 1890–1906; naturalization records of minors, 1892–1906; naturalization depositions, 1911–53; naturalization certificate stubs, 1907–25; and statements of fact for petitions, 1911–14.

Naturalization records of the U.S. District Court for the Western District of Washington (Tacoma) include declarations of intention, 1907–57; naturalization records, 1896–1900; naturalization petitions, 1913–19; naturalization petition and record documents, 1912–52; orders of the court in naturalization, 1929–59; military naturalization petitions, 1918–19; overseas naturalization petitions, 1954–55; repatriation petitions, 1936–43; and soldiers' repatriation petitions, 1919–43.

Records of the U.S. Circuit Court for the Western District of Washington (Tacoma) include declarations of intention, 1892–1906, and naturalization records, 1890–1904.

There are also records relating to naturalizations from territorial and other courts in King, Pierce, Snohomish, and Thurston Counties. For King County, these include deposition case files, 1868–1924; declarations of intention, 1854–89 and 1889–1910; stub books relating to declarations of intention, 1893–96 and 1897–1906; naturalization petitions, 1906–28; an index to declarations of intention and naturalization petitions, 1906–24; final certificates, 1889–1906; stub books for naturalization certificates, 1897–1906; stub books for naturalization certificates for minors, 1897–1906; and a naturalization journal for minors, 1903–6.

The records for Pierce County include declarations of intention, 1853–89 and 1889–1924; records of citizenship, 1854–81; certificates of citizenship, 1889–1906; an index to declarations and final decrees of citizenship, 1854–1919; naturalization petitions, 1906–24; and naturalization indexes, 1906–22.

For courts in Snohomish County, the records include declarations of intention, 1876–90 and 1890–1973; deposition case files, 1896–1929; naturalization petitions, 1906–74; citizenship records, 1890–1906; stub books for certificates of naturalization, 1907–26; lists of citizenship petitions granted and denied, 1929–75; a general index to naturalizations, 1892–1975; a card index to naturalizations, 1950–74; repatriation petitions, 1939–55; and transferred naturalization petitions, 1948–73.

For courts in Thurston County, the records include deposition case files, 1844–1907; declarations of intention, 1883–1974; petitions for naturalization, 1906–74; naturalization journals of adults, 1891–1905; naturalization journals of minors, 1903–6; stub books for certificates of naturalization, 1907–24; recommendations and court orders, 1930–74; a card index to naturalizations, 1850–1973; repatriation oaths of allegiance, 1940–64; and transferred naturalization petitions, 1952–74.

Wisconsin

The archives branch, FARC Chicago, has records of the U.S. District Court for the Western District of Wisconsin (Madison). Records relating to naturalizations include declarations of intention, 1902–04 and 1920–21, created by the Superior, Wis. office; declarations of intention, 1870–1900, created by the LaCrosse, Wis. office; docket, 1866–1900, created by the LaCrosse, Wis. office; declarations of intention, 1876–1920, not inclusive; naturalization dockets, 1855–84; naturalization petition and record documents, 1910–18; and naturalization certificates, 1910–13.

3.2 Naturalization Information in Other Federal Records

Other federal records that provide naturalization information are **passport applications**, among the General Records of the Department of State, Record Group 59, and **homestead applications**, in the Records of the Bureau of Land Management, Record Group 49. If a naturalized citizen applied for a passport before 1906, records of his or her naturalization are usually in the passport application file. Homestead applicants had to present evidence that they were citizens or had applied for citizenship, so naturalization papers are often in a homestead applicant's file. For more information about passports, see page 246; for more about homestead applications, see page 229.

In addition, there are **photocopies of naturalization records for New York City and New England** in the Records of the Immigration and Naturalization Service (Record Group 85) resulting from a WPA project designed to centralize, photocopy, and index information in naturalization records scattered among federal, state, and local courts. The WPA was terminated before the project was completed.

Photocopies of and an index to naturalization documents filed in the courts of New York City, 1792–1906, are in the archives branch, FARC New York, arranged by court name and thereunder numerically by volume, bundle number, or page or record number. Photocopies of and an index to naturalization documents filed in courts in Connecticut, Maine, Massachusetts, New Hampshire, and Rhode Island are in the National Archives in Washington, DC. They are arranged by state, thereunder by court, and thereunder by date of naturalization. The index contains some cards for New York and Vermont, but the records to which they refer are not among this series of photocopies.

The records in both of these sets of files from the WPA project consist of 5″ × 8″ photographic copies of naturalization documents, usually two pages for each naturalization, with some or all of the following information: petition for citizenship, oath of allegiance, record of previous citizenship, place and date of birth, occupation, place and date of arrival in the United States, name of the ship, place of residence at the time of application, and name and address of a witness to these statements. Earlier records contain less information than later ones.

The indexes for both sets of files from the WPA project are 3″ × 5″ cards, arranged by name of petitioner, arranged according to the soundex system described on page 31. The index refers to the name and location of the court that granted the certificate of naturalization and to the volume and page number of the naturalization record. The printed cards have spaces, often left blank, for other information from the naturalization papers.

Finally, a volume entitled "List of Naturalization Certificates Sent to the U.S. Attorney for Review, and Returned by Him to the Board of Civil Service Examiners, of Persons Taking Civil Service Examinations, 1905–06" is part of Records of the United States Civil Service Commission, Record Group 146. References to naturalization certificates for persons taking federal civil service examinations in New York State are entered under the initial letter of the surname and thereunder chronologically by date the certificate was sent to the U.S. attorney. The list shows the name of the court that issued each naturalization certificate, the kind of civil service examination taken and where, and the date the certificate was returned by the attorney.

3.3 Naturalization Records Not in the National Archives

To obtain information about naturalization records that are not in the custody of the National Archives, the researcher should write to the appropriate court official—usually the clerk of the court that issued the certificate of naturalization. If the subject of research is a person who was naturalized after September 27, 1906, inquiries should be sent to the Immigration and Naturalization Service, 425 Eye Street N.W., Washington, DC 20536.

CHAPTER 4

Section B. Military Records

Records of the Regular Army

Military records make up a large part of the National Archives of the United States. Those that relate to military personnel constitute a rich source for genealogical research. They fall into two categories: evidence of military service, and evidence of veterans' benefits. The service, of course, preceded the benefits. In this chapter, sections describing the service records of the regular army, volunteer army, U.S. Navy, Marine Corps, and Coast Guard precede sections about pension files, bounty land warrant applications, and records of homes for veterans.

A researcher might well begin, however, with the pension files. A veteran's or his widow's application for a pension may provide most of the genealogical information sought: the veteran's age and residence at date of application, the names of his wife and children, and the dates of marriage and death. A pension application may provide information about the veteran's military service—the name of his unit and dates, for example—and other essential keys to the search for other evidence of his service. To use the service records, the researcher must know when and where in the armed forces his ancestor served and whether he was an officer or an enlisted man. These distinctions are less important for searches in the pension applications.

Records of military service may provide an individual's date of birth or age, possibly place of birth and date of death. Usually, however, military service records will simply document a serviceman's activities during a particular war, giving evidence of where he served, perhaps his physical condition, and possibly an account of wounds or capture. Unfortunately, for members of the regular army, navy, or Marine Corps, no central records were kept. For volunteer soldiers during the nineteenth century, there are several series of compiled military service records; they are described on pages 97–119. These compilations were prepared in the late nineteenth century by War Department clerks who abstracted the information from original muster rolls, returns, and medical and prison records. A comparable service record for a member of the regular military establishment must be pieced together from registers of enlistments and commissions, muster rolls, returns, descriptive books, War Department and Navy Department correspondence, and many other types of records. Such a search should not be undertaken unless pension files or family records have revealed the dates of the veteran's service.

By an act of 7 August 1789 (1 Stat. 49–50), Congress created the War Department; the Secretary of War was at its head, in charge of military and naval activities and organizations. Congress also created the permanent military establishment under an act of September 29, 1789 (1 Stat. 95–6) by authorizing the reenlistment of the 700 men in troops raised in compliance with an act of October 3, 1797 (34 J.C.C. 578–9). The act further provided for the commissioning of officers.

War Department jurisdiction over naval matters ceased when the Navy Department was established on 30 April 1798 (2 Stat. 553). The Department of Defense was established by the National Security Act of 1947 (61 Stat. 502–4) to include the Department of the Army, the Department of the Navy, and the Department of the Air Force.

Among the responsibilities initially assigned to the War Department was the establishment of an academy for the training of officers. The U.S. Military Academy was created at West Point in 1802 under the direction of the U.S. Army Corps of Engineers. The administration of pensions, land grants based on military service, and Indian affairs originally handled by the War Department were transferred to the Department of the Interior when it was created on 3 March 1849 (9 Stat. 395–7). Pension matters were transferred again in July 1930, when the Veterans Administration came into being (45 Stat. 1016–18).

The Secretary of War assigned to the Adjutant General responsibility for maintaining the archives of the Revolutionary War and the records of federal military service in the postwar period. The pre–1801 records were destroyed by fire at the War Department offices on 8 November 1800. Other nineteenth-century records were lost in various disasters, incuding the British invasion of Washington in 1814.

4.1 Records Relating to Officers and Enlisted Men

Because the Adjutant General's Office maintained the principal body of official U.S. Army records, the central files of that office have a large number of records about matters relating to individual servicemen. In addition, each War Department office, bureau, branch, and division maintained its own records, as did each individual command and some officers assigned to special duties. Such records may duplicate, supplement, or complement the Adjutant General's Office records and are usually arranged in a similar manner.

Until 1890, records were arranged under a system like the one described in the introduction on page 16, into letters sent and letters received, with registers and occasional indexes.

Administrative changes led to the adoption of new record-keeping systems in 1890, when a record card system was established. In addition to replacing the registers and letter books, it permitted summarization of all communications about the same person or subject. Further, the system eliminated the need to retain each piece of correspondence received; only a report of the communication and any action taken was kept, and many communications were returned to the inquirer with the reply. Communications received and sent, 1890–1917, make up the Document File of the General Correspondence of the Adjutant General's Office, Record Group 94.

The record-keeping systems are described in *Records of the Adjutant General's Office*, Preliminary Inventory 17, compiled by Lucille H. Pendell and Elizabeth Bethel (Washington: National Archives, 1949), and in various publications relating to the War Department, including *Struggle for Supremacy: The Career of General Fred C. Ainsworth*, by Mabel E. Deutrich (Washington: Public Affairs Press, 1962). The correspondence series themselves are described in more detail in the following paragraphs, and their availability as microfilm publications is noted where applicable.

Registers of letters received, 1812–89, serve as an index to communications received in the Office of the Adjutant General. The registers identify the correspondent, subject, and the disposition of the communication (that is, sent to another War Department office or bureau, or to another executive office). Appropriate cross-references to other persons and subjects mentioned in the correspondence sometimes are entered in the registers. The registers are chronogolically arranged, with one or more registers serving a given calendar year or group of years. They are unindexed for the period 1812–60, except for the year 1846. Entries in the registers are arranged by initial letter of the surname of the sender, office, agency, or business firm. The registers have been microfilmed as *Registers of Letters Received, Office of the Adjutant General, 1812–89*, M711, 85 rolls.

In **indexes to letters received**, 1846 and 1861–89, entries identify the correspondent or subject of the correspondence, with appropriate cross-references to other persons mentioned in the inquiry and other subjects of importance. Entries in an index volume for a single calendar year identify all communications received from the same person or office and, in some instances, show appropriate file consolidation numbers (the numbers assigned to the communications). The indexes have been microfilmed as *Indexes to Letters Received, Adjutant General's Office, Main Series, 1846, 1861–1889*, M725, 9 rolls.

Indexes to the general correspondence of the Adjutant General's Office for the period January 1890–March 1891 are contained in three volumes. Volume 1 contains entries for the letters "A–L" and volume 2, "M–Z." Volume 3 is a supplemental volume containing some entries not duplicated in volumes 1 or 2. Beginning April 1891, entries were made on index cards using name of soldier, person making inquiry; title of business firm; geographical location, military post, or organizational unit of the army; or subject. If any inquiry relates to a soldier, the index card generally also gives the title of the organization in which he served, the name of the person or office making the inquiry, the subject of the inquiry, and the file number. Most of the cards have been filed alphabetically according to a modified soundex system (see page 31 for an explanation of the soundex system). The indexes are available as *Index to General Correspondence of the Adjutant General's Office, 1890–1917*, M698, 1,269 rolls.

Letters received, 1805–21, contain letters originally received by War Department officers, offices, and bureaus and military units, divisions, districts, and departments. They include letters from officers, enlisted men, the President, Congress, private persons, and business firms. The letters deal with the appointment, recruitment, transfer, pay, promotion, leave, discharge, and other actions affecting officers and enlisted men of the army; orders, regulations, and other issuances of the War Department; Indian affairs; military organizations; military installations; and other subjects.

The general arrangement of the series of letters is chronological by year and thereunder alphabetical by the name, office, or title of the person who wrote the letter or to whom the letter chiefly relates, with some consolidations of correspondence for a single year or from a single individual for one or more years; and a few letters are arranged by subject. Many imperfections exist in the general arrangement. The records are now arranged in one continuous numerical series. The letters are reproduced as *Letters Received by the Office of the Adjutant General, 1805–1821*, M566, 144 rolls.

Letters received, 1822–89, were received from similar sources and relate generally to the same kinds of subjects or topics as the earlier letters. In this series, the letters are arranged to correspond with the arrangement of entries in the registers of letters received (described above) and are numbered in a separate sequence under each letter of the alphabet for each year. Some consolidations of correspondence on a given subject were assembled. Cross-references to consolidated files and to correspondence filed in records of other War Department offices and bureaus appear in the series. The letters are reproduced as *Letters Received by the Office of the Adjutant General, Main Series, 1822–1860*, M567, 636 rolls; *1861–1870*, M619, 828 rolls; *1871–1880*, M666, 593 rolls; and *1881–1889*, M689, 740 rolls.

The document file and record cards that make up the **general correspondence** of the Adjutant General's Office, 1890–1917, contain both letters received and copies of letters sent, interfiled, as well as reports and related papers. The records originated in or were received by the Principal Records Division, the Adjutant General's Office, 1890–June 1894; the Adjutant General's Office, July 1894–June 1904; the Military Secretary's Office, July 1904–7; and the Adjutant General's Office, 1908–17. The functions of these offices were essentially the same duties assigned to the Adjutant General's Office upon its creation, with some additions and modifications. The offices were reponsible for conducting the business of the permanent military establishment, including pensions, pay and bounties, and the military and medical histories of former officers and enlisted men. Beginning in July 1894, personal information relating to the military service of officers, which had been filed separately from 1863 to June 30, 1894, in Appointment, Commission, and Personal Branch files, was included among the records of the Adjutant General's Office. Additional descriptions of the duties of the successor offices are given in the introduction to M698.

The records in the document file for the period 1890–30 June 1894 are arranged by year, and thereunder by the number assigned to the communication upon its receipt. For the period 1 July 1894–30 June 1917, records are arranged in one continuous numerical series, with some gaps in the numbers. Not all communications received by the respective offices for the period 1890–1917 were retained; sometimes the inquiry and the reply were returned to the sender. In such instances, the only evidence of the communication and the reply is a record card. A record card was prepared for each communication received and sent; on it were entered a digest of the incoming communication, a copy of the reply, and appropriate memorandums, endorsements, and other notations to show what action was taken. Except for the period 1890–30 June 1894, when various arrangements were used, the record cards are arranged numerically and parallel the document file and the index; related items in each bear the same file number and office designation.

Letters sent, 1800–90, constitute the main or central series of letters sent by the Adjutant General's Office. The Appointment, Commission, and Personal Branch; Volunteer Service Branch; Colored Troops Division; Bounty and Claims Division; and the Military Prison Record Division maintained their own series of outgoing correspondence during their existence. Copies of some replies sent by the various War Department offices and branches are filed with related letters in the letters received series described above. The letters have been reproduced as *Letters Sent by the Office of the Adjutant General, Main Series, 1800–1890*, M565, 63 rolls. Most of the volumes have an index, which has been microfilmed preceding the letters.

Muster rolls, 1791–31 October 1912, are another kind of record useful for identifying individual officers and enlisted men. A muster roll is a list of all troops actually present on parade or otherwise accounted for on the day of muster or review of troops under arms. Muster rolls were made to take account of the number of soldiers assigned to the unit, to inspect their arms and accoutrements, and to examine their condition.

The muster roll from which the names were called was also the voucher from which the paymaster issued pay. The several types include descriptive rolls; muster-in rolls; the regular muster-for-pay rolls for individuals, detachments, companies, and regiments; and muster rolls for field, staff, and band. Muster-for-pay rolls, the larger series, include the names of personnel of the organization, with names of commissioned officers and noncommissioned officers coming first, followed by names of privates in alphabetical order. Given are date and place of enlistment, by whom enrolled and for what period, date of muster into service, date and amount of last pay and for what period, and remarks that may include disposition of any absentees, notes of desertions, and deaths. Regular army troops mustered for pay on the last day of February, April, June, August, October, and December. Muster and descriptive rolls give additional information, including place of birth, age at date of muster, previous occupation, color of hair, color of eyes, complexion, bounty paid and amounts due, clothing accounts, and remarks. Special musters of troops were taken at various times, and such records may include all or much of the information contained on the muster-for-pay rolls.

The muster roll used before 1918 contained a "record of events" column, which gives valuable historical information relating to military activities; it was replaced in 1918 by a **roster**, which gives only a list of names together with rank and changes in status.

To use muster rolls, the researcher needs to know which units a serviceman was assigned to and the dates of his service. Muster rolls are arranged by arm of service, thereunder numerically by regiment, thereunder alphabetically by company or troop or other unit, and thereunder chronologically. Muster rolls for special units are filed at the end of the series. Included with some of the earlier muster rolls are inspection returns, various papers relating to pay, bounty books, order books, and other materials. Similar records for the later period are separately filed, if extant, in various other series.

Among other series of War Department records are additional records relating to officers and enlisted personnel of the regular army who were prisoners of war, served in special capacities, were ill or wounded, received decorations or awards, or were court-martialed.

Carded medical records, 1821–84 and 1894–1912, contain information relating to regular army personnel admitted to hospitals for treatment. Each card includes name, rank, organization, cause for admission, date admitted and discharged (or date deserted or died if applicable), transfers, and remarks. The 1821–84 records are arranged by regiment number, and thereunder by initial of surname. The 1894–1912 records are arranged by arm of service, thereunder by number of regiment, and thereunder by initial letter of surname.

Original medical records from which the carded abstracts were prepared are extant, as are records that were not included in the abstracting project but that contain varying amounts of information relating to the treatment of individuals at specific hospitals. There are also records relating to medical activities in specific wars in the records of the Adjutant General's Office for the period 1821–1912 and in the records of the Office of the Surgeon General for later periods. Because of the volume, arrangement, and specialized topics of such records, researchers should consult

NARS inventories and then seek the advice of the archivists familiar with such records for information relating to a specific person, unit, and period of service.

Records relating to officers and enlisted **medical personnel**, as well as those who served in civilian capacities, are contained in Records of the Office of the Surgeon General (Army), Record Group 112, and in Records of the Office of the Adjutant General, Record Group 94. The following series in Record Group 112 are generally alphabetically arranged and contain varying amounts of information: military service cards of Revolutionary War medical officers, 1775–1819; registers of medical officers, 1806–20 and 1849–1902; military service cards of medical officers, 1812–62; military service cards of retired or deceased medical officers (A–R), 1813–1914; medical service cards of medical officers, 1860–1917; registers of military service of medical officers and contract surgeons, 1876–79; military service cards of regular army officers of the Medical Corps, 1894–1917; military service cards of dental surgeons, 1911–17; personnel data cards of Civil War contract surgeons, 1862–1914; service history cards of contract surgeons, 1898–1915; service data cards of contract dentists who were commissioned dental surgeons in 1911 (1901–11); summary data cards showing the service history of contract dental surgeons, 1911–16; and personal data cards of Spanish-American War contract nurses, 1898–1939. Of particular interest is the consolidated correspondence file, which contains information about medical officers and nurses. The correspondence was received after 1889, but the records contain some references to the period 1818–90.

In Record Group 94 are personal papers of medical officers and physicians before 1912. These records include extracts of orders, appointment information, personal reports, information concerning duty stations, records of promotions, and, for contract medical officers, information relating to the contract terms and duty stations. The series is arranged alphabetically by name of medical officer. Files are included in this series for officers who served with volunteer units before 1903.

There are also papers relating to medical cadets in the Civil War. This series contains information relating to appointments, discharges, and the service of medical cadets. Some information relating to pre-Civil War service is included in some files. The files are arranged alphabetically by name of cadet.

A three-volume "Address Book" shows the name, rank, organization, post office address, and date of death of Civil War medical officers. One volume identifies surgeons and assistant surgeons serving in volunteer organizations; another, surgeons; and the third, surgeons and assistant surgeons serving with the U.S. Army. The entries, arranged alphabetically by surgeon's name, are dated from the 1860s to 1894.

Papers relating to hospital stewards, 1862–93, consist of orders; correspondence concerning appointments, discharges, and service; and the personal reports of hospital stewards. The records are arranged alphabetically by name of steward.

The **court-martial records** in Records of the Office of the Judge Advocate General (Army), Record Group 153, are dated 1808–1939. Of greatest genealogical significance in these records is a large series of case files for general courts-martial, courts of inquiry, and military commissions. These files are arranged by case number. A name index for the period 1891–1917 gives name and rank of defendant, army unit, case number, and date. A similar index to the earlier case files is currently being prepared by the National Archives. These records will be of greatest use to the researcher who knows when and where the subject of research was court-martialed.

Each case file generally includes a copy of the trial transcript; other related documents, such as correspondence or orders pertaining to the case are sometimes included. The trial transcript usually indicates the charges and specifications, pleas and arraignments of defendants, testimony of defendants and witnesses, findings and sentencings of the court, and, upon occasion, reviewing authorities' reports and statements of action by the Secretary of War and the President. Case files also indicate names, ranks, and units of soldiers court-martialed, and, in some instances, their dates of birth and places of residence.

Records relating to wars are separate series of records relating to military activities during a given emergency. They are included in the records of the Adjutant General's Office, in the records of the various War Department offices and bureaus, and in records relating to military units. Examples of such records are correspondence series with name and subject indexes; records of regular army units maintained by the units; and special correspondence series relating to particular situations or circumstances, such as the records relating to persons gassed during World War I, records relating to persons who served in civilian capacities during war and peacetime, and records relating to persons who initially served in a military capacity and were subsequently discharged and hired as civilians in the same capacity. These series usually contain more information about officers then enlisted men. Many include indexes from about 1861.

The names and descriptions of specific records series relating to officers or enlisted men are given in NARS inventories of the records. For example, Preliminary Inventory 17, *Records of the Adjutant General's Office*, includes the indexed series of post-Revolutionary War manuscripts; War of 1812 "miscellaneous records"; Mexican War letters received; unindexed Civil War staff papers; generals' papers and books; and generals' reports of service.

There are also **records relating to regular army military units** in Records of U.S. Regular Army Mobile Units, 1821–1942, Record Group 391; Records of U.S. Army Coast Artillery Districts and Defenses, 1901–42, Record Group 392; Records of U.S. Army Commands, 1784–1821, Record Group 98; Records of U.S. Army Continental Commands, 1821–1920, Record Group 393; Records of U.S. Army Overseas Operations and Commands, 1898–1942, Record Group 395; to a limited extent, Records of the Headquarters of the Army, Record Group 108; and other record groups containing records incidental to military service.

4.2 Records of Officers

Researching an officer's military career during the period

before 1917 is difficult, because few histories of officers were kept, and officers' papers were put in consolidated files only during a short period after 1863. Accordingly, the researcher should first consult published biographies and histories to identify the period of the officer's service, the units to which he was attached, and any other particulars of his service that can be gleaned from secondary sources. Among such publications are *Historical Register and Dictionary of the United States Army from its Organization, September 29, 1789, to March 2, 1903*, by Francis B. Heitman, 2 vols. (Washington, 1903; Congressional Serial 4535 and 4536), which was reprinted by the University of Illinois Press, Urbana, 1965; *Biographical Register of the Officers and Graduates of the U.S. Military Academy*, by George W. Cullum, 9 vols. (various publishers, 1850–91); *U.S. Army Register*, published biannually since 1815; and the various registers of volunteer officers mentioned in tables 10, 13, 15, and 16.

Heitman's *Historical Register* is a complete list of commissioned officers of the army, including officers of the volunteer staff and brevet majors and generals or brigadier generals of volunteers. It gives their full names and shows their service as cadets, officers, or enlisted men, either in the regular army or volunteer service. A list of Confederate officers who served in the U.S. Army is included.

The U.S. Army Register, a published list of regular army officers, begins with the year 1813. The early editions provide name, rank, military specialty, date of commission, staff appointments and brevets, and regiment and military district (W3.11:813). *A Compilation of Registers of the Army of the United States from 1815 to 1837* comprises most of the early registers in a single volume (W3.11:815–37). Annual editions of the register were published in this same series until 1945. Complete army registers for the years 1813–38 can also be found in the *American State Papers, Class 5, Military Affairs* (ASP 016–022). For the years 1891–1943, an alphabetical *Army Directory* published by the Adjutant General's Office is also available (W3.10:891–945). The Congressional Serial Set contains transcripts of lists of officers composed for fiscal reports with the name, rank, date of commission, brevets or commissions of prior date, the number of months for which pay accounts were received, annual pay, rations, allowance for servants, cost of forage, fuel and quarters as follows:

1848 (Ser. 543–56)
1849 (Ser. 577–54)
1850 (Ser. 679–48)
1851 (Ser. 679–50)
1852 (Ser. 679–58)
1853 (Ser. 721–59)
1854 (Ser. 783–58)
1855 (Ser. 851–22)
1856 (Ser. 897–24)
1857 (Ser. 955–66)
1858 (Ser. 1006–58)
1859 (Ser. 1048–35)
1860 (Ser. 1100–54)

The most recent edition of the *U.S. Army Register* in Record Group 287 was issued in three volumes for 1976. (Sup Docs No. M108.8:, D102.9:)

Basic evidence of an officer's service consists of documents relating to his appointment and to the termination of his service. This usually includes a letter of appointment, an oath of office, a letter of acceptance of the appointment, and records or documents relating to the termination of his service by resignation, dismissal, death, or retirement.

The most accessible sources of information about officers are in the records of the Adjutant General's Office and its subdivisions. The War Department fire of 1800 destroyed much of the documentation pertaining to officers who served in the regular army from 1784 to 1800. There are compiled military service records for the officers who served in the few organizations that were predecessors of the regular army, principally the First American Regiment, First U.S. Regiment, Battalion of Artillery, and U.S. Levies. Service in other organizations may be documented in muster rolls and returns. The most important series for information about regular army officers who served during the period 1800–62 are the correspondence files, muster and payrolls, and returns in Record Group 94. Information about some officers who served during the period 1800–21 can be obtained from the registers of enlistments.

The Commission Branch was organized in the Office of the Adjutant General on 1 January 1863, to handle such matters as appointments, promotions, resignations, discharges, retirements, assignments, and details of commanding officers of the regular army, volunteer officers in staff corps, officers appointed by the President, officers in the District of Columbia Militia, veterinary surgeons, post traders, and noncommissioned staff officers up to 1882. On 1 January 1871, the branch was designated the Appointment, Commission, and Personal (ACP) Branch of the Adjutant General's Office and continued as such until 1894. Because the branch, in addition to creating records of its own, drew from the central files of the Adjutant General's Office earlier papers dealing with appointments and commissions, its records are a good resource for documenting the service of officers. A detailed description of the various record series of the branch is given in Preliminary Inventory 17, *Records of the Adjutant General's Office*. Records of the branch include letters sent and received, registers of letters received, indexes, registers of applications for appointments, commissions, and many other documents, some of which have been microfilmed as *Letters Received by the Commission Branch of the Adjutant General's Office, 1863–70*, M1064, 527 rolls; and *Name and Subject Index to the Letters Received by the Appointment Commission, and Personal Branch of the Adjutant General's Office, 1871–94*, M1125, 4 rolls.

Applications for appointment to positions in the U.S. Army and War Department, 1871–80, were made to the President, the Secretary of War, and others. They are arranged chronologically by year, thereunder numerically. Entries in twelve volumes of registers of applications identify the correspondent or applicant, the position applied for, date received, by whom recommended, and the action on the application. Indexes identify the correspondent or applicant and give the file number assigned to the consolidation of papers relating to the individual in the ACP file of letters received.

The records of the ACP Branch include various series relating to army commissions, including original commissions that were never delivered, copies of commissions issued, and copies of letters of appointment and promotion.

Original commissions, signed by the President, that were never delivered, are arranged chronologically, 1812–1902, and thereunder alphabetically by name of officer. Registers of commissions vary, but usually show the name of the officer, rank, date of commission, date of acceptance, and remarks. Registers of appointment include name, residence, rank, organization, and date of appointment. In addition, some registers include date and place of birth. The commission and appointment records are variously dated, and some relate to type of appointment.

Three **historical registers** of commissioned officers of the line of the army show name, place of birth, military unit, date of commission, date of resignation, date of death, and sometimes other information and remarks. Volume 1 covers the period 1799–1860, volume 2, 1861–1900, and volume 3, 1901–15. Within each volume, the arrangement is alphabetical by initial letter of surname of officer, and thereunder chronological by year. (Similar registers are in the records of the Ordnance Department, Paymaster's Department, Quartermaster's Office, and the Signal Corps.)

In 1816, every officer made a personal **report of place of birth**. The records of these reports are arranged alphabetically by initial letter of surname of officer.

A one-volume **roster of officers**, 1783–1826, gives officer's name, place of residence, date of acceptance of first commission, date and change of each rank held during the period indicated, and remarks. The remarks consist of pertinent information relating to the individual's military service. The entries are arranged alphabetically by initial letter of the officer's surname.

Most of the U.S. Military Academy **cadet application papers**, 1805–66, are arranged by year and thereunder numerically by file number. The file designation consists of the year in which the application was received and the number assigned to the file, with a few unnumbered applications at the end of each calendar year arranged alphabetically by the name of the candidate. No applications for the year 1811 are extant. An index to this series is arranged alphabetically by the initial letter of the surname of the applicant, thereunder by initial vowel sound of the surname, and thereunder chronologically by date of application. The index entries show the name of the applicant, year of application, state from which the candidate applied, and file number of the application papers. Some of these applications contain a considerable amount of information about the family background of the applicants. Some incorrect spellings of names have been noted in the index, but no corrections have been made. A list of early applications, 1804–9, that were forwarded to the Record and Pension Office in 1896 appears at the beginning of the name index. Many of the papers to which the list refers are now filed among the records microfilmed as *Letters Received by the Secretary of War, Main Series, 1801–1870*, M221, 317 rolls.

The application papers have been reproduced as *U.S. Military Academy Cadet Application Papers, 1805–1866*, M688, 242 rolls. Roll 1 contains the index. In addition, a list of applicants for whom no papers have been found in this series has been prepared and is filmed after the introductory remarks to the microfilm publication.

The Volunteer Service Branch was established in the office of the Adjutant General in October 1861. It was charged with all matters pertaining to the authorization, recruiting, organization, service, and discharge of volunteer troops as organizations, together with the officers. The branch was transferred to the Record and Pension Office when that office was created in 1889.

Some regular army officers initially entered the military service as volunteers, resigned their regular commission in favor of higher volunteer commissions during wartime, or were assigned to duty with volunteers. Evidence of this service is contained in the compiled military service records of volunteers. Information about such officers can be found among the records of the Volunteer Service Branch, which consist primarily of letters sent, letters received, and alphabetical name indexes to letters sent and letters received showing the register numbers assigned to communications. The index volumes are chronologically arranged, and some indexes to letters received contain briefs of the communications. The compiled military service records contain cross-references to the appropriate Volunteer Service Branch records.

Because the records relating to volunteers also contain information about regular army personnel, researchers may locate material about an ancestor who was a regular army officer in the general correspondence of the Record and Pension Office.

Every commander of a body of troops was required to furnish **returns** (or official reports) to the adjutant general at specified intervals, usually monthly, on forms provided by that office. The station of troops, the strength of each unit, and the names of commissioned personnel and their whereabouts were thus kept currently available in the Adjutant General's Office. This body of records, used in conjunction with the muster rolls, constitutes a valuable source of historical information. Separate series of returns are available for departments, divisions, posts, and military organizations. The most useful returns for genealogical research are the post and military organization returns.

Post returns, early 1800s–December 1916, are monthly returns of many military posts, camps and stations. Returns generally show the units that were stationed at a particular post and their strength, the names and duties of the officers, the number of officers present and absent, a list of official communications received, and a record of events. These records have been reproduced as *Returns from United States Military Posts, 1800–1916*, M617, 1,550 rolls. They are arranged alphabetically by name of post and thereunder chronologically.

In connection with post returns, *Historical Information Relating to Military Posts and Other Installations, ca. 1700–1900*, M661, 8 rolls, may be useful. Reproduced on this microfilm is the twenty-seven-volume "Outline Index of Military Forts and Stations." Also reproduced are a few sixteenth-, seventeenth-, and twentieth-century references.

The purpose of **returns of military organizations** was to report unit strength in total numbers of men present, absent, sick, or on extra or daily duty, and to give a specific accounting of officers and enlisted men by name. Additional information was required on returns from time to time. These returns, 1821–1916, are arranged by arm of service, thereunder numerically by regiment, and thereunder chronologically by date of return.

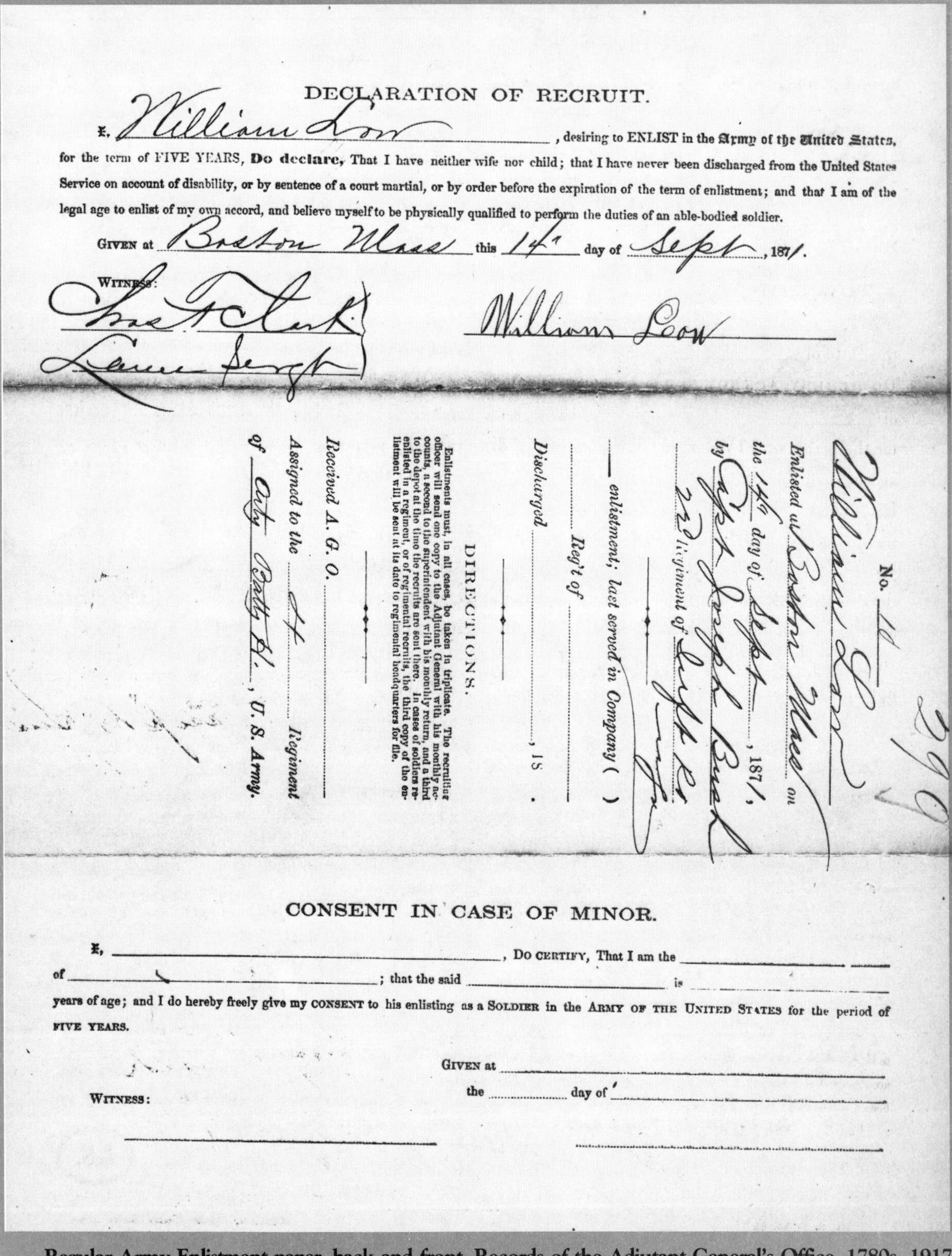

DECLARATION OF RECRUIT.

I, William Low, desiring to ENLIST in the Army of the United States, for the term of FIVE YEARS, **Do declare,** That I have neither wife nor child; that I have never been discharged from the United States Service on account of disability, or by sentence of a court martial, or by order before the expiration of the term of enlistment; and that I am of the legal age to enlist of my own accord, and believe myself to be physically qualified to perform the duties of an able-bodied soldier.

GIVEN at Boston Mass this 14th day of Sept, 1871.

WITNESS: Chas F Clark
Lance Sergt

William Low

No. 11

William Low

Enlisted at Boston Mass on the 14th day of Sept, 1871, by Capt Joseph Beck 22 Regiment of Infy

___ enlistment; last served in Company ( )

___ Reg't of ___

Discharged ___, 18 .

DIRECTIONS.

Enlistments must, in all cases, be taken in triplicate. The recruiting officer will send one copy to the Adjutant General with his monthly accounts, a second to the superintendent with his monthly return, and a third to the depot at the time the recruits are sent there. In case of soldiers re-enlisted in a regiment, or of regimental recruits, the third copy of the enlistment will be sent at its date to regimental headquarters for file.

Received A. G. O.

Assigned to the 4 Regiment of Arty Batty H, U. S. Army.

CONSENT IN CASE OF MINOR.

I, ___, DO CERTIFY, That I am the ___ of ___; that the said ___ is ___ years of age; and I do hereby freely give my CONSENT to his enlisting as a SOLDIER in the ARMY OF THE UNITED STATES for the period of FIVE YEARS.

GIVEN at ___

the ___ day of ___

WITNESS:

Regular Army Enlistment paper, back and front. Records of the Adjutant General's Office, 1780s–1917, Record Group 94.

Residence Lawrence Mass.

THE UNITED STATES OF AMERICA.

OATH OF ENLISTMENT AND ALLEGIANCE.

STATE OF Massachusetts }
TOWN OF Boston } ss:

I, William Low, born in Haverhill in the State of Massachusetts, and by occupation a Laborer, Do hereby acknowledge to have voluntarily enlisted this fourteenth day of September, 1871, as a **Soldier** in the Army of the United States of America, for the period of FIVE YEARS, unless sooner discharged by proper authority: And do also agree to accept from the United States such bounty, pay, rations, and clothing as are, or may be established by law. And I do solemnly swear, that I am twenty one years and — months of age, and know of no impediment to my serving honestly and faithfully as a Soldier for five years under this enlistment contract with the United States. And I, William Low do also solemnly swear, that I will bear true faith and allegiance to the **United States of America**, and that I will serve them honestly and faithfully against all their enemies or opposers whomsoever; and that I will observe and obey the orders of the President of the United States, and the orders of the officers appointed over me, according to the Rules and Articles of War.

William Low (L.S.)

Subscribed and duly sworn to before me, this 14th day of Sept, A. D. 1871.

Joseph Bush
Capt 22d Inft
Recruiting Officer. U.S.A.

I CERTIFY, ON HONOR, That I have carefully examined the above-named recruit, agreeably to the General Regulations of the Army, and that, in my opinion, he is free from all bodily defects and mental infirmity which would, in any way, disqualify him from performing the duties of a soldier.

A. A. McLaren
Surgeon. U.S.A.
Examining Officer.

I CERTIFY, ON HONOR, That I have minutely inspected the above-named recruit, William Low, previously to his enlistment, and that he was entirely sober when enlisted; that, to the best of my judgment and belief, he is of lawful age; and that I have accepted and enlisted him into the service of the United States under this contract of enlistment as duly qualified to perform the duties of an able-bodied soldier, and, in doing so, have strictly observed the Regulations which govern the Recruiting Service. This soldier has gray *eyes*, dark *hair*, ruddy *complexion*, is five *feet* seven ½ *inches high.*

Joseph Bush (L.S.)
Capt 22d Inft
Recruiting Officer, United States Army

[A. G. O. No. 73.]

Station books of officers and organizations of the regular army, 1861–1915, show officer's name, letter of company, station, whereabouts at last report, date of information, and remarks about such matters as special assignments and leaves. For cadets at the U.S. Military Academy, residence and date and place of birth are included. Place and date of marriage of officers are often mentioned, and addresses, occupations, and date of death of retired officers are given. The 186 volumes are arranged generally chronologically by year under arm of service, thereunder by number of regiment, and thereunder by rank for the following groups for the periods indicated: infantry, 1862–1913 (61 vols.); infantry, 1861, and cavalry and artillery, 1861–1906 (51 vols.); cavalry, 1907–13 (6 vols.); artillery, 1907–13 (7 vols.); general staff officers, 1861–1913 (50 vols.); retired officers, 1891–1915 (10 vols.); unattached, 1870–71 and 1911 (2 vols.); and Signal Corps and hospital chaplains, 1864–67 (1 vol.).

Typescript volumes of **officers' histories**, ca. 1861–1904, may also be useful. Entries in the five volumes of this series are arranged roughly by arm of service and thereunder alphabetically. In addition to information about military service, they contain extracts from officers' efficiency reports, summaries of Civil War volunteer service, and information about honors awarded. Military histories of some regular army and volunteer officers, chiefly those who served in the Civil War, were prepared between 1875 and 1890 and were bound in two volumes. They contain citations to the consolidated files upon which they are based. Each volume contains an index. In addition to the records of the Adjutant General's Office, several other record groups contain information about officers of the regular army.

Records of the Office of the Chief of Engineers, Record Group 77, include four volumes of military service **registers of officers of the Engineer Corps**, 1857–94. Among Records of the Office of the Quartermaster General, Record Group 92, are eight volumes of personal histories of regular officers in the Quartermaster's Department, 1846–1905.

Records of the Office of the Surgeon General (Army), Record Group 112, includes eleven volumes of **registers of military service of officers**, 1806–20 and 1849–1902, as well as a single volume of lists showing the service and stations of medical officers, 1829–33. There are eight volumes of military service histories of ordnance officers, ca. 1815–1922, and a single volume of military service histories of ordnance officers serving at field establishments, 1838–82, among Records of the Office of the Chief of Ordnance, Record Group 156. Records of the Office of the Paymaster General, Record Group 99, includes a register of paymasters, 1815–68, and nine volumes of personal histories of paymasters, 1848–1910.

Records of the Office of the Chief Signal Officer, Record Group 111, includes one volume of synopses of military histories of officers, 1860–67, and two volumes of military histories of officers, 1861–65. A number of the regular army regiments also maintained volumes of officers' histories, which can be found in Records of the United States Regular Army Mobile Units, 1821–1942, Record Group 391. A few officers' histories are in Records of United States Army Continental Commands, 1821–1920, Record Group 393; one collection of some consequence consists of nine volumes of military histories of officers in the Department of Texas, 1869–99.

There is considerably more information about West Point cadets and the officers in charge at West Point in the Records of the United States Military Academy, RG 404, described in Preliminary Inventory 185. The original records are in the U.S. Military Academy Archives, West Point, NY.

4.3 Records of Enlisted Men

Researching the career of an enlisted man is generally less complicated than researching the career of an officer, but only because there are fewer records relating to enlisted personnel. As with officers' records, most records of enlisted men are in the Records of the Adjutant General's Office, Record Group 94. Genealogists will find useful the information to be gleaned from the enlistment papers and registers of enlistment.

An **enlistment paper** was a contract required of every enlisted man who served in the regular army. The records are arranged in three series: 1784–1815; 1798–14 July 1894; and 15 July 1894–31 October 1912. The first series is arranged in a drop file by the initial letter only of the surname. The second and third series are arranged alphabetically by name of soldier, and thereunder chronologically by date of enlistment. Enlistment papers for persons who served two or more enlistments have sometimes been consolidated.

Enlistment papers generally show soldier's name, place of enlistment, date, by whom enlisted, age, occupation, personal description, regimental assignment, and certification of the examining surgeon and recruiting officer. The papers relating to enlistments after 15 July 1894 include descriptive and assignment cards, prior service cards, certificates of disability, final statements, inventories of effects, and records of death and interment, if appropriate. The highest of the handwritten numbers on the front side of each enlistment paper, at the top center, identifies the enlistment register entry for the soldier.

Enlistment papers for Indian scouts are discussed on page 171.

Registers of enlistment, 1798–1913 generally contain information relating to the enlistment and termination of service of enlisted personnel. The registers for the period 1798–30 June 1821, volumes 1–35, also contain information about officers in service during that period. A register entry spans two pages and varies in content.

The register entries for the period 1798–30 June 1821 contain soldier's name, military organization, physical description, date and place of birth, enlistment information, and remarks. Entries in the remarks column contain cryptic references to the source record from which the information was obtained. A partial key to the references, generally a two-initial abbreviation of the title of the original record, appears in volume 1 of the enlistment registers. The source documents cannot now be identified in all cases. Complete service information is not given for every soldier; in particular, the date or reason for termination of service may not be supplied.

The registers for the period 1 July 1821–1913 are uniform in content. A two-page entry contains the same information that appears on the enlistment paper, as well as information relating to the termination of service. The left-hand page gives the enlisted man's name; date and place of enlistment; by whom enlisted; period of enlistment; place of birth; age; civilian occupation at the time of enlistment; and personal description.

The right-hand page gives the number and arm of service, company, and information relating to separation from service. If the individual was discharged, the date, place, and reason for discharge are given, as well as rank. Varying additional information, such as on courts-martial or desertions, appears in the remarks column. For the period 1821–1913, the remarks column does not show the source of the information. The enlistment information was copied from the enlistment papers; the termination information came from muster rolls and other records.

Separate registers are found for mounted rangers, 1832–33; Indian scouts, 1866–1914; post quartermasters, 1884–90; sergeants appointed under an act of 5 July 1884; ordnance sergeants, 1832–90; commissary sergeants, 1873–91; Philippine scouts, October 1901–13; Puerto Rican provisional infantry, 1901–14; and hospital stewards, 1887–99. To locate the enlistment register of a particular serviceman, a researcher should know approximately when he served. It is helpful to know the department or arm of service in which he served. The enlistment registers, except those for hospital stewards, quartermaster sergeants, and ordnance sergeants, have been reproduced as *Registers of Enlistments in the U.S. Army, 1798–1914*, M233, 47 rolls. The registers for 1798–30 June 1821 are arranged in strict alphabetical order. The later registers are arranged by initial letter of the surname, and thereunder chronologically by month and year of enlistment. Some volumes in the later registers are arranged in groups of months for a period of several years during the Mexican War, July 1846–October 1850.

There are a few **military histories** of enlisted personnel. Resumes of retiring enlisted personnel and those of principal musicians and drum majors are generally found in the correspondence files of the Adjutant General's Office. Separate histories of quartermaster sergeants, 1884–93, are contained in the Records of the Quartermaster General, Record Group 92; separate registers and lists of ordnance personnel, 1832–1917, are contained in Records of the Office of the Chief of Ordnance; and separate registers, lists, and descriptive books, 1856–87, of hospital stewards are contained in the Records of the Office of the Surgeon General, Record Group 112.

Additional details of a soldier's service may be found on the muster rolls of his military unit, in medical records, and in court-martial records, as noted above on pages 86–87. Occasionally, information may be found in the numerous correspondence files of the Adjutant General's Office and other War Department offices and bureaus, but searching these files is seldom rewarding in proportion to the time required. One exception is the records of the Record and Pension Office, for which there is a consolidated name index, 1775–1904. The Enlisted Branch of the Adjutant General's Office, 1848–89, and the Colored Troops Branch, 1863–89, also handled matters relating to enlisted personnel, but the absence of consolidated name indexes hampers research.

Certificates of disability, 1812–99, are certificates issued by surgeons recommending discharges for soldiers. They contain statements about types of disabilities. Complete information relating to the individual is given, including name; rank; organization; when, where, and by whom enlisted; period of enlistment; age; place of birth; personal description; and station. The papers are variously arranged.

Final statements, 1862–99, are papers relating to the deaths of soldiers. Each contains a record of death and burial, an inventory of personal effects, and a final statement relating to the military service of the individual that includes personal description, cause and place of death, and an account of the soldier's financial affairs. The records are arranged generally by organization for various groups of years.

Reports of **medical examination of recruits**, 1884–1912, are in the records relating to the sick and wounded in the medical records of the Record and Pension Office of the Adjutant General's Office. They show name; residence; date and place of birth; occupation; race; marital status; previous employment; father's nationality; citizenship status; previous military service; name and address of dependants; personal description and remarks; report of physical examination; date and place of acceptance; and enlistment or rejection. The records are arranged alphabetically by the name of the recruit and thereunder by the date of enlistment.

Information about the service of enlisted men may also be found in the records of the Enlisted Branch of the Adjutant General's Office, which was created in December 1862 to handle recruitment, discharge, transfers, furloughs, and other matters relating to enlisted men. The office inherited the "Addison File" relating to the military service of enlisted men, a file created or kept by a clerk in the War Department. The papers in the file are dated 1848–62. In 1889, the functions of the Enlisted Branch were transferred to the Record and Pension Office.

The **correspondence files of the Enlisted Branch** consist of letters sent, 1851–52, 1860–62, and 1863–89; registers of letters received, 1862–89; and letters received, 1848–62 and 1863–89. Letters sent, arranged chronologically by the date sent, are indexed for the period 1863–89. Letters received are arranged chronologically by year and thereunder by symbol assigned in the register of letters received, with varying other arrangements. Name indexes, 1863–89, and subject indexes, 1863–81, serve to locate communications in the letters received series. References to communications contained in this and other series of records relating to regular army personnel are sometimes contained on the jackets of the enlistment papers, 1894–1912, and in the registers of enlistment.

Military records described in other sections of this chapter relate also to officers and enlisted men of the regular army. See pages 135–142 for pension records, page 145 for bounty land warrant records, and pages 155–157 for records of veterans' homes and soldiers' burials. See also page 245 for descriptions of records of genealogical value about military dependents.

CHAPTER 5

Service Records of Volunteers

CHAPTER

5

Service Records of Volunteers

5.1 Introduction: Compiled Military Service Records

5.1 Introduction: Compiled Military Service Records

In wars in which there were not enough free enlistments in the regular army and militia, men were conscripted to serve in **volunteer** (non-regular) military units. The military service records of volunteers cover service during the Revolutionary War, 1775–83; the post-Revolutionary War period, 1784–1811; the War of 1812, 1812–15; Indian Wars, 1816–60; the Mexican War, 1846–48; the Civil War, 1861–65; and the Spanish-American War and the Philippine Insurrection, 1898–1903. Volunteers also served during Indian disturbances, civil disorders, and disputes with Canada and Mexico.

The military service records of volunteer soldiers were abstracted onto cards from muster and pay rolls, rank rolls, returns, hospital records, prison records, accounts for subsistence, and other records. The card abstracts for each individual soldier were placed into a jacket-envelope bearing the soldier's name, rank, and military unit. The jacket-envelope, containing one or more abstracts and, in some instances, including one or more original documents relating specifically to one soldier, is called a **compiled military service record.**

A compiled military service record is as complete as the records of an individual soldier or his unit. A typical record shows the soldier's rank, military unit, and dates of entry into service, discharge or separation by desertion, and death or dismissal. It may also show age, place of birth, and residence at enlistment.

The compiled military service records are arranged by war or period of service, thereunder by state or other designation, thereunder by military unit, and thereunder alphabetically by surname of the soldier. To consult the compilation for a particular soldier's record, the researcher must find out, either from an appropriate index or from family records, in which military unit (usually a regiment) the soldier served.

The compiled military service records were prepared under a War Department program begun some years after the Civil War to permit more rapid and efficient checking of military and medical records in connection with claims for pensions and other veterans' benefits. The abstracts were so carefully prepared that there is virtually no need to consult the original records from which they were made. The original records will not contain additional information about particular soldiers.

A researcher may fail to locate the record of an individual's military service for several reasons. A soldier may have served, for instance, in the regular army (see pages 83–93) or in a unit from a state other than the one where he lived. He may have served under more than one name, or used more than one spelling of his name. Proper records of his service may not have been made; or, if made, they may have been lost or destroyed in the confusion that often attended mobilization, military operations, and disbandment of troops. It is also possible that references to the soldier in the records may be so vague that his correct name or unit cannot be determined.

The name on the jacket-envelope was chosen from one of the abstracts contained in a soldier's compiled military service record. It is not necessarily the correct name of the soldier; nor is it necessarily the way his name was most frequently spelled in the original records. The rank shown at termination of a soldier's service may not be the highest rank he attained while in service and it may not show any brevet (honorary) rank that may have been conferred after service.

If a soldier served in more than one unit, there may be more than one jacket-envelope for him, and his other service may not be cross-referenced in the record or on the jacket. Additional service by the same soldier rendered in a state militia unit that was never mustered into federal service will not be documented in the records at the National Archives.

General indexes containing the names of all the soldiers for whom there are compiled military service records are available for each of the segments in which the compiled military service records are arranged; that is, for the Revolutionary War, post-Revolutionary War period, War of 1812, Mexican War, Indian wars, Confederate army, Spanish-American War, and Philippine Insurrection, but not for the Union army in the Civil War. These general indexes include cross-references to variants of soldiers' names.

The compiled military service records of soldiers serving in a unit bearing a state name as a part of its official unit designation (for example, 1st Virginia Militia) were also indexed in **state indexes**, except for records of the Mexican War and the Philippine Insurrection.

Each index card contains the soldier's name, rank, and military unit. Cross-references are made to the final unit designation if a unit was known by more than one name, and the various names are shown on one or more abstracts. In addition, cross-references are made to the appropriate unit designation if the records of the soldier's service in different units are consolidated into a single record.

A pension or bounty land warrant application file also contains evidence of the service of a veteran. These records are described on pages 133–140.

There may be information about a serviceman in records other than his compiled military service record or pension application file, such as documents relating to the service of his unit, his officers, or other military units participating in the same disturbance.

A rough chronology of the stations and movements of a military unit can be developed by using **record-of-events cards** that were compiled at the same time as the service records for individuals. The information on them was abstracted from the record-of-events sections of muster rolls and returns. They are filed by military unit in jacket-envelopes along with the compiled military service records for the personnel of that military organization. There are record-of-events cards for units that served in the Mexican War and later wars, and for some units in Indian wars; there are none for organizations in the Revolutionary War, the post-Revolutionary War period, or the War of 1812. The record-of-events cards do not document the service of an individual.

Records of U.S. Continental Commands, 1821–1920, Record Group 393, include series of correspondence, orders, returns, and other records relating to military operations and the personnel who conducted them. Searching the

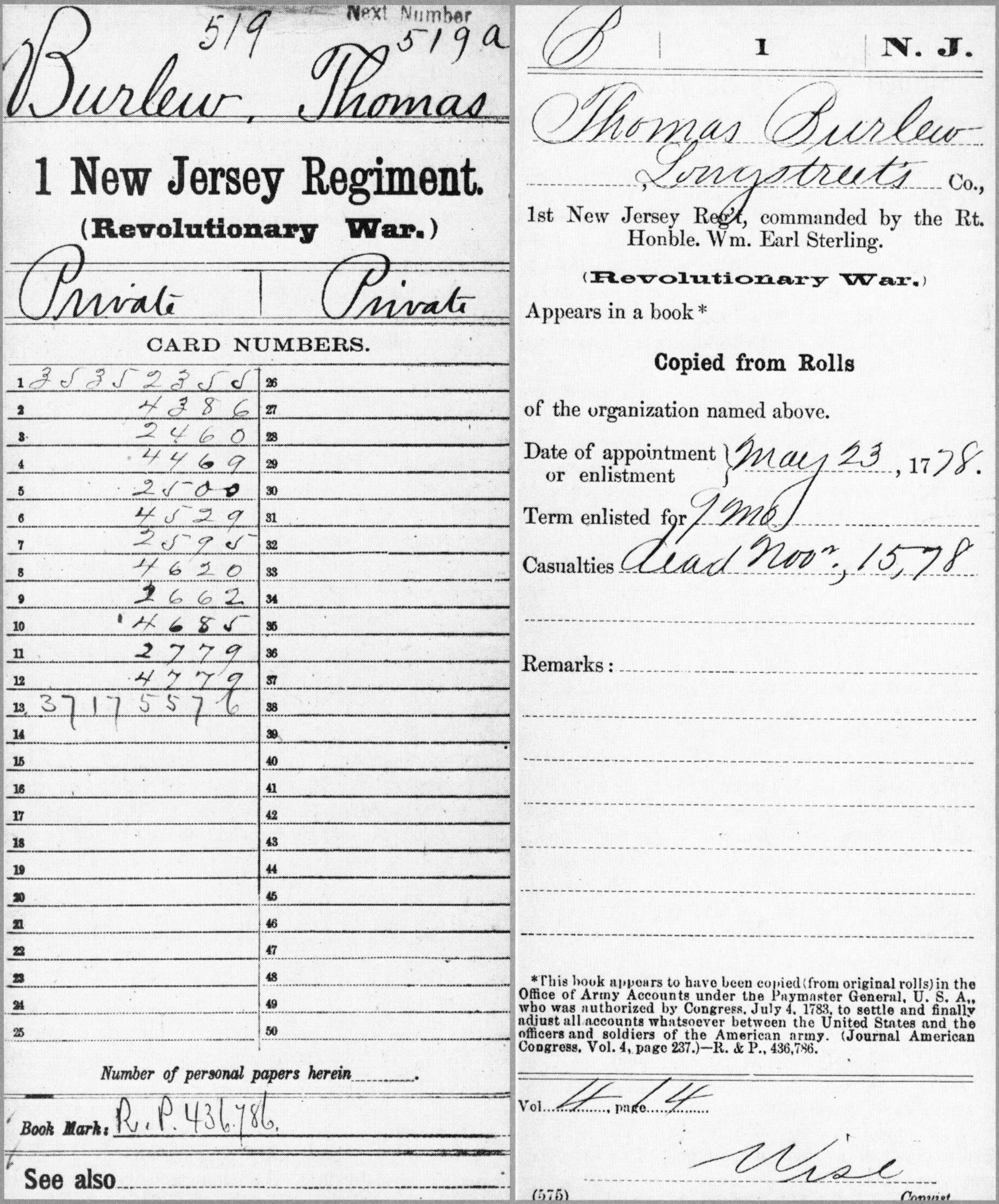

519 Next Number 519a

Burlew, Thomas

1 New Jersey Regiment.

(Revolutionary War.)

Private | Private

CARD NUMBERS.

1	35352355	26	
2	4386	27	
3	2460	28	
4	4469	29	
5	2500	30	
6	4529	31	
7	2595	32	
8	4620	33	
9	2662	34	
10	4685	35	
11	2779	36	
12	4779	37	
13	37175576	38	
14		39	
15		40	
16		41	
17		42	
18		43	
19		44	
20		45	
21		46	
22		47	
23		48	
24		49	
25		50	

Number of personal papers herein ....

Book Mark: R. P. 436,786.

See also ....

B | 1 | N. J.

Thomas Burlew

Longstreets Co.,

1st New Jersey Reg't, commanded by the Rt. Honble. Wm. Earl Sterling.

(Revolutionary War.)

Appears in a book*

Copied from Rolls

of the organization named above.

Date of appointment or enlistment May 23, 1778.

Term enlisted for 9 mo

Casualties dead Nov. 15, 78

Remarks: ....

*This book appears to have been copied (from original rolls) in the Office of Army Accounts under the Paymaster General, U. S. A., who was authorized by Congress, July 4, 1783, to settle and finally adjust all accounts whatsoever between the United States and the officers and soldiers of the American army. (Journal American Congress, Vol. 4, page 237.)—R. & P., 436,786.

Vol. 4, page 14

Wise

(575) Copyist

Revolutionary War compiled military service record. War Department Collection of Revolutionary War Records, Record Group 93. National Archives Microfilm Publication M881.

B | 1 (3d Establishment, 1777-83.) | N. J.

Thos Burlew

Pvt., { Capt. Elias Longstreet's Co., 1st New Jersey Regiment, commanded by Col. Matthias Ogden.*

Appears on (**Revolutionary War.**)

Company Pay Roll

of the organization named above for the month

of June, 1778.

Commencement of time ...., 17 .

Commencement of pay June 1, 17 .

To what time paid ...., 17 .

Pay per month 6 2/3 dolls

Time of service 1 mo.

Whole time of service ....

Subsistence ....

Amount of pay £ 2-10s

Amt. of pay and subsistence ....

Pay due to sick, absent ....

Casualties ....

Remarks: ....

*This company was designated at various times as Captain Elias Longstreet's, Capt. Peter V. Voorhies', Capt. Jacob Piatt's, Capt. William Piatt's and 7th Company.

T. Jones
Copyist.

(545)

B | 1 (3d Establishment, 1777-83.) | N. J.

Thomas Burlew

pvt, { Capt. Elias Longstreet's Co., 1st New Jersey Regiment, commanded by Col. Matthias Ogden.*

(**Revolutionary War.**)

Appears on

Company Muster Roll

of the organization named above for the month

of June, 1778.

Roll dated Elisabeth Town July 14, 1778.

Appointed ...., 17 .

Commissioned ...., 17 .

Enlisted ...., 17 .

Term of enlistment 9 mos.

Time since last muster or enlistment ....

Alterations since last muster ....

Casualties ....

Remarks: ....

*This company was designated at various times as Captain Elias Longstreet's, Capt. Peter V. Voorhies', Capt. Jacob Piatt's, Capt. William Piatt's and 7th Company.

Howell
Copyist.

(543)

command records for information about specific individuals, however, is difficult. The records are fragmentary and poorly indexed. The command in which a soldier served must be established before any research at all is undertaken, and a considerable knowledge of military history is necessary to use these records.

There may also be useful records in one of the many series of correspondence in Records of the Adjutant General's Office, 1780's–1917, Record Group 94, and the jacket of the compiled military service record may carry notations of or cross-references to them. The most important series and related indexes are described in the section of this chapter on the regular army, pages 83–93. A more comprehensive description of the record group is in *Records of the Adjutant General's Office,* Preliminary Inventory 17, by Lucille H. Pendell and Elizabeth Bethel (Washington: National Archives and Records Service, 1949).

For information about wars and battles through the nineteenth century, *Alphabetical List of Battles . . .*, by Newton A. Strait (Washington, 1900), may be consulted.

Copies of compiled military service records can be ordered by mail using NATF Form 26, Order and Billing for Copies of Veterans' Records, which may be obtained from the Reference Services Branch (NNIR), General Services Administration, Washington, DC 20408.

5.2 Volunteer Service Records by War

5.2.1 Revolutionary War

Compiled military service records for men who fought in the Revolutionary War were abstracted from records in the War Department Collection of Revolutionary War Records, Record Group 93. This record group resulted from the War Department's attempts to find substitutes for the records that were destroyed in 1800 and 1814. The department purchased several private collections, such as the papers of Timothy Pickering, who served George Washington as adjutant general and quartermaster general during the Revolutionary War and who held various cabinet posts under Presidents Washington and John Adams. In this record group are also military records of the Revolutionary War that were transferred to the War Department in the latter parts of the nineteenth century from other executive departments.

Descriptions of the various records series included in the collection are contained in *War Department Collection of Revolutionary War Records*, Preliminary Inventory 144, revised edition, compiled by Mable E. Deutrich and Howard H. Wehmann (Washington: National Archives and Records Service, 1970). Entry 13 in the preliminary inventory refers to a "Catalogue of State and Continental Organizations, Revolutionary War"; this volume names each organization and its commanding officer.

Records for individual soldiers are available on microfilm as *Compiled Service Records of Soldiers Who Served in the American Army During the Revolutionary War*, M881, 1097 rolls. Some of the Revolutionary War compiled service records for persons other than soldiers appear on microfilm as *Compiled Service Records of American Naval Personnel and Members of the Departments of the Quartermaster General and the Commissary General of Military Stores Who Served During the Revolutionary War*, M880, 4 rolls.

The compiled service records are arranged under the designation "Continental Troops" or under a state name, thereunder by organization, and thereunder alphabetically by soldier's surname. The military organizations designated "Continental Troops" were generally state units adopted by the Continental Congress in the first years of the Revolutionary War, or units raised in more than one state. Regular units of the Continental army that were raised in only one state are generally listed with that state's military organizations.

The most comprehensive name index is the *General Index to Compiled Military Service Records of Revolutionary War Soldiers, Sailors, and Members of Army Staff Departments*, M860, 58 rolls. This index may refer the user to more than one jacket-envelope if a soldier served in more than one unit. In addition to the general index, the following state indexes are available: *Index to Compiled Service Records of Volunteer Soldiers Who Served During the Revolutionary War in Organizations from the State of North Carolina*, M257, 2 rolls; *Index to Compiled Service Records of Revolutionary War Soldiers Who Served With the American Army in Connecticut Military Organizations*, M920, 25 rolls; *Index to Compiled Service Records of Revolutionary War Soldiers Who Served With the American Army in Georgia Military Organizations*, M1051, 1 roll; and additonal indexes (which are not microfilmed) to the names of soldiers serving in organizations from the states of Delaware, Maryland, Massachusetts, New Hampshire, New Jersey, New York, Pennsylvania, Rhode Island, South Carolina, Vermont, and Virginia.

The original records and copies of records from which the Revolutionary War compiled service records were made are available on microfilm: *Revolutionary War Rolls, 1775–1783*, M246, 138 rolls, and *Numbered Record Books Concerning Military Operations and Service, Pay and Settlement of Accounts, and Supplies in the War Department Collection of Revolutionary War Records*, M853, 41 rolls. Notations in the lower left corner of the card abstracts frequently indicate the volume number of the original record copied.

Miscellaneous Numbered Records (The Manuscript File) in the War Department Collection of Revolutionary War Records, 1775–1790's, M859, 125 rolls, also contain information about civilians who are included in the compiled service records, because they performed some other service, furnished supplies, or were mentioned in correspondence files for other reasons. The records relating to civilians were not compiled; they include information about paymasters, chaplains, medical personnel, judges, quartermasters, wagonmasters, teamsters, and others. The miscellaneous numbered records, approximately 35,500 items, generally contain originals and copies pertaining to Revolutionary War military operations, service of individuals, pay, and settlement of accounts and supplies, 1775–1790s, but they include some nineteenth-century documents relating to the settling of accounts and pension matters.

In this varied collection there are lists of persons on various pension rolls; records removed from pension files and transferred to the War Department; copies of commissions, resignations, enlistment papers, orders, and accounts; and correspondence that includes various lists of persons. The records relating primarily to military service have been examined, copied, and included in the compiled military service records. A name index to persons mentioned has been microfilmed as *Special Index to Numbered Records in the War Department Collection of Revolutionary War Records, 1775–1783,* M847, 39 rolls.

Record Group 93 contains photostatic copies of records that are in the custody of public and private institutions and individuals in Virginia, North Carolina, and Massachusetts; the copies were made in accordance with an act of 1913 (37 Stat. 723). They include correspondence of the State Boards of War, minutes of the boards, and, for Virginia, county court records. For identification of the records copied, including the names of the Virginia counties from which records were copied, see H. C. Clark's "Report on Publication of Revolutionary Military Records," *Annual Report of the American Historical Association for the Year 1915*, pp. 193–199. The photostats for Virginia and some of those for Massachusetts are numbered and are included in the index microfilmed as M847. A separate card index to the photostats for Virginia is more nearly complete, but is not on microfilm.

Related records include muster rolls, strength returns, payrolls, military lists of various sorts, journals, correspondence, and other records in Records of the Continental and Confederation Congresses and the Constitutional Convention, Record Group 360. These records have been microfilmed as *Papers of the Continental Congress, 1774–1789*, M247, 204 rolls, and *Miscellaneous Papers of the Continental Congress, 1774–1789*, M332, 10 rolls. A comprehensive personal name and major subject index to documents in Record Group 360 is *Index to the Papers of the Continental Congress*, compiled by John P. Butler, 5 vols. (Washington: National Archives and Records Service, 1978).

Central Treasury Records of the Continental and Confederation Governments Relating to Military Affairs, 1775–1789, M1015, 7 rolls, includes military pay records that could be used as evidence of service. The company record of the 1st Pennsylvania Regiment, dated March 1779–August 1780, is filmed on roll 4. The payrolls and muster rolls are arranged by type of record and thereunder chronologically. The records are not indexed, but they consist of about fifty pages that can easily be scanned for particular names. The similar account book of James Johnston, Paymaster of the 2d Pennsylvania Regiment, 17 March 1777–11 August 1779, is also filmed on roll 4. This volume is part of Records of the United States General Accounting Office, Record Group 217.

The company book of Capt. Aaron Ogden, 1st New Jersey Regiment, dated February 1782–March 1783, is also on roll 4. It includes copies of size rolls, muster rolls, and returns. A size roll shows the name; age; personal description; trade; town, county, and state of birth; place of residence; and date of enlistment of each soldier. For information about particular soldiers, the researcher must search the whole volume, which is not indexed. This volume is part of Records of the Bureau of the Public Debt, Record Group 53.

Annotated copies of the printed *Register of the Certificates Issued by John Pierce, Esquire, Paymaster General, and Commissioner of the Army Accounts, for the United States* (New York: Francis Childs, 1786) are also part of Record Group 53, filmed on roll 6. The *Register* names officers and men of the Continental army (except South Carolinians) to whom certificates of indebtedness were issued between 1783 and 1787 under the Continental Congress resolution of 4 July 1783 empowering the paymaster "to settle and finally adjust all accounts whatsoever, between the United States and the officers and soldiers of the American army." An alphabetized index to the *Register*, showing the number of each certificate, to whom issued, and the amount, was published in the DAR's *Seventeenth Report, 1913–14*, pp. 149–712 (63d Cong., 3d sess., S. Doc. 988, serial 6777). This index was filmed on roll 5; it was also reprinted by the Genealogical Publishing Co., Baltimore, 1973.

5.2.2 Post-Revolutionary War Period

Record Group 94 contains military service records of soldiers who served in the various Indian campaigns, insurrections, and disturbances that occurred in the post-Revolutionary period; they are available as *Compiled Service Records of Volunteer Soldiers Who Served From 1784 to 1811*, M905, 32 rolls.

The compiled service records are arranged by U.S. organization, including the 1st and 2d Regiments of U.S. Levies, by state organizations alphabetically, and by territoral organizations alphabetically. The records are further arranged according to military unit and thereunder alphabetically by surname of soldier. Researchers who do not know the unit in which the subject of their research served may find the *Index to Compiled Military Service Records of Volunteer Soldiers Who Served From 1784 to 1811*, M694, 9 rolls, helpful. Each index card gives the name of a soldier, his rank, his unit, and the general dates he served. There are cross-references for names that appear in the records under more than one spelling and for service in more than one unit or organization.

Also in Record Group 94 are indexes for soldiers who served in units supplied by a single state or territory. Each of these indexes, composed of cards that duplicate the ones contained in the general index, is arranged alphabetically by name of soldier. In addition, correspondence, records of accounts, and other records created by the early military establishment pertain to the mustering, equipping, provisioning, and paying of the volunteer forces.

The *War Department Collection of Post-Revolutionary War Manuscripts*, M904, 4 rolls is also from Record Group 94. Dated 1784–1811, the documents consist of miscellaneous muster rolls, accounts, and related materials. There is a name index on cards. Some documents show such information as the name, rank, and military organization of a soldier; most are dated.

In addition to records in Record Group 94, several numbered record books in Record Group 93 include material relating to military affairs after the Revolutionary War. They are available as *Numbered Record Books Concerning Military Operations and Service, Pay and Settlement of Accounts, and Supplies in the War Department Collection of Revolutionary War Records*, M853, 41 rolls.

TABLE 9

Selected Genealogical Research Aids: Revolutionary War

Many publications contain information identifying Revolutionary War soldiers and showing their service. Some of these publications show the name and military organization of each soldier named and are based in whole or in part on state service records or state and national service records. They often supply identifying information that will make possible effective searches in the records of the National Archives, or they supplement the incomplete records in the National Archives.

General

Heitman, Francis B. *Historical Register of Officers of the Continental Army During the War of the Revolution, April 1775–December 1783*. Rev. ed. Washington: Rare Book Shop Publishing Co., 1914.

Saffell, William T. R. *Records of the Revolutionary War: Containing Military and Financial Correspondence of Distinguished Officers*. New York: Pudney and Russell, 1858.

Peterson, Clarence Stewart *Known Military Dead During the American Revolutionary War, 1775–1783* . . . . Baltimore, 1959. Reprinted by Genealogical Publishing Co., Baltimore, 1967.

Revolutionary War Pensions

Index of Revolutionary War Pension Applications in the National Archives ("Hoyt's Index"). Rev. ed. NGS Special Publication 40. Washington: National Genealogical Society, 1966.

Ainsworth, Mary Govier, comp. "Recently Discovered Records Relating to Revolutionary War Veterans Who Applied for Pensions Under the Act of 1792," *National Genealogical Society Quarterly* 46 (1958):8–13, 73–78.

War Department. *Letter From the Secretary of War, Communicating a Transcript of the Pension List of the United States* . . . . Washington: A. & G. Way, 1813. Reprinted in *Collections of the Minnesota Historical Society* 6 (1894):502–539, and by the Genealogical Publishing Co., Baltimore, 1959.

War Department. . . . *Report of the Names, Rank, and Line, of Every Person Placed on the Pension List* . . . . [Acts of 1818 and 1820], 16th Cong., 1st sess., H. Exec. Doc. 55, serial 34. Reprinted by the Southern Book Co., Baltimore, 1955.

War Department. *Report From the Secretary of War . . . in Relation to the Pension Establishment of the United States*, [1835] 23d Cong., 1st sess., S. Exec. Doc. 514, serials 249–251. Reprinted in 4 volumes by the Genealogical Publishing Co., Baltimore, 1968.

State Department. *A Census of Pensioners for Revolutionary or Military Services; With Their Names, Ages, Places of Residence* . . . . Washington: State Department, 1841. Available on roll 3 of microfilm publication T498, the 1790 census, and also reprinted by the Southern Book Co., Baltimore, 1954, and the Genealogical Publishing Co., Baltimore, 1967.

Genealogical Society. *A General Index to a Census of Pensioners . . . 1840*. Baltimore: Genealogical Publishing Co., 1965.

Pension Bureau. *List of Pensioners on the Roll January 1, 1883,* . . . . 47th Cong., 2d sess., S. Exec. Doc. 84, serials 2078–2082. Reprinted by the Genealogical Publishing Co., Baltimore, 1970.

Report of the Secretary of the Interior, With a Statement of Rejected or Suspended Applications for Pensions, 32d Cong., 1st sess., S. Exec. Doc. 37, serial 618. Reprinted with an index by the Genealogical Publishing Co., Baltimore, 1969.

American State Papers, Claims. Washington: Gales and Seaton, 1834.

Alabama

Owen, Thomas McAdory. *Revolutionary Soldiers in Alabama*. Montgomery: Alabama Department of Archives and History, 1911. Reprinted by the Genealogical Publishing Co., Baltimore, 1967.

Connecticut

Smith, Stephen R. et al. *Record of Service of Connecticut Men in the I.—War of the Revolution. II.—War of 1812. III.—Mexican War*. Hartford: Connecticut Adjutant General's Office, 1889.

Lists and Returns of Connecticut Men in the Revolution, 1775–1783. In *Collections of the Connecticut Historical Society* 8(1901) and 12(1909).

Delaware

Delaware Archives, Military and Naval. vols. 1–3, *Revolutionary War*. Wilmington: Delaware Public Archives Commission, 1911–19. Reprinted by AMS Press, New York, 1974.

Whiteley, William G. *The Revolutionary Soldiers of Delaware*. Wilmington: Historical Society of Delaware, 1896.

Florida

Fritot, Jessie Robinson, comp. *Pension Records of Soldiers of the Revolution Who Removed to Florida*. Jacksonville: Jacksonville Chapter, Daughters of the American Revolution, 1946.

CHAPTER 5 Service Records of Volunteers

5.2 Volunteer Service Records by War

Georgia

Knight, Lucian Lamar, comp. *Georgia's Roster of the Revolution*. Atlanta: Georgia Department of Archives and History, 1920.

Candler, Allen D. *The Revolutionary Records of the State of Georgia . . . 1769–1782*. Atlanta: Georgia Legislature, 1908.

Illinois

Meyer, Virginia M. (Mrs. Harold S.). *Roster of Revolutionary War Soldiers and Widows Who Lived in Illinois Counties*. Chicago: Illinois Daughters of the American Revolution, 1962.

Maryland

Archives of Maryland, vol. 18, *Muster Rolls and Other Records of Service of Maryland Troops in the American Revolution, 1775–1783*. Baltimore: Maryland Historical Society, 1900. Reprinted by the Genealogical Publishing Co., Baltimore, 1972.

Massachusetts

Massachusetts Soldiers and Sailors of the Revolutionary War. 17 vols. Boston: Secretary of the Commonwealth, 1896–1908. This publication is incomplete; more names are on file at the Massachusetts State Archives. The volumes do, however, cover Maine.

New Hampshire

Hammons, Isaac W., ed. *State and Provincial Papers*, vols. 14–17, *Rolls and Documents Relating to Soldiers in the Revolutionary War*. Concord: New Hampshire Legislature, 1885–89, vol. 30, *Miscellaneous Revolutionary Documents*. Manchester, 1910.

New Jersey

Stryker, William S., comp. *Official Register of the Officers and Men of New Jersey in the Revolutionary War*. Trenton: New Jersey Adjutant General's Office, 1872. The *Index* for this register was prepared and published by the New Jersey Historical Records Survey, Newark, 1941. The *Index* has been reprinted by the Genealogical Publishing Co., Baltimore, 1965.

New York

Fernow, Berthold, ed. *Documents Relating to the Colonial History of the State of New York*. 15 vols. Albany: New York State University, 1853–1887.

Mather, Frederick G., *The Refugees of 1776 From Long Island to Connecticut*. New York: J. B. Lyon Co. 1913. Reprinted by the Genealogical Publishing Co., Baltimore, 1972.

New York State Comptroller's Office. *New York in the Revolution as Colony and State*. 2 vols. Albany: J. B. Lyon Co., 1901–4. The earlier editions of volume 1 were compiled by James A. Roberts. Volume 2 has cover title: *New York in the Revolution. Supplement*.

North Carolina

Clark, Walter, ed. *The Colonial and State Records of North Carolina*. vol. 16, *1782–83*. Goldsboro: Nash Brothers, 1899. *Index*, edited by Stephen B. Weeks. 4 vols. 1909–14.

Roster of Soldiers from North Carolina in the American Revolution. Durham: North Carolina Daughters of the American Revolution, 1932. Reprinted by the Genealogical Publishing Co., Baltimore, 1967.

Ohio

Henderson, Frank D., Rea, John R., and Dailey, Jane Dowd (Mrs. Orville D.), comps. *The Official Roster of the Soldiers of the American Revolution Buried in the State of Ohio*. Columbus: F. J. Heer Printing Co., 1929.

Dailey, Jane Dowd, comp. *Soldiers of the American Revolution Who Lived in the State of Ohio*. Greenfield: Ohio Daughters of the American Revolution, 1938.

Pennsylvania

Pennsylvania Archives. 2d series, vols. 10–11, *Pennsylvania in the War of the Revolution, Battalions and Line, 1775–1783*. Edited by John B. Linn and William H. Egle. Harrisburg: Secretary of the Commonwealth, 1895–96. Vols. 13–14, *Pennsylvania in the War of the Revolution, Associated Battalions and Militia, 1775–1783*. Edited by William H. Egle (1895–96). Vol. 15, *Journals and Diaries of the War of the Revolution with Lists of Officers and Soldiers, 1775–1783*. Edited by William H. Egle, 1892. 3d series, vol. 23, *Muster Rolls of the Navy and Line, Militia and Rangers, 1775–1783*. Edited by William H. Egle (1898). 5th series, vols. 2–8, and 6th series, vols. 1–2. Edited by Thomas L. Montgomery (1906). There are general indexes within the series, especially 1st series, vol. 14, 3d series, vol. 27, and 6th series, vol. 15. See also *Guide to the Published Archives of Pennsylvania . . . .* Compiled by Henry Howard Eddy. Harrisburg: Pennsylvania Historical and Museum Commission, 1949.

(table continued on following page)

TABLE 9 (CONTINUED)

Selected Genealogical Research Aids: Revolutionary War

South Carolina

Salley, A. S., Jr., ed. *Documents Relating to the History of South Carolina During the Revolutionary War*. Columbia: Historical Commission of South Carolina, 1908.

DeSaussure, Wilmot G., comp. . . . *Officers Who Served in the South Carolina Regiments* . . .. Charleston, 1894.

Boddie, William Willis. *Marion's Men—A List of Twenty-five Hundred*. Charleston: Heisser Printing Co., 1938.

Revill, Janie. *Copy of the Original Index Book Showing the Revolutionary Claims Filed in South Carolina Between August 20, 1773–August 31, 1776*. Columbia, 1941. Reprinted by the Genealogical Publishing Co., Baltimore, 1969.

South Carolina Treasury. *Stub Entries to Indents Issued in Payment of Claims Against South Carolina Growing Out of the Revolution*. Edited by A. S. Salley, Jr. 11 vols. Columbia: Historical Commission of South Carolina, 1910–57.

Pruitt, Jayne Conway Garlington. *Revolutionary War Pension Applicants Who Served From South Carolina*. Fairfax County, Va., 1946.

Tennessee

Allen, Penelope Johnson. *Tennessee Soldiers in the Revolution*. Bristol: Tennessee Daughters of the American Revolution, 1935. Reprinted by the Genealogical Publishing Co., Baltimore, 1975.

Vermont

Goodrich, John E., ed. *Rolls of the Soldiers in the Revolutionary War, 1775 to 1783*. Rutland: Tuttle Co., 1904.

Virginia

Pay Rolls of Militia Entitled to Land Bounty—Virginia. Richmond: Virginia Auditor of Public Accounts, 1851.

McAllister, Joseph Thompson. *Virginia Militia in the Revolutionary War*. Hot Springs, Va.: McAllister Publishing Co., 1913.

Gwathmey, John H. *Historical Register of Virginians in the Revolution, Soldiers, Sailors, Marines, 1775–1783*. Richmond: Dietz Press, 1938. Reprinted by the Genealogical Publishing Co., Baltimore, 1973.

Burgess, Louis A., ed. *Virginia Soldiers of 1776*. Richmond: Richmond Press, 1927. Reprinted by the Reprint Co., Spartanburg, S.C.

Eckenrode, H. J., comp. *List of Revolutionary Soldiers of Virginia*. Special Report of the Department of Archives and History. 2 vols. Richmond: Virginia State Library, 1912–13.

Brumbaugh, Gaius Marcus. *Revolutionary War Records: Virginia*. Washington, D.C., and Lancaster, Pa.: Lancaster Press, 1936. Reprinted by the Genealogical Publishing Co., 1967.

Wilson, Samuel Mackay, comp. *Catalogue of Revolutionary Soldiers and Sailors of the Commonwealth of Virginia to Whom Land Bounty Warrants Were Granted by Virginia for Military Services in the War of Independence*. Lexington: Kentucky Sons of the Revolution, 1913. Reprinted by the Southern Book Co., Baltimore, 1953, and by the Genealogical Publishing Co., Baltimore, 1967.

A List of Claims for Bounty-Land for Revolutionary Services. Governor of Virginia, Document 35. Richmond, 1835.

West Virginia

Johnston, Ross B., ed. *West Virginians in the American Revolution*. West Virginia Historical Soceity Publication 1. Parkersburg, W.Va.: West Augusta Historical and Genealogical Society, 1959.

Special Categories

Duncan, Louis Caspar. *Medical Men in the American Revolution, 1775–1783*. Army Medical Bulletin 25. Carlisle Barracks, Pa.: Medical Field Service School, 1931.

Dandridge, Danske. *American Prisoners of the Revolution*. Baltimore: Genealogical Publishing Co., 1967.

Dickoré, Maria, comp. and trans. *Hessian Soldiers in the American Revolution—Records of Their Marriages, and Baptisms of Their Children in America Performed by the Rev. G. C. Cöster, 1776–1783, Chaplain of Two Hessian Regiments*. Cincinnati: C. J. Krehbiel Co., 1959.

Ford, W. C., comp. *British Officers Serving in the American Revolution, 1774–1783*. Brooklyn: Historical Printing Club, 1897.

O'Brien, Michael J. *A Hidden Phase of American History: Ireland's Part in America's Struggle for Liberty*. New York: Dodd, Mead and Co., 1919.

Les Combattants Francais de la Guerre Américaine, 1778–1783, 58th Cong., 2d sess., S. Doc. 77, serial 4595. This is an incomplete list, relating chiefly to men who returned to France, based on French records and published by the Ministère des affaires étrangères. The 1905 Senate document was indexed. Reprinted by the Genealogical Publishing Co., Baltimore, 1969.

5.2.3 War of 1812

When the United States declared war against Great Britain in 1812, Congress authorized the President to increase the size of the regular military establishment, to accept and organize volunteers, to raise units of Rangers and Sea Fencibles, and to create a Flotilla Service. The Ranger units were raised for the protection of the frontier along the Mississippi River and in the adjacent states. The Sea Fencibles was the first organization of the U.S. Army charged exclusively with coastal defense; with the Flotilla Service, it protected ports, harbors, and the coast.

Some confusion arose as to whether service in the Rangers, the Sea Fencibles, and some of the volunteer units had been rendered in the regular establishment or in the volunteers. The War Department, while abstracting and compiling these military service records decided that the units of Rangers, Sea Fencibles, Flotillas, and some volunteer units that include the name "United States" or the initials "U.S." as part of their official designation were volunteer units and not units of the regular establishment. As a result of the confusion, records about members of these services are found in records of the regular army (and navy and Marine Corps for the Sea Fencibles and Flotilla Service) as well as in compiled military service records.

Regulars, volunteers, and militia units were also fighting Indians during the period 1812–15. Records of service in the Florida or Seminole War of 1812, the Peoria (Illinois) Indian War of 1813, and the Creek Indian War of 1813–14 are found in the War of 1812 segment of the compiled military service records in Record Group 94. Records relating to service in the regular army, except as mentioned above, are described on pages 83–93.

Many of the War of 1812 volunteer units were mustered into service for short periods of time (30, 60, 90, and 120 days; 6, 9, and 12 months). Consequently, many persons served more than one enlistment in the same unit or different units. There may be two or more compilations relating to the service of the same soldier. Generally, the records in the War of 1812 segment of the compiled military service records do not refer to service in other units or to earlier or later service in the same unit.

Members of volunteer units in the War of 1812 may also have served in federal units before and after that war, either in volunteer units or the regular military or naval establishments. Some veterans whose records are in this segment served in the Revolutionary War and the War of 1812, and a few served in the Civil War as well as the War of 1812. Most War of 1812 soldiers, however, performed their other service in the 1784–1811 period or in the Indian wars after the War of 1812.

Most of the compiled military service records for the War of 1812 are arranged by state or territory and thereunder by unit; the others are for units whose complements were not limited to a single state or territory, or whose designation did not include the name of a state, such as the U.S. Volunteers; U.S. Rangers; Sea Fencibles; Cherokee, Chickasaw, Choctaw, and Creek Indian regiments; 1st Battalion U.S. Volunteers (Louisiana); 1st Regiment U.S. Volunteers (Mississippi Territory); 2d Regiment Artillery (New York); and Captain Booker's Company, U.S. Volunteers (Virginia). Under the name of each unit, the compiled military service records are arranged alphabetically by surname of soldier.

Records of Mississippi soldiers are available as *Compiled Service Records of Volunteer Soldiers Who Served During the War of 1812 in Organizations From the Territory of Mississippi*, M678, 22 rolls.

The name index has been reproduced as *Index to Compiled Service Records of Volunteer Soldiers Who Served During the War of 1812*, M602, 234 rolls. In addition to the general index, there are separate indexes for persons who served in units from particular states and territories, and indexes for persons who served in miscellaneous units not attributed to a state or territory. The indexes for Louisiana, North Carolina, and South Carolina have been microfilmed as M229, 3 rolls; M250, 5 rolls; and M652, 7 rolls.

The indexes, the compiled service records, and the original records from which the compiled records were abstracted are in Record Group 94. Related records that were not abstracted during the compilation project include numerous rolls known as **receipts for pay**. They are arranged by state, thereunder numerically by regiment, thereunder by name of commanding officer, thereunder chronologically for various periods of service, and thereunder alphabetically by surname of soldier. There are separate series of rolls for volunteers serving in Indian wars, 1811–58.

There is also a series of miscellaneous records or **"manuscripts" of the War of 1812**. Most are dated 1812–15, but some of a later date describe events or transactions that occurred during the war. The manuscripts are arranged numerically in jacketed files; an extensive card index to names is available. Many of the files relate to state militia organizations and to claims of persons who served in them. Other files pertain to civilians who rendered services such as transporting troops and supplies or labor on fortifications, or who furnished various goods for army use, including forage, foodstuffs, tents, carts, and horses. Few of the documents provide any detailed information about particular individuals, but some may indicate names and residences of civilians and names, ranks, and military organizations of soldiers.

Prisoner-of-war records, 1812–15, relating to both British and American prisoners, include miscellaneous correspondence arranged in numbered bundles, each with a separate card index; correspondence and lists of prisoners sent from the Treasury Department to the Adjutant General's Office, arranged numerically with separate card indexes; unarranged and unindexed lists of prisoners sent from the Navy Department to the Adjutant General's Office; a list of American prisoners of war held in Quebec, and at Halifax, Nova Scotia, and in the West Indies, with entries arranged alphabetically by place of imprisonment and with two alphabetical sequences under Halifax; a list of American prisoners who died in British custody, arranged alphabetically by prisoner's surname; a list of American prisoners in the West Indies and Bermuda, arranged alphabetically by prisoner's name, but with entries for names beginning with A through S only; and a list of American prisoners captured or held in England, Upper Canada, Newfoundland, Fort Sullivan in the District of Maine, Madeira, and Bladensburg, Maryland, arranged according to location and thereunder alphabetically by prisoner's surname. In this last volume

TABLE 10

Selected Genealogical Research Aids: War of 1812

General

Pension Bureau. *List of Pensioners on the Roll January 1, 1883, . . .* 47th Cong., 2d sess., S. Exec. Doc. 84, serials 2078–2082. Reprinted by the Genealogical Publishing Co., Baltimore, 1970.

Connecticut

Smith, Stephen R., et al. *Record of Service of Connecticut Men in the I.—War of the Revolution. II.—War of 1812. III.—Mexican War.* Hartford: Connecticut Adjutant General's Office, 1889.

Delaware

Delaware Archives, Military and Naval. Vols. 4–5, *War of 1812.* Wilmington: Delaware Public Archives Commission, 1916. Reprinted by AMS Press, New York, 1974.

Maryland

Dielman, Louis Henry, ed. "Maryland Roster, War of 1812." In William Matthew Marine. *The British Invasion of Maryland 1812–1815*, pp. 195–495. Baltimore: Society of the War of 1812 in Maryland, 1913. Reprinted by Tradition Press, Hatboro, Pa., 1965, and by the Genealogical Publishing Co., Baltimore, 1977.

Maine

See Massachusetts.

Massachusetts

Baker, John, comp. *Records of the Massachusetts Volunteer Militia . . . War of 1812–14.* Boston: Massachusetts Adjutant General's Office, 1913. This volume also covers Maine.

New Jersey

Records Of Officers and Men of New Jersey in Wars 1791–1815. Trenton: New Jersey Adjutant General's Office, 1909. Reprinted by the Genealogical Publishing Co., Baltimore, 1970.

Pennsylvania

Pennsylvania Archives, 2d series, vol. 12. *Muster Rolls of the Pennsylvania Volunteers in the War of 1812–14.* Edited by John B. Linn and William H. Egle. Harrisburg: Secretary of the Commonwealth, 1896. 6th series, vols. 7–9. *War of 1812–14.* Edited by Thomas L. Montgomery (1907).

Vermont

Johnson, Herbert T., comp. *Roster of Soldiers in the War of 1812–14.* St. Albans: Vermont Adjutant and Inspector General's Office, 1933.

is a list of the crews of the USS *Essex* and the brig *Vixen*, which were captured by the British. The list includes only names beginning with the letters A and B. The records vary considerably as to detail, but include such information as the name, rank, and military organization of the prisoner, date and place of capture, and date of release. Table 10 lists published works treating military service in the War of 1812.

5.2.4 Indian Wars

In the decades after the War of 1812, volunteer units often served during Indian hostilities, either assisting units of the regular army or acting independently. The compiled military service records, 1815–58, reflect volunteer service in the Seminole or Florida Wars, 1817–18, 1835–42, and 1855–58; Winnebago War, 1827; Sac and Fox War, 1831; Black Hawk War, 1832; Creek War, 1836–37; Indian wars in Texas, 1849–51; the Indian removal, 1835–41; and various other disturbances.

The War Department did not recognize some Indian campaigns as "wars," even though the Treasury Department under various legislative acts reimbursed the states and territories for the services of volunteer units, and the men who served in such units, or their heirs, received bounty land and sometimes pensions. Notable examples are the Osage War, 1832; Patriot and Aroostock War, 1838–39; Heatherly War, 1836; and Cayuse War, 1848.

Although most of the persons who served during this period were free citizens of the United States, Indians also served in the U.S. interest at various times, especially Choctaw, Creek and Friendly Creek (Apalachicola), Menominee, Potawatomi, Delaware, Shawnee, and Winnebago Indians.

Compiled military service records of volunteer soldiers serving in the various Indian campaigns generally do not contain personal papers for officers or enlisted men. Records for Indian units are generally separate.

The designations of volunteer units generally include the name of the state or territory from which they served, but it should be noted that boundaries have changed. Service records of volunteers in units of the militia mustered in from Green Bay (Wisc.) in the Black Hawk War, for example, are found under Michigan Territory, not under Wisconsin.

The *Index to Compiled Service Records of Volunteer Soldiers Who Served During Indian Wars and Disturbances*, 1815–58, M629, 42 rolls, contains a card for each person who served during the period for whom a compiled military service record was prepared. The card shows name, rank, regiment, and war and is especially useful to the researcher who does not know the campaign or unit in which the subject of research served. In addition to the general index, there are indexes for persons who served in units from various states and territories, although separate indexes are not available for each state or territory for each disturbance. Some entries for several states or territories have been combined into a single index; for example, the index for Illinois troops in the Black Hawk War includes the names of persons who served from Michigan and the names of persons who served in the Potawatomi Indian units. Nevertheless, knowing the state in which the subject of research served and the name of the disturbance will expedite the researcher's attempt to determine the designation of his unit from one of these smaller indexes. Some of them have been microfilmed, as shown in table 11.

Record Group 393 includes series of correspondence, orders, returns, and other records relating to the various Indian wars and disturbances and the military activities and personnel connected with these operations. Many of the records are fragmentary and poorly indexed, however, and research in them is difficult. The researcher must know the command in which the subject of research served before any search can be undertaken. A considerable knowledge of military history is necessary to make use of these records.

TABLE 11

Microfilmed Indexes to Compiled Military Service Records of Volunteers During the Indian Wars

State	Disturbance and Date	Microfilm Publication	Number of Rolls
Alabama	Creek War 1836–37	M244	2
Alabama	Cherokee Removal 1838	M243	1
Alabama	Florida War 1836–38	M245	1
Florida	Florida War 1835–38	M1086	63
Georgia	Cherokee Disturbances and Removal 1836–38	M907	1
Louisiana	Florida War 1836	M239	1
Louisiana	War of 1836–38	M241	1
Michigan	Patriot War 1838–39	M630	1
New York	Patriot War 1838	M631	1
North Carolina	Cherokee Disturbances and Removal 1837–38	M256	1
Tennessee	Cherokee Disturbances and Removal, and Field and Staff of the Army of The Cherokee Nation	M908	2

5.2.5 Mexican War

War with Mexico was declared on 13 May 1846, less than six months after Texas had been admitted to the Union. Even during the congressional debates concerning the admission of the new state, the United States, in anticipation of war with Mexico, had ordered units of volunteers into service. One unit came from Louisiana, and five units came from Texas. The Texas units commenced service in the fall of 1845, and some Texas units served until the end of the war. Such service was not continuous, but many of the units were mustered out at the end of one enlistment and mustered in again a day or so later.

The act of Congress by which war was declared specified the service of the regular military and naval establishment and the use of volunteers and the militia. Militia service was limited to no more than six months of continuous service, while the volunteers could be mustered for twelve months or until the end of the war. Volunteer units came from twenty-four states, California, and the District of Columbia. One unit was composed of Indians, and a separate battalion of about 500 men was formed of members of the Church of Jesus Christ of Latter-Day Saints, known as the Mormon Battalion. An additional unit, called the Santa Fe Battalion, Missouri Mounted Volunteers, was organized in New Mexico.

Some of the volunteers who served in the Mexican War had also served in the earlier Indian wars or would later serve in the Civil War. Some of the Texas volunteers were retained in service after the war to protect the frontier areas of Texas from Indian attack. The service of these units is documented in records relating to the Indian wars, 1816–58.

Evidence of the federal service of volunteer and militia units, 1846–48, is in compiled military service records. They are arranged alphabetically by state or territory, followed by the compilations for soldiers who served in Mormon organizations. The records are further broken down by organization, ending with the regiment or the independent battalion or the company. Under each unit, the service records are arranged alphabetically by surname of soldier. The compiled service records of volunteer soldiers who served in organizations from Mississippi have been microfilmed as M863, 9 rolls; from Pennsylvania, as M1028, 13 rolls; from Tennessee, as M638, 15 rolls; from Texas, as M278, 19 rolls; and in Mormon organizations, as M351, 3 rolls.

The name index has been reproduced as *Index to Compiled Service Records of Volunteer Soldiers Who Served During the Mexican War*, M616, 41 rolls.

For an alphabetical list of volunteer officers in the Mexican War, showing rank and organization, see *Historical Register and Dictionary of the United States Army*, by Francis B. Heitman (Washington, 1903), 2:43–73.

5.2.6 Civil War—Union

President Lincoln's proclamation of April 15, 1861, called for 75,000 militiamen from the loyal states and territories to suppress the rebellion in the southern states. Subsequent proclamations and acts of Congress provided for additional increases in the size of the regular army and navy and called forth additional volunteers and militiamen. The states and territories met the requirements through activating the militia, voluntary enlistments, and the draft. The federal draft system, created by Congress in 1863, superseded the state and territorial draft systems; draft records are described in this section on page 118.

During the first two years of the war, many units were mustered for short periods (30, 60, and 90 days and 6, 9, and 12 months), but normal enlistments were for one to three years. Most soldiers served in units formed within their neighborhoods or states or territories of residence. Some enlisted in the regular army or were assigned to regular army units. Others joined units formed at a previous residence or place of birth. Some soldiers were assigned to units composed of persons from a different state or territory, or to units composed of soldiers from several states or territories. Others were detailed or transferred to special units created to serve a particular need or to units created for persons having special talents, such as the U.S. Sharpshooters, Mississippi Gunboat Flotilla, Mississippi Ram Fleet, Pontoon Brigade, Engineers, Signal Corps, Marines (army), U.S. Colored Troops, Indian Brigade, or Balloon Corps. Blacks and Indians were prohibited from serving in separate units before 1863 by orders of the War Department, but individual blacks and Indians did serve in the various units before 1863 and throughout the war. The U.S. Colored Troops and Indian regiments are discussed in later chapters devoted to records about blacks and records about Indians, respectively.

A reenlisting soldier was not necessarily assigned to the same unit in which he had previously served, or even to the same branch of service, or arm of service. Disabled soldiers still capable of performing a service were assigned to the Veteran Reserve Corps. Before 1863, a Confederate soldier who was taken prisoner could ask to serve in the Union army, in which case he might be assigned to a regular army or volunteer unit. After 1863, such former Confederate prisoners of war were assigned to one of the six numbered regiments of U.S. Volunteers specifically to fight Indians in the western part of the United States. Some units included civilian personnel as part of their complements. Soldiers serving in the Signal Corps as telegraphers were discharged and rehired as civilians in 1863. Soldiers serving the Mississippi Ram Fleet were transferred to the U.S. Navy in 1862.

Many units upon organization adopted or used a unique name, generally the name by which the unit had been known as a militia unit. When the unit was mustered into the Union army, the name was changed to conform with regulations of the Union army. A unit designation generally consisted of a number, the state or territory name, and the arm of service; for example, 1st Iowa Cavalry. Some unit designations included the name of the officer who formed the company, or its commanding officer. Unit designations were changed for a variety of reasons while units were in service, sometimes several times. Some units had two or more successive designations: for example, 1st Pennsylvania Cavalry and 44th Pennsylvania Volunteers. State and territory names were not used for units composed of soldiers from several states or territories or for special units. Records are generally filed under the final designation for a particular unit. A compilation of the various names for units, *List of Synonyms of Organizations in the Volunteer Service of the United States During the Years 1861, '62, '63, '64, and '65* (Washington: Adjutant General's Office, 1885), compiled by John T. Fallon, permits identification of the final designation from any of the names of a given unit.

There are compiled military service records for nearly all soldiers who were accepted for service in the Union army as militiamen or volunteers, 1861–65, whether or not they actually served. Records relating to soldiers who participated in actions that occurred between 1861 and 1865 are included in the records of the Civil War, even if the actions, such as Indian warfare, were unrelated to the war. The compiled military service records for Civil War soldiers are similar to those for other periods of service.

Records of enlisted men sometimes include information about age, residence at the time of enlistment, occupation at the time of enlistment, and physical description. Personal papers occasionally give additional information about residence, family, or business of officers and enlisted men. Information about heirs is sometimes found in records of hospitalization or death in service.

The records generally refer to federal service in other units during, before, and after the Civil War. The records may also refer to related files among the various correspondence series of the records of the Adjutant General's Office (listed on page 93 and described in the chapter about the regular army). Genealogical researchers should look for both types of cross-references when using the compiled military service records; they are normally found on the lower part of the file jackets, the unit references appearing in the "See Also" section, and the file references in the "Book Mark" section, but similar cross-references may appear elsewhere on the jacket.

Table 12 gives microfilm publication numbers for compiled service records of those states and territories whose records have been microfilmed.

In addition to the compiled military service records in jacket-envelopes, there are separate series of card abstracts and personal papers that are not in jacket-envelopes. These series were accumulated by the War Department, but were not interfiled with the regular compilations for various reasons, usually, because the information was insufficient or contained discrepancies and could not be positively identified with any soldier for whom there was a compiled service record. Sometimes no compiled service record had been established on the basis of other records, and the item did not provide enough evidence to justify establishing one. Unjacketed card abstracts are arranged alphabetically or in the same general regimental order as the jacket-envelopes. The unfiled personal papers are arranged alphabetically.

To locate the compiled service record of a Union army soldier, the researcher must determine the name of the unit in which he served. No general comprehensive name index to the compiled service records for Union army volunteer soldiers exists. Separate indexes are available for each state and territory except South Carolina, which furnished no white troops to the Union army. Separate indexes are also available for the compiled service records of soldiers who served in units formed from several states and territories, such as the Veteran Reserve Corps, U.S. Colored Troops, U.S. Volunteers (including former Confederate prisoners of war), U.S. Veteran Volunteer Engineer and Infantry units, U.S. Sharpshooters, Indian Home Brigade, Mississippi Marine Brigade, Prisoners of War (partial index to

TABLE 12

Microfilmed Indexes and Compiled Service Records for Union Army Volunteers

State	Index: Microfilm publication	Index: Number of rolls	Compiled Military Service Records: Microfilm publication	Compiled Military Service Records: Number of rolls
Alabama	M263	1	M276	10
Arizona Territory	M532	1		
Arkansas	M383	4	M399	60
California	M533	7		
Colorado Territory	M534	3		
Connecticut	M535	17		
Dakota Territory	M536	1		
Delaware	M537	4		
District of Columbia	M538	3		
Florida	M264	1	M400	11
Georgia	M385	1	M403	1
Idaho Territory (see Washington Territory)				
Illinois	M539	101		
Indiana	M540	86		
Iowa	M541	29		
Kansas	M542	10		
Kentucky	M386	30	M397	515
Louisiana	M387	4	M396	50
Maine	M543	23		
Maryland	M388	13	M384	238
Massachusetts	M544	44		
Michigan	M545	48		
Minnesota	M546	10		
Mississippi	M389	1	M404	4
Missouri	M390	54	M405	854
Montana (see Washington Territory)				
Nebraska Territory	M547	2		
Nevada	M548	1		
New Hampshire	M549	13		
New Jersey	M550	26		
New Mexico Territory	M242	4	M427	46
New York	M551	159		
North Carolina	M391	2	M401	25
Ohio	M552	122		
Oklahoma (see Dakota Territory)				
Oregon	M553	1		
Pennsylvania	M554	136		
Rhode Island	M555	7		
South Carolina	None			
Tennessee	M392	16	M395	220
Texas	M393	2	M402	13
Utah Territory	M556	1	M692	1
Vermont	M557	14		
Virginia	M394	1	M398	7
Washington Territory	M558	1		
West Virginia	M507	13	M508	261
Wisconsin	M559	33		
Wyoming (see Washington Territory)				
U.S. Colored Troops	M589	98		
U.S. Volunteers (1st–6th Regiments only)			M1017	65
Veteran Reserve Corps	M636	44		

Confederate prisoners who enlisted in the Union army), Pioneer Brigade, U.S. Signal Corps, Captain Turner's Company Volunteer Pioneers, Brigade and Post Bands, Departmental Corps, and Varner's Battalion of Infantry. Table 12 gives microfilm publication numbers for indexes that have been filmed. There are no index cards for those soldiers mentioned in unjacketed abstracts or unfiled personal papers.

To locate the record of service of a particular soldier, the researcher may need to consult several indexes. A soldier may have enlisted in or been assigned to a unit from a different state or territory from the one the researcher expects, or to a special unit composed of persons from several different areas. For example, the index for regiments of U.S. Colored Troops may contain entries for the service records of white officers.

Some of the officers who served in Union army volunteer units are listed in the *Official Army Register of the Volunteer Force of the United States Army for the Years 1861, '62, '63, '64, '65* (Washington: Adjutant General's Office, 1865–67). A list of the field officers of volunteers and militia in the service of the United States during the Civil War and other lists of officers appear in *Historical Register and Dictionary of the United States Army* by Francis B. Heitman, and in the numerous rosters of Union army troops prepared by the adjutant generals of the various states and territories. The rosters are listed in table 13.

Abstracts of medical records were prepared for soldiers treated at medical facilities in posts and camps, and in the field. Particulars of the length of stay at a facility and the reason for confinement are generally mentioned in the abstracts. (A few of the cards relate to treatment during the Mexican War and the Spanish-American War.) The cards are arranged by state or territory, thereunder by unit number, and thereunder in rough alphabetical order by surname of soldier. A miscellaneous series following the cards for the state or territory contains abstracts for persons who served in units that did not have a number as part of the official designation and for other persons whose full unit designation could not be identified. In some instances, the abstracts relating to a particular soldier have been interfiled in his compiled military service record.

Records relating to volunteer general officers and officers serving in staff capacities not attached to a particular unit are generally not found with the compilation for a state or territory, but are in a separate series of abstracts.

Additional information about some Union army officers and soldiers is in a number of series of correspondence files among the records of the Adjutant General's Office. Correspondence relating to officers is generally found among the records of the Volunteer Service Division, 1861–89; the Record and Pension Office, 1889–1904; and the letters received series, 1800–1917. Correspondence relating to enlisted personnel is generally found among records of the Enlisted Branch, 1848–89; the Record and Pension Office, 1889–1904; and the correspondence series, 1800–1917. Correspondence relating to officers and enlisted personnel of the U.S. Colored Troops is contained in the records of the Colored Troops Division, 1863–89; the Record and Pension Office, 1889–1904; and the main correspondence series, 1800–1917. In nearly every instance, proper cross-references to additional files have been noted on the compiled service record. Descriptions of these series and their indexes are given in the section of this chapter relating to the regular army. (Pages 83–93).

At the same time that service records of individual Union soldiers were compiled, the War Department compiled **service histories of volunteer units of the Union army**, similar to those described on page 108. Those for units that served in the Civil War have been microfilmed as *Compiled Records Showing Service of Military Units in Volunteer Union Organizations*, M594, 225 rolls.

Other records of the various War Department offices and bureaus may contain information about specific soldiers and Civil War activities in general. Records of United States Army Continental Commands, 1821–1920, Record Group 393, include correspondence, reports, orders, and returns relating to Civil War military operations and the personnel who conducted them. For various commands, there may also be such personnel-related records as registers or lists of furloughs, leaves of absence, and discharges; troop rosters and station books or lists; and registers of officers. These records are rarely rewarding in genealogical research, however. Most are not arranged by name, and indexes are few and incomplete. Furthermore, information about specific soldiers may be duplicated in the compiled military service records.

A comprehensive description of the various records available is given in *Guide to Federal Records Relating to the Civil War*, compiled by Kenneth W. Munden and Henry P. Beers (Washington: National Archives and Records Service, 1962). Some information also appears in *War of the Rebellion: A Compilation of the Official Records of the Union and Confederate Armies*, 128 vols. (Washington: War Department, 1880–1901). This publication is available on microfilm as *Official Records of the Union and Confederate Armies, 1861–1865*, M262, 128 rolls, and it was also reprinted by The National Historical Society, Gettysburg, Pa., 1971–72. Libraries may shelve it among federal government documents under SuDocs. No. W45.5.130 or in Serial Set 4209–558. The name index may enable researchers to discover actions in which their ancestors participated.

As the Civil War entered its third year, it became increasingly apparent that recruiting systems for the Union forces were inadequate. To remedy this, Congress passed the First Conscription Act on 3 March 1863 (12 Stat. 731). It made all men aged 20 to 45 subject to military service, although service could be avoided by payment of $300 or procuring a substitute to enlist for three years. State quotas that were proportionate to total population were also established under the act.

The Civil War **draft records** include consolidated lists and descriptive rolls of enrollment districts, in Records of the Provost Marshal General's Bureau, Record Group 110, and case files on drafted aliens, in the General Records of the Department of State, Record Group 59.

The **consolidated lists** are the principal records of the Washington office of the Provost Marshal General's Bureau that relate to individual men. They are arranged by state and thereunder by enrollment or congressional district. Most are bound in volumes. They are divided into three classes:

men between the ages of 20 and 35 subject to military duty and unmarried men above 35 and under 45 subject to military duty; married men above 35 and under 45; and volunteers. Entries in each class are arranged in rough alphabetical order by initial letter of surname.

Each entry shows name; place of residence; age on 1 July 1863; occupation; marital status; state, territory, or country of birth; and, if a volunteer, in what military organizations he served.

Descriptive rolls or lists are the principal records of the enrollment districts that relate to individual men. They are arranged by state and thereunder by number of enrollment or congressional district. The rolls are chiefly in bound volumes. Arrangement of the entries varies considerably from district to district. Some are not indexed; some are indexed by initial letter of surname; and some are indexed by place of residence.

An entry often shows, in addition to the information in the corresponding consolidated list, physical description, place of birth, and whether accepted or rejected for military service. Entries in many volumes, however, are not complete.

It is difficult to find a particular serviceman in either the consolidated lists or the descriptive rolls, unless the congressional district in which he lived is known. If the researcher knows the county in which the serviceman lived in 1863, the number of the congressional district can be ascertained from *Congressional Directory for the Second Session*

TABLE 13

Selected Genealogical Research Aids: Civil War—Union

General

Official Army Register of the Volunteer Force of the United States Army for the Years 1861, '62, '63, '64, '65. 8 vols. Washington: Adjutant General's Office, 1865.

Henry, Guy Vernor. *Military Record of Civilian Appointments in the United States Army*. Vol. 1, New York: Carleton, 1870. Vol. 2, New York: D. Van Nostrand, 1873.

Heitman, Francis B. *Historical Register and Dictionary and Register of the United States Army, From Its Organization, September 29, 1789, to March 2, 1903*. 2 vols. Washington, 1903. Published as 57th Cong., 2d sess., H. Doc. 446, serial 4536, and reprinted by the University of Illinois Press, Urbana, 1965.

Strait, Newton A. and Wells, J. W., comps. *Alphabetical List of Battles of the War of the Rebellion With Dates . . . and a roster of All Regimental Surgeons*. Washington: N. A. Strait, 1882.

War College Division, U.S. General Staff. *Bibliography of State Participation in the Civil War, 1861–1866*. 3d ed. Washington: War Department, 1913.

California

Orton, Richard H., comp. *Records of California Men in the War of the Rebellion, 1861–1867*. Sacramento: California Adjutant General's Office, 1890.

List of Electors, Resident of California, in the Military Service. . . . Sacramento: California Adjutant General's Office, 1865.

Connecticut

Smith, Stephen R., comp. *Record of Service of Connecticut Men in the Army and Navy of the United States During the War of the Rebellion*. Hartford: Connecticut Adjutant General's Office, 1889.

Morse, Horace J., comp. *Catalog of Connecticut Volunteer Organizations, With Additional Enlistments and Casualties to July 1, 1864*. Hartford: Connecticut Adjutant General's Office, 1864.

Ingersoll, C. M., comp. *Catalog of Connecticut Volunteer Organizations (Infantry, Cavalry, and Artillery) in the Service of the United States, 1861–1865 . . . .* Hartford: Connecticut Adjutant General's Office, 1869.

Illinois

Reece, J. N., comp. *Report of the Adjutant General of the State of Illinois*. Rev. ed. 9 vols. Springfield: Illinois Military and Naval Department, 1900–02.

Indiana

Terrell, W. H. H., comp. *Report of the Adjutant General of the State of Indiana*. 8 vols. Indianapolis: Indiana Adjutant General's Office, 1869.

Iowa

Alexander, William L., comp. *List of Ex-Soldiers, Sailors, and Marines Living in Iowa*. Des Moines: Iowa Adjutant General's Office, 1886.

Baker, N. B., comp. *Report of the Adjutant General and Acting Quartermaster General of the State of Iowa, January 1, 1865, to January 1, 1866*. Des Moines: Iowa Adjutant General's Office, 1866.

Thrift, William H. and Logan, Guy E., comps. *Roster and Record of Iowa Soldiers in the War of the Rebellion . . . .* 6 vols. Des Moines: Iowa Adjutant General's Office, 1908–11.

(table continued on following page)

of the Thirty-Eighth Congress of the United States of America (Washington: U.S. House of Representatives, 1865).

Under the terms of the Conscription Act, the President, on 8 May 1863, issued a proclamation announcing that aliens who had declared their intention to become citizens and who were in the United States sixty-five days after that date would not be allowed to avoid the draft on the plea of alienage. The State Department became involved in the release from military service of aliens who were drafted from 1862 onward. The records of this activity in Record Group 59 include an alphabetical case file containing draft notices, depositions of aliens regarding their foreign citizenship, and correspondence. Other correspondence of the Secretary of State regarding the release of aliens is in separate letter books (indexed) and in files of loose papers. An alphabetical list of draft cases shows the states and counties from which the aliens were drafted.

5.2.7 Civil War—Confederate

As the Confederate government evacuated Richmond in April 1865, the central military records of the Confederate army were taken to Charlotte, N.C., by the adjutant and inspector general, who then transferred them to a Union officer. The records were taken to Washington, where, along with other Confederate records captured by the Union army, they were preserved by the U.S. War Department. In 1903, the Secretary of War persuaded the governors of

TABLE 13 (CONTINUED)

Selected Genealogical Research Aids: Civil War—Union

Kansas

Noble, P. S., comp. *Report of the Adjutant General of the State of Kansas . . . 1861–1865*. 2 vols. Leavenworth: Kansas Adjutant General's Office, 1867–70. Volume 1 was reprinted by the Kansas State Printing Co., Topeka, 1896.

Louisiana

Burt, W. G., comp. *Annual Report of the Adjutant General of the State of Louisiana for the Year Ending December 31st, 1889*. New Orleans: Louisiana Adjutant General's Office, 1890.

Maine

Hodsdon, John L., comp. *Annual Report of the Adjutant General of the State of Maine, for the Year Ending December 31, 1863*. Augusta: Maine Adjutant General's Office, 1863.

Annual Report, 1861–66. 7 vols. Augusta: Maine Adjutant General's Office, 1862–67, with supplement, *Alphabetical Index of Maine Volunteers, Etc., Mustered Into the Service of the United States During the War of 1861*.

Hodsdon, John L., comp. *Returns of Desertions, Discharges, and Deaths in Maine Regiments . . . .* Augusta: Maine Adjutant General's Office, 1864.

Maryland

Williams, L. Allison, Jarrett, J. H., and Vernon, George W. F. *History and Roster of Maryland Volunteers, War of 1861–65*. Baltimore: Commission on the Publication of the Histories of the Maryland Volunteers During the Civil War, 1898–99.

Massachusetts

Record of the Massachusetts Volunteers, 1861–65. Boston: Massachusetts Adjutant General's Office, 1868–70.

Massachusetts Soldiers, Sailors, and Marines in the Civil War . . . . 8 vols. Norwood and Brookline: Massachusetts Adjutant General's Office, 1931–35. A ninth volume, subtitled *Index to Army Records* and published in Boston in 1937, pertains to vols. 1–6 and part of vol. 7.

Michigan

Brown, Ida C. *Michigan Men in the Civil War*. Michigan Historical Collections Bulletin 9. Ann Arbor: University of Michigan, 1959.

Robertson, John, comp. *Michigan in the War*. Rev. ed. Lansing: Michigan Adjutant General's Department, 1882.

Turner, George H., comp. *Record of Service of Michigan Volunteers in the Civil War, 1861–1865*. 46 vols. Kalamazoo: Michigan Adjutant General's Department, 1905.

Robertson, John *Annual Report of the Adjutant General of the State of Michigan for the Year 1864*. Lansing: Michigan Adjutant General's Department, 1865. And . . . *For the Years 1865–66*. Lansing, 1866.

Michigan Adjutant General's Department, *Alphabetical General Index to Public Library Sets of 85,271 Names of Michigan Soldiers and Sailors Individual Records*. Lansing: Michigan Secretary of State, 1915.

Minnesota

Minnesota in the Civil and Indian War, 1861–65. 2 vols. St. Paul: Minnesota Board of Commissioners on Publication of History of Minnesota in Civil and Indian Wars, 1890–93.

Warming, Irene B., comp. *Minnesotans in the Civil and Indian Wars, an Index to the Rosters in Minnesota in the Civil and Indian Wars, 1861–1865*. St. Paul: Minnesota Historical Society, 1936.

most southern states to lend the War Department the Confederate military personnel records, which were in the possession of the states, for copying. These records are part of the War Department Collection of Confederate Records, Record Group 109.

The **compiled military service records** of Confederate officers, noncommissioned officers, and enlisted men consist of cards on which the War Department, between 1903 and 1927, recorded information abstracted from Union prison and parole records and from captured and other surviving Confederate records. They are similar to those described on page 108. In addition to the usual information found on compiled military service records, some of these show facts about a soldier's imprisonment. If he was captured, they may show the date of his release and parole, or if he died in prison, the date of his death. References to the original records are included on the cards. Table 14 gives the microfilm publication number for the compiled service records for each state.

There are also two other series. One consists of jacket-envelopes for men who served in military units raised directly by the Confederate government (such as the 1st Confederate Infantry, Morgan's Cavalry, and the Cherokee Mounted Rifles), arranged by organization and thereunder alphabetically by name. These records have been reproduced as *Compiled Service Records of Confederate Soldiers Who Served in Organizations Raised Directly by the Confederate Government*, M258, 123 rolls.

Missouri

Simpson, Samuel P. *Annual Report of the Adjutant General of Missouri . . . 1865*. Jefferson City: Missouri Adjutant General's Office, 1866.

Nebraska

Roster of Soldiers, Sailors, and Marines of the War of 1812, the Mexican War, and the War of the Rebellion Residing in Nebraska June 1, 1893. Lincoln: Iowa Department of State, 1893, . . . *June 1, 1895*. York, 1895. And . . . *December 1, 1897*. Lincoln, 1898.

Patrick, John R. *Report of the Adjutant General of the State of Nebraska*. Des Moines: Iowa Adjutant General's Office, 1871.

New Hampshire

Ayling, Augustus D., comp. *Revised Register of the Soldiers and Sailors of New Hampshire in the War of the Rebellion, 1861–66*. Concord: New Hampshire Adjutant General's Office, 1895.

New Jersey

Stryker, William S., comp. *Record of Officers and Men of New Jersey in the Civil War, 1861–1865*. 2 vols. Trenton: New Jersey Adjutant General's Office, 1876.

New York

Irvine, William, comp. *A Record of the Commissioned and Non-commissioned Officers and Privates of the Regiments Organized in the State of New York . . . .* 8 vols. Albany: New York Adjutant General's Office, 1864–68.

Phisterer, Frederick, comp. *New York in the War of the Rebellion, 1861 to 1865*. 6 vols. 3d ed. Albany, 1912.

Ohio

Reid, Whitelaw. *Ohio in the War*. Cincinnati and New York: Moore, Wilstach, and Baldwin, 1868. Reprinted by the Eclectic Publishing Co., Columbus, Ohio, 1893.

Official Roster of the Soldiers of the State of Ohio in the War of the Rebellion, 1861–66. 12 vols. Akron: Ohio Roster Commission, 1886–95.

Pennsylvania

Bates, Samuel P. *History of Pennsylvania Volunteers, 1861–65*. 5 vols. Harrisburg: Pennsylvania State Legislature, 1869–71.

Russell, A. L. *Annual Report of the Adjutant General of Pennsylvania, 1863*. Harrisburg: Pennsylvania Adjutant General's Office, 1864.

Rhode Island

Dyer, Elisha. *Annual Report of the Adjutant General of Rhode Island and Providence Plantations for the Year 1865*. 2 vols. Rev. ed. Providence: Rhode Island Adjutant General's Office, 1893–95.

Vermont

Peck, Theodore S., comp. *Revised Roster of Vermont Volunteers and Lists of Vermonters Who Served in the Army and Navy of the United States During the War of the Rebellion, 1861–66*. Montpelier: Vermont Adjutant and Inspector General's Office, 1892.

Wisconsin

Chapman, Chandler P., comp. *Roster of Wisconsin Volunteers, War of the Rebellion, 1861–65*. 2 vols. Madison: Wisconsin Adjutant General's Office, 1886.

Wisconsin Volunteers, War of the Rebellion, 1861–65, Arranged Alphabetically. Madison: Wisconsin Adjutant General's Office, 1914.

TABLE 14

Microfilmed Indexes and Compiled Military Service Records for Confederate Army Volunteers

	Index	Compiled Military Service Records		
State	**Microfilm Publication**	**Number of rolls**	**Microfilm Publication**	**Number of rolls**
Alabama	M374	49	M311	508
Arizona Territory	M375	1	M318	1
Arkansas	M376	26	M317	256
Florida	M225	9	M251	104
Georgia	M226	67	M266	607
Kentucky	M377	14	M319	136
Louisiana	M378	31	M320	414
Maryland	M379	2	M321	22
Mississippi	M232	45	M269	427
Missouri	M380	16	M322	193
North Carolina	M230	43	M270	580
South Carolina	M381	35	M267	392
Tennessee	M231	48	M268	359
Texas	M227	41	M323	445
Virginia	M382	62	M324	1,075
Organizations Raised Directly by the Confederate Government			M258	123
General and Staff Officers			M331	275
Consolidated Index	M818	26		

The other series consists of jacket-envelopes known as the general and staff officers' papers, which include records not only for officers occupying staff positions, but also for noncommissioned officers and enlisted men performing staff services. These records are arranged alphabetically by name. They have been reproduced as *Compiled Service Records of Confederate General and Staff Officers and Nonregimental Enlisted Men*, M331, 275 rolls.

Card indexes, arranged alphabetically by name of soldier can be used to locate the name of a unit in which a soldier served. The *Consolidated Index to Compiled Service Records of Confederate Soldiers*, M253, 535 rolls, refers to the records for the individual states and the records in the two other series. Each card gives a soldier's name, rank, and unit, and there is often a statement concerning the origin or background of the unit. In addition to the consolidated index, there is a separate index to the records for each state. Table 14 gives the microfilm publication numbers of these indexes.

"Unfiled Papers and Slips Belonging in Confederate Compiled Service Records" were accumulated by the War Department to be interfiled with the compilations, but they were never interfiled. Items most commonly included are card abstracts and personal papers similar to those found in compiled service records of Confederate soldiers. The card abstracts contain entries taken from sources like those used to create the compiled military service records. References to original records, letters, vouchers, requisitions, paroles, and oaths of allegiance are included. The personal papers are the originals of documents relating solely to the particular soldier.

In general, papers were placed in the unfiled papers series when their proper filing was uncertain or there was no other place to file them because the information was insufficient or contained discrepancies and could not be positively identified with any soldier for whom there was a compiled service record. Sometimes, no compiled service record had been established on the basis of regular service records, and the item did not provide enough evidence to justify establishing one. In some cases, a soldier may have served in a home guard unit or another state organization never called into the service of the central government of the Confederate States. It is sometimes difficult to tell whether some items refer to a soldier, a civilian employee, or a private individual.

The papers relating to Confederate civilians are similar to many of the documents in the Confederate papers relating to citizens or business firms described on page 217, but the identity of each person was not always clearly indicated. Civilian records include employment information about hospital attendants, clerks and other employees. Also included are some papers relating to Confederate sympathizers, some of whom are the same persons whose names appear in the Union Provost Marshals' files described on page 162.

The records are arranged alphabetically by surname with cross-references to spelling variations, and guide cards show how similar-sounding names are placed together. Researchers should be aware that it may be necessary to search for a name under a number of different spellings. The records included in this series generally are not covered by any of the indexes relating to Confederate compiled service records or to any other records relating to Confederate service or civilians. The series is available as *Unfiled Papers and Slips Belonging in Confederate Compiled Service Records*, M347, 442 rolls.

Included in the series are some cross-references to records or documents contained in other series of Confederate records, some of which have not been microfilmed, and to compiled service records. Some correspondence originally filed in other series has been included in this series.

Compiled military service records that give histories of Confederate military units consist of jacket-envelopes bearing the names of the units and the title "Captions and Record of Events." These jacket-envelopes typically contain cards showing captions that were copied from original muster rolls and certificates of the mustering officer verifying the accuracy of the rolls. They also contain record-of-events cards like those for Union military units described on page 97. The amount of information varies from card to card. Some cards give only date and name of station. Other cards give detailed accounts of a unit's operation and activities.

Because some records of the Confederate army were lost or destroyed during the war and at its close, the compiled military histories of most units are incomplete. There are no record-of-events cards for a few state units that were mustered into Confederate service or for militia units that were never mustered into service.

The service records of Confederate military units and the service records of Confederate soldiers were compiled at the same time. Abstracts were made from documents in the War Department's collection and from documents borrowed mostly from southern states by the War Department in an effort to obtain as complete military histories of units as possible. The original muster rolls and returns were the principal sources of information abstracted on the caption cards, but rosters, payrolls, hospital registers, casualty lists, Union prison registers and rolls, parole rolls, and inspection reports were also examined. Abstracts were verified by separate comparison, and every precaution was taken to ensure their accuracy. The carded abstracts have been reproduced as *Compiled Records Showing Service of Military Units in Confederate Organizations*, M861, 74 rolls.

Most of the compiled records are arranged alphabetically by state and thereunder by type of unit: cavalry, artillery, and infantry followed by reserve, militia, local defense, conscript, prison guard, instruction, or other organizations. Other names by which units were known, and related information, are shown on the records. The arrangement of compiled records for units raised directly or otherwise formed by the Confederate government is similar except that they are not arranged by state.

Lists of **Confederate soldiers and civilians who died in federal prisons** were compiled in compliance with a statute of 1906 (34 Stat. 56) that provided "for the appropriate marking of the graves of the soldiers and sailors of the Confederate Army and Navy who died in Northern prisons and were buried near the prisons where they died." The burial lists (in Record Group 92) are generally arranged alphabetically by name of the prison camp or other location where the deaths occurred. Each list is alphabetical by name of deceased and usually gives the name, rank, company, regiment, date of death, and number and location of grave for each person interred, including a few private citizens. Available on microfilm is *Register of Confederate Soldiers, Sailors, and Citizens Who Died in Federal Prisons and Military Hospitals in the North, 1861–1865*, M918, 1 roll. There are also records of cemeteries in Record Group 92 that contain burial registers and lists.

Among the War Department Collection of Confederate Records, Record Group 109, are other registers of Confederates who died in Union prisons, which have been reproduced as *Selected Records of the War Department Relating to Confederate Prisoners of War, 1861–1865*, M598, 145 rolls. Particularly useful is a two-volume series of registers of prisoner deaths compiled by the Office of the Commissary General of Prisoners (rolls 5 and 6) and a five-volume series of registers of prisoner deaths, compiled by the Surgeon General's Office (rolls 11–12).

Among the records of the Confederate Secretary of War and Adjutant and Inspector General's Offices in Record Group 109 are a number of **records of appointments** and subsequent careers of military personnel. Much of the information contained in the records, however, may already be available in more convenient form in the compiled military service records for individual officers. Many of the volumes consist of registers of applications and recommendations for appointments, registers and lists of appointments, and registers of applications and recommendations for promotions. Volumes are variously arranged: chronologically by date of appointment or application, alphabetically by surname of appointee, or by type of appointment. Some of the books are individually indexed, but there is also a master alphabetical card index to appointments of officers, which was prepared by the U.S. Adjutant General's Office. The card index covers entries in many of the significant volumes. Appointment registers give such information as name; rank; dates of appointment, rank, confirmation, and acceptance; arm of service; state; to whom the officer or appointee reported; and subsequent personnel actions. Rosters of commissioned officers of regiments and battalions contain information similar to that found in the appointment registers. Other records of military personnel include registers of resignations, discharges, and deaths, which show name, rank, organization, and dates and places of resignation, discharge, or death.

Information about Confederate officers and other soldiers is also interpersed among the various correspondence series of the Confederate War Department. These are available as *Letters Received by the Confederate Secretary of War, 1861–1865*, M437, 151 rolls; *Letters Received by the Confederate Adjutant and Inspector General, 1861–1865*, M474, 164 rolls; and *Letters Received by the Confederate Quartermaster General, 1861–1865*, M469, 14 rolls. Alphabetical card indexes to names of correspondents and persons mentioned in the letters are available as *Index to Letters Received by the Confederate Secretary of War, 1861–1865*, M409, 34 rolls and *Index to Letters Received by the Confederate Adjutant and Inspector General and the Confederate Quartermaster General, 1861–1865*, M410, 41 rolls.

Information about the confirmation of appointments of Confederate officers is given in *Journal of the Congress of the Confederate States of America, 1861–65* (58th Cong., 2d sess., S. Doc. 234, serials 4610–4616). A general index is in the last volume.

Some Confederate soldiers are named in *War of the Rebellion: A Compilation of the Official Records of the Union and Confederate Armies*, 128 vols. (Washington: War Department, 1880–1901). The last volume is a general index. The voluminous publication, including the index, has been microfilmed as *Official Records of the Union and Confederate Armies, 1861–1865*, M262, 128 rolls. It has also been reprinted by the National Historical Society, Gettysburg, Pa., 1971–72.

5.2.8 Spanish-American War

During the Spanish-American War in 1898, volunteer soldiers served in existing state militia units accepted into federal service, in additional units raised in states and territories, and in units raised directly by the federal government. Because the methods of enlistment varied, the compiled military service records for these soldiers are arranged in four subseries: records of state units arranged alphabetically by state; records of volunteers from the continental territories; records of volunteers raised directly by the federal government; and records of volunteers from Puerto Rico. The compiled service records are further arranged by an organizational breakdown ending with the regiment or the independent battalion or company. Under each unit the service records are arranged alphabetically by surname of soldier.

A general comprehensive index identifies the compiled service records of volunteer soldiers regardless of their military units. It has been reproduced as *General Index to Compiled Service Records of Volunteer Soldiers Who Served During the War with Spain*, M871, 126 rolls. Each index card gives name, rank, and unit in which the soldier served. There are cross-references to names that appeared in the records under more than one spelling.

Some index cards refer to "miscellaneous personal papers"; there are no compiled service records for persons whose index card contains this entry. The papers themselves follow the jacket-envelopes for most units. The War De-

TABLE 15

Selected Genealogical Research Aids: Civil War—Confederate

General

Wright, Marcus G. *General Officers of the Confederate Army* . . . . New York: Neale Publishing Co., 1911.

Estes, Claude. *List of Field Officers, Regiments, and Battalions in the Confederate States Army, 1861–65.* Macon, Ga.: J. W. Burke Co., 1912.

Alabama

McMorries, Edward Young. *History of the First Regiment Alabama Infantry, Volunteer Infantry, C.S.A.* Montgomery: Brown Printing Co., 1904.

Georgia

Candler, Allen D., ed. *The Confederate Records of the State of Georgia.* 5 vols. Atlanta: Georgia Legislature, 1909–11.

Henderson, Lillian. *Roster of the Confederate Soldiers of Georgia, 1861–65.* 6 vols. Hapeville, Ga.: Longino and Porter, 1959–64.

Kansas

Fox, S. M., comp. "Roll of the Officers and Enlisted Men of the Third, Fourth, Eighteenth and Nineteenth Kansas Volunteers, 1861," *13th Biennial Report*, appendix. Topeka: Kansas Adjutant General's Office, 1902.

Kentucky

Harris, Abner, comp. *Reports of the Adjutant General of the State of Kentucky—Confederate Kentucky Volunteers, War 1861–1865.* 2 vols. Frankfort: Kentucky Adjutant General's Office, 1915–18.

Lindsey, D. W., comp. *Report of the Adjutant General of the State of Kentucky, 1861–1866.* 2 vols. Frankfort: Kentucky Adjutant General's Office, 1866–67.

Louisiana

Booth, Andrew B. *Records of Louisiana Confederate Soldiers and Louisiana Confederate Commands.* New Orleans: Military Record Commission, 1920.

North Carolina

Moore, John W. *Roster of North Carolina Troops in the War Between the States.* Raleigh: Ashe and Gatling, 1882.

Jordan, Weymouth T., Jr., and Manarian, Louis H. *North Carolina Troops, 1861–1865: A Roster.* Raleigh: North Carolina Department of Archives and History, 1966– .

Tennessee

Tennesseans in the Civil War. 2 vols. Nashville: Tennessee Civil War Centennial Commission, 1964.

Wright, Marcus J. *Tennessee in the War, 1861–65.* New York: Ambrose Lee Publishing Co., 1908.

TABLE 16

Selected Genealogical Research Aids: Spanish-American War and Philippine Insurrection

General

Heitman, Francis B. *Historical Register and Dictionary of the United States Army . . .* (Washington, 1903), 2:185–272. A separate list of acting assistant or contract surgeons, U.S. Army, in service at any time between April 17, 1898, and January 1, 1903, appears on pages 273–279 of this volume.

Official Register of Officers and Volunteers in the Service of the United States . . . March 2, 1899, . . . June 1, 1900. Washington: Adjutant General's Office, 1900.

Peterson, Clarence Stewart. *Known Military Dead During the Spanish-American War and the Philippine Insurrection, 1898–1901.* Baltimore, 1958.

Mawson, Harry P. and Buel, J. W., comps. *Leslie's Official History of the Spanish-American War.* Washington, 1899.

Correspondence Relating to the War with Spain . . . With an Appendix Giving . . . a Brief History of the Volunteer Organizations. . . . Washington: Adjutant General's Office, 1902.

Connecticut

Connecticut Volunteers Who Served in the Spanish-American War, 1898–1899. Hartford: Connecticut Adjutant General's Office, 1899.

Illinois

Reece, Jasper N. *Report of the Adjutant General of the State of Illinois. . . .* Springfield: Illinois Adjutant General's Office, 1900–02.

Indiana

Gore, James K. *Record of Indiana Volunteers in the Spanish-American War, 1898–1899.* Indianapolis: Indiana Adjutant General's Office, 1900.

Kansas

Fox, S. M. *13th Biennial Report of the Adjutant General of the State of Kansas, 1901–2.* Topeka: Kansas Adjutant General's Office, 1902.

Minnesota

Eleventh Biennial Report . . . Including Military Operations . . . up to November 30, 1900. St. Paul: Minnesota Adjutant General's Department, 1901.

Nebraska

Pool, Charles H. *Roster of Veterans of the Mexican, Civil, and Spanish-American Wars, Residing in Nebraska, 1915.* Lincoln: Nebraska Secretary of State, 1915.

New Jersey

Report of the Adjutant General of New Jersey . . . . Somerville: New Jersey Adjutant General's Office, 1899.

New York

New York, Adjutant General's Office. *New York in the Spanish-American War, 1898.* 3 vols. Rev. ed. Albany: J. B. Lyon, 1902. Herrick, Chauncey W., comp. *Index.* 1914.

North Carolina

Roster of the North Carolina Volunteers in the Spanish-American War. Raleigh: North Carolina Adjutant General, 1900.

Ohio

Hough, Benson W., et al. comps. *Official Roster of Ohio Soldiers in the War With Spain, 1898–1899.* Columbus: Ohio Adjutant General's Department, 1916.

Oregon

Gantenbein, C. U., comp. *The Official Records of the Oregon Volunteers in the Spanish War and Philippine Insurrection.* 2d ed. Salem: Oregon Adjutant General's Office, 1903.

Pennsylvania

Stewart, Thomas J., comp. *Record of Pennsylvania Volunteers in the Spanish-American War, 1898.* 2d ed. Harrisburg: Pennsylvania Adjutant General's Office, 1901.

West Virginia

Biennial Report of the Adjutant General of West Virginia, 1899–1900. Charleston: West Virginia Adjutant General's Office, 1900.

partment apparently accumulated these papers to be interfiled with the regular series of compiled service records, but never interfiled them.

There is a separate index for the organizations from each state. The index for Louisiana is available as M240, 1 roll, and for North Carolina as M413, 2 rolls. There is also a separate index for units of U.S. Volunteers. *Compiled Service Records of Volunteer Soldiers Who Served in the Florida Infantry During the War with Spain*, M1087, 13 rolls, is the only microfilm publication of compiled military service records for the Spanish-American War.

Information about volunteers during the Spanish-American War is found in the general correspondence of the Adjutant General's Office. An extensive name and subject index is available on microfilm as *Index to General Correspondence of the Adjutant General's Office, 1890–1917*, M698, 1,269 rolls. Operational records for the army and its subcommands are in Records of U.S. Army Overseas Operations and Commands, 1898–1942, Record Group 395. Published research aids are listed in Table 16.

5.2.9 Philippine Insurrection

The acts of Congress authorizing the raising of troops to fight in the Philippine Insurrection, 1899–1902, allowed for the recruitment of volunteers from all the continental states and territories and from the Philippines. Some units were composed of persons from a single place, but many were made up of men from more than one place. Accordingly, units of volunteers accepted into federal service for the Philippine Insurrection did not include the name of the state or territory as part of their official designations, as had been customary in previous wars. Designations, therefore, do not provide a clue as to the state or territory of residence of persons serving in the unit, even if the unit was formed in a single state.

The compiled military service records are arranged by regiment number and regiment name without reference to the state or territory in which the unit was formed; thereunder, the jacket-envelopes are arranged alphabetically by surname of soldier. Only Americans who served in regiments formed in the United States and in the Philippines are represented. No records relating to Filipinos are included. Records relating to the Puerto Rican Regiment, U.S. Volunteers, which was organized for service in the Philippines but remained in Puerto Rico, are filed and indexed with the compiled service records of the Spanish-American War.

A general comprehensive index was published as *Index to Compiled Service Records of Volunteer Soldiers Who Served During the Philippine Insurrection*, M872, 24 rolls. There is no compiled service record for a soldier whose index card contains a cross-reference to the miscellaneous papers. This is a separate series of personal papers following the compiled service records. It was apparently accumulated by the War Department for interfiling that never took place.

The *Index to General Correspondence of the Adjutant General's Office, 1890–1917*, M698, 1,269 rolls, may lead to other information about volunteers and enlisted men. Operational records for the army and its subcommands are among the Records of U.S. Army Overseas Operations and Commands, 1898–1942, Record Group 395.

Historical sketches of volunteer organizations were prepared in response to the Adjutant General's instructions of 19 October 1900, which were distributed in Circular No. 23 of 23 December 1900, Headquarters, Division of the Philippines. The histories are arranged by arm of service, and thereunder numerically by regiment. The histories for all the regiments that participated in the war are not in this file, but the typescripts comprise detailed unit histories of the 26th–49th U.S. Volunteer Infantry Regiments in the Philippine Insurrection. No history was found for the 11th U.S. Volunteer Cavalry and the miscellaneous units of volunteers arranged by unit number.

5.3 Records of Military Service in the Twentieth Century

5.3.1 World War I: Draft Records

The archives branch, FARC Atlanta, has World War I draft records. They are part of Records of the Selective Service System (World War I), Record Group 163.

Draft registration cards (Series 1 PMGO Form 1) contain information supplied by each registrant, including name, address, date of birth, age, race, citizenship status, birthplace, occupation and employer, dependent relative, marital status, father's birthplace, and name and address of nearest relative. They are arranged alphabetically by state, thereunder by local board, and thereunder by individual registrant.

Docket books (Series 2 PMGO Form 178) and **classification lists** (Series 3 PMGO Form 1000) show for each registrant dates of each step in the induction process through acceptance or rejection at mobilization camps.

Appeals to the President from district boards include decisions affirmed and returns of record on appeal. They detail the reasons for appeal (such as dependents) and physical, marital, and draft status of members of the family. An index is available.

There are also records of American registrants in England, a list of registrants living in Canada, and a list of registrants living abroad in other nations. These records show names, ages, and addresses of registrants; an index as available.

5.3.2 Other Records

Records relating to the following groups of military personnel are at the **National Personnel Records Center** in St. Louis, Mo.:

- U.S. Army officers and enlisted personnel completely separated after 1956. Personnel jackets of officers separated between 30 June 1917, and 1956 were destroyed by fire in 1972, as were jackets of enlisted men separated between 30 October 1912, and 1956.
- U.S. Air Force officers and enlisted men completely separated after 1956. Earlier jackets of the Army Air Corps and the U.S. Air Force were destroyed by fire in 1972.
- Marine Corps officers and enlisted members completely separated after 1895.
- U.S. Navy officers completely separated after 1902 and enlisted men completely separated after 1885.

- U.S. Coast Guard officers completely separated after 1928 and enlisted personnel completely separated after 1914.

Requests for information about veterans should be submitted to the National Personnel Records Center (MPR), 9700 Page Blvd., St. Louis, MO 63132, using Standard Form 180, Request Pertaining to Military Records. This form is available from the St. Louis Center, Government Printing Office, Federal Information Centers, local Veterans Administration offices, veterans service organizations, and the Reference Services Branch (NNIR), General Services Administration, Washington, DC 20408.

The release of information from these military personnel records is subject to restrictions imposed by the military departments consistent with provisions of the Freedom of Information Act of 1967 (as amended in 1974) and the Privacy Act of 1974. Under these regulations, most information of a personal nature may be furnished only with the written consent of the veteran, or of his next of kin if the veteran is deceased. Further details about the release of information from personnel records are provided on Standard Form 180 or may be obtained from the St. Louis Center.

CHAPTER 6

Naval and Marine Service Records

6.1 Introduction

Responsibility for naval matters was vested in the Secretary of War until an act of 1798 established the Department of the Navy. The act empowered the Secretary of the Navy "to take possession of all the records, books and documents, and all other matters and things appertaining to this department . . . ." Most of the records of officers and enlisted men are in two record groups, Records of the Bureau of Naval Personnel, Record Group 24, and Naval Records Collection of the Office of Naval Records and Library, Record Group 45. Established originally to collect and prepare for publication manuscripts dealing with naval affairs in the Civil War, the Naval Records and Library Office became for a time the de facto archival unit of the Office of the Secretary of the Navy.

The U.S. Marine Corps was also established in 1798, but until 1834, no one knew whether the corps was more akin to the navy or to the army, for the 1798 act placed the marines under navy regulations when afloat, and under the army when ashore. An act of 1834 adopted the concept that the Marine Corps should be part of the Navy Department.

6.2 U.S. Navy Records

6.2.1 Revolutionary War

The naval and marine service records of the Revolutionary War are fragmentary. In addition to those in Record Group 24 and Record Group 45 mentioned above, there are records assembled by the War Department in War Department Collection of Revolutionary War Records, Record Group 93, and in Records of the Continental and Confederation Congresses and the Constitutional Convention, Record Group 360.

The **record books** assembled by the Navy Department include the payroll of the Continental Ship *Confederacy*, 1780–81, in one volume; a photostatic copy of the rosters of officers and men of the *Bonhomme Richard*, the *Pallas*, and the *Vengeance*, 1779, in one volume; and a photostatic copy of the log of the Continental Ship *Ranger*, 1778–80, in one volume. There is a separate typewritten index to each volume. The information varies from volume to volume, but generally shown are the names of individuals and the vessels on which they served and sometimes other service or payment data.

Some of the **unbound papers** assembled by the Navy Department form part of a large series called the **area file** because the papers therein are arranged by geographical regions or areas. The papers vary widely in form and content. Documents that contain references to naval men of the Revolutionary War, along with other early parts of the area file, are covered by a card index. Some records may show such information as the name and rank of a naval man of the Revolutionary War, the vessel on which he served, and a date.

The area file includes photostatic copies of letters and other documents from the period of the American Revolution that were copied from originals in manuscript collections of the states of Massachusetts, Virginia, and North Carolina. The documents are microfilmed on *Area File of the Naval Records Collection, 1775–1910,* M625, 414 rolls. An alphabetical card index to names of vessels, American and foreign naval officers and privateersmen, and other individuals mentioned in the documents is available, but not microfilmed.

There are also three lists of captured American naval personnel and other prisoners and individuals entitled to prize money for service under John Paul Jones. Each list is an alphabetically arranged set of 3″ × 8″ printed cards captioned "War of the Revolution, Navy and Privateer Records," containing information derived from several sources. The first subseries of cards pertains to persons taken to Forton Prison in England: officers and men of captured American vessels (including Continental warships, privateers, and prizes) and a few passengers. The cards show the name of the individual and often state of residence, date committed to prison, rank, name of the vessel on which captured and port from which it sailed, date of capture, name of the vessel making the capture, and whether the prisoner escaped or died in prison.

The second subseries of cards pertains to prize money due to the "heirs" of John Paul Jones. The entries were taken from Senate Executive Document 11, 37th Congress, 2d session. Each card shows the name of an individual, rank, vessel on which he served (*Bonhomme Richard* or *Alliance*), the amount of prize money due, and sometimes nationality (French or American).

The third subseries of cards relates to persons sent to Mill Prison in England. The cards are similar in content to those in the first list; some also show city or town of residence of prisoners, if exchanged, and if joined the British Navy. The information was taken from "A List of the Americans Committed to Old Mill Prison Since the American War," *New England Historical and Genealogical Register* 19 (1865):74–75, 136–141, and 209–213, and *A Relic of the Revolution,* by Charles Herbert (Boston: C. H. Pierce, 1847), which has been reprinted by the New York Times, New York, 1968.

A 5″ × 8″ card index, prepared by the Office of Naval Records and Library cites names mentioned in documents of Record Group 45 relating to the Revolutionary War. The index is incomplete, but it is more comprehensive than the index to the area file. The index consists mainly of names of American naval officers and enlisted men, but it also includes names of Marine Corps officers and men, officers and men of the Virginia State Navy, officers and men of privateers, French volunteers, and American military officers.

The War Department collected only a few naval records of the Revolutionary War and transferred most of them to the Navy Department in 1906. Before that time, however, **compiled service records** for naval personnel were created. This series of card abstracts is available on rolls 3 and 4 of *Compiled Service Records of American Naval Personnel and Members of the Departments of the Quartermaster General and Commissary General of Military Stores Who Served During the Revolutionary War,* M880, 4 rolls. The most comprehensive name index to the Revolutionary War compiled service records is *General Index to Compiled Service Records of Revolutionary War Soldiers,* M860, 58 rolls. A separate index to names of naval personnel is *Index to Compiled*

Service Records of American Naval Personnel Who Served During the Revolutionary War, M879, 1 roll. The names appearing in M879 are generally duplicated in M860.

The information on the cards in the compiled service records was carefully transcribed from lists of American sailors and vessels, payrolls, portage bills, and assignments of pay relating to ships of the Continental navy and state navies, the frigate *Alliance*, brigantines *Dartmouth* and *Polly*, sloops *Independence* and *Montgomery*, the schooner *Putnam*, and the ship *Raleigh*; lists of American prisoners taken by the British ships *Gibraltar*, *Hunter*, and *Felicity*; lists of vessels arriving and departing from Tribel's Landing in October 1781; and entries in volume 175 of the numbered record books, which includes the names of many sailors from the states of New York and Virginia.

A five-volume published name and subject index to the Papers of the Continental Congress makes it easy to determine whether a reference to the individual being researched exists in that part of Record Group 360.

6.2.2 Records of Commissioned Officers

Several series in Record Group 45 relate to commissioned officers of the regular navy and acting or volunteer officers who served during the Civil War and the Spanish-American War.

Among the earliest records in Record Group 45 is a **register of officers** of the navy, May 1815 to June 1821. The register is alphabetical by first letter of surname, and thereunder chronological. Each entry gives the officer's name, rank, date of appointment to the rank, age, and remarks of his superior in regard to his promotion potential.

Also for this early period are two series of **statements of place of birth** of officers. Those for 1816 are largely records for officers whose names began with the letters "C" and "D" and provide under the name the officer's age and place of birth. Similar statements for 1826 are on printed forms, arranged alphabetically. Those relating to chaplains and pursers are in a separate volume. Each record shows the name of the officer and the name of the state or territory in which he was born, from which he was appointed, and of which he was a citizen.

A record of **officers serving in 1829** is in one indexed volume. Each entry shows the name of the officer and his service record from the date of his appointment to 1829.

Acceptances were letters from men accepting appointments as officers, often with oaths of allegiance enclosed. Commissioned and warrant officers' acceptances, 1804–64, are arranged chronologically and thereunder alphabetically; those for volunteer officers, 1861–71, are arranged chronologically in subseries according to rank. Dates of coverage vary within each rank. Many of the letters or accompanying oaths of allegiance contain statements of birthplace or residence. Some subseries are indexed. There is also a series of acceptances for acting engineers, 1862–65, with oaths of allegiance enclosed.

Statements of service of officers are available in several record series. In Record Group 45 one series consists of two volumes, indexed by name, containing statements of service submitted by officers, 1842–44, in response to a navy questionnaire. Another series, also indexed by name, contains tabular summaries of these statements. These 1842–44 statements give name, date of entry into service, and dates and descriptions of subsequent orders and service, including the names of vessels to which the officer was assigned. A separate series, in Record Group 24, contains similar statements of service submitted by officers in 1865–66. They are also indexed by name and give name, place (and sometimes date) of birth, state from which appointed, state of residence, date of entry into service, date of present commission, naval battles in which engaged, and other details of service.

The **age certificates** of naval and marine officers, were prepared as a result of the retirement provisions of an act of 1861 (12 Stat. 329). The certificates are in four volumes, two for 1862, and two for 1863. The entries in each series are arranged alphabetically by surname of officer and are indexed. Each certificate is signed by the officer and shows his name, rank, and date of birth. These volumes are in Record Group 24.

Abstracts of service of officers, 1798–1924, are in lettered and numbered volumes in Record Group 24. They relate to most naval and Marine Corps officers, volunteer officers of the Civil War, some noncommissioned officers, and a few professors and teachers at the U.S. Naval Academy. The abstracts in the lettered series refer to letters sent conveying appointments, to orders and letters accepting resignations, and to applications for appointment as midshipmen or cadets, 1798–1893. A list of the lettered volumes, with the inclusive dates covered by each, follows. Because the abstracts are filed chronologically, a particular officer can only be located if the approximate date of his commission is known.

A 1798–1801
B 1801–3
C 1804–8
D 1809–13
E 1813–17
F 1818–25
G 1825–31
H 1832–40
I 1840–45
J 1846–58
K 1859–63
L 1864–71
M 1872–78
N 1879–88
O 1889–93

There are two parts to volumes J–O; each part is separately bound. Part 1 relates to officers above the rank of master, and Part 2, to officers of the rank of master or below. Some volumes are indexed; in others, the entries are arranged alphabetically. An entry shows the name of the officer, the date of his appointment, the date and nature of changes in rank, and, where pertinent, the date and nature of the termination of his service. These records are reproduced as *Abstracts of Service of Naval Officers ("Records of Officers"), 1798–1893*, M330, 19 rolls.

Abstracts of service in the numbered volumes have not been microfilmed. They are in thirty-eight numbered volumes and relate to officers of the regular navy, chiefly those who were appointed 1846–1902, although some are as late as 1924.

There is a loose-leaf index to the names in these volumes. The records often show such information as the name of the officer, the date and place of his birth, the date of his entrance on duty, the ranks he held, the names of the stations to which he was assigned, his place of residence, the date and place of his death, and, if he was serving in 1908 or later, the names and addresses of beneficiaries. In addition, there is a single, indexed volume covering 1799–1829 that summarizes service records of officers of certain ranks.

There are several series of miscellaneous records of volunteer officers in the Civil War and later. These records are variously arranged, usually alphabetically by surname, or chronologically in volumes with name indexes. Correspondence concerning volunteer officers, 1861–67, contains letters of application, recommendation, and appointment, together with many lists of officers. Letters sent transmitting appointments and orders, 1861–79, also include notifications of promotion and approvals of requests for leave. A register of volunteer officers, 1861–87, gives date of original entry into service, name, state of birth, state of which a resident, and duty station. The entries in this register are arranged by rank, and thereunder alphabetically by initial letter of surname. Registers of volunteer officers honorably discharged, 1861–70, include the officer's permanent address at the time of discharge. A list of volunteer officers dismissed from service, 1861–65, whose surnames began with A or B, gives the officer's name, rank, and date of dismissal.

A **register of engineer officers** in one indexed volume, 1843–99, in Record Group 45, relates to the officers who served in the Engineer Corps of the navy until the corps was abolished in 1899 (30 Stat. 1004). Each entry shows the name of the officer, date and place of birth, date of appointment to the Engineer Corps, a detailed service record, and date and place of death or date of retirement.

Also in Record Group 45 is an incomplete three-volume compilation of biographical data for some officers who served in the War of 1812, the Mexican War, and the Civil War. There are name indexes to the series. Included are date of birth, date of appointment, and information concerning war service.

Personnel record cards of officers of the Naval Auxiliary Service, chiefly 1907–17, in Record Group 24, are arranged alphabetically by name of officer. Each card shows the name of the officer, place of residence, place and date of birth, name and address of next of kin, and a summary of service record.

6.2.3 Records of Midshipmen and Cadets

The records relating to midshipmen or cadets concern chiefly those who served from the time of the establishment of the U.S. Naval Academy at Annapolis, Md., in 1845. They include registers of admissions and records of appointees. Information about the relatively few midshipmen in the navy during the years 1798–1848 is meager; however, there is some information concerning midshipmen in letters received from officers by the Secretary of the Navy and in the navy "Subject File" in Record Group 45. Other facts may be garnered from the abstracts of service records of naval officers in lettered volumes, described on page 123, and from Navy Department general correspondence files.

Records of the U.S. Naval Academy, Record Group 405, contain **registers of candidates for admission** to the academy, 1849–1930, with some gaps, arranged chronologically according to date of appointment. Most entries show candidate's name, residence, date and place of birth, and signature, and name, residence, and occupation or profession of his parent or guardian. Names of parents or guardians are also included in the data about each cadet in a **list of cadets,** 1864–68, and in a **register of names and addresses of parents and guardians of cadets,** 1871–76. The records reproduced in *U.S. Naval Academy Registers of Delinquencies, 1846–50 and 1853–82, and Academic and Conduct Records of Cadets, 1881–1908,* M991, 45 rolls, provide further personal information about cadets enrolled in the academy at those dates. These series and others are described in *Records of the U.S. Naval Academy,* Inventory 11, compiled by Geraldine N. Phillips and Aloha South (Washington: National Archives and Records Service, 1975).

In Records of the Bureau of Naval Personnel, Record Group 24, are **letters of appointment, naval cadets,** 1894–1940, 12 volumes. The letters show name of appointee, date of issuance and effective date of appointment, and congressional district from which the cadet was appointed. **Jackets of naval cadets,** 1862–1910, are principally records of cadets who failed in examinations, resigned, or were dismissed for disciplinary reasons. Arranged numerically, each jacket includes such documents as letter of nomination from a member of Congress, letter of acceptance, testimonial letters, reports of examining boards, an oath, and in the case of those who successfully completed the course, a letter of promotion to ensign. Other information that may be in the jackets includes cadet's residence, father's name, and where appropriate, the date of appointment and date of commission.

The Bureau of Naval Personnel, Washington, DC 20370, retains the index for this series, but the file numbers of the jackets of midshipmen or cadets for the period 1862–93 can be obtained from the records of officers in the lettered volumes of abstracts of service described on page 123. The archives of the Naval Academy in Annapolis, Md., has microfilm copies of the jackets of midshipmen who entered the academy after 1906, but they are largely restricted under privacy considerations.

6.2.4 Records of Enlisted Men

Records about navy enlisted men are dated 1798–1956. Muster and pay rolls of ships and shore establishments through 1859 are in Record Group 45. Records for the years 1860–1900 are in Record Group 24 and are described in *Records of the Bureau of Naval Personnel,* Preliminary Inventory 123, compiled by Virgil E. Baugh (Washington: National Archives and Records Service, 1960).

There are several series of bound volumes of **muster rolls and payrolls** of ships and stations. Muster rolls generally show the name of the enlisted man, the ship or station on which he was serving, his dates of service, and, in some cases, the ship or station from which he had transferred. Payrolls generally show the name of the enlisted man, his station or rank, date of commencement of his service, and terms of service. To use muster rolls and payrolls, researchers should know where the subject of research was stationed during the time pertinent to the research.

Muster and pay rolls of vessels, 1798–1859, are arranged alphabetically by name of ship, and thereunder chronologically. For each of the first three volumes of records of the frigate *Constitution*, 1798–1815, there is a typewritten name index. Muster and pay rolls of shore establishments, 1805–49 and 1859–69, are also arranged alphabetically by name of station, and thereunder chronologically.

Muster rolls of vessels, 1860–1900, make up 366 volumes arranged chronologically in three separate series, and thereunder alphabetically by name of vessel. The volumes contain, for each person aboard, information concerning enlistment, whether entitled to an honorable discharge, personal description, date received on board, and applicable data concerning transfer, discharge, desertion, or death. There are eleven volumes of muster rolls, 1861 and 1863, for ships that captured prize vessels during the Civil War. These rolls were probably used as a basis for awarding prize money. They show the name, rank, and pay for each officer and member of the crew.

Muster rolls of ships and stations, 1891–1900, make up 154 volumes arranged in two groups: rolls of naval vessels and rolls of naval stations, torpedo boats, and vessels of the U.S. Coast and Geodetic Survey. The first group is arranged alphabetically by name of ship and thereunder alphabetically by initial letter of the individual's last name. The second group is unarranged. Information contained in these volumes includes, when applicable, name of individual, time of enlistment, period of service on the vessel or station, and applicable data on transfer, discharge, desertion, or death.

Muster rolls of ships and shore establishments, 1898–1939, make up 3,539 volumes arranged in chronological periods, and thereunder alphabetically by name of vessel or shore establishment. The rolls contain the names of individuals serving on the vessel or shore establishment, the period of their service, and information of their transfer, discharge, desertion, or death.

Muster rolls for ships, stations, and other naval activities, 1939–56, are microfilmed on 21,120 rolls. They are arranged alphabetically by name of vessel or symbol of unit, and thereunder chronologically. The rolls for the period 1941–56 are indexed by name of vessel or unit. The microfilmed rolls contain copies of several documents: the quarterly roll, an alphabetical list of enlisted personnel attached to a ship, station, or other naval unit; the report of changes, an alphabetical list of enlisted personnel showing changes relating to rating and transfers; a list of any passengers on board submitted at the time of sailing; and the recapitulation sheet, a summary of all changes in the status of personnel aboard ship or in a naval unit.

Registers of enlistments provide the chief source of information about enlisted men for the years 1845–54. The registers are in three volumes (two volumes for 1845–53, and one volume for 1854) with entries that have been copied in part from records later destroyed. Each entry shows the name of individual, date and place of enlistment, place of birth, and age. In some entries, a column for remarks is filled out with such information as the name of the ship or station assigned, or the date of discharge. The entries are arranged alphabetically by initial letter of surname. The records were indexed, and the index was incorporated into the *Index to Rendezvous Reports, Before and After the Civil War, 1846–61 and 1865–84,* T1098, 32 rolls.

Weekly returns of enlistments at naval rendezvous (or recruiting stations), 1855–91, provide the chief source of information about enlisted men for the years 1855–65 and an important source for the years 1866–85. Returns are arranged in volumes chronologically by week, thereunder by name of naval rendezvous, and thereunder by date of enlistment. The returns for each year are numbered consecutively. Most entries in the weekly returns of enlistments show, under the name of the naval rendezvous, the name of the enlisted man, date and term of enlistment, rating, a reference to any previous naval service, place of birth, age, occupation, and personal description. Some entries show place of residence. The records for the period 1855–84 were indexed, and the index entries were incorporated into either T1098 or *Index to Rendezvous Reports, Civil War, 1861–65,* T1099, 31 rolls. Also on microfilm are *Index to Rendezvous Reports, Naval Auxiliary Service, 1846–84,* T1100, 1 roll, and *Index to Rendezvous Reports, Armed Guard Personnel, 1846–84,* T1101, 3 rolls. For 1885, a key to enlistment returns contains entries arranged alphabetically by initial letter of surname.

Quarterly returns of enlistments of vessels, 1866–91, are also an important source for data about enlisted men, 1866–84. Returns are in 43 volumes, which are arranged by year; within each volume, returns are arranged by number, thereunder by quarter, thereunder by name of vessel, and thereunder by date of enlistment. Most entries show, under the name of the vessel, the name of the enlisted man, date and term of enlistment, rating, a reference to any previous naval service, place of birth, age, occupation, and personal description. Some entries show place of residence. The returns for the years 1866–84 were indexed, and the index entries were incorporated into T1098.

Jackets for enlisted men relate to service of enlisted men between 1842 and 1885. The jackets, which are arranged alphabetically, were prepared between 1885 and 1941 and contain documents assembled or created in connection with pension claims, requests for service records, and requests for copies of honorable discharge. A jacket usually shows the name of the enlisted man, his full service record, and the place of his residence after service.

Continuous service certificates are dated 1865–99 and are arranged alphabetically by surname of enlisted man. Given for each man are name, date of entry for pay, vessels on which service was performed, rating, professional qualifications, dates of transfer to and discharge from vessels, character of discharge, age, description, health record, and dates of reenlistment.

Personnel record cards for enlisted men of the Naval Auxiliary Service in Record Group 24 are dated chiefly 1901–17. They are arranged alphabetically by name. A card shows, for each enlisted man: name, rating, name of vessel on which he served, year and place of birth, occupation, personal description, name of next of kin, date and nature of separation from service, and place of residence.

Also in Record Group 24 are **card abstracts of World War I service records**, which are on 5″ × 8″ cards and are dated 1917–19. They are arranged alphabetically by name of state, and thereunder alphabetically by surname of enlisted man. A card shows, for each enlisted man: name, serial number, date and place of enrollment or enlistment, age and rating, home address, dates and places of service, and date and place of discharge.

Records of Naval Apprentices

The naval apprentice system was set up under authority of an act of 2 March 1837 (5 Stat. 153), to supply the navy with disciplined and well-trained seamen. The first real training program for apprentices was set up in 1864, but after the Civil War, the crews of naval vessels had more foreign-born seamen than Americans. Another apprentice system, therefore, was established in 1875 for boys between the ages of 16 and 18 to serve until they were 21. By the close of the Spanish-American War, the apprentice system had reduced the number of foreign seamen in the U.S. Navy to a small percentage of the enlisted men.

Certificates of consent, 1838–40, in Record Group 24, arranged chronologically and not indexed, reflect the first use of the system. A certificate shows the name of the boy, date of birth, and name of parent or guardian.

Apprenticeship papers, 1864–89, are in individual folders arranged alphabetically by the first two letters of surname. They consist of forms filled out by parents or guardians and, for the years 1864–69, testimonials of character. Each apprenticeship paper shows the name of the apprentice, place of service, date of entrance into service, place and date of birth, and name, residence, and relationship of parent or guardian.

A register of naval apprentices, 1864–75, concerns service aboard the training ships *Sabine, Portsmouth,* and *Saratoga*. An entry shows the name of the apprentice, date and place of birth, date and place of enlistment, name of parent or guardian, and date of detachment from the service. The single volume is indexed by initial letter of surname.

6.2.5 Records of Officers and Enlisted Men

Court-martial and other personnel records in Records of the Office of the Judge Advocate General (Navy), Record Group 125, are dated 1799–1943. The records include name indexes and registers to some of the court-martial records, transcripts of proceedings of general courts-martial and courts of inquiry, records for summary courts-martial and deck courts, records of proceedings of boards of investigation and inquest, proceedings and registers of examining and retiring boards, personnel reports of commanding officers, and correspondence relating to desertions and discharges. These series are usually arranged in numerical order. To find information about a particular court-martial, the researcher must know the approximate date; in some cases, it may be necessary to know the type of offense as well.

The information given in the records includes, when applicable: name of the sailor charged; his rating, ship or station, and other service information; the alleged offense; place and date of trial; and the sentence. Medical information used in evaluating a sailor's fitness for duty is in the records of examining and retiring boards. The reports of the commanding officers include punishment lists and lists of men who were in naval prisons. The correspondence relating to desertions pertains to the efforts of individuals to have their discharge status changed from dishonorable to honorable.

Earlier records are available on *Records of General Courts-Martial and Courts of Inquiry of the Navy Department, 1799–1867,* M273, 198 rolls.

The **claims files for special naval awards** relate chiefly to claims for prize money. Although naval servicemen were in some instances entitled to bounty land warrants, their principal benefit in addition to their pay was prize money awarded on the basis of prizes captured on the high seas during the time of war. These claims files are interfiled with Treasury Department payment records, in the large "Miscellaneous Account" file. For a description of the part of the files that relates to prize money, see Edward H. West's "Applications for Prize Money," *National Genealogical Society Quarterly* 32(1944):65–68.

In certain cases, special funds were put aside to satisfy claims of the heirs of men lost at sea. In Records of the Veterans Administration, Record Group 15, are records relating to the U.S. brig *Epervier* and the U.S. schooner *Grampus*. The *Epervier* mysteriously disappeared after sailing through the Straits of Gibraltar on 14 July 1815. Claims were based on an act of 1817, which provided, for the heirs of the men lost, the equivalent of six months' pay in addition to the pay due the deceased on 14 July 1815. The documents relating to a claim include a receipt acknowledging payment; a copy of the marriage record of the deceased, or an affidavit identifying his orphans; power of attorney; and related correspondence. The claims are in two large envelopes, arranged alphabetically by name of naval servicemen. A claim shows such information as the maiden name of the wife of the naval serviceman, date and place of their marriage, place of her residence, and names of orphans or other heirs.

The *Grampus* was last seen near Charleston on 14 March 1843. Claims made on the basis of a fund raised for the relief of the heirs are dated 1843–45. The documents in the claims files include receipts, copies of marriage records, applications, and correspondence. The claims are arranged alphabetically in two large envelopes. A claims file shows the maiden name of the wife of the naval serviceman, date and place of their marriage, place of her residence, and the identification of orphans or other heirs by name and place of residence and dates of birth.

Files for claims for half pay of Virginia naval officers of the Revolutionary War are described with pension records on page 138.

6.2.6 Related Records

Biographical information about enlisted men is found in conduct reports and shipping articles in Record Group 24. There is also scattered personnel documentation in records relating to medical officers and patients in Records of the Bureau of Medicine and Surgery, Record Group 52; in records relating to inmates of the Naval Asylum (later U.S.

Naval Home) in Record Group 24; in records relating to officers and apprentices in Records of the Bureau of Yards and Docks, Record Group 71; and in records relating to personnel assigned to navy yards in Records of Naval Districts and Shore Establishments, Record Group 181. Published research aids are listed in table 17.

There are also registers of French and American prisoners of war held by the British at Halifax, Barbados, and Jamaica, 1805–15, and at Quebec, 1813–15. Part of Record Group 45, the register entries include name and number of each prisoner, ship that captured him, date and location of capture, name and type of vessel on which he served before capture, and dates and conditions of the beginning and end of imprisonment.

6.3 Records of the U.S. Marine Corps

6.3.1 Introduction

The U.S. Marine Corps was created in 1798 (1 Stat. 594). In 1834 (4 Stat. 712), the corps was made a part of the U.S. Navy, but in 1952 (66 Stat. 282), the Marine Corps was made a distinct service, with its commandant enjoying coequal status with other members of the Joint Chiefs of Staff. The National Archives has service records relating to officers and enlisted men of the Marine Corps, chiefly for the years 1798–1895, with a few as early as 1776 and some as late as 1945. Most records relating to U.S. Marine Corps personnel after 1895 are at the National Personnel Records Center, St. Louis, Mo. (see page 118).

Many of the records described in this section are part of Records of the U.S. Marine Corps, Record Group 127. If the subject of research was a marine, the navy sections of this guide may be useful; some records relating to marines are part of the navy series, and some of the published research aids listed on page 129 apply to both services. Some records described in this section are part of Records of the Bureau of Naval Personnel, Record Group 24, and of Naval Records Collection of the Office of Naval Records and Library, Record Group 45, but unless otherwise indicated in the descriptions, the records are in Record Group 127. The most useful finding aid for Marine Corps records, regardless of location, is *Records of the United States Marine Corps,* Inventory 2, compiled by Maizie Johnson (Washington: National Archives and Records Service, 1970).

6.3.2 Records of Officers

The records of appointments and military service of Marine Corps officers are widely scattered among many small series in Record Groups 127, 24, and 45, in many of which information is arranged chronologically. They cannot be used to ascertain whether a particular person was a commissioned officer or when he served. Edward Callahan's *List of Officers of the Navy of the United States and of the Marine Corps, From 1775 to 1900* (New York: L. R. Hamersly, 1901) or other sources will provide dates of appointment and service. With this knowledge, a researcher can seek documentation in the records for a person's commission or an abstract of his service. In some cases, the records show place of birth.

In Record Group 45 are letters of acceptance of appointments, 1805–12; letters of resignation, 1804–20; confirmations of appointments, 1814–42; a register of some Marine Corps and civilian personnel, 1799–1854; lists of officers of shore establishments, 1855–97; and records of promotions, 1909–20.

In Record Group 24 are confirmations of appointments, 1843–1909; lists of officers of shore establishments, 1878–1909; copies of commissions, 1844–1918; abstracts of officers' service in lettered volumes, described on page 123 and microfilmed on M330, contain abstracts of marine officers' service, 1798–1802 and 1809–13 in volumes A and D; and letters of resignation, 1878–86.

Series in Record Group 127 are the best sources of documentation of the **military service** of Marine Corps officers. A one-volume register shows the name, rank, and state of birth of commissioned officers of the Marine Corps in each year, 1819–48. A similar register for each year, 1849–58 (contained in the front part of the first of two volumes of abstracts of military service of Marine Corps officers), shows the same information and date of entry into service, state from which appointed, and state of residence. The remainder of that first volume pertains to officers serving during the period 1869–73, and the second volume, to officers serving during the period 1899–1904. Entries are arranged by rank, but there are name indexes in the volumes. The entries give information about promotions, appointments to boards, assignments and transfers, and retirement. The second volume also shows, for each officer: date and place of birth, state from which appointed, state of residence, and date of commission. Another series of two volumes contains press copies of military histories and statements of service of officers that were prepared by the Marine Corps during the 1904–11 period in response to inquiries from military officials. The records are arranged chronologically, but there are name indexes. Certificate books of officers and enlisted men (described on page 128) contain similar information.

For an officer of the Marine Corps who served during the Civil War, there may be information in the **age certificates** of navy and marine officers in Record Group 24. These certificates were prepared as a result of the retirement provisions of an act of 1861 (12 Stat. 329), and are in four volumes, two for 1862 and two for 1863. The entries in each series are arranged alphabetically by surname of the officer indexed. Each certificate is signed by the officer and shows his name, rank, and date of birth. Similar records—statements of place of birth of officers in 1816 and 1826—are in Record Group 45 and are described on page 123.

For a marine officer who served during the Spanish-American War, information may be found in the **register of living and retired officers,** 1899–1904, in Record Group 127. It lists each officer serving in 1899 and each officer commissioned during the years 1899–1904. An entry shows the name of the officer; date and place of his birth; state from which he was appointed; state in which he was born; and service record, 1899–1905.

An alphabetical **card list** of officers shows only name, and "reserve" if applicable, for persons who served before 1900 and for persons who served thereafter, date of entry into service and a serial number.

6.3.3 Records of Enlisted Men

Enlisted men of the Marine Corps, 1798–1941, are identified by an alphabetical **card list**. Each card gives name and date and place of enlistment or last reenlistment. Date of enlistment is a useful date for researchers examining any military service records, making this series a good starting point for research.

Service records of enlisted men are dated 1798–1895. They are arranged chronoloically by year of enlistment or latest reenlistment, thereunder alphabatically by initial letter of surname, and thereunder chronologically by date of enlistment or reenlistment. A service record may contain one or more of the following: conduct record, descriptive list, enlistment papers, notice of discharge, report of medical survey, service report, and military history.

Size rolls, 1798–1901, contain the name, rank, age, place of birth, date and place of enlistment, personal appearance, and occupation of enlisted men. **Descriptive lists,** 1879–1906, contain the same information as well as family and service history. These series are variously arranged; to use them, the researcher must know at least the approximate date the subject of research enlisted.

Five different series relate to **discharges** of enlisted men, 1829–1927. These registers, certificates, and lists generally give name, rank, date of enlistment, and date and place of discharge. These series are variously arranged; to use the records the researcher must know approximately when a particular marine was discharged.

Entries in a one-volume **list of retired enlisted men,** 1885–1906, give date of last enlistment, location when retired, and date and place of death if the marine died before July 1906. The entries are arranged chronologically by date of retirement.

Death registers of enlisted men consist of five volumes with overlapping dates, 1838–1942. Entries are arranged by time period, thereunder by initial letter of surname, and thereunder generally chronologically by date of death. To use the records, the researcher must know the approximate date of death of his subject. Each entry shows name of marine, rank, serial number (if any), date of enlistment or last reenlistment, and occasionally, regiment, date, place, and cause of death.

6.3.4 Records of Officers and Enlisted Men

Muster rolls, 1789–1945, are arranged chronologically by month, and thereunder by detachment or other unit, except for periods during World War I and World War II, when they are arranged in two subseries: (1) posts and stations and (2) mobile units. There are indexes in the volumes to the names of ships and stations. A muster roll generally shows name of ship or station and, for officers and enlisted men: name, rank, date of enlistment or reenlistment, and, if applicable, date of desertion or apprehension, sentence of court-martial (and the offense), injuries sustained or illness and type of treatment, and date of death or discharge. To use muster rolls, the researcher must know where the subject of research was stationed.

Certificate books of officers and enlisted men contain certified statements of military service, showing such information as dates of service, appointments, enlistments and reenlistments, promotions, transfers, duty assignments, wounds, debts, troops commanded, desertions, discharges, and physical characteristics. The information was abstracted from other records of the Marine Corps about persons who served in the general period 1837–1911.

Research in this series is laborious. There are fifteen volumes of statements, and most of them are press copies. The statements are arranged chronologically by date of certification, and there are name indexes to only a few of the volumes.

Information about an officer or enlisted man who was wounded or died in service with the U.S. Marine Corps, can be found in the **card list of casualties**. Each card generally shows name, rank, and military organization of a marine; injury sustained or date and place of death; and often such additional information as date of birth and name and address of next of kin. Most of the lists consist of more than one part; that is, duplicate sets of cards are arranged more than one way. The most common arrangement is alphabetical by surname of marine, but arrangement by date of casualty, by type of casualty (killed in action, died of wounds, died of disease, for example), by place of casualty, by state of residence, and by regiment are also used. In parts of lists where the primary arrangement is by type of casualty, geography, and name of officer or enlisted man, the subarrangement is often alphabetical.

There are about twenty lists. The most comprehensive are officers who died in service, 1776–1930, and enlisted men who died in service, 1776–1930. There are also lists of casualties in the War of 1812; casualties in the Civil War; casualties in the Spanish-American War; casualties in the Philippine Islands, Samoa, and Puerto Rico, 1899–1901; casualties in overseas expeditions, 1900–31, including the Boxer Rebellion and in Nicaragua, Veracruz, Haiti, and the Dominican Republic; overseas burials, 1898–1918; aviation casualties, 1918–33; casualties from explosions and earthquakes, 1924–37; and casualties from miscellaneous causes, 1889–1945.

Several of the lists relate to Marine Corps casualties during World War I. They include lists of officers wounded in France, enlisted men wounded in Europe, enlisted men who died in Europe, Marine Corps personnel who died in the United States, and enlisted men who suffered from shellshock.

An additional **register of deaths** in World War I consists of a single volume in two parts, one part for officers and one for enlisted men. Entries in each part are arranged alphabetically by surname. Each entry gives the marine's name, rank, company, regiment, cause of death, date and place of death, and name and address of next of kin.

Information about **courts-martial** is found in four series in Record Group 27. Proceedings of general courts-martial for officers and enlisted men of the Marine Corps are dated 1816–52 and are arranged chronologically. Charges and specifications prepared by the Navy Department and the commandant of the Marine Corps against officers and enlisted men of the Marine Corps are dated 1823–55 and are arranged chronologically. Orders for courts-martial and most sentences are contained in orders issued and received, 1798–1866, and in orders and circulars issued by the commandant, 1805–60; both series are arranged chronologically.

TABLE 17

Selected Genealogical Research Aids: U.S. Navy and U.S. Marine Corps

Callahan, Edward W., ed. *List of Officers of the Navy of the United States and of the Marine Corps, From 1775 to 1900.* New York: L. R. Hamersly & Co., 1901. An alphabetical list of the names of officers of the regular navy and Marine Corps and of the acting or volunteer officers of the Civil War, with dates of appointment. Reprinted by Haskell House, 1969.

Bureau of Naval Personnel. *Register of Commissioned and Warrant Officers of the United States Navy and Marine Corps.* The best source of information about officers who served after 1900. This register has varied in title and frequency since it first appeared in 1798.

Smith, Charles R. *Marines in the Revolution.* Washington, 1975. Reproduces selected muster, pay, and prize rolls and contains brief biographies of Continental marine officers.

Office of Naval Records and Library. *Register of Officer Personnel, United States Navy and Marine Corps and Ships' Data, 1801–1807.* Washington: Navy Department, 1945. Gives the name and brief service record for each commissioned, warrant, and acting officer in the navy and Marine Corps during the years of the Barbary Wars. Supplements Office of Naval Records and Library, *Naval Documents Related to the United States Wars With the Barbary Powers.* Washington: Navy Department, 1939–44.

Official Records of the Union and Confederate Navies in the War of the Rebellion: General Index. Washington: Navy Department, 1927. Consists in part of a personal name index to 30 volumes of transcripts of official records. It was also published as 69th Cong., 1st sess., H. Doc. 113, serial 8603, and on roll 31 of NARS microfilm publication M275.

Office of Naval Records and Library. *Register of Officers of the Confederate States Navy, 1861–65.* Washington: Navy Department, 1931. Identifies Confederate naval officers alphabetically by surname.

Register of Alumni, Graduates and Former Naval Cadets and Midshipmen. Published since 1886 by the U.S. Naval Academy Alumni Association. Gives for each graduate the name, date of graduation, state of birth, highest rank at time of publication, and, where appropriate, date of retirement or death.

Annual Register of the United States Naval Academy, Annapolis, Maryland. 50 vols. Washington: U.S. Naval Academy, 1858–1918.

Hamersly, Lewis R. *The Records of Living Officers of the United States Navy and Marine Corps.* 7 editions. Philadelphia: J. B. Lippincott & Co., 1870, 1878, 1884, 1890, 1894, 1898, 1902.

Bureau of Navigation. *Navy Directory: Officers of the United States Navy and Marine Corps.* Washington: Navy Department, 1908–42.

Drury, Clifford Merrill, comp. *The History of the Chaplain Corps, United States Navy.* Vols. 3, 4, and 5. Washington: Bureau of Naval Personnel, 1949–60. Biographical sketches and service-record data about navy chaplains.

Medal of Honor, 1861–1949, The Navy. Washington: Bureau of Naval Personnel, 1950. Officers and enlisted men who received the medal of honor.

Therefore, the researcher must know the date of a particular court-martial to locate the records.

The court-martial records in Records of the Office of the Judge Advocate General (Navy), Record Group 125, relate also to officers and enlisted men of the Marine Corps. The records include transcripts of proceedings of general courts-martial. A name index identifies the case file of a particular person and the records relating to a court of inquiry. Each dossier, when complete, contains the precept appointing the court; letters detailing or detaching its several members; a letter dissolving the court; the charges and specifications; minutes of the court consisting chiefly of a verbatim transcript of testimony; the plea of the defendant (often printed); copies of correspondence introduced as part of the minutes; the finding of the court; the sentence in case of a finding of guilty; the endorsements of the Judge Advocate General (beginning in 1880), the Secretary of the Navy, and the President; and documents introduced in evidence and collected in an appendix, often designated by numbers or letters by which they are referred to in the minutes. The earlier records are available as *Records of General Courts-Martial and Courts of Inquiry of the Navy Department, 1799–1867,* M273, 198 rolls.

6.4 Confederate Naval and Marine Corps Records

The records of service in the Confederate Navy and Marine Corps consist of carded service records and carded hospital and prison records in the War Department Collection of Confederate Records, Record Group 109, and a few shipping articles, muster rolls, payrolls, and subject files in the Naval Records Collection of the Office of Naval Records and Library, Record Group 45.

Naval and Marine Corps **service records,** which are known to be incomplete, consist of cards prepared by the U.S. War Department, probably in the late nineteenth century, referring to vessel papers, payrolls, muster rolls, and other documents relating to service in the Confederate Navy and Marine Corps. Filed with them sometimes are original documents relating solely to particular persons. The records are in two series—one for naval personnel and one for marine personnel—and they are arranged alphabetically by surname in each series. The records show the name and rank of the sailor or marine, and sometimes they lead to other information about his service. The records are available as *Records Relating to Confederate Naval and Marine Personnel,* M260, 7 rolls.

Hospital and prison records consist of cards on which the War Department, when it was compiling the military service records, abstracted information about naval and marine personnel from Union and Confederate hospital registers, prescription books, and other records and from Union prison and parole rolls. Filed with these are original papers, primarily from prison records, relating to individuals. The records are arranged alphabetically by name of sailor or marine with appropriate cross-references to other series. The records are also available on M260. The cards and papers show the name of the person and his ship or station, and such other information as date and place of capture, release, or parole; place of confinement; date, place, and cause of admission to a hospital; and date of discharge. References to the original records are included on the cards.

The few **shipping articles** for enlisted men in the Confederate Navy, 1861–65, are bound in one volume, which contains a typed index. A typical article shows the name of the enlisted man, rating, signature, and date of enlistment.

The National Archives has some **muster rolls and payrolls** of ships and shore establishments of the Confederate Navy. They are unindexed, but National Archives staff members have prepared lists of vessels and shore establishments for which there are such records. To use the records, the researcher must know where the subject of research was stationed. An entry in the rolls shows the name and rank of the naval serviceman or marine.

Related muster rolls and payrolls, as well as papers on such personnel-related topics as battle and accident casualties, admissions to medical facilities, courts-martial, heroic acts, commendations, and memorials, are found in the **Confederate Navy subject files**. These records are arranged according to a subject classification scheme, and thereunder chronologically. It has been reproduced as *Subject File of the Confederate States Navy, 1861–1865,* M1091, 61 rolls.

6.5 Records of the U.S. Coast Guard

The U.S. Coast Guard, established in the Department of the Treasury in 1915, was formed by consolidating the Revenue Cutter Service and the Life Saving Service. The Light-house Bureau was added in 1939. The Coast Guard, which operates on the high seas and navigable waters of the United States and its territorial possessions, operates as part of the navy in time of war or when the President directs. Record Group 26 is made up of the records of the U.S. Coast Guard since 1915 and of its three predecessor services.

The most valuable records of the Coast Guard for genealogical research are the **service records of the officers and crews** of the three services of which it is composed. However, the abundance of records overlapping in date makes searching for the record of a particular individual difficult.

Light-house keepers were nominated by Collectors of Customs until 1895 and thereafter by inspectors designated by the **Light-house Board**. They were placed under Civil Service in 1896. Correspondence concerning keepers and their assistants, 1821–1902, contains nominations of these officials, testimonials in their behalf, notifications of appointment, oaths of office, resignations, and other personnel records. The series is indexed. Another series of records about light-house keepers, 1853–1907, gives the name of the keeper, title, residence, and dates of employment. These records are difficult to search unless the researcher knows the district and light where a person was stationed.

There are also lists, records of service, and notices of appointments for light-house keepers and other employees of the Light-house Bureau, such as the crews of vessels and tenders. When the Light-house Bureau was placed under the U.S. Coast Guard, a record was prepared of the proceedings for induction, 1939–40, giving detailed records about each employee of the Light-house Bureau at that time. The records include age, marital status, qualifications, and previous service.

The **Revenue Cutter Service** originated under an act of 4 August 1790. It was intended to enforce laws governing the collection of customs and tonnage duties. Records in Record Group 26 relating to officers of the Revenue Cutter Service include **records of officer personnel,** 1791–1919, in fifteen volumes arranged alphabetically by name of officer. They provide dates of service, citations to pertinent correspondence, and charges. There are also copies of commissions, 1791–1910, in two series. One, for 1791–1848, is arranged chronologically as commissions were issued; the other, for 1815–1910, is arranged chronologically, and thereunder alphabetically by surname of officer. In the latter series and another small volume covering 1850–60, there are also applications for commissions.

Applications for appointment as cadet engineer, 1861–65, and other positions in the Revenue Cutter Service, 1844–80, are also available. Ships' rosters, 1819–1904, provide names of officers on board the cutters; they are arranged alphabetically by name of vessel and thereunder chronologically.

The records relating to **enlisted crew members** of the Revenue Cutter Service include muster rolls, payrolls, and shipping articles. In one series of muster rolls are unbound monthly reports, 1848–1910, arranged by name of vessel and thereunder chronologically. They are not indexed, so they can be searched only by name of vessel and the individual's approximate date of service. Muster rolls and payrolls show the name, and, when appropriate, signature or mark of each crew member. There are also 160 volumes of **muster rolls,** 1833–1932, compiled for Revenue Cutter Service Headquarters that give, for each crew member: name, rating, date and place of enlistment, place of birth, age, occupation, personal description, and number of days served during the reported month, along with notes if the crewman was detached, transferred, or discharged or if he deserted or died during the report period. The records are arranged alphabetically by name of vessel.

The **shipping articles,** 1863–1915, are bound in thirty-two volumes arranged alphabetically by name of vessel; the volumes are not indexed. Use of these records requires knowledge of the name of the ship and the approximate date of crewman's service. Information includes crew member's name, rating, wages, date and place of enlistment, place of birth, age, occupation, personal description, and signature or mark. Some dated 1907 and later give the name and address of the nearest relative or beneficiary.

The Life Saving Service was set up as a bureau of the Treasury Department in 1878, although cruisers and life-saving stations to aid the shipwrecked had been previously authorized for several ports along the northeastern Atlantic coast. Employees of the service were station keepers and surfmen. The service was organized into twelve districts, expanded to thirteen by 1915 when it was made a part of the U.S. Coast Guard.

Useful records of the Life Saving Service include registers, service record cards, and disability correspondence. The **registers of station masters and surfmen,** 1878–1913, usually show name of employee, post office address, previous occupation, year of birth, year when employee would reach age 55, present age, military service, if any, state from which appointed, date of appointment, compensation, date discharged, and reason for leaving. The registers are bound volumes arranged by district and station. Two volumes are name indexes.

The **service record cards,** 1900–14, show name of employee, legal residence, place of birth, place and status of employment, changes of status, and salary. The cards are arranged alphabetically.

Records of Life Saving Service employees who were injured on the job are documented in the **disability correspondence**, 1878–1910, arranged by district, and thereunder alphabetically by name of employee.

Articles of engagement for surfmen, 1878–1914, are arranged chronologically, and thereunder by district. The article shows a list of surfmen, terms of engagement and compensation. They may include reports of changes in crew along with the reason for the change, and biographical information on new crew members. Frequently, medical inspection reports providing physical descriptions of the surfmen examined are also included.

CHAPTER 7

Pension Records

CHAPTER

7

Pension Records

7.1 Introduction

7.2 Pension Application Files

7.1 Introduction

For more than a century before the Revolutionary War, British colonies in North America provided pensions for disabled soldiers and sailors. During and after the Revolutionary War, the U.S. government continued this practice and expanded it to include other kinds of pensions. Because the applications for pensions by veterans and their dependents often contain personal and family information, the pension records have long been a primary source for genealogical research.

The National Archives has pension applications and records of pension payments for veterans, their widows, and other heirs. They are based on service in the armed forces of the United States between 1775 and 1916, but not duty in the service of the Confederate States of America, 1861–65. In a few cases, the federal government assumed responsibility for pensions based on service in state militia and other state military organizations, and records of these pensions are also in the National Archives. Most pension records are in Record Group 15, Records of the Veterans Administration.

Three principal types of pensions were provided to servicemen and their dependents by the federal government. Disability or invalid pensions were awarded to servicemen for physical disabilities incurred in the line of duty; service pensions were awarded to veterans who served for specified periods of time; and widows' pensions were awarded to women and children whose husbands or fathers had served in war for specified periods of time or had been killed.

Applications for pensions were made under numerous public and private acts of Congress. Public acts, under which the majority of pensions were authorized, encompassed large classes of veterans or their dependents who met common eligibility requirements. Private acts concerned specific individuals whose special services or circumstances merited consideration but who could not be awarded pensions under existing public acts.

Application procedures followed by would-be pensioners varied according to the act under which benefits were sought. Generally, the process required an applicant to appear before a court of record in the state of his or her residence to describe under oath the service for which a pension was claimed. A veteran's widow was required to provide information concerning the date and place of her marriage. The application statement, or declaration, as it was usually called, with such supporting papers as property schedules, marriage records, and affidavits of witnesses, was certified by the court and forwarded to the official, usually the Secretary of War or the Commissioner of Pensions, responsible for administering the specific act under which the claim was being made. If an applicant was eligible, his name was placed on the pension list. Payments were usually made semiannually through pension agents of the federal government in the states. An applicant rejected under the terms of an early pension act often reapplied for benefits under later, more liberal laws.

7.2 Pension Application Files

Initially, the documents relating to an individual claim for a pension were folded and placed in an annotated jacket. Later these documents were flattened and filed with the jackets in large envelopes. The jacket, now obsolete as a container, was kept because of the annotations. The envelopes with their contents are called **pension application files**.

The number and nature of documents in a file vary considerably. A single claim file consists of the application of the claimant, supporting documents of identity and service, and evidence of the action taken by the government on the claim. When there were two or more claims relating to the service of the same veteran in the same war, all claims are filed together. For example, a veteran might apply for a pension, citing his military service; after his death, his widow might apply for a pension on the basis of the same service. A file with a widow's application normally contains more genealogical information than a veteran's file.

Pension applications submitted by widows of veterans are filed under the name of the veteran on whose service the application is based. If the widow remarried, there are "former widow" and "remarried widow" cross-reference cards showing the state or organization in which her deceased first husband served, his name, and the surname his widow acquired upon remarriage. These cards are interfiled according to the widow's latest surname, but the papers will be found under the name of the veteran. There are also cross-reference cards for variations in spelling of a veteran's name.

The pension files in the National Archives number many millions. They are divided into the following major series: Revolutionary War, Old Wars, War of 1812, Indian wars, Mexican War, and Civil War and later. The records in each series are arranged alphabetically by name of veteran, except those in the Civil War and later series, which are arranged numerically by application, certificate, or file number. All series of pension application files have alphabetical name indexes.

The information below is typical of what may be found in applications for pensions or bounty land based on a veteran's service at any period:

A. Veteran's application

1. Name
2. Rank
3. Military unit
4. Period of service
5. Residence
6. Birthplace
7. Date of birth or age
8. Property (when claims were made on basis of need)

B. Widow's application

1. Most of the above
2. Her name
3. Her age
4. Residence
5. Maiden name
6. Marriage date and place
7. Husband's death, date, and place

C. Children's or heirs' applications

1. All of the above
2. Heirs' names

Baptismal fraktur of Henry Muskenug, submitted as documentation as part of a pension application. Revolutionary War Pension and Bounty-Land-Warrant Application Files, Records of the Veterans Administration, Record Group 15. National Archives Microfilm Publication M804.

3. Dates and places of their births
4. Residence
5. Date of their mother's death

In application files, there are often supporting documents such as discharge papers, affidavits and depositions of witnesses, narratives of events during service (to prove that veteran had served at a particular time even though he might not have documentary evidence), marriage certificates, birth records, death certificates, pages from family Bibles, and other papers.

In addition to the information about individual applicants, historical information pertaining to the organization of military units, movement of troops, details of battles and campaigns, and activities of individuals may also be obtained from application statements of veterans, from affidavits of witnesses, and from the muster rolls, diaries, orders, or orderly books that were occasionally submitted as proofs of service if they had not been sent by the Bureau of Pensions to other government departments. Naval and privateer operations are documented by applications, affidavits, and in some files, orders based on service at sea. A few files contain letters written to or by soldiers and sailors during the Revolutionary War that give firsthand accounts of land and sea engagements and civil events and conditions. Furloughs, passes, pay receipts, enlistment papers, commissions, warrants, and other original records of the period from 1775 to 1783 are also in some of the files.

The rest of this chapter contains descriptions of pension application records for the veterans and widows of particular wars and other periods of military service. *Only exceptions to the typical list will be noted.*

Copies of pension application files can be ordered by mail by using NATF Form 26, Order and Billing for Copies of Veterans' Records. Copies of NATF Form 26 may be obtained from the Reference Services Branch (NNIR), General Services Administration, Washington, DC 20408.

7.2.1 Revolutionary War

During the Revolutionary War, Congress used pension legislation and the promise of free land to encourage enlistment and the acceptance of commissions. After the war, such legislation constituted a reward for service already rendered. As years passed and the number of Revolutionary War veterans, widows, and their heirs decreased, pensions became increasingly generous, and qualifications for pensions increasingly less stringent. Most Revolutionary War pension application files are in envelopes containing applications and other records pertaining to claims for pensions or bounty land warrants. They may also appear in the form of summary cards with information about claimants for whom no original application papers exist or cross-reference cards to envelopes and summary cards.

A file can therefore be a single card or an envelope containing many pages of records. Each file pertains to one or more claims by one or more persons for pensions or bounty land warrants, based on the participation of one individual in the Revolution, along with an occasional file relating to claims based on later service.

The records are arranged in alphabetical order by surname of the veteran. When two or more veterans have the same surname and given name, the further arrangement of the files based on their service is generally alphabetical by state or organization in which a veteran served, or by the word "Continental," "Navy," or some other designation placed in the heading of some files above or before the name of a state. Within each file the records are unarranged.

All of the contents of all of the files are reproduced on *Revolutionary War Pension and Bounty-Land-Warrant Application Files,* M804, 2,670 rolls. An introduction to this microfilm publication is reproduced on each roll and is also printed in the accompanying descriptive pamphlet. This introduction contains an excellent explanation of the eligibility requirements of the various resolutions and acts of Congress, 1776–1878, establishing pensions for Revolutionary War service. Also explained are the symbols and numbers on the envelopes. Understanding the symbols is not essential to use the records, however, because the files are now arranged in alphabetical order.

A second microfilm publication, *Selected Records From Revolutionary War Pension and Bounty-Land-Warrant Application Files,* M805, 898 rolls, reproduces all records from envelope files containing up to 10 pages of records, but only significant genealogical documents are microfilmed from larger files.

A fire in the War Department in 1800 destroyed Revolutionary War pension applications and related papers submitted before that date. Consequently, if a veteran applied for a disability or invalid pension before 1800, the envelope of his file will show his name, the state or organization in which he served, and a file symbol. In place of the missing papers, most of the files contain one or more small cards giving such information as rank, unit, date of enlistment, nature of disability, residence, and amount of pension. The information was transcribed by the Bureau of Pensions from *American State Papers, Claims* (Washington: Gales and Seaton, 1834). This volume contains transcriptions of the eight War Department pension reports based on original applications and submitted to Congress, 1792–95. The volume is indexed. The reports themselves are in Records of the U.S. House of Representatives, Record Group 233, and Records of the U.S. Senate, Record Group 46. A report dated 1792 is in the second volume of a House publication entitled, "Reports War Department 1st Cong. 3rd Sess., to 2nd Cong. 2nd Sess." The seven reports for 1794 and 1795 are in a Senate volume entitled "War Office Returns of Claims to Invalid Pensions." Each report identifies many applicants for invalid pensions. Entries are arranged by date of report, thereunder by state, and thereunder by name of applicant.

Similar reports, 1794–96, were retained by the War Department and are now among the Records of the Office of the Secretary of War, Record Group 107. They constitute pages 526–612 of a War Department record book, the backstrip inscription of which reads "War Office Letter Book 1791–97." The entries duplicate many entries in the reports submitted to Congress, but some entries are unique.

The reports are microfilmed on *Correspondence of the War Department Relating to Indian Affairs, Military Pensions, and Fortifications, 1791–1797,* M1062, 1 roll.

The 1796 reports were transcribed and printed in "Recently Discovered Records Relating to Revolutionary War Veterans Who Applied for Pensions Under the Act of

1792," *National Genealogical Society Quarterly* 46 (March 1958): 8–13 and (June 1958): 73–78.

Most pension rolls published by the federal government before the Civil War were printed only in the Congressional Serial Set. In 1817, the War Department published a list of approximately 1,000 invalid pensions, providing name, state, rank, and annual allowance of each pensioner. The same volume of the Congressional Serial Set has a list of 300 half-pay pensions derived from land relinquishments, showing the number of the pension certificate, names of the guardians of heirs of deceased soldiers, names of original claimants, rank, annual allowance, and state (Ser. 6–34, 35). In 1818, a list of 7,300 invalid pensioners was issued with similar information (Ser. 3–170). And in 1820, the War Department issued an extensive list of over 15,000 American Revolutionary pensioners, showing name, rank, and line (Ser. 34–55). Other pension lists printed before the Civil War in the Congressional Serial Set are as follows:

1823 (74–43)
1828 (171–24 and 185–68)
1831 (208–86 and 219–120)
1835 (249, 250, 251–514)
1849 (579–74)
1857 (959–119)

The 1835 report was issued to replace papers and applications for invalid pensions submitted after 1800 that were destroyed in another War Department fire, in 1814. The transcribing was not systematic, but was apparently done only to answer inquiries about specific veterans. The report, however, does contain names appearing on annual lists of invalid pensioners prepared by the states in response to a 1785 resolution of the Congress of the Confederation. The volumes are not indexed.

Information from the files and from other sources about the Virginia military and naval forces has been published in Gaius Marcus Brumbaugh's *Revolutionary War Records: Virginia* (Washington, D.C., and Lancaster, Pa.: Lancaster Press, 1936). The volume has been reprinted by the Genealogical Publishing Co., Baltimore, 1967.

In addition, cross-reference slips in the files published on M804 describe those diaries, account books, muster rolls, returns, and other records of historical value that were transferred to other bureaus of the War Department and the Library of Congress between 1894 and 1913.

While the U.S. Congress was enacting laws granting increasingly generous pensions to Revolutionary War soldiers and veterans, the states were also passing legislation to encourage or reward military service. In May 1779, the Virginia General Assembly authorized the payment of half pay for life to the state's naval officers and militia officers who would serve for the rest of the war in state units within the state's borders or in the Continental army. After the cessation of hostilities, Virginia was unable to satisfy all claims brought and sought to have the U.S. government assume the obligation, stating that the cession to the United States of large tracts of Virginia land northwest of the Ohio River had reduced the state's expected revenues. A federal act of 1832 directed the Secretary of the Treasury to reimburse the state of Virginia for half pay pension payments made to officers of the Virginia State Navy and certain designated units of the Virginia Line. The secretary was further to assume any additional pension payments due to officers in these units.

The pension records reproduced on M804 include cross-references to these **Virginia half pay files**. The files themselves have been reproduced on *Virginia Half Pay and Other Related Revolutionary War Pension Application Files,* M910, 18 rolls.

Another source of genealogical data about Revolutionary War pensioners are the **final payment vouchers** in the Records of the U.S. General Accounting Office, Record Group 217. A final payment voucher is the record of the payment made to the heirs of the pensioner after his death. If the heirs did not file for the money that was due the pensioner from the time he received his last payment until the time of his death, there is no final payment, only a last payment. Vouchers for both last and final payments were filed among the pension agents' accounts where they were difficult to find, so the National Archives staff removed some 55,000 of them from the pension agents' accounts and arranged them by state and thereunder alphabetically by surname of pensioner. An alphabetical index was also prepared.

From the registers of payments to United States pensioners (available on microfilm as *Ledgers of Payments, 1818–72, to United States Pensioners Under Acts of 1818 through 1858, From Records of the Office of the Third Auditor of the Treasury,* T718, 23 rolls), the name of every Revolutionary War veteran paid under the appropriate acts was placed on a 3″ × 5″ card along with location of the pension agent's office, act authorizing payment, date of pensioner's death, and date of either the last or final payment. Cards for which vouchers were located were annotated with an asterisk. The same procedure was followed for widows and invalid pensioners, if the ledgers indicated that a final payment had been made after their deaths.

These cards and vouchers are not available to researchers. The Reference Services Branch Staff of the National Archives will search the index cards and the segregated vouchers. If the voucher requested by a researcher (in person or by letter) is not among these files, no further search will be made unless the researcher has examined microfilm publication T718 and found evidence that a final payment was made. In this case, the researcher must furnish the name of the pensioner, the act under which the pension was paid, date of death, and date of final payment. Final payment vouchers of pensioners paid by agencies in Alabama, Arkansas, California, and some of those paid by Connecticut agencies were consolidated with the related Revolutionary War pension application files.

An alphabetical name index to the Revolutionary War pension application files has been published as *Index of Revolutionary War Pension Applications in the National Archives,* Rev. ed. NGS Special Publication 40 (Washington: National Genealogical Society, 1976). The index shows the name of the veteran; the state from which he served, except for service in the naval forces; the name of his widow, if appropriate; and the pension application file number and bounty land warrant if appropriate. Other published works dealing with Revolutionary War pensions are listed in table 9 on page 102.

Using available pension records of veterans of the Revolutionary War, interviews, and an early camera, the Reverend E. B. Hilliard produced a book, *The Last Men of the Revolution* (Hartford, Conn.: N.A. and R.A. Moore, 1864), containing a brief biography and a photograph of each surviving veteran. The book was reprinted by Barre (MA) Publishers in 1968.

7.2.2 Old Wars

The "Old Wars" series of pension application files relates chiefly to claims based on death or disability incurred in service in the regular establishment between the end of the Revolutionary War in 1783 and the outbreak of the Civil War in 1861. The claims concern service in the regular army, navy, or Marine Corps during the War of 1812, Mexican War, Indian wars, and in some cases the Civil War. A few Old Wars pension application files have been consolidated with the files in the separate series for the War of 1812, Mexican War, Indian wars, and Civil War.

The files in the Old Wars series are arranged alphabetically by name of veteran. The alphabetical *Old War Index to Pension Files, 1815–1926,* T316, 7 rolls, shows the name of the veteran; name and class of dependent, if any; service unit; application, file, and certificate number; and state from which the claim was made. Cross-references to files in other series are included when appropriate.

Related records, the YI series, once a part of the records of the Navy Department, pertain to naval and marine personnel. This alphabetical file contains papers maintained by pension agents in the field, 1815–37, and correspondence between the Navy Department and the Bureau of Pensions concerning pension claims, 1880–91.

7.2.3 War of 1812

The War of 1812 series of pension application records relates to claims based on service performed between 1812 and 1815. The records chiefly concern pensions granted by acts of 1871 (16 Stat. 411) and 1878 (20 Stat. 27). The former provided pensions to veterans who had been cited by Congress for specific service if they did not later support the Confederate cause during the Civil War, and to many widows of such veterans if the marriage had taken place before the treaty of peace in 1815. The 1878 act provided for pensions to veterans who had served fourteen days in any engagement, and to widows of such veterans.

Interfiled or consolidated with the files in the series are some War of 1812 pension application files that previously formed a part of the Old Wars pension series. Likewise interfiled or consolidated with the files in this series are some War of 1812 bounty land warrant application files from the post-Revolutionary War series described on page 145.

A file includes such documents as a veteran's or widow's application or declaration for pension, a report from the Third Auditor of the Treasury Department containing a summary of the veteran's service record, and a statement showing action on the claim.

The files in the War of 1812 series are arranged alphabetically by name of veteran. The alphabetical name index is available as *Index to War of 1812 Pension Application Files,* M313, 102 rolls. Each frame shows the face side of a jacket-envelope containing relevant documents. Given are the name of a veteran; the name of his widow, if any; service data; pension application and certificate numbers; and/or a bounty land warrant application number, if any. Certain pension application files in the War of 1812 series can be located through the use of the Remarried Widows Index.

7.2.4 Indian Wars

The Indian wars series of pension application records relates to service performed in the Indian campaigns between 1817 and 1898. Consolidated with this series are some Indian wars pension application files that were formerly filed in the Old Wars series.

In addition to the usual types of records found in pension applications, the Indian wars records contain a family questionnaire and, for the veteran, a personal history questionnaire. The family questionnaire shows the maiden name of the wife; date and place of the marriage of the couple and the name of the person who performed the ceremony; name of a former wife, if any, and date and place of her death or divorce; and names and dates of birth of living children.

The files are arranged alphabetically by name of veteran. An alphabetical name index is contained in *Index to Indian Wars Pension Files, 1892–1926,* T318, 12 rolls. Entries in this index show the name of the veteran; name and class of dependent, if any; service data; application number and, for an approved claim, pension certificate number and state from which the claim was made.

For pension application files concerning men who were disabled or killed in Indian wars and in whose behalf no service claims were made, see the records in the Old Wars series. For pension applications relating to persons who served in an Indian campaign during the War of 1812, Mexican War, or Civil War, see the pension indexes relating to claims based on service in that war.

7.2.5 Mexican War

The Mexican War series of pension application records relates to claims based on service performed in 1846–48. An act of Congress approved 29 January 1887 (24 Stat. 371), provided pensions for veterans who had served sixty days, or for their unremarried widows.

Consolidated with this series are some pension application files, formerly filed in the Old Wars series, that relate to men who were disabled or killed in the Mexican War. Like pension applications for Indian wars veterans, the Mexican War pension files contain a family questionnaire.

The files are arranged alphabetically by name of veteran. An alphabetical name index is contained on *Index to Mexican War Pension Files, 1887–1926,* T317, 14 rolls. Entries in this index show name of the veteran; name and class of dependent, if any; service data; and application number and, for an approved claim, pension certificate number and state from which the claim was made. Certain pension application files in the Mexican War series can be located through the Remarried Widows Index.

For pension application files concerning men who were disabled or killed in the Mexican War and in whose behalf no service claims were made, see the records in the Old Wars series.

7.2.6 Civil War and Later

The Civil War and later series of pension application files relates chiefly to army, navy, and Marine Corps service performed between 1861 and 1916. Excluded, however, are records of service in Confederate forces, certain records relating to service in the Indian wars, and records of pensioners still on the rolls in 1934, the date of termination of claims in this series. Most of the records relate to Civil War service; some relate to earlier service by a Civil War veteran; others relate to service in the Spanish-American War, the Philippine Insurrection, the Boxer Rebellion, and the regular establishment. A few files relating to naval service of men who were killed or disabled during the Civil War are interfiled with the Old Wars series of pension application files. For information about Confederate pensions, write the appropriate archival depository of the state for which service was rendered or in which the veteran lived after the war.

The number and type of documents in the Civil War and later series vary greatly from file to file; they are often numerous. The documents of the greatest genealogical interest include the declaration of the veteran, the declaration of the widow, the statement of service from the War or Navy Department, the personal history questionnaire, the family questionnaire, and documents relating to the termination of pensions.

Five acts, 1862–1907, provided pensions based on Civil War service, each extending benefits on more liberal terms.

The information in the files varies depending on the act under which the pension was applied for, the number of years the veteran survived after the war, and whether or not he was survived by a widow or other dependent.

The records are arranged numerically by application, certificate, or file number. Index cards arranged alphabetically by surname of veteran have been microfilmed as *General Index to Pension Files, 1861–1934,* T288, 544 rolls. A card shows the name of the veteran; name and class of dependent, if any; service data; application number or file number; and, for an approved claim, certificate number or file number and state from which the claim was filed.

Because the alphabetical index often shows several veterans with the same name, it may be difficult to identify the file desired without time-consuming research. This difficulty can be resolved if the researcher knows the military or naval unit the veteran served in or the given name of the veteran's widow. It is also helpful to know, in addition, the residence or date of birth of the veteran. Such information appears on the award cards described on page 142.

Other index cards known as the **organization index,** have been microfilmed as *Organization Index to Pension Files of Veterans Who Served Between 1861 and 1900,* T289, 765 rolls. These index cards contain entries for men in army organizations in service chiefly between 1861 and 1917. The cards are arranged alphabetically by state, thereunder by arm of service (infantry, cavalry, artillery), thereunder numerically by regiment, thereunder alphabetically by company, and thereunder alphabetically by the veteran's surname. The informational content and format of the organization index cards is virtually the same as that of the alphabetical index described above.

7.3 Other Records

In addition to pension application files, certain other related records contain material for genealogical research. Documentation of pension payments appears in two record groups. In Records of the Veterans Administration, Record Group 15, are Pension Office record books of **payments to invalid pensioners,** 1801–15, and to other Revolutionary War pensioners; **field record books,** 1805–1912; and **award cards,** 1907–33. In the Records of the U.S. General Accounting Office, Record Group 217, are **Treasury Department pension payment vouchers** for pensioners, including naval and privateer pensioners. The segregated **last and final payment vouchers** of Revolutionary War pensions were discussed above, page 138.

Because they are not arranged by name of pensioner, pension payment records are difficult to use and in most cases are consulted only as a last resort, when other series have not yielded the information sought.

Pension Office record books include one volume for payments to invalid pensioners labeled "Revolutionary War and Acts of Military Establishment, Invalid Pensioners Payments, March 1801 through September 1815." Many of the pensioners were Revolutionary War veterans whose papers were presumably destroyed in the War Department fires of 1800 and 1814. The entries, which record semiannual payments, are arranged by state, and thereunder alphabetically by initial letter of surname.

An entry shows name and rank of pensioner, state in which payment was made, and amount paid in March and September of each year. If the pensioner died or moved to another state during the period of the records, the fact is indicated, and in some cases, the date of death is shown.

Pension Office records of payments to other Revolutionary War pensioners pursuant to acts of Congress approved between 1818 and 1853 are in fourteen unnumbered volumes. They cover pensioners in states or territories as follows: Maine; New York (acts of 1818–32); New York (acts of 1836–53); Rhode Island, New Jersey, Delaware, District of Columbia, and Nebraska; Virginia and Tennessee; Kentucky, Missouri, and Mississippi; Massachusetts (part); Massachusetts (part) and Ohio; Pennsylvania, Maryland, and Illinois; New Hampshire and Indiana; Connecticut; Vermont and Georgia; North Carolina, South Carolina, Louisiana, Alabama, and Michigan; and Arkansas, Florida, Wisconsin, Iowa, Texas, California, Minnesota, and Oregon.

Searches should be made in the volume for the state or territory where the veteran or widow lived while receiving the pension. Entries are arranged by state or territory of residence of the pensioner, thereunder by date of the act under which the pension was paid, and thereunder alphabetically by initial letter of the surname of the pensioner. An entry shows name of the agency through which payment was made, name of pensioner, and amount of pension. Many entries show also the date of pensioner's death.

Pension Office **field record books** document the periodic payment of pensions, 1805–1912. The volumes are arranged alphabetically by the name of the city in which the last pension agency having jurisdiction over a specific area was located.

DECLARATION FOR WIDOW'S PENSION

ACT OF APRIL 19, 1908—AMENDED BY ACT OF SEPTEMBER 8, 1916, AND ACT OF MAY 1, 1920

State of Minnesota, County of Otter Tail, ss:

On this 3d day of June, 1922, personally appeared before me, a Notary Public within and for the County and State aforesaid, Luella E. Shaw who, being duly sworn by me according to law, declares that she is 66 years of age and that she was born Sept 10th 1855, at New York State

That she is the widow of Darius N. Shaw, who enlisted Oct 12th 1861, at Lansing, Minn under the name of Darius N. Shaw, as a Private (Rank) in Company "E" 4th Regiment, Minnesota

(Here state company and regiment, if in the Army; or vessels, if in the Navy.)

and was honorably discharged Oct 15th 1862, having served ninety days or more or was discharged for or died in service of a disability incurred in the service and in the line of duty during the Civil War.

That he also served as private in Company "B" 2nd Regiment of Minnesota Calvalry and was honorable discharged of Dec 1865

(Here give a complete statement of all other military, naval, or coast guard service, if any, at whatever time rendered.)

That she was married to said soldier (or sailor) August 4, 1891 under the name of Luella E. Taylor, at Grand Forks N. Dak, by Alex McGregor, Pastor, M. E. Church that she had been previously married; that he had been previously married, to Milton W. Taylor, & was divorced and Darius N. Shaw had previously married Sylvia Wood and that she died Jan 7, 1891

(Here state all prior marriages of either, and give the names and dates and places of death or divorce of all former consorts.)

and that neither she nor said soldier (or sailor) was ever married otherwise than as stated above.

(If any *former* husband rendered military or naval service, here describe same and give number of any pension claim based thereon.)

That said soldier (or sailor) died May 2d, 1922, at Ottertail, Minn; that she was not divorced from him; and that she has not remarried since his death.

That the following are the ONLY children of the soldier (or sailor) under sixteen years of age NOW living, namely:

None, born ____, 1___, at None
____, born ____, 1___, at ____
____, born ____, 1___, at ____
____, born ____, 1___, at ____
____, born ____, 1___, at ____

That the above-named child____ of the soldier (or sailor) {is / are} ____ now receiving a pension, and that such child ____ {is a / are} member____ of her family and ____ cared for by her.

That she has not heretofore applied for pension, the number of her former claim being ✓; that said soldier (or sailor) was ____ a pensioner, the number of his pension certificate being 289563.

That she makes this declaration for the purpose of being placed on the pension roll of the United States under the provisions of the ACT OF APRIL 19, 1908, as amended by the ACT OF SEPT. 8, 1916, and ACT OF MAY 1, 1920.

She hereby appoints M. Elliott Waggaman & Co. (De Lapointe Rice and M. Elliott Waggaman), Washington, D. C., her true and lawful attorneys.

(Two attesting and identifying witnesses.)

(1) G. H. Schultz (Signature of first witness.) — Luella E. Shaw (Claimant's signature in full.)
Ottertail Minn (Address of first witness.) — Ottertail Minn. (Claimant's address in full.)
(2) H. G. Schultz (Signature of second witness.)
Ottertail Minn (Address of second witness.)

Subscribed and sworn to before me this 3 day of June, 1922, and I hereby certify that the contents of the above declaration were fully made known and explained to the applicant before swearing, including the words ____ erased, and the words ____ added; and that I have no interest, direct or indirect, in the prosecution of this claim.

(SEAL.)

A. H. Brutlag (Signature.)
H. BRUTLAG, Notary Public, Ottertail Co. Minn. My Commission Expires Jan. 24, 1925.
(Official character.)

ATTORNEY FILED — W. L. S. — LAW DIVISION

U. S. PENSION OFFICE JUN 8 1922

Declaration accepted as widow's claim under Act of May 1, 1920. Power of attorney ...

Two witnesses sign here

Executing officer should not act as witness

Declaration for widow's pension based on Civil War service. Civil War and Later Pension Application Files, Records of the Veterans Administration, Record Group 15.

The entries show for each pensioner: date of the payments made, sometimes the name of county of residence or the post office address of the pensioner, date the pension was discontinued, if appropriate, and sometimes the date of death or of remarriage of the widow. To use these records, it is necessary to obtain from the related pension application file the certificate number and the name of the agency through which payment was last made.

A card index to these volumes is arranged alphabetically by the name of the city in which the pension agency was located, and thereunder by class of pensioner. An index card shows city, class of pensioner and volume designation. Sometimes the date of the act under which the pension payment was made also appears on the card. The researcher must know the city where the pension agency served the veteran.

Pension Office **award cards** record payments to pensioners on the rolls, 1907–33, except World War I pensioners. Arranged alphabetically by surname of pensioner, they were on microfilmed as *Veterans Administration Pension Payment Cards, 1907–1933,* M850, 2,539 rolls.

Each card shows name of pensioner, name of military unit, date of the act and certificate or file number under which payment was made, and date the pension began. Some cards show place of residence and date of death of a pensioner, names of the pension agencies from or to which jurisdiction was transferred, and name of widow or other recipient of death benefits.

The cards are sometimes useful in identifying Civil War or other pension application files that cannot be identified from the microfilmed indexes.

Treasury Department **pension payment volumes** record semiannual payments from 1819 to 1871. They have been microfilmed as *Ledgers of Payments, 1818–1872, to U.S. Pensioners Under Acts of 1818 Through 1858, From Records of the Office of the Third Auditor of the Treasury,* T718, 23 rolls. The entries are arranged by act of Congress under which payment was made, and thereunder by name of pension agency. Pensioners' names appear in rough alphabetical order by initial letter of surname. Following each name is a record of payments made to the pensioner. Each volume contains a record of payments made for a specific time period. Succeeding payments are in the next volume. Some entries terminate abruptly in 1820, because a number of pensioners who applied for pensions under the 1818 act were dropped from the rolls. Other entries terminate because the pensioners died or failed to claim payments.

An entry shows name of pensioner, name of veteran (if different), name of pension agency through which payment was made, and quarter and year of last payment to the pensioner. When an heir or a legal representative claimed an unpaid balance due the pensioner at the time of death, the date of death of the pensioner is given and the date the final payment was made to the family or heirs.

To locate an entry, the following information from the pensioner's pension application file should be obtained: the name of the veteran and, if the pensioner was the widow, the name of the widow; the date of the latest act of Congress under which payment was authorized; the name of the last pension agency through which payment was made; and the amount of the periodic pension payment. A typescript "Key to the Pension Payment Volumes Relating to Revolutionary War Pensioners," a copy which is available at the National Archives building, will identify the volumes and pages on which are found entries relating to payments made by a specific pension agency under the appropriate act.

Most vouchers for last and final payments for Revolutionary War pensions have been placed in the separate series described on page 138, but some vouchers for last and final payments to veterans of other wars remain interfiled in a large series of vouchers arranged alphabetically by name of state, thereunder by name of pension agency, thereunder by quarter year of payment, thereunder by date of act under which payment was made, and thereunder numerically or alphabetically by surname.

Final payment vouchers show the date and place of death of the pensioner and the names of heirs. These vouchers usually exist only if the date of death of the pensioner appears in one of the pension payment volumes described above. Last payment records indicate the date the pensioner was last paid.

Other Treasury Department **records of payment to naval pensioners** concern men who were disabled in service with the navy or Marine Corps or as privateers, chiefly between 1798 and 1865, and widows of men who died in such service. Related pension application files are, for the most part, in the Old Wars series or the Civil War and later series of the pension application files.

Three pension payment volumes cover the following periods: 1815–38, 1838–63, and 1846–73 (primarily 1848–66). Entries in the volumes are arranged by state, and thereunder in rough alphabetical order by initial letter of surname of pensioner. An entry shows name of pensioner, rank of veteran, date the pension began, the amount of the monthly allowance and the quarterly or semiannual dates of payment, and, in some instances, the name of the vessel on which the veteran was injured or the date of his death.

Finally, the federal government has published several **lists of pensioners**. A five-volume list of persons on the pension roll in 1883, giving name of pensioner, reason for the pension, post office address, rate of pension per month, and date of original allowance is available in both the departmental set (I24.6:883) and the Serial Set (Ser. 2078–2082). Names and addresses of U.S. pensioners in Canada (I24.6:899/1) and other foreign countries in 1899 (I24.6:899/2) along with their class, service, rate of allowance, type of disability, and number of certificate can also be found in the departmental publications. John G. Ames provided a list of approximately 2,300 names of pensioners in the *Index to Publications of the U.S. Government* 1881–1893, II, 1036–59 (Ser. 4745–754).

On 1 March 1883, the Secretary of Interior, H.M. Teller, submitted to the U.S. Senate a list of approximately 270,000 pensioners, giving the name of each pensioner, the reason for the pension, the pensioner's post office address, the rate of pension per month, and the date of the original allowance. All of this information is arranged by state, and thereunder alphabetically by county and post office. This most comprehensive and useful list of pensioners can be found in the U.S. Serial Set (Ser. 2078, 2079, 2081, and 2082).

CHAPTER

8

Bounty Land Warrant Records

CHAPTER 8

Bounty Land Warrant Records

8.1 Introduction

8.2 Revolutionary War and Post-Revolutionary War Period

8.1 Introduction

A bounty land warrant was a right to free land on the public domain. In 1776, during the Revolutionary War, the Continental Congress promised bounty land as an inducement to enter and remain in military service. For that conflict and other wars in which the United States was engaged during the years 1812–1855, the federal government continued to issue bounty land warrants to veterans or their heirs as a reward for service.

Depending on the period in which a claim was made, claimants for bounty land warrants sent applications to the Secretary of War, the Commissioner of Pensions, or the Secretary of the Interior. Affidavits of witnesses, marriage records, and other forms of evidence of identity and service were also forwarded. A claimant whose application was approved was issued a warrant for a specified number of acres. He could then "locate" his warrant; that is, he could select part of the public domain in exchange for the warrant. The Treasury Department and, after 1849, the Interior Department, accepted the warrants and issued patents, which gave actual title to the land. Most recipients of bounty land warrants did not choose to locate the warrants and to settle on the public domain; instead, they remained in their old homes and sold the warrants.

This process produced two kinds of records valuable for genealogical research: bounty land warrant application files, in Records of the Veterans Administration, Record Group 15, and various series of the warrants themselves, as well as registers and indexes to warrants, in Records of the Bureau of Land Management, Record Group 49.

A **bounty land warrant application file** contains the documents relating to claims for bounty land: an application by the veteran or his widow for a warrant, sometimes a discharge certificate submitted by the veteran or his heirs as evidence of service, and a jacket showing whether the claim was approved or disapproved.

A file containing an approved bounty land warrant application is identified by a number made up as follows: the abbreviation B.L. Wt., the number of the warrant, the number of acres granted, and the year (often represented by the last two digits) of the act under which the claim was submitted. In the example B.L. Wt. 79615–160–55, 79615 is the number of the warrant, 160 the number of acres, and 55 stands for the 1855 act. This information—warrant number, acreage, and act—is sufficient to identify the related land-entry papers, described on page 227. Because most bounty land warrant claimants sold their warrants to others, the land-entry papers seldom refer to the veteran or his family. Infrequently, the recipient of the warrant died before he sold it, and the land-entry papers may reveal the names of his heirs.

The envelope containing a disapproved bounty land warrant application is identified by the abbreviation B.L. Reg. or Rej., the register number assigned to the application, and the year, or last two digits of the year, of the act under which the claim was made. Rejected applications are similar in content to those that were approved.

A file contains such information as the name, age, residence, military or naval unit, and period of service of the veteran. If the applicant was an heir, the file also shows the name, age, and place of residence of the widow or other claimant and the date of the veteran's death. If the application was approved, the file shows also the warrant number, number of acres granted, date issued, and, where appropriate, name of the assignee. Two or more claims may be filed together if they relate to the service of the same veteran.

Copies of bounty land warrant application files can be ordered by mail by using NATF Form 26, Order and Billing for Copies of Veterans' Records. Copies of this form are available from the Reference Services Branch (NNIR), General Services Administration, Washington, DC 20408.

8.2 Revolutionary War and Post-Revolutionary War Period

8.2.1 Revolutionary War Applications

Bounty land warrant application files for Revolutionary War veterans are arranged alphabetically and are interfiled in the series of pension application files described on pages 135–139. This large series has been microfilmed as *Revolutionary War Pension and Bounty-Land-Warrant Application Files,* M804, 2,670 rolls. The pension index described on page 138 also contains entries for veterans whose service was the basis for bounty land warrant claims, except veterans whose surnames begin A–Del.

Fire destroyed the application files relating to more than 14,000 numbered warrants issued between 1789 and 1800. However, information from each file has been transcribed on a large record card. The card shows the name of the veteran, his rank, his military or naval unit, warrant number, number of acres granted, date issued, and, where appropriate, name of the assignee. The record cards are interfiled alphabetically with complete files in the series of pension and bounty land warrant applications and are microfilmed on M804.

8.2.2 Post-Revolutionary War Applications

Congress passed numerous acts providing bounty land benefits for veterans who served after the Revolutionary War or their heirs. The last and most liberal was the act approved 3 March 1855 (10 Stat. 702), which authorized the issuance of bounty land warrants for at least 160 acres of land if the veteran had served fourteen days or in a battle. These benefits were also extended to wagonmasters and teamsters who were employed in time of war in the transportation of military stores and supplies.

The post-Revolutionary War series of bounty land warrant applications relates to claims based on service from 1790 to 1855, mostly in the War of 1812, the Indian wars, and the Mexican War. Congress did not authorize bounty land warrants for service after 1855, so there are no bounty land warrant records for veterans of the Union army in the Civil War. However, Union veterans were given special consideration when they applied for homesteads.

The files are arranged alphabetically by name of veteran. Each file consists of the application of the veteran or his widow, sometimes a discharge certificate submitted as evidence of service, and the jacket, which shows whether the claim was approved or disapproved.

Bounty land warrant application files and pension application files for War of 1812 veterans were consolidated and filed with the pension applications, which are described on page 139.

8.2.3 Records of Surrendered Bounty Land Warrants

In addition to bounty land warrant application files, the National Archives has records relating to the warrants that were surrendered to the federal government for tracts of land in the public domain. Except for some issued for service in the War of 1812, warrants were assignable, so most veterans sold them on the open market and did not settle on public lands.

Most Revolutionary War warrants issued under acts before 1855 were converted into tracts of land in the U.S. Military District of Ohio, and early warrants issued for service in the War of 1812 limited the location of the warrants to military reservations in Arkansas, Illinois, and Missouri. Later acts, however, enabled warrant owners to exchange warrants for scrip that could be used to acquire land elsewhere on the public domain. Warrants surrendered beginning in 1842 were not limited to specific areas of the public domain.

Congress greatly increased bounty land benefits through acts of 1847 (9 Stat. 125), 1850 (9 Stat. 520), 1852 (10 Stat. 4), and 1855 (10 Stat. 701). They provided for bounty land or additional bounty land for veterans and heirs of veterans of the Revolutionary War or later service between 1790 and 1855. As a result, veterans and other persons such as wagonmasters who served fourteen days during wartime were entitled to bounty land. The benefits were increasingly generous. The 1855 act provided that anyone who had received less than 160 acres under previous acts could get another warrant for enough additional acres to total the amount. The acts after 1847 differ from the earlier acts in that the warrants were granted as a reward for service rather than as an inducement to serve. Nearly all these warrants were sold on the market for what they could bring, and the purchasers used them as payment or partial payment for tracts of land.

The National Archives has records relating to U.S. Revolutionary War warrants surrendered for land in the U.S. Military District of Ohio; records relating to Virginia Revolutionary War warrants surrendered for land in the Virginia Military District of Ohio; records relating to warrants issued for service in the War of 1812; and records relating to warrants issued for unspecified land. All these records are in Record Group 49.

The first warrants surrendered for land in the **U.S. Military District of Ohio** were issued under an ordinance of 1788 (*Journals of the Continental Congress,* vol. 34, p. 397–8) and an act of 1803 (2 Stat. 236), as extended in 1806 (2 Stat. 378). Under an act of 1796 (1 Stat. 490), as amended, the U.S. Military District of Ohio was reserved for holders of these warrants.

The 1796 act specified that the land was to be distributed in minimum quantities of quarter townships or 4,000 acres. For this reason, it was necessary for persons possessing warrants totaling less than that amount to entrust their warrants to an agent who located the land and received a patent. The land was then distributed among the original warrant holders, and a deed was issued to each one by the agent. The act of 1796 also provided that the Secretary of the Treasury should give public notice in the states and territories and then register warrants for nine months. After this period, the priority of location of the registered warrants was determined by lottery. A warrant holder could then select the specific quarter township he desired, and a person who had failed to register within the specified time could make his selection from any land still available. Originally, the lands in the U.S. Military District of Ohio were to be distributed by 1 January 1800; but in 1803, 1806, and later years, Congress extended the time limit for registering and locating the warrants.

The records include warrants and related papers and two registers with indexes. The warrants and related papers are arranged by date of act and thereunder by warrant number. The first series includes U.S. military bounty land warrants issued under an act of 1788; they are numbered 1–14220. A warrant shows the date of issuance, name and rank of the veteran, state from which he enlisted, and, when applicable, name of heir or assignee. If the warrant was sold by the veteran or bequeathed to heirs, notes on the reverse of the warrant indicate subsequent transfers of ownership.

Most of the warrants numbered 1 to 6912 in this first series were destroyed during War Department fires in 1800 and 1814; generally, the only existing documents in the files relating to these warrants are a few copies of patents granted for land claims. Beginning with warrant 6913, most of the actual warrants are intact. Those that are missing are presumed to be lost or not surrendered by the veteran or his heirs. In the few instances where a warrant was exchanged for scrip, a cross-reference sheet indicates the scrip application number and the appropriate act.

Finding aids for these warrants are the "Index to the Register of Army Land Warrants" and the "Register of Army Land Warrants per Acts of 1796 and 1799." The index contains entries arranged alphabetically by initial letter of surname of the warrant holder who registered and located the warrant on land in the U.S. Military District of Ohio between 1799 and 1805. An entry also shows warrant number, number of acres, and page number in the register where the name of the veteran or warrant holder is cited. The register contains entries arranged chronologically by date of warrant registration from 11 April 1799 to 20 March 1805. Each entry gives the registration date, name of patentee, and name and service rank of the warrantee. Because land could be granted only in quarter townships, warrants are registered in 4,000-acre groupings, and a legal description is provided only for each located quarter township. Additional information for each quarter township includes the lottery numbers drawn and the number of land certificates surrendered for the 4,000 acres.

The second series of warrants are those issued under the acts of 1803 and 1806. The warrants are numbered 1–272 under the act of 1803, and continue 273–2119 under the act of 1806. Eighteen warrants issued under later acts are also included. A warrant in this second series shows the date of issuance, name and rank of the veteran, state from which he enlisted, and name of the heir or assignee. Most of the individual warrants are extant, along with a certificate

BOUNTY LAND CLAIM.

FORM OF DECLARATION FOR SURVIVING OFFICER OR SOLDIER.

State of Illinois,
County of Coles. }

On this 26 day of March A. D. one thousand eight hundred and fifty five personally appeared before me W. W. Bishop a Justice of the peace, duly authorized to administer oaths within and for the County and State aforesaid, David Dryden aged 61 years, a resident of Coles County in the State of Illinois who being duly sworn according to law, declares that he is the identical David Dryden who was a private in the Company commanded by Captain Wily Jones in the 5th Regiment of Va Militia commanded by Col Preston in the war 1812 that he volunteered at Abington Va on or about the 1st day of October A. D. 1813 for the term of six months and continued in actual service in said war for the term of six months and was honorably discharged at Norfolk Va on the 15th day of March A. 1814 on account of expiration of term of service as will appear by the muster rolls of said Company

He makes this declaration for the purpose of obtaining the bounty land to which he may be entitled under the "act granting additional bounty land to certain officers and soldiers who have been engaged in the military service of the United States," approved March 3, 1855. And refers to his former declaration made under act of 1850 upon which he obtained a Land Warrant No. , for 80 acres, which he having legally transferred and disposed of, is not within his power now to return

He further declares that he has not received a warrant for bounty land under any other act of Congress, nor made any application therefor, than the one above referred to, under act of 1850 upon which he obtained the said Land Warrant, No. for 80 acres, and the one now presented.

David Dryden ....

Swern to and subscribed before me the day and year above written; and I hereby certify that I believe the said David Dryden who signed and executed the above declaration, and is now present, to be the identical man who served as aforesaid, and that he is of the age above stated, and that I have no interest in said claim.

W. W. Bishop .... J. P.

State of Illinois,
County of Coles. }

Personally appeared Byrd Monroe and George B. Balch citizens of the said County and State aforesaid, who being duly sworn, depose and say that they are personally acquainted with David Dryden and that he is the person now present who signs and executes the within declaration.

Byrd Monroe ....

George B. Balch ....

Sworn to and subscribed before me this 26 day of March A. D., 1855 ; and I certify that the said Byrd Monroe and George B. Balch are credible and respectable citizens.

W. W. Bishop .... J. P.

Bounty land claim, form of declaration for surviving officer or soldier. War of 1812 Bounty Land Warrant Application Files, Records of the Veterans Administration, Record Group 15.

BOUNTY LAND UNITED S

Department of

No

OFFICE OF THE

It is hereby Certified,

granting Bounty Land to certain officers

United States" Robert G. Mitch

EIGHT

any land office of the United States in one b

upon any

this

Danforth, Bald & Co. Philada. & New York.

To

or it will be located for you by the General Land Off

State and Land District in which you wish the locati

To the Register of the Land Office

at

Section in Tow

Attest

Michael McClarke

Notary

Military Bounty Land Warrant No. 8816-80-50, based on service in the Mexican War. Records of the Bureau of Land Management, Record Group 49.

316

ATES OF AMERICA

BOUNTY LAND

the Interior

8816

MISSIONER OF PENSIONS.

nder the Act of September 28th 1850 entitled "An Act

oldiers who have been engaged in the military service of the

1st Lieutenant in Capt Jones' Company ("E")

Volunteers

ican War

ACRES

is entitled to locate Eighty Acres at

d in conformity to the legal subdivisions of the public lands,

public lands subject to entry at private sale.

Given under my hand and the seal of the Department

th day of June Eighteen hundred and fifty one

J E Heath Commissioner

You can locate this Certificate at any of the United States land offices

he return of it with your request to that effect endorsed thereon specifying the

If you locate it fill up and sign the following application

Locate this Certificate on the quarter of

of Range

Register

Robert G. Mitchell

of location that indicates where the bounty land was located in the U.S. Military District of Ohio. Occasionally, there are also such documents as an affidavit, a power of attorney, or a deed of conveyance showing transfer of warrant ownership. When there is no certificate of location, a legal description is usually provided on the front or reverse of the warrant by a series of numbers indicating lot, quarter section, township, and range.

Finding aids for these warrants include an index prepared by the National Archives staff and the "Register of Military Land Warrants Presented at the Treasury for Locating and Patenting, 1804–35." The index was prepared from the warrant files and from the register. An entry usually indicates the veteran's name, warrant number, and the act under which the warrant was issued; it may contain a cross-reference to the scrip application number. For those entries extracted from the register, the page containing the information is given.

Entries in the register are arranged chronologically by date of warrant registration, 1804–35. Each entry provides registration date; name of the person presenting the warrant for registration; warrant number; number and the service rank of the warrantee; number of acres shown on the warrant; location of the land selected by lot, township, and range in the U.S. Military District of Ohio; date on which a patent for the land was received; and to whom the patent was delivered. There are also entries for warrants registered in exchange for scrip.

Both series of warrants and related papers and the registers and indexes have been reproduced as *U.S. Revolutionary War Bounty Land Warrants Used in the U.S. Military District of Ohio and Related Papers (Acts of 1788, 1803, 1806)*, M829, 16 rolls.

8.2.4 Virginia Military District Warrants

The National Archives also has Revolutionary War bounty land warrants issued by the Commonwealth of Virginia and converted into tracts of land in the Virginia Military District of Ohio. Application files for these Virginia warrants are not among records at the National Archives; for information about Virginia applications, write the Virginia State Library, Richmond, VA 23219.

Revolutionary War veterans of service in the Continental Line of Virginia, and their heirs or assignees, were eligible for the Virginia warrants. Originally the warrants were issued for land on the south side of the Green River in Kentucky. But, as a result of an agreement between Virginia and the United States, Virginia agreed to cede its western lands to the United States; Congress, by an act of 1794 (1 Stat. 394), enabled holders of Virginia Continental Line warrants to surrender their warrants for tracts of land in a specific area in the Northwest Territory. This area, between the Scioto and Little Miami Rivers, became known as the Virginia Military District of Ohio. Unused warrants could be exchanged for scrip in 1830 or later.

The records include entry papers and a map of part of the Virginia Military District of Ohio. The entry papers are dated chiefly 1782–1892. A file includes such documents as a survey, a surrendered warrant, an assignment, a certificate of location, an affidavit concerning the heirs of the veteran, and correspondence. A file may also show date and place of death of warrantee, names of heirs, and place of residence. Often a person had several warrants and requested that one large tract be surveyed to satisfy them; in such cases, a file will contain more than one warrant. On the other hand, sometimes one warrant was used to acquire more than one tract. In such cases the original warrant will be in one file and the others based on it will contain no warrant or only a copy of the original.

The jacket of each file cites the volume and page number of the record copy of the patent, which is kept by the Bureau of Land Management, Alexandria, Va., and the files are arranged by these numbers.

Finding aids include an alphabetical index to names of warrantees that gives the warrant number; a register entitled "Virginia Military Warrants—Numerical—Continental and State Lines," which is arranged by warrant number and gives the survey number; and a register entitled "Surveys for Land in Virginia Military District, Ohio," which is arranged by survey number and gives the volume and page number that identifies the case file. If only the name of the warrantee is known, it is necessary to use all three finding aids in succession. It should be noted that the first two of these finding aids include entries for U.S. warrants and Virginia State Line warrants as well as Virginia Continental Line warrants.

There are related records in the custody of the Virginia State Library, Richmond. These include **military certificates,** which were issued after an individual presented proof of his Revolutionary War service. The bounty land warrants were then issued for these certificates. Also in the Virginia State Library are a "Register of Military Certificates Located in Ohio and Kentucky"; record copies of warrants 1–9969, with gaps; and registers of military warrants.

The names of warrantees have been published in *Revolutionary War Records: Virginia,* by Gaius Marcus Brumbaugh (Washington, D.C., and Lancaster, Pa.: Lancaster Press, 1936), pp. 387–525; the volume has been reprinted by the Genealogical Publishing Co., Baltimore, 1967. For information about the Virginia Revolutionary War warrants used to patent land in Kentucky, 1782–93, see *Old Kentucky Entries and Deeds,* by Willard Rouse Jillson (Louisville: Standard Printing Co., 1926), pp. 313–392; the volume has been reprinted with a new preface by the Genealogical Publishing Co., Baltimore, 1969.

8.3 War of 1812

War of 1812 bounty land warrants resulted from an act of May 6, 1812 (2 Stat. 729), and other legislation. A noncommissioned officer or soldier who served in the regular army for the duration of the War of 1812 was entitled to bounty land in one of three bounty land districts. These districts, containing 6 million acres in all, were eventually located in Arkansas, Illinois, and Missouri. Until 1842, the warrants could not be used for land outside these districts, and until 1852 they were not assignable except by inheritance. Each soldier was entitled to 160 acres, except for a few soldiers who were entitled to 320 acres, or double bounty, in accordance with an act of 1814 (3 Stat. 147).

The warrants were not actually delivered to the veterans, but were retained by the General Land Office. A veteran received a notification that a warrant had been issued in his name. Most of the warrants were kept in bound volumes in two series, one for 160-acre warrants and one for 320-acre warrants.

The warrants give the following information: name of veteran; his rank on discharge from military service; his company, regiment, and branch of service; date the warrant was issued; and, usually, date the land was located and the page on which the location is recorded in the abstracts. (The abstracts of military bounty land warrant locations were kept by the General Land Office. They are chronological lists of locations of sites for which patents—documents conveying title to land—were granted on the basis of bounty land warrants.) Issue dates extend from 19 August 1815 to 2 June 1858 for the 160-acre warrants, and from 23 August 1815 to 1 April 1839 for the 320-acre warrants.

Warrants 1–2519 of the first series and 1–79 of the second series were detached from the volumes and are now included in two series of notifications. For these warrants, stubs remaining in the volumes provide warrant number; veteran's name, rank, and regiment; and, in many cases, date of location and citation from the abstracts. Warrants 27116–28085 under the act of 1814 and warrants 1077–1101 are missing from the records of the General Land Office, but there are copies of them in Record Group 15.

There are indexes to patentees in Missouri, Arkansas, and Illinois, and an index for patentees under the 1842 act that permitted the warrants to be used for any available public land. Warrants also may be identified through the bounty land warrant application files.

The warrants, stubs, and indexes are available as *War of 1812 Military Bounty Land Warrants, 1815–1858,* M848, 14 rolls; however, only a partial index was available for Illinois when the filming was done.

8.4 Other Warrants Through 1855

Warrants issued for **unspecified land** are dated chiefly 1847–59, with some as late as 1915. A file contains such documents as a surrendered bounty land warrant or a certificate that a bounty land warrant would be filed in the General Land Office, a power of attorney, an assignment, an affidavit required of a preemption claimant who had bought the warrant, and a certificate of location by which the person surrendering the warrant specified the land wanted. The files are arranged by date of the act under which the warrants were issued, thereunder by number of acres awarded (usually 40, 80, 120, or 160 acres), and thereunder by number of warrant.

The alphabetically arranged bounty land warrant application files serve as keys to the warrantees, or persons who received the warrants, named in these files. If a warrant was surrendered on the basis of an application made under one of these acts, the symbols in the file numbers of the related bounty land warrant application file indicate enough information to locate an entry file. The names of the patentees are not indexed.

Most files contain no information of genealogical interest about the warrantee, because most warrants were sold shortly after they were acquired. In the infrequent cases where the warrantee died possessing the warrant, the file contains the names and places of residence of the warrantee's heirs.

The files identify the patentees by name. They show where the tract acquired by the warrant was located and when it was acquired. In the numerous instances where a patentee purchased a warrant to be applied against a tract in which he had a preemption claim, the file shows when the patentee settled on the land, the size of the household, and the nature of the improvements on the land.

CHAPTER 9

Other Records Relating to Military Service

Other records that may document military service include records of soldiers' homes for aged and needy veterans, records of burials at soldiers' homes and in military cemeteries, applications for headstones, and records of soldiers who died overseas or were listed missing in action.

CHAPTER 9
Other Records Relating to Military Service
9.1 Records of Soldiers' Homes

9.1 Records of Soldiers' Homes

The National Homes for Disabled Volunteer Soldiers were established by Congress in 1866 (14 Stat. 10) to provide residences for needy veterans. Honorably discharged officers, sailors, soldiers, or marines who served in the regular, volunteer, or other forces of the United States (or in the organized militia or the National Guard called into federal service) were eligible if they were disabled by disease or wounds, without adequate means of support, and incapable of earning a living. Women who had served as nurses or in other capacities were admitted to the homes under later laws. The branches of the homes, their locations, and the years of their creation are shown in table 18. After 1930, when the homes were consolidated with other agencies to form the Veterans Administration, the branches became known as Veterans Administration Homes.

Records of the homes are dated 1866–1938 and are part of Records of the Veterans Administration, Record Group 15. The records of greatest genealogical value generally consist of historical registers of residents (called "members") of the homes and, for some homes, hospital and death records. The National Archives has no records for the Biloxi, St. Petersburg, or Tuskegee homes.

TABLE 18

Branches of the National Homes for Disabled Volunteer Soldiers

Locations and Dates Founded

Eastern Branch, Togus, Maine, 1866
Central Branch, Dayton, Ohio, 1867
Northwestern Branch, Wood, Wis., 1867
Southern Branch, Kecoughtan, Va., 1870
Western Branch, Leavenworth, Kan., 1885
Pacific Branch, Sawtelle, Calif., 1888
Marion Branch, Marion, Ind., 1888
Roseburg Branch, Roseburg, Oreg., 1894, successor to the Oregon State Home at Roseburg
Danville Branch, Danville, Ill., 1898
Mountain Branch, near Johnson City, Tenn., 1903
Battle Mountain Sanitarium, Hot Springs, S. Dak., 1907
Bath Branch, Bath, N.Y., 1929, successor to the New York State Home at Bath
St. Petersburg Home, St. Petersburg, Fla., 1930
Biloxi Home, Biloxi, Miss., 1930
Tuskegee Home (formerly a hospital), Tuskegee, Ala., 1933

A record of veterans admitted to the homes was kept in the **historical registers** maintained at the various branches. A home number was assigned to each individual upon admission. The member retained this number even if he was discharged and later readmitted to the branch. Each page of the register is divided into four sections: military history, domestic history, home history, and general remarks. The veteran's military history gives the time and place of each enlistment, rank, company and regiment, time and place of discharge, reason for discharge, and nature of disabilities when admitted to the home. The domestic history gives birthplace, age, height, various physical features, religion, occupation, residence, marital status, and name and address of nearest relative. The home history gives the rate of pension, date of admission, conditions of readmission, date of discharge, cause of discharge, date and cause of death, and place of burial. Under general remarks is information about papers relating to the veteran, such as admission paper, army discharge certificate, and pension certificate; information also was entered about money and personal effects if the member died while in residence at the branch.

The only **registers of deaths** extant pertain to the former New York State Home at Bath, 1879–1937, and to the former Oregon State Home at Roseburg, 1894–1937. An entry shows name, service rendered in the armed forces, place of birth, age, date and place of death, and place of burial. If the place of burial was in the home cemetery, the grave number is given. An entry may include the name and address of the relative notified of the veteran's death.

Entries are arranged chronologically, but each of the three New York volumes has a rough alphabetical index to the initial letter of surnames.

There are also **funeral records** at the Bath Home, 1918–21, and reports relating to the value of personal belongings of deceased members of the Danville Home, 1923–29. **Burial registers** are also available for the Togus Home, 1892–1932 and 1935–38. Each entry in these registers includes the decedent's name, regiment and company, date of death, and section of row of the home cemetery where buried or remarks if buried elsewhere. There are **hospital registers** for the Togus Home, 1873–83. An entry contains the veteran's name, military organization, nature of disability when admitted to the home, age, physical description, occupation, marital status, number of children, place of birth, amount of veteran's pension, and remarks. Remarks generally include date of discharge from the hospital or date of death.

The U.S. Soldiers' and Airmen's Home, originally named the United States Military Asylum, was created by Congress in 1851 (9 Stat. 595). Under that act, three temporary homes were established: East Pascagoula Asylum (also called Greenwood's Island), East Pascagoula, Miss.; New Orleans Asylum, New Orleans, La.; and the Washington Asylum, Washington, D.C. Under a different act, a fourth home called the Western Military Asylum was established in 1853 at Harrodsburg, Ky. The New Orleans Asylum was in operation about one year. The East Pascagoula Asylum operated until 1855, when its members were transferred to the Western Military Asylum, which was closed in 1858. The Washington Asylum was renamed the U.S. Soldiers' Home in 1859, and the name was subsequently changed to the U.S. Soldiers' and Airmen's Home in 1972; it began admitting disabled and retired members of the U.S. Air Force in 1942.

Records of greatest genealogical value in Records of the U.S. Soldiers' Home, Record Group 231, consist of general and monthly registers of members, hospital records, and death records. To use the records, the researcher must know which home the subject of research lived in and the approximate date of admission, hospital treatment, or death.

For the East Pascagoula Asylum, the records consist of lists of veterans admitted, June 1853 and March–August 1855. Only the names of members are given. The lists are arranged chronologically.

For the Western Military Asylum, there are monthly reports of members and civilian employees, June 1853–September 1858. Only the names of members and employees are given. The records are arranged chronologically.

There is also one volume of monthly registers of members admitted to the Western Military Asylum and the Washington Asylum, 1853–58. Entries are arranged chronologically, and thereunder alphabetically by initial letter of member's surname. An entry usually shows the name of the resident, name of the home, date of admission, military history, physical description, date and place of birth, occupation at the time of admission, marital status, size of family, and remarks. Additional members' registers, dated 1852–1941, showing the same information, are available for the Washington Asylum/U.S. Soldiers' Home.

For the Soldiers' Home, there are also muster rolls and returns that in part duplicate the information in the members' registers. They show names of veterans assigned to the home and their status—whether present, sick in the hospital, in prison, on furlough, discharged, or died. The muster rolls, dated February 1870–November 1879, are arranged chronologically by month, and thereunder generally alphabetically by surname of member. The returns, January 1879–December 1908, are arranged chronologically, and there is a name index for June 1904–08. Additional lists, 1886–87 and 1898–1912, show members admitted, suspended, readmitted, and dismissed. They are arranged chronologically by type of list.

Hospital records for the U.S. Soldiers' Home consist of registers of persons admitted to the hospital, 1872–1943. They give the member's name; age; date and place of birth; military unit; diagnosis; date of admission, discharge, or death; and remarks. In addition there are registers of members reporting to the hospital, registers of the sick, and the daily registers of patients admitted and discharged. The records are generally arranged by type of record and thereunder chronologically.

The **death records** for the Soldiers' Home include registers and certificates of death. The registers, 1852–1942, show the number assigned to the entry, date, name of the deceased member, age, nativity, and cause of death. Certificates of death, 1876–89 and 1913–29, are copies of the official record of death prepared by the District of Columbia Health Department; they vary in content according to the date of death. Generally they include the name of the deceased; date, place, and cause of death; date and place of birth; marital status; and name of the person reporting the death. The registers and certificates are chronologically arranged.

Other records relating to members of the U.S. Soldiers' and Airmen's Home, 1880–1942, consist of **case files for deceased members** of the home. Included in a case file are the member's military and home history; date, place, and cause of death; and date and place of burial. These records are alphabetically arranged by name of the member. Records of residents since 1942 are in the custody of the home. Information about such members and access to the records may be requested by writing to the Superintendent, U.S. Soldiers' and Airmen's Home, Rock Creek Road and Upshur Steets, N.W., Washington, DC 20011.

9.2 Soldiers' Burial Records

The National Archives does not have a record of the burial of every soldier who died in service. There are registers and lists of burials at national cemeteries and post cemeteries of military installations in the United States, Cuba, the Philippines, Puerto Rico, and China. There are a few burial registers for private cemeteries; but in most cases, if a soldier was buried in a private cemetery, no record of the burial was kept by the federal government. The burials recorded in the registers were generally those of soldiers on active duty, except those of family members and civilian dependents who were buried in the cemeteries of frontier army posts. Most of the extant soldiers' burial records before 1962 are in Records of the Office of the Quartermaster General, Record Group 92. They are dated chiefly 1861–1914, with some as early as 1807 and a few as late as 1939. To use these records to document a burial, one must know where the subject of research was buried and the approximate date. Beginning in 1962, burial records are in Records of the Office of the Chief of Support Services, Record Group 410.

There are approximately 200 **burial registers for national cemeteries and post cemeteries**. One register has been microfilmed as *Register of Confederate Soldiers, Sailors, and Citizens Who Died in Federal Prisons and Military Hospitals in the North, 1861–65,* M918, 1 roll.

The arrangement, inclusive dates, and contents of the burial registers vary considerably. At a minimum, they show, for each soldier: name, military organization, and date and place of burial. The most detailed registers are four volumes for the U.S. Soldiers' Home Cemetery. The first two volumes are dated 1861–63, and the second two, 1864–68. Each volume is indexed by initial letter of the surname of the interred soldier. Entries in these volumes also show rank; place of residence before enlistment; name and residence of widow or other relative; age; cause, place, and date of death; and date of burial.

There are, in addition, compiled **lists of Union soldiers buried at the U.S. Soldiers' Home,** 1861–1918. The entries are arranged alphabetically by initial letter of surname. There is a separate set of lists arranged by state from which the soldiers served. An entry usually shows the name of the soldier, military organization, date of death, and place of burial. Other records of deaths at the U.S. Soldiers' Home are described in the previous section.

Other lists were compiled of **Union soldiers buried at national cemeteries**. These lists relate chiefly to burials during the years 1861–65, but to some as late as 1886. They are arranged alphabetically by state of burial. For each state, there are three kinds of lists: on one the names are arranged by cemetery, on another by military organization, and on another alphabetically by initial letter of surname of soldier. There are lists arranged by surname, however, only for Connecticut, Delaware, District of Columbia, Iowa, Maine, Maryland, Massachusetts, Michigan, New Hampshire, New Jersey, Pennsylvania, Rhode Island, Vermont, and Wisconsin. An entry usually shows the name of the soldier, military organization, date of death, and place of burial.

Lists of Union soldiers who were buried in public and private cemeteries during the Civil War are published in *Roll of Honor . . .*, 27 vols. (Washington: U.S. Quartermaster Department, 1865–71). Entries are arranged by name of cemetery, thereunder alphabetically by name of soldier; they show the date of death. An accompanying *Alphabetical Index to Places of Interment of Deceased Union Soldiers* (Washington: U.S. Quartermaster Department, 1868) pertains to volumes 1–13. The National Archives has an unpublished place index to all volumes.

Also in Record Group 92 are letters received relating to buried soldiers, 1864–90, and quartermaster's notifications, 1863–66, which alerted post or station quartermasters to make preparations for the interment of remains in post or station cemeteries. There are reports of the sexton of Arlington National Cemetery, 1864–67, pertaining to burials and reinterments mainly in that cemetery but also in other federally owned cemeteries.

The Cemetery Service, National Cemeterey System, Veterans Administration, 810 Vermont Ave. N.W., Washington, DC 20422, has an alphabetically arranged 5″ × 8″ card record identifying practically all **soldiers who were buried in national cemeteries** and other cemeteries under federal jurisdiction from 1861 to the present.

9.3 Headstone Applications

Applications for headstones, 1879–1964, relate only to servicemen who were buried in private cemeteries and whose heirs applied for a government-furnished headstone. Under terms of an act of 1879 (20 Stat. 281), headstones were to be erected at the unmarked graves of Union servicemen, Revolutionary War soldiers, and servicemen from other wars in which the United States engaged.

Applications for headstones were made by relatives of the deceased veteran, by veterans associations, by local or state governments, or by civic groups. An application shows the name and address of the applicant for the headstone, name of veteran, military organization, rank, and years of service, place and date of burial, and sometimes date and cause of death.

The applications are arranged in several series. Most are arranged by state of burial, thereunder by county, and thereunder by cemetery. Applications for headstones for the graves of soldiers, sailors, and marines buried outside the United States, 1911–24, are arranged alphabetically by country of burial and thereunder by name of deceased. A few of the applications that relate to servicemen who were buried at branches of the National Home for Disabled Volunteer Soldiers are arranged by name of the home and thereunder by date of application.

Alphabetically arranged 3¼″ × 4″ cards identify the applications dated 1879–1903. Each card shows name of serviceman, military organization, name and location of cemetery where buried, date and place of death, and date of the application.

Applications for headstones for Confederate veterans are included in the records. Many applications or copies of applications are interfiled with the case files described following.

9.4 Other Records

Case files, 1915–39, consist of correspondence and filled-out forms in folders, each folder relating to an existing or proposed burial place of a serviceman. The folders are arranged alphabetically. Although most of the folders relate to servicemen who died during the period covered by the files, some relate to servicemen who died before 1915, and some relate to soldiers who were living when the documents were dated. The files include many types of documents relating to burial, including copies of applications for headstones. Each file shows such information as name of soldier, military organization, place of residence, date of death, and place of burial.

Records of World War I **soldiers who died overseas** 1917–22, are on 5″ × 8″ cards arranged in several series alphabetically by name of soldier or name of cemetery. Most of the cards are **grave registrations,** each showing the name of a soldier, military organization, cause and date of death, date and place of burial, and name and address of nearest kin or guardian. Some of the cards record American names in European chapels. A card usually shows name of soldier, military organization, date of death, a statement of death in action, name and address of nearest kin or guardian, and name of the chapel.

In Records of the American Battle Monuments Commission, Record Group 117, 1923–60, are **lists of soldiers missing in action** that were compiled from missing-in-action lists supplied by the various branches of the armed services. The lists include names of missing soldiers, units with which they served, and dates on which they disappeared. These missing soldiers are memorialized at war monuments and cemeteries maintained by the commission.

War crimes investigation records of World War II in the Records of the Office of the Judge Advocate General (Army), Record Group 153, are dated 1942–54. They consist of card indexes, case files and trial records, and reports of interviews with U.S. soldiers and airmen who were **prisoners of war**.

The indexes are alphabetically arranged 3″ × 5″ cards that refer to all individuals connected—as alleged perpetrators, victims, or witnesses—with war crimes in Europe and the Far East. A card shows the name of the individual and the number that refers to the case files and trial records. Sometimes a brief description of the incident is given.

The case files are arranged numerically. Use the indexes to locate pertinent records. The testimony of victims of or witnesses to German and Japanese atrocities in the case files and trial records contains information about the experiences of individuals in concentration camps.

The interviews contain information about name, rank, military unit, hometown, marital status, education, and employment of former prisoners of war. Some of the same information, as well as date and place of death if known, was recorded for U.S. soldiers who died in action while being captured, or while prisoners of war. Some interviews are arranged alphabetically by name, some are arranged by area, and some are unarranged.

Medal of Honor Recipients, 1863–1973, is available as Committee Print Number 15 of the Committee on Veterans' Affairs, United States Senate, 93rd Congress, 1st Session. It lists the names of all those awarded the Medal of Honor from the time that this medal was created during the Civil War to 1973. The book provides the rank and organization of each of the approximately 3,400 medal winners, as well as an account of the act of heroism for which the medal was awarded (Y4.V64/4: M46/3/863–973).

CHAPTER

10

Section C. Records Relating to Particular Groups

Records of Civilians During Wartime

Genealogists may be most familiar with the records of ancestors who served in U.S. military forces during the Revolutionary War, the Civil War, and other American conflicts, but records in the National Archives may also document the activities of civilian ancestors during wartime. Among the records described in this chapter are fiscal records of the Revolutionary War; several series relating to aliens during the War of 1812; several series relating to Confederate civilians during the Civil War, including amnesty records; and several series relating to persons of Japanese ancestry in the United States during World War II.

10.1 Revolutionary War

The National Archives has several series of fiscal records relating to the Revolutionary War that may be used for genealogical research, including **records of Continental loan offices** in Records of the Bureau of the Public Debt, Record Group 53.

Continental loan offices were authorized by a resolution of the Congress of 3 October 1776 to receive subscriptions for loans to help finance the Revolutionary War and to issue interest-bearing certificates to the subscribers. The National Archives has Continental loan office records for Connecticut, Delaware, Maryland, New Hampshire, New Jersey, New York, Pennsylvania, Rhode Island, and Virginia. They show the creation of a part of the U.S. domestic public debt generated during the Revolutionary War.

The records consist mainly of registers of loan office certificates and liquidated debt certificates. The loan certificate represents an early effort to fund the war and circulate the currency; the liquidated debt certificate was an instrument used to consolidate the public debt by settling the claims of individual citizens. In the absence of a circulating medium, certificates of interest (or "indents") were issued on these obligations. Other types of records include registers of interest certificates, indexes, journals, ledgers, and accounts current.

Many of these records have been microfilmed; they are *Records of the Massachusetts Continental Loan Office, 1777–1791,* M925, 4 rolls; *Records of the Connecticut, New Hampshire, and Rhode Island Continental Loan Offices, 1777–1789,* M1005, 2 rolls; *Records of the New Jersey and New York Continental Loan Offices, 1777–1790,* M1006, 2 rolls; *Records of the Pennsylvania Continental Loan Office, 1776–1788,* M1007, 3 rolls; and *Records of the Delaware and Maryland Continental Loan Offices, 1777–1790,* M1008, 1 roll. The records for the Virginia Continental Loan Office will be filmed on M1009. There are no records for North Carolina, South Carolina, or Georgia.

Efficient research in these records requires knowledge of the state where the subject of research lived when the debt was collected, although the microfilm publications for all the states could be consulted. Loan certificate registers typically consist of entries under specific denominations, arranged chronologically by date of issue, and giving the name of the subscriber and serial number of the note. This arrangement makes a search for a particular name tedious, but the process merely involves reading down the name column. Some registers of interest certificates show the signatures of subscribers, but the records seldom show their addresses or other identifying information. The certificates were transferred freely from one person to the next and, to a limited extent, passed in trade.

Two other National Archives publications related to this record group may also be useful: *Card Index to "Old Loan" Ledgers of the Bureau of the Public Debt, 1790–1836,* M521, 15 rolls, and *"Old Loans" Records of the Bureau of the Public Debt,* Preliminary Inventory 52, compiled by Philip D. Lagerquist, Archie L. Abney, and Lyle J. Holverstott (Washington: National Archives and Records Service, 1953). Both publications, however, also concern the U.S. public debt for many years after the Revolutionary War.

The miscellaneous numbered records described on page 100 pertain to some civilians during the Revolutionary War as well as military matters.

10.2 War of 1812

"An Act respecting Alien Enemies" of 6 July 1798 (1 Stat. 577), one of the infamous alien and sedition acts, was the basis for restrictions on aliens during the War of 1812. That law defined all male citizens of a nation formally at war with the United States age 14 or older as alien enemies; it was extended to apply to the War of 1812 by an act of 1812 (2 Stat. 781). Under provisions of these laws, the Department of State, on 7 July 1812, issued a public notice requiring all British subjects to report to U.S. marshals in their state or territory: name, age, length of residence in the United States, names of members of their families, place of residence, occupation, and whether they had applied for naturalization. The marshals were instructed to make returns of these reports to the department.

The National Archives has these **U.S. marshals' returns**, 1812–15, and letters from marshals, 1812–14, relating to enemy aliens. Included with the returns are some lists of prisoners of war who were delivered to marshals from U.S. ships. The marshals' returns are arranged for the most part by marshal's district, and thereunder chronologically, so that to use them the researcher must know the place of residence of the subject of research during the War of 1812. The letters are arranged for the most part chronologically; the prisoner-of-war lists are arranged chronologically. Some of the letters and returns are in General Records of the Department of State, Record Group 59, and these have been microfilmed on rolls 1–4 of *"War of 1812 Papers" of the Department of State, 1789–1815,* M588. Other letters and returns are in the Naval Records Collection of the Office of Naval Records and Library, Record Group 45.

The returns list male aliens only and usually give name, age, occupation, length and places of residence in the United States, names of dependent family members, and date of application for naturalization.

The letters contain evidence, pleas, and recommendations for the exemption of certain aliens from the regulations applicable to them. The prisoner lists show name, age, years in the United States, names of dependent family members, residence, and occupation.

Also in Record Group 59 are **lists of persons authorized to sail** from the United States during the war, generated primarily at the port of Philadelphia. The lists are arranged chronologically, so that searching for particular names involves a document-by-document inspection. They list only adults and provide each person's name and nationality and, in some cases, occupation, age, date of arrival in the United States, and physical characteristics.

In Record Group 45 is a **register of alien enemies** reported by the U.S. marshal at New York City and of alien enemies removed from New York City, March–July 1813[?]. This register consists of two parts. In the first part, entries are arranged alphabetically by initial letter of surname and thereunder chronologically; in the last part, entries are arranged chronologically. Recorded in the first part of the register are the permit number issued to the alien; name; height; age; color of skin, eyes, and hair; place of residence and occupation; a date, presumably the one on which the permit was issued; and the name of the person who recommended the alien for surveillance. The last part of the register provides the following information for each alien removed: name; height and age; color of skin, eyes, and hair; place to which transferred after removal from New York City; and date of removal.

Under a July 1812 order, 380 aliens reported to the marshal of New York; the number who reported under a February 1813 order was about 272. Even though the year is not stated in the register, it seems probable that the entries were made in 1813. This volume may originally have been part of the "War of 1812 Papers" of the Department of State.

A **register of persons removed** from the Atlantic coast during the War of 1812, May–September 1813, is also in Record Group 45. Entries are arranged alphabetically by initial letter of surname, and thereunder chronologially by date of the order for removal. A note on the front cover of the register states that the volume contains the names of persons "whose requests for indulgence [permission to remain] were granted or rejected. They were not suspects but persons who were removed from the coast because of their nativity, etc." The officers responsible for issuing the orders for removals and for preparing this register are not identified. The information about each alien includes name and residence, whether or not indulgence was granted, place of relocation, date of the order for removal, and remarks, which usually include reason for removal or for indulgence. The volume of letters sent referred to in the remarks column is unidentified. The register may originally have been part of the "War of 1812 Papers" of the Department of State.

The miscellaneous records, or "manuscripts," of the War of 1812 described on page 105 pertain to some civilian as well as military matters.

10.3 Civil War

Because the Civil War was fought almost entirely in the South, there are many more records relating to Confederate civilians than to civilians in the North.

10.3.1 Civilians in the North

The Internal Revenue Act of July 1862 (12 Stat. 432) was supposed "to provide Internal Revenue to support the Government and to pay Interest on the Public Debt." Monthly, annual, and special taxes were levied on personal property such as yachts and carriages, and on the receipts of certain businesses; licenses were required for all trades and occupations. The assessment lists prepared for every state and territory are in the Records of the Internal Revenue Service, Record Group 58. Many of the lists have been microfilmed; see page 162.

The National Archives has case files that relate to **aliens drafted** into the U.S. Army and released, 1862–64. Included are draft notices, depositions, and correspondence relating to releases. The case files are arranged alphabetically by surname of alien, and the National Archives staff will search for the file of a particular alien. The records are in Record Group 59. Each file contains the name of the alien, district from which drafted, country of citizenship, and, in some cases, date of release. Some files also give age, length of time in the United States, and physical description of the alien.

10.3.2 Civilians in the South

Much information about the effect of the war on the southern population is in the records of the provost marshals of the Union army who were assigned as military police to the various territorial commands, armies, and corps. The records of their activities are in the **Union provost marshals' files**. Their duties included maintaining law and order among the civilian population, maintaining the Union army's prisons, and, to a certain extent, settling disputes caused by the war itself. They sought out and arrested deserters from the Union army, some Confederate deserters, Confederate spies, and civilians suspected of disloyalty; investigated the theft of government property; controlled the passage of civilians in military zones and those using government transportation; confined prisoners; and maintained records of paroles and oaths of allegiance. Provost courts were established in some territorial commands to try civilian violators of military orders and the laws of war or to handle other offenses arising under the military jurisdiction. They also tried military personnel accused of civil crimes.

Because many of these records deal with Confederate citizens, they have been placed in the War Department Collection of Confederate Records, Record Group 109. They are arranged in two series: (1) papers relating to one named person and (2) papers relating to two or more named persons. Papers in the first series vary from a single document to a complete dossier on an individual. Papers in the second series consist of documents, lists, and papers generally numbered or chronologically arranged. While the records for the most part relate to civilians, some information in them relates to Confederate servicemen, foreigners, and the soldiers in the Union army who conducted the activities of the provost marshal's various bureaus. The records may relate to some of the same persons for whom papers are found in the unfiled papers and slips belonging in Confederate compiled service records (see page 113) and in Confederate papers relating to citizens and business firms, but they are generally not similar in content. In some instances, there may be compiled service records for Confederate soldiers mentioned in this series.

The Union provost marshals' file of papers relating to individual civilians consists of correspondence, provost court papers, orders, passes, parole records, oaths of allegiance, transportation permits, and claims for compensation for property used or destroyed by military forces. The information in the records relates to Confederate sympathizers, deserters, guerrillas, civilian and Confederate military prisoners, persons accused of violations of military and civil law, citizens residing in areas occupied by Union forces who wished to travel across Union lines to visit relatives or friends in prison or in other areas, persons taking the oath of allegiance to the Union, merchants and others wishing to transport merchandise, and persons living in Union states who were considered to be involved in treasonable activities.

The records are arranged alphabetically by name of the civilian or soldier concerned. They are available as *Union Provost Marshals' File of Papers Relating to Individual Civilians,* M345, 300 rolls. Some cross-reference slips in the series identify some of the persons for whom documents appear in the Union provost marshals' file of papers relating to two or more civilians and in other series in Record Group 109.

The Union provost marshals' file of papers relating to two or more civilians are similar in content to the papers relating to individual civilians, and documents are generally located through the cross-references in the first series. The series is composed of several parts: (1) an incomplete place and subject index, (2) documents numbered 1 to 22737, which are also chronologically arranged, March 1861–December 1866, (3) unnumbered documents arranged chronologically, January–October 1867, (4) lists of civilian and some military prisoners confined at various military prisons, arranged by the name of the prison, and thereunder chronologically, which include information about status (received, released, transferred, or died), and (5) documents relating to the confiscation and destruction of property. The records are available as *Union Provost Marshals' File of Papers Relating to Two or More Civilians,* M416, 94 rolls.

Information about Confederate civilians is also interspersed among the various **War Department correspondence** series in Record Group 109. They are available on microfilm as *Letters Received by the Confederate Secretary of War, 1861–1865,* M437, 151 rolls; *Letters Received by the Confederate Adjutant and Inspector General, 1861–1865,* M474, 164 rolls; and *Letters Received by the Confederate Quartermaster General, 1861–1865,* M469, 14 rolls. Alphabetical card indexes to names of correpondents and persons mentioned in the bodies of the letters are available as *Index to Letters Received by the Confederate Secretary of War, 1861–1865,* M409, 34 rolls, and *Index to Letters Received by the Confederate Adjutant and Inspector General and the Confederate Quartermaster General, 1861–1865,* M410, 41 rolls. Correspondence and other documents as well as card abstracts relating to Confederate citizens and civilian employees are included on *Confederate Papers Relating to Citizens or Business Firms,* M346, 1,158 rolls, and *Unfiled Papers and Slips Belonging in Confederate Compiled Service Records,* M347, 442 rolls, described on page 115.

Records of the **Confederate Bureau of Conscription,** mostly for the state of Virginia, are in Record Group 109. Included are registers of individuals exempted from military service and registers of persons detailed to agricultural and other jobs. There are several registers of free blacks detailed to jobs in Virginia. Entries show names of individuals, occupations, dates exempted or detailed, and, in some instances, physical descriptions and places of residence. Registers are alphabetically or chronologically arranged and generally unindexed. Locating information about a particular individual may entail reading all the entries.

Records of civilian employees of the Confederate government are described on page 217. Records of blacks on payrolls of civilian personnel at Confederate shore establishments are described on page 189.

For South Carolina, there is material in Record Group 109 pertaining to the sequestration of **alien-enemy property,** including a minute book of proceedings, account books, writs of garnishment, and a docket of cases. These bound records contain information about individuals whose property was affected, and a number are indexed by name. Sequestration case files, 1861–62, are arranged alphabetically by name of individual, company, or other organization and contain numerous cross-reference cards prepared by the U.S. War Department.

There are reports of abandoned or confiscated land in the headquarters records, Land Division, in Records of the Bureau of Refugees, Freedmen, and Abandoned Lands, Record Group 105. From Records of District Courts of the United States, Record Group 21, there are available on microfilm *Case Papers of the U.S. District Court for the Eastern District of Virginia, 1863–1865, Relating to the Confiscation of Property,* M435, 1 roll; and *Confederate Papers of the U.S. District Court for the Eastern District of North Carolina, 1861–1865,* M436, 1 roll. Maps relating to property abandoned by its owners and captured by federal forces during the Civil War are described on page 262.

There are several small series of records relating to the sale and destruction of cotton, 1862–65, which document transactions between individual cotton sellers and the Confederate States of America. The records are part of Treasury Department Collection of Confederate Records, Record Group 365, and they are described in *Treasury Department Collection of Confederate Records,* Preliminary Inventory 169, compiled by Carmelita S. Ryan (Washington: National Archives and Records Service, 1967).

Some of the information in the records is transcribed in *Cotton Sold to the Confederate States* (62d Cong., 3d sess., S. Doc. 987, serial 6348). The entries are arranged by name of seller in two alphabetical sequences, one for sellers in Alabama, Arkansas, Florida, Georgia, Louisiana, Mississippi, and South Carolina, and one for sellers who sold through the Texas Cotton Bureau at Houston.

10.3.3 Amnesty and Pardon Records

Early in the Civil War, the Congress authorized the President to extend pardon and amnesty to participants in the rebellion (12 Stat. 592). Presidential proclamations of 8 December 1863, 29 May 1865, and 7 September 1867 granted pardon and amnesty to increasingly larger groups of individuals upon the condition that they take an oath of allegiance. President Andrew Johnson's proclamation of 4 July 1868 granted pardon and amnesty to virtually all remaining participants without the requirement of an oath. Amnesty and pardon records in the National Archives are in Record Group 59 and are described in *General Records of the Department of State,* Preliminary Inventory 157, com-

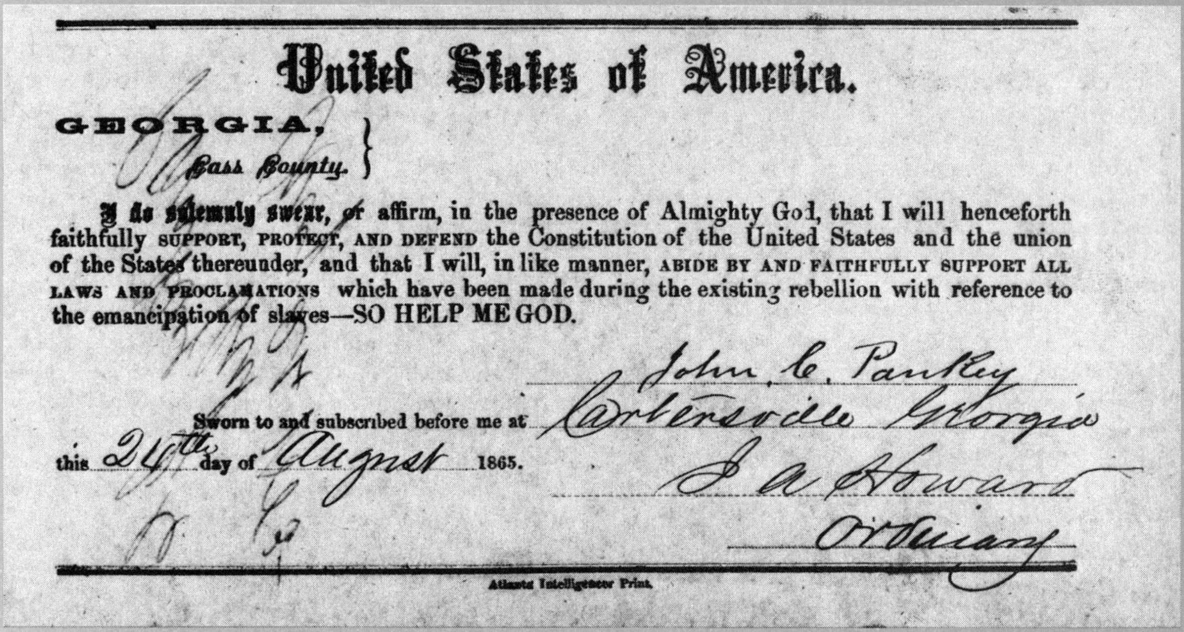

United States of America.

GEORGIA,
Cass County.

I do solemnly swear, or affirm, in the presence of Almighty God, that I will henceforth faithfully SUPPORT, PROTECT, AND DEFEND the Constitution of the United States and the union of the States thereunder, and that I will, in like manner, ABIDE BY AND FAITHFULLY SUPPORT ALL LAWS AND PROCLAMATIONS which have been made during the existing rebellion with reference to the emancipation of slaves—SO HELP ME GOD.

John C. Pankey

Sworn to and subscribed before me at Cartersville Georgia

this 24th day of August 1865.

J. A. Howard

Ordinary

Atlanta Intelligencer Print.

Amnesty oath of John C. Pankey, 1865. Amnesty Oaths, 1864–66, Civil War Amnesty and Pardon Records, General Records of the Department of State, Record Group 59.

piled by Daniel T. Goggin and H. Stephen Helton (Washington: National Archives and Records Service, 1963).

The several series of **amnesty oaths,** 1863–66, relate to a vast number of southerners who wished to gain or regain U.S. citizenship. Usually, the oath, a single document, is all that relates to one person. Filed with the oaths, in appropriate instances, are acknowledgments of warrants of Presidential pardons and agreements to accept conditions of pardon. One series consists of documents relating to one person arranged by name of state, and thereunder usually alphabetically by the first two letters of the surname. To use the records, the researcher must know the state where the subject of research took the oath of allegiance. Another series of documents relating to more than one person is arranged numerically, usually under the name of a state. There are cross-references in the series of documents relating to one person to the names on documents in the series of papers relating to more than one person.

An oath shows the name of the person; the place the oath was taken, which was often the place of residence; the date the oath was taken; and usually the signature of the person taking the oath. Sometimes an oath gives the age and description of the person taking the oath and, in appropriate instances, his Confederate military organization.

Many of the oaths show specific places of residence, and for many persons, the places of residence were the same in 1860 and 1870. An effective search of the amnesty oaths may provide a county name, which in turn can lead to the population census schedules.

The series of **amnesty papers** in Record Group 94 are dated chiefly 1865–67. President Andrew Johnson's 1865 proclamation of amnesty excluded most persons who had held high civilian or military rank under the Confederacy, as well as all southerners with property valued at $20,000 or more; these persons were required to apply directly to the President for pardon. The application files of 14,000 such individuals are included in this series. The files, which include oaths of allegiance and other supporting documents, are arranged by state and thereunder alphabetically by name of applicant. A general name index to the entire collection has been prepared by National Archives staff members. An application file gives the name, age, occupation, and place of residence of the applicant, together with biographic data. The files and the index are available as *Case Files of Applications From Former Confederates for Presidential Pardons ("Amnesty Papers"), 1865–1867,* M1003, 73 rolls.

The series of **pardons** in Record Group 59 consists of copies of Presidential pardons for Confederates, 1865–66. They are arranged chronologically. There are also lists of persons accepting amnesty pardons, 1865–67. There is a consolidated name index to the pardons, as well as indexes in the separate volumes.

The copies of pardons contain the name and address of the person pardoned and the date of the pardon. The consolidated index contains the name and county for each person pardoned. The lists of acceptances contain names and, in some cases, addresses.

Lists of the names of most of the persons who received pardons in the years 1865–67 were published in various congressional documents: *Message of the President . . .* [4 May 1866] (39th Cong., 1st sess., H. Doc. 99, serial 1263); *Message of the President . . .* [8 Jan. 1867] (39th Cong., 2d sess., H. Doc. 31, serial 1289); *Message of the President . . .* [2 Mar. 1867] (39th Cong., 2d sess., H. Doc. 116, serial 1293); *Message of the President . . .* [8 July 1867] (40th Cong., 1st sess., H. Ex. Doc. 32, serial 1311); *Impeachment of the President* [25 Nov. 1867] (40th Cong., 1st sess., H. Rept. 7, serial 1314); and *Final Report of the Names of Persons Engaged in Rebellion Who Have Been Pardoned by the President* [4 Dec. 1867] (40th Cong., 2d sess., H. Ex. Doc. 16, serial 1330).

The first of these lists the names of persons with property worth more than $20,000 who were pardoned, as well as the amount of property seized and returned. The messages of 8 January, 2 March, and 8 July 1867 responded to the House resolution of 10 December 1866. House Report 7, by the House Judiciary Committee, includes a reprint of the list of 2 March 1867. The message of 4 December 1867, was the final report of persons pardoned between 15 April 1865 and the date of the report.

10.3.4 Claims Arising from the Civil War

Another source of geneaological information about civilians in the Civil War period is the series of case files of the Southern Claims Commission. The commission (1871–80) was established to examine and recommend action on claims for property seized for use by the U.S. Army from citizens in southern states who remained loyal to the Union. The approved claims files are in Record Group 217, arranged alphabetically by state, thereunder alphabetically by county, and thereunder alphabetically by name of claimant. A typical Civil War claim file includes the petition of the claimant, formal report of the commission, testimony of the claimant and of other persons supporting or opposing the granting of the claim, and sometimes additional documents submitted in evidence, such as proof of title to the property, proof of relationship to the owner, or proof of other legal interest in the property.

The *Consolidated Index of Claims Reported by the Commissioners of Claims to the House of Representatives from 1871–1880* (Washington: U.S. House of Representatives, 1892) facilitates the use of these records. It gives an alphabetical listing of claimants who appeared before the Southern Claims Commission, and for each claimant the state of residence, claim number, and action taken.

Other records, including disallowed claims, are in Records of the U.S. House of Representatives, Record Group 233. Claims brought before the quartermaster general by loyal citizens in loyal states are very similar; they are described on page 230.

10.4 World War II: Evacuees

During World War II, about 110,000 persons of Japanese ancestry were evacuated from parts of California, Oregon, Washington, Arizona, Alaska, and Hawaii that were designated as military areas. At first, evacuation was voluntary, and all persons of Japanese descent were advised to move outside the military zone. During this voluntary phase of the evacuation, approximately 9,000 Japanese-Americans moved inland. Shortly thereafter, however, a new order established assembly centers under the Wartime Civil Control Administration (WCCA), and the War Relocation Authority (WRA) was set up to carry out the removal, relocation, maintenance, and supervision of persons excluded from military areas. The Japanese-Americans were eventually transferred to ten inland centers administered by the WRA. As early as July 1942, the evacuees were permitted to leave the relocation centers to resettle in nonrestricted areas of the country. On 17 December 1944, the west coast general exclusion order was revoked, and by 1946 all the relocation centers had been closed.

The WRA and WCCA accumulated much personal information about the evacuees, now in Records of the War Relocation Authority, Record Group 210.

Files less than 50 years old may be examined only by authorized representatives of federal and state government agencies officially concerned with them, or by evacuees or their legal representatives. No information based on these records except a summary statement of internment and employment will be furnished without the written consent of the person concerned, his legal representative, or (after his or her death) the next of kin.

One roll of accessioned microfilm contains **change of residence cards** submitted by persons of Japanese descent who moved from their former residence during the voluntary migration phase of the evacuation program. The cards contain the following information for each individual: name, previous address, new address or destination, sex, age, race, citizenship, and alien registration number.

Two **social data registration forms** were used by WCCA for initial registration of evacuees. These forms were microfilmed and contain the following information for each evacuee family: address at the time of evacuation, number of persons in the family moving and therefore registering together, and family number. The forms give the following information for each individual evacuee: name, relationship to head of family, sex, age, place of birth, education, occupation, alien registration number, and physical condition. Arrangement is in two sets: (1) by civilian exclusion number, 1–108, and thereunder by family number and (2) by family number.

WCCA and WRA evacuee transfer lists are photostatic copies of lists of evacuees transferred from WCCA assembly centers to war relocation centers. Each list contains the names of the assembly and relocation centers involved; the name, age, sex, and, occasionally, family number or assembly center number for each evacuee; and a memorandum of transmittal.

The WCCA **master index of evacuees** is an accessioned microfilm copy of 4″ × 6″ cards. The following information is given for each evacuee: name, age, sex, place of birth, family number, alien registration number, occupation, name of nearest relative, previous address, and assembly center address.

Evacuee case files contain interview records, basic family factsheets, health records, property records, leave records, and school records. The following information is given for each individual: name, individual and family numbers, birthplace, birthdate, religion, marital status, educational level, linguistic ability, employment history, military service record, previous addresses (including any abroad), dates of entrance into assembly and relocation centers, parents' and relatives' names and countries of origin, illnesses and treatments during residence in the relocation center, stored personal property, real property, relocation center employment earnings, and leave.

There are IBM punched **summary data cards** for all evacuees at relocation centers. Given for each individual evacuee are (a) name, individual number, last permanent address, date of entrance into relocation center, relocation center address, and miscellaneous notations and (b) place and date of birth, sex, marital status, religion, highest school grade attained, language schools attended, languages spoken, occupations, assembly center address, residence in Japan (if any), extent of education in Japan (if any), parents' birthplaces, and father's occupations. The (a) items are typed or written; the (b) items are punched in code. A guide to the code is available.

Cards for institutionalized evacuees were made for persons who, under WRA jurisdiction, were confined to such institutions as general hospitals, mental hospitals, tuberculosis sanatariums, and orphanages. Some of these persons had entered these institutions from a relocation center; others had been admitted before evacuation occurred. A typical card contains the following information regarding an individual: name, family number, alien registration number, date of birth, age, marital status, citizenship, preevacuation address, name and type of institution, dates of admission and release, type of release, and destination after release.

A typical **basic family card** contains the following information for each family: name of head of the family, family number, names of family members and others in the household, their relationship to the family head, their birthdates and birthplaces, their occupations or other status at the center, address of the family at the center, and record of the family earnings and compensation there. The 8″ × 11″ cards are arranged alphabetically by center and thereunder alphabetically by name of family head. There are no cards for the Jerome Center.

Final accountability rosters list all evacuees at each relocation center. A typical entry contains the following information for each evacuee: name, family number, sex, date of birth, marital status, citizenship status, alien registration number, method of entry into relocation center (from an assembly center, other institutions, Hawaii, another relocation center, or birth), date of entry, preevacuation address, center address, type of final departure (indefinite leave, internment, repatriation, segregation, relocation, or death), date of departure, and final destination. Included also in each roster are summary figures on evacuees at each center and on total admissions and departures.

Vital statistics records are microfilm copies of photostats of birth, stillbirth, and death certificates for persons of Japanese descent. The certificates originated in public health departments in California, Oregon, Washington, and Arizona.

Records relating to persons, other than individuals of Japanese ancestry, who were excluded from sensitive domestic military areas during World War II are in Records of the Office of the Judge Advocate General (Army), Re-

Japanese-Americans, grandfather and grandchildren, awaiting transportation to a relocation camp. Hayward, California, 8 May 1942. Photograph No. 210-G-C160 by Dorothea Lange. Records of the War Relocation Authority, Record Group 210.

cord Group 153. The records, dated 1941–48, include the individual **exclusion case files**, which document the relocation of German and Italian aliens and U.S. citizens of German and Italian extraction from militarily sensitive areas to other parts of the country. The records show the name of the person excluded, date and place of birth, marital status, education, employment record, military service record, date of order of exclusion, and information about legal proceedings and appeals. Most are arranged alphabetically by name of person excluded.

CHAPTER 11

Records of American Indians

11.1 Introduction

The records of many executive, legislative, and judicial agencies of the federal government may include information about specific tribes and individual Indians, just as they do about non-Indians. There is documentation of Indian activities in the military records of volunteer and regular army service, and in bounty land warrant applications, pension applications, claims, and census schedules described in other chapters in this guide. In some cases Indians are specifically identified.

For example, there is a separate series of enlistment papers in Record Group 94 for **Indian scouts** who served in the regular army, 1866–1914. It is arranged in two parts: enlistment papers, and jackets containing consolidated personal papers for each scout. Both files are arranged by initial letter of the surnames of the scouts, and thereunder according to enlistment numbers. Volume indexes pertain to these enlistment papers and to the separate Indian scout enlistment registers. The volumes are identified as New Mexico, 1866–74; Indian Territory and Oklahoma, n. d.; Northern, 1874–1914; and Arizona, 1866–1914. The **bounty land warrant application files** relating to military service from the Revolutionary War also include a segregated, alphabetically arranged series relating to Indians, 1812–55, showing name of Indian, military organization, and dates of service.

The federal census population schedules described in chapter 1 include the names of Indians who had severed their tribal affiliations, but there is seldom a way to identify such Indians in the census before 1870. Not until 1890 do the decennial census schedules in Record Group 29 enumerate the Indian population with any accuracy. In this record group, however, there are four volumes of schedules of a **special 1880 enumeration of Indians** living near military installations in Washington and Dakota Territories and in California. See also "A Note About Indians" on page 20.

Maps of Indian reservations are described in Chapter 20 beginning on page 263.

General descriptions of Indian records in the National Archives are given in *Guide to the National Archives of the United States* (Washington: National Archives and Records Service, 1974) and in Oliver W. Holmes's "Indian-Related Records in the National Archives and Their Use," *Indian-White Relations: A Persistent Paradox* (Washington: National Archives and Records Service, 1976), pp. 13–32. More specific descriptions of record series are found in *Guide to Records in the National Archives Relating to American Indians,* compiled by Edward E. Hill (Washington: National Archives and Records Service, 1982), and in *Records of the Bureau of Indian Affairs,* Preliminary Inventory 163, also compiled by Edward E. Hill, 2 vols. (Washington: National Archives and Records Service, 1965). The last two publications are useful for understanding the administrative structure of the Bureau of Indian Affairs and are indispensable for extensive genealogical research in Indian records.

The records described below deal specifically with Indians. After a discussion of the general types of records held by the National Archives in Washington and in the regional archives branches, there is a list of Indian agencies represented in the holdings of each of these depositories.

11.2 The Bureau of Indian Affairs

Most of the records in the National Archives about Indians are in the Records of the Bureau of Indian Affairs (BIA), Record Group 75. However, the responsibility of the Bureau never extended to all Indians, but was confined to those living on reservations or to Indians maintaining their tribal affiliation in some manner. Some tribes, particularly in the East, have been under state authority rather than federal. Consequently, the National Archives has few holdings concerning eastern tribes. In addition, many persons with some degree of Indian blood may not be covered by records relating to Indians; they may never have been enrolled as Indians or may have severed their tribal connections before records were kept.

11.2.1 Central Office Records

The records of the BIA in the National Archives in Washington are those of the central office of the Bureau, which has been primarily responsible for administration. Field officials maintain actual contact with Indian people and carry out functional operations. The records of their work are located in the archives branches of the Federal Archives and Records Centers (FARCs). There is necessarily much duplication between the records of the central office and those of field offices, because officials in the field report their activities to and receive direction from Washington. During the nineteenth century there were two principal types of BIA officials in the field: superintendents, each of whom had general responsibility for a particular geographical area; and agents, who were immediately responsible for relations with one or more tribes.

Over the years of conducting the government's business with Indians, the Bureau of Indian Affairs often prepared enumerations of Indian tribes. The early rolls were not continuous in coverage, and the names of all members were not always listed.

In 1885, however, pursuant to an act of 1884 (23 Stat. 98), each Indian agent began submitting annual census lists of the Indians in his charge. These **census rolls** constitute one record series from 1885 to 1940, perhaps the most useful single series for Indian genealogy. They are available on microfilm as *Indian Census Rolls, 1885–1940,* M595, 692 rolls.

The census rolls are arranged alphabetically by name of Indian agency, thereunder by name of tribe, and thereunder by year. A tribe may have been successively under the jurisdiction of several Indian agencies, so it is important to find out which agency had jurisdiction for a particular tribe during the life of the subject of research. The names of individual Indians on the rolls before about 1916 are not arranged alphabetically; locating a particular name may require scanning all entries for the tribe. After 1916 most agents alphabetized the names of individuals on the annual census lists.

The post-1885 rolls usually show, for each Indian, the Indian or English name and sometimes both; sex; age; relationship to the head of family; and sometimes relationship to other Indians named on the same roll. A name is often assigned two numbers on a roll, one representing the order in which the name appears on the roll and the other the number assigned to the name on the roll of a previous year. A few rolls show the names of persons who were born or died during the year and their dates of birth and death; after 1924 such information was recorded on separate rolls now interfiled.

No census rolls were submitted for the Five Civilized Tribes of Oklahoma. There are rolls for the Cherokee of North Carolina for most years, 1898–1939, and for the Choctaw in Mississippi for 1926–39.

The records of earlier enumerations are listed in the appendix of *Vital Statistics in the National Archives Relating to the American Indian*, Reference Information Paper 61, by Carmelita S. Ryan (Washington: National Archives and Records Service, 1973), and the records are described in Preliminary Inventory 163, *Records of the Bureau of Indian Affairs*, 2 vols. (Washington: National Archives and Records Service, 1965). Because census rolls are among the records of the Indian agency that had jurisdiction over a tribe, and are also in the central office of the BIA, most of the archives branches have census rolls, some earlier than 1885 and later than 1940. Except for the few censuses taken before and after the dates covered by M595, the census rolls in the archives branches largely duplicate those reproduced on M595.

From 1830 to the mid-1860s, it was the policy of the federal government to persuade the Indians east of the Mississippi River to sign treaties giving up their ancestral lands and accepting land in the West. The resulting **Indian removal records,** primarily 1830–52, chiefly concern the Cherokee, Chickasaw, Choctaw, Creek, and Seminole, both before and after their removal to the West. Some of the records are tribal census lists taken before emigration, while others are muster rolls of the parties of emigrating Indians. The muster rolls are arranged chronologically by date of emigration and are, for the most part, not indexed. Unless the date on which a particular Indian emigrated is known, it is virtually impossible to locate his or her name on a muster roll. The census rolls are arranged by agency, reservation, or other jurisdiction, and are indexed.

The records vary in content. Some show only the names of the heads of families. Others show, in addition, the number of persons, by age group and sex, in each family, and, for some tribes that moved westward, the original place of residence of each head of family.

Emigration-related census rolls available on microfilm are *1832 Census of Creek Indians Taken by Parsons and Abbott in 1832,* T275, 1 roll; *Census Roll, 1835, of the Cherokee Indians East of the Mississippi and Index to the Roll,* T496, 1 roll; and *Old Settler Cherokee Census Roll, 1895, and Index to Payment Roll, 1896,* T985, 2 rolls.

Special **enrollments of Eastern Cherokee** were prepared to determine the eligibility of individual members of that tribe for reimbursement for land and land improvement. The records are dated 1848, 1851–52, 1867–69, 1884, 1907–08, and 1928. Entries on the rolls are usually alphabetized or indexed. All the rolls give the name and age of each member of the tribe. Some indicate relationships to other enrolled members. For further details, see Gaston Litton's "Enrollment Records of the Eastern Band of Cherokee Indians," in *North Carolina Historical Review,* 17 (July 1940): 199–231.

Probably the most extensive enrollment of the Cherokee was the one made in 1907–8. Pursuant to an act of 1902 (32 Stat. 726), the Cherokee filed three suits in the U.S. Court of Claims to press their claims for funds due them under their treaties of 1835, 1836, and 1845 with the United States. The court awarded more than $1 million to be distributed to all Eastern Cherokee alive on 28 May 1906, who could prove that they were members of the Eastern Cherokee tribe at the time of the treaties or were descended from members who had not been subsequently affiliated with any other tribe.

In 1906 Guion Miller was appointed by the Court of Claims to be Special Commissioner to determine who was eligible to participate in the award. Miller submitted his report and roll on 28 May 1909, and a supplementary report and roll on 5 January 1910. The report consists of ten volumes of findings on individual applications, arranged for the most part chronologically. Miller submitted as exhibits copies of Bureau of Indian Affairs census rolls and indexes used in determining the eligibility of the Cherokee. This material has been reproduced as *Records Relating to the Enrollment of Eastern Cherokees by Guion Miller, 1908–1910,* M685, 12 rolls.

The applications filed by Cherokee who wished to participate in the Court of Claims award are particularly rich in genealogical information. Each applicant was asked for such information as full English and Indian name, residence, age, place of birth, name of husband or wife, names of children, place of birth and date of death of parents and grandparents, names and ages of brothers and sisters, and names of uncles and aunts. The applications are in Records of the U.S. Court of Claims, Record Group 123, and are arranged by application number. The appropriate case number can be ascertained from a two-volume index arranged alphabetically by name (usually English) of the applicant. The index is available on roll 1 of M685. The case files have been filmed as *Eastern Cherokee Applications of the U.S. Court of Claims, 1906–09,* M1104, 348 rolls. More detailed information about the applications, Miller's reports and rolls, and the copies and indexes of earlier special rolls appear in *Preliminary Inventory to the Records of the United States Court of Claims,* compiled by Gaiselle Kerner, Preliminary Inventory 58 (Washington: National Archives and Records Service, 1953).

In 1893 the Dawes Commission was charged with securing agreements with the Choctaw, Chickasaw, Cherokee, Creek, and Seminole Indians to extinguish tribal title to all their lands in Indian Territory and to allot their lands in severalty. As provided for in several acts of Congress, the Dawes Commission prepared **final rolls of the Five Civilized Tribes** listing the members of each tribe, and submitted the rolls to the Secretary of the Interior for approval. The names of those approved as eligible to receive land and those disapproved were included on the rolls. Most rolls give name, age, sex, degree of Indian blood, and the

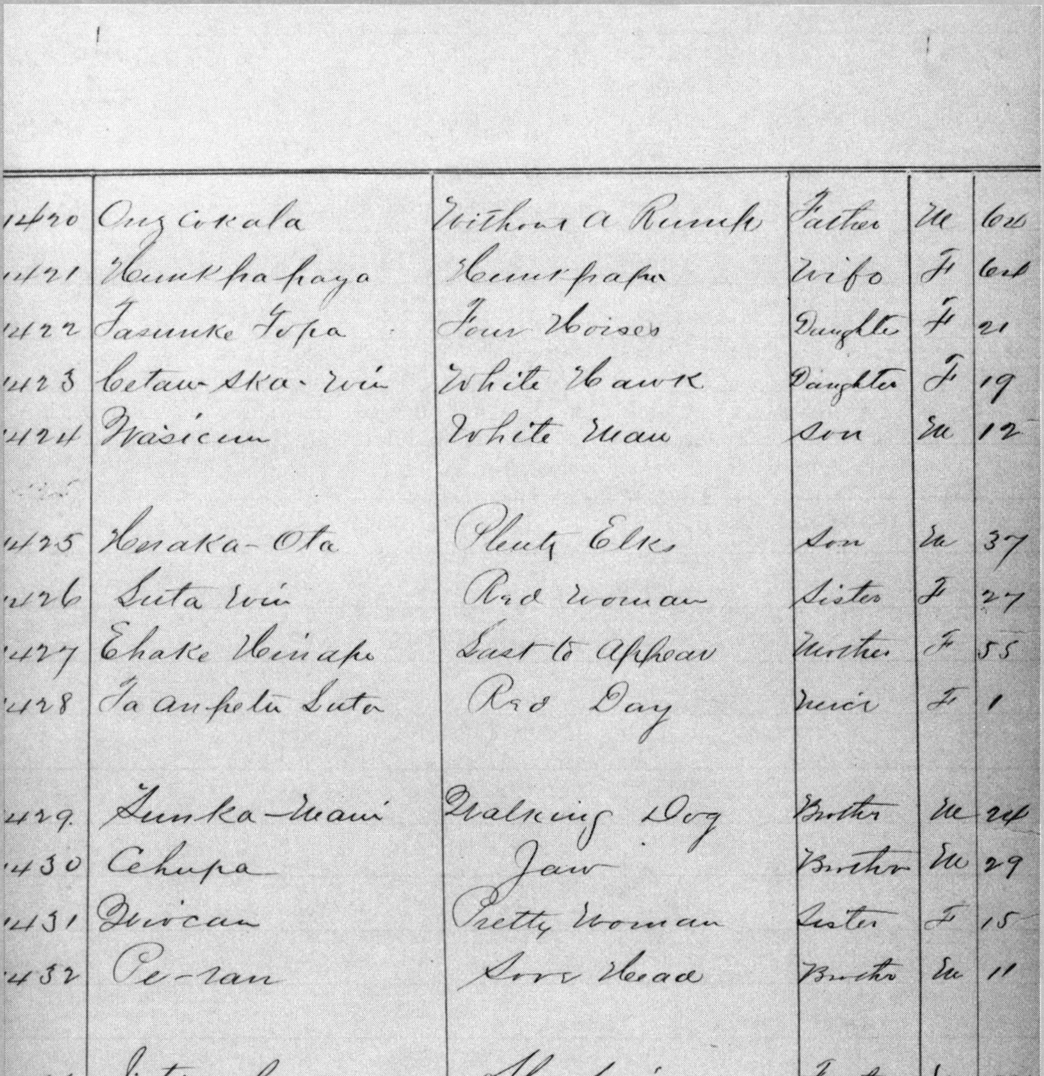

1420	Ongcokala	Without a Rump	Father	M	Old
1421	Hunkpapaya	Hunkpapa	Wife	F	Old
1422	Tasunke Topa	Four Horses	Daughter	F	21
1423	Cetan-ska-win	White Hawk	Daughter	F	19
1424	Wasicun	White Man	Son	M	12
1425	Hehaka-Ota	Plenty Elks	Son	M	37
1426	Luta win	Red woman	Sister	F	27
1427	Ehake Hinape	Last to Appear	Mother	F	55
1428	Taanpetu Luta	Red Day	Niece	F	1
1429	Sunka-mani	Walking Dog	Brother	M	24
1430	Cehupa	Jaw	Brother	M	29
1431	Iwican	Pretty Woman	Sister	F	15
1432	Pe-san	Sore Head	Brother	M	11
1433	Istimela	Sleeping	Father	M	57
1434	Ta-anpetu waste	Pretty Day	Wife	F	38
1435	Ogle wanbli	Eagle Frock	Daughter	F	5
1436	Sinte sna	Rattling Tail	Daughter	F	1
1437	Wasicun wakan	Holy White Man	Father	M	34
1438	Nakoton win	Tramp Noise	Wife	F	27
1439	Blotanhunka	Leader of War Party	Daughter	F	1
1440	Ktela	Kill	Brother In Law	M	17
1441	Tatanka Iyotake (Chief)	Sitting Bull	Father	M	51
1442	Oyate wanyakapi	Seen by the Nation	Wife	F	46

Page from 1885 Hunkpapa Sioux census at Standing Rock Agency showing entry for Chief Sitting Bull. Records of the Bureau of Indian Affairs, Record Group 75. National Archives Microfilm Publication M595.

roll and census-card number for each individual. The rolls are arranged by name of tribe and thereunder by separate categories for citizens by blood, citizens by marriage, and freedmen. There are also final rolls for the Mississippi Choctaw and the Delaware Cherokee. There are separate rolls in some of the groups for minor children and newborn babies. The names on the final rolls are arranged numerically in the order in which they were recorded, and locating information about a particular Indian requires scanning the entire roll for his or her tribe. The rolls are part of the Records of the Office of the Secretary of the Interior, Record Group 48.

The original rolls are reproduced as *Final Rolls of Citizens and Freedmen of the Five Civilized Tribes in Indian Territory*, T529, 3 rolls. The Choctaw and Chicasaw rolls are reproduced on roll 1, the Cherokee rolls on roll 2, and the Creek and Seminole rolls on roll 3. The rolls were also published by the commission as *Final Rolls of Citizens and Freedmen of the Five Civilized Tribes in Indian Territory*, with an index volume in which the appropriate number for a particular name can be found.

The original enrollment cards prepared by the commission are held by the archives branch, FARC Fort Worth. In addition to the information provided in the lists, each enrollment card contains references to earlier tribal rolls, parents' names and places of residence, and references to decisions by the Secretary of the Interior. Each card also includes the names of related enrollees—husband, wife, children, and sometimes grandchildren and wards. Similar enrollment cards originating with the Realty Branch of the Bureau of Indian Affairs in Muskogee, Oklahoma, are available on seventy-four rolls of accessioned microfilm at the archives branch, FARC Kansas City.

Annuity payrolls resulted from treaties or acts of Congress providing the federal government would make annual payments to tribal members for stated periods of time. The rolls, which are in Record Group 75, are usually in bound volumes arranged by name of tribe and thereunder chronologically. To locate a particular name, it may be necessary to scan the entire roll for each appropriate year. As a minimum the annuity payrolls show the name of each head of family; usually they show the name, age, sex, amount of payment, and signature or mark of each member. Those among the records of the central office of the BIA in the National Archives are dated 1848–1940.

Most archives branches have annuity payrolls, but many of them are duplicated in the central office records. The annual census rolls are more useful than annuity payrolls for genealogical research in the period after 1885.

Land allotment records were created when, under the terms of various treaties and acts of Congress, the federal government extinguished title to reservations and alloted land to individual members of tribes. These records are arranged by tribe and thereunder by enrollment number. The content of the records varies from tribe to tribe, but usually includes applications for allotment, plat maps designating the allotted land, registers of names of allottees and descriptions of their allotments, and information about contested allotments and improvements made to the land before selection. There is also, for some tribes, information about sales and leases of allotted land. Applications for allotment sometimes include information about an individual's places of residence and enrolled relatives.

11.2.2 Field Office Records

Besides the records of the central office of the Bureau of Indian Affairs, there are records created by field offices of the BIA, chiefly agencies and schools. Most of the field office records that are part of the National Archives of the United States are in the archives branches of the Federal Archives and Records Centers (FARCs). Field office records are typically kept in a less orderly manner than central office records, so there are great variations in what has survived and how it is arranged. The kinds of records maintained did not vary much from one jurisdiction to another of the same type. To avoid repetition, the principal types of field office records that are helpful for genealogical research are described below. Table 19 lists principal Indian agencies and the location of records.

Census rolls are described on page 171 above.

Allotment payrolls are described above.

Agency employee records often relate to Indian judges and Indian police, as well as to teachers in both boarding and day schools, who may have been either Indian or white. The records are usually arranged by date of employment, necessitating a search of the entire list for a particular name if there is no index. About individuals, some of the information that may appear in the records of an employee are name, position, salary, date and place of employment, sex, race, age, marital status, birthplace, legal residence, previous occupation, and date and cause of termination.

Individual history cards relating to students usually show name, tribe, sex, birthdate, and names and census or allotment numbers of parents, brothers, sisters, uncles, and aunts.

Marriage cards usually give Indian and English name; sex; tribe; census or allotment number; how married (by tribal custom or U.S. law); name of spouse; if divorced, when, where, and how; and names, sex, and birth and death dates of children born of the marriage.

Marriage registers may include names of principals, age, nationality, tribe, father's and mother's names, and previous marriages. Occasionally a divorce decree has been entered.

Individual Indian index cards, prepared pursuant to the Indian Office Circular 652, 29 June 1912, show, of males, name; address; allotment number, if any; and tribal affiliation.

Vital statistics generally consist of records, arranged chronologically, of births and deaths. Birth records may include parents' names, child's name, sex, degree of Indian blood, tribe, and residence. Death registers often consist of name of deceased; age; sex; degree of Indian blood; tribe; place, date, and cause of death; and residence.

Sanitary records of the sick and injured usually show name, age, and sex of patient; disease; date taken sick; and when recovered or deceased. There is often a separate list of births and deaths associated with sanitary records. The entries are usually arranged chronologically.

Heirship records often included correspondence with inheritance examiners and listings of heirs to allotments. Heirship ledgers may show name of land allotted, date of

TABLE 19

Bureau of Indian Affairs Field Office Records

(Note: Names in parentheses are agencies under which the listed agency is mentioned in E. Hill's *Guide to Records in the National Archives Relating to American Indians.*)

School or Agency	Location
Aberdeen Area Office	FARC Kansas City
Abiquiu and Cimarron Agencies	FARC Denver
Albuquerque Indian School	FARC Denver
Anadarko Area Office	FARC Fort Worth
Arapaho, Cheyenne and, Agency	FARC Fort Worth
Bannock, Shoshone and, Agency	
(Wind River Agency)	FARC Denver
(Fort Hall Agency)	FARC Seattle
Billings Area Office	FARC Seattle
Birch Cooley School (Pipestone Indian School)	FARC Kansas City
Bismarck Indian School	FARC Kansas City
Blackfeet Agency	FARC Seattle and FARC Denver
California Agency (Sacramento Area Office)	FARC San Francisco
California Agency (Riverside Area Field Office)	FARC Los Angeles
Camp Apache Agency (Fort Apache Agency)	FARC Los Angeles
Camp McDowell Agency (Pima Agency)	FARC Los Angeles
Canton Asylum for Insane Indians (Pipestone Indian School)	FARC Kansas City
Cantonment Agency (Conho Agency)	FARC Fort Worth
Carlisle Indian Industrial School	National Archives
Carson School and Agency	FARC San Francisco
Carter and Laona Agencies	FARC Chicago
Charles G. Burke Indian School	FARC Denver
Chamberlain Indian School	National Archives
Chemawa Indian School	FARC Seattle
Cherokee Agency, East	National Archives
Cherokee Agency, North Carolina	FARC Atlanta
Cherokee Agency, West	National Archives
Cheyenne and Arapaho Agency (Concho Agency)	FARC Fort Worth
Cheyenne River Agency	FARC Kansas City
Chickasaw Agency, East	National Archives
Chilocco Indian School	FARC Fort Worth
Choctaw Agency, East	National Archives
Cimarron Agency (Abiquiu Agency)	FARC Denver
Coeur d'Alene Agency (Colville Agency)	FARC Seattle
Colorado River Agency	FARC Los Angeles
Colville Agency	FARC Seattle
Concho Agency	FARC Forth Worth
Consolidated Chippewa Agency	FARC Kansas City and National Archives
Choctaw and Chickasaw Agency (Muskogee Area Office)	National Archives
Creek Agency, East	National Archives
Crow Creek Agency	FARC Kansas City
Cushman School (Puyallup Agency)	FARC Seattle
Devil's Lake Agency (Fort Totten Agency)	FARC Kansas City
Digger Agency	FARC San Francisco
Fallon School and Agency	FARC San Francisco
Five Civilized Tribes Agency (Muskogee Area Office)	FARC Forth Worth
Flandreau School and Agency	FARC Kansas City
Flathead Agency	FARC Seattle
Fond du Lac Agency (Red Lake Agency)	FARC Kansas City and FARC Chicago
Fort Apache Agency	FARC Los Angeles
Fort Belknap Agency	FARC Seattle
Fort Berthold Agency	FARC Kansas City
Fort Bidwell School and Agency	FARC San Francisco
Fort Bridger Agency (Wind River Agency)	FARC Denver
Fort Defiance Subagency (Navajo Agencies)	FARC Los Angeles
Fort Hall Agency	FARC Seattle
Fort Lapwai Agency (Northern Idaho Agency)	FARC Seattle

(table continued on following page)

TABLE 19 (CONTINUED)

Bureau of Indian Affairs Field Office Records

School or Agency	Location
Fort Lewis Indian School	FARC Denver
Fort Peck Agency	FARC Seattle
Fort McDermitt Agency (Reno Agency)	FARC San Francisco
Fort Mohave School (Colorado River Agency)	FARC Los Angeles
Fort Shaw Indian School	National Archives
Fort Totten Agency	FARC Kansas City
Fort Yuma Agency	FARC Los Angeles
Fox Day School (Sac and Fox Agency)	FARC Chicago
Gila River Agency (Pima Agency)	FARC Los Angeles
Grand Portage School (Consolidated Chippewa Agency)	National Archives
Grand Rapids Agency	FARC Chicago
Grand River Agency (Standing Rock Agency)	FARC Kansas City
Grand Ronde-Siletz Agency	FARC Seattle
Great Lakes Consolidated Agency	FARC Chicago
Great Nemaha Agency (Potawatomi Agency)	FARC Kansas City
Green Bay Agency (Menominee Agencies)	FARC Chicago
Greenville School and Agency	FARC San Francisco
Haskell Institute	FARC Kansas City
Hayward Indian School	FARC Chicago
Hoopa Valley Agency	FARC San Francisco
Hope School (Springfield School)	National Archives
Hopi Agency	FARC Los Angeles
Horton Agency (Potawatomi Agency)	FARC Kansas City
Jicarilla Agency	FARC Denver
Juneau Area Office	FARC Seattle
Kansas Agency (Potawatomi Agency)	FARC Kansas City
Kaw Agency (Pawnee Agency)	FARC Fort Worth
Keshena Agency (Menominee Agency)	FARC Chicago
Kickapoo Agency (Potawatomi Agency)	FARC Kansas City
Kiowa Agency (Anadarko Area Office)	FARC Fort Worth
Klamath Agency	FARC Seattle
Lac du Flambeau Agency and School	FARC Chicago
Laguna Sanatorium	FARC Denver
Laona Agency (Great Lakes Consolidated Agency)	FARC Chicago
LaPointe Agency (Hayward Indian School and Lac du Flambeau Agency)	FARC Chicago
Leech Lake Agency	National Archives and FARC Kansas City
Lemhi Agency (Fort Hall Agency)	FARC Seattle
Leupp Training School (Navajo Agencies)	FARC Denver
Lovelocks School (Fallon School)	FARC San Francisco
Lower Brulé Agency	FARC Kansas City
Mackinac Agency	FARC Chicago
Malheur Agency	National Archives
Menominee Agencies, Minneapolis Area Office	FARC Kansas City
Menominee Agencies in Wisconsin	FARC Chicago
Mescalero Agency	FARC Denver
Mesquakie Day School (Sac and Fox Agency)	FARC Chicago
Miami Agency	FARC Fort Worth
Milk River Agency (Fort Peck Agency)	FARC Seattle
Minneapolis Area Office	FARC Kansas City
Minnesota Agency	FARC Kansas City
Mission Tule River Agency (Pala Subagency)	FARC Los Angeles
Moqui Pueblo Agency	National Archives
Mount Pleasant Indian School	FARC Chicago
Muskogee Area Office	FARC Fort Worth and National Archives
Navajo Agencies	FARC Denver and Los Angeles
Neah Bay Agency (Taholah Agency)	FARC Seattle
Neosha Agency (Miami Agency)	FARC Fort Worth

(table continued on following page)

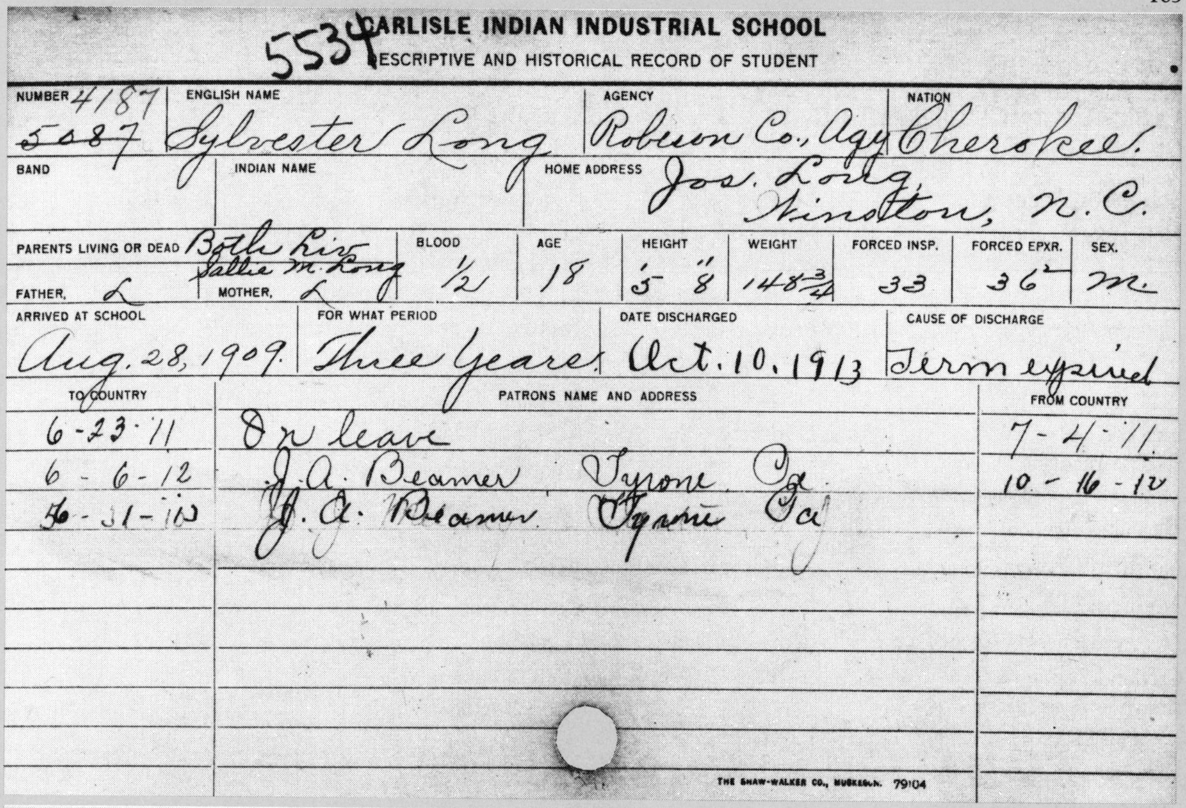

5534

CARLISLE INDIAN INDUSTRIAL SCHOOL

DESCRIPTIVE AND HISTORICAL RECORD OF STUDENT

NUMBER	ENGLISH NAME	AGENCY	NATION
4187 ~~5087~~	Sylvester Long	Robeson Co., Agy	Cherokee.

BAND	INDIAN NAME	HOME ADDRESS
		Jos. Long, Winston, N. C.

PARENTS LIVING OR DEAD	BLOOD	AGE	HEIGHT	WEIGHT	FORCED INSP.	FORCED EPXR.	SEX.
Both Liv. FATHER, L MOTHER, Sallie M. Long L	1/2	18	5' 8"	148 3/4	33	36 2	M.

ARRIVED AT SCHOOL	FOR WHAT PERIOD	DATE DISCHARGED	CAUSE OF DISCHARGE
Aug. 28, 1909.	Three Years.	Oct. 10, 1913	Term expired

TO COUNTRY	PATRONS NAME AND ADDRESS	FROM COUNTRY
6-23-11	On leave	7-4-11
6-6-12	J. A. Beamer Tyrone Pa	10-16-12
5-31-13	J. A. Beamer Tyrone Pa	

THE SHAW-WALKER CO., MUSKEGON. 79104

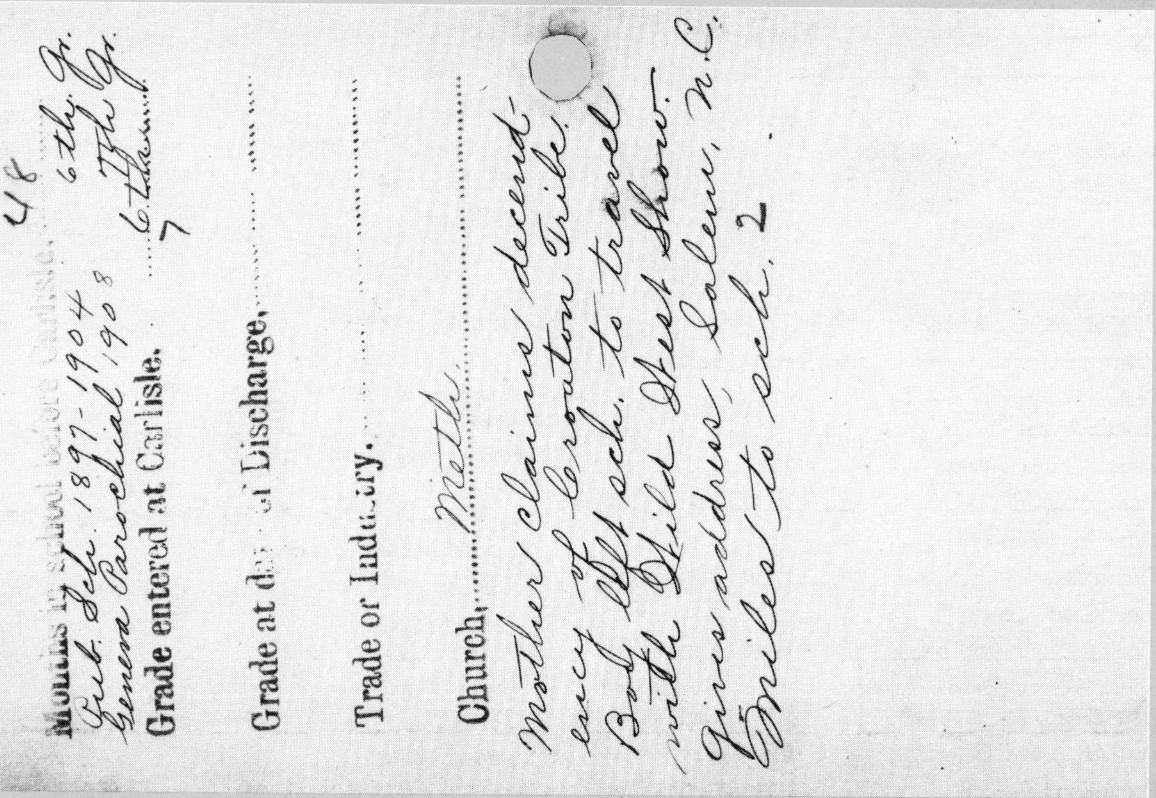

Months in school before Carlisle. 48

Pub. Sch. 1897-1904 6th Gr.

Genesa Parochial 1908 7th Gr.

Grade entered at Carlisle. 6th ... 7

Grade at date of Discharge, ...

Trade or Industry. ...

Church, Meth.

Mother claims descendency of Croaton Tribe.

Boy left sch. to travel with Wild West Show.

Gives address, Salem, N.C.

2 miles to sch.

Individual history card for student at Carlisle Indian School. The student later became the show business celebrity "Chief Buffalo Long Lance." Records of the Bureau of Indian Affairs, Record Group 75.

TABLE 19 (CONTINUED)

Bureau of Indian Affairs Field Office Records

School or Agency	Location
Nett Lake Agency	National Archives and FARC Kansas City
Nevada Agency	FARC San Francisco
New York Agency	National Archives
Nez Perce Agency (Northern Idaho Agency)	FARC Seattle
Nisqually and Skokomish Agency (Puyallup Agency)	FARC Seattle
Northern Cheyenne Agency	FARC Seattle
Northern Idaho Agency	FARC Seattle
Northern Pueblos Agency	FARC Denver
Oakland Agency (Pawnee Agency)	FARC Fort Worth
Omaha Agency (Winnebago Agency)	FARC Kansas City
Oneida School and Agency	FARC Chicago
Osage Agency	FARC Fort Worth
Otoe Agency (Pawnee Agency)	FARC Fort Worth
Ouray Agency (Uintah and Ouray Agency)	FARC Denver
Pala Subagency	FARC Los Angeles
Palm Springs Agency	FARC Los Angeles
Papago Agency	FARC Los Angeles
Paiute Agency (Uintah and Ouray Agency)	FARC Denver
Pawnee Agency	FARC Fort Worth
Pechanga Agency (Pala Subagency)	FARC Los Angeles
Phoenix Area Office	FARC Los Angeles
Pierre Agency	FARC Kansas City
Pierre Indian School	FARC Kansas City
Pima Agency	FARC Los Angeles
Pine Ridge Agency	FARC Kansas City
Pipestone Indian School	FARC Kansas City
Ponca Agency (Pawnee Agency) (Winnebago Agency)	FARC Forth Worth FARC Kansas City
Portland Area Office	FARC Seattle
Potawatomi Agency	FARC Kansas City
Prairie du Chien Agency (Winnebago Agency)	FARC Kansas City
Pueblo and Pueblo and Jicarilla Agencies	FARC Denver
Pueblo Day Schools at Albuquerque and Santa Fe	FARC Denver
Pueblo Indian Agency and Pueblo Day Schools	FARC Denver
Puget Sound District Agency	FARC Seattle
Puyallup Agency and Cushman School	FARC Seattle
Quapaw Agency (Miami Agency)	FARC Fort Worth
Quinaielt Agency (Puyallup Agency)	FARC Seattle
Rapid City Indian School	FARC Kansas City
Red Cliff School and Agency	FARC Chicago
Red Cloud Agency (Pine Ridge Agency)	FARC Kansas City
Red Lake Agency	FARC Kansas City
Red Moon Agency (Concho Agency)	FARC Fort Worth
Reno Agency	FARC San Francisco
Rice Boarding School (San Carlos Agency)	FARC Los Angeles
Riggs Institute (Flandreau School)	FARC Kansas City
Riverside Area Field Office	FARC Los Angeles
Rosebud Agency	FARC Kansas City
Roseburg Agency	FARC San Francisco
Round Valley Agency	FARC San Francisco
Sac and Fox Agency and Sanatorium	FARC Chicago
Sacramento Agency and Area Office	FARC San Francisco
Salem (Chemawa) School (Grand Ronde-Siletz Agency)	FARC Seattle
San Carlos Agency	FARC Los Angeles
San Jacinto Agency (Tule River Agency)	FARC San Francisco
Santa Fe Indian School	FARC Denver
Santee Agency (Flandreau Agency)	FARC Kansas City
Seger Agency (Concho Agency)	FARC Fort Worth
Seminole Agency, Florida	FARC Atlanta
Seneca School (Miami Agency)	FARC Fort Worth
Shawnee Agency in Oklahoma	FARC Fort Worth

School or Agency	Location
Sherman Institute	FARC Los Angeles
Shiprock Boarding School (Navajo Agencies)	FARC Denver
Shiprock Subagency (Navajo Agencies)	FARC Los Angeles
Shoshone and Bannock Agency (Wind River Agency)	FARC Denver
Siletz Agency (Grand Ronde-Siletz Agency)	FARC Seattle
(Roseburg Agency)	FARC San Francisco
Sioux Sanatorium	FARC Kansas City
Sisseton Agency	FARC Kansas City
Six Nations Agency (New York Agency)	National Archives
Skokomish Agency (Tulalip Agency)	FARC Seattle
Southern Apache Agency	National Archives
Southern Mission Agency (Pala Subagency)	FARC Los Angeles
Southern Pueblos Agency	FARC Denver
Southern Ute and Consolidated Ute Agencies	FARC Denver
Spokane Agency	FARC Seattle
Spotted Tail Agency (Rosebud Agency)	FARC Kansas City
Springfield (Hope) Indian School	National Archives
Standing Rock Agency	FARC Kansas City
Taholah Agency	FARC Seattle
Toadlena Day School	FARC Denver
Tomah Indian School and Agency	FARC Chicago
Tongue River Agency (Northern Cheyenne Agency)	FARC Seattle
Truxton Canyon Agency	FARC Los Angeles
Tuba City Subagency	FARC Los Angeles
Tulalip Agency	FARC Seattle
Tule River Agency	FARC San Francisco
Turtle Mountain Agency	FARC Kansas City
Unitah and Ouray Agency	FARC Denver
Umatilla Agency	FARC Seattle
United Pueblos Agency	FARC Denver
Union Agency (Muskogee Area Office)	National Archives
Utah Agency (Abiquiu Agency)	FARC Denver
Upper Arkansas Agency (Concho Agency)	FARC Fort Worth
Upper Missouri Agency (Crow Creek Agency)	FARC Kansas City
Upper Platte Agency (Rosebud Agency)	FARC Kansas City
Vermillion Lake Agency	FARC Chicago
Vermillion Lake School (Nett Lake Agency)	National Archives
Wahpeton Indian School	FARC Kansas City
Walker River Agency	FARC San Francisco
Warm Springs Agency	FARC Seattle
Western Shoshone Agency	FARC San Francisco
Western Washington Agency (Taholah and Tulalip Agencies)	FARC Seattle
Whetstone Agency (Rosebud Agency)	FARC Kansas City
White Earth Agency	National Archives and FARC Kansas City
White River Agency (Lower Brulé Agency)	FARC Kansas City
Wichita Agency (Anadarko Area Office)	FARC Fort Worth
Window Rock Area Office (Navajo Agencies)	FARC Denver and FARC Los Angeles
Wind River Agency	FARC Denver
Winnebago Agency	FARC Kansas City
Wittenberg Indian School	National Archives
Yakima Agency	FARC Seattle
Yankton Agency	FARC Kansas City
Zuni Agency	FARC Denver

Group of Indian boys in cadet uniforms, Carlisle Indian School, Pennsylvania. Photograph No. 75-IP-1-9 by J. N. Choate, ca. 1880.

allotment, date of allottee's death, and names of approved heirs.

Registers of Indian families include Indian name, English name, age, blood or nationality, tribe or allegiance, marital status, date of marriage, how married, and parents' names and register numbers.

Most **Indian school records** are among the field records for various Indian agencies, to be noted on table 19. They usually contain school reports, individual pupil records, and school censuses in which students are listed by name. In addition there were nonreservation boarding schools, some of which are noted also in table 19.

School census records in the early twentieth century were the means of determining the amount of federal payment to the school, at a certain amount per student per day of attendance. The record for each student usually shows name, sex, age, percent of Indian blood, names of parents, name of school, and number of grades.

School reports may report attendance, pupil examination and promotion, and records of supervisory visits to homes of adult students. Quarterly school reports often describe each student by name, age, tribe, degree of Indian blood, name of home agency, date entered, grade, subjects of study, and attendance. Monthly reports are usually only statistical summaries.

Public school contracts and reports contain much the same information for comparable time periods.

In table 19, an alphabetical listing of Indian agencies and schools of the Bureau of Indian Affairs, only the location of the records is given. The frequent reorganizations of the BIA, as well as many transfers of tribes from one agency and place to another, make it impossible to designate one agency as holding the records of a particular tribe. The researcher should consult pages 117–194 of Edward E. Hill's *Guide to Records in the National Archives Relating to American Indians* for a detailed account of each field office and of the Indians under its jurisdiction at various times. Where an agency or school name is followed by another agency name in parenthesis, the name in parenthesis is the heading under which Hill describes that agency.

CHAPTER 12

Records of Black Americans

CHAPTER
12
Records of Black Americans
12.1 Introduction
12.2 Census Records
12.3 Military Service and Related Records

12.1 Introduction

For the most part, the records in the National Archives relating to blacks are not found as separate entities, but are interspersed among various record series. In many records, the race of individuals is indicated, but in most it is not. Generally, however, from the close of the Civil War to the present, genealogy for blacks follows the same research paths as does genealogy for others. Researchers of black genealogy should first gather the information available from living relatives, in family records, and in cemeteries. The same county, state, and federal sources, libraries, historical and genealogical societies, and other records usually consulted in genealogical research are useful to researchers in the genealogy of blacks.

The federal records generally useful for genealogical research are thus also useful for black genealogy. The most helpful series in the census, military, and Freedmen's Bureau records are described in this chapter. Other series of records contain information relating to blacks, but are not generally useful for genealogy because of their arrangement, the lack of indexes, or the fact that they relate only to a few people, a specific geographical area, or a particular occupation or class. Among such records are the peonage case records of the Justice Department, relating to people enslaved after the Civil War, records of the Bureau of Customs and other federal agencies that administered programs for the free blacks and former slaves before the Freedmen's Bureau was established, records relating to the suppression of the slave trade, records relating to labor and the employment of blacks before, during, and after the Civil War, and records relating to federal employment in general. A distinction has also been made between records documenting the history of blacks as a group (black history) and those providing information about individuals (genealogy).

The series of records that are described in the following paragraphs either include racial descriptions or comprise separate series of records that relate specifically to blacks. The records described in the various chapters and sections of this guide relating to military service, bounty land, pensions, land records, Indians, court records, civilian personnel records, and passenger lists are all pertinent to black research; consequently, the entire guide should be studied by researchers of black genealogy. For supplemental reading, see *Who Do You Think You Are, Digging for Your Family Roots?* by Suzanne Hilton (Philadelphia: Westminster Press, 1976); *Black Genealogy: How To Begin,* by James D. Walker (Athens: University of Georgia Center for Continuing Education, 1977); *A Guide to Documents in the National Archives for Negro Studies,* compiled by Paul Lewinson (Washington: Committee on Negro Studies, American Council of Learned Societies, 1947); and *Guide to Federal Archives Relating to Africa,* by Aloha South (Honolulu: Crossroads Press, 1977.)

12.2 Census Records

The first listing of all blacks by name in a federal census was made in 1870, in the first federal census taken after the Civil War. In 1850 and 1860, slave statistics were gathered, but the census schedules did not list slaves by name; they were tallied unnamed in age and sex categories. These slaves schedules are useful, however, as circumstantial evidence that a slave of a certain age and sex was the property of a particular owner in 1850 or 1860.

Free blacks who were heads of households were enumerated by name in the censuses from 1790 to 1840, and the names of all free household members were included in the censuses of 1850 and 1860. Slaves, however, were listed in total numbers or recorded in age and sex categories, 1790–1840. *List of Free Black Heads of Families in the First Census of the United States, 1790,* Special List 34, compiled by Debra L. Newman (Washington: National Archives and Records Service, rev. 1974), lists roughly 4,000 free blacks recorded as heads of families. Chapter 1 in this guide describes in detail the contents of the various census schedules, including what is available regarding slaves and free blacks.

12.3 Military Service and Related Records

12.3.1 Revolutionary War and After

Blacks have served in all the wars of the United States, sometimes in all-black units. Records of their service and of their applications for veteran's benefits are contained in the series of military records fully described in Chapters 4–9.

Some blacks who served in the Revolutionary War are noted in *List of Black Servicemen Compiled From the War Department Collection of Revolutionary War Records,* Special List 36, compiled by Debra L. Newman (Washington: National Archives and Records Service, 1974). Additional information about servicemen in the Revolutionary War can be obtained from the pension application files available as *Revolutionary War Pension and Bounty Land Warrant Application Files,* M804, 2,670 rolls. Selections from the files are available on M805, 898 rolls.

Another part of the experience of blacks during the Revolutionary War is documented in Records of the Continental and Confederation Congresses and the Constitutional Convention, Record Group 360. When the British evacuated New York in 1783, they took with them many former slaves. Lists of those who left with the British, called **inspection rolls,** were created so that reparation could be made to former owners under the terms of the Treaty of Paris of 1783. Consequently, carefully accurate information was recorded for each evacuee. Given are name, sex, sometimes age, and brief physical description of each individual; name and residence of former owner; and additional information in a "remarks" column. The lists are available on roll 7 of *Miscellaneous Papers of the Continental Congress, 1774–1789,* M332, and roll 66 of *Papers of the Continental Congress, 1774–1779,* M247.

Blacks served as enlisted men and occasionally as officers during wars of the late nineteenth and early twentieth centuries. At various times, there were blacks in the regular army, volunteers, navy, Marine Corps, and Coast Guard. Although race is not always noted in the records, physical descriptions are sometimes given. It may be helpful to consult *Data Relating to Negro Military Personnel in the 19th*

Century, Reference Information Paper 63, by Aloha South (Washington: National Archives and Records Service, 1973).

12.3.2 Civil War

During the Civil War, black soldiers served with Union forces in regiments of **U.S. Colored Troops (U.S.C.T.)** and also in the navy and Marine Corps. As with other compiled military service records of the Civil War, the records are in Record Group 94. They are arranged according to military organization with an alphabetical index that is available as *Index to Compiled Service Records of Volunteer Union Soldiers who Served with the United States Colored Troops,* M589, 98 rolls. Historical information about volunteer organizations is available on rolls 204–217 of *Compiled Records Showing Service in Volunteer Union Organizations,* M594. Regimental records, including correspondence, orders, descriptive books and morning reports, are described in *Tabular Analysis of the Records of the U.S. Colored Troops and Their Predecessor Units in the National Archives of the United States,* Special List 33, compiled by Joseph B. Ross (Washington: National Archives and Records Service, 1973). The Colored Troops Division of the Adjutant General's Office was responsible for recruiting and other matters relating to black soldiers; records of the division are dated 1863–89 and are part of Records of the Adjutant General's Office, 1780's–1917, Record Group 94. The letters received, 1863–88, contain consolidated files pertaining to individual black soldiers. In most instances, a reference to the correspondence file is on the jacket of the compiled military service record of the particular soldier. Colored Troops Division records also include fifty-four volumes of descriptive lists of colored volunteers who enlisted in Missouri, 1864, arranged chronologically, with name indexes. The lists give name, age, eye and hair color, complexion, height, place of birth, occupation, and date of enlistment. In the cases of former slaves, former owners' names may be entered. Information about the various colored troop regiments, including lists of officers, combats, and casualties, can be found in volume 8 of *Official Army Register of the Volunteer Force of the United States Army for the Years 1861, '62, '63, '64, '65* (Washington: Adjutant General's Office, 1867); in *A Compendium of the War of the Rebellion,* by Frederick H. Dyer (Des Moines: Dyer Publishing Co., 1908, and New York: T. Yoseloff, 1959); in *War of the Rebellion, A Compilation of the Official Records of the Union and Confederate Armies,* 128 volumes (Washington: War Department, 1880–1902), which has been microfilmed on M262, 128 rolls, and has been reprinted by the National Historical Society, Gettysburg, Pa., 1972; and in *Official Records of the Union and Confederate Navies in the War of the Rebellion,* 31 volumes (Washington: Navy Department, 1894–1927), which has been microfilmed on M275, 31 rolls.

Blacks also served in the **Confederate states military forces** as members of otherwise white units, with the exception of the Regiment of Native Guards mustered for the defense of New Orleans. The identification of these men as blacks must generally be made from sources outside the National Archives, as the military records do not usually show race.

Following the Civil War, some blacks applied for (and in a few instances were granted) admission to the **U.S. Military Academy**. Records relating to these applications are available as *Selected Documents Relating to Blacks Nominated for Appointment to the U.S. Military Academy During the 19th Century, 1870–87,* M1002, 21 rolls.

Records relating to blacks granted the **Medal of Honor** during the late nineteenth century are similarly available as *Documents Relating to the Military and Naval Service of Blacks Awarded the Congressional Medal of Honor From the Civil War to the Spanish-American War,* M929, 4 rolls.

Regimental histories and other information concerning black troops in the Spanish-American War and the Philippine Insurrection can be found in volume 1 of *Correspondence Relating to the War with Spain . . .* (Washington: War Department, 1902), and also in unpublished historical accounts in Record Group 94.

After the Civil War, blacks served in the regular army during war and peace. The 9th and 10th Cavalry and 38th, 39th, 40th, and 41st Infantry Regiments were organized as all-black units in July 1866. In 1869, the four infantry units were consolidated to form the 24th and 25th Regiments. Published works on this subject are *The Buffalo Soldiers: A Narrative of the Negro Cavalry in the West,* by William H. Leckie (Norman: University of Oklahoma Press, 1967); *The Black Infantry in the West, 1869–1891,* by Arlen L. Fowler (Westport, Conn.: Greenwood Publishing Corp., 1971); *The Black Soldier and Officer in the United States Army, 1891–1917,* by Marvin Fletcher (Columbia: University of Missouri Press, 1974); *Under Fire With the Tenth U.S. Cavalry,* by Hershel V. Cashin (New York: Arno Press, 1969); and *The Colored Regulars in the United States Army . . .,* by Theophilus G. Steward (Philadelphia: A.M.E. Book Concern, 1904; reprinted by Arno Press, New York, 1969).

In Records of the U.S. General Accounting Office, Record Group 217, are disallowed **military claims** of persons who served in the U.S. Colored Troops (U.S.C.T.), including cavalry (U.S.C.C.) and artillery (U.S.C.A.) units, 1864–93. The records of the Office of the Second Auditor of the Treasury Department document the claims filed by such soldiers or their heirs for bounty or other pay and allowances due. Typically, a claim file consists of a petition, affidavits, and correspondence directly relating to the claim, but some files include discharge papers and proof of origin or identity. These records are arranged by unit number—there are some for the 15th and 21st U.S.C.T.; 22nd to 138th U.S.C.T.; 1st to 6th U.S.C.C.; 1st to 14th U.S.C.A.; 5th, 10th, and 55th Massachusetts volunteers; 29th Connecticut volunteers; and files for persons in miscellaneous units—and are further arranged thereunder alphabetically by name of soldier. These records appear to be related to the records of the Colored Troops Division of the Adjutant General's Office, 1863–89, in Record Group 94, and many letters passed between the offices in attempts to decide claims. The allowed claims of this type were not segregated by unit but were filed with the large, comprehensive series of Second Auditor's accounts, which were destroyed with congressional approval in the 1950s.

12.3.3 Naval Records

Records of the U.S. Navy include information about blacks who enlisted in this service. The pre-1840 records are unindexed, and, in general, all of the records are difficult to

SCHEDULE 2.—Slave Inhabitants in The Eleventh District **in the County of** Carroll **State of** Georgia **, enumerated by me, on the** 15 **day of** Sept **, 1850.** T S Martin **Ass't Marshal.**

NAMES OF SLAVE OWNERS.	Number of Slaves.	DESCRIPTION. Age.	Sex.	Colour.	Fugitives from the State.	Number manumitted.	Deaf & dumb, blind, insane, or idiotic.
1	2	3	4	5	6	7	8
L S Chapman	10	8	M	B			
	11	7	M	B			
	12	6	F	B			
	13	4	M	B			
	14	3	M	B			
√	15	1	F	B			
A H Harrison	1	60	F	B			
	2	28	M	B			
	3	26	F	B			
	4	26	M	B			
	5	19	F	B			
	6	6	M	B			
	7	4	M	B			
	8	11	M	B			
	9	11	M	B			
	10	9	F	B			
√	11	6	F	B			
Wm H Robards √	1	32	M	M			
J H Cantright √	1	11	F	B			
Andw McMullin	1	18	M	M			
√	2	15	F	B			
F M Richards √	1	25	F	B			
E W Holland	1	22	F	M			
	2	4	M	B			
	3	3	F	B			
	4	1	F	M			
	5	36	F	M			
	6	7	F	M			
	7	13	F	M			
	8	12	M	M			
	9	19	M	M			
	10	25	M	B			
	11	17	M	B			
	12	19	M	B			
	13	18	M	B			
	14	18	M	B			
	15	18	M	B			
	16	18	M	B			
	17	25	M	B			
	18	12	M	M			
	19	16	M	B			
	20	10	M	B			

NAMES OF SLAVE OWNERS.	Number of Slaves.	DESCRIPTION. Age.	Sex.	Colour.	Fugitives from the State.	Number manumitted.	Deaf & dumb, blind, insane, or idiotic.
1	2	3	4	5	6	7	8
	21	9	M	B			
	22	9	M	B			
	23	12	F	B			
	24	9	M	B			
	25	18	M	M			
	26	4/12	F	M			
	27	18	F	B			
√	28	15	M	B			
Wm V Bailey	1	53	F	B			
	2	27	M	B			
	3	21	F	B			
	4	2	F	B			
√	5	1	F	B			
A H Green	1	30	F	B			
	2	12	M	B			
	3	10	M	B			
√	4	10	F	M			
B. L Little √	1	8	M	B			
Wm H Awtry	1	35	M	B			
	2	32	M	B			
	3	28	M	B			
√	4	10	F	B			
Quincy McCorkle	1	30	M	B			
	2	20	F	B			
	3	4	F	M			
√	4	2	F	M			
A N M Robinson √	1	22	M	B			
Ephraim Jackson √	1	70	M	B			
Jas. Aldridge	1	35	F	B			
	2	29	M	B			
	3	15	M	B			
	4	8	F	B			
√	5	2	F	B			
Geo H Palmore	1	23	M	B			
	2	23	M	B			
	3	18	F	B			
Wyatt Moore √	1	20	M	B			
Thos W Burton	1	45	F	B			
	2	30	F	M			
	3	26	F	B			
	4	17	M	B			
	5	11	M	B			

Schedule of slave inhabitants, 1850 Census. Records of the Bureau of the Census, Record Group 29.

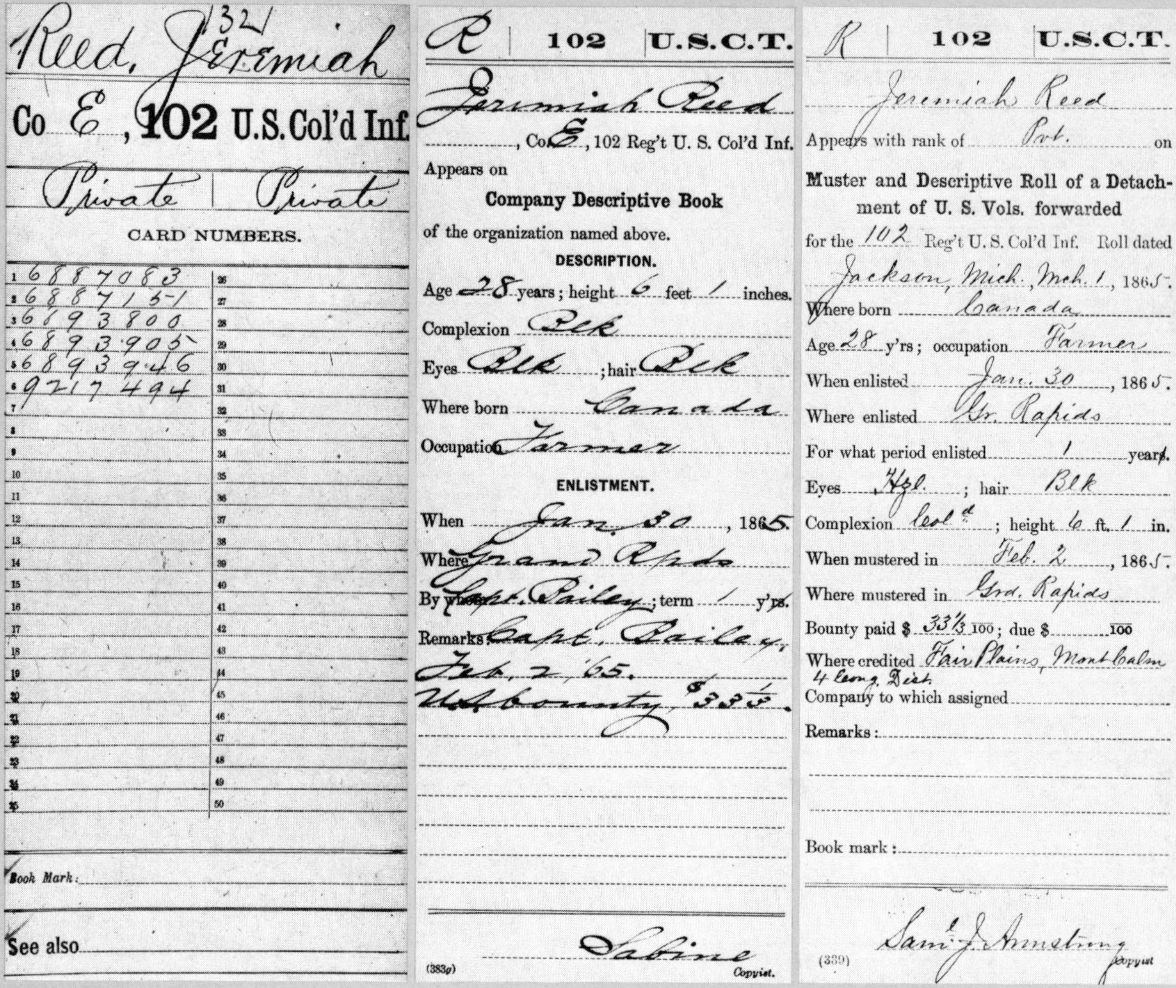

Reed, Jeremiah 132

Co E, 102 U.S. Col'd Inf.

Private | Private

CARD NUMBERS.

1 6887083
2 6887151
3 6893800
4 6893905
5 6893946
6 9217494

Book Mark:

See also

R | 102 | U.S.C.T.

Jeremiah Reed

, Co. E, 102 Reg't U. S. Col'd Inf.

Appears on

Company Descriptive Book

of the organization named above.

DESCRIPTION.

Age 28 years; height 6 feet 1 inches.

Complexion Blk

Eyes Blk ; hair Blk

Where born Canada

Occupation Farmer

ENLISTMENT.

When Jan. 30, 1865.

Where Grand Rpds

By whom Capt. Bailey ; term 1 y'rs.

Remarks: Capt. Bailey, Feb. 2, '65. U.S. bounty, $33⅓.

(383g) Sabine Copyist.

R | 102 | U.S.C.T.

Jeremiah Reed

Appears with rank of Pvt. on

Muster and Descriptive Roll of a Detachment of U. S. Vols. forwarded

for the 102 Reg't U. S. Col'd Inf. Roll dated

Jackson, Mich. Mch. 1, 1865.

Where born Canada

Age 28 y'rs; occupation Farmer

When enlisted Jan. 30, 1865.

Where enlisted Gr. Rapids

For what period enlisted 1 years.

Eyes Hzl. ; hair Blk

Complexion Col'd ; height 6 ft. 1 in.

When mustered in Feb. 2, 1865.

Where mustered in Grd. Rapids

Bounty paid $ 33⅓/100 ; due $ /100

Where credited Fair Plains, Montcalm 4 Cong. Dist.

Company to which assigned

Remarks:

Book mark:

(339) Sam'l J. Armstrong Copyist

Three cards from a compiled military service record of a volunteer soldier, U.S. Colored Troops. Records of the Adjutant General's Office, 1780s–1917, Record Group 94.

search. **Ships' muster rolls** in Records of the Bureau of Naval Personnel, Record Group 24, for example, may indicate race, beginning with the Civil War, or contain a description of the enlisted man ("Negro" or "mulatto") in addition to name, rating, date and place of enlistment, and state of birth. But in this instance, to locate the information about a particular black seaman, the researcher must know the date and place of enlistment or the name of the vessel on which he served.

Fragmentary records relating to African slaves and blacks who were prisoners of war, declared contraband or refugees, or wartime civilian laborers may be found in Naval Records Collection of the Office of Naval Records and Library, Record Group 45. Some of the more significant series are noted below.

Blacks are among the persons mentioned in a register of American and French **prisoners of war** held by the British at Halifax, Barbados, and Jamaica, 1805–15, and at Quebec, 1813–15. The register entries show name, rank, and number of each prisoner; ship that captured him; date and location of capture (usually at sea); name and type of vessel (man of war, privateer, merchant) on which he served before capture; vessel that delivered him to Halifax, Barbados, or Jamaica and date of delivery; and dated notations about his exchange, discharge, death, or escape.

The register for prisoners held at Quebec also shows prisoner's place of birth; age; height; weight; color of hair, skin, and eyes; distinguishing marks or wounds; and supplies and clothing furnished.

Blacks are identified on the payrolls of **civilian personnel at Confederate shore establishments,** May 1861–December 1864. Among the payrolls is a pay and receipt roll of personnel employed, including slaves, at Fluvanna County, Va., July 1863–March 1864; pay and receipt rolls of slaves at Moseley's Farm, Powhatan County, Va., August–September 1862, at Keswick, Powhatan County, Va., July–August 1862, and in Powhatan County, Va., November 1862–December 1863; a payroll of slaves employed at Richmond, Va., July 1862–December 1863; and a payroll of slaves employed on board the C.S.S. *Cotton* at Shreveport, La., January–February 1864.

Lists and a **register of slaves** received by the Engineer Office at Charleston and Georgetown Harbors, S.C., to work on the fortifications for the city of Charleston, August 1862–September 1863, show dates on which the slaves were received, districts from which they were received, names of slaveholders, first names of the slaves, and the total number of slaves received from each slaveholder. Also included in the register are notes concerning slaves who ran away from the fortifications and a small number of entries for slaves who were hired to work on the fortifications during January through June 1864.

Black enlisted men who served in the Union or regular navy are mentioned in the letters received concerning Union and Confederate **naval prisoners of war,** May 1862–March 1865, including the place where Union naval prisoners were held and arrangements were made for their exchange. They are frequently accompanied by lists of Union naval prisoners paroled by the Confederates, announced as exchanged, or still held in the South. Also included are other lists of Union naval prisoners held in the South during the years 1863–65, extracts of declarations of exchange of prisoners, and general orders announcing exchanges, 1862–65.

In the journal kept by Capt. George Emmons while commanding the U.S.S. *Lackawanna* is a list of black refugees and others given passports to enter or depart from Galveston, Tex., 1864–65. The letters received by the commandants of the Boston and Washington navy yards for 1862 contain reports of arrivals of "contrabands" (free Negroes or slaves) at those yards; similar reports are included in the letters received by the commandant of the Portsmouth navy yard in 1864. Usually the names of the vessels or the names of the army officers by whom the contrabands were delivered to the yards are given.

12.4 Freedmen's Bureau and Related Records

After the Civil War, Congress created the Freedmen's Bureau (officially designated the Bureau of Refugees, Freedmen, and Abandoned Lands) by an act of 1865 (13 Stat. 507). The Bureau was a part of the War Department and was assigned responsibilities that included "the control of all subjects relating to refugees and freedmen from rebel States, or from any district . . . within the territory embraced in the operations of the Army." The Bureau helped former slaves make the transition to citizenship.

The period of the Bureau's greatest activity extended from June 1865 to December 1868. Bureau activities included aiding in legalizing marriages consummated during slavery, witnessing labor contracts, issuing rations and clothing to destitute freedmen and refugees, leasing land, operating hospitals and freedmen's camps, and providing transportation to refugees and freedmen returning to their homes or relocating them in other parts of the country. Included are records relating to freedmen and white citizens, military employees, teachers, and agents of civic and religious organizations. As the Bureau developed, it became involved in helping former Union servicemen file and collect claims for bounties, pay arrears, and pensions. Congress later authorized additional funds, and the Bureau began issuing and distributing food and supplies to destitute people in the South. Much of the work of the Bureau ended in early 1869, and it was abolished in 1872 (17 Stat. 366). The unfinished business of the Bureau—claims, arrears, pension and bounty actions—was turned over to the Freedmen's Branch, Office of the Adjutant General. The records contain information useful to researchers of black genealogy, including, in some instances, names of persons, residences, occupations, and dates. In general, however, the nature and arrangement of the records and the lack of name indexing precludes easy access to specific genealogical data. The records commonly are administrative or statistical in nature; many of them consist of official communications or issuances. The researcher should, therefore, bring as much knowledge as possible to his or her research and be prepared to make a substantial item-by-item search in correspondence files using the indexes and registers.

The Bureau records, Record Group 105, are subdivided into two major groups, the first consisting of the records of Commissioner Oliver Otis Howard and other staff officers

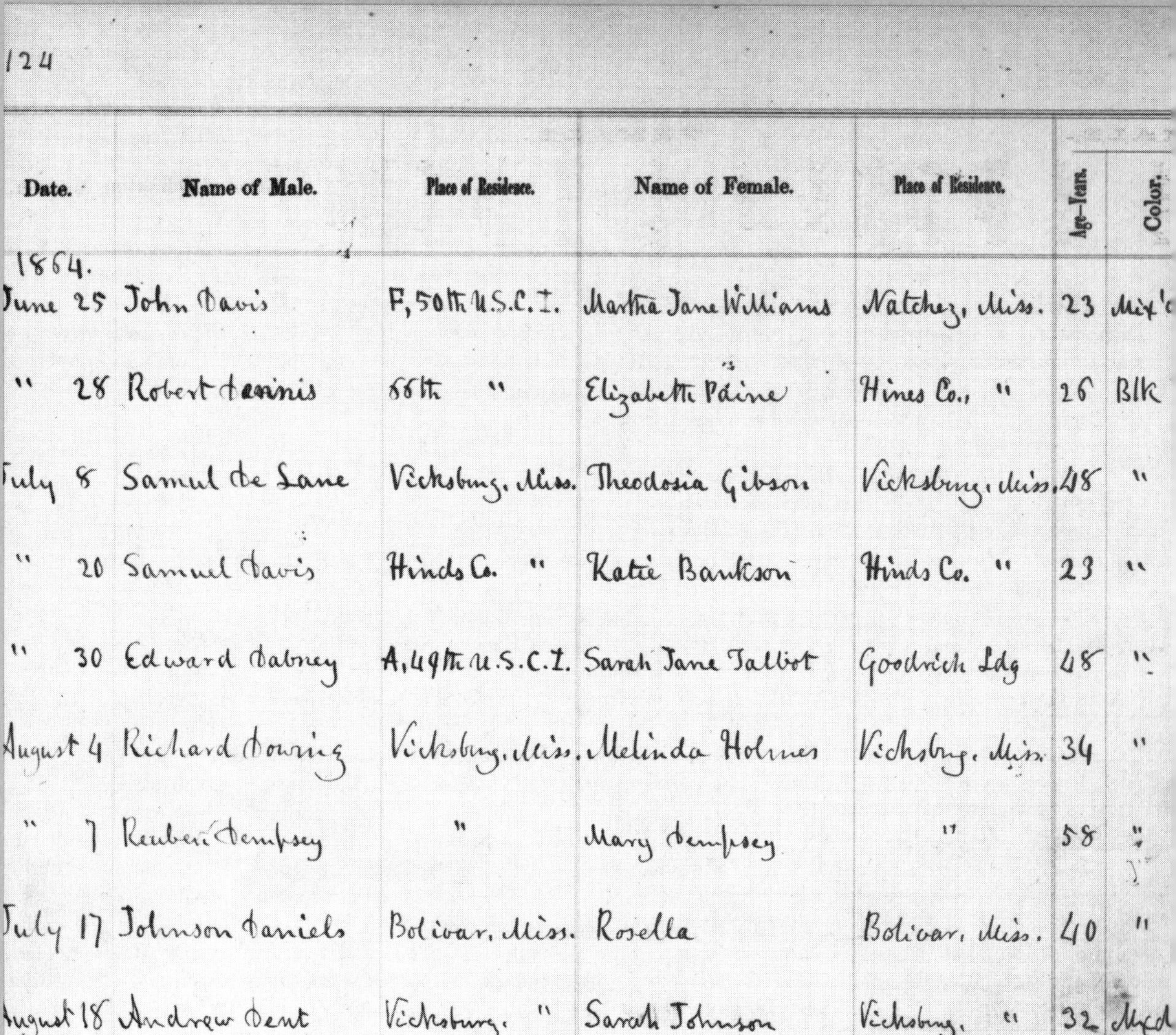

124

Date.	Name of Male.	Place of Residence.	Name of Female.	Place of Residence.	Age—Years.	Color.
1864.						
June 25	John Davis	F, 50th U.S.C.I.	Martha Jane Williams	Natchez, Miss.	23	Mix'd
" 28	Robert Dennis	58th "	Elizabeth Paine	Hines Co., "	26	Blk
July 8	Samuel De Lane	Vicksburg, Miss.	Theodosia Gibson	Vicksburg, Miss.	48	"
" 20	Samuel Davis	Hinds Co. "	Katie Bankson	Hinds Co. "	23	"
" 30	Edward Dabney	A, 49th U.S.C.I.	Sarah Jane Talbot	Goodrich Ldg	48	"
August 4	Richard Downing	Vicksburg, Miss.	Melinda Holmes	Vicksburg, Miss.	34	"
" 7	Reuben Dempsey	"	Mary Dempsey	"	58	"
July 17	Johnson Daniels	Bolivar, Miss.	Rosella	Bolivar, Miss.	40	"
August 18	Andrew Dent	Vicksburg, "	Sarah Johnson	Vicksburg, "	32	Mxd
" 18	Richard Dimit	47 U S C I	Eliza Sherka	Greenwood "	41	"
June 4	William Davis	49 " "	Alice William	Vicksbg Miss	21	Bl
Sept 1	Edward Dodson	66 " "	Eliza Dodson	" "	48	"
" 4	Humphry Deason	47th U.S.C.I.	Mary McPherson	Lake Providence La	37	Mxd
" 8	Edmond Douglas	E 49th U.S.C.I.	Hannah Williams	Vicksburg Miss	37	Blk
" 10	Raphael Devers	I., 52nd U.S.C.I.	Mary Wild	Issaquena Co "	36	"

Register of marriages of freedmen. Records of the Assistant Commissioner for the State of Mississippi, v. 43, pp. 124–125. Records of the Bureau of Refugees, Freedmen, and Abandoned Lands, Record Group 105. National Archives Microfilm Publication M826.

12

MALE.					FEMALE.								
Do. of Father.	Do. of Mother.	Lived with another Woman. Years.	Separated by.	No. of Children by Previous Connection.	Age—Years.	Color.	Do. of Father.	Do. of Mother.	Lived with another Man. Years.	Separated by.	No. of Children by Previous Connection.	No. of Children Unitedly.	Name of Officiating Ministe[r] and Witness.
Mix'd	Mixed				21	Blk	Blk	Blk	–				James Peet John A. Davis
Blk	Blk				24	"	"	"					Walter C. Yancy S. C. Feemster
"	"	4	Force	2	16	"	"	"					Joseph Warren L. B. Eaton
"	"				21	"	"	"					R. L. Howard Adin Mann
"	"	11	Death		27	"	"	"	7	death	1 1		Joseph Warren Patsy Monson
"	"				23	Mixed	Mixed	Mixed					Page Tyler Robert McCary
"	"	1			57	Blk	Blk	Blk	6	Force	6		Joseph Warren S. A. Dickey
"	"	5	"		39	Mixed	Mixed	Mixed	18	death			G. N. Carruthers John Edmonson
"	Mxd	2	Her desertion		18	Blk	Blk	Blk					Joseph Warren Adam Bowie
uisa	"				35	Mxd	"	Mxd					C. W. Buckley Luther P. Fitch
Blk	Blk				18	Brown	"	Brown					J. G. Edwards [illegible]
"	"				35	Blk	"	Blk	8	Force	4		J. A. Hawley Morrison King
Mxd	"	1	force	1	30	Mxd	Mxd	"				4	C. W. Buckley. Luther P. Fitch
Blk	"	11	death	1	25	Blk	Blk	"	1	death			James A. Hawley. Louisa Woodin
	"	2	"	2	30	"	"	"	5	desertion	4		Joseph Warren Sallie A. Dickey

of the Washington, D.C., headquarters, 1865–72. These records are described in *Records of the Bureau of Refugees, Freedmen, and Abandoned Lands, Washington Headquarters,* Preliminary Inventory 174, compiled by Elaine Everly (Washington: National Archives and Records Service, 1973), and some of them are available on the following microfilm publications: *Selected Series of Records Issued by the Commissioner of the Bureau of Refugees, Freedmen, and Abandoned Lands, 1865–1872,* M742, 7 rolls, consisting of letters and endorsements sent and circulars and special orders; *Registers and Letters Received by the Commissioner of the Bureau of Refugees, Freedmen, and Abandoned Lands, 1865–1872,* M752, 74 rolls; and *Records of the Education Division of the Bureau of Refugees, Freedmen, and Abandoned Lands, 1865–1871,* M803, 35 rolls.

The second major group contains records of the various district or field offices in the southern states, which include, for each district, records of the assistant commissioner in charge. The field office records are incomplete, but for most districts there are also records of the superintendents of education and other staff officers and for subordinate officers and agents serving in the subdistricts. Table 20 shows the availability of these records as microfilm publications. Bureau headquarters and field office records are discussed below with primary emphasis on the series with more genealogical significance.

Bureau headquarters records. The records of the Washington, D.C., headquarters include about two linear feet of freedmen's marriage certificates, 1861–69. The series also includes marriage licenses, monthly reports of marriages from bureau offices, and other proofs of marriage. The documents are arranged alphabetically by state in which the marriage was performed, and thereunder in general alphabetical order by the initial letter of surname of the bridegroom. Therefore, the researcher must know where the marriage that interests him was performed. Most of the records are dated 1865–68, but included are some reports of marriages performed before the war and some performed at contraband camps during the war.

The collection is fragmentary; the number of certificates for each state vary from several hundred each for Louisiana, Mississippi, and Tennessee to one for Alabama and none for other states. Certificates frequently include such information as names and residences of brides and grooms, dates and places of marriages, and names of persons who performed ceremonies. Certificates may also indicate ages and complexions of brides and grooms, complexions of parents, periods of time brides and grooms lived with previous spouses and causes for separation, and numbers of children by present and previous unions.

Records of district or field offices contain fragmentary records of marriages. Most of these records consist of registers of marriages maintained by local superintendents and agents. Knowledge of the place and date of a particular marriage is necessary to locate it in the records. Registers generally give the names of the couples and the dates marriages were registered. Many registers also provide information about previous marriages, numbers of children, and names of ministers or others who performed the ceremonies. Entries in the registers may be arranged chronologically or alphabetically by surname. Most of the records are for the states of Arkansas, Kentucky, Louisiana, and Mississippi, with a few scattered items for several other states. A series of consolidated registers for the state of Mississippi is available on roll 42 of *Records of the Assistant Commissioner for the State of Mississippi, Bureau of Refugees, Freedmen and Abandoned Lands, 1865–1869,* M826, 50 rolls. Additional records relating to marriages performed by Freedman's Bureau personnel are among records maintained by the counties in which the marriages were performed.

Other field office records of possible genealogical significance include scattered census returns, fairly extensive series of labor contracts and registers, hospital and transportation records, records of complaints registered by freedmen, and records relating to the administration of relief. The labor contract records exist at both the state and local levels and provide information such as dates of contracts, periods of service, names of contracting parties and/or family members, types of work performed, and rates of wages. Included among records of the Assistant Commissioner for the District of Columbia are descriptive lists of freed people for whom transportation was requested by employment agents, 1867–68, showing names, heights, complexions, names of former owners, and former and present residences. Scattered applications and certificates for relief, 1866–68, list heads of families who had received relief, and give race; number of men, women, and children in the family; signatures of head of family and witnesses; and, in some instances, age, sex, and cause of destitution.

Congress incorporated the **Freedman's Savings and Trust Company** in 1865 primarily for the benefit of former slaves. The main office was in Washington, but there were branches in a number of cities in the states of New York, Pennsylvania, Mississippi, Louisiana, Arkansas, Tennessee, Florida, and Texas. The bank branches maintained **registers of depositors,** most of whom were blacks, in which they recorded some personal and family information. Not all branches asked for the same information, and not all forms were completed. However, the information in the registers includes account number; name; age; complexion; place of birth; place raised; name of former master and mistress; residence; occupation; names of parents, spouse, children, brothers, and sisters; remarks; and signature. The registers are arranged alphabetically by name of state; entries in the registers are arranged alphabetically by name of city where the bank was located, thereunder chronologically by date the account was opened, and thereunder numerically by account number. The registers are in Records of the Office of the Comptroller of the Currency, Record Group 101. They have been reproduced as *Registers of Signatures of Depositors in Branches of the Freedman's Savings and Trust Company, 1865–1874,* M816, 27 rolls. In the same record group are 42 volumes of indexes to the deposit ledgers that serve as an index to the registers. Some of the index volumes are incomplete, while others index only special accounts or other records. The indexes are arranged alphabetically by name of state, and thereunder by city where the branch was located. The names in the indexes are arranged by initial letter of surname and thereunder by sound of the name. The indexes have been reproduced as *Indexes to Deposit Ledgers in Branches of the Freedman's Savings and Trust Company, 1865–1874,* M817, 5 rolls.

To use these records of the Freedman's Savings and Trust Company, the researcher must know the city where the subject of research had an account. Researchers should determine the account number from M817 and use it to locate the appropriate entry in the registers on M816.

The Treasury Department established **special agencies** in 1861 to trade in the insurgent areas of the South controlled by the U.S. military and in adjacent areas in loyal states. The agencies, in addition to other responsibilities, were responsible for the employment and welfare of freedmen until the establishment of the Bureau of Refugees, Freedmen, and Abandoned Lands. The records are similar to those of the Freedmen's Bureau. Included in Records of Civil War Special Agencies of the Treasury Department, Record Group 336, are reports relating to labor contracts and to food and other supplies furnished to individuals and families; there are also records relating to the disposition of confiscated and abandoned property. The records (for the period 1861–66) are arranged by agency, thereunder by subject, and generally thereunder chronologically. Because the boundaries and duties of the special agencies often changed, the researcher must have a good knowledge of the administrative history of the agencies. Some of this background information is given in *Guide to Federal Archives Relating to the Civil War,* compiled by Kenneth W. Munden and Henry P. Beers (Washington: National Archives and Records Service, 1962), pp. 233–240.

Because some of the programs for blacks later administered by the Freedmen's Bureau were initially carried out by the army commands headquartered in various southern states, there are records relating to blacks in Records of U.S. Army Continental Commands, Record Group 393. The army involvement continued, although to a somewhat lesser extent, into the Reconstruction period. Army command records relating specifically to blacks are few, fragmentary, and generally unindexed. Information relating to specific black individuals can be obtained from general record series only through painstaking research performed with the assistance of experienced archivists. Like the Freedmen's Bureau, the army commands supervised the employment of blacks as agricultural laborers on farms and plantations. Records of the Department of the Gulf and Louisiana, for example, include payrolls of laborers employed on plantations, 1864–67, and a small collection of descriptive lists ("registers") of laborers employed on plantations, 1864. The latter indicate age, sex, type of labor, former owner, and former residence. The military commands were also concerned, like the Bureau, with abuses perpetrated by whites upon freedmen. Records of the Departments of the South and South Carolina and the Second Military District include several series of reports of such "outrages," 1865–68, with registers, 1867–68. Provost marshals in various commands occasionally took censuses of black and white inhabitants in their respective areas. Fragmentary censuses for 1864 are among records of the Department of the Gulf, mostly for Plaquemines Parish, La., indicating name, age, sex, occupation, place of birth, and number of children. Among records of the Department of the South are similar 1864 censuses for Florida, including the Jacksonville and St. Augustine areas. Entries indicate name; height; eye, skin, and hair color; age; last residence; former owner; and date individual entered the military department.

Confederate records relating to black civilian laborers, 1861–65, in the War Department Collection of Confederate Records, Record Group 109, are described on page 205. For a general monograph, see *The Confederate Negro, Virginia's Craftsmen and Military Laborers, 1861–1865,* by James H. Brewer (Durham, N.C.: Duke University Press, 1969).

12.5 Records of Slaves in the District of Columbia

There are several series of records relating to slaves and the emancipation of slaves in the District of Columbia. If the

TABLE 20

Microfilmed Freedmen's Bureau Field Office Records

	Assistant Commissioner		Superintendent of Education	
State	Microfilm publication	Number of rolls	Microfilm publication	Number of rolls
Alabama	M809	23	M810	8
Arkansas	M979	52	M980	5
District of Columbia	M1055	21	M1056	24
Georgia	M798	36	M799	28
Louisiana	M1027	36	M1026	12
Mississippi	M826	50		
North Carolina	M843	38	M844	16
South Carolina	M869	44		
Tennessee	M999	34	M1000	9
Texas	M821	32	M822	18
Virginia	M1048	67	M1053	20

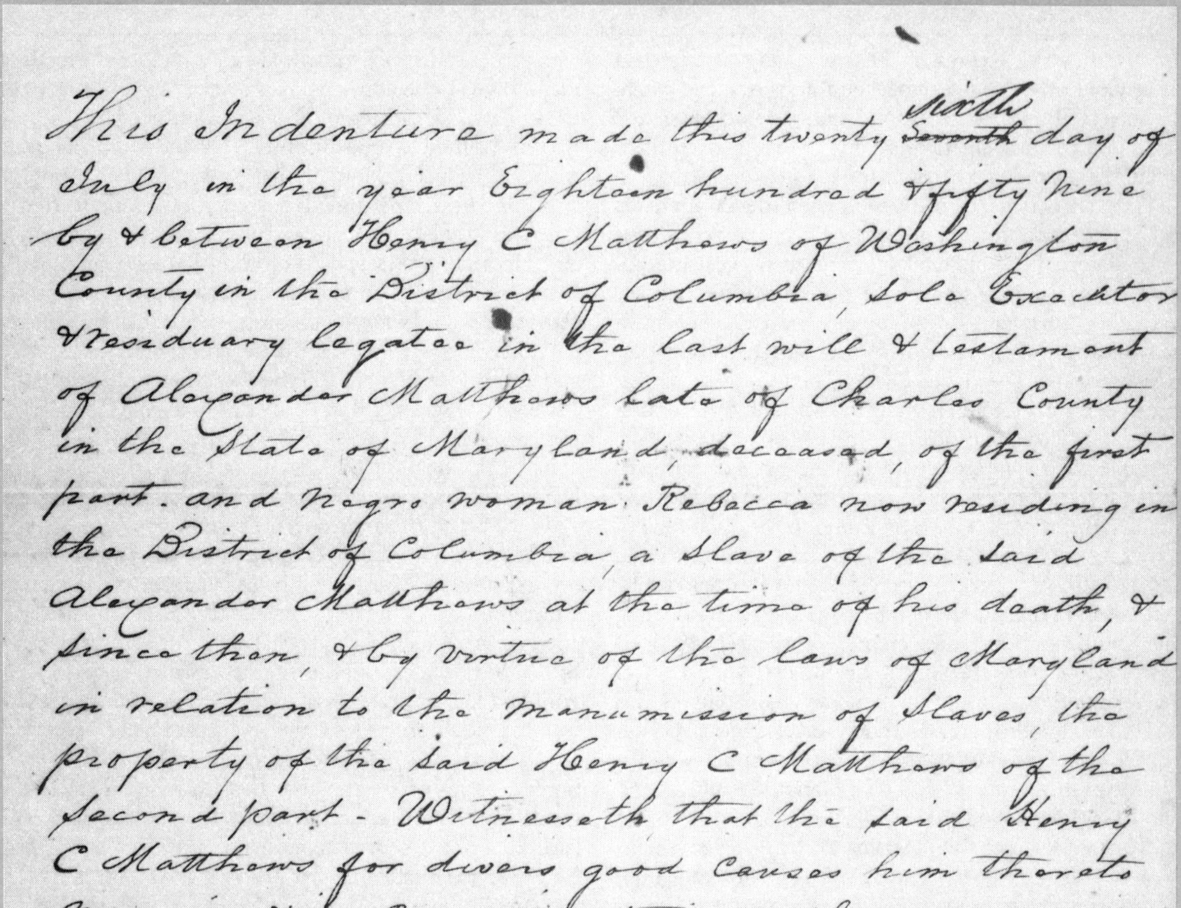
This Indenture made this twenty ~~seventh~~ sixth day of
July in the year Eighteen hundred & fifty nine
by & between Henry C Matthews of Washington
County in the District of Columbia, sole Executor
& residuary legatee in the last will & testament
of Alexander Matthews late of Charles County
in the State of Maryland, deceased, of the first
part. and Negro woman Rebecca now residing in
the District of Columbia, a slave of the said
Alexander Matthews at the time of his death, &
since then, & by virtue of the laws of Maryland
in relation to the manumission of slaves, the
property of the said Henry C Matthews of the
second part - Witnesseth, that the said Henry
C Matthews for divers good causes him thereto
moving, & in consideration of the sum of One
Dollar to him paid by the said Negro Woman
Rebecca, at the ensealing & delivery of these presents,
the receipt of which is hereby acknowledged,
hath liberated set free manumitted & discharged
from slavery & from every species of servitude to
him, either in his private right, or as Executor
aforesaid, the said Negro woman Rebecca. She
being of the age of Twenty two years, in good health,
& capable of maintaining herself by labour - and
doth hereby declare & pronounce the said Negro
woman Rebecca to be from henceforth a free Woman

Manumission record, Henry C. Matthews, for "Negro Woman Rebecca," 9 July 1859.
Records of the District Courts of the United States, Record Group 21.

In testimony whereof the said Henry C Matthews hath hereunto set his hand & seal, the day & year first aforesaid -

Signed sealed & delivered in our presence - } H. C. Matthews (Seal)

Anthy Hyde
W S Matthews

Washington County District of Columbia -

On this twenty Seventh day of July in the year Eighteen hundred & fifty Nine, Personally appeared before the Subscriber a Justice of the Peace in & for the County aforesaid, Henry C Matthews, party of the first part, named in the aforegoing instrument of writing, & acknowledged the same to be his act and deed; Witness my hand and Seal.

Anthy Hyde
J.P. (Seal)

subject of research was a resident of the District, the researcher should also see chapter 18.

Persons alleged to be fugitive slaves are the subject of most of the *Habeas Corpus Case Records, 1820–1863, of the United States Circuit Court for the District of Columbia,* M434, 2 rolls. This series consists of writs of habeas corpus (orders to produce a prisoner and show cause for his capture and detention) and related documents filed in habeas corpus proceedings. The records are arranged chronologically; to use them, the researcher must know the year of the case, although both rolls of film can be searched. Similar records are among those of other U.S. district courts.

Other papers, 1851–63, relating to claims under the 1850 law to recover fugitive slaves then living in the District of Columbia are available on *Records of the United States District Court for the District of Columbia Relating to Slaves, 1851–1863,* M433, 3 rolls. Many cases contain only the warrant for the negro's arrest; others contain documents and papers related to proof of ownership. The records are arranged chronologically.

An 1862 act (12 Stat. 376) abolished slavery in the District of Columbia. Slave owners were required to free their slaves with compensation. By an act of July 1862 (12 Stat. 536) slaves whose owners refused or neglected to free them could petition for their freedom. Also on M433 are **emancipation papers,** 1862–63, that consist of schedules or lists of slaves filed by owners and former slaves pursuant to the acts. The schedules show when the court issued certificates of freedom to the former slaves; they are arranged chronologically. **Manumission papers,** 1857–63, also filmed on M433, consist of similar schedules but relate only to masters' voluntary freeing of slaves. They are arranged chronologically. There are six volumes of unmicrofilmed manumission and emancipation records, 1821–62, in the records of the same court. They are arranged alphabetically by owner, guardian, trustee, or administrator.

A board of commissioners was appointed to receive petitions for compensation under the 1862 acts. The records of the board consist of a volume of minutes, 28 April 1862–14 January 1863, with a name and subject index in the front of the volume; a volume containing a record of petitions filed (which includes the petition number, name of the petitioner, and names of slaves and their value), arranged chronologically with an index by name of petitioner in the front of the volume; various other records relating to the administration of the 1862 acts; a series of 900 petitions filed under the act of April 16; and other petitions filed under the act of July 12.

These records have been reproduced as *Records of the Board of Commissioners for the Emancipation of Slaves in the District of Columbia, 1862–1863,* M520, 6 rolls. They are part of Record Group 217.

12.6 Other Records

12.6.1 Cherokee Freedmen

There are a few records relating to blacks among the Records of the Bureau of Indian Affairs, Record Group 75.

The Cherokee citizenship of many ex-slaves of the Cherokee of Indian Territory and of some Shawnee and Delaware Indians who claimed Cherokee citizenship was disputed by the Cherokee. The establishment of their status was important in determining their right to live on Cherokee land and to share in certain annuity and other payments.

A series of investigations was conducted in order to compile rolls of Cherokee freedmen and other claimants to Cherokee citizenship. They were begun (1889–90) by Commissioner John W. Wallace, and though the resulting rolls were frequently revised in later years, they were called the **Wallace rolls**. Claimants presented affidavits which were divided into "Free Negroes," who had been free at the beginning of the Civil War, "Admitted Cherokee Freedmen," who had not previously been recognized as Cherokee citizens, "Authenticated Cherokee Freedmen," who had been recognized previously, and "Rejected Cherokee Freedmen," with similar designations for other applicants. Among the records are letters received, supplements and revisions, and an index to revised copies of the Wallace Rolls of Cherokee Freedmen. The final report prepared by Wallace is numbered 21833–90 in letters received, 1881–1907. The last revision of the "Roll of Cherokee Freedmen" was completed in 1896–97; it lists family groups and their descendants under authenticated and admitted freedmen.

Also in Record Group 75 are reports on appraisement of improvements by persons considered by the Cherokee to be intruders, including some freedmen on Cherokee lands.

In Record Group 217 there are also annuity payment rolls, often duplicating those in Record Group 75.

Among the Records of the Office of the Secretary of the Interior, Record Group 48, are rolls created by the Indian Territory Division that contain the names of some persons identified as freedmen. These rolls are available as *Final Rolls of Citizens and Freedmen of the Five Civilized Tribes in Indian Territory . . .,* T529, 3 rolls. These records are more fully described in the chapter about Indians, page 157. The original enrollment cards are in the archives branch, FARC Ft. Worth.

12.6.2 Records Relating to the Slave Trade and African Colonization

Correspondence of the Secretary of the Navy Relating to African Colonization, 1819–1844, M205, 2 rolls, provides much information concerning arrangements made by the Navy Department for the return of Africans captured from slave vessels bound for the United States to reception centers at Sherbro Island, Cape Mesurado, and Liberia, West Africa. Also discussed in these letters are arrangements made by U.S. district attorneys and other federal officials for the temporary placement of the Africans in the southern states. Letters received by the Secretary of the Navy from commanding officers of the African Squadron, 1843–61, are reproduced as rolls 101–112 of *Letters Received by the Secretary of the Navy From Commanding Officers of Squadrons ("Squadron Letters"), 1841–1886,* M89, 300 rolls. *Letter Books of Commodore Matthew C. Perry, 1843–45* (filmed as M206, 1 roll), and letter books of Commodore William C. Bolton, 1847–49, commanding officers of the African Squadron are also available. All these series are in Record Group 45.

Diplomatic correspondence pertaining to the slave trade is scattered through *Despatches from United States Ministers to Great Britain, 1791–1906,* M30, 200 rolls; . . . *Brazil, 1809–1906,* M121, 74 rolls; . . . *Liberia, 1863–1906,* M170, 14 rolls; and *Despatches from United States Consuls in Monrovia, Liberia, 1852–1906,* M169, 7 rolls. *Domestic Letters of the Department of State, 1784–1906,* M40, 171 rolls, and *Miscellaneous Letters of the Department of State, 1789–1906,* M179, 1,310 rolls, include scattered correspondence with various colonization societies. These series are in Record Group 59.

The records in each series are arranged chronologically. These records are of marginal value for genealogical research, but they are useful to help place black family history in the context of the nineteenth century.

Records of the Office of the Secretary of the Interior Relating to the Suppression of the African Slave Trade and Negro Colonization, 1854–1872, M160, 10 rolls, consists of three bound volumes and a quantity of unbound records relating to the suppression of the African slave trade and the colonization of recaptured and free blacks. These records, dated between 10 August 1854 and 3 February 1872 are part of Record Group 48.

Certain correspondence pertaining to the suppression of the slave trade and to colonization projects has been published: *Liberated Africans* . . . (37th Cong., 3d sess., H. Ex. Doc. 28, serial 1161); . . . *Transportation, Settlement, and Colonization of Persons of the African Race* (39th Cong., 1st sess., S. Ex. Doc. 55, serial 1238); and . . . *Operations of the United States Squadron on the West Coast of Africa, the Condition of the American Colonies There* . . . (28th Cong., 2d sess., S. Doc. 150, serial 458), which includes "Roll of Emigrants That Have Been Sent to the Colony of Liberia, Western Africa, by the American Colonization Society and Its Auxiliaries, to September, 1843," pp. 152–307, and "Census of the Colony of Liberia, September 1843," pp. 308–393.

In Records of District Courts of the United States, Record Group 21, are case files concerning admiralty and criminal matters pertaining to the slave trade. The admiralty cases in district courts were largely proceedings in rem (against the ship, her cargo, and tackle); they are related to the seizure, condemnation, and sale of ships engaged in the slave trade. The criminal cases in district and circuit courts concerning the slave trade pertain to charges of outfitting slave ships and to the service of masters and crews. To locate the records of a specific case, the researcher must know the court, the date, and the name of the defendant. The records of Record Group 21 are in the custody of the various regional archives branches.

General Records of the Department of Justice, Record Group 60, contain scattered correspondence concerning the slave trade; Records of the Foreign Service Posts of the Department of State, Record Group 84, contain material supplementing that in Record Group 59; and Records of U.S. Attorneys and Marshals, Record Group 118, contain scattered correspondence of the U.S. attorney for the Southern District of Alabama, 1830–60 (in the archives branch, FARC Atlanta), dealing with the laws prohibiting the further importation of slaves.

Slave manifests in Records of the U.S. Customs Service, Record Group 36, are of marginal value in genealogical research about black families. Masters of ships bringing cargoes into the United States from abroad had to submit a manifest or list of all of the goods they were importing. The National Archives has the manifests of a few of the ships that bought in slaves between 1789 and 1808, before foreign slave trade became illegal. The manifests give the number of slaves, the African port or area from which the ship sailed, the U.S. port it entered, the shipper, and the name and address of the recipient of the cargo. Because no names appear on the lists, these manifests are useful only for circumstantial evidence.

Masters of ships carrying slave cargoes between domestic ports were required to submit a manifest of their human cargoes. The manifests generally include the slave's name (almost always a given name, not a surname), sex, age, and height. They also contain the name of the shipper and the person or firm to whom the slaves were shipped. There are about 13 feet of inward and outward manifests for several ports, including Savannah, Mobile, and New Orleans. They are arranged by port, and thereunder chronologically. To locate information about a particular slave, a researcher must know where, when, and by whom the slave was sold.

CHAPTER 13

Records of Merchant Seamen

CHAPTER 13

Records of Merchant Seamen

13.1 Impressed American Seamen

13.2 Seamen's Protection Certificates

The records in the National Archives pertaining to merchant seamen include series relating to impressed American seamen and to seamen's protection certificates as well as crew lists, shipping articles, and logbooks of merchant vessels.

13.1 Impressed American Seamen

The unbound letters received by the State Department relating to American seamen impressed by Great Britain before the War of 1812 or imprisoned during the war are dated 1794–1815 and are arranged alphabetically by name of seaman. They include letters from collectors of customs, impressed seamen and their relatives and friends, and U.S. agents in such cities as London and Liverpool. Some letters report cases of impressment; others transmit requests for the release of individual seamen, for seamen's certificates, and for affidavits of U.S. citizenship.

Bound registers of applications for the release of impressed seamen, 1793–1802, are arranged chronologically, but they are indexed by the first letter of the surname of the seaman. Each entry in the registers shows the name of the seaman and such related information as date of capture, date of application for release, name of vessel from which taken, name of vessel on which impressed or place of imprisonment, and, occasionally, the number of the seaman's protection certificate and the name of the port where it was issued. Similar registers for 1804–17 were maintained by the U.S. consulate in London; these are also arranged chronologically, but there is a separate name index.

The letters and bound applications for release of impressed seamen are in Record Group 59. In the same record group is a list of impressed seamen prepared by the Department of State in October 1805. It has been indexed by Elizabeth Pearson White in "Impressed American Seamen," *National Genealogical Society Quarterly* 60 (1972): 125–131, 188–193. The registers that were maintained by American diplomats in London are in Records of the Foreign Service Posts of the Department of State, Record Group 84.

Several lists of impressed seamen were published in *American State Papers*. The first includes over 700 names of seamen impressed between 1 September 1804 and 18 May 1805, giving for each seaman the date of his impressment, the ship of war into which he was impressed, and remarks relating to proof of citizenship (ASP 02–196). The second, dated 2 March 1808 contains 697 names (ASP 03–212). In 1816, Secretary of State James Monroe provided Congress with two final lists of impressed American seamen. The first shows the names of 1,421 seamen impressed into the service of British public ships, and transferred to and confined in English prisons as prisoners of war. The information was taken from official lists furnished by the British authorities to the American agent for prisoners in London. The second shows the names of 219 American seamen impressed and finally transferred to prisons in the West Indies or Nova Scotia. Both lists provide the names of seamen impressed, their rank, the name of the British man-of-war that impressed them, the place confined, the date of release, the vessel in which they returned to the United States, and their date of arrival. There is a name index (ASP 04–282).

Also in 1816, President James Madison sent to the House of Representatives three lists of American seamen impressed by British vessels. The lists were published in 1816 in Washington with the title, *Message from the President of the United States, Transmitting A Report of the Secretary of State, in Obedience to a Resolution of the House of Representatives, of the Twenty-Eight of February Last, of the Number of Impressed American Seamen Confined in Dartmoor Prison; the Number Surrendered, Given Up, or Taken on Board British Vessels Captured during the Late War: Together with their Places of Residence.*

List A gives the names of 1,421 impressed seamen, the names of the British men-of-war responsible and the circumstances of the impressments, the places of confinement, the dates of release, the vessels on which the seamen returned to the Untied States, and the dates of arrival.

List B provides the same information for 158 American seamen confined in prisons in the West Indies.

List C provides the names of 219 American seamen impressed on British ships and discharged in England after the peace treaty. This final list was furnished by American agents in London. (Z4.14/1: HD4).

13.2 Seamen's Protection Certificates

Attempts to protect American seamen from impressment by Great Britain and other powers during the eighteenth and early nineteenth centuries led to the creation of records now useful to genealogists. The famous case of the *Lydia*, from which five American seamen were impressed on the high seas in February 1796, caused great outrage in the country and the Congress. As a result, an act of 1796 (1 Stat. 477) required each district collector of customs to keep a register of seamen who applied for seamen's protection certificates and presented evidence of citizenship such as a birth certificate, a passport, an old seaman's protection certificate issued in another port, or an oath taken before a notary public, alderman, or other official. Collectors or deputy collectors of customs received applications, issued the certificates to the seamen, kept the proofs of citizenship on file in the districts, and regularly sent lists of registered seamen to the Secretary of State.

Registers of seamen who received certificates are available at the archives branch, FARC Boston, for the districts of Fall River, Mass., 1837–69; New London, Conn., 1796–1827, 1833–78; New Haven, Conn., 1793–1801, 1803–41; and Newport, R.I., 1835–55. Because the certificates were used for identification, the registers include the following information about individual seamen: name, certificate number and date of issue, age, place of birth, how citizenship was obtained (birth or naturalization), physical description including height, weight, complexion, color of hair and eyes, and in some cases identifying marks such as scars, limps, or deformed limbs. The names are arranged in rough alphabetical order by the initial letter of the surname, and thereunder chronologically.

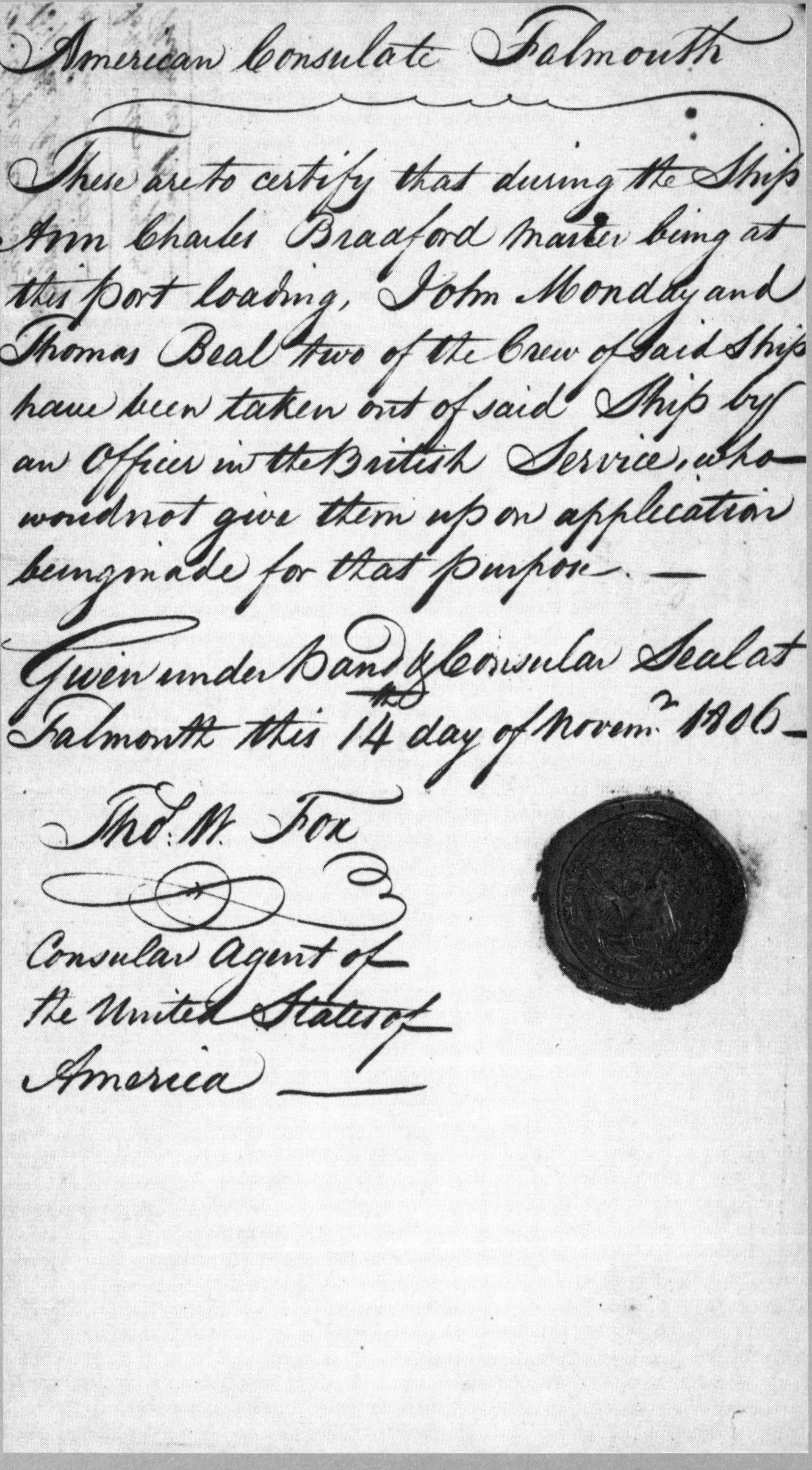

American Consulate Falmouth

These are to certify that during the Ship
Ann Charles Bradford master being at
this port loading, John Monday and
Thomas Beal two of the Crew of said Ship
have been taken out of said Ship by
an Officer in the British Service, who
would not give them up on application
being made for that purpose. —

Given under Hand & Consular Seal at
Falmouth this 14th day of Novem.r 1806 —

Thos. W. Fox

Consular Agent of
the United States of
America —

Certificate of impressment of two American merchant seamen, 1806. Letters Received Regarding Impressed Seamen, Records of Impressed Seamen, General Records of the Department of State, Record Group 59.

TABLE 21
Crew Lists on Microfilm

Port	Period covered	Microfilm publication	Number of rolls
Baton Rouge, La.	1 Jan. 1919–31 Mar. 1924		1
Boston, Mass.	1916–43	T938	269
Brunswick, Ga.	1 Jan. 1904–31 Dec. 1938		2
Charleston, S.C.	1 Jan. 1910–31 Dec. 1945		38
Fort Lauderdale, Fla.	1 Dec. 1939–Dec. 1945		11
Gloucester, Mass.	1918–43	T941	13
Gulfport, Miss.	19 Oct. 1904–30 Mar. 1945		7
Gulfport, Miss. (alien changes)	1919–45		5
Hartford, Conn.	Feb. 1929–Dec. 1943		4
Jacksonville, Fla.	1906–45		39
Key West, Fla.	1 Aug. 1914–31 Dec. 1945		19
Lake Charles, La.	1 Oct. 1940–31 Dec. 1945		1
Miami, Fla.	1920–45		123
Mobile, Ala.	1 Aug. 1903–31 Dec. 1945		59
Mobile, Ala. (Form 689: aliens)	1 Jan. 1925–31 Dec. 1931		4
New Bedford, Conn.	1917–43	T942	2
New Orleans, La.	1910–45	T939	311
New York, N.Y.	16 June 1897–31 Dec. 1942	T715	6,674*
Pascagoula, Miss.	1 Jan. 1907–5 Sept. 1928		3
Pensacola, Fla. (Form 689: aliens)	1 Jan. 1907–31 Dec. 1939		5
Pensacola, Fla.	1905–45		13
Philadelphia, Pa.	May 1917–31 Dec. 1945		220
Philadelphia, Pa. (alien changes)	1918		1
Portland, Maine	1 May 1917–Jan. 1944		37
Providence, R.I.	Aug. 1918–31 Dec. 1943		22
Savannah, Ga.	1910–31 Dec. 1945		32
Tampa, Fla.	1 Jan. 1904–31 Dec. 1945		72
West Palm Beach, Fla.	21 Sept. 1925–31 Dec. 1945		12

* Includes passenger lists.

The certificates themselves were carried by the seamen; certificates did not become federal records except in those infrequent cases when a seaman turned in an old, worn certificate and applied for another. Few applications or files of supporting documents and proofs of citizenship are extant. The National Archives has original applications for only three ports and files of supporting documents for only two.

Original applications exist for Philadelphia, 1796–1861, New Haven, 1801–41, and Mobile, 1819–34. They are arranged chronologically, and they are not indexed. An application shows the name, age, physical description, place of birth, and signature or mark of each seaman and the signature or mark of witnesses, who sometimes were relatives. The two series of supporting documents submitted by seamen are for Salem and Beverly, Mass., 1796–1807, arranged chronologically, and New York, 1797–1850, arranged by state of birth of the seaman. These records require the genealogist to know when and where the subject of research went to sea.

The applications for Philadelphia for the war period, 1812–15, were thoroughly analyzed by Ira Dye, and the results are available as *Computer-Processed Tabulations of Data From Seamen's Protective Certificate Applications to the Collector of Customs for the Port of Philadelphia, 1812–1815,*

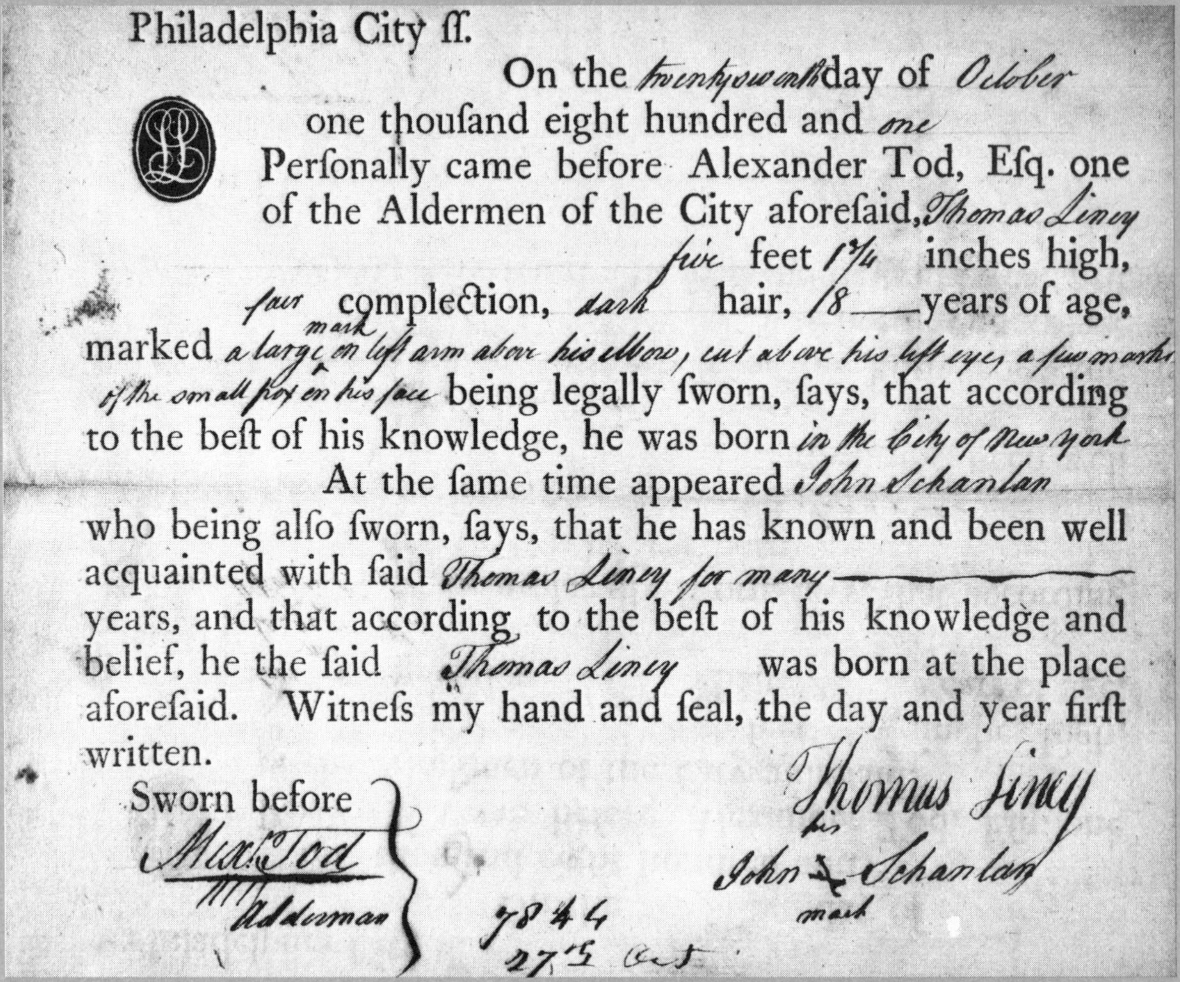

Philadelphia City ſſ.

On the twentyseventh day of October one thouſand eight hundred and one Perſonally came before Alexander Tod, Eſq. one of the Aldermen of the City aforeſaid, Thomas Liney five feet 1 3/4 inches high, fair complection, dark hair, 18 years of age, marked a large mark on left arm above his elbow, cut above his left eye, a few marks of the small pox on his face being legally ſworn, ſays, that according to the beſt of his knowledge, he was born in the City of New York

At the ſame time appeared John Schanlan who being alſo ſworn, ſays, that he has known and been well acquainted with ſaid Thomas Liney for many years, and that according to the beſt of his knowledge and belief, he the ſaid Thomas Liney was born at the place aforeſaid. Witneſs my hand and ſeal, the day and year firſt written.

Sworn before
Alex. Tod
Alderman

Thomas Liney
John his X mark Schanlan

7844
27th Oct

Seaman's protection certificate, issued to merchant seamen in attempt to thwart British press gangs. (Few of these certificates are in the National Archives.) Records of the U.S. Customs Service, Record Group 36.

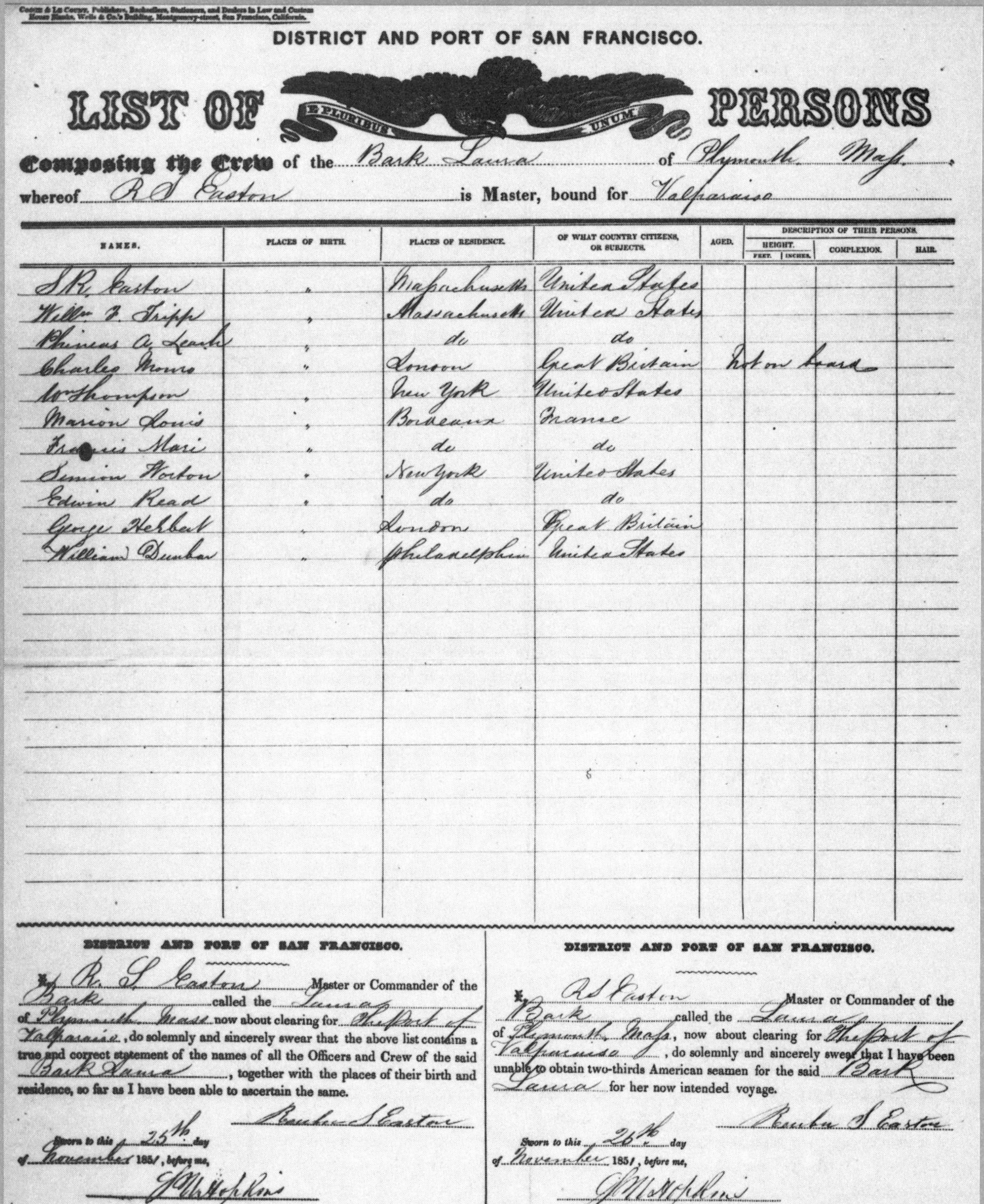

Cooke & Le Count, Publishers, Booksellers, Stationers, and Dealers in Law and Custom House Blanks, Wells & Co's Building, Montgomery-street, San Francisco, California.

DISTRICT AND PORT OF SAN FRANCISCO.

LIST OF PERSONS

Composing the Crew of the Bark Laura of Plymouth Mass.

whereof R S Easton is Master, bound for Valparaiso

NAMES.	PLACES OF BIRTH.	PLACES OF RESIDENCE.	OF WHAT COUNTRY CITIZENS, OR SUBJECTS.	AGED.	DESCRIPTION OF THEIR PERSONS. HEIGHT. FEET.	INCHES.	COMPLEXION.	HAIR.
S R Easton	,	Massachusetts	United States					
Willm F. Tripp	,	Massachusetts	United States					
Phineas A Leach	,	do	do					
Charles Morris	,	London	Great Britain	Not on board				
Wm Thompson	,	New York	United States					
Marion Louis	,	Bordeaux	France					
Francis Marie	,	do	do					
Simon Horton	,	New York	United States					
Edwin Read	,	do	do					
George Hebbert	,	London	Great Britain					
William Dunbar	,	Philadelphia	United States					

DISTRICT AND PORT OF SAN FRANCISCO.

I, R. S. Easton Master or Commander of the Bark called the Laura of Plymouth Mass now about clearing for the Port of Valparaiso, do solemnly and sincerely swear that the above list contains a true and correct statement of the names of all the Officers and Crew of the said Bark Laura, together with the places of their birth and residence, so far as I have been able to ascertain the same.

Reuben S Easton

Sworn to this 25th day of November 1851, before me,

G W Hopkins

Deputy Collector.

DISTRICT AND PORT OF SAN FRANCISCO.

I, R S Easton Master or Commander of the Bark called the Laura of Plymouth Mass, now about clearing for the Port of Valparaiso, do solemnly and sincerely swear that I have been unable to obtain two-thirds American seamen for the said Bark Laura for her now intended voyage.

Reuben S Easton

Sworn to this 25th day of November 1851, before me,

G W Hopkins

Deputy Collector.

Crew list of vessel departing from San Francisco, 1851. Records of the U.S. Customs Service, Record Group 36.

M972, 1 roll. Information from the records is arranged in several different ways, including alphabetically by name of seaman.

There are, in addition, abstracts of applications for most ports, and this series is the most fruitful for genealogical research.

Abstracts for the port of Baltimore, 1808–67, and the district of Fairfield, Conn., 1801–80, are bound. Other abstracts date from 1815 to 1866. Abstracts show the name, age, physical description, and place of birth of each seaman. There are two 3" × 5" card indexes to these abstracts: one relates to New York City, and the other to most other ports. The indexes are arranged alphabetically by surname of seaman.

In general, the applications and proofs are less rewarding for research than the abstracts, because they pertain to fewer places and require more information to search. Their value as documentary evidence is, however, greater than the abstracts, because they bring the researcher one step closer to the life of the seaman.

All of the records described thus far in this section are in Record Group 36.

Applications for seamen's protection certificates for the years 1916–40 are in Records of the Bureau of Marine Inspection and Navigation, Record Group 41. They are arranged by port and thereunder usually chronologically. Those for San Francisco, however, are arranged alphabetically, and those for New Orleans, in rough alphabetical order. Applications for Boston, New York, and Philadelphia are indexed.

These later applications show name of seaman, age, or date of birth, often place of birth, photograph or personal description, signature or mark, and, if naturalized, date of naturalization and name of court that granted it. Fingerprints are often included in both the application files and the copies of the certificates.

13.3 Crew Lists

An act of 1803 (2 Stat. 203) "for the further protection of American seamen" required masters of American vessels leaving U.S. ports for foreign voyages or arriving at U.S. ports from foreign voyages to file crew lists with collectors of customs. This law did not apply to foreign vessels or to American vessels on coastal voyages. A crew list shows the name, place of birth and residence, and description of each member of the crew.

In Record Group 36 are crew lists for New York, 1803–1919; New Orleans, 1803–1902; Philadelphia, 1803–99; and San Francisco, 1851–99. Crew lists exist for some other ports, mostly for shorter periods in the nineteenth century. The lists are arranged by port, thereunder chronologically, and thereunder by ship. To use crew lists, the researcher must know which ports a particular crew sailed from and approximate dates. Vessel arrival and clearance registers are available for many ports, but they do not necessarily cover the same years as the crew lists for any given port. The registers may help to establish the exact date of arrival or departure of a particular ship and will also supply the name of the master.

Information on the New Orleans crew lists, 1803–25, is also available in Record Group 36 in fifteen volumes of typescripts of the records. The lists show the name of the seaman, rank, state or country of birth, and country of citizenship. In each of the fifteen volumes is a composite alphabetical index to the names of the seamen, names of masters, and names of ships mentioned in the lists in that volume. The indexes and the typescript form of these records make the New Orleans lists for these two decades easier to use than other crew lists.

Two other volumes in this series of typescripts may be valuable if the subject of research was a merchant seaman working in or out of New Orleans. "Flatboats on the Mississippi in 1807" contains typescripts of manifests of vessels for the month of May; they show the name of the master, name of vessel, names of crew members, and cargo. "Returns of Seamen for Marine Hospital Tax" shows names of vessels, masters, and crew members and the length of time crew members were employed. The typescripts of these returns are arranged chronologically and cover the years 1805–33. They pertain to coastal as well as foreign voyages.

Some twentieth-century crew lists in the Records of the Immigration and Naturalization Service (INS), Record Group 85, were microfilmed and destroyed by INS before they were placed in the National Archives, so the microfilm is now the only record. These lists can be used in the Microfilm Research Room of the National Archives Building.

Table 21 shows the ports for which there are crew lists, dates of the lists, and numbers of rolls. Table 21 also shows ports for which there are lists of manifests of aliens employed on vessels as members of the crew. For lists that consist of accessioned microfilm only, no microfilm numbers appear in the table.

13.4 Shipping Articles

Shipping articles are another useful series of records for genealogical information about merchant seamen. Shipping articles are legal contracts between the seaman and the owners of vessels, specifying wages and some working conditions. Shipping articles were required as early as 1790 (1 Stat. 131), but they were not regularly filed with collectors of customs at ports of engagement or discharge until 1840 (5 Stat. 394). An act of 1872 (17 Stat. 262) made shipping commissioners in certain ports responsible for superintending the shipping and discharge of seamen, and these officials largely took over the function of filing the articles from the collectors of customs. In general, shipping articles through 1872 are in Record Group 36, and articles from later years are in Record Group 41, but the dividing date varies from port to port.

Shipping articles show, for each seaman: name, signature or mark, state or country of birth, age, personal description, shipboard occupation, monthly wages, date and place the articles were signed, date and place the seaman was paid (on the "paid-off" copy of the articles only), and, sometimes, name and address of next of kin or some other designated person.

Shipping articles are extant for many ports for varying parts of the overall period 1840–1938. They are arranged

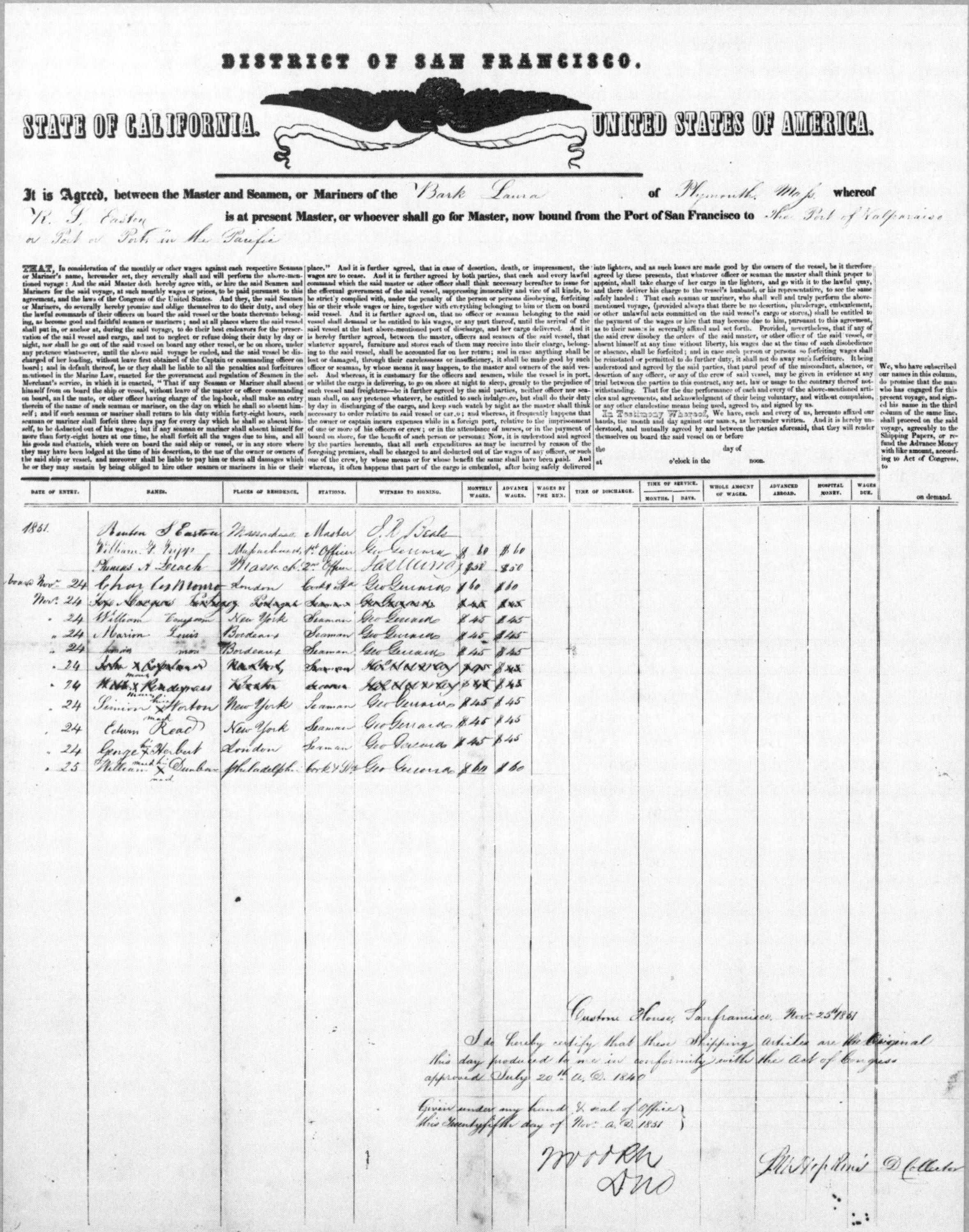

DISTRICT OF SAN FRANCISCO.

STATE OF CALIFORNIA. UNITED STATES OF AMERICA.

It is Agreed, between the Master and Seamen, or Mariners of the Bark Laura of Plymouth Mass. whereof R. S. Easton is at present Master, or whoever shall go for Master, now bound from the Port of San Francisco to the Port of Valparaiso or Port or Ports in the Pacific

THAT, In consideration of the monthly or other wages against each respective Seaman or Mariner's name, hereunder set, they severally shall and will perform the above-mentioned voyage: And the said Master doth hereby agree with, or hire the said Seamen and Mariners for the said voyage, at such monthly wages or prices, to be paid pursuant to this agreement, and the laws of the Congress of the United States. And they, the said Seamen or Mariners, do severally hereby promise and oblige themselves to do their duty, and obey the lawful commands of their officers on board the said vessel or the boats thereunto belonging, as become good and faithful seamen or mariners; and at all places where the said vessel shall put in, or anchor at, during the said voyage, to do their best endeavors for the preservation of the said vessel and cargo, and not to neglect or refuse doing their duty by day or night, nor shall he go out of the said vessel on board any other vessel, or be on shore, under any pretence whatsoever, until the above said voyage be ended, and the said vessel be discharged of her loading, without leave first obtained of the Captain or commanding officer on board; and in default thereof, he or they shall be liable to all the penalties and forfeitures mentioned in the Marine Law, enacted for the government and regulation of Seamen in the Merchant's service, in which it is enacted, "That if any Seaman or Mariner shall absent himself from on board the ship or vessel, without leave of the master or officer commanding on board, and the mate, or other officer having charge of the log-book, shall make an entry therein of the name of such seaman or mariner, on the day on which he shall so absent himself; and if such seaman or mariner shall return to his duty within forty-eight hours, such seaman or mariner shall forfeit three days pay for every day which he shall so absent himself, to be deducted out of his wages; but if any seaman or mariner shall absent himself for more than forty-eight hours at one time, he shall forfeit all the wages due to him, and all his goods and chattels, which were on board the said ship or vessel, or in any store where they may have been lodged at the time of his desertion, to the use of the owner or owners of the said ship or vessel, and moreover shall be liable to pay him or them all damages which he or they may sustain by being obliged to hire other seamen or mariners in his or their place." And it is further agreed, that in case of desertion, death, or impressment, the wages are to cease. And it is further agreed by both parties, that each and every lawful command which the said master or other officer shall think necessary hereafter to issue for the effectual government of the said vessel, suppressing immorality and vice of all kinds, to be strictly complied with, under the penalty of the person or persons disobeying, forfeiting his or their whole wages or hire, together with everything belonging to him or them on board said vessel. And it is further agreed on, that no officer or seaman belonging to the said vessel shall demand or be entitled to his wages, or any part thereof, until the arrival of the said vessel at the last above-mentioned port of discharge, and her cargo delivered. And it is hereby further agreed, between the master, officers and seamen of the said vessel, that whatever apparel, furniture and stores each of them may receive into their charge, belonging to the said vessel, shall be accounted for on her return; and in case anything shall be lost or damaged, through their carelessness or insufficiency, it shall be made good by such officer or seaman, by whose means it may happen, to the master and owners of the said vessel. And whereas, it is customary for the officers and seamen, while the vessel is in port, or whilst the cargo is delivering, to go on shore at night to sleep, greatly to the prejudice of such vessel and freighters—be it further agreed by the said parties, neither officer nor seaman shall, on any pretence whatever, be entitled to such indulgence, but shall do their duty by day in discharging of the cargo, and keep such watch by night as the master shall think necessary to order relative to said vessel or cargo; and whereas, it frequently happens that the owner or captain incurs expenses while in a foreign port, relative to the imprisonment of one or more of his officers or crew; or in the attendance of nurses, or in the payment of board on shore, for the benefit of such person or persons: Now, it is understood and agreed by the parties hereunto, that all such expenditures as may be incurred by reason of the foregoing premises, shall be charged to and deducted out of the wages of any officer, or such one of the crew, by whose means or for whose benefit the same shall have been paid. And whereas, it often happens that part of the cargo is embezzled, after being safely delivered into lighters, and as such losses are made good by the owners of the vessel, be it therefore agreed by these presents, that whatever officer or seaman the master shall think proper to appoint, shall take charge of her cargo in the lighters, and go with it to the lawful quay, and there deliver his charge to the vessel's husband, or his representative, to see the same safely landed: That each seaman or mariner, who shall well and truly perform the above-mentioned voyage, (provided always that there be no desertion, plunderage, embezzlement, or other unlawful acts committed on the said vessel's cargo or stores,) shall be entitled to the payment of the wages or hire that may become due to him, pursuant to this agreement, as to their names is severally affixed and set forth. Provided, nevertheless, that if any of the said crew disobey the orders of the said master, or other officer of the said vessel, or absent himself at any time without liberty, his wages due at the time of such disobedience or absence, shall be forfeited; and in case such person or persons so forfeiting wages shall be reinstated or permitted to do further duty, it shall not do away such forfeiture. It being understood and agreed by the said parties, that parol proof of the misconduct, absence, or desertion of any officer, or any of the crew of said vessel, may be given in evidence at any trial between the parties to this contract, any act, law or usage to the contrary thereof notwithstanding. That for the due performance of each and every of the above-mentioned articles and agreements, and acknowledgment of their being voluntary, and without compulsion, or any other clandestine means being used, agreed to, and signed by us.

In Testimony Whereof, We have, each and every of us, hereunto affixed our hands, the month and day against our names, as hereunder written. And it is hereby understood, and mutually agreed by and between the parties aforesaid, that they will render themselves on board the said vessel on or before

the day of

at o'clock in the noon.

We, who have subscribed our names in this column, do promise that the man who has engaged for this present voyage, and signed his name in the third column of the same line, shall proceed on the said voyage, agreeably to the Shipping Papers, or refund the Advance Money with like amount, according to Act of Congress, to

DATE OF ENTRY.	NAMES.	PLACES OF RESIDENCE.	STATIONS.	WITNESS TO SIGNING.	MONTHLY WAGES.	ADVANCE WAGES.	WAGES BY THE RUN.	TIME OF DISCHARGE.	TIME OF SERVICE. MONTHS.	TIME OF SERVICE. DAYS.	WHOLE AMOUNT OF WAGES.	ADVANCED ABROAD.	HOSPITAL MONEY.	WAGES DUE.	on demand.
1851.	Reuben S Easton	Massachusetts	Master	S. R. Beale											
	William F. Tripp	Massachusetts,	1st Officer	Geo Gerrard	$ 60	$ 60									
	Francis A. Leach	Massach.	2nd Officer	[illegible]	$ 50	$ 50									
[illegible] Nov. 24	Charles Monro	London	Cook & Stw	Geo Gerrard	$ 60	$ 60									
Nov. 24	[illegible]	Portugal	Seaman	[illegible]	$ 45	$ 45									
" 24	William Thompson	New York	Seaman	Geo Gerrard	$ 45	$ 45									
" 24	Marion Louis	Bordeaux	Seaman	Geo Gerrard	$ 45	$ 45									
" 24	Louis [illegible]	Bordeaux	Seaman	Geo Gerrard	$ 45	$ 45									
" 24	John X [illegible]	[illegible]	Seaman	[illegible]	$ 45	$ 45									
" 24	[illegible] X [illegible]	[illegible]	Seaman	[illegible]	$ 45	$ 45									
" 24	Simon his X mark Horton	New York	Seaman	Geo Gerrard	$ 45	$ 45									
" 24	Edwin Read	New York	Seaman	Geo Gerrard	$ 45	$ 45									
" 24	George his X mark Herbert	London	Seaman	Geo Gerrard	$ 45	$ 45									
" 25	William his X mark Dunbar	Philadelphia	Cook & Stw	Geo Gerrard	$ 60	$ 60									

Custom House, Sanfrancisco, Nov. 25th 1851

I do hereby certify that these Shipping Articles are the Original this day produced to me in conformity with the Act of Congress approved July 20th A. D. 1840

Given under my hand & seal of Office this Twentyfifth day of Nov. A. D. 1851

[illegible] Hopkins D Collector

Shipping articles, San Francisco. Records of the U.S. Customs Bureau, Record Group 36.

by port, and thereunder chronologically, with some variations. To use them, the researcher must know where and when the subject of research was hired as a merchant seaman. Shipping articles after 1872 for New York, Philadelphia, Boston, Baltimore, and San Francisco are indexed by ship or arranged in rough alphabetical order.

Shipping articles and crew lists for the port of San Francisco in the periods 1854–56, 1861–62, 1883–86, and 1900–50 are at the archives branch, FARC San Francisco. They are arranged chronologically, and thereunder alphabetically by name of ship. The branch also has a register of discharges, 1883–84, that lists in chronological order discharges of seamen at the completion of voyages.

Crew bonds were required of each master of vessels as an assurance that, at the time of the vessel's return to a U.S. port, he would account for all persons named on a verified list that had been delivered to the collector of customs when the vessel departed from the United States. The San Francisco branch has bonds for San Francisco for 1896, arranged chronologically.

13.5 Logbooks

Official logbooks of U.S. flag vessels, primarily ships engaged in foreign trade from the late nineteenth century through 1938, are in Record Group 41. The logbooks contain names, occupations, and ratings of the performance or ability of the crew members, and slop accounts, or expenditures of crew members for personal items while on board.

Also required by law to be entered in logbooks were records of offenses committed by crew members; inquiries, illnesses, deaths, and births that occurred during a voyage; changes in crew, and deductions from seamen's wages or sale of their effects.

Typically, logbooks are arranged by port of arrival, and thereunder sometimes by date of deposit and sometimes alphabetically by name of vessel. To use the logbooks, researchers should know the name of the ship and the port and approximate date of arrival. Access to the logbooks requires the permission of the U.S. Coast Guard.

13.6 Other Records

In Record Group 26 at the archives branch, FARC Kansas City, are records relating to the enrollment of vessels and licensing of crews at several inland ports. Vessel documentation may sometimes be useful in establishing the name and residence of the owner, master, or captain of the vessel at the time of enrollment. Casualty reports or investigations may also contain some personal information.

For the port of Duluth, there are masters' oaths for renewal, 1901–40. Included in the oaths is the citizenship status of the master; if naturalized, the state, court, and date of naturalization are given.

For the port of Dubuque, there are indexes, 1870–1910, to various types of individual licenses; individual license files, 1917–55, arranged alphabetically; and stubs, 1905–59, from licenses of engineers, masters, pilots, mates, and operators.

For the port of Galena, there are operators' license stubs, 1870–1910; for the port of St. Louis, masters' oaths for renewal, 1870–1948; and for the port of St. Paul, operators' license stubs, 1879–1895.

Reports of persons hired for ships of the Quartermaster Department and the U.S. Army Transport Service are described on page 216. The records from the Office of the U.S. Shipping Commissioner at San Francisco include shipping articles for U.S. Army transports for 1898–1920. They are in Records of the U.S. Shipping Board, Record Group 32.

CHAPTER 14

Records of Civilian Government Employees

14.1 Introduction

The National Archives has many records relating to civilian employees of the executive and judicial branches of the federal government. Personnel records are in many record groups, often in the record group set up for the general headquarters records of an executive department, such as the General Records of the Department of State, Record Group 59. There are no consolidated civilian personnel files among the records of the National Archives.

The types and dates of records vary from agency to agency. They include letters of application, recommendation or endorsement, and acceptance; registers of appointment; oaths of office; surety bonds for bonded officials; commissions; and letters of resignation. Most are dated from the time of the establishment of the agency to about 1910.

For many years, the federal government issued an annual or biennial list of its employees, civilian and military, at first including every person on federal payrolls down to the lowest paid laborer or charwoman. The earliest issue of this *Official Register*, or Blue Book, was entitled *Register of Officials and Agents* and was published in 1816 by the State Department. From 1816 to 1907, the official register was generally issued under varying titles but in the same form, showing the officials and employees by departments and divisions in tabular arrangement, with a name index, and often listing such information as office, place of birth, place of appointment, place employed, and financial compensation. The number of names listed increased steadily from 6,327 in 1816 to 349,000 in 1907. In 1921, the Bureau of the Census issued the last comprehensive edition of the *Official Register* listing all employees in the civil service (C3.10:921). After 1921, the *Official Register* listed only those civil servants in administrative positions, and in 1959 the publication was discontinued altogether. (S1.11:, I1.25:, C3.10:, CS1.31).

The National Personnel Records Center, Civilian Personnel Records (NCPC), 111 Winnebago Street, St. Louis, MO 63118, maintains most extant personnel folders for federal employees whose employmet ended after about 1910. Records less than 75 years old are closed to public examination. A researcher requesting a record from NCPC should provide the full name of the employee, date of birth, social security number if known, name of the agency where last employed, and place and approximate date of employment.

Most records relating to civilian employees give full name, position held, agency, and place and terminal dates of employment. Some also show state, territory, or country of birth; age; place from which appointed; and salary. Letters of application and letters of recommendation may include considerable biographical information, such as the name of a relative of the applicant and the nature of the applicant's previous employment and political activity. The amount of material in a file varies considerably and sometimes is voluminous if the position sought was an important one.

The arrangement of civilian personnel records is usually complex. Surety bonds, other than those relating to postmasters, are filed together. Record cards for bonds dated 1789–1910 and for those dated 1911–15 are arranged alphabetically by name of bonded official. A few agencies filed letters of application with letters of recommendation or other personnel records in separate name files. In other cases, letters of application and recommendation are interfiled in large correspondence series that may be inadequately indexed. Many other records relating to employment with a government agency are arranged by type of record and thereunder chronologically; they are generally not indexed. Even in the best research circumstances, where good indexes or finding aids exist, the researcher must know which department or agency employed the subject of research and the approximate dates of service.

Described in this chapter are letters of application and recommendation of the State and Treasury Departments, appointment files and other records of the Justice Department, appointment records of postmasters, Interior Department appointment papers, Internal Revenue Service rosters, records of applicants and civilian employees of the War Department, records of medical personnel who served the War Department, reports of persons and articles hired and other records of the Quartermaster Department, records of civilian employees of the navy, and records of employees of the Confederate government. Records of employees of the government of the District of Columbia are described in chapter 18. Records of employees of some Indian agencies are in the custody of the various archives branches; these records are described in chapter 11.

14.2 U.S. Government Employees

14.2.1 Department of State

State Department **letters of application and recommendation** relate to appointments under the jurisdiction of the Department, 1797–1901, and to Foreign Service officers, 1901–24. There are also letters related to positions in other executive departments in the early years of the federal government. The letters are arranged by Presidential administration, and thereunder alphabetically by applicant's name. Letters from 1901 to 1924 are arranged alphabetically. They are part of Record Group 59.

Applications and recommendations for office during the presidency of George Washington are in the custody of the Manuscript Division of the Library of Congress. State Department application and recommendation files for the administrations of John Adams through Ulysses S. Grant are available as microfilm publications, as shown in table 22. The descriptive pamphlet that accompanies each microfilm publication lists the name of each person for whom there is a file and cites the roll on which the file is filmed.

A useful publication issued by the Department of State is the Foreign Service list. Beginning in 1898, the *Diplomatic and Consular Service of the United States* gives, for each member: name, rank, residence, place of birth, place appointed from, date of the commission, annual compensation, and to what country accredited. Each issue of this publication contains an index of places and an index of names. After 1929, the title in this series changed to the *Foreign Service List*. The list provides information on assignments of Foreign Service and other U.S. personnel in the field. It includes chiefs of missions, Foreign Service officers, and consular agents as well as the Agency for In-

TABLE 22

Microfilmed State Department Letters of Application and Recommendation

Presidential Administration	Dates	Microfilm publication	Number of rolls
John Adams	1797–1801	M406	3
Thomas Jefferson	1801–9	M418	12
James Madison	1809–17	M438	8
James Monroe	1817–25	M439	19
John Quincy Adams	1825–29	M531	8
Andrew Jackson	1829–37	M639	27
Martin Van Buren, William Henry Harrison, and John Tyler	1837–45	M687	35
James Polk, Zachary Taylor, and Millard Fillmore	1845–53	M873	98
Franklin Pierce and James Buchanan	1853–61	M967	50
Abraham Lincoln and Andrew Johnson	1861–69	M650	53
Ulysses S. Grant	1869–77	M968	69

ternational Development, the Peace Corps, the U.S. Information Agency and others (S1.7:).

The *Register of the Department of State* (S1.6) can also be consulted.

14.2.2 Department of the Treasury

Letters of application and recommendation for positions in the Treasury Department date from about 1833 to 1910. Files for bureau heads and other headquarters staff are arranged alphabetically by personal name. Files for field staff are arranged by name of bureau or title of position (such as Bureau of Internal Revenue or Collector of Customs), thereunder by state, thereunder by district or city, and thereunder alphabetically by personal name. To use them, you must first know the name and location of the position for which the subject of your research applied. Both series of records are part of Record Group 56.

In Records of the Internal Revenue Service, Record Group 58, at the archives branch, FARC Chicago, is a roster of officers and employees of the 1st District of Michigan (Detroit). The roster gives the name, rank, post office address, compensation, date of appointment, date and cause of termination of service, birthplace and date, military service, and names of relatives employed by the government and where employed.

The archives branch, FARC Kansas City, has rosters of officers and employees of the 6th Collection District of Missouri (Kansas City), 1881–1921. Included are each person's name, rank (job title), post office address, compensation, date of appointment, date and cause of termination of employment, date and place of birth, period and nature of civil service, information concerning military service, and names of relatives employed by the government and the places of their employment.

14.2.3 Department of Justice

Two series of appointment files for the Department of Justice, Record Group 60, contain information about applicants for positions in the Justice Department. **Appointments of federal judges, marshals, and attorneys,** 1853–1901, are primarily applications and endorsements for positions in the judicial districts. They are arranged by judicial district and thereunder chronologically by Presidential administration and then alphabetically by name. To use them, the researcher must know where and when the subject of research sought a position. Parts of this series are available as microfilm publications: *Records Relating to the Appointment of Federal Judges, Attorneys, and Marshals for the Territory and State of Idaho, 1861–99,* M681, 9 rolls; . . . *Oregon, 1853–1903,* M224, 2 rolls; . . . *Utah, 1853–1901,* M680, 14 rolls; and . . . *Washington, 1853–1902,* M198, 17 rolls.

The pamphlet that accompanies each microfilm publication contains an alphabetical list of persons for whom files are extant. In a similar series, **applications and endorsements,** 1901–33, are files about federal judges, marshals, attorneys, and other field staff arranged by judicial district and thereunder by office and alphabetically by personal name. To locate a particular name, the researcher must know the position the person applied for, its location, and the date of application.

Two microfilm publications are useful to the genealogist searching for records relating to U.S. marshals and deputy marshals. *Index to Names of United States Marshals, 1789–1960,* T577, 1 roll, is an alphabetical list giving dates and places of service, information required for the use of most of the other pertinent series in Record Group 60. *Letters Sent by the Department of Justice: Instructions to U.S. Attorneys and Marshals, 1867–1904,* M701, 212 rolls, is also available.

The correspondence of U.S. marshals occasionally includes lists of deputies, oaths of office, and other references to deputies. Other than the *Annual Reports of the Attorney General,* which from 1897 to 1921 contain lists of office and field deputies, and the *Registers of the Department of Justice,* which frequently list office deputies, there is no general name index for deputy marshals. The one major Department of Justice series relating to deputies is appointment correspondence about U.S. deputy marshals, 1898–1937. These records are arranged by judicial district, and thereunder chronologically. The researcher must be able to supply the dates and place of the subject's service as a deputy marshal.

Although the majority of letters described in the following five series pertain to substantive issues and cases, there is considerable information about individual marshals and deputies, including oaths of office, resignations, and requests for leave.

Attorney general's papers, 1789–1870, are letters received by the attorney general, most dating after 1818. They are arranged by source of correspondence such as the President, Senate and House of Representatives, various executive offices, and judicial district officials, including U.S. marshals. Chronological registers of letters received can be searched to locate references to particular letters. A few of the registers are indexed.

Source chronological files, 1871–84, are letters received by the Department of Justice, arranged by source of correspondence. Registers of letters received are available. Parts of this series have been microfilmed: *Letters Received by the Department of Justice from the State of Louisiana, 1871–1884,* M940, 6 rolls; *Letters Received by the Department of Justice From the State of South Carolina, 1871–1884,* M947, 9 rolls; and *Letters Received by the Department of Justice From Mississippi, 1871–1884,* M970, 4 rolls.

Year files, 1884–1903, are letters received by the Department of Justice, primarily from judicial district officials. They are arranged numerically by subject or case file number with registers and indexes available.

Numerical files, 1904–37, are letters received and copies of letters sent by the Department of Justice. The series overlaps the classified subject files, described next. Most of the correspondence is from judicial district officials. The letters are arranged numerically by subject or case file number. Finding aids include volume indexes to 1908; a card index to letters received and sent, 1908–10; a card index for persons, concerns, and subjects, 1910–20; a card index for persons, 1917–33; and record slips of correspondence, 1910–46, arranged by source.

Classified subject files, 1914–41 and 1945–49, are letters received and sent; the series overlaps the numerical files, 1904–37. The letters are arranged numerically by class number; for example, class 5 relates to tax violations, and class 60, to antitrust violations. Finding aids for numerical files also are used for this series.

The *Register of the Department of Justice and the Judicial Officers of the United States; Including Instructions to Marshalls, District Attorneys, and Clerks of the United States Courts (1885–1970)* was compiled by authority of the attorney general. The forty-six volumes in this series in the Publications of the U.S. Government, Record Group 287, list the name, office, place of birth, place appointed from, where employed, annual compensation, and date of appointment for virtually all civil servants in the Justice Department for the given year. (J1.7:).

14.2.4 Post Office Department

The appointments of postmasters are documented in a **record of the first returns** (quarterly account statements) received from postmasters by the postmaster general, 1789–1818, and in **registers of the appointment of postmasters,** 1815–30 September 1971. The records are in Records of the Post Office Department, Record Group 28.

The first returns give the dates of the returns, the names of the post offices and the states in which they were situated, and the names of the postmasters. The approximate dates of appointment of the postmasters can sometimes be found in the letter books of the postmaster general. The appointment registers give the names of the post offices, their states and counties, the dates of establishment and discontinuance of the post offices, and the names and dates of appointment of the postmasters. The registers for the period 1832–1971 are arranged alphabetically by state and county and are available on microfilm: *Records of Appointment of Postmasters, 1832–September 30, 1971,* M841, 145 rolls. The earlier registers are arranged alphabetically by post office and are available on microfilm: *Records of Appointment of Postmasters, October 1789–1832,* M1131, 4 rolls.

The earliest listing of postmasters, a general term which apparently described persons performing all the functions necessary to a local post office, including mail carriers, can be found in the *Official Register* for 1816. On 18 January 1820, Postmaster General R. J. Meigs, presented to the House of Representatives a list of twenty-one clerks employed in the post office at salaries from $800 to $1,700 and a list of contracts for carrying the mail, drawn up by the postmaster general in the year 1819. This second list shows the names of 312 contractors for carrying mail, indicates their state, the sums paid to them, and the locality and numbers of their routes (Serial 33). Later lists of mail contractors or mail carriers continued to be published in the Congressional Serial Set with additional information as late as 1841. (Serial 33–54, 53–87, 66–64, 82–104, 103–159, 118–99, 140–171, 153–121, 167–177, 174–258, 187–135, 197–77, 209/1–117, 220–212, 242–408, 274–175, 290–203, 299–222, 304–182, 326–139, 341–254, 392–54).

For the years following 1841, the *Official Register* will provide lists of postmasters.

14.2.5 Department of the Interior

Appointment papers of the Interior Department date from 1849 to 1907. The files are arranged by name of state or territory, thereunder by name of bureau, thereunder by name of place, and thereunder by personal name. There are some indexes. The files are part of Record Group 48. Interior Department appointment papers for some states are available as microfilm publications, as shown in table 23.

14.2.6 War Department

Records of the Office of the Secretary of War, Record Group 107, includes a number of series relating to applications for civilian jobs in the War Department, appointments to positions, and careers of employees. Arrangement of the different series varies considerably; many are not indexed. To use them, a researcher needs to know approximately when and where the subject of research worked for the War Department and sometimes the subject's legal state of residence.

Registers of applications and application papers are dated 1820–1903. Entries in the registers generally show the applicant's name and place of birth, position desired, names of persons submitting letters of recommendation on behalf of the applicant, and whether the application papers were filed in the Office of the Secretary of War or forwarded to another War Department bureau.

The application files themselves vary greatly in size and in the quantity of genealogical information they contain. Some simply consist of a single letter from the applicant requesting a civilian position in the War Department or a commission in the army. Other more extensive files may contain letters of recommendation, oaths of allegiance, letters of appointment, and copies of replies the War Department sent to the applicant or to persons recommending him. Such files might show the applicant's name, place of birth, current residence, and information concerning education, former military service, general character, profession, political ties, health, previous job experience, and the military service or political affiliation of relatives.

Series containing applications for civilian appointments in the War Department include the following: applications for War Department appointments, 1820–46; applications for commissions and civilian appointments, 1847–70 and 1872–82; applications for civilian positions in the War Department, 1898–1902; and applications for positions as laborers and charwomen, 1901–3. Files are generally arranged alphabetically by surname of applicant and pertain to requests for such positions as Indian agents, sutlers, watchmen, pension agents, clerks, messengers, copyists, librarians, scouts, guides, surveyors, stenographers, bookkeepers, and typists.

Entries in **registers and lists of appointments** and employees, 1863–1913, may show the employee's name, state from which appointed, date of appointment, position, office to which appointed, and remarks that indicate dates of promotions, transfers, details, reductions in salary, resignation, discharge, or death. The series include registers of civilian War Department employees stationed in Washington, D.C., 1863–94 and 1898–1908; registers of civilian War Department employees, 1885–94 and 1898–1913; printed annual registers of civilian War Department employees in Washington, D.C., 1885–1909; registers of appointments and changes in the status of civilian War Department employees, 1894–1901, 1903–9, and 1911–13; lists of civilian War Department appointments in Cuba, Puerto Rico, and the Philippine Islands, 1898–1900; and registers of appointments and changes in the status of temporary employees in the War Department, 1902–5.

Lists and registers of applications and appointments for civilian employees similar to these described for Record Group 107 are also found among the records of the various War Department bureaus, including those of the Chief of Engineers, Record Group 77; the Quartermaster General, Record Group 92; the Adjutant General, Record Group 94; the Surgeon General (Army), Record Group 112; the Freedmen's Bureau, Record Group 105; the Provost Marshal (Civil War), Record Group 110; the Paymaster General, Record Group 99; and the Chief of Ordnance, Record Group 156. The records for each of these offices generally include lists and registers of applications and appointments as described above. This guide does not describe these records for each office.

Some of the **records of the Appointment, Commission, and Personal Branch** in Record Group 94 relate to civilian employees of the army and the War Department. There are applications for appointments, 1871–80, twelve volumes of registers of these applications, and a two-volume name index to the registers and applications. Most of these records concern applications for military commissions, but there are applications for some civilian positions such as post trader and military cemetery superintendent. The index will supply appropriate entries in the registers of applications. A register entry gives the name of the applicant, rank or residence, date of the application, position applied for, who recommended the applicant, and the action taken. The actual applications are arranged by year and thereunder numerically; the file numbers are given in the registers of applications.

Other records of civilian employment. There are personal histories of civilian War Department employees stationed in Washington, D.C., 1882–94. The histories are on standard forms and include name, birthplace, and legal voting residence (state, county, and congressional district) of employee; past military service; disabilities; marital status; number of dependents; date of original appointment in the War Department; names of persons submitting letters of recommendation; age and occupation when appointed; current position title and grade; home address in Washington, D.C.; the War Department bureau and building to which assigned; and names and places of employment of relatives in government service. Because the records are arranged by state and thereunder by name, a researcher must know the state of legal residence to locate the history for a specific employee.

Information about civilians and civilian employees is also interspersed among the Secretary of War's letters received and general correspondence. Available on microfilm are *Letters Received by the Secretary of War, Main Series, 1801–1870,* M221, 317 rolls, and *Letters Received by the Secretary of War, Unregistered Series, 1789–1861,* M222, 34 rolls. The corresponding registers of letters received, containing abstracts of the letters, are available on microfilm as *Registers of Letters Received by the Office of the Secretary of War, Main Series, 1800–1870,* M22, 134 rolls. Book indexes are reproduced as *Indexes to Letters Received by the Secretary of War, 1861–1870,* M495, 14 rolls. There is also a card

TABLE 23

Microfilmed Interior Department Appointment Papers

State or territory	Dates	Microfilm publication	Number of rolls
Arizona	1857–1907	M576	22
California	1849–1907	M732	29
Colorado	1857–1907	M808	13
Florida	1849–1907	M1119	6
Idaho	1862–1907	M693	17
Mississippi	1849–1907	M849	4
Missouri	1849–1907	M1058	9
Nevada	1860–1907	M1033	3
New Mexico	1850–1907	M750	18
New York	1849–1906	M1022	5
North Carolina	1849–92	M950	1
Oregon	1849–1907	M814	10
Wyoming	1869–1907	M830	6

index to the general correspondence for the period 1890–1913 that is not microfilmed.

Additional records relating to civilian employees are scattered throughout the letters received and general correspondence of the Adjutant General's Office in Record Group 94. To make a thorough search of these files, however, it is generally necessary to know where and for whom the subject of research worked and the period of employment. The letters received have been microfilmed and are available as *Letters Received by the Office of the Adjutant General (Main Series), 1805–1821,* M566, 144 rolls; *1822–1860,* M567, 636 rolls; *1861–1870,* M619, 828 rolls; *1871–1880,* M666, 593 rolls; and *1880–1889,* M689, 740 rolls. Available indexes and other finding aids for the letters received include *Registers of Letters Received by the Office of the Adjutant General (Main Series), 1812–1889,* M711, 85 rolls, and *Indexes to Letters Received by the Office of the Adjutant General (Main Series),' 1846, 1861–1889,* M725, 9 rolls. An extensive name and subject index to the general correspondence has been reproduced as *Index to General Correspondence of the Adjutant General's Office, 1890–1917,* M698, 1,269 rolls.

Record Group 94 includes several series relating to **civilian medical personnel**. In the nineteenth and early twentieth centuries, the U.S. Army frequently relied on the services of civilian physicians and surgeons to supplement the small number of regular army medical officers. The **personal papers** of these contract medical officers and surgeons, ca. 1820–1917, is a large series that constitutes an important genealogical resource. Arranged in individual jackets alphabetically by name of physician, the files include copies of contracts into which the physicians entered (showing date, salary, assignment, and contracting parties); personal reports giving duty station and responsibility by months; correspondence relating to applications for appointment, for renewal of contract, or for termination of employment (annulment of contract); and miscellaneous biographical information, such as postemployment residences and date of death. The volume and value of the documentation vary considerably among the various jackets, the majority of which are for physicians who served during the Civil War, 1861–65.

Several smaller series can be used to search for a physician whose approximate dates of service are known. They deal with contract surgeons including seven volumes of chronologically arranged copies of contracts, 1839–49 and 1861–65; alphabetically arranged pay accounts, ca. 1820–94, but primarily 1861–65; eleven numerically arranged volumes pertaining to contracts, with two accompanying name index volumes, 1847–92; station cards of acting assistant surgeons, 1862–68, and 1898–1901, arranged alphabetically by name of physician, which provide information on dates of contract and service and duty stations; a one-volume record of Civil War contract surgeons arranged by hospital, which provides name of surgeon, dates of contract and service, and post office address; and a one-volume chronologically arranged record of accounts, 1865. One volume in a three-volume series of alphabetically arranged address books, 1860–94, pertains to contract surgeons.

The researcher who knows the name of the command in which a contract surgeon served, as well as the approximate dates of service, can use three series of monthly returns of medical officers: sixty-four volumes, 1859–86, arranged by command and thereunder chronologically; twenty-five feet of unbound records, 1861–65, arranged by state or command, and thereunder chronologically; and seventeen feet of unbound records, 1898–1909, arranged by command, and thereunder chronologically. The records give the name of the surgeon, date of contract, post or station, and organization of troops with which he served—information that may only make previous knowledge more exact.

Records relating to contract surgeons, 1862–1915, are also in Record Group 112.

There is a series of cards containing service records of **hospital attendants, matrons, and nurses,** 1861–65. The cards are arranged by initial letter of surname and include information on dates of employment, capacity in which hired, salary, and place of employment. Female personnel are represented by returns of hospital matrons, 1876–87, arranged by post, department, or division, and thereunder chronologically; these provide name of individual matron and, for posts only, date of appointment. Other records relating to contract nurses during the Spanish-American War and to matrons, cooks, and laundresses during the Civil War and during the period 1893–1904 are also found in Record Group 112.

Quartermaster officers throughout the United States were required to submit to the Quartermaster General in Washington monthly reports, listing by name all persons employed by them and all articles hired. These **reports of persons and articles hired,** covering the period 1818–1913, are perhaps the single most important source of information about civilian employees of the Quartermaster Department found in the National Archives. They are part of Record Group 92. The report forms were originally drawn by hand, but printed blanks were introduced in 1856 and by 1861 had entirely superseded the handwritten forms. The format and content of the reports were remarkably uniform throughout the entire period, generally providing in columns the following information about each employee: full name, inclusive dates of monthly service, number of days employed, rate of compensation, date of contract, amount paid or due, and occupation. The rate of compensation was normally based on a uniform time segment (day, month, or year), but occasionally a different basis, such as (in the case of dispatch riders) the number of trips made or packages carried, was used. Various occupations are listed, but most fall under a few broad categories, such as office employees (clerks); construction workers (carpenters, joiners, masons, laborers); blacksmiths, farriers, hostlers, and other occupations related to the care of horses and draft animals; transport workers (teamsters, wagonmasters, draymen); and certain specialized occupations (scouts, guides, interpreters, telegraph operators).

The main series of persons and articles hired consists of more than 1,500 feet of records dated 1818–1905. It is arranged chronologically by year, and thereunder alphabetically by surname of the reporting officer, 1818–60, or numerically, 1861–1905. Genealogical research in this series is difficult because to use it the researcher must know the name of the employing quartermaster. A researcher who knows the post or station at which the subject of research was hired and the approximate dates of employment, however, may find that several finding aids, though incomplete, can help identify the quartermaster: a one-volume register of reports, 1834–60, arranged by year, thereunder alphabetically by name of reporting officer to 1849, and then alphabetically by station; a seventeen-volume reporting officer index for the period 1861–94, arranged by time period, and thereunder alphabetically; an incomplete two-volume index to stations, 1861–67, arranged by station (but not alphabetically), and thereunder chronologically; and a card index to names of reporting officers, ca. 1898–1905, arranged by station in two subseries (Philippine Islands and non-Philippines), and thereunder chronologically.

Direct access by name of employee is possible for a few brief time periods through specialized finding aids, which are also incomplete. For the years 1898–1902, there is an alphabetical card index to employees entered in the reports, and there is an alphabetical card index to names of men employed as scouts and in related occupations. There is an alphabetical card index to men employed in the Mississippi Marine Brigade and Ram Fleet, July–September 1863, and a similar one-volume list for the period May–July 1864. The index entries give the names of reporting officers. For 1861 only, the Quartermaster Department compiled individual employment service cards (similar to compiled military service records) for the civilian employees listed in the reports of persons and articles hired. These **"Record of Personal Services" cards** are arranged alphabetically by name of employee.

Additional reports of persons and articles hired are found among the quartermaster records of the Mexican War, 1846–48, arranged by name of reporting officer, and among the surviving records of individual quartermaster officers, 1837–97, generally arranged chronologically. Again, the researcher must know the name of the quartermaster and dates. Additional reports, arranged chronologically, are sometimes found among the quartermaster records of the geographical departments into which the post-Civil War army was divided; for example, the Department of Dakota, 1872–1900, and the Department of the Platte, 1866–96. To use them, the researcher must know which army command hired the subject of research.

The reports of persons and articles hired for the ships of the **Army Transport Service,** 1898–1913, were removed by the Quartermaster Department from the main series and are now maintained separately with other related records. They are arranged in three subseries by type of vessel (mine planters, short-term transports, major transports), thereunder alphabetically by name of vessel, and thereunder chronologically by date of report. To find information about an individual serving aboard ship, the researcher must know the type and name of the vessel and the approximate period of employment.

There are two finding aids to the quartermaster ships mentioned in the reports. For the Civil War period, 1861–65, there is a one-volume alphabetical index to names of vessels, while for the period 1898–1901, there is a similar alphabetical card index. Both finding aids were prepared before the segregation of the Army Transport Service reports and, therefore, refer to file numbers in the main series. However, cross-references in the main series direct researchers to the Army Transport Service reports of persons and articles hired.

Other records of the U.S. Army Transport Service relate to individuals. There is a vessel card index to correspondence relating to crews of the service, which refers to the general correspondence (or "Document File") of the Office of the Quartermaster General, 1890–1914. Also available are one list of crews and "Persons and Articles Transferred on or Between Army Transports, 1906–09," on which entries are arranged alphabetically by name of vessel; lists of vessels and crews, 1898–1913, arranged alphabetically by name of vessel; unarranged records entitled "Name of Ships Officers and Time of Entering Service, 1898–1899"; lists of officers, engineers, masters, and stevedores employed in the U.S. Army Transport Service, 1899–1900, unarranged; a list of applications for positions on U.S. Army transports and notes on former employees ineligible to be rehired, 1900–1, chronologically arranged; a record of employees discharged from the U.S. Army Transport Service, 1907–13, arranged alphabetically by name of discharged employee; shipping articles or articles of agreement between masters and seamen in the Merchant Service of the United States, 1898–1906, arranged alphabetically by U.S. Army Transport Service vessel, and thereunder chronologically; and crew lists of the U.S. Army Transport Service and correspondence relating to them, 1899–1901, unarranged. (Also, among the records of the U.S. Shipping Commissioner at San Francisco are shipping articles for U.S. Army transports for 1898–1920. They are in Records of the Bureau of Marine Inspection and Navigation, Record Group 41.)

Another large series of records of the Office of the Quartermaster General, the **consolidated correspondence file,** 1784–1890, also contains information about regular employees of the Quartermaster Department, as well as records about many other diverse subjects. Using the series is easier because it is arranged alphabetically by name and subject. If there is a file about the subject of your research, it might contain such records as applications for employment; requests for promotion, transfer, and reinstatement; reports of disciplinary action and investigation; oaths of appointment providing age, date of birth, marital status, or residence; and receipts for wages.

For the period 1891–1914, there is a **general correspondence file relating to personnel**. Record cards for that correspondence provide summaries or full texts of the letters or documents pertaining to an individual. These series are arranged chronologically under one or more file numbers. You will find information similar to that in the earlier consolidated correspondence file, 1794–1890. However, because arrangement is numerical rather than alphabetical, the researcher must first consult the alphabetical name and subject card index to the general correspondence to obtain the file designations for the correspondence or record cards relating to the subject of research.

14.2.7 Department of the Navy

Many series in Record Group 45 and Record Group 80 contain records of civilian employees of the Navy Department. These series are variously arranged, but some of them contain name indexes. To use the records, the researcher must know approximately when the subject of research held or applied for a position.

Records of applicants usually show name of applicant, date of application, and type of position applied for. Registers of applications for civilian positions, 1834–71, also show the applicant's state of residence and contain name indexes, except for the period January 1854–May 1864. There are letters of application and recommendation for civilian positions at navy yards, 1839–42, arranged by date of application. There are lists for 1849 and abstracts and information for 1853 concerning applicants for civilian positions, with an incomplete name index. In a register pertaining to clerkships, 1872–74, entries are arranged according to type (applications received, candidates eligible for examination, and candidates examined). Additional information in an entry in this register includes the applicant's age and state of residence.

Records of appointment and discharge contain letters of appointment sent to civilian employees, 1825–55; lists of appointments of acting assistant paymasters, 1861–65; press copies of letters sent appointing and discharging civilian employees, 1882–86; and notices of appointments sent by the chief clerk to the auditor for the navy, 1904–11. There are name indexes to the letters of appointment, except for letters for the period 1882–86, which are arranged chronologically. The records contain names of employees and types of positions to which they were appointed or from which they were discharged. The records are in Record Group 45 and Record Group 80.

Registers of employees consist of a register of Marine Corps and civilian personnel, 1799–1854, and a register of captain's clerks, commander's clerks, paymaster's clerks, and pay stewards, 1844–71. Both contain name indexes. An entry in the first series shows the name of employee, state of residence, and dates of appointment, promotion, resignation, orders, and leaves of absence. An entry in the later series shows name of clerk, vessel on which served, and dates of service.

There are also returns of civilian employees in shore establishments, 1887–1910, arranged by shore establishment, and service records of civilian employees, 1917–23, arranged by place of employment and thereunder by name. To use these three groups of records, the researcher must know where the subject of research worked. Other records of civilian employees, 1900–51, are at the National Personnel Records Center in St. Louis.

14.3 Members of Congress

For information about senators and representatives in Congress, the most readily available source is the *Biographical Directory of the American Congress, 1774–1971,* (1972 pages, 92d Congress, 1st sess., Sen Doc. 92–8). The directory provides reliable biographical information on more than 10,800 members of Congress. First issued for the period 1774–1788, these biographical sketches have been revised, updated, and improved in the light of information made available by historical associations and individuals interested in family genealogy. (Serial 12938)

14.4 Records of the Confederate Government

Record Group 109 includes some records pertaining to civilian workers of the Confederate government. Much of the documentation, however, is for War Department employees, most of whom were hired on a temporary basis. One of the largest and most significant series is among records of the Quartermaster General's Office and consists of unbound **payrolls** for hired civilian workers, 1861–65. The rolls are arranged numerically (1–16239) and include some other types of records, principally reports of persons and articles hired. Most of the rolls were prepared by local quartermaster or commissary officers in the field, but a number were also submitted by engineer, medical, and ordnance officers and superintendents of niter and mining districts. Types of workers hired included arms fabricators and finishers, blacksmiths, carpenters, cartridge makers, clerks, clothing cutters, couriers, foragemasters, hospital matrons and stewards, laborers on military defenses, nurses, packers, plumbers, seamstresses, shoemakers, teamsters, wagoners, and wagonmasters. Payrolls or reports of persons and articles hired generally show names of employing officers, places of employment, periods of service, rates of pay, and signatures of payees and witnesses. A smaller series of unbound slave payrolls is also arranged numerically (1–5889). It pertains largely to slaves employed on military defenses, but also in ordnance establishments, quartermaster depots, and elsewhere. In addition to the information appearing on the other payrolls, slave payrolls often show names of owners and names and occupations of slaves. Both unbound series of payrolls are covered by a single alphabetical card index prepared by the U.S. War Department.

For more detailed information about the employment of slaves by the Confederate government, see page 177.

Records of civilian employees are also found among those for various offices of the Confederate government. Records of some Confederate hospitals, for example, contain lists of both black and white workers, including stewards, matrons, and cooks. Arsenal or ordnance establishment records include time books and lists of men hired. These records, however, are widely scattered and often unindexed. In addition, they generally contain minimal information, perhaps only the names of persons employed. In a few instances, information may be available about the nature of duties performed and dates of work.

One of the most useful and readily accessible sources of information for all types of civilian government personnel is a large file of Confederate papers relating to citizens or business firms, more commonly known as the **Citizens File**. Available as *Confederate Papers Relating to Citizens or Business Firms,* M346, 1,158 rolls, the series consists of some 650,000 vouchers and other related documents filed in more than 350,000 alphabetically arranged jackets. The file was artificially assembled by the U.S. War Department employees during the late nineteenth century from original Confederate records and relates mostly to domestic business or commercial transactions between individuals, companies, or industries and the Confederate government. A number of files pertain to individuals who furnished forage, food, slaves for labor, horses, wagons, building supplies, and various types of equipment, or who rendered services such as hauling supplies or provisions, transporting prisoners, building or repairing equipment, and grazing livestock. Other files pertain to civilian government employees and officials and include those for detectives, hospital matrons, clerks, depot laborers, messengers, and purchasing agents. These files will normally consist of vouchers, bills, or receipts relating to pay or work expenses. Files for government officials may also include copies or drafts of letters, endorsements or memorandums, letters of application or recommendation, copies of regulations, copies of printed government documents, and worksheets. Files for individuals often indicate the dates of transactions, and some may contain information about the person's place of residence. In addition to original documents, a number of files include information recorded by the U.S. War Department, particularly in the form of cross-references to related materials among other Confederate records.

There are **other records** relating to civil servants in the Confederate government. These, however, pertain to a relatively limited group of persons. Available records are also rather sparse and often unindexed. Records of the Office of the Secretary of War include monthly lists of War Department employees and their salaries, March 1861–March 1865, arranged chronologically. The lists are found in a volume of War Department requisitions on the Treasury Department for funds to pay salaries of civilian officers and employees; this volume is identified as Chapter IX, vol. 98. Also available is a volume of payrolls of War Department civilian officers and employees, July 1862–March 1865 (Ch. IX, vol. 88) and a quarterly payroll of the same, January–March 1865 (Ch. IX, vol. 87). These bound payrolls are generally arranged chronologically by month, and thereunder by War Department office. Records relating to civilian appointments in the Confederate War Department include a register of applications and recommendations for military and civil appointments (Ch. IX, vol. 90), arranged chronologically. Entries give names of prospective employees, the nature of the position sought, and names of recommending persons. Among the records of the Adjutant and Inspector General's Office is a one-volume listing of civil and military officers, 1861–64 (Ch. I, vol. 121). The unarranged entries show names of appointees and dates of appointments and resignations. There are three registers of applications for clerkships and other positions in the Treasury Department, 1861–65 (Ch. X, vols. 156, 156 1/2, and 157). Entries are arranged alphabetically in two of the volumes and numerically in the other; the numerically arranged volume contains a name index. Entries show names and residences of applicants, dates of applications, positions applied for, and, sometimes, names of references.

Other records of civilian employment include payrolls of civilian navy personnel at Confederate shore establishments, 1861–64, in Record Group 45. These records are unindexed, but lists prepared by the National Archives staff indicate shore establishments for which there are such records. Payrolls for slave laborers are noted for some establishments; they are listed on page 189.

CHAPTER 15

Section D. Other Useful Records

Land Records

CHAPTER 15

Land Records

15.1 Introduction

Much of the present-day United States was once a part of the public domain, that is, land owned by the federal government and subject to sale or other transfer of ownership under laws passed by Congress. The states that were formed from the public domain are called **public land states;** they are listed in table 24. The records of transactions whereby the government transferred land to individuals, either by sale or by grant, are **land entry papers,** and the document that guarantees title to such land is a **patent**. Some early settlers in the public domain exercised the right of **preemption,** by which without permission they built a house and made other improvements on public land and were allowed to purchase the land later at a minimum price when surrounding land was put up for public sale.

The United States has used the public domain for several purposes. The military bounty land has been noted above on pages 145–151. In Florida, Oregon, and Washington State before the Civil War, the government gave land to persons who would make their homes on the land, because settlement by actual settlers was a means of confirming a claim to the territory when ownership had been disputed by another nation. These grants were known as **donation entries,** because the government gave some of its land to individuals free. For details about this kind of claim see page 228. Some land grants were made to ensure that land would be used in a certain way, such as for timber culture; others, such as grants to railroads, were made to encourage development.

The land records in the National Archives consist principally of documents relating to the disposal of land in the public land states. Dated chiefly 1800–1973, but with some as early as 1685, land entry records consist of patents or other claims documents that were prepared and submitted before patents were issued by the federal government. Until the Homestead Act was passed in 1862, most land entry papers contain very little genealogical information. In most cases, there is only the name of the entryman and his place of residence at the time he made his purchase or entry. Files of donation entries and preemption claims for cash purchase are more likely to give personal information about the patentee.

Private land claims files may also be rich in genealogical information. Some of these claims arose when the United States acquired inhabited territory from another country. For example, when California was acquired from Mexico at the end of the Mexican War, the settlers who had been granted land by the Mexican government were required to prove the legality of their Mexican titles. Because some of the owners of ranchos in 1850 were probably descendants of the original grantee, the files of these private land claims may be useful to the genealogist. Such claims are described in detail on page 257.

The records described in this chapter are in the Records of the Bureau of Land Management, Record Group 49, unless otherwise indicated. Township survey plats, private land claim plats, and U.S. land district maps are described in chapter 20.

A good general survey of public land policy is Paul W. Gates's *History of Public Land Law Development* (Washington, 1968). A good source for information about the uniform records of land disposal is Robert W. Harrison's "Public Land Records of the Federal Government," in *Mississippi Valley Historical Review* 41 (Sept. 1954): 277–288.

Title to a tract of land could be obtained only after it had been surveyed. Under the provisions of the land ordinance of 1785 (*J.C.C.* 28: 375–381), land in the public domain was to be sold by the government through the loan offices of the Board of Treasury. The first such land, located in areas included in present-day Ohio, was surveyed and sold in 1787. With the exception of surveys of a part of Ohio, the surveys followed a uniform pattern, providing standard **land descriptions**.

The surveys depend upon east-west base lines and north-south meridians. Parallel to the meridians are ranges of townships. Each township is six miles square and usually consists of thirty-six numbered sections. A section consists of 640 acres and is divided into quarter sections of 160 acres each. A tract is normally described in terms of a fractional section, section, township, and range: for example, "Northeast quarter of section 15, township 2 north, range 8 east of the sixth principal meridian." Such a land description is often needed to locate the records relating to a land transaction.

For information about the system of identifying individual tracts, see plate 87 in *Atlas of American History,* edited by James Truslow Adams and Roy V. Coleman (New York: Charles Scribner's Sons, 1943).

Records of the disposition of each tract of land were kept in **tractbooks**. These registers, arranged geographically, include the following column headings: land description, number of acres, date of sale, name of purchaser, land office, and entry number. Other information of a varied nature may appear in the tractbooks as annotations or remarks.

Sets of tractbooks were kept in the central office of the General Land Office (and its successor, the Bureau of Land Management), in Washington, D.C., and in the offices located in the many land districts that were eventually created. The tractbooks maintained in the district offices remained with those offices as long as they existed; afterward, many were placed in the custody of successor field offices, such as the state and area offices of the Bureau of Land Management. Eventually, some were turned over to

TABLE 24

Public Land States

Alabama	Iowa	New Mexico
Alaska	Kansas	North Dakota
Arizona	Louisiana	Ohio
Arkansas	Michigan	Oklahoma
California	Minnesota	Oregon
Colorado	Mississippi	South Dakota
Florida	Missouri	Utah
Idaho	Montana	Washington
Illinois	Nebraska	Wisconsin
Indiana	Nevada	Wyoming

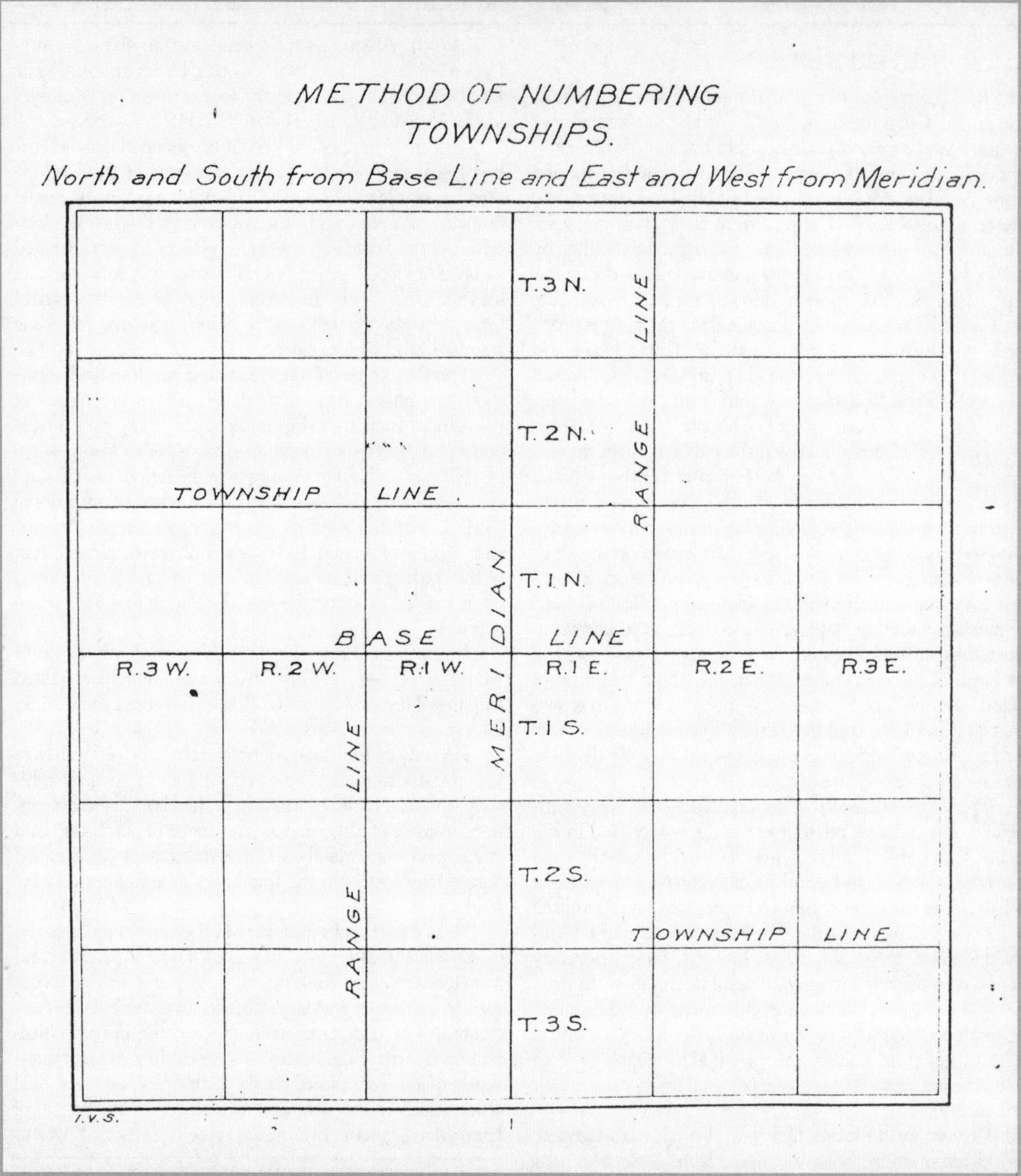

Townships six miles square were numbered according to their position relative to a meridian (running vertically, north and south) and a base line (running horizontally, east and west). In the diagram above, the townships immediately south of the base line and east of the meridian would be numbered "Township 1 South, Range 1 East" or T1S R1E.

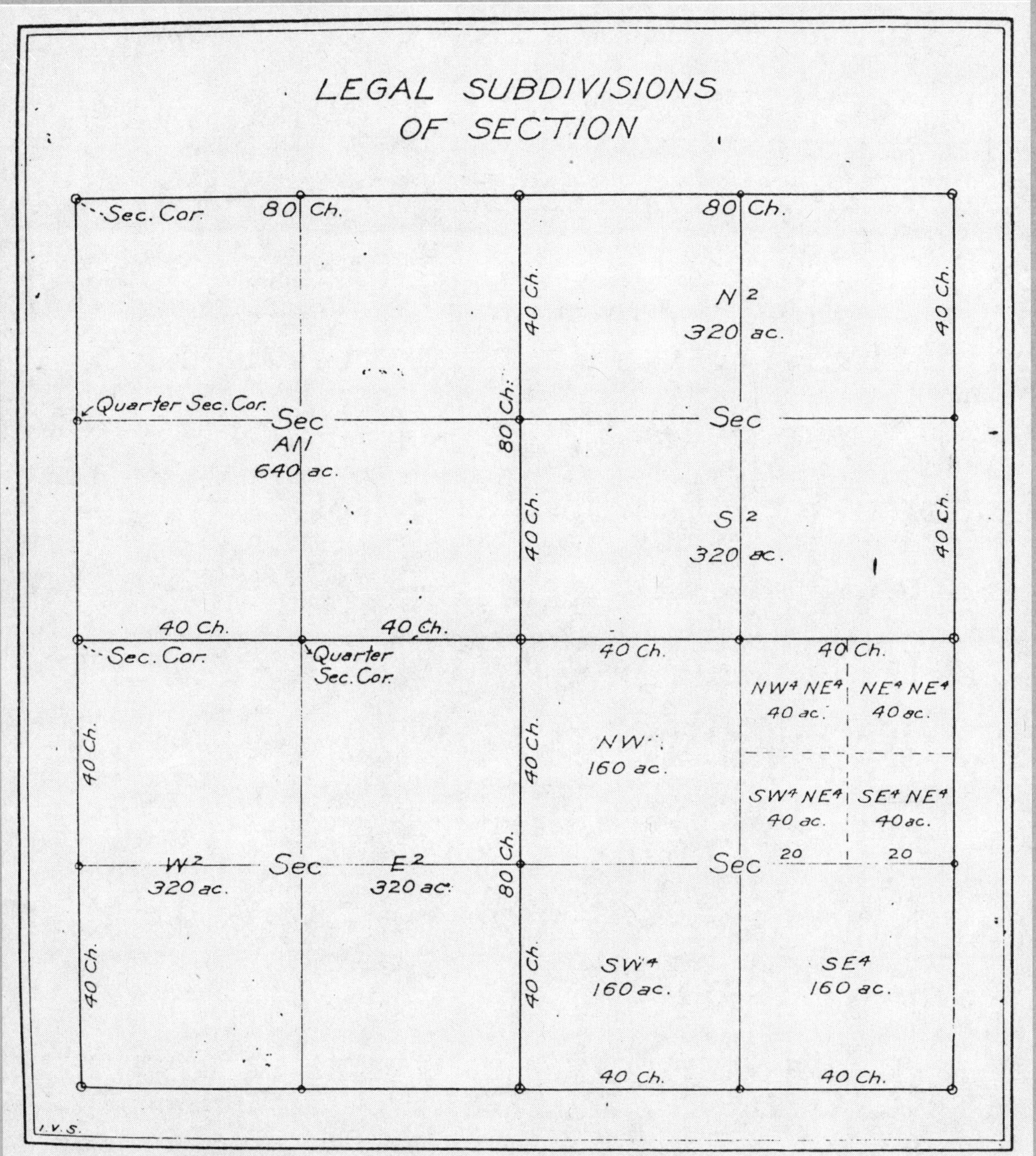

3

Each six-square-mile township was divided into 36 sections of 640 acres each, four of which are represented in the diagram above. In the upper left is one complete section, undivided. The upper right section has been divided into half sections, designated "half section north" (N^2) and "half section south" (S^2). A section could also be split vertically, creating "half section east" (E^2) and "west" (W^2) shown in the lower left portion of the diagram. Quarter sections, shown in the lower right section, were designated "quarter section northwest" (NW^4), "quarter section southwest" (SW^4), "southeast (SE^4) or "northeast" (NE^4). When a quarter section was divided into 40 acre lots, the descriptions indicated both the quarter section and the position of the lot in the quarter section. Thus "NW^4 NE^4" means the northwest quarter lot in the northeast quarter section.

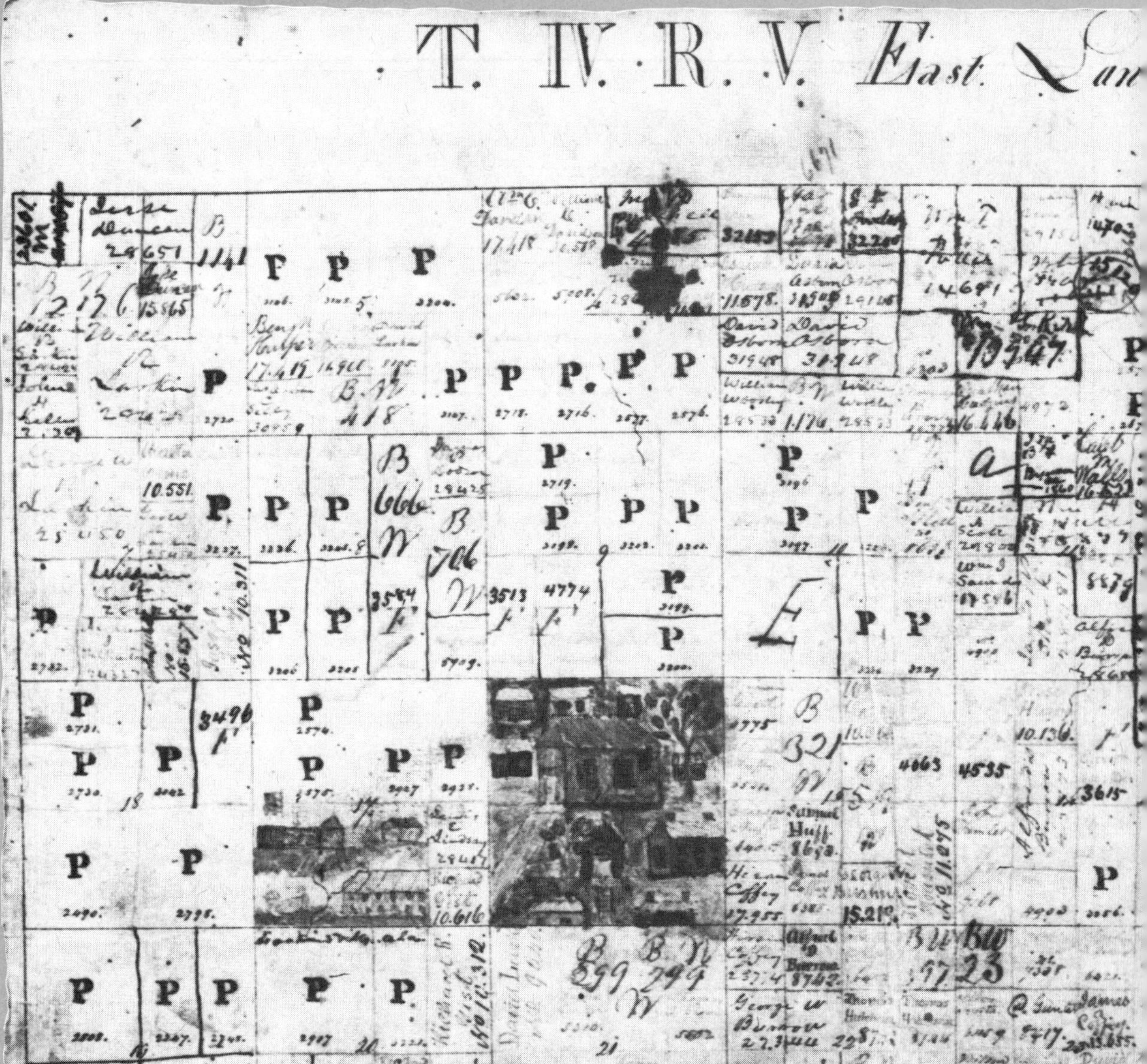
T. IV. R. V. East.

strict. Northern Part. of Alabama
Table of Contents
1. 635. 36. 19. 640 96.
2. 640 80 20 636 32
3. 639 60 21. 641 84
4. 638 00 22. 637. 56
5. 641. 56 23. 640 08
6. 640 00 24. 639. 44
7. 638 96 25. 639. 04
8. 638 56 26. 641 20
9. 637 84 27. 639. 36
10. 637. 76 28. 638 40
11. 641 92 29. 639. 28
12. 629. 68 30. 641. 44
13. 634 72 31. 645. 76.
14. 639 60. 32. 647. 28
15. 636. 72. 33. 644. 96.
16. 641 68 34. 652. 24.
17. 636 00. 35. 651. 88
18. 639. 52 36. 645. 52
Surveyed in the 4th Qr of 1822.
by
Wm Graves Bouldin
Deputy Surveyor

Survey map of Township IV, Range V, East Land District, Northern Part of Alabama. Alabama, Huntsville, S & E, R5E, T4S, Records of the Bureau of Land Management, Record Group 49. The map shows names of landowners, with the section set aside for support of a school containing a picture of a little red schoolhouse. The "F's" and "P's" were notations of the local land office, probably meaning patent pending and final patent. The table at right shows the actual acreage of each section, more or less than the standard 640 acres because of irregularities of the terrain.

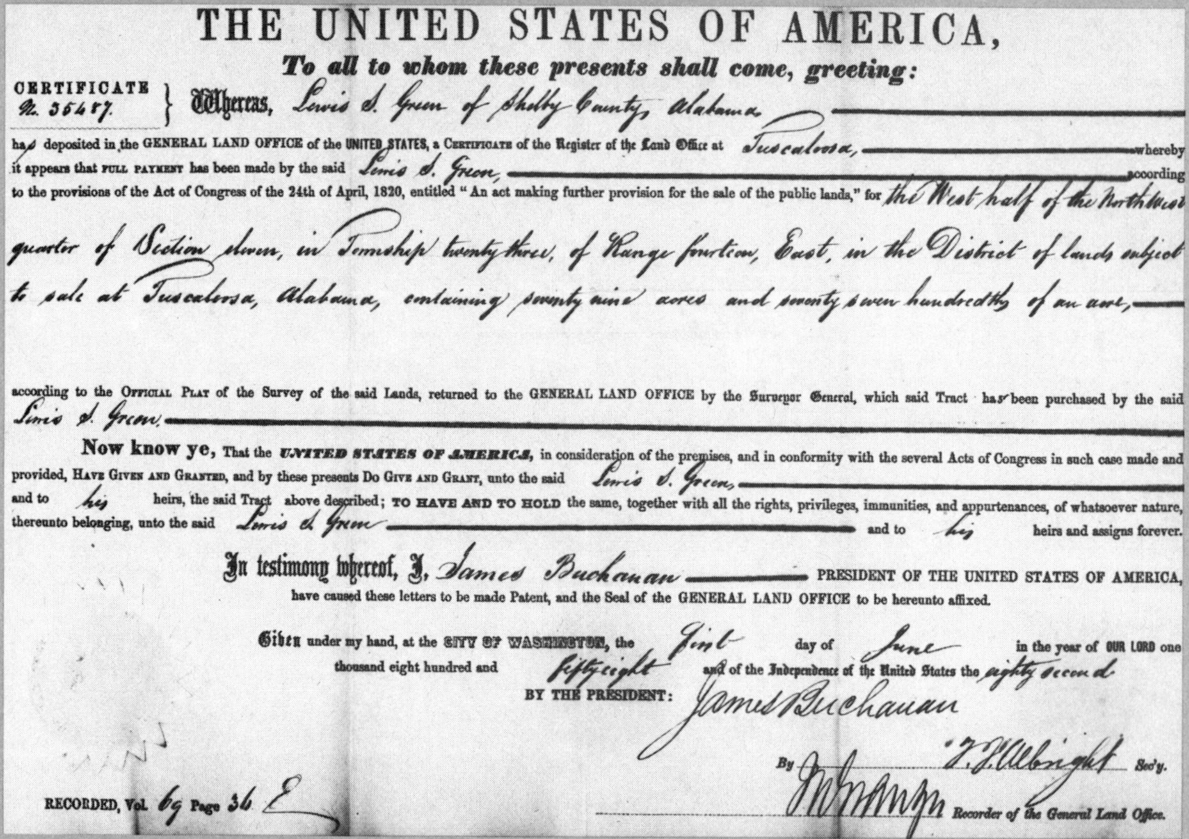

THE UNITED STATES OF AMERICA,

To all to whom these presents shall come, greeting:

CERTIFICATE No. 35487. } Whereas, Lewis S. Green of Shelby County, Alabama

has deposited in the GENERAL LAND OFFICE of the UNITED STATES, a Certificate of the Register of the Land Office at Tuscaloosa, whereby it appears that FULL PAYMENT has been made by the said Lewis S. Green, according to the provisions of the Act of Congress of the 24th of April, 1820, entitled "An act making further provision for the sale of the public lands," for the West half of the North West quarter of Section eleven, in Township twenty three, of Range fourteen, East, in the District of lands subject to sale at Tuscaloosa, Alabama, containing seventy nine acres and seventy seven hundredths of an acre,

according to the Official Plat of the Survey of the said Lands, returned to the GENERAL LAND OFFICE by the Surveyor General, which said Tract has been purchased by the said Lewis S. Green.

Now know ye, That the UNITED STATES OF AMERICA, in consideration of the premises, and in conformity with the several Acts of Congress in such case made and provided, Have Given and Granted, and by these presents Do Give and Grant, unto the said Lewis S. Green, and to his heirs, the said Tract above described; TO HAVE AND TO HOLD the same, together with all the rights, privileges, immunities, and appurtenances, of whatsoever nature, thereunto belonging, unto the said Lewis S. Green and to his heirs and assigns forever.

In testimony whereof, I, James Buchanan PRESIDENT OF THE UNITED STATES OF AMERICA, have caused these letters to be made Patent, and the Seal of the GENERAL LAND OFFICE to be hereunto affixed.

Given under my hand, at the CITY OF WASHINGTON, the First day of June in the year of OUR LORD one thousand eight hundred and fifty eight and of the Independence of the United States the eighty second.

BY THE PRESIDENT: James Buchanan

By J. F. Albright Sec'y.

RECORDED, Vol. 69 Page 36 E

Recorder of the General Land Office.

Cash patent certificate No. 35487, Tuscaloosa, Alabama. Records of the Bureau of Land Management, Record Group 49.

state and local historical societies or state archives. Some are now in the regional archives branches.

The central office set of tractbooks is now divided between the Eastern States Office of the Bureau of Land Management and the National Archives. The Bureau of Land Management has the tractbooks for the public land states east of the Mississippi River and the first tier of states west of that river (Minnesota, Iowa, Missouri, Arkansas, and Louisiana); the National Archives has those for states farther west. Microfilm copies (1,340 rolls) of all tractbooks are available for use at the Bureau of Land Management and can be purchased from that office. The National Archives does not have a copy of this extensive microfilm set.

The Bureau of Land Management has five volumes of indexes to Ohio tractbooks relating to the years 1800–20, with a few entries for transactions of later dates. The books are for the following land offices: Canton (Wooster), Chillicothe, Cincinnati, Marietta and Zanesville, and Steubenville. Entries in the indexes are arranged alphabetically by the first letter of the surname. From the description of the tracts in the tractbooks, it is possible to locate the related entry file in the National Archives.

Most record copies of **land patents** issued to persons who acquired land up to 1908 are in volumes arranged by state, and thereunder by land office. The volumes are divided between the Bureau of Land Management and the National Archives in the same way as the central office tractbooks. Some patents not arranged by state, such as those issued in exchange for military bounty land warrants, are also kept by the Bureau of Land Management. Later patents (described on page 229) are all held by the Bureau of Land Management. Patents give name of patentee, location of land, land office, land entry identification, and date of patent.

The township and range number can be determined from an atlas and the census population schedules; the location of the tract can be determined from the entries in the tractbook covering the approximate area concerned. If the date of the entry and an approximate location of the land are known, the chronologically arranged entries in one of the abstract books in the National Archives can be searched for the appropriate land office. Abstracts were made from the records created in the local land offices and submitted as montly reports from the local register and receiver to the central office in Washington. They contain information similar to that contained in the tractbooks. The abstracts are harder to use, because most land entries involved more than one transaction, and there may be abstract entries for more than one date. In tractbooks, on the other hand, all the information for one tract is together.

The National Archives has abstracts from all public land states, although the collection is not complete. Also in the National Archives is a four-volume index called "Index List of Offices," which helps to identify the land office with responsibility for a given area at a given time.

The genealogical use of land entry papers is complex. The requirements for a search vary, depending upon the nature of the facts available. If a person received a patent to land after 30 June 1908, there should be an entry in the indexes described under the numerical series, 1908–73, on page 229. If a person was entitled to a patent between 1800 and 30 June 1908 on the basis of purchase or condition of settlement, and the land was located in Alabama, Alaska, Arizona, Florida, Louisiana, Nevada, or Utah, there should be an entry in the 3″ × 5″ card index to those patents in the National Archives. If a person received a patent to land in Ohio through a district land office, 1800–20, there should be an entry in the book index relating to that land office in the Bureau of Land Management in Alexandria, Va. If, for military service, a person received a patent to land in the Virginia Military District of Ohio, the U.S. Military District of Ohio, or one of the War of 1812 bounty land districts, the researcher should see the indexes pertaining to those respective districts described on pages 150 and 151 in this guide.

If the subject of research received a patent to land, and the researcher has an accurate description of the land in terms of subdivision, section, township, and range, the related land entry file can be ascertained by using the tractbooks in the National Archives or in the Bureau of Land Management. If the researcher does not have a description of the tract, it is often possible to obtain the description from the recorder of deeds for the county where the tract is located.

15.2 Public Land Records, 1800–1908

Pursuant to an act of 1800 (2 Stat. 73), four district land offices were established in that part of the Northwest Territory that became Ohio. Gradually, other land offices were set up throughout the public domain to handle requests for land. Normally, documents relating to a request for land were transmitted to Washington after the file had been completed or the request abandoned. The records of land purchases or of land distributed under special conditions of settlement were arranged by state, thereunder by name of land office, thereunder by series, and thereunder numerically. A list of the land offices together with the principal series for each land office is given in *Land-Entry Papers of the General Land Office,* Preliminary Inventory 22, compiled by Harry P. Yoshpe and Philip P. Bower (Washington: National Archives and Records Service, 1949).

Nearly all the land sold by the federal government between 1800 and 30 June 1820 was sold on credit through the few land offices then in operation at no less than $2 an acre. The records of these transactions are in the **credit entry files**. Sale of land on credit was discontinued after 30 June 1820, but many purchasers of land previously bought on which installments were overdue were able to obtain title to their tracts through relief acts beginning in 1821.

Of genealogical interest in the credit entry files are **credit entry final certificates,** 1800–35, and a few of later date, which were issued when purchases were completed. A certificate states that the individual has met all the requirements to purchase the land and is entitled to a patent. These certificates are filed among the papers of each appropriate land office in two numerical series. One is for certificates issued for purchases made before 1 July 1820, called **credit prior certificates;** the other is for certificates that became effective after that date under relief legislation, called **credit under certificates**.

Normally, the receipts for purchases (documents merely stating that the individual paid an amount of money) are not filed with the related final certificates, but are in separate series. Occasionally, a document such as an assignment (a sale of the land to another person) is filed with the final certificate.

A final certificate normally shows name and place of residence of entryman as given at the time of purchase, date of purchase, number of acres in the tract, description of the tract (subdivision, section, township, and range), a summary of the payments made, and a citation to the record copy of the patent in the Bureau of Land Management.

Nearly all the land sold by the federal government to individual settlers on and after 1 July 1820 was sold for cash at no less than $1.25 an acre, pursuant to an act of 24 April 1820 (3 Stat. 566). The **cash entry files,** which are arranged by name and land office, are dated 1820–30 June 1908, but the series for a specific land office usually covers only a part of this period. A file includes the receipt for moneys paid and a final certificate authorizing the claimant to obtain a patent. If the tract paid for was claimed on the basis of a preemption claim, the file may include a preemption proof or similar document. If the tract paid for was entered as a homestead, and the homestead entry had been commuted to a cash entry, the cash entry file includes the documents for the homestead entry.

There is a master 3″ × 5″ card index, alphabetically arranged by name of entryman, to the cash entry files for Alabama, Alaska, Arizona, Florida, Louisiana, Nevada, and Utah. (This master index includes homesteads, credit purchases, timber culture lands, and other types of land entries before 1908, but not military bounty lands or private land claims.) An index card gives the name of entryman, date of entry, state and land office, land description (section, township, and range), type of entry, and certificate number.

Each final certificate shows name of entryman, place of residence at time of purchase, description of tract (in terms of subdivision, section, township, and range), number of acres in the tract, date of the patent, and volume and page number of the record copy of the patent in the Bureau of Land Management or the National Archives. The testimony of the claimant in a preemption proof may include the name of the claimant, age, citizenship, date of entry on the tract, number and relationship of members of the household, and nature of the improvements on the tract.

The **donation entry files** concern land given away in return for certain conditions of settlement. They include files for Florida, Oregon, and Washington.

Under terms of the Florida Armed Occupation Act of 1842 (5 Stat. 502), as amended, men able to bear arms were entitled to apply for 160 acres of land in certain unsettled areas of East Florida and were given patents to the land upon fulfilling the condition of five years' settlement.

The **Florida donation entry files,** mainly 1842–50, for each appropriate land office are filed in a single numerical series. The documents in each file vary, depending upon the extent to which title had been perfected. A complete file includes a permit to settle, an application for a patent, a report by the land agent, and a final certificate authorizing the claimant to obtain a patent. The master card index described above includes references to files containing final certificates. If a final certificate was not issued, there is no index card in the file.

A permit to settle shows the name of the applicant, marital status, month and year he became a resident of Florida, and a description of the land in terms of subdivision, section, township, and range. An application for a patent shows the name of applicant, a description of the land, name of settler, and period of settlement. A final certificate shows the name of applicant, a description of the land, date of the patent, and the volume and page number of the recorded copy of the patent in the Bureau of Land Management.

Under terms of an act of 1850 (9 Stat. 496), certain white settlers and Indians of mixed blood in Oregon Territory (which then included Washington), and certain settlers arriving there between 1 December 1850 and 1 December 1853, were entitled to land. The number of acres granted depended upon the marital status of the settler and the date of settlement; it varied from 160 to 640. Settlers were required to live on the land and cultivate it for four years.

The **Oregon and Washington donation files** for each appropriate land office are filed in two numerical series. One relates to complete entries, the other to incomplete or canceled entries. The files for both complete and incomplete entries have been reproduced on microfilm as *Oregon and Washington Donation Land Files, 1851–1903,* M815, 108 rolls.

Registers with indexes for both the Oregon and the Washington donation land claims are available on microfilm: *Abstracts of Oregon Donation Land Claims, 1852–1903,* M145, 6 rolls, and *Abstracts of Washington Donation Land Claims, 1855–1902,* M203, 1 roll. The registers fully identify each claim by name, land office, and certificate number, and can be used to locate files on M815. An alphabetical index to the Oregon donation claims is also available on a roll of microfilm prepared by the Oregon State Library.

This information was published by the Genealogical Forum of Portland, Oregon, under the title "Index to Oregon Donation Land Claims." Each index card gives the name of the entryman, name of the land office, certificate number, number of acres, township, range, and section of each approved claim. On another roll, this information is arranged by location of land.

Documents in a file for a completed entry include the notification of settlement, which describes the land either by legal description (range, township, section, and fraction of section) or by natural features (metes and bounds), sometimes accompanied by a plat; an affidavit of settlement, which includes date and place of birth and, if applicable, of marriage; proofs of cultivation; an oath that the land had been used for cultivation only; for naturalized persons, proof of citizenship (not filmed on M815); and the donation certificate, which shows name of entryman, place of residence, description of land, date of patent, and volume and page number of the recorded patent in the National Archives.

Under the Homestead Act of 1862 (12 Stat. 392), citizens and persons who had filed their intentions to become citizens were given 160 acres of land in the public domain if they fulfilled certain conditions. In general, an applicant had to build a home on the land, reside there for five years, and cultivate the land. Some later acts modified or waived some of these conditions. An act of 1872 (17 Stat. 333), for example, provided special benefits for Union veterans or their widows and orphans.

The **homestead entry papers** filed by name of land office are dated 1863–30 June 1908. In general, there are two separately numbered series for each land office, one relating to complete, and the other relating to incomplete, homestead entries. A complete homestead entry file includes such documents as the homestead application; the certificate of publication of intention to make a claim; the homestead proof, consisting of testimonies of two witnesses and the testimony of the claimant; the final certificate authorizing the claimant to obtain a patent; and, when appropriate, a copy of naturalization proceedings or a copy of a Union veteran's discharge certificate.

A **homestead application** shows the name of the entryman, place of residence at the time of application, description of the tract, and number of acres in the tract. The testimony of claimant on a **homestead proof** shows a description of the tract; name, age, and post office address of the claimant; description of the house and date when residence was established therein; number and relationship of members of the family; nature of the crops; and number of acres under cultivation. A **final certificate** shows the location of the tract, name and post office address of the claimant, date the patent was issued, and volume and page number of the recorded copy of the patent in the Bureau of Land Management or in the National Archives. A copy of naturalization proceedings relating to a naturalized citizen or an alien who had declared his intention of becoming a citizen shows the name of immigrant, name of court, date of naturalization or declaration, and country of previous allegiance; it does not generally give town of birth or previous residence, the name of ship on which he came to the United States, or date and port of arrival.

Some entrymen who applied for homesteads wanted to obtain possession of the tracts before the passage of the time required by law. Such persons purchased the tracts for cash at the established price instead of fulfilling the homestead conditions. The homestead entry documents in such cases are filed with the cash entry files for the same land office.

15.3 Public Land Records, 1908–73

Land entry files based on patents that were issued between 1 July 1908 and 16 May 1973 are in the **numerical series**. Arranged in numerical order by patent number, these files contain records of cash, homestead, and other types of entries completed within this period. A 3″ × 5″ card index lists the names of the applicants alphabetically with the corresponding land office and serial application number. Another 3″ × 5″ card index, arranged by land office, and thereunder by serial application number, indicates the patent numbers assigned to perfected patents.

Each file shows the name of the patentee, place of residence, a description of the tract (subdivision, section, township, and range), date of the patent, and number of the file, which is also the number of the record copy of the patent in the Bureau of Land Management. The type of land entry determines the nature of additional information in the file.

Files relating to land entries that were canceled, relinquished, or rejected during this period have been retained in the legal custody of the Bureau of Land Management and are stored in the records center sections of the various Federal Archives and Records Centers.

15.4 Private Land Claims

Private land claims, 1789–30 June 1908 are claims based on grants, purchases, or settlements that took place before the United States acquired sovereignty over the land. The term "private land claim" is sometimes used to apply to land claims based on other considerations. For example, French emigrants claimed land at Gallipolis, Ohio, on the basis of a special act of Congress. Although such claims are not described separately, they are occasionally included or referred to among the records described here.

Private land claims were made by persons who claimed to have grants from foreign sovereigns, to descendants of such persons, to pioneers from the United States who settled in these lands with the permission of the foreign governments, and to U.S. citizens who bought up rights to lands acquired under foreign sovereignty and presented them to federal agencies for the purpose of acquiring title.

Much land in what is now the United States was granted or settled between 1685 and 1853, while it was under the rule of France, Great Britain, Mexico, or Spain. This land was often described according to the indiscriminate method of surveying by natural features in terms of metes and bounds; it was usually confirmed in terms of metes and bounds, rather than in terms of subdivision, township, and range.

Whenever the United States acquired land from a foreign government, it established a board of commissioners or other agency to adjudicate private land claims. The agencies that were originally established rarely completed their work; and the unfinished business was referred to other federal agencies such as the district land offices, the U.S. district courts, the Court of Claims, the Supreme Court, the General Land Office, and (for lands deeded by Mexico) the Court of Private Land Claims.

There are records of private land claims in the National Archives for land in parts of the following states: Alabama, Arizona, Arkansas, California, Colorado, Florida, Illinois, Indiana, Iowa, Louisiana, Michigan, Mississippi, Missouri, New Mexico, and Wisconsin. Each of these states was originally in one of the following areas: the Northwest Territory (Illinois, Indiana, Michigan, and Wisconsin); Mississippi Territory (Alabama and Mississippi); the Louisiana Purchase (Louisiana and the following states of Missouri Territory: Arkansas, Iowa, and Missouri); the Florida Cession (Florida); and the Mexican Cession (Arizona, California, Colorado, and New Mexico).

Records relating to individual claims presented before boards of commissioners or other federal agencies, 1790–1837, were reported to Congress and transcribed and indexed in *American State Papers, Public Lands* (Washington: Gales and Seaton, 1832–61). Claims presented, 1790–

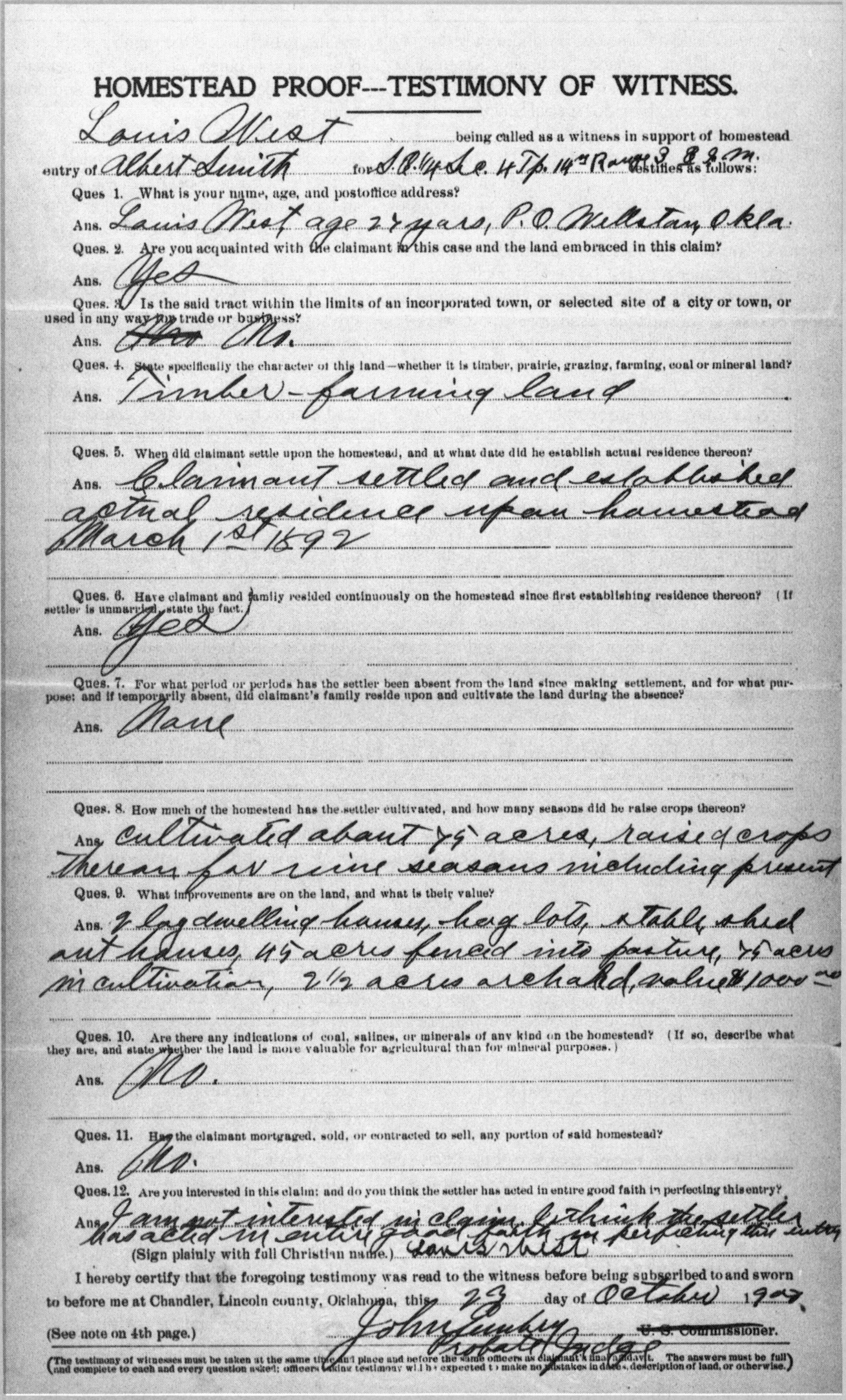

HOMESTEAD PROOF---TESTIMONY OF WITNESS.

Louis West being called as a witness in support of homestead entry of Albert Smith for S.E.¼ Sec. 4 Tp. 14 N. Range 3 E. I.M. testifies as follows:

Ques. 1. What is your name, age, and postoffice address?

Ans. Louis West, age 27 years, P.O. Wellston, Okla.

Ques. 2. Are you acquainted with the claimant in this case and the land embraced in this claim?

Ans. Yes

Ques. 3. Is the said tract within the limits of an incorporated town, or selected site of a city or town, or used in any way for trade or business?

Ans. ~~No~~ No.

Ques. 4. State specifically the character of this land—whether it is timber, prairie, grazing, farming, coal or mineral land?

Ans. Timber-farming land

Ques. 5. When did claimant settle upon the homestead, and at what date did he establish actual residence thereon?

Ans. Claimant settled and established actual residence upon homestead March 1st 1892

Ques. 6. Have claimant and family resided continuously on the homestead since first establishing residence thereon? (If settler is unmarried, state the fact.)

Ans. Yes

Ques. 7. For what period or periods has the settler been absent from the land since making settlement, and for what purpose: and if temporarily absent, did claimant's family reside upon and cultivate the land during the absence?

Ans. None

Ques. 8. How much of the homestead has the settler cultivated, and how many seasons did he raise crops thereon?

Ans. cultivated about 75 acres, raised crops thereon for nine seasons including present

Ques. 9. What improvements are on the land, and what is their value?

Ans. 2 log dwelling houses, hog lots, stable, shed out houses, 45 acres fenced into pasture, 75 acres in cultivation, 2½ acres orchard, value $1000.00

Ques. 10. Are there any indications of coal, salines, or minerals of any kind on the homestead? (If so, describe what they are, and state whether the land is more valuable for agricultural than for mineral purposes.)

Ans. No.

Ques. 11. Has the claimant mortgaged, sold, or contracted to sell, any portion of said homestead?

Ans. No.

Ques. 12. Are you interested in this claim; and do you think the settler has acted in entire good faith in perfecting this entry?

Ans. I am not interested in claim. I think the settler has acted in entire good faith in perfecting this entry

(Sign plainly with full Christian name.) Louis West

I hereby certify that the foregoing testimony was read to the witness before being subscribed to and sworn to before me at Chandler, Lincoln county, Oklahoma, this 23 day of October 1901.

(See note on 4th page.) John Embry ~~U.S. Commissioner.~~ Probate Judge

(The testimony of witnesses must be taken at the same time and place and before the same officers as claimant's final affidavit. The answers must be full and complete to each and every question asked; officers taking testimony will be expected to make no mistakes in dates, description of land, or otherwise.)

Homestead proof, testimony of claimant and of a witness, Guthrie, Oklahoma Homestead FC 4480. Records of the Bureau of Land Management, Record Group 49.

HOMESTEAD PROOF—TESTIMONY OF CLAIMANT.

Albert Smith being called as a witness in his own behalf in support of homestead entry No. .... for S.E.1/4 Sec. 4 Tp. 14 N R. 3 E testifies as follows:

Ques. 1. What is your name, age, and postoffice address?

Ans. Albert Smith, age 44 years, P.O. Warwick, Okla.

Ques. 2. *Are you a native born citizen of the United States, and, if so, in what state or territory were you born?

Ans. Yes, born in Missisippi

Ques. 3. Are you the identical person who made homestead entry No. .... at the Guthrie Okla. land office on the 9th day of November 1891 and what is the true description of the land now claimed by you?

Ans. Yes. S.E.1/4 Sec. 4 Township 14 N of Range 3 E I.M.

Ques. 4. When was your house built on the land, and when did you establish actual residence therein? (Describe said house and other improvements which you have placed on the land, giving the total value thereof.

Ans. Log dwelling house 14 x 10 ft, built January 1892 I established actual residence therein March 1st 1892
Other improvements 2 log houses, 45 acres pasture fenced with wire, 75 acres in cultivation, 2 1/2 acres orchard, out houses, hog lots all of the value of $1500.00

Ques. 5. Of whom does your family consist; and have you and your family resided continuously on the land since first establishing residence thereon? (If unmarried, state the fact.)

Ans. Myself, wife and six children, and we have resided continuously on land since first establishing residence thereon

Ques. 6. For what period or periods have you been absent from the homestead since making settlement, and for what purpose; and if temporarily absent, did your family reside upon and cultivate the land during such absence?

Ans. None

Ques. 7. How much land have you cultivated each season, and for how many seasons have you raised crops thereon?

Ans. cultivated 3 acres 1892, 10 acres 1894, [illegible] acres 1896, 56 acres in 1899, [illegible] 1897, 75 acres 1898, 1899, 1900
Raised crops thereon nine seasons including present

Ques. 8. Is your present claim within the limits of an incorporated town, or selected site of a city or town, or used in any way for trade or business?

Ans. No

Ques. 9. What is the character of the land? Is it timber, mountainous, prairie, grazing, or ordinary agricultural land? State its kind and quality, and for what purpose it is most valuable.

Ans. Timber, ordinary agricultural land, most valuable for valuable for farming

Ques. 10. Are there any indications of coal, salines, or minerals of any kind on the land? (If so, describe what they are, and state whether the land is more valuable for agricultural than for mineral purposes.)

Ans. No.

Ques. 11. Have you ever made any other homestead entry? (If so, describe the same.)

Ans. No

Ques. 12. Have you sold, conveyed, or mortgaged any portion of the land, and if so, to whom and for what purpose?

Ans. No

Ques. 13. Have you any personal property of any kind elsewhere than on this claim? (If so, describe the same, and state where the same is kept.)

Ans. No

Ques. 14. Describe the legal subdivisions, or by number, kind of entry, and office where made, any other entry or filing (not mineral), made by you since August 30, 1890.

Ans. Made None

(Sign plainly with full Christian name.) Albert Smith

~~*In case the party is of foreign birth a certified transcript from the court records of his declaration of intention to become a citizen, or of his naturalization, or a copy thereof, certified by the officer taking this proof, must be filed with the case. Evidence of naturalization is only required in final (five year) homestead cases.~~

I hereby certify that the foregoing testimony was read to the witness before being subscribed to and was sworn to before me at Chandler, Lincoln county, Oklahoma, this 23d day of October 1900

[illegible] ~~U.S. Commissioner.~~
Probate Judge

Holding Down A Lot In Guthrie.
26

Turn-of-the-century Land Booms
"Holding Down a Lot in Guthrie." Photograph No. 48-RST-7B-6 by C. P. Rich, ca. 1889.

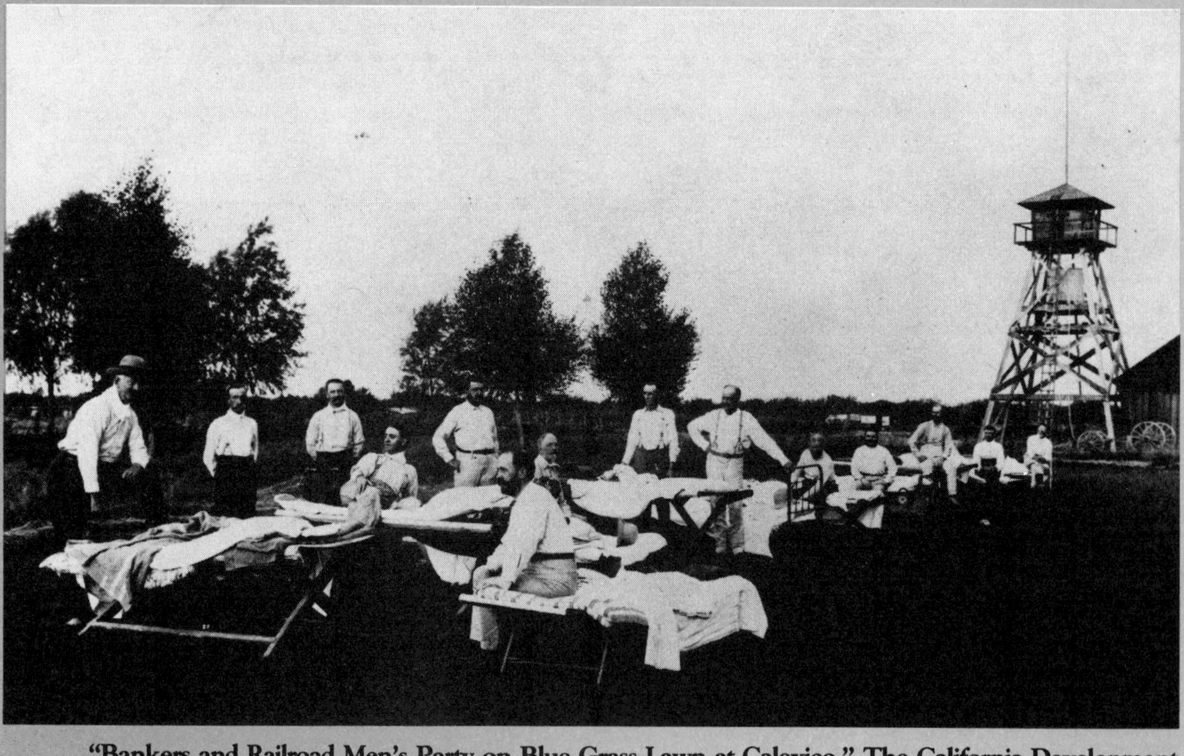

"Bankers and Railroad Men's Party on Blue Grass Lawn at Calexico." The California Development Company hoped that this campout would persuade the men to invest in Imperial Valley schemes, ca. 1904. Photograph No. 48-RST-7-17.

Both photographs, Records of the Office of the Secretary of the Interior, Record Group 48.

"First train [and wagons] leaving the line north of Orlembo [Orlando] for Perry [Oklahoma Territory], Sept. 16, 1893." Photograph No. 49-AR-7.

"In line at the Land Office, Perry, Sept. 23, 1893. 9 o'clock AM. waiting to file." Photograph No. 49-AR-32.

Both photographs, Records of the Bureau of Land Management, Record Group 49.

1809, are in volume 1; 1809–15, in volume 2; 1815–24, in volume 3; 1824–28, in volume 4; 1827–29, in volume 5; 1829–34, in volume 6; 1834–35, in volume 7; and 1835–37, in volume 8. Each volume is indexed by name of claimant. A consolidated index has been published under the title *Grassroots of America,* edited by Phillip W. McMullin (Salt Lake City: Gendex Corp., 1972). Most of the reports published by Gales and Seaton were also published in the less complete edition of the *American State Papers* (1834) by Duff Green.

Originals of the committee reports to Congress on private land claims are among Records of the U.S. Senate, Record Group 46, and Records of the U.S. House of Representatives, Record Group 233. They are filed by Congress, thereunder by name of committee, and thereunder chronologically.

Committee reports on individual land claims considered from 1826 to 1876 by the two congressional committees on private land claims are collected and published in *Reports of the Committees on Private Land Claims of the Senate and House of Representatives,* 2 volumes (45th Cong., 3d sess. Misc. Doc. 81, serial 1836). Each volume is indexed by name of claimant or subject, but many names were omitted. There is also an "Index to Reports of Committee on Private Land Claims, House of Representatives" on pages 5–20 of *House Index to Committee Reports* by T. H. McKee (Y1.3:C73/2). The Congressional Serial Set provides digested summaries and alphabetical lists of private claims presented to the U.S. Congress from the 1st to 51st Congress (1789–1891). See table 25.

Private land claims **case files** in Record Group 49 are arranged by state or other geographic area, and thereunder by docket number, with indexes for most areas. Types of records include correspondence, reports, maps and plats, petitions, affidavits, transcripts of court decisions, and deeds and abstracts of title. Because proof of title was required, wills, deeds, marriage certificates, and assignments may be found among these records; for the most part, they are certified copies of original documents. Most of the records were created during the adjudication of claims by agencies of the United States; they do not include the original grant or other documents of the previous government, except perhaps some copies in translation. For California, however, there are records, for the most part in Spanish, concerning claims presented to the Mexican government during the years 1822–46.

The following microfilm publications reproduce some of the records and indexes to private land claims in California: *Private Land Grant Cases in the Circuit Court of the Northern District of California, 1852–1910,* T1207, 28 rolls; *Index to Private Land Grant Cases, U.S. District Court, Northern District of California, 1853–1910,* T1214, 1 roll; *Index by County to Private Land Grant Cases, U.S. District Court, Northern and Southern Districts of California,* T1216, 1 roll; and *Index to Private Land Grant Cases, U.S. District Court, Southern District of California,* T1215, 1 roll.

Genealogical information in the claims varies. Some claims mention only the name of the claimant and the location of the land; others show such additional information about the claimant as place of residence at the time the claim was made and the names of relatives, both living and dead. Often there is more information about heirs than about the original claimant.

15.5 Land Records at Regional Archives Branches

Some of the records of the Bureau of Land Management are held by the various archives branches located in Federal Archives and Records Centers. They are listed in this section by state. The arrangement of the records is usually chronological, or, in the case of final certificates, numerical. Where indexes exist, they are alphabetical by surname or, for mineral lands, by name of mine. Not all land offices have all the series listed or all of the time spans indicated.

Arizona

Tractbooks, Gila and Salt River Meridian, ca. 1875–1959 and Phoenix serial register books, 1908–1970, are at the archives branch, FARC Denver.

At the archives branch, FARC Los Angeles are the following records of the suveyor general, Arizona, and of land offices at Phoenix, Prescott, Tucson, and Florence: applications for mineral surveys, 1904–14; applications for mineral surveys, 1887–1920; registered mining claims, 1871–1902; register of entries on mining lands, 1892–1905; register of applications for mining patents, 1905–8; orders for homestead surveys, 1909–25; register of homestead entries, 1871–1908; abstracts of final desert land certificates, 1887–1905; register of timber culture entries, 1883–91; register of final timber culture certificates, 1884–1903; abstracts of public land sold, 1871–97; and register of applications from Indians for nonreservation lands, 1888–91.

California

At the archives branch, FARC Los Angeles, are these records of the land office at Los Angeles: homestead applications, 1886–95; register of homestead entries, 1869–1908; register of final homestead certificates issued, 1873–1906; applications for desert land entries, 1887–93; register of applications for mining patents, 1873–81; declaratory statements of intention to claim lands, 1863–90; and register of timber culture entries, 1875–92.

Colorado

At the archives branch, FARC Denver, are records of the Central City, Del Norte, Denver, Durango, Glenwood Springs, Gunnison, Hugo, Lamar, Leadville, Montrose, Pueblo, and Sterling land offices: land entry registers and tractbooks, ca. 1864–1908; serial register books, ca. 1908–49; enlarged homestead designations, 1911–21; stockraising homestead designations, 1930–36; record of patents delivered, 1918 and before; mineral survey index, 1885–1950; surveyor general's mineral claim index, 1875–1907; and alphabetical listing by claim, "L–Z," 1887–1908.

Iowa

At the archives branch, FARC Kansas City, are land entry abstracts: warrant books, cashbooks, receipts, homestead entries, and other abstracts of lands granted by land offices in Burlington, 1840–97; Chariton, 1853–59; Kanesville

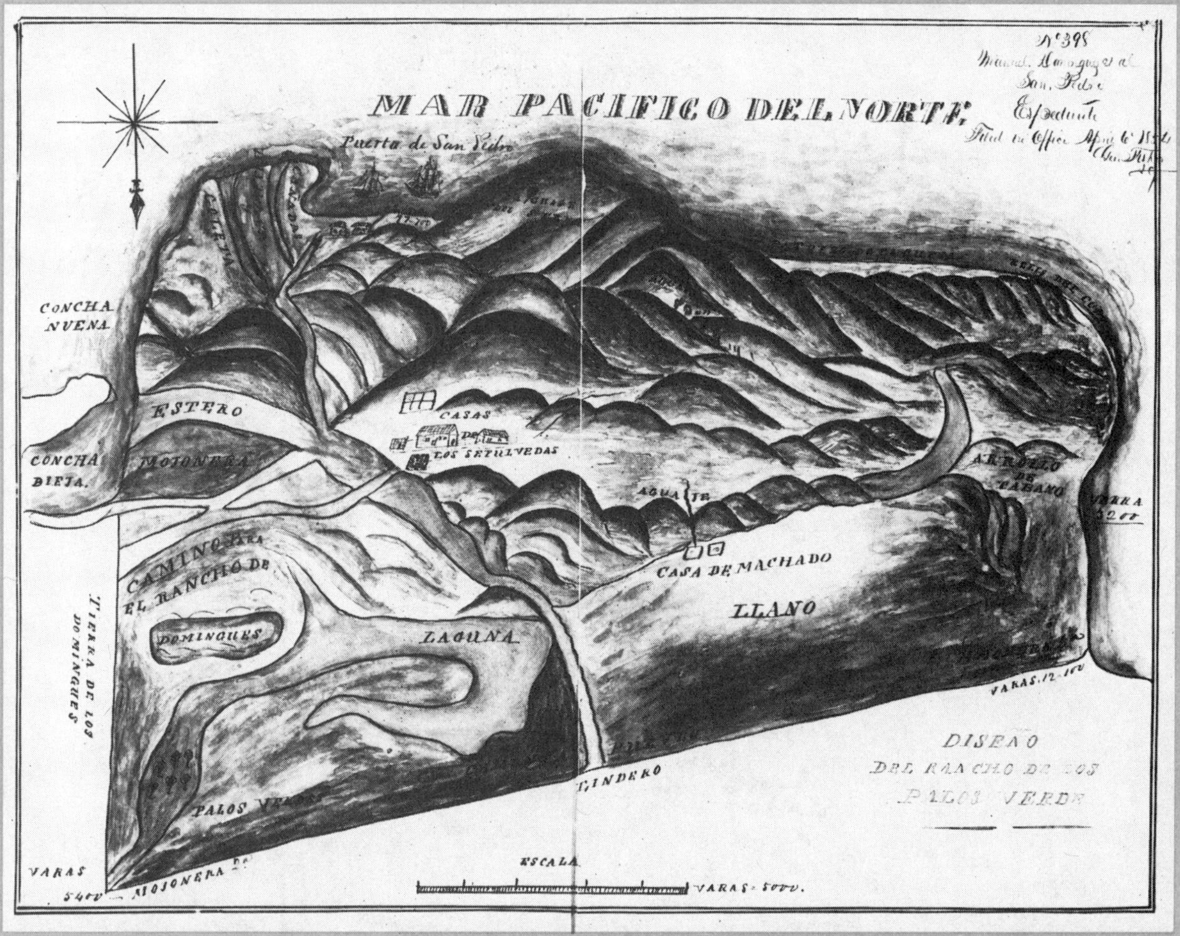

Diseño No. 398. Map submitted in support of a private land claim in California, 1854. Records of the Bureau of Land Management, Record Group 49.

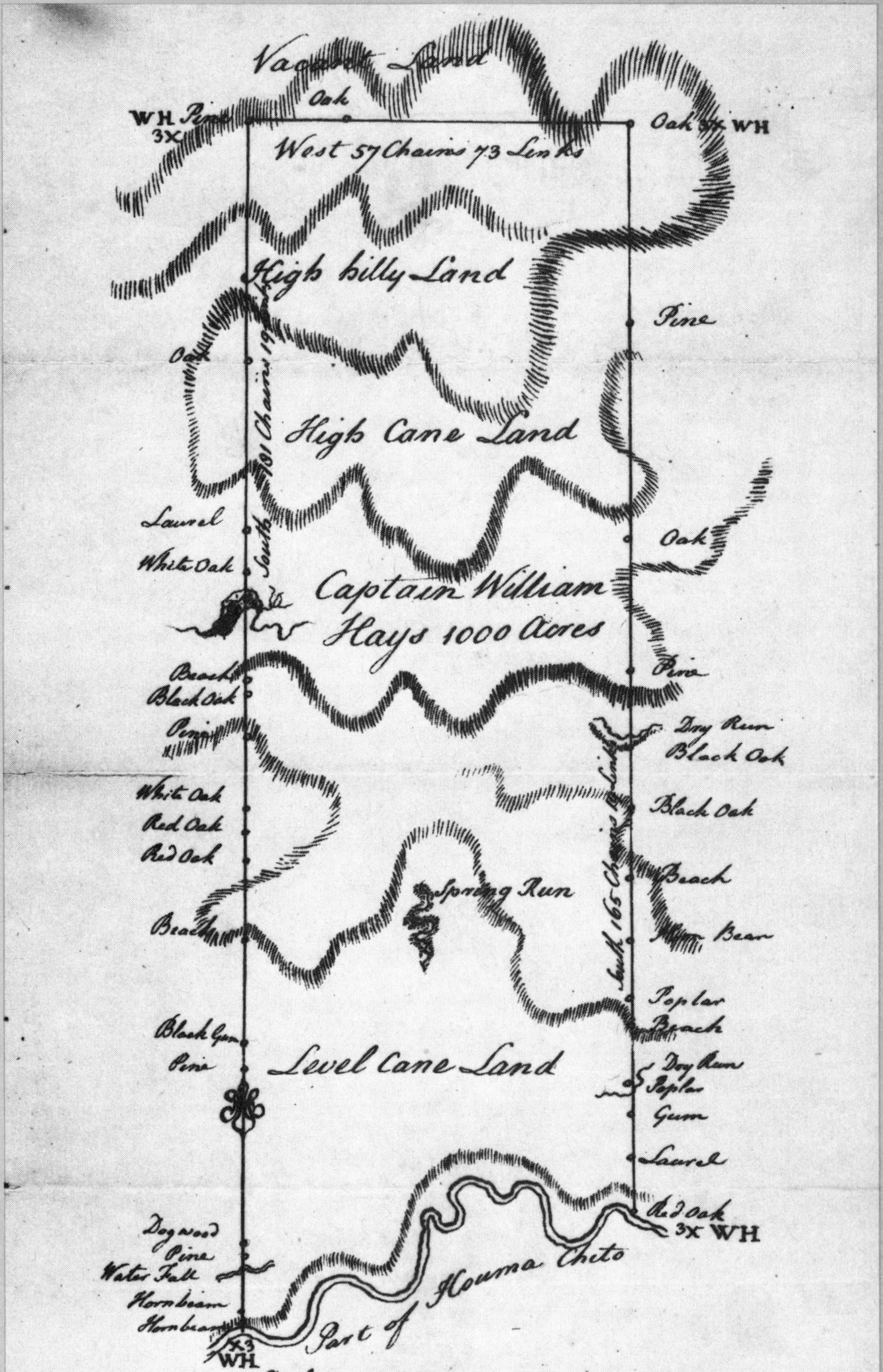

Survey plat of a 1773 British Florida land grant in support of a private land claim in Florida. Records of the Bureau of Land Management, Record Group 49.

and Council Bluffs, 1853–73; Decorah, 1855–59; Des Moines, 1852–1909; Dubuque, 1838–59; Fairfield, 1842–59; Fort Des Moines, 1853–90; Fort Dodge, 1855–86; Iowa City, 1851–73; and Sioux City, 1855–78.

Kansas
At the archives branch, FARC Kansas City, are the following land entry abstracts: register of absentee Wyandotte Indian selections and homestead entries from land offices in Dodge City, 1905, and Junction City, 1863–74.

Montana
At the archives branch, FARC Denver, are records of the Billings, Bozeman, Glasgow, Great Falls, Havre, Helena, Kalispell, Lewistown, Miles City, and Missoula land offices: tractbooks, 1850–1933; abstracts of cash entries, 1868–1908; registers of mineral entries, 1868–1908; registers of applications for mineral patents, 1870–1908; registers of homestead entries and homestead final certificates, 1868–1908; abstracts of desert land and timber culture entries and final certificates, 1877–1908; abstracts of various scrip entries, 1870–1908; abstracts of declaratory statements, 1885–91; record of patents delivered, 1871–1916; register of rejected entries, 1890–1908; and serial register books, 1908–50.

Nevada
At the archives branch, FARC San Francisco, are the following records of the Carson City, Elko, Eureka, and Reno land offices: township tractbooks, 1864–1964; original township survey plats, 1861–1962; record of patents delivered, 1884–1909; register of homestead entries filed under the act of 1862, 1864–1908; register of final homestead certificates, 1869–1908; register of mining land entries, 1862–1908; register of receipts for mineral lands sold, 1868–93; abstract of desert land entries, 1877–1908; register of timber culture entries, 1876–88; and unpatented land entry serial case files, 1881–1968.

New Mexico
At the archives branch, FARC Denver, are the following records of Clayton, Folsom, Fort Sumner, La Mesilla, Las Cruces, Roswell, Santa Fe, and Tucumcari land offices: registers of donation notifications and entries, 1855–71; registers of homestead entries, 1868–1904; registers of homestead final certificates, 1875–1907; registers of mineral entries, 1869–1903; registers of mining patent applications, 1876–1904; registers of desert land and timber entries, 1875–1908; timber culture final certificates, 1892–1903; desert land final certificates, 1883–1907; registers of receipts for lands sold, 1868–96; preemptions, 1878–88; homesteads, 1868–1906; mineral lands, 1874–1906; timber culture, 1875–91; coal land, 1868–88, and desert land, 1882–1906; registers of declaratory statements, 1888–1908; registers of soldiers' homestead declaratory statements, 1879–1908; and serial register books, 1908–56.

CHAPTER 16

Claims Records

16.1 Introduction

For most of the nineteenth century, many claims against the U.S. Government were settled by the Treasury Department. If a claim was rejected by the Treasury Department, the claimant's only recourse was to appeal directly to Congress. Petitions to that body for relief had become so numerous by mid-century that Congress was finding it impossible to make proper and necessary investigations for action on them. Although the U.S. Court of Appeals was established in 1855, it was not until the late 1880s that Congress ceased entirely to serve in an appellate capacity on private claims. Claims relating to services, supplies, or transportation furnished to or requisitioned for the army were heard by the quartermaster general.

The papers relating to an individual claim are often in a single folder or jacket and consist of a filled-out form, correspondence, and supporting documents. The records relating to an individual claim vary considerably in the information they contain, depending on the nature of the claim. Almost any claim record shows the name of the claimant, age, and place of residence at the date of filing; some contain the names of parents, grandparents, or other family members and other personal information.

Discussed in this chapter are nonmilitary claims adjudicated by the Treasury Department and appealed to Congress, claims against the U.S. Army settled by the quartermaster general, and two special kinds of claims: French spoliation claims and Indian depredation claims. Disallowed claims of U.S. Colored Troops are discussed on page 186, Southern Claims Commission claims on page 165, pension and bounty land warrant applications on pages 135 and 145, and Cherokee Indian claims on page 172.

16.2 Claims Brought Before Congress

Congressional claims records often contain information about local political, social, and economic affairs. The private claims brought before Congress consist of petitions and memorials, sometimes with related papers, presenting claims against the government for military service; for confirmation of land grants; for damages to persons or property committed by agents of the government, by foreign governments, or by Indian tribes; and for other forms of private relief such as the removal of political disabilities imposed on certain former Confederates by section three of the Fourteenth Amendment. The records of the House of Representatives also include papers relating to claims rejected by the Southern Claims Commission.

One group of claims brought before Congress was published in *American State Papers* (036–216): "Claims Barred by the Statute of Limitations but Adjusted and Allowed, 1810." On 12 December 1810, Secretary of the Treasury Albert Gallatin sent to the Senate a statement of all the claims which had been adjusted and allowed at the Treasury Department and for which certificates of registered debt had been issued under "An act providing for the settlement of claims of persons under particular circumstances barred by limitations heretofore established," passed 27 March 1792. The statement provides the names of nearly 1,500 men who served during the Revolutionary War, the date of certificate, the number of the statement, the type of service performed, the date on which interest commenced, and the amount of money allowed. There is a name index.

Lists of private claims brought before the Senate and the House of Representatives were printed as congressional documents. Each list is arranged alphabetically by name of claimant and shows the nature or object of the claim, the Congress and session before which it was brought, the nature and number or date of the committee report, and additional information. Table 24 shows the coverage of each list and cites the congressional document.

TABLE 25

Lists of Private Claims Brought Before Congress

Congress	**Dates**	**Congressional document containing list**
Senate		
14th–46th	1815–81	46th Cong., 3d sess., S. Misc. Doc. 14, serials 1945–46
47th–51st	1881–91	53d Cong., 2d sess., S. Misc. Doc. 266, serial 3175
52d–55th	1891–99	56th Cong., 1st sess., S. Doc. 449, serial 3881
56th and 57th	1899–1903	57th Cong., 2d sess., S. Doc. 221, serial 4433
58th	1903–5	59th Cong., 1st sess., S. Doc. 3, serial 4917
59th and 60th	1905–9	60th Cong., 2d sess., S. Doc. 646, serial 6165
House of Representatives		
1st–31st	1789–1851	32d Cong., 1st sess., H. Misc. Doc. (unnumbered), serials 653–655
32d–41st	1851–71	42d Cong., 3d sess., H. Misc. Doc. 109, serial 1574
42d–46th	1871–81	47th Cong., 1st sess., H. Misc. Doc. 53, serial 2036
47th–51st	1881–91	53d Cong., 2d sess., H. Misc. Doc. 213, serial 3268

These lists were compiled from entries in the *Journals* of the Senate and House. They do not accurately reflect the actual content of the claims files because individual files were often forwarded by Congress to the various executive agencies for implementation or returned to the petitioners or their congressional representatives.

The claims brought before the Senate are in Record Group 46; those brought before the House of Representatives are in Record Group 233.

Records more than fifty years old in the files of the Senate are open to researchers, with some exceptions. Records or reproductions of records of the House of Representatives may be made available to researchers only with the authorization of the Clerk of the House.

16.3 Quartermaster Claims

Claims records, 1839–1914, but principally 1861–90, are in Record Group 92. They normally consist of claims registers, correspondence, and other loose papers relating to individual claims. They are arranged by type of service rendered, and thereunder by the number assigned to each claim by the third auditor of the treasury. Most of the individual registers include name indexes, and there are, in addition, some separate name indexes that cover several registers. In many instances, the loose documentation pertaining to an individual claim has been removed from the quartermaster files and transferred to the third auditor's office as part of the settlement process and may not be extant.

For the pre-Civil War period, 1839–60, there are four volumes of registers: claims examined in the Quartermaster General's Office, 1839–42, one volume, arranged numerically; claims received relating chiefly to the Mexican War, 1847–58, one volume, arranged generally chronologically; and claims received from civilians (mostly Mexican War teamsters) for services performed, 1848–60, two volumes, the first volume arranged alphabetically by initial letter of surname of claimant, and the second arranged chronologically by date of receipt of claim. All four volumes include name indexes.

Claims arising from the Civil War and settled in the following decades constitute the bulk of the quartermaster claims records. An act of 4 July 1864 (13 Stat. 381), made the quartermaster general responsible for investigating and recommending settlement of "all claims of loyal citizens in states not in rebellion, for quartermaster's stores" furnished to or seized by the Union army, whether or not receipts had been issued for them. For the period 1861–70, these **"Fourth of July claims"** for horses and mules, forage and fuel, quarters, building materials, rent, personal services, mileage, extra duty, damages, and supplies are registered by auditor's number in sixty-eight volumes of claims registers. Also entered in these registers are rejected claims pertaining to services, horses, and property, 1866–86, and to horses and forage, 1864–90. The correspondence and related papers constituting the claims files are arranged by register volume, and thereunder by auditor's number. There are name indexes in each register volume.

For the period 1871–89, claims relating to rent, forage, and fuel and other Fourth of July claims are registered by year, and thereunder by auditor's number in twenty-nine volumes, for which there is a partial name index in five volumes. The claims files parallel the arrangement of the registers. There are cross-references in the registers to Fourth of July claims considered and rejected by the quartermaster general. The rejected claims files, 1871–90, are arranged according to the numbers of the boxes, and thereunder the packages in which they were originally stored. There is an incomplete register of these rejected claims in two volumes, 1878–90, arranged by box and package number.

The registers and claims files for these Fourth of July claims are a good resource for genealogists, because they pertain to a large number of individuals and the information is generally interesting. Using the series, however, is so difficult that the search may not be worthwhile unless there is good reason to think the subject of research did in fact file a claim. He must have been a loyal citizen of a loyal state. It may also be necessary to know approximately when the claim was filed and for what type of goods or service. For the earlier 1861–70 period, the name indexes in all sixty-eight register volumes must be checked. For the 1871–89 period, the index is consolidated, but incomplete. For rejected claims, all the entries in the two-volume register must be searched, even though this register is also incomplete.

Other Civil War claims records include a one-volume register of claims received relating to transportation, 1861–62, and to personal services by persons later deceased, 1864–68, arranged by type of claim, and thereunder numerically, with a name index; a one-volume register of claims received relating to horses and mules, March–December 1864, arranged chronologically, and thereunder numerically; a one-volume register of claims received relating to national cemeteries, 1869–70, arranged by auditor's number, with a name index; and a one-volume register of claims received concerning mileage, extra-duty pay, final pay, arrears, and bounty, January 1867–October 1870, arranged alphabetically by initial letter of surname of claimant. Two series of claims files, one relating to property damage by Union troops, 1861–65, and the other to claims for public animals, which were submitted to the Cavalry Bureau in 1864, are arranged numerically. To use the records, researchers must first search the registers of letters received by the quartermaster general, 1818–70 (142 vols.).

Claims for remuneration for extra duty, mileage, quarters and fuel, and services, 1871–78, are represented by seven volumes of registers and by claims files arranged by year and thereunder by auditor's number. There are two volumes of registers for claims received relating to supplies originating after the Civil War and to rents originating during and after the war, 1875–78, with claims files, arranged by volume and auditor's number, and with two volumes of name indexes.

For the period 1879–90, there are eleven volumes of registers for claims received pertaining to personal services and allowances, and claims files arranged by year and auditor's number, with a one-volume incomplete name index; and four volumes of registers, 1879–94, relating to claims received for regular supplies, with claims files 1879–90, arranged by time period and thereunder by auditor's number, and a four-volume name index.

There are 131 separately maintained registers of **transportation claims,** 1861–87, arranged by type of claim, and thereunder by volume, consisting of fifteen volumes of registers relating to ocean and lake transportation claims and to claims for services and vessels, 1861–70, with vessel indexes; three volumes dealing with claims relating to transportation, value and services of vessels of western rivers, ferriages, tolls, and services on military railroads, 1861–70, with name and vessel indexes included; and 113 volumes relating to railroad transportation accounts, 1861–87.

By an act of 1902 (32 Stat. 43), Congress authorized the quartermaster general to spend $50,000 to reimburse paroled Confederate soldiers of the Army of Northern Virginia for horses, sidearms, and baggage seized by Union soldiers; the Union soldiers had acted under orders that violated the terms of surrender. Documentation generated, 1902–14, in support of these "Confederate horse claims" includes registers of claims paid, 1901–10, twelve pads arranged by time period, with name indexes, 1901–6; claims files, 1902–14, arranged by file numbers from the correspondence of the quartermaster general, 1890–1914; a few record cards for rejected claims, arranged by name of claimant; and unarranged press copies of lists of claims submitted to the secretary of war, 1902–10.

16.4 Other Claims

In 1872, the **Alabama claims** were described in a Department of State publication *Revised List of Claims Filed with the Department of State, Growing Out of the Acts Committed by the Several Vessels, which have Given Rise to the Claims Generically Known As the Alabama Claims* (S3.13/1:C52/2). The list provides information on losses to Confederate privateers such as the *Alabama,* the *Shenandoah,* the *Florida,* the *Tallahassee,* and an index of the names of ships and individuals involved.

A facsimile of the manuscript of the index to the Alabama claims was issued some time after 1872 under the title, *List of the Documents and Correspondence in the Cases of the United States and of Great Britain* (S3.13/1:D65).

The **French spoliation case files** are legal and evidentiary documents relating to claims arising from depredations committed by French warships and privateers on American commerce during the period 1793–1801. Included are shipping records and other documents dated as early as 1783. The case files are in Records of the U.S. Court of Claims, Record Group 123. They are arranged by case number.

Indexes to the files are in Records of the Court of Claims Section (Justice), Record Group 205. Among them is *French Spoliation Awards by the Court of Claims of the United States Under the Act of January 20, 1885* (Washington: U.S. Court of Claims, 1934), which gives the name of each original claimant, vessel, master, and case file number. The work is arranged alphabetically by name of original claimant. The "List of Vessels, With the Docket Number of Cases, Filed in the Court of Claims Under the Act of 20 January 1885," an alphabetical list of vessels that shows names of masters and case numbers of all pertinent cases, can also be consulted. These claims provide genealogical information because of the long period between the time an American merchant or shipowner suffered loss in the 1793–1801 period and the time when his heirs filed claims in the 1880s. Claimants under the 1885 act had to prove descent from the original claimants.

Further information about French spoliation claims is found in *Records of the United States Court of Claims,* Preliminary Inventory 58, compiled by Gaiselle Kerner (Washington: National Archives and Records Service, 1953), and *Records of the Court of Claims Section of the Department of Justice,* Preliminary Inventory 47, compiled by Gaiselle Kerner and Ira N. Kellogg, Jr. (Washington: National Archives and Records Service, 1952).

Indian depredation case files contain legal documents and correspondence relating to claims for property taken or destroyed by Indians of tribes at peace with the United States. The incidents on which the claims were based took place in the period from roughly 1814 through the Sioux uprising of 1890–91, although most of them occurred during the hostilities of the 1860s and 1870s. The documents used as evidence in the cases often present colorful pictures of frontier life, which could add an interesting note to the genealogy of a descendant of one of the claimants. The case files, arranged by case number, are in the Records of the U.S. Court of Claims, Record Group 123.

Closely related material in Record Group 205 is described in Preliminary Inventory 47. Perhaps the most useful record in this record group is a one-volume index to names of claimants and claimants' representatives and to names of Indian tribes committing the depredations. The alphabetical index entries refer to the appropriate case numbers. A list of tribes without case numbers is in appendix II of Preliminary Inventory 58, *Records of the United States Court of Claims.*

CHAPTER 17

Court Records

17.1 Introduction

Described in this chapter are Records of District Courts of the United States, Record Group 21, except naturalization records, which are discussed in detail in chapter 3; records of pardons and paroles; extradition records; and records of persons apprehended by the U.S. Secret Service. Records of courts-martial are described in chapter 4.

17.2 Records of U.S. District Courts

The records of U.S. district courts are in the custody of the various regional archives branches. They include criminal, civil, admiralty, and bankruptcy dockets and case files; indexes; and related records. Depending on when the court was established, the records are dated from 1789 to the mid-1950s.

A **docket** is a volume containing brief abstracts of the successive proceedings in a case. Over the years, courts have created a number of different kinds of dockets, such as appearance dockets, bar dockets, execution dockets, and judgment dockets. These volumes are usually arranged by case file number. Many dockets contain alphabetical indexes to names of persons involved in the actions.

Case files consist of original unbound papers filed in connection with court proceedings. Depending on the type of action, they include pleadings, criminal indictments, civil complaints, depositions, jury verdicts, transcripts of testimony, exhibits, and other formal court records. Occasionally, case files (admiralty, civil, criminal, and bankruptcy) were maintained together without regard for the type of action.

Record books and final record books contain brief descriptions of court proceedings and copies of papers filed in connection with specific cases. Entries in record books are usually arranged chronologically; it is therefore possible for entries concerning a specific case to be found in a number of different volumes. Final record books usually contain copies of papers filed in connection with a case; the data are usually consolidated in one volume. Because original papers are often missing from case files, these volumes may contain the only extant record of certain actions.

Very few archives branches have custody of the alphabetical name indexes to case files that were created by the courts. Where they exist, they have usually been retained by the courts.

In addition to the records mentioned above, some archives branches have British vice-admiralty records, U.S. circuit court records, Confederate district court records, and U.S. territorial court records. Branches have also accessioned records of U.S. attorneys and marshals, which are closely related to the U.S. district court records.

Some of the holdings of the archives branches of Record Group 21 are described by state in the following pages. Questions about the existence of records for other U.S. district courts should be directed to the chief of the appropriate archives branch. You can determine the appropriate branch and mailing address by using table 2 on page 18.

17.3 Pardon and Parole Records

Early pardon records are in General Records of the Department of State, Record Group 59. **Petitions for pardon,** 1789–1860, request pardons for persons convicted of federal crimes. They are arranged by Presidential administration, and thereunder numerically if the pardon was granted and alphabetically if the pardon was not granted. The cover sheet for each case shows the case number, name of criminal, and location in the series of pardons and remissions where a copy of the pardon is bound.

Copies of **pardons and remissions,** 1793–1893, are arranged chronologically in sixteen volumes; each volume is indexed.

A **register of pardons,** 1793–1871, is arranged by Presidential administration, and thereunder by pardon number. The part covering the period 1844–71 also contains an alphabetical list. An entry shows name, case number, place where the case arose, nature of the crime, President who issued the pardon, and location of the pardon in the series of pardons and remissions. Name **indexes to pardons and remissions** are in one volume (incomplete) for 1847–48 and one volume for 1847–71.

To use these records, the researcher must know the approximate date of the pardon. The case file number can be found in the register and used to locate the petition for pardon.

Other records relating to federal prisoners who appealed to the President for pardon are in Records of the Office of the Pardon Attorney, Record Group 204.

Case files, 1853–1946, consist of applications, correspondence, and reports on the case or prisoner. They are arranged by case number, which is made up of a number or a letter and the number of the page of the docket volume where the case is entered.

The **docket of pardon cases,** 1853–1923, records in forty-one volumes the formal steps in the history of each case, from the time the petition was filed until final action was taken. The information shown for each case includes name of prisoner, judicial district where convicted, nature of the crime, sentence and date, place of incarceration, and action by the President and date. Each volume contains an alphabetical index.

Entries in an **index for pardon cases,** 1853–89, are arranged alphabetically by applicant for case files and docket volumes. Shown is name, judicial district, case number, and action taken.

Pardon warrants, 1893–1936, are copies of warrants for pardons that were granted by the President. Warrants before 1929 show case numbers. They are arranged by date of pardon in twenty-nine volumes. Each volume includes an index to persons pardoned.

Also in Record Group 204 are records of pardons denied, files on pardons of political prisoners of World War I, and correspondence about pardon matters. See *Records of the Office of the Pardon Attorney,* Preliminary Inventory 87, compiled by Gaiselle Kerner (Washington: National Archives and Records Service, 1955).

17.4 Extradition Records

The main series of extradition records is in Record Group 59 and consists of chronologically arranged case files, 1836–1906. Later cases are part of the central numerical and decimal files of the Department of State. The case files include applications of the United States to foreign governments for extradition of fugitives from U.S. justice, applications of foreign governments to the United States for extradition of fugitives from justice of those countries, and related court papers. Extradition case files include the name of the person to be extradited, the country involved, and the nature, place, and date of the crime of which the person sought is accused. Cases before 1877 contain references to related correspondence in other State Department records. The index to Presidential pardons for the years 1843–68 also shows which cases involved extradition.

To use these records, the researcher must know the date the warrant for extradition was issued for the person being researched.

17.5 U.S. Secret Service Records

Records relating to criminals and suspects in Records of the U.S. Secret Service, Record Group 87, are dated 1863–1971. They are mainly case files for persons arrested for counterfeiting U.S. currency and registers of persons suspected of this crime. Information in the case files includes, when applicable, time, place, and reason for arrest; date of trial; sentence; and the physical appearance and personal history of the accused person. Photographs of the accused are usually included. The records are arranged in rough chronological order, but there are indexes in some volumes.

CHAPTER 18

Records of the District of Columbia

CHAPTER 18

Records of the District of Columbia

18.1 Introduction

The District of Columbia was created by acts of 16 July 1790 and 3 March 1791 from lands ceded to the federal government by Maryland and Virginia. Originally, it included the town and county of Alexandria, Va., and the city of Georgetown. The area ceded by Virginia was retroceded in 1846, and in 1878 Georgetown was annexed, giving the city its present limits and making the city of Washington coextensive with the District of Columbia. Until 1879, the area within the District but outside both Georgetown and Washington City was known as Washington County.

In Record Group 21 are federal court records relating to the District of Columbia (except for the part returned to Virginia). They include transcripts of wills, administration papers relating to estates of decedents, guardianship papers, and identures of apprenticeship. Emancipation papers are described on page 184; naturalization records are described on page 76. For records of residents of the District of Columbia who were civilian employees of the federal government, see chapter 14.

In Record Group 351 are several series relating to applications and appointments to positions within the D.C. government. There are also assessment and taxation records and deeds pertaining to ownership of real property in the cities of Washington and Georgetown and the county of Washington.

18.2 Court Records

Transcripts of wills probated in the District of Columbia, 1801–88, are arranged chronologically in twenty-five volumes. A second series of transcripts, 1801–1919, and the original wills are deposited with the Register of Wills and Clerk of the Probate Court, U.S. Courthouse, Washington, DC 20001.

A one-volume "General Index to Recorded Wills," arranged by name of maker of the will, gives the volume and page numbers to both series. A two-volume index labeled "Probate Index to Wills Filed and Wills Recorded," gives the volume and page numbers for the second series only.

A will normally shows the name and address of the maker, dates of the will and its probate, name of the executor, and often names of children or other family members.

Administration records, 1801–78, relate to the estates of decedents. They include bound administration dockets, of which those between 1837 and 1853 are missing, and unbound administration case files. A volume entitled "Probate Index" indexes both the dockets and the case files by surname of decedent.

A docket shows the name of the administrator, or if the deceased had made a will, the name of the executor; name and residence of the decedent; names of sureties; and date letters of administration were granted. A case file usually contains the inventory of the estate, the account or periodical accounts of the administrators or executors, related vouchers, and sometimes a petition for administration and related correspondence. It normally shows the name of the decedent, the nature and value of the estate, and the amount distributed to each named heir. It sometimes shows the date of death of the decedent and the names of heirs at law.

Guardian records, 1801–78, relate to estates inherited by wards of the court, chiefly minors. They include bound guardian dockets and the unbound case files of guardian papers. The only complete index to the names of the wards is the same one-volume "Probate Index" as for the administration records. It indexes both the dockets and the case files.

A docket shows the names of the guardian and the sureties; name and residence of the decedent; names of wards, and if they were minors, usually their dates of births or ages; and value of the estate. A case file normally contains the account or periodical accounts of the guardian, related vouchers, and often related correspondence. A case file usually shows the name of the guardian and the amounts distributed periodically to each ward.

Indentures of apprenticeship, 1801–74, are arranged chronologically. The originals are unbound, but copies, which exist for 1801–11 only, are bound in one volume. Both the unbound originals and the bound copies are indexed. An indenture of apprenticeship is a single document that shows the name and usually the age of the apprentice, name of one parent, name and trade of the master, and terms of the apprenticeship.

18.3 Records of D.C. Government Employees

Registers of appointments in the District of Columbia government, 1871–80, relate to appointments as commissioners, trustees of the public schools, physicians to the poor, Metropolitan Police Force, justices of the peace, commissioners of the Washington Asylum, and to the offices of the collector, treasurer, assessor, and engineers. The entries relate primarily to appointments made during the period 1871–80, but they include appointments to the metropolitan police force as early as 1861. Entries usually show the name of the appointee, position, salary, amount of bond, date of removal or resignation, and remarks. Most entries are arranged by office, and thereunder chronologically by date of appointment. They are indexed by name.

A **roster of employees** in local government offices, 1876–78, includes employee's name, position, salary, and remarks concerning dismissal, resignation, salary changes, appointment, and other data. The roster is arranged alphabetically by name of office.

Applications for employment in the Bureau of Streets, Avenues, and Alleys are dated 1871–74. Entries include file number, name of applicant, residence, date of application, position desired, by whom recommended, and notations on action taken. They are arranged by file number and indexed.

A **register of appointments to the Metropolitan Police Force,** 1861–1930, covers men appointed between 1861 and 1906 and documents their careers on the force through 1930. Entries show name; date and place of birth; date and place of naturalization, if applicable; former occupation; marital status and number in the family; home

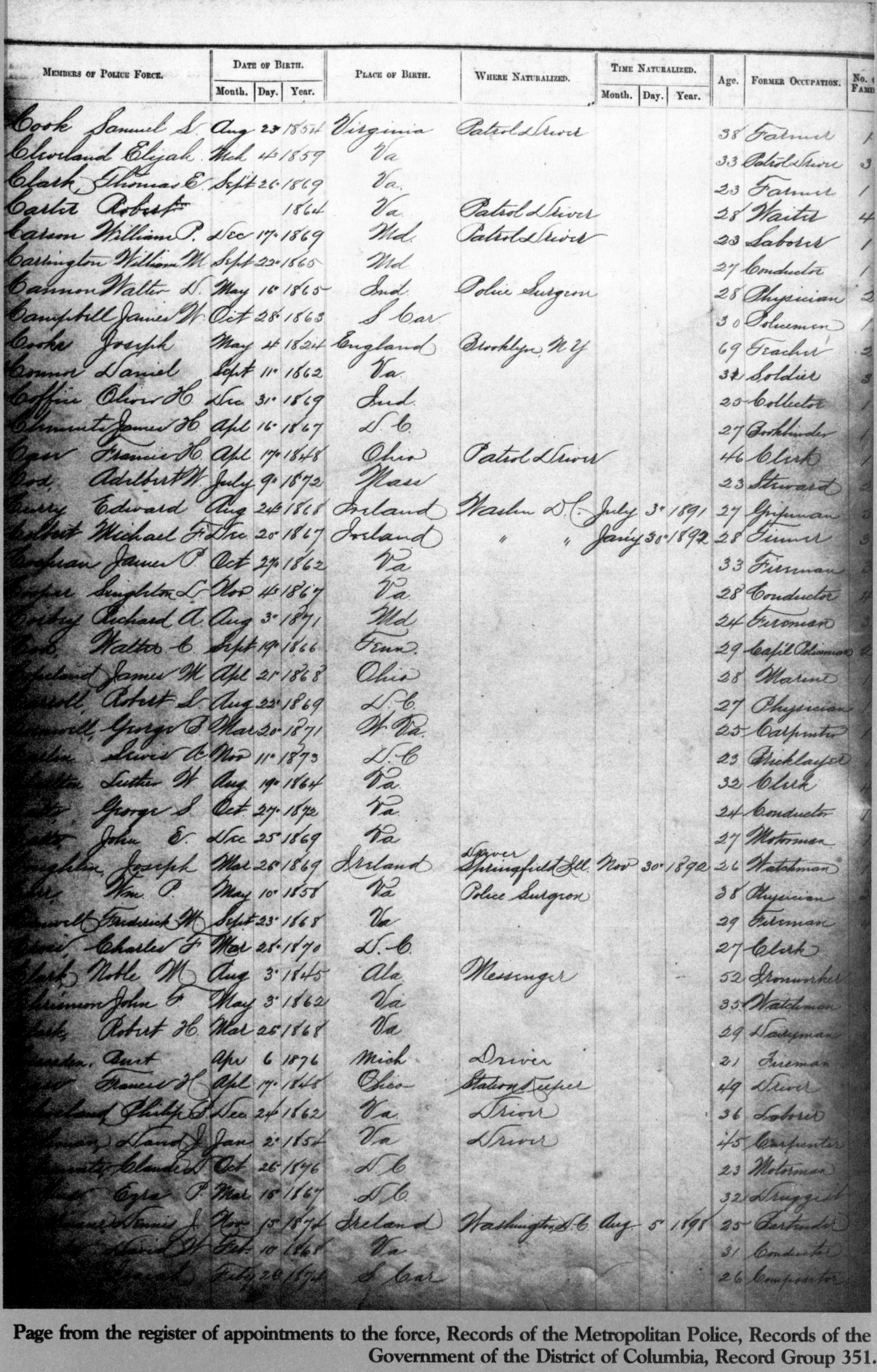

Members of Police Force.	Date of Birth. Month.	Day.	Year.	Place of Birth.	Where Naturalized.	Time Naturalized. Month.	Day.	Year.	Age.	Former Occupation.	No. of Fam…
Cook Samuel S.	Aug	23	1854	Virginia	Patrol Driver				38	Farmer	1
Cleveland Elijah	Mch	4	1859	Va					33	Patrol Driver	3
Clark Thomas E.	Sept	26	1869	Va.					23	Farmer	1
Carter Robert			1864	Va	Patrol Driver				28	Waiter	4
Carson William P.	Dec	17	1869	Md	Patrol Driver				23	Laborer	1
Carrington William M.	Sept	22	1865	Md					27	Conductor	1
Cannon Walter D.	May	16	1865	Ind.	Police Surgeon				28	Physician	2
Campbell James W.	Oct	28	1863	S Car					30	Policeman	1
Cooke Joseph	May	4	1824	England	Brooklyn, N.Y.				69	Teacher	2
Connor Daniel	Sept	11	1862	Va					31	Soldier	1
Coffin Oliver H.	Dec	31	1869	Ind.					25	Collector	1
Clements James H.	Apl	16	1867	D.C.					27	Bookbinder	1
Carr Francis H.	Apl	17	1848	Ohio	Patrol Driver				46	Clerk	1
Cod Adelbert W.	July	9	1872	Mass					23	Steward	
Curry Edward	Aug	24	1868	Ireland	Washn D.C.	July	3	1891	27	Gripman	
Colbert Michael F.	Dec	20	1867	Ireland	"	Jany	30	1892	28	Tinner	
Cochran James P.	Oct	27	1862	Va					33	Fireman	
Cooper Singleton L.	Nov	4	1867	Va					28	Conductor	
Cosby Richard A.	Aug	3	1871	Md					24	Fireman	
... Walter C.	Sept	19	1866	Tenn.					29	[illegible]	
Copeland James M.	Apl	21	1868	Ohio					28	Marine	
Carroll Robert S.	Aug	22	1869	D.C.					27	Physician	
Cromwell George B.	Mar	20	1871	W. Va.					25	Carpenter	
... Lewis A.	Nov	11	1873	D.C.					23	Bricklayer	
...ton Luther W.	Aug	19	1864	Va					32	Clerk	
... George S.	Oct	27	1872	Va					24	Conductor	
... John E.	Dec	25	1869	Va					27	Motorman	
...ughlin Joseph	Mar	26	1869	Ireland	Driver Springfield Ill.	Nov	30	1892	26	Watchman	
... Wm. P.	May	10	1858	Va	Police Surgeon				38	Physician	
...well Frederick M.	Sept	23	1868	Va					29	Fireman	
... Charles F.	Mar	25	1870	D.C.					27	Clerk	
Clark Noble M.	Aug	3	1845	Ala	Messenger				52	Ironworker	
... John F.	May	3	1862	Va					35	Watchman	
... Robert H.	Mar	25	1868	Va					29	Dairyman	
... Burt	Apr	6	1876	Mich	Driver				21	Fireman	
... Francis H.	Apl	17	1848	Ohio	Station Keeper				49	Driver	
...land Philip S.	Dec	24	1862	Va	Driver				36	Laborer	
... David J.	Jan	2	1854	Va	Driver				45	Carpenter	
... Claude D.	Oct	26	1876	D.C.					23	Motorman	
... Ezra P.	Mar	18	1867	D.C.					32	Druggist	
... Dennis J.	Nov	15	1874	Ireland	Washington D.C.	Aug	5	1898	25	Bartender	
... David W.	Feb	10	1868	Va					31	Conductor	
...	Feby	26	1874	S Car					26	Compositor	

Page from the register of appointments to the force, Records of the Metropolitan Police, Records of the Government of the District of Columbia, Record Group 351.

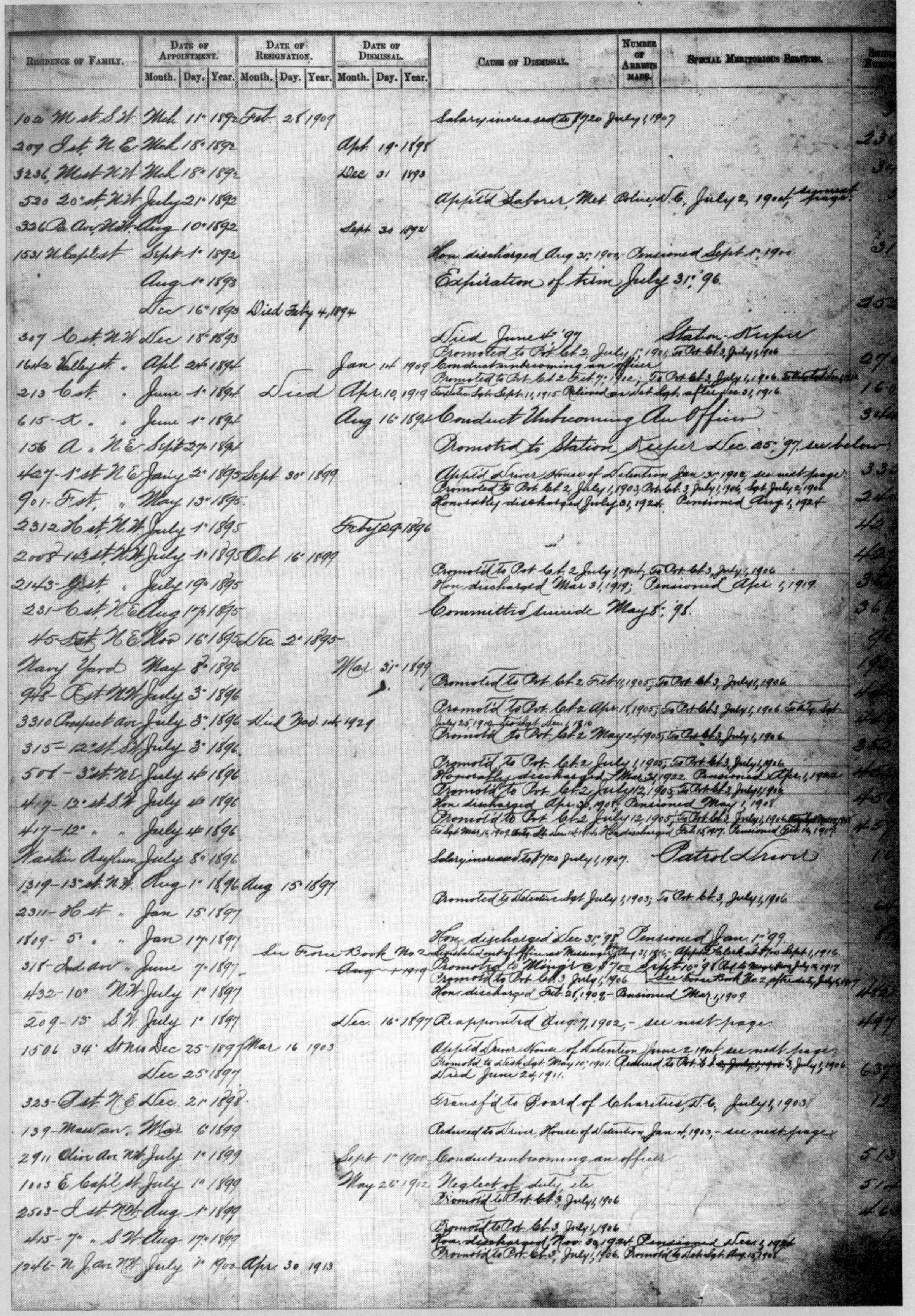

Residence of Family.	Date of Appointment. Month.	Day.	Year.	Date of Resignation. Month.	Day.	Year.	Date of Dismissal. Month.	Day.	Year.	Cause of Dismissal.	Number of Arrests made.	Special Meritorious Services.	Serial Number
102 M st. S.W.	Mch.	11th	1892	Feb.	28	1909				Salary increased to $720 July 1, 1907			[illegible]
207 I st. N.E.	Mch	18th	1892				Apr.	19th	1898				23[illegible]
3236 M st. N.W.	Mch	18th	1892				Dec	31	1893				34[illegible]
520 20th st. N.W.	July	21st	1892							Appt'd Laborer, Met. Police, D.C., July 2, 1904, see next page.			[illegible]
336 Pa. Ave. N.W.	Aug	10th	1892				Sept	30	1892				
1531 Whapple st.	Sept	1st	1892							Hon. discharged Aug 31, 1900 - Pensioned Sept 1, 1900			31
	Aug	1st	1893							Expiration of term July 31st 96.			
	Dec	16th	1893	Died Feby 4, 1894									25[illegible]
307 C st. N.W.	Dec	18th	1893							Died June 4th '97		Station-Keeper	
1642 Valley st. "	Apl	24th	1894				Jan	14	1909	Promoted to Pvt. Cl. 2, July 1st 1901, To Pvt. Cl. 3, July 1, 1906 Conduct unbecoming an officer			27[illegible]
213 C st. "	June	1st	1894	Died			Apr.	10,	1919	Promoted to Pvt. Cl. 2 Feb 7, 1902; To Pvt. Cl. 3, July 1, 1906. [illegible] To Detective Sgt. Sept. 11, 1915. Retired as Det. Sgt. after Dec. 31, 1916.			16[illegible]
615 - K " "	June	1st	1894				Aug	16th	1894	Conduct Unbecoming An Officer			34[illegible]
156 A " N.E.	Sept	27th	1894							Promoted to Station Keeper Dec. 25, '97, see below			
427 - 1st st. N.E.	Jany	2nd	1895	Sept	30th	1899				Appt'd Driver, House of Detention Jan 3rd 1902, see next page			33[illegible]
901 - F st. "	May	13th	1895							Promoted to Pvt. Cl. 2, July 1, 1903, Pvt. Cl. 3 July 1, 1906, Sgt. July 2, 1906 Honorably discharged July 31, 1924. Pensioned Aug 1, 1924			24[illegible]
2312 H st. N.W.	July	1st	1895				Feby	29th	1896				42[illegible]
2008 14th st. N.W.	July	1st	1895	Oct	16th	1899							4[illegible]
2143 - G st. "	July	19th	1895							Promoted to Pvt. Cl. 2 July 1, 1901; To Pvt. Cl. 3, July 1, 1906 Hon. discharged Mar 31, 1919; Pensioned Apr 1, 1919			3[illegible]
231 - C st. N.E.	Aug	17th	1895							Committed suicide May 8, '98.			36[illegible]
45 - ~~I st.~~ N.E.	Nov	16th	1895	Dec.	2nd	1895							[illegible]
Navy Yard	May	8th	1896				Mar	31st	1899				19[illegible]
948 - R st. N.W.	July	3rd	1896							Promoted to Pvt. Cl. 2 Feb 11, 1905; To Pvt. Cl. 3, July 1, 1906			4[illegible]
3310 Prospect Ave	July	3rd	1896	Died Nov. 14 1929						Promoted To Pvt. Cl. 2 Apr. 15, 1905; To Pvt. Cl. 3 July 1, 1906. To Acty. Sgt. July 25, 1910. To Sgt. Dec 1, 1910			4[illegible]
315 - 12th st. S.W.	July	3rd	1896							Promoted to Pvt. Cl. 2 May 2, 1905; to Pvt. Cl. 3, July 1, 1906.			35[illegible]
508 - 3rd st. N.E.	July	4th	1896							Promoted to Pvt. Cl. 2 July 1, 1905; To Pvt. Cl. 3, July 1, 1906 Honorably discharged Mar 31, 1922. Pensioned Apr 1, 1922			4[illegible]
417 - 12th st. S.W.	July	4th	1896							Promoted to Pvt. Cl. 2 July 12, 1905; To Pvt. Cl. 3, July 1, 1906 Hon. discharged Apr. 30, 1908. Pensioned May 1, 1908.			45[illegible]
417 - 12th " "	July	4th	1896							Promoted to Pvt. Cl. 2 July 12, 1905; To Pvt. Cl. 3, July 1, 1906 [illegible] To Sgt. Mar 16, 1909. [illegible] Hon. discharged Feb. 15, 1917. Pensioned Feb. 16, 1917			45[illegible]
Washington Asylum	July	8th	1896							Salary increased to $720 July 1, 1907.		Patrol Driver	1[illegible]
1319 - 13th st. N.W.	Aug	1st	1896	Aug	15th	1897							
2311 - H st. "	Jan	15th	1897							Promoted to Detective Sgt. July 1, 1903; To Pvt. Cl. 3, July 1, 1906			6[illegible]
1809 - 5th " "	Jan	17th	1897							Hon. discharged Dec 31st 98 Pensioned Jan 1st '99.			[illegible]
318 - Ind. Ave "	June	7th	1897	See Force Book No 2			~~Aug 1 1919~~			Legislated out of Office as Messenger Aug 31, 1916. Appt'd Clerk at $900 Sept 1, 1916. Promoted to Mesngr @ $700 Sept 10th '98 [illegible] July 1, 1917			
432 - 10th N.W.	July	1st	1897							Promoted to Pvt. Cl. 3 July 1, 1906 See Force Book No 2, [illegible] July 1, 1917 Hon. discharged Feb. 28, 1908 - Pensioned Mar 1, 1909			48[illegible]
209 - 15 S.W.	July	1st	1897				Dec.	16th	1897	Reappointed Aug 7, 1902, - see next page			44[illegible]
1506 34th St N.W.	Dec	25th	1897	Mar	16	1903				Appt'd Driver House of Detention June 2, 1904, see next page			
	Dec	25th	1897							Promoted to Desk Sgt. May 10, 1901. Reduced to Pvt. Cl. ~~2, July 1, 1906~~ 3, July 1, 1906 Died June 24, 1911.			63[illegible]
323 - P st. N.E.	Dec.	21st	1898							Transf'd to Board of Charities, D.C., July 1, 1903			12[illegible]
139 - Mass. Ave. "	Mar	6	1899							Reduced to Driver, House of Detention, Jan 4, 1903, - see next page			
2911 Olive Ave N.W.	July	1st	1899				Sept	1st	1900	Conduct unbecoming an officer			513
1003 E Cap'l St.	July	1st	1899				May	26th	1902	Neglect of duty etc			51[illegible]
2503 - I st. N.W.	Aug	1st	1899							Promoted to Pvt. Cl. 3, July 1, 1906			46[illegible]
415 - 7th " S.W.	Aug	17th	1899							Promoted to Pvt. Cl. 3 July 1, 1906 ~~Hon. discharged Nov 30, 1924. Pensioned Dec 1, 1924~~			
1246 - N. Jer. Av. N.W.	July	1st	1900	Apr.	30	1913				Promoted to Pvt. Cl. 3, July 1, 1906. Promoted to Det. Sgt. Aug 15, 1908			

address; dates of appointment, resignation, or dismissal; pensions; and remarks concerning promotion or reasons for dismissal. Many are closed with date of death. Entries are arranged in rough alphabetical order by the initial letter of surname.

Metropolitan police service records, 1861–1930, cover men appointed between 1861 and 1917. The records show, for each name: date, position, and summary of service, including promotions, resignations, discharge, suspensions, fines, and other official personnel actions. They are arranged in rough alphabetical order by initial letter of surname.

Metropolitan Police Force personnel case files, 1861–1930, are alphabetically arranged records of men appointed between 1861 and 1900, with a few as late as 1926. The content of a file varies; a typical file may include application for appointment, recommendations, physical and medical information, summary of assignments, and records relating to complaints, disciplinary actions, and final board actions. Documents in these files are restricted.

Registers of oaths administered to members of the Metropolitan Police Force, 1862–65 and 1868–78, include name of officer, date, and signature of appointee as a patrolman, an additional patrolman, or a special patrolman. This series covers only temporary appointments and is arranged in rough chronological order.

18.4 Land and Property Records

Records relating to land and property in the District of Columbia include **deed books,** 1792–1869, that consist of handwritten copies of deeds that record the transfer of titles to real property. Also recorded are other legal documents such as bills of sale, mortgages, deeds of manumission of slaves, certificates of freedom establishing the free status of blacks in the antebellum period. Indexes to the records are maintained at the D.C. Recorder of Deeds' Office.

D.C. building permits, 1877–1949, consist of applications for permits, and permits issued for private construction, repairs to existing structures, erecting fences and signs, razing of buildings, installation of equipment, etc. The completed application forms include name of owner, location of construction, names and addresses of the architect and builder, purpose of construction, cost estimates, and details concerning the nature of the work and materials utilized. Sometimes, plans and sketches are included. They are arranged chronologically and numbered sequentially. The building permits are now being microfilmed as *D.C. Building Permits, 1877–1949,* M1116. The publication includes a card index, 1877–1958, arranged by number of square (block), name of street, or name of subdivision.

There are also *maps, plans, and atlases,* 1792–1915. The records consist primarily of manuscript and annotated maps, but also include plats and survey descriptions for various dates. Plat books, 1793–96, 1809, and 1853–83, show subdivisions of squares. Also included is the "Brewer Collection," which consists of plats, surveys, and related material pertaining primarily to Georgetown, 1809–91.

Assessment books, city of Washington, 1814–1940, consist of periodic compilations of assessors' valuations of real property in the city of Washington. Lists for 1902–40 include data for the city of Georgetown, and lists for 1908–40 include information for the county of Washington. Entries vary, but usually they show square and lot number, square footage, rate of taxation, value of land, and name of owner. Some volumes, especially later ones, show the assessed value of improvements. The volumes are arranged by number of square.

Tax books for the city of Washington are dated 1824–79. These are annual records of tax payments on real property in the city. A typical entry shows name of property owner, square and lot number, and assessed value of land and improvements. Some volumes include information about assessed value of personal property. Arrangement is mainly in rough alphabetical order by surname of owner.

There are also records relating to land and property in Georgetown. Entries in general **assessment books for Georgetown,** 1878–1897, show square and lot number, lot size, and name of owner. Some volumes show assessed value of land and improvements. The records are arranged by block or square number.

In **tax books for Georgetown,** 1800–19 and 1835–97, there are periodic lists of assessments on real property. The content varies, but typical entries give information on the name of the landholder, location of the property, assessed value of land, and frequently, assessed value of improvements. Arrangement varies from volume to volume. There are some name indexes to earlier volumes. The volumes covering the period 1800–19 and 1865–79 have been microfilmed as *Records of the City of Georgetown (D.C.), 1800–79,* M605, 49 rolls.

General **assessment books for the county of Washington,** 1875–1900, are lists of assessments of real property, done at three-year intervals. Entries usually show name of owner, location of property, number of acres, and value of land and improvements. The volumes are usually arranged by name of subdivision (but not alphabetized), or by plat number. Some volumes contain an index to names of locations in the front of the volume.

Taxbooks for Washington County, 1855–79, are lists of payments of assessments on real property. Entries vary, but usually give name of person assessed, location of the property, number of acres, value of land and improvements, and amount of tax due. Lists for 1855 and 1868 include entries for assessments on personal property. There are gaps in the records. Arrangement varies. The lists for 1855–64 and 1868 are in no discernible order, but the volume for 1855–64 contains an alphabetical index to names. Beginning with 1871, most of the volumes are arranged in rough alphabetical order by surname of owner.

CHAPTER 19

Miscellaneous Records

CHAPTER 19

Miscellaneous Records

19.1 Introduction

This chapter discusses several miscellaneous groups of records. Documentation of births, marriages, and deaths (except for Indians) is relatively scarce among the holdings of the National Archives. Some series pertaining to these vital statistics for civilians at army posts and for U.S. citizens abroad do exist, however, and are described here.

Federal tax records do not contain what is considered to be genealogical information—that is, information about family relationships. Some tax assessment lists, however, may lead to interesting information about a family's financial circumstances.

The chapter also contains descriptions of passport records, records of the government of American Samoa, Historical Records Survey publications, and *Territorial Papers of the United States*.

19.2 Civilian Records from Army Posts

Births, marriages, and deaths of civilians at U.S. Army posts are recorded on cards dated 1884–1912. These cards consist of abstracts of reports sent by the posts to the Adjutant General's Office and are in Record Group 94. The cards recording each type of event are filed separately and arranged alphabetically by surname. Each birth card shows the name and sex of the baby; name, rank, and military organization of the father; maiden name of the mother; number of children by the marriage; and date and place of birth. Each marriage card shows the name and rank or occupation of the husband; name, age, and place of birth of the wife; and date and place of marriage. Each death card shows the name of the civilian who died; name, and where appropriate, rank and military organization of the husband or nearest relative; sex and age of the civilian who died; and date, place, and cause of death.

Other records supplement the carded files and provide information for earlier and later periods. Record Group 94 includes hospital registers, monthly reports of sick and wounded, and medical histories of posts, where information about births and deaths may be recorded. Records containing this type of information are less frequently found in Records of U.S. Army Continental Commands, 1821–1920, Record Group 393. Birth and death certificates are also found in some of the later army post records in Records of U.S. Army Continental Commands, 1920–1942, Record Group 394. Most of the records are arranged chronologically; there are no name indexes. Registers of burials at army posts are found in Record Group 92 and are described on page 156.

In Records of the Office of the Chief of Chaplains, Record Group 247, are 134 rolls of negative microfilm documenting **marriages, baptisms, and funerals performed by army chaplains,** 1917–64. (The chief of chaplains retains the positive microfilm and handles reference requests on it.) In the same record group are twenty-nine volumes of chapel registers, 1902–23 and 1939–51. These are arranged alphabetically by name of military installation, and thereunder by type of service (baptism, marriage, funeral). There are name indexes in each volume.

From the late nineteenth century to 1917, there are chaplains' reports that document baptisms, marriages, and funerals performed. The reports, however, do not form a separate series but instead are interspersed in the letters received and general correspondence of the Adjutant General's Office in Record Group 94. The correspondence is indexed by name and is further described on page 85.

19.3 Records of Americans Abroad

One of the responsibilities of American consuls abroad is to keep records of registrations, births, deaths, and marriages of U.S. citizens residing or traveling in foreign countries. The most extensive are death notices, made in accordance with an act of 1792 (1 Stat. 255).

Many of the reports, especially **death notices,** are found in despatches from U.S. consular, and sometimes diplomatic, officials abroad. They are interfiled with despatches dealing with many other subjects and are in many different series from the 1790s through the 1940s in Record Group 59. To use these records, the researcher must know the place and approximate date of the registration or death of the subject of research. Diplomatic and consular despatches dated through mid-1910 are available on microfilm as many different publications, listed on pages 13–56 of the *Catalog of National Archives Microfilm Publications* (Washington: National Archives and Records Service, 1974).

A more useful series in Record Group 59 is a set of bound volumes for the period 1857–1922 containing copies of death notices sent by the Department of State to newspaper publishers, informing them of the deaths of U.S. citizens in foreign countries and requesting that the notices be published. These volumes pertain only to deaths and are not available on microfilm, but most of the volumes are indexed so that researchers can use them if they know the date of death of the subject of research.

Reports of births, deaths, marriages, and registrations are also found among the records of U.S. consular and diplomatic posts abroad in Records of the Foreign Service Posts of the Department of State, Record Group 84. The completeness of these records varies from post to post. The names of posts and dates of the records are given in *List of Foreign Service Post Records in the National Archives,* Special List 9, rev. ed., compiled by Mark G. Eckhoff and Alexander P. Marvo (Washington: National Archives and Records Service, 1967). To use these records, the researcher must know the place and date of the registration or death of the subject of research. Registrations of U.S. citizens abroad who are less than 75 years old may not be used without permission.

Registrations of U.S. citizens abroad usually include the name of the registrant, date and place of birth, last place of residence in the United States, date of arrival in the foreign country, place of residence in the foreign country, reasons for foreign residence, marital status, and names and information about births of spouses and children. Birth registrations include the name and sex of the child, date and place of birth, and names and residence of the parents. Certificates of marriage usually include only the names and ages of the couple and the date of marriage. Death notices normally show the name, place of former residence in the

United States, date and place of death, and name and post of the reporting official. Death notices were sometimes accompanied by information about the estate of the deceased.

19.4 Other Vital Statistics

The archives branch, FARC Los Angeles, has one roll of microfilm containing baptismal records of Los Angeles County, 1771–1873, and the Thomas Workman Temple collection of baptismal records from the San Gabriel Mission and the Plaza Church, 1945. These records came from the California State Society, Daughters of the American Revolution.

Some of the extant birth, marriage, and death records of Indians are described in chapter 6. Marriage certificates among records of the Freedmen's Bureau are described on page 192. Records of deaths and burials of soldiers and residents of veterans homes are described on pages 155–157. Information about marriages and deaths of veterans may appear in pension files, described in chapter 4.

19.5 Passport Records

Except for a short time during the Civil War, passports were not required of U.S. citizens traveling abroad before World War I. They were frequently obtained when not required, however, because of the added protection they might afford. The National Archives has passport applications received by the Department of State, with related records, 1791–1925. The records are in Record Group 59 or Record Group 84. Passport applications less than 75 years old may not be used without permission.

A passport application varies in content, the information being ordinarily less detailed before the Civil War than afterward. It usually contains the name, signature, place of residence, age, and personal description of the applicant; names or number of persons in the family intending to travel; the date; and, where appropriate, the date and court of naturalization. It sometimes contains the exact date and place of birth of the applicant and of spouse and minor children, if any, accompanying the applicant, and, if the applicant was a naturalized citizen, the date and port of arrival in the United States, name of vessel on which applicant arrived, and date and court of naturalization.

For the period 1906–25, each application includes name of applicant, date and place of birth, name and date and place of birth of spouse or children (when applicable), residence and occupation at time of application, immediate travel plans, physical description, and photograph. Often accompanying applications are transmittal letters and letters from employers, relatives, and others attesting to the applicant's purpose for travel abroad.

Passport applications are arranged chronologically, and the main series, 1830–1925, is in bound volumes. The various finding aids listed in table 26 facilitate a search for a particular application. Sometimes the indexes contain helpful genealogical information, as can be seen from the illustrated examples.

Emergency passport applications, 1877–1905, are also in bound volumes. These applications for passports or renewals of passports were made at U.S. Foreign Service posts abroad. They are arranged by name of post, and thereunder chronologically, but an index to applicants cites the name of the post. Emergency passport applications, 1906–25, are in varying arrangements; there is an index for 1906–18, with entries arranged alphabetically as far as the first two letters of the surname.

TABLE 26

Finding Aids for Passport Applications

Dates	**Characteristics**
1834–59	Overlapping book registers, usually alphabetical by initial letter of surname
1850–52 and 1860–80	3″ × 5″ card index, alphabetical
1881–1905	Book indexes, alphabetical by first three letters of surname
1906–23	3″ × 5″ card index, alphabetical

For some periods during the years 1907–25, there are separate applications for U.S. Foreign Service personnel and their dependents, military personnel and civilian government employees and their dependents, residents of Puerto Rico and the Philippine Islands, aliens who had applied for citizenship, and persons who intended to visit China. The applications are covered by the indexes for the main series.

Other series include a register of passports issued, 1810–17; bound record copies of passports issued, 1817–34; a register of passports issued to persons destined for Santo Domingo Island, 1799–1801; applications and certificates, 1907–25, filed at U.S. Foreign Service posts by persons who intended to stay in a particular country for an extended period, and an index for the years 1907–21; and post-World War I applications for certificates of identity filed by wives of members of the American Expeditionary Forces and U.S. citizens who were residents of Germany.

In addition, there are passport records in the National Archives that were maintained by diplomatic and consular posts abroad. Those records before 1874 were not always duplicated in the Department's own files. For the most part, they are scattered and contain relatively little information.

19.6 Tax Records

19.6.1 Direct Tax Lists for Pennsylvania

The National Archives has only a small part of the records created under the first federal direct tax, a 1798 levy on real property and slaves. The records in the National Archives pertain only to Pennsylvania; they are in Records of the Internal Revenue Service, Record Group 58, and have been filmed as *United States Direct Tax of 1798: Tax Lists for the State of Pennsylvania,* M372, 24 rolls.

The records consist mainly of assessment and collection lists, with a few other kinds of lists that were made from them to comply with various aspects of these laws and subsequent ones. The lists are in more than 700 volumes arranged in a complicated geographical scheme by division, district, county, and township; thereunder, they are arranged by type of list. On roll 1 of M372, however, is an alphabetical list of place names that appear in the records and the number of the roll on which the information is filmed. To use the lists, the researcher must know where in Pennsylvania the subject of research lived as of 1 October 1798, then search the appropriate roll for the pertinent list.

The lists most useful for genealogical research are Particular Lists A, B, and C. Particular List A relates to dwellings (with outbuildings) of more than $100 in value on lots not exceeding two acres. It shows, for most dwellings, the name of the occupant, name of owner, location and dimensions of the dwelling and outbuildings, building materials used, number of stories and windows, and value.

Particular List B relates to lands, lots, wharves, and buildings, except those described in A. Particular List B generally shows, for each occupant of such land, lot, wharf or building, the name of occupant, name of owner, number and dimensions of dwelling and outbuildings, number and description of all other buildings and wharves, location and name of adjoining proprietors, acreage, and value.

Particular List C usually shows the name of the superintendent or owner of slaves, total number owned, number exempt from the tax, and number subject to the tax. There are very few slave lists in the Pennsylvania records.

Some records, of varying amounts and arrangements, of the 1798 tax in other states are in the custody of the following depositories: the Connecticut Historical Society, Historical Society of Delaware, Maryland Historical Society (Maryland and District of Columbia), New England Historic Genealogical Society (Maine, Massachusetts, and New Hampshire), Rhode Island Historical Society, Tennessee State Library and Archives, and Vermont Historical Society.

19.6.2 Tax Assssment Lists

Extensive and detailed tax lists were made under the supervision of district assessors appointed in each state or territory under the provisions of an act of 1862 (12 Stat. 432). The law provided for specific monthly and annual taxes to be assessed on goods and services at the level of production and distribution, including taxes on licenses, income, and personal property. An act of 1872 (17 Stat. 401) abolished the offices of assessors as of 1 July 1873 and greatly reduced the number of taxes to be collected. The lists in Washington, D.C., are dated 1862–73; lists in some of the regional archives branches include some records created under other tax laws and are dated as late as 1917. Other lists, 1874–1910, were compiled by district collectors for taxes on alcohol and tobacco products. All of the lists are in Record Group 58.

Assistant assessors of divisions prepared the lists in alphabetical order on large sheets. The pages for each division within an assessment district were later bound into yearly books by the district assessor. The amount of territory assigned to each division varied, depending on the population, from part of a city or county to several counties in a state. The majority of the lists are monthly returns of specific or ad valorem taxes on products owned by individual manufacturing companies or vendors. The next largest category

TABLE 27

Microfilmed Internal Revenue Assessment Lists for the Civil War Period

State or Territory	Dates	Microfilm publication	Number of rolls
Alabama	1865–66	M754	6
Arkansas	1865–66	M755	2
	1867–74	T1208	4
California	1862–66	M756	33
Colorado	1862–66	M757	3
Connecticut	1862–66	M758	23
Delaware	1862–66	M759	8
District of Columbia	1862–66	M760	8
Florida	1865–66	M761	1
Georgia	1865–66	M762	8
Idaho	1865–66	M763	1
	1867–74	T1209	1
Illinois	1862–66	M764	63
Indiana	1862–66	M765	42
Iowa	1862–66	M766	16
Kansas	1862–66	M767	3
Kentucky	1862–66	M768	24
Louisiana	1863–66	M769	10
Maine	1862–66	M770	15
Maryland	1862–66	M771	21
Michigan	1862–66	M773	15
Mississippi	1865–66	M775	3
Montana	1864–72	M777	1
Nevada	1863–66	M779	2
New Hampshire	1862–66	M780	10
New Mexico	1862–70 1872–74	M782	1
New York and New Jersey	1862–66	M603	217
North Carolina	1864–66	M784	2
Pennsylvania	1862–66	M787	107
Rhode Island	1862–66	M788	10
South Carolina	1864–66	M789	2
Texas	1865–66	M791	2
Vermont	1862–66	M792	7
Virginia	1862–66	M793	6
West Virginia	1862–66	M795	4

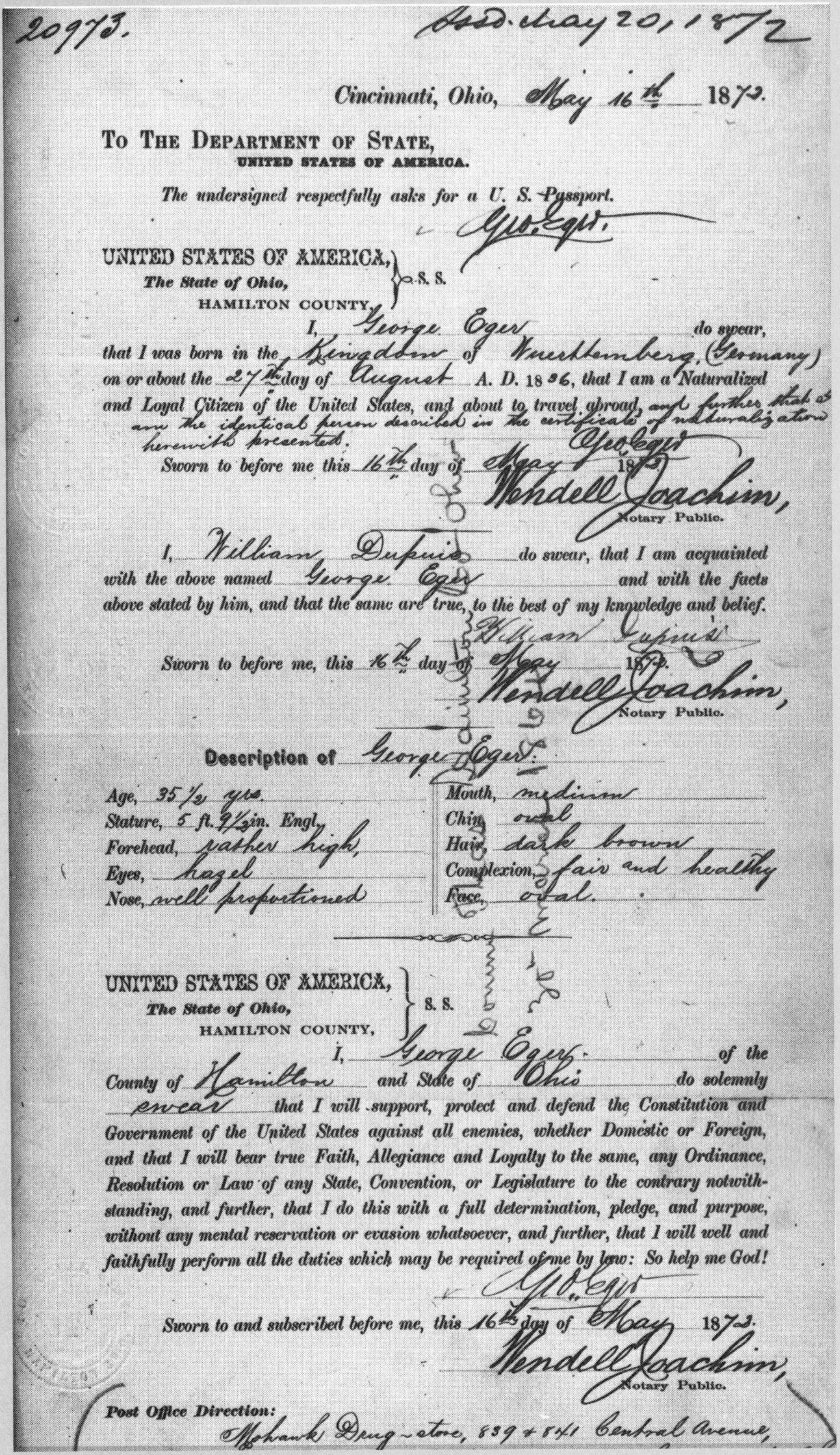
20973. Issd. May 20, 1872

Cincinnati, Ohio, May 16th 1872.

To The Department of State,
UNITED STATES OF AMERICA.

The undersigned respectfully asks for a U. S. Passport.

Geo. Eger.

UNITED STATES OF AMERICA,
The State of Ohio, } S. S.
HAMILTON COUNTY,

I, George Eger *do swear, that I was born in the,* Kingdom *of* Wuerttemberg, (Germany) *on or about the* 27th *day of* August *A. D. 18*36, *that I am a Naturalized and Loyal Citizen of the United States, and about to travel abroad,* and further that I am the identical person described in the certificate of naturalization herewith presented.

Geo. Eger.

Sworn to before me this 16th *day of* May *18*72.

Wendell Joachim,
Notary Public.

I, William Dupuis *do swear, that I am acquainted with the above named* George Eger *and with the facts above stated by him, and that the same are true, to the best of my knowledge and belief.*

William Dupuis

Sworn to before me, this 16th *day of* May *18*72.

Wendell Joachim,
Notary Public.

Description of George Eger.

Age, 35 1/2 yrs.	*Mouth,* medium
Stature, 5 *ft.* 9 1/2 *in. Engl.*	*Chin,* oval
Forehead, rather high,	*Hair,* dark brown
Eyes, hazel	*Complexion,* fair and healthy
Nose, well proportioned	*Face,* oval.

UNITED STATES OF AMERICA,
The State of Ohio, } S. S.
HAMILTON COUNTY,

I, George Eger *of the County of* Hamilton *and State of* Ohio *do solemnly* swear *that I will support, protect and defend the Constitution and Government of the United States against all enemies, whether Domestic or Foreign, and that I will bear true Faith, Allegiance and Loyalty to the same, any Ordinance, Resolution or Law of any State, Convention, or Legislature to the contrary notwithstanding, and further, that I do this with a full determination, pledge, and purpose, without any mental reservation or evasion whatsoever, and further, that I will well and faithfully perform all the duties which may be required of me by law: So help me God!*

Geo. Eger

Sworn to and subscribed before me, this 16th *day of* May *18*72.

Wendell Joachim,
Notary Public.

Post Office Direction:
Mohawk Drug-store, 839 + 841 Central Avenue,

Eger, George

Place of birth: Würtemberg, Germany
Date of birth: Aug. 27, 1836

Place of naturalization: Court Common Pleas, Hamilton Co., Ohio
Date of naturalization: Mar. 30, 1864

No.: 20973 Date: May 20, 1872 Vol.: 395

THE NATIONAL ARCHIVES
Form I-3

DIVISION OF CATALOGING
GPO 16—7094

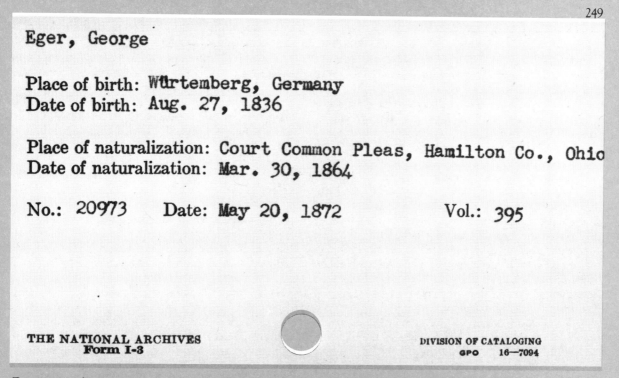

Passport application with the index card to it. Records of the Passport Division, General Records of the Department of State, Record Group 59.

of tax lists are annual returns of income of more than $600, personal property, and license fees. Lists are not included for every division for every month, nor are there lists of annual taxes for every year in a district or a state.

The alphabetical lists for each division show the names of persons, partnerships, firms, associations, or corporations; post office addresses; amounts of annual income, value of articles subject to the special tax or duty, or quantities of goods made or sold that were charged with a specific or ad valorem tax or duty; and amounts of duty or tax due.

Assessment lists for the Civil War period, 1862–66, are available on microfilm. (The 1866 records are included because the annual taxes were collected for 1865.) To use the records, the researcher must search the lists for the place where the subject of research lived or owned property subject to the tax. Table 27 lists the dates and microfilm publication numbers for each state. The descriptive pamphlet for each microfilm publication shows the counties assigned to each assessment district or division.

The archives branch, FARC Denver, has original monthly assessment lists for Colorado, 1873–1917; New Mexico, 1885–1917; and Wyoming, 1874–79.

The archives branch, FARC Kansas City, has original monthly assessment lists for Iowa, 1873–1917; Minnesota, 1866–1917; Nebraska, 1906–17; and South Dakota, 1915–17.

The archives branch, FARC Chicago, also has assessment lists. The majority of the volumes contain corporation tax lists, but there are some lists for individuals, giving names, addresses, and amounts paid. The records relate to Springfield, Ill., 1908–17; Detroit, Mich., 1870–1917; Columbus, Ohio, 1906–17; and Milwaukee, Wis., 1876–1917.

At the archives branch, FARC San Francisco, are records of individual tax assessments, 1914–17; corporation taxes (individuals, firms, and corporations), 1909–17; corporations, joint stock companies, and associations, 1911–12 and 1915–17; and U.S. and foreign corporation taxes, 1917.

The archives branch, FARC Los Angeles, has assessment lists for individuals, 1914–17. These alphabetical listings show the amount owed, at that time 1 percent of an individual's gross income. The volumes originated in the 6th District of California (Los Angeles).

19.7 Other Records

The second Bank of the United States, chartered in 1816, was the subject of a congressional investigation in 1818. The *Report of the Committee to Inspect the Bank of the United States* contains alphabetical lists of approximately 6,400 **stockholders of the Bank of the United States** at the time of the first dividend in July 1818. The statement shows the number of shares owned by, and the place of residence of, each stockholder.

Three groups of **records about American Samoa** may be useful to genealogical researchers in this specialized area. They are located at the archives branch, FARC San Francisco, and are part of Records of the Government of American Samoa, Record Group 284.

Records of the high court include wills, 1906–61, arranged by number; probate cases, 1902–45, dealing mainly with estate matters; and divorce files, 1900–62, including petitions for divorce, divorce orders, and documents in evidence, arranged chronologically by year, and thereunder by number. These are **census returns** for 1900, 1903, 1908–9, 1912, 1916, 1920, 1922, 1923, 1926, and 1945. The reports include population figures for villages, lists of village residents, numbers of foreign residents, and births and deaths. They are arranged chronologically. There are also alien **registration forms,** 1940–44, arranged by serial number, and preliminary forms for **petitions of naturalization,** 1946.

Coded administrative files in the records of the Governor's office contain several files related to Matai names. Correspondence, 1920–40, is arranged alphabetically by Matai name and concerns Matai name claims and case decisions by the high court. The Matai name registrations, 1935–57, are arranged roughly in chronological order and give name of registrant, Matai title assigned, village of residence, petition signed by family members over 14 years old, application to high or talking chief, and date. The Matai name resignations, 1936–55, give the name of the resignee, title resigned, date of petition, and sometimes the recommendation of the resignee or high court for the new titleholder. The Matai name removals, 1925–55, are arranged chronologically and give the name of the titleholder, title, and reason for removal given by the high court or family. The Matai name lists, 1940–50, give the name of the titleholder, name of title held, and the district.

Records of the Attorney General's Office include **immigration and emigration records,** 1937–65. This series contains letters of identity, affidavits of birth and identity in support of those letters, passenger lists, and correspondence regarding visas and travel permits. The records are arranged chronologically. Also in the series is a bound register of letters of identity, 1955–57, and a bound record of arrivals in American Samoa, 1955–61.

An imaginative and potentially useful program in the Work Projects Administration (WPA) of the New Deal was the **Historical Records Survey**. Affording employment for many professionals in the social sciences and the humanities and for clerical workers left idle by the Depression, its goal was to locate and describe records at the county level across the United States. It also did some work in church and municipal records. The onset of World War II, solving the unemployment problem by siphoning workers off into defense work and the armed forces, meant that few of the projects were completed, and much of what was accomplished has since been lost or destroyed by local government officials with little appreciation of the usefulness of the inventories.

The National Archives has record copies of most of the printed publications of the Historical Records Survey, including some of genealogical interest, 1936–43. The extant records are in Records of the Work Projects Administration, Record Group 69. The National Archives does not have the microfilm publications or the unpublished project material of the Historical Records Survey.

The publications of the Historical Records Survey are listed in the Work Projects Administration *Bibliography of Research Projects Reports, Check List of Historical Records Survey Publications,* Technical Series, Research and Records

Bibliography 7 (Washington: Work Projects Administration, 1943). The bibliography has been reprinted by the Genealogical Publishing Co., Baltimore, 1969. The names and addresses of the state depositories for the unpublished project material appear in an appendix to this bibliography. *The WPA Historical Records Survey: A Guide to the Unpublished Inventories, Indexes, and Transcripts,* compiled by Loretta Hefner (Chicago: Society of American Archivists, 1980), contains lists of the specific holdings of HRS materials in each repository where they have been located.

Other available Historical Records Survey materials in the National Archives include mimeographed copies of inventories of many county archives in the United States. These inventories give a description, with total volume and terminal dates, of records such as wills, land records, birth and death certificates, marriage licenses, and naturalization records located in courthouses and other depositories within the county. The contents vary depending on the subject. The proportion of counties in a state for which inventories were completed varies from complete coverage for the counties of North Carolina to no inventories for any of the counties of Connecticut, Maine, or Rhode Island.

There are also copies of inventories of federal archives in the states; copies of inventories of state, municipal, town, and church archives; church directories; guides to vital statistics records; transcripts of records, including those relating to Spanish land grants in Florida; and other inventories and miscellaneous publications.

At the archives branch, FARC Los Angeles, is one roll of microfilm consisting of an Arizona WPA inventory of federal archives in Tucson, 1939.

The Territorial Papers of the United States is a multivolume documentary historical publication containing archival materials selected from many record groups of the National Archives. The objective of the series is to document the administrative history of the U.S. territories with texts that are annotated, exact, representative, and particularly significant. In addition to governmental operations, the records relate to genealogy, economic development, Indian affairs, geographical features, and partisan politics.

The volumes are highly selective, representing perhaps 5 percent of the total material about a territory. Microfilm supplements whose purpose is to reproduce substantially all textual and cartographic materials in the National Archives bearing on each territory have been created for some territories. Certain categories are excepted, such as some Indian and military records that are included in other microfilm publications and repetitive accounting and land records. The microfilmed records have not been annotated or indexed, but published volumes serve as guides to the microfilm supplements. Many documents reproduced in the supplements are cited or printed in the volumes, and related materials can often be located through the detailed index in each volume. In addition to indexed items in the volumes, genealogists may wish to devote special attention to the memorials and petitions reproduced in the microfilm supplements. This form of documentation serves to fix the residence of many territorial settlers at the given date of the record, provides an image of their signatures, and gives the settlers' opinions on varied subjects. The microfilmed records are arranged first by governmental branch (legislative, executive, or judicial), and thereunder by department and agency. This hierarchical arrangement brings together for the researcher, logically and conveniently, much of the pertinent documentation for specific areas of territorial life and history.

Volumes in this series have been published for: territories northwest of the Ohio River, territories south of the Ohio River, Mississippi, Indiana, New Orleans, Michigan, Louisiana-Missouri, Illinois, Alabama, Arkansas, and Florida. Some of these volumes are no longer available for purchase, but they have been microfilmed as *The Territorial Papers of the United States,* M721, 15 rolls.

There are also two published volumes for the territory of Wisconsin, with a microfilm supplement, *The Territorial Papers of the United States: The Territory of Wisconsin, 1836–48,* M236, 122 rolls. There are also microfilm publications of *The Territorial Papers of the United States: The Territory of Iowa, 1838–46,* M325, 102 rolls; *The Territorial Papers of the United States: The Territory of Minnesota, 1849–1858,* M1050, 11 rolls; and *The Territorial Papers of the United States: The Territory of Oregon, 1848–1859,* M1049, 12 rolls. The last two of these are incomplete and work is progressing on them.

CHAPTER

20 Cartographic Records

20.1 Introduction

Maps and related cartographic records are often useful for genealogical research. They provide important information on contemporary place names and localities; show changing political boundaries, such as counties and minor civil subdivisions; and sometimes include names of individual landowners or residents. The National Archives has custody of almost 2 million maps. Those accessioned through 1966 are described in general terms in the *Guide to Cartographic Records in the National Archives* (Washington: National Archives and Records Service, 1971). A general discussion of their value for genealogists is included in Ralph E. Ehrenberg's "Cartographic Records of the National Archives," *National Genealogical Society Quarterly,* 64 (June 1976): 83–111.

The following cartographic series have particular significance to genealogists and may be used in the cartographic search room of the National Archives now located in Alexandria, Va. Photostat and large electrostatic reproductions can be purchased for a nominal price.

20.2 Census Records

Census **enumeration district maps** were prepared by the Bureau of the Census decennially from 1880 to 1960. They consist of approximately 130,000 printed, photocopied, and manuscript maps of cities, counties, lesser political units, and unincorporated areas. Only three maps are extant for 1880, but the number of available maps increases with each succeeding census. The maps, arranged alphabetically by name of state, and thereunder by name of county and locality, are in Record Group 29. The genealogist using the later nineteenth- and early twentieth-century censuses will find that knowing the enumeration district for a particular town or other political unit will make access to the required records easier.

These maps are usually annotated to show the boundaries and the numbers of enumeration districts. Wards, precincts, incorporated areas, urban unincorporated areas, townships, census supervisors' districts, and congressional districts are also shown on some maps.

Occasionally, enumeration districts are annotated on maps that indicate the names of residents or landowners, primarily in rural areas. Enumeration districts in several Texas counties are displayed on maps that also show land grants to individuals in Texas during the 1820s and 1830s.

The enumeration district maps for 1880–1940 are listed in *Cartographic Records of the Bureau of the Census,* Preliminary Inventory 103, compiled by James B. Rhoads and Charlotte M. Ashby (Washington: National Archives and Records Service, 1958).

Enumeration district descriptions, 1850–1950, are also useful. From 1850 to 1870, the Bureau of the Census collected data according to two designated units, the district and the subdivision. The district usually corresponded to a state or part of a state, and the subdivision corresponded to a county or a part thereof. Beginning with 1880, the smallest unit was redesignated as the enumeration district, which corresponded frequently to a minor civil division. Written descriptions of districts and subdivisions, 1850–70, exist in three manuscript volumes. Similar descriptions of enumeration districts, 1880–1950, are found in four manuscripts and 489 typescript volumes.

The enumeration district descriptions for 1880 are incomplete, pertaining only to the following states and territories: Dakota (part), Delaware (part), District of Columbia, Florida, Georgia, Idaho, Illinois, Indiana, Iowa, Kansas, Kentucky, Louisiana, Maine, Maryland, Massachusetts, Michigan, Minnesota, Mississippi, Missouri, Nebraska, Nevada, New Hampshire, New Jersey, New Mexico, New York, North Carolina, Rhode Island, South Carolina, Tennessee, Texas, Utah, Vermont, Virginia, Washington, West Virginia, and Wyoming.

These volumes are arranged by census, and thereunder generally alphabetically by name of state. Within individual volumes, the descriptions are usually arranged numerically by supervisors' districts, and thereunder by enumeration districts, usually conforming to an alphabetical arrangement of counties. To locate a description of a particular enumeration district, the researcher must know at least the name of the county. In these volumes, census enumeration district and subdivision boundaries are described in terms of counties, geographical parts of counties, townships, wards, precincts, blocks, and streets. Also included for some, but not all, censuses are the names and addresses of enumerators and special instructions to them.

Descriptions are available on microfilm as *Descriptions of Census Enumeration Districts, 1830–1890 and 1910–1950,* T1224, 146 rolls, and *Census Enumeration District Descriptive Volumes for 1900,* T1210, 10 rolls.

Civil division outline maps among the records of the Bureau of the Census are approximately 500 printed and annotated maps of the United States and individual states from 1920 to 1970. They show county or municipality and minor civil division boundaries and names and locations of incorporated places. They are arranged chronologically, and thereunder alphabetically by state.

20.3 General Land Office Records

The National Archives has approximately 20,000 headquarters office **township survey plats** retained by the General Land Office in Washington, D.C. and more than 22,000 local office plats used by the local land office having jurisdiction over specified townships. Among the holdings are manuscript headquarters plats for the states of Illinois, Indiana, Iowa, Kansas, Missouri, and parts of Ohio, including the "Old Seven Ranges," 1785–87. Local office plats are available for Alabama, Illinois, Indiana, Iowa, Kansas, Mississippi, Missouri, Wisconsin, and parts of Ohio, Oklahoma, Oregon, and Washington.

These plats, arranged by state, principal meridian, and range and township number have been consolidated into one series and are available on microfilm as *Township Plats of Selected States,* T1234, 69 rolls. The researcher needs the legal descriptions from these plats to use the land records most efficiently.

Headquarters office plats show section numbers and boundaries, physical features, and any cultural features that

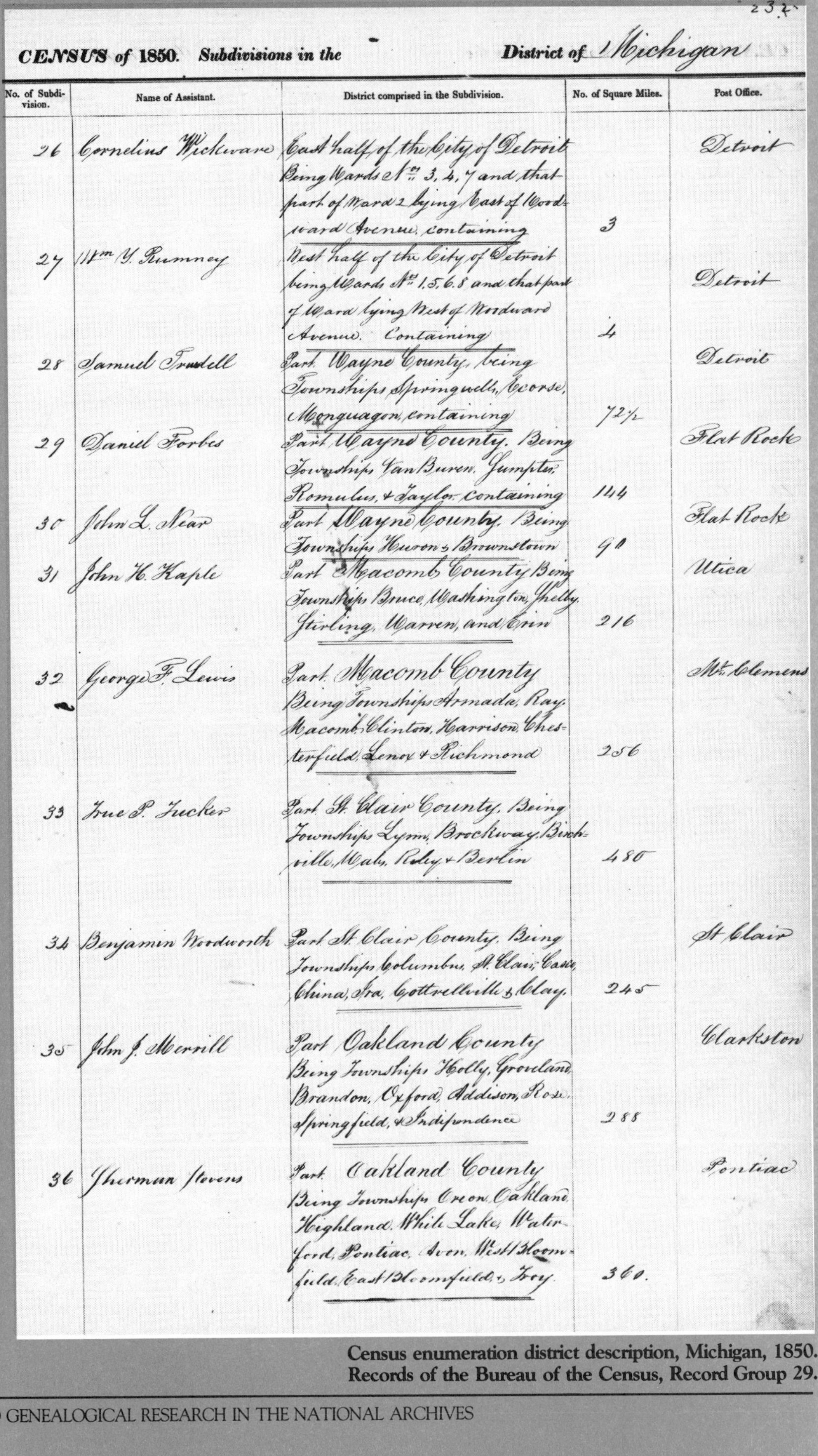

CENSUS of 1850. Subdivisions in the **District of** Michigan

No. of Subdivision.	Name of Assistant.	District comprised in the Subdivision.	No. of Square Miles.	Post Office.
26	Cornelius Wickware	East half of the City of Detroit Being Wards No. 3, 4, 7 and that part of Ward 2 lying East of Woodward Avenue, containing	3	Detroit
27	Wm Y. Rumney	West half of the City of Detroit being Wards No. 1, 5, 6, 8 and that part of Ward lying West of Woodward Avenue. Containing	4	Detroit
28	Samuel Trudell	Part Wayne County, being Townships Springwells, Ecorse, Monguagon, containing	72½	Detroit
29	Daniel Forbes	Part Wayne County. Being Townships Van Buren, Sumpter, Romulus, & Taylor, containing	144	Flat Rock
30	John L. Near	Part Wayne County. Being Townships Huron & Brownstown	90	Flat Rock
31	John H. Kaple	Part Macomb County Being Townships Bruce, Washington, Shelby, Sterling, Warren, and Erin	216	Utica
32	George F. Lewis	Part Macomb County Being Townships Armada, Ray, Macomb, Clinton, Harrison, Chesterfield, Lenox & Richmond	256	Mt. Clemens
33	True P. Tucker	Part St. Clair County. Being Townships Lynn, Brockway, Birchville, Wales, Riley & Berlin	480	
34	Benjamin Woodworth	Part St. Clair County. Being Townships Columbus, St. Clair, Cass, China, Ira, Cottrellville & Clay.	245	St Clair
35	John J. Merrill	Part Oakland County Being Townships Holly, Groveland, Brandon, Oxford, Addison, Rose, Springfield, & Independence	288	Clarkston
36	Sherman Stevens	Part Oakland County Being Townships Orion, Oakland, Highland, White Lake, Waterford, Pontiac, Avon, West Bloomfield, East Bloomfield, & Troy.	360.	Pontiac

Census enumeration district description, Michigan, 1850.
Records of the Bureau of the Census, Record Group 29.

preceded the federal survey of the township, such as the improvements and fields of the pre-survey settlers. The surnames of such settlers, who were few in number, are usually given. The names and addresses of early patentees, such as "Isaac Craig of Pittsburgh" are indicated on some of the plats of the "Old Seven Ranges." Private land claim boundaries and the names of claimants also appear in some areas. Local office plats may show the names of patentees, but more often they merely show land entry symbols and numbers.

Typical symbols shown are "E" for entry, "HE" for homestead entry, "AP" for application pending, "P" for patent, "FP" for final proof, "FC" for final certificate, and "SL" for school land.

The source and nature of private land claims is explained on page 229.

Private land claim records include manuscript and annotated lithographed plats in bound volumes of private land claims in the states and territories of Arizona (1 vol.), California (28 vols.), Colorado (1 vol.), Florida (4 vols.), Illinois (1 vol.), and New Mexico (8 vols.). Most of these plats were compiled from surveys made by the General Land Office after the claims were finally confirmed. Three of the California volumes contain plats of disapproved claims. Additional unbound plats relate to claims in Florida, Louisiana, Michigan, Missouri, Ohio, and Wisconsin. Other maps and plats of private land claims in California, Florida, Illinois, Indiana, Louisiana, Michigan, New Mexico, and Wisconsin are found in the "Old Map File"; some claims are documented on township survey plats.

Additional records relating to private land claims in California consist of approximately 820 expedientes, 1822–46; three volumes of bound records of the California Board of Commissioners, 1852–56; nearly 300 unbound maps relating to claims papers (dockets) of the General Land Office; and standard published General Land Office maps of the state at intervals from 1876 to 1944.

The expedientes are case files consisting of petitions for land, reports, concessions, patents, disenos (rough sketch maps), and papers relating to boundary litigation. Such documents, which are usually in Spanish, document claims based on Spanish or Mexican grants and were used by the California Board of Commissioners to adjudicate claims.

The bound records of the California Board of Commissioners consist of copies of approximately 785 disenos. This set of disenos is more complete than the one filed with the expedientes.

Private land claims records are arranged by state, and thereunder by sequences unique to each series.

The names of claims or claimants are usually shown, either within the boundaries of the claims or in tabular lists coordinated with claim locations. Claim acreages and numbers, buildings, topography, names of surrounding property owners, and other cultural and physical features may also be indicated.

Typewritten and photocopied indexes list private land claims by name of claim and correlate the various records pertaining to specific claims. *List of Cartographic Records of the General Land Office,* Special List 19, compiled by Laura E. Kelsay (Washington: National Archives and Records Service, 1964), is helpful. Also useful are J. N. Bowman's "Index of the Spanish-Mexican Private Land Grant Records and Cases of California" (typewritten, 1958), available in the research room, and *Annual Report of the Commissioner of the General Land Office for the Fiscal Year Ending June 30, 1880* (Washington: General Land Office, 1881), pp. 395–495.

U.S. land district maps consist of manuscript and published maps of states, territories, and individual land districts. The individual land district maps pertain primarily to Ohio, Indiana, and Illinois. A map of the Virginia Military Tract in Ohio is included. Most of the maps were compiled from official sources during the nineteenth century; they document the changing locations of land districts and land offices. Many are arranged alphabetically by state with the subsequent arrangement being chronological. Those maps filed among the records of the U.S. Senate are arranged by Congress and session numbers; they can be searched by date only.

Commonly shown on the state and territory maps are locations of land offices and boundaries of land districts, private land claims, counties, and federal land reserves. The maps of individual land districts are more detailed; some show townships with the names of landowners in numbered sections or parts thereof. In addition to the name of each patentee, the map of the Virginia Military Tract also indicates an entry number and amount of acreage within the limits of each tract.

Many of the maps relating to land districts are described in Special List 19 and in *List of Selected Maps of States and Territories,* Special List 29, compiled by Janet T. Hargett (Washington: National Archives and Records Service, 1971).

20.4 Military Records

Manuscript, annotated, and printed maps, plans, and charts were compiled or collected by various military organizations. They are chiefly dated ca. 1770–1925. Of foremost importance are the records of the U.S. Army Corps of Engineers, the organization responsible for most of the military mapping pertaining to civil works, exploration, and military campaigns and fortifications in the United States during the eighteenth, nineteenth, and twentieth centuries. Map coverage is most heavily concentrated in, but not limited to, areas of substantial federal activity. Notable are detailed area and county maps of parts of Arkansas, Georgia, Louisiana, Maryland, Texas, and Virginia during the 1860s; maps of colonies, states, and territories; city plans; and maps of canals and roads. These records are usually arranged by state or region (by subject for canals and roads), and thereunder chronologically with some exceptions.

These records frequently indicate roads, canals, and waterways that could have been migration routes; land ownership or the names of residents; the boundaries of civil divisions and their names or numbers; and additional place name information including inns, mills, churches, mountains, and other cultural and physical features.

Card catalogs, registers, and typed lists prepared by the Corps of Engineers and the National Archvies staff constitute a comprehensive guide to these records. References and descriptions of many of the records are in the National Archives publications listed in table 28.

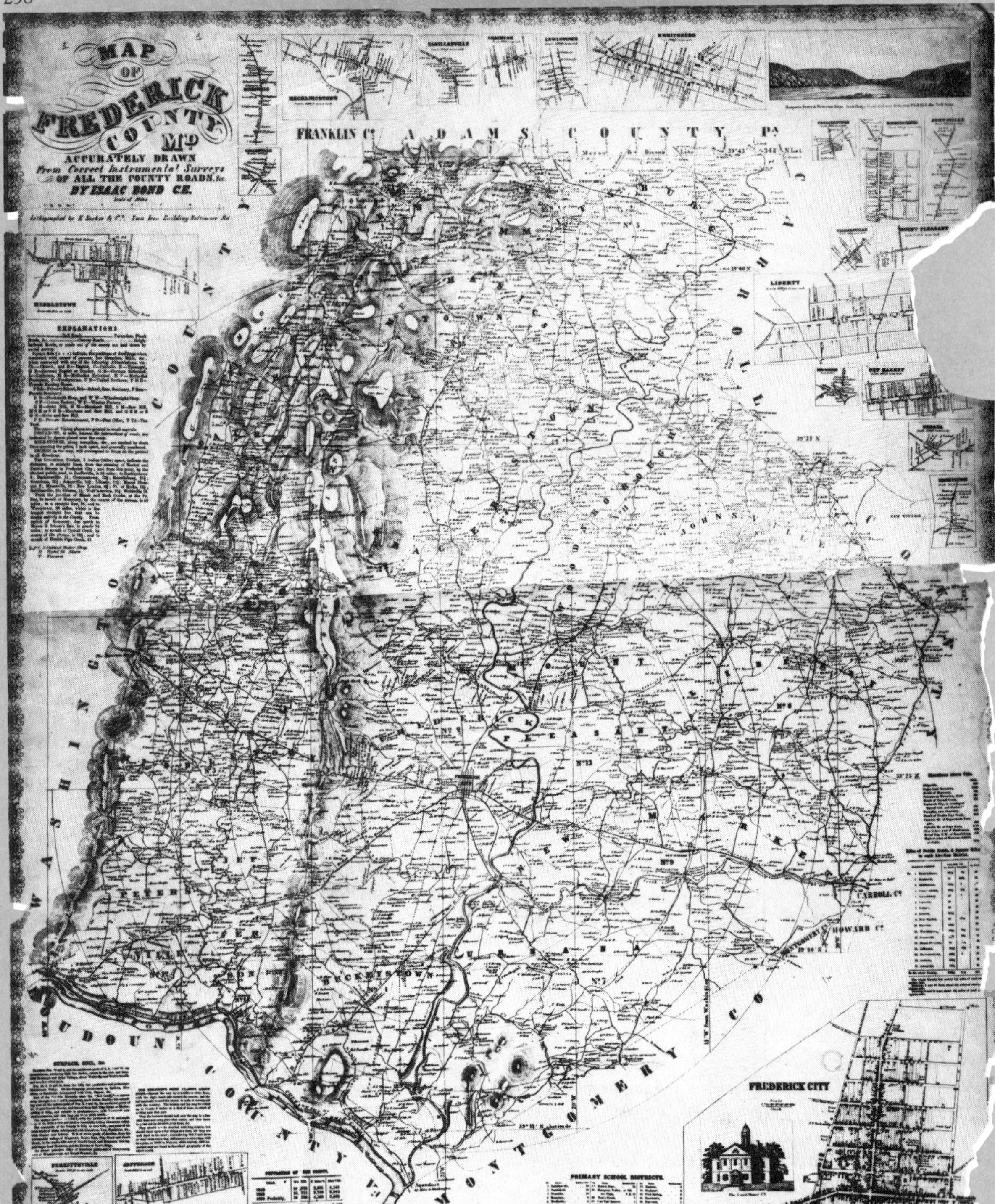

Map of Frederick County, Maryland, c. 1867, with map details showing names of property owners in various parts of the county. Records of the Office of the Chief of Engineers, Record Group 77.

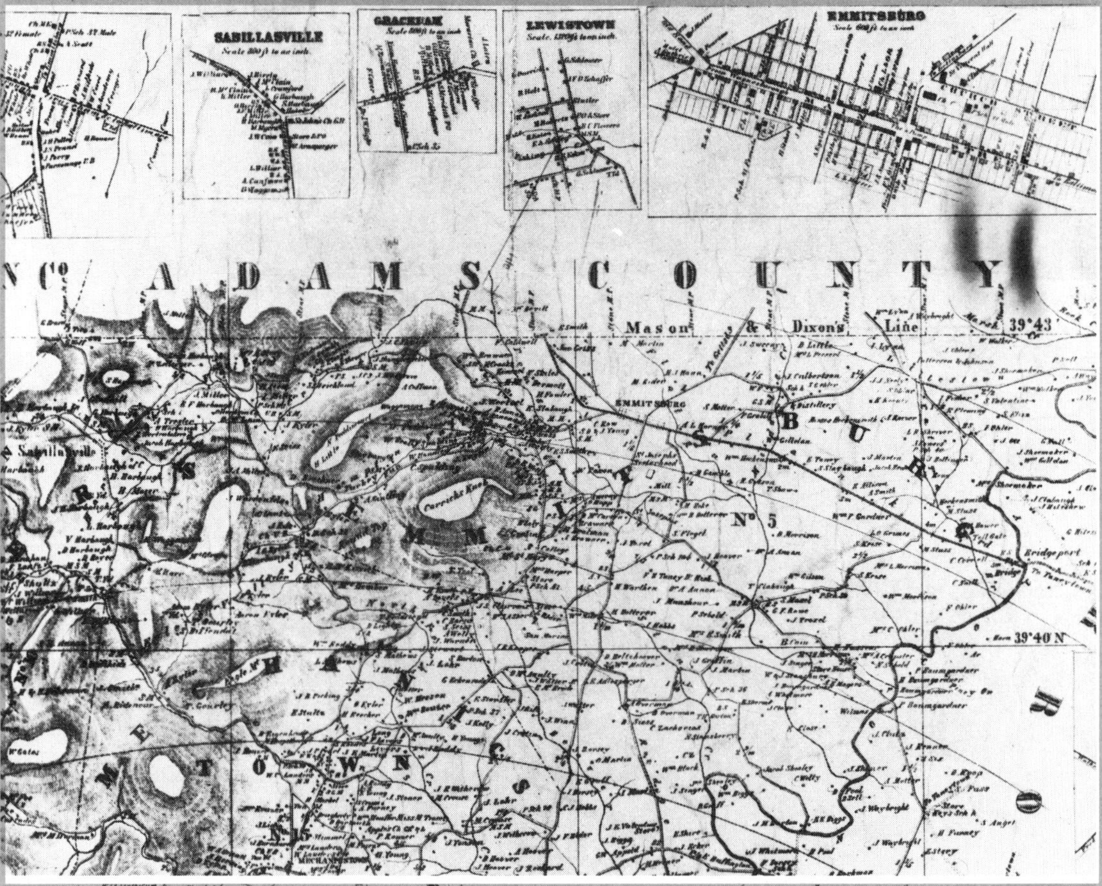
SABILLASVILLE
GRACEHAM
LEWISTOWN
EMMITSBURG
ADAMS COUNTY
Mason & Dixon's Line
39°43'
EMMITSBURG
No 5
Bridgeport
39°40'N

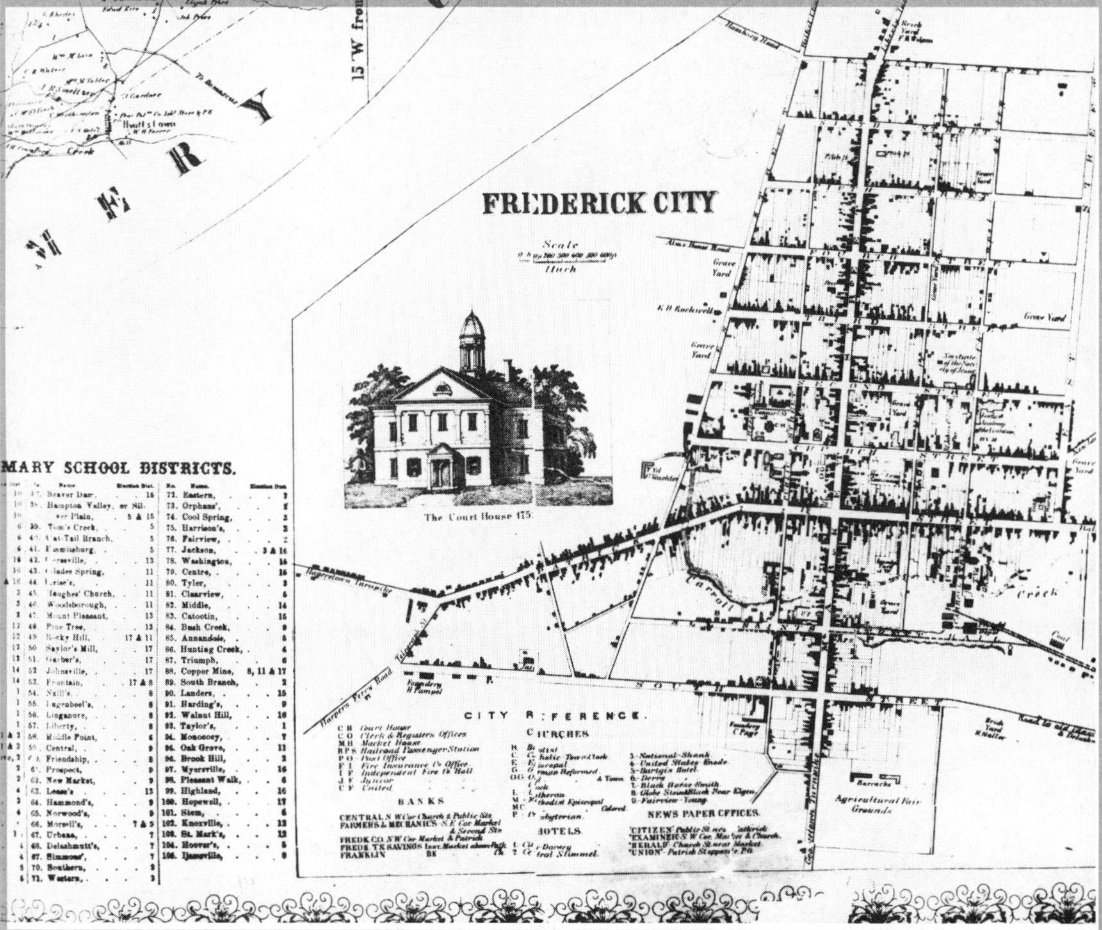
FREDERICK CITY
Scale
The Court House
MARY SCHOOL DISTRICTS.
CITY REFERENCE.
CHURCHES
BANKS
HOTELS
NEWS PAPER OFFICES
Agricultural Fair Grounds
Grave Yard

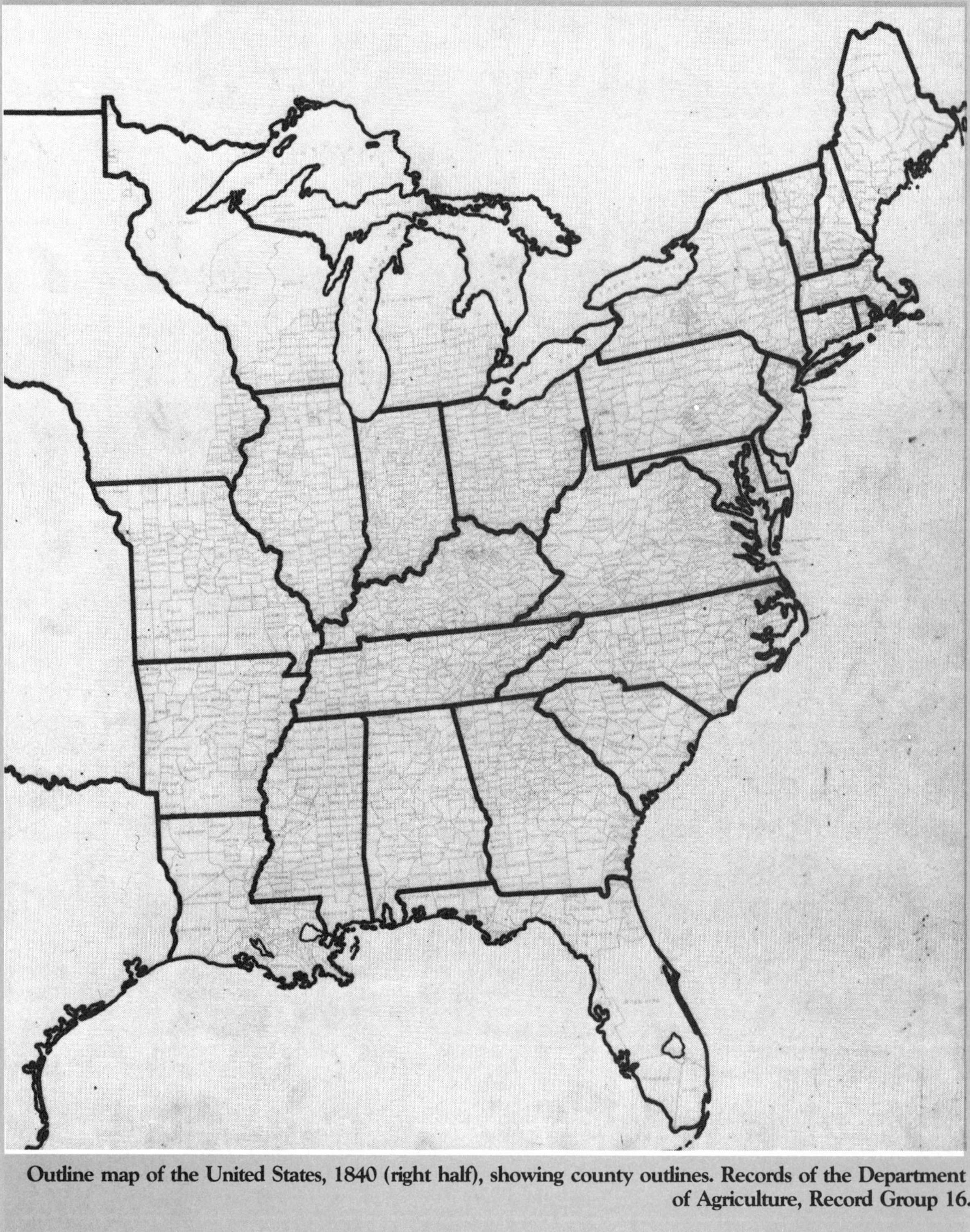

Outline map of the United States, 1840 (right half), showing county outlines. Records of the Department of Agriculture, Record Group 16.

20.5 Other Cartographic Records

The Department of Agriculture prepared and published **small-scale civil division maps** of the United States decennially for the years 1840–1900. Similar maps are also available for 1909, 1915, 1920, 1931, 1935, and 1940. The maps indicate county boundaries and names as they existed for the specific year within all organized states and territories of the continental United States.

During the 1930s, approximately 2,200 civil division maps spanning the period 1789–1932 were prepared in conjunction with the congressional vote analysis atlas, a Work Projects Administration (WPA) study based upon congressional voting districts. Small outline maps of states showing county boundaries and names during the various Congresses compose the bulk of this group of maps. A few maps show municipal ward boundaries and numbers in some major cities. Most of these civil division outline maps are found in two series of state maps designated "preliminary" and "approved," respectively. Many of the maps in the preliminary series are not professionally drawn; some are unfinished and may include inaccurate information. All states are not represented in this series. The approved series is more reliable, but does not include maps for the entire period, 1789–1932. The preliminary series is arranged alphabetically by state, and thereunder mostly chronologically; the approved series is arranged by Congress number (1st–53d and 76th–77th).

The early series, 1839, of **postal route maps** in the Records of the U.S. Post Office Department, Record Group 28, is arranged chronologically; the later series, 1894–1960, is arranged by state, and thereunder chronologically. Rural delivery route maps, 1900–37, are arranged alphabetically by state, and thereunder by name of county and locality. Postal route maps show county names and boundaries, post offices, and routes and distances between post offices. Names of individuals are sometimes shown on rural delivery maps.

Postal route maps made before 1895 are listed in *Records and Policies of the Post Office Department Relating to Place-Names,* Reference Information Paper 72, compiled by Arthur Hecht and William J. Heynen (Washington: National Archives and Records Service, 1975), and *Transportation in Nineteenth-Century America: A Survey of the Cartographic Records in the National Archives of the United States,* Reference Information Paper 65, compiled by Patrick D. McLaughlin (Washington: National Archives and Records Service, 1975). A card catalog lists rural delivery route maps. See also *Records of the Post Office Department,* Preliminary Inventory 168, revised edition, compiled by Arthur Hecht et al. (Washington: National Archives and Records Service, 1967).

The Geological Survey records contain manuscript and published **topographical quadrangle maps**, 1888–present. They indicate extensive cultural and physical features such as county and township names and boundaries, towns, roads, railroads, houses, schools, churches, cemeteries, mountains, valleys, streams, and lakes. Quadrangles are arranged by scale, then by state, and thereunder by name of map sheet.

Current and historical graphic indexes are available for the published Geological Survey quadrangle maps; there is a card catalog for the manuscript maps among them. Geological Survey state gazetteers and dictionaries, 1894–1906, are among the textual records of the U.S. Government Printing Office.

The published **area and county soil maps** are dated from 1900 to about 1945. The information shown on some of them is similar to that found on the quadrangle maps. Certain soil maps surpass the quadrangle maps, however, in providing obscure and obsolete place names. The soil maps are arranged by state, and thereunder by area or county, and the county soil maps are listed in a card catalog.

Because property taxes are assessed at local levels, very few **tax assessment maps** have become federal records. One of the few exceptions is a series of manuscript plats of St. Helena Parish, S.C., 1865–66. These plats were compiled by the Direct Tax Commission in the District of South Carolina after that area came under federal control during the Civil War. Tax sale certificate numbers and names of individuals appear within the limits of land tracts.

TABLE 28

Checklist of National Archives Publications Relating to Cartographic Records

Guide to Cartographic Records in the National Archives (1971).

Civil War Maps in the National Archives (1964).

Hargett, Janet T., comp. *List of Selected Maps of States and Territories,* Special List 29 (1971).

Hecht, Arthur and Heynen, William J. *Records and Policies of the Post Office Department Relating to Place-Names,* Reference Information Paper 72 (1975).

Kelsay, Laura E., comp. *Cartographic Records in the National Archives of the United States Relating to American Indians,* Reference Information Paper 71 (1974).

Kelsay, Laura E., comp. *Cartographic Records of the Bureau of Indian Affairs,* Special List 13 (1977).

Kelsay, Laura E. and Pernell, Frederick W., comps. *Cartographic Records Relating to the Territory of Iowa, 1838–1846,* Special List 27 (1971).

Kelsay, Laura E. and Ashby, Charlotte M., comps. *Cartographic Records Relating to the Territory of Wisconsin, 1836–1848,* Special List 23 (1970).

Kelsay, Laura E., comp. *List of Cartographic Records of the General Land Office,* Special List 19 (1964).

McLaughlin, Patrick D., comp. *Pre-Federal Maps in the National Archives: An Annotated List,* Special List 26 (rev. 1975).

McLaughlin, Patrick D., comp. *Transportation in Nineteenth-Century America: A Survey of the Cartographic Records in the National Archives of the United States,* Reference Information Paper 65 (1975).

Rhoads, James B. and Ashby, Charlotte M., comps. *Preliminary Inventory of the Cartographic Records of the Bureau of the Census,* Preliminary Inventory 103 (1958).

Maps relating to captured and abandoned property during the Civil War are in the records of the Department of the Treasury. Manuscript and printed maps compiled or used by Treasury agents pertain to land in parts of Desha and Chicot Counties, Ark.; (East) Carroll, Madison, and Tensas Parishes, La.; and Bolivar, Washington, Issaquena, Warren, Claiborne, Jefferson, Adams, and Wilkinson Counties, Miss. The names of plantations, their boundaries, acreage, and names of owners are indicated.

Maps pertaining to American Indians include manuscript, annotated, printed, and photocopied maps of states and territories, counties, townships, towns, and Indian reservations, mostly in the western United States, ca. 1800–1944. Most items are arranged numerically by a file number assigned by the Bureau of Indian Affairs. One volume of manuscript maps of grants and reserves in Indiana, Michigan, and Ohio, 1807–49, is filed with the records of the General Land Office. A substantial number of these maps show the names of individual persons within the boundaries of the lands granted or allotted to them. Considerable place name information also appears on these maps. A card index lists these maps by number, by subject, and by area of state, and thereunder by tribe or reservation.

Pertinent publications are *Cartographic Records of the Bureau of Indian Affairs*, Special List 13, compiled by Laura E. Kelsay (Washington: National Archives and Records Service, 1977), and *Cartographic Records in the National Archives of the United States Relating to American Indians*, Reference Information Paper 71, compiled by Laura E. Kelsay (Washington: National Archives and Records Service, 1974).

The David Dale Owen map of southern Wisconsin was the result of a detailed 1839 geographical and geological survey of the part of Wisconsin Territory between the Wisconsin River and the Illinois–Wisconsin boundary. The survey was conducted for the U.S. Treasury Department under the personal supervision of David Dale Owen to locate and research mineral lands. One of the results was a manuscript map of the 4,000-square-mile area. This map has a scale of one inch to one mile and dimensions of sixty-eight by ninety-four inches. It is filed among the records of the U.S. Senate.

Mines, mills, furnaces, smelters, and the names of their owners or operators are indicated on the map. Physical features, roads, settlements, and houses with the names of residents also appear. Overall, the names and locations (by township, range, and section numbers) of more than 500 individuals are documented on this map.

See Herman R. Friis's "The David Dale Owen Map of Southwestern Wisconsin," *Prologue: The Journal of the National Archives* (Spring 1969): 9–28. Landowners appearing on this map are listed in Herman R. Friis's and Alison Wilson's "Individuals Identified by David Dale Owen as Living or Working in Southwestern Wisconsin, Autumn 1839," *National Genealogical Society Quarterly* 58(Dec. 1970): 243–251.

APPENDIX

I

Record Groups Cited

List of Record Groups Cited

RG 15 Records of the Veterans Administration
RG 21 Records of District Courts of the United States
RG 24 Records of the Bureau of Naval Personnel
RG 26 Records of the U.S. Coast Guard
RG 28 Records of the U.S. Postal Service
RG 29 Records of the Bureau of the Census
RG 32 Records of the U.S. Shipping Board
RG 36 Records of the U.S. Customs Service
RG 41 Records of the Bureau of Marine Inspection and Navigation
RG 45 Naval Records Collection of the Office of Naval Records and Library
RG 46 Records of the U.S. Senate
RG 48 Records of the Office of the Secretary of the Interior
RG 49 Records of the Bureau of Land Management
RG 52 Records of the Bureau of Medicine and Surgery
RG 53 Records of the Bureau of the Public Debt
RG 56 General Records of the Department of the Treasury
RG 58 Records of the Internal Revenue Service
RG 59 General Records of the Department of State
RG 60 General Records of the Department of Justice
RG 69 Records of the Work Projects Administration
RG 71 Records of the Bureau of Yards and Docks
RG 75 Records of the Bureau of Indian Affairs
RG 77 Records of the Office of the Chief of Engineers
RG 80 General Records of the Department of the Navy, 1798–1947
RG 84 Records of the Foreign Service Posts of the Department of State
RG 85 Records of the Immigration and Naturalization Service
RG 87 Records of the U.S. Secret Service
RG 92 Records of the Office of the Quartermaster General
RG 93 War Department Collection of Revolutionary War Records
RG 94 Records of the Adjutant General's Office, 1780's–1917
RG 98 Records of U.S. Army Commands, 1784–1821
RG 99 Records of the Office of the Paymaster General
RG 101 Records of the Office of the Comptroller of the Currency
RG 105 Records of the Bureau of Refugees, Freedmen, and Abandoned Lands
RG 107 Records of the Office of the Secretary of War
RG 108 Records of the Headquarters of the Army
RG 109 War Department Collection of Confederate Records
RG 110 Records of the Provost Marshal General's Bureau (Civil War)
RG 111 Records of the Office of the Chief Signal Officer
RG 112 Records of the Surgeon General (Army)
RG 118 Records of U.S. Attorneys and Marshals
RG 123 Records of the U.S. Court of Claims
RG 125 Records of the Office of the Judge Advocate General (Navy)
RG 127 Records of the U.S. Marine Corps
RG 146 Records of the U.S. Civil Service Commission
RG 153 Records of the Office of the Judge Advocate General (Army)
RG 156 Records of the Office of Chief of Ordnance
RG 163 Records of the Selective Service System (World War I)
RG 181 Records of the Naval Districts and Shore Establishments
RG 204 Records of the Office of the Pardon Attorney
RG 205 Records of the Court of Claims Section (Justice)
RG 217 Records of the U.S. General Accounting Office
RG 231 Records of the U.S. Soldiers' Home
RG 233 Records of the U.S. House of Representatives
RG 247 Records of the Office of the Chief of Chaplains
RG 284 Records of the Government of American Samoa
RG 287 Publications of the U.S. Government
RG 351 Records of the Government of the District of Columbia
RG 360 Records of the Continental and Confederation Congresses and the Constitutional Convention
RG 365 Treasury Department Collection of Confederate Records
RG 366 Records of Civil War Special Agencies of the Treasury Department
RG 391 Records of the U.S. Regular Army Mobile Units, 1821–1942
RG 392 Records of U.S. Army Coast Artillery Districts and Defenses, 1901–1942

RG 394	Records of U.S. Army Continental Commands, 1920–1942
RG 393	Records of U.S. Army Continental Commands, 1821–1920
RG 395	Records of U.S. Army Overseas Operations and Commands, 1898–1942
RG 404	Records of the U.S. Military Academy
RG 405	Records of the U.S. Naval Academy
RG 410	Records of the Office of Chief of Support Services

APPENDIX

Microfilm Publications Cited

2

List of Microfilm Publications Cited

GR1 Mortality Census Schedules, North Carolina, 1850–1880. 5 rolls.

GR3 Population Census Schedules, 1810, Washington County, Ohio. 1 roll.

GR4 Population Census Schedules, 1800, 1803, Washington County, Ohio. 1 roll.

GR6 Mortality Census Schedules, Montana, 1870–1880. 1 roll.

GR7 Mortality Census Schedules, Utah, 1870, and Vermont, 1870. 1 roll.

GR20 Wisconsin Territorial Census, 1836–1842, 1846, 1847. 3 rolls.

GR21 Mortality Schedules, New Jersey, 1850–1880 (negative). 4 rolls.

GR22 Mortality Schedules (census), South Carolina, 1850–1880. 3 rolls.

GR24 First Territorial Census of Oklahoma (negative): Logan, Oklahoma, Cleveland, Canadian, Kingfisher, Payne, and Beaver Counties. 1 roll.

GR27 South Dakota State Historical Society (incomplete). 5 rolls.

GR28 Kansas Territorial Census Records, 1859. 3 rolls.

M19 Fifth Census of the United States, 1830. 201 rolls.

M22 Registers of Letters Received by the Office of the Secretary of War, Main Series, 1800–1870. RG 107. 134 rolls.

M30 Despatches from United States Ministers to Great Britain, 1791–1906. RG 59. 200 rolls.

M32 Second Census of the United States, 1800. 52 rolls.

M33 Fourth Census of the United States, 1820. 142 rolls.

M40 Domestic Letters of the Department of State, 1784–1906. RG 59. 171 rolls.

M89 Letters Received by the Secretary of the Navy from Commanding Officers of Squadrons ("Squadron Letters"), 1841–1886. RG 45. 300 rolls.

M121 Despatches From United States Ministers to Brazil, 1809–1906. RG 59. 74 rolls.

M123 Schedules Enumerating Union Veterans and Widows of Union Veterans of the Civil War, 1890. RG 15. 118 rolls.

M145 Abstracts of Oregon Donation Land Claims, 1852–1903. RG 49. 6 rolls.

M158 Schedules of the Colorado State Census of 1885. 8 rolls.

M160 Records of the Office of the Secretary of the Interior Relating to the Suppression of the African Slave Trade and Negro Colonization, 1854–1872. RG 48. 10 rolls.

M169 Despatches from United States Consuls in Monrovia, Liberia, 1852–1906. RG 59. 7 rolls.

M170 Despatches from United States Ministers to Liberia, 1863–1906. RG 59. 14 rolls.

M179 Miscellaneous Letters of the Department of State, 1789–1906. RG 59. 1310 rolls.

M198 Records Relating to the Appointment of Federal Judges and United States Marshals for the Territory and State of Washington, 1853–1902. RG 60. 17 rolls.

M203 Abstracts of Washington Donation Land Claims, 1855–1902. RG 49. 1 roll.

M205 Correspondence of the Secretary of the Navy Relating to African Colonization, 1819–1844. RG 45. 2 rolls.

M206 Letter Books of Commodore Matthew C. Perry, 1843–1845. RG 45. 1 roll.

M221 Letters Received by the Secretary of War, Registered Series, 1801–1870. RG 107. 317 rolls.

M222 Letters Received by the Secretary of War, Unregistered Series, 1789–1861. RG 107. 34 rolls.

M224 Records Relating to the Appointment of Federal Judges, Attorneys, and Marshals for Oregon, 1853–1903. RG 60. 3 rolls.

M225 Index to Compiled Service Records of Confederate Soldiers Who Served in Organizations From the State of Florida. RG 109. 9 rolls.

M226 Index to Compiled Service Records of Confederate Soldiers Who Served in Organizations From the State of Georgia. RG 109. 67 rolls.

M227 Index to Compiled Service Records of Confederate Soldiers Who Served in Organizations From the State of Texas. RG 109. 41 rolls.

M229 Index to Compiled Service Records of Volunteer Soldiers Who Served During the War of 1812 in Organizations From the State of Louisiana. RG 94 and RG 407. 3 rolls.

M230 Index to Compiled Service Records of Confederate Soldiers Who Served in Organizations From the State of North Carolina. RG 109. 43 rolls.

M231 Index to Compiled Service Records of Confederate Soldiers Who Served in Organizations From the State of Tennessee. RG 109. 48 rolls.

M232 Index to Compiled Service Records of Confederate Soldiers Who Served in Organizations From the State of Mississippi. RG 109. 45 rolls.

M233 Registers of Enlistments in the U.S. Army, 1798–1914. RG 94 and RG 407. 47 rolls.

M236 A Microfilm Supplement to the Territorial Papers of the United States: Wisconsin, 1836–1848. No single RG. 122 rolls.

M237 Passenger Lists of Vessels Arriving at New York, 1820–1897. RG 36. 675 rolls.

M238 Consular Trade Reports, 1943–1950. RG 59. 681 rolls.

M239 Index to Compiled Service Records of Volunteer Soldiers Who Served During the Florida War in Organizations From the State of Louisiana. RG 94 and RG 407. 1 roll.

M240 Index to Compiled Service Records of Volunteer Soldiers Who Served During the War With Spain in Organizations From the State of Louisiana. RG 94 and RG 407. 1 roll.

M241 Index to Compiled Service Records of Volunteer Soldiers Who Served During the War of 1837–1838 in Organizations From the State of Louisiana. RG 94 and RG 407. 1 roll.

M242 Index to Compiled Service Records of Volunteer Union Soldiers Who Served in Organizations From the State of New Mexico. RG 94 and RG 407. 4 rolls.

M243 Index to Compiled Service Records of Volunteer Soldiers Who Served During the Cherokee Removal in Organizations From the State of Alabama. RG 94 and RG 407. 1 roll.

M244 Index to Compiled Service Records of Volunteer Soldiers Who Served During the Creek War in Organizations From the State of Alabama. RG 94 and RG 407. 2 rolls.

M245 Index to Compiled Service Records of Volunteer Soldiers Who Served During the Florida War in Organizations From the State of Alabama. RG 94 and RG 407. 1 roll.

M246 Revolutionary War Rolls, 1775–1783. RG 93. 138 rolls.

M247 Papers of the Continental Congress, 1774–1789. RG 360. 204 rolls.

M248 Publications of the National Archives. No single RG. 24 rolls.

M250 Index to Compiled Service Records of Volunteer Soldiers Who Served During the War of 1812 From the State of North Carolina. RG 94 and RG 407. 5 rolls.

M251 Compiled Service Records of Confederate Soldiers Who Served in Organizations From the State of Florida. RG 109. 104 rolls.

M252 Third Census of the United States, 1810. RG 29. 71 rolls.

M253 Consolidated Index to Compiled Service Records of Confederate Soldiers. RG 109. 535 rolls.

M255 Passenger Lists of Vessels Arriving at Baltimore, 1820–1891. RG 36. 50 rolls.

M256 Index to Compiled Service Records of Volunteer Soldiers Who Served During the Cherokee Disturbances and Removal in Organizations From the State of North Carolina. RG 94 and RG 407. 1 roll.

M257 Index to Compiled Service Records of Volunteer Soldiers Who Served During the Revolutionary War in Organizations From the State of North Carolina. RG 93. 2 rolls.

M258 Compiled Service Records of Confederate Soldiers Who Served in Organizations Raised Directly by the Confederate Government. RG 109. 123 rolls.

M259 Passenger Lists of Vessels Arriving at New Orleans, 1820–1902. RG 36. 93 rolls.

M260 Records Relating to Confederate Naval and Marine Personnel. RG 109. 7 rolls.

M261 Index to Passenger Lists of Vessels Arriving at New York, 1820–1846. RG 36. 103 rolls.

M262 Official Records of the Union and Confederate Armies, 1861–1865. No single RG. 128 rolls.

M263 Index to Compiled Service Records of Volunteer Union Soldiers Who Served in Organizations From the State of Alabama. RG 94 and RG 407. 1 roll.

M264 Index to Compiled Service Records of Volunteer Union Soldiers Who Served in Organizations From the State of Florida. RG 94 and RG 407. 1 roll.

M265 Index to Passenger Lists of Vessels Arriving at Boston, 1848–1891. RG 36. 282 rolls.

M266 Compiled Service Records of Confederate Soldiers Who Served in Organizations From the State of Georgia. RG 109. 607 rolls.

M267 Compiled Service Records of Confederate Soldiers Who Served in Organizations From the State of South Carolina. RG 109. 392 rolls.

M268 Compiled Service Records of Confederate Soldiers Who Served in Organizations From the State of Tennessee. RG 109. 359 rolls.

M269 Compiled Service Records of Confederate Soldiers Who Served in Organizations From the State of Mississippi. RG 109. 427 rolls.

M270 Compiled Service Records of Confederate Soldiers Who Served in Organizations From the State of North Carolina. RG 109. 580 rolls.

M272 Quarterly Abstracts of Passenger Lists of Vessels Arriving at New Orleans, 1820–1875. RG 36. 17 rolls.

M273 Records of General Courts-Martial and Courts of Inquiry in the Navy Department, 1799–1867. RG 125. 198 rolls.

M275 Official Records of the Union and Confederate Navies, 1861–1865. No single RG. 31 rolls.

List of Microfilm Publications Cited

M276 Compiled Service Records of Volunteer Union Soldiers Who Served in Organizations From the State of Alabama. RG 94 and RG 407. 10 rolls.

M277 Passenger Lists of Vessels Arriving at Boston, 1820–1891. RG 36. 17 rolls.

M278 Compiled Service Records of Volunteer Soldiers Who Served During the Mexican War in Organizations From the State of Texas. RG 94 and RG 407. 19 rolls.

M279 Records of the 1820 Census of Manufactures. RG 29. 27 rolls.

M311 Compiled Service Records of Confederate Soldiers Who Served in Organizations From the State of Alabama. RG 109. 508 rolls.

M313 Index to War of 1812 Pension Application Files. RG 15. 102 rolls.

M317 Compiled Service Records of Confederate Soldiers Who Served in Organizations From the State of Arkansas. RG 109. 256 rolls.

M318 Compiled Service Records of Confederate Soldiers Who Served in Organizations From the Territory of Arizona. RG 109. 1 roll.

M319 Compiled Service Records of Confederate Soldiers Who Served in Organizations From the State of Kentucky. RG 109. 136 rolls.

M320 Compiled Service Records of Confederate Soldiers Who Served in Organizations From the State of Louisiana. RG 109. 414 rolls.

M321 Compiled Service Records of Confederate Soldiers Who Served in Organizations From the State of Maryland. RG 109. 22 rolls.

M322 Compiled Service Records of Confederate Soldiers Who Served in Organizations From the State of Missouri. RG 109. 193 rolls.

M325 The Territorial Papers of the United States: The Territory of Iowa, 1838–1846. No single RG. 102 rolls.

M326 Index to Passenger Lists of Vessels Arriving at Baltimore, 1833–1866 (City Passenger Lists). RG 36. 22 rolls.

M327 Index to Passenger Lists of Vessels Arriving at Baltimore, 1820–1897 (Federal Passenger Lists). RG 36. 171 rolls.

M330 Abstracts of Service of Naval Officers ("Records of Officers"), 1798–1893. RG 24. 19 rolls.

M331 Compiled Service Records of Confederate General and Staff Officers and Nonregimental Enlisted Men. RG 109. 275 rolls.

M332 Miscellaneous Papers of the Continental Congress, 1774–1789. RG 360. 10 rolls.

M334 A Supplemental Index to Passenger Lists of Vessels Arriving at Atlantic and Gulf Coast Ports (Excluding New York), 1820–1874. RG 36. 188 rolls.

M345 Union Provost Marshal's File of Papers Relating to Individual Civilians. RG 109. 300 rolls.

M346 Confederate Papers Relating to Citizens or Business Firms. RG 109. 1,158 rolls.

M347 Unfiled Papers and Slips Belonging in Confederate Compiled Service Records. RG 109. 442 rolls.

M351 Compiled Service Records of Volunteer Soldiers Who Served During the Mexican War in Mormon Organizations. RG 107. 3 rolls.

M352 Schedules of the Nebraska State Census of 1885. RG 29. 56 rolls.

M360 Index to Passenger Lists of Vessels Arriving at Philadelphia, 1800–1906. RG 36. 151 rolls.

M372 United States Direct Tax of 1798: Tax Lists for the State of Pennsylvania. RG 58. 24 rolls.

M374 Index to Compiled Service Records of Confederate Soldiers Who Served in Organizations From the State of Alabama. RG 109. 49 rolls.

M375 Index to Compiled Service Records of Confederate Soldiers Who Served in Organizations From the Territory of Arizona. RG 109. 1 roll.

M376 Index to Compiled Service Records of Confederate Soldiers Who Served in Organizations From the State of Arkansas. RG 109. 26 rolls.

M377 Index to Compiled Service Records of Confederate Soldiers Who Served in Organizations From the State of Kentucky. RG 109. 14 rolls.

M378 Index to Compiled Service Records of Confederate Soldiers Who Served in Organizations From the State of Louisiana. RG 109. 31 rolls.

M379 Index to Compiled Service Records of Confederate Soldiers Who Served in Organizations From the State of Maryland. RG 109. 2 rolls.

M380 Index to Compiled Service Records of Confederate Soldiers Who Served in Organizations From the State of Missouri. RG 109. 16 rolls.

M381 Index to Compiled Service Records of Confederate Soldiers Who Served in Organizations From the State of South Carolina. RG 109. 35 rolls.

M382 Index to Compiled Service Records of Confederate Soldiers Who Served in Organizations From the State of Virginia. RG 109. 62 rolls.

M383 Index to Compiled Service Records of Volunteer Union Soldiers Who Served in Organizations From the State of Arkansas. RG 94 and RG 407. 4 rolls.

M384 Compiled Service Records of Volunteer Union Soldiers Who Served in Organizations From the State of Maryland. RG 94 and RG 407. 238 rolls.

M385 Index to Compiled Service Records of Volunteer Union Soldiers Who Served in Organizations From the State of Georgia. RG 94 and RG 407. 1 roll.

M386 Index to Compiled Service Records of Volunteer Union Soldiers Who Served in Organizations From the State of Kentucky. RG 94 and RG 407. 30 rolls.

M387 Index to Compiled Service Records of Volunteer Union Soldiers Who Served in Organizations From the State of Louisiana. RG 94 and RG 407. 4 rolls.

M388 Index to Compiled Service Records of Volunteer Union Soldiers Who Served in Organizations From the State of Maryland. RG 94 and RG 407. 13 rolls.

M389 Index to Compiled Service Records of Volunteer Union Soldiers Who Served in Organizations From the State of Mississippi. RG 94 and RG 407. 1 roll.

M390 Index to Compiled Service Records of Volunteer Union Soldiers Who Served in Organizations From the State of Missouri. RG 94 and RG 407. 54 rolls.

M391 Index to Compiled Service Records of Volunteer Union Soldiers Who Served in Organizations From the State of North Carolina. RG 94 and RG 407. 2 rolls.

M392 Index to Compiled Service Records of Volunteer Union Soldiers Who Served in Organizations From the State of Tennessee. RG 94 and RG 407. 16 rolls.

M393 Index to Compiled Service Records of Volunteer Union Soldiers Who Served in Organizations From the State of Texas. RG 94 and RG 407. 2 rolls.

M394 Index to Compiled Service Records of Volunteer Union Soldiers Who Served in Organizations From the State of Virginia. RG 94 and RG 407. 1 roll.

M395 Compiled Service Records of Volunteer Union Soldiers in Organizations From the State of Tennessee. RG 94 and RG 407. 220 rolls.

M396 Compiled Service Records of Volunteer Union Soldiers Who Served in Organizations From the State of Louisiana. RG 94 and RG 407. 50 rolls.

M397 Compiled Service Records of Volunteer Union Soldiers Who Served in Organizations From the State of Kentucky. RG 94 and RG 407. 515 rolls.

M398 Compiled Service Records of Volunteer Union Soldiers Who Served in Organizations From the State of Virginia. RG 94 and RG 407. 7 rolls.

M399 Compiled Service Records of Volunteer Union Soldiers Who Served in Organizations From the State of Arkansas. RG 94 and RG 407. 60 rolls.

M400 Compiled Service Records of Volunteer Union Soldiers Who Served in Organizations From the State of Florida. RG 94 and RG 407. 11 rolls.

M401 Compiled Service Records of Volunteer Union Soldiers Who Served in Organizations From the State of North Carolina. RG 94 and RG 407. 25 rolls.

M402 Compiled Service Records of Volunteer Union Soldiers Who Served in Organizations From the State of Texas. RG 94 and RG 407. 13 rolls.

M403 Compiled Service Records of Volunteer Union Soldiers Who Served in Organizations From the State of Georgia. RG 94 and RG 407. 1 roll.

M404 Compiled Service Records of Volunteer Union Soldiers Who Served in Organizations From the State of Mississippi. RG 94 and RG 407. 4 rolls.

M405 Compiled Service Records of Volunteer Union Soldiers Who Served in Organizations From the State of Missouri. RG 94 and RG 407. 854 rolls.

M406 Letters of Application and Recommendation During the Administration of John Adams, 1797–1801. RG 59. 3 rolls.

M407 Eleventh Census of the United States, 1890. RG 29. 3 rolls.

M409 Index to the Letters Received by the Confederate Secretary of War, 1861–65. RG 109. 34 rolls.

M410 Index to Letters Received by the Confederate Adjutant and Inspector General and by the Confederate Quartermaster General, 1861–1865. RG 109. 41 rolls.

M413 Index to Compiled Service Records of Volunteer Soldiers Who Served During the War With Spain in Organizations From the State of North Carolina. RG 94 and RG 407. 2 rolls.

M416 Union Provost Marshal's File of Papers Relating to Two or More Civilians. RG 109. 94 rolls.

M418 Letters of Application and Recommendation During the Administration of Thomas Jefferson, 1801–1809. RG 59. 12 rolls.

M425 Passenger Lists of Vessels Arriving at Philadelphia, 1800–1882. RG 36. 108 rolls.

M427 Compiled Service Records of Volunteer Union Soldiers Who Served in Organizations From the Territory of New Mexico. RG 94 and RG 407. 46 rolls.

List of Microfilm Publications Cited

M432 Seventh Census of the United States, 1850. RG 29. 1,009 rolls.

M433 Records of the United States District Court for the District of Columbia Relating to Slaves, 1851–1863. RG 21. 3 rolls.

M434 Habeas Corpus Case Records, 1820–1863, of the United States Circuit Court for the District of Columbia. RG 21. 2 rolls.

M435 Case Papers of the United States District Court for the Eastern District of Virginia, 1863–1865, Relating to the Confiscation of Property. RG 21. 1 roll.

M436 Confederate Papers of the United States District Court for the Eastern District of North Carolina, 1861–1865. RG 21. 1 roll.

M437 Letters Received by the Confederate Secretary of War, 1861–1865. RG 109. 151 rolls.

M438 Letters of Application and Recommendation During the Administration of James Madison, 1809–1817. RG 59. 8 rolls.

M439 Letters of Application and Recommendation During the Administration of James Monroe, 1817–1825. RG 59. 19 rolls.

M469 Letters Received by the Confederate Quartermaster General. RG 109. 14 rolls.

M474 Letters Received by the Confederate Adjutant and Inspector General. RG 109. 164 rolls.

M495 Indexes to Letters Received by the Secretary of War, 1861–1878. RG 107. 14 rolls.

M496 Index to the Eleventh Census of the United States, 1890. RG 29. 2 rolls.

M507 Index to Compiled Service Records of Volunteer Union Soldiers Who Served in Organizations From the State of West Virginia. RG 94 and RG 407. 13 rolls.

M508 Compiled Service Records of Volunteer Union Soldiers Who Served in Organizations From the State of West Virginia. RG 94 and RG 407. 261 rolls.

M520 Records of the Board of Commissioners for the Emancipation of Slaves in the District of Columbia, 1862–1863. RG 217. 6 rolls.

M521 Card Index to "Old Loan" Ledgers of the Bureau of the Public Debt, 1790–1836. RG 53. 15 rolls.

M531 Letters of Application and Recommendation During the Administration of John Quincy Adams, 1825–1829. RG 59. 8 rolls.

M532 Index to Compiled Service Records of Volunteer Union Soldiers Who Served in Organizations From the Territory of Arizona. RG 94 and RG 407. 1 roll.

M533 Index to Compiled Service Records of Volunteer Union Soldiers Who Served in Organizations From the State of California. RG 94 and RG 407. 7 rolls.

M534 Index to Compiled Service Records of Volunteer Union Soldiers Who Served in Organizations From the Territory of Colorado. RG 94 and RG 407. 3 rolls.

M535 Index to Compiled Service Records of Volunteer Union Soldiers Who Served in Organizations From the State of Connecticut. RG 94 and RG 407. 17 rolls.

M536 Index to Compiled Service Records of Volunteer Union Soldiers Who Served in Organizations From the Territory of Dakota. RG 94 and RG 407. 1 roll.

M537 Index to Compiled Service Records of Volunteer Union Soldiers in Organizations From the State of Delaware. RG 94 and RG 407. 4 rolls.

M538 Index to Compiled Service Records of Volunteer Union Soldiers Who Served in Organizations From the District of Columbia. RG 94 and RG 407. 3 rolls.

M539 Index to Compiled Service Records of Volunteer Union Soldiers Who Served in Organizations From the State of Illinois. RG 94 and RG 407. 101 rolls.

M540 Index to Compiled Service Records of Volunteer Union Soldiers Who Served in Organizations From the State of Indiana. RG 94 and RG 407. 86 rolls.

M541 Index to Compiled Service Records of Volunteer Union Soldiers Who Served in Organizations From the State of Iowa. RG 94 and RG 407. 29 rolls.

M542 Index to Compiled Service Records of Volunteer Union Soldiers Who Served in Organizations From the State of Kansas. RG 94 and RG 407. 10 rolls.

M543 Index to Compiled Service Records of Volunteer Union Soldiers Who Served in Organizations From the State of Maine. RG 94 and RG 407. 23 rolls.

M544 Index to Compiled Service Records of Volunteer Union Soldiers Who Served in Organizations From the State of Massachusetts. RG 94 and RG 407. 44 rolls.

M545 Index to Compiled Service Records of Volunteer Union Soldiers Who Served in Organizations From the State of Michigan. RG 94 and RG 407. 48 rolls.

M546 Index to Compiled Service Records of Volunteer Union Soldiers Who Served in Organizations From the State of Minnesota. RG 94 and RG 407. 10 rolls.

M547 Index to Compiled Service Records of Volunteer Union Soldiers Who Served in Organizations From the State of Nebraska. RG 94 and RG 407. 2 rolls.

M548 Index to Compiled Service Records of Volunteer Union Soldiers Who Served in Organizations From the State of Nevada. RG 94 and RG 407. 1 roll.

M549 Index to Compiled Service Records of Volunteer Union Soldiers Who Served in Organizations From the State of New Hampshire. RG 94 and RG 407. 13 rolls.

M550 Index to Compiled Service Records of Volunteer Union Soldiers Who Served in Organizations From the State of New Jersey. RG 94 and RG 407. 26 rolls.

M551 Index to Compiled Service Records of Volunteer Union Soldiers Who Served in Organizations From the State of New York. RG 94 and RG 407. 157 rolls.

M552 Index to Compiled Service Records of Volunteer Union Soldiers Who Served in Organizations From the State of Ohio. RG 94 and RG 407. 122 rolls.

M553 Index to Compiled Service Records of Volunteer Union Soldiers Who Served in Organizations From the State of Oregon. RG 94 and RG 407. 1 roll.

M554 Index to Compiled Service Records of Volunteer Union Soldiers Who Served in Organizations From the State of Pennsylvania. RG 94 and RG 407. 136 rolls.

M555 Index to Compiled Service Records of Volunteer Union Soldiers Who Served in Organizations From the State of Rhode Island. RG 94 and RG 407. 7 rolls.

M556 Index to Compiled Service Records of Volunteer Union Soldiers Who Served in Organizations From the Territory of Utah. RG 94 and RG 407. 1 roll.

M557 Index to Compiled Service Records of Volunteer Union Soldiers Who Served in Organizations From the State of Vermont. RG 94 and RG 407. 14 rolls.

M558 Index to Compiled Service Records of Volunteer Union Soldiers Who Served in Organizations From the Territory of Washington. RG 94 and RG 407. 1 roll.

M559 Index to Compiled Service Records of Volunteer Union Soldiers Who Served in Organizations From the State of Wisconsin. RG 94 and RG 407. 33 rolls.

M565 Letters Sent by the Office of the Adjutant General (Main Series), 1800–1890. RG 94 and RG 407. 63 rolls.

M566 Letters Received by the Office of the Adjutant General, 1805–1821. RG 94 and RG 407. 144 rolls.

M567 Letters Received by the Office of the Adjutant General (Main Series), 1822–1860. RG 94 and RG 407. 636 rolls.

M575 Copies of Lists of Passengers Arriving at Miscellaneous Ports on the Atlantic and Gulf Coasts and at Ports on the Great Lakes, 1820–1873. RG 36. 16 rolls.

M576 Interior Department Appointment Papers: Arizona, 1857–1907. RG 48. 22 rolls.

M589 Index to Compiled Service Records of Volunteer Union Soldiers Who Served with United States Colored Troops. RG 94 and RG 407. 98 rolls.

M593 Ninth Census of the United States, 1870. RG 29. 1,748 rolls.

M594 Compiled Records Showing Service of Military Units in Volunteer Union Organizations. RG 94 and RG 407. 225 rolls.

M595 Indian Census Rolls, 1884–1940. RG 75. 692 rolls.

M596 Quarterly Abstracts of Passenger Lists of Vessels Arriving at Baltimore, 1820–1869. RG 36. 6 rolls.

M598 Selected Records of the War Department Relating to Confederate Prisoners of War, 1861–1865. RG 109. 145 rolls.

M602 Index to Compiled Service Records of Volunteer Soldiers Who Served During the War of 1812. RG 94 and RG 407. 234 rolls.

M603 Internal Revenue Assessment Lists for New York and New Jersey, 1862–1866. RG 58. 217 rolls.

M605 Records of the City of Georgetown (D.C.), 1800–1879. RG 351. 49 rolls.

M617 Returns from U.S. Military Posts, 1800–1916. RG 94 and RG 407. 1,550 rolls.

M619 Letters Received by the Office of the Adjutant General (Main Series), 1861–1870. RG 94 and RG 407. 828 rolls.

M625 Area File of the Naval Records Collection, 1775–1910. RG 45. 414 rolls.

M629 Index to Compiled Service Records of Volunteer Soldiers Who Served During Indian Wars and Disturbances, 1815–1858. RG 94 and RG 407. 42 rolls.

M630 Index to Compiled Service Records of Volunteer Soldiers Who Served From the State of Michigan During the Patriot War, 1838–1839. RG 94 and RG 407. 1 roll.

M631 Index to Compiled Service Records of Volunteer Soldiers Who Served From the State of New York During the Patriot War, 1838. RG 94 and RG 407. 1 roll.

M636 Index to Compiled Service Records of Volunteer Union Soldiers Who Served in the Veteran Reserve Corps. RG 94 and RG 407. 44 rolls.

M637 First Census of the United States, 1790. RG 29. 12 rolls.

List of Microfilm Publications Cited

M638 Compiled Service Records of Volunteer Soldiers Who Served During the Mexican War in Organizations From the State of Tennessee. RG 94 and RG 407. 15 rolls.

M639 Letters of Application and Recommendation During the Administration of Andrew Jackson, 1829–1837. RG 59. 27 rolls.

M650 Letters of Application and Recommendation During the Administrations of Abraham Lincoln and Andrew Johnson, 1861–1869. RG 59. 53 rolls.

M652 Index to Compiled Service Records of Volunteer Soldiers Who Served During the War of 1812 in Organizations From the State of South Carolina. RG 94 and RG 407. 7 rolls.

M653 Eighth Census of the United States, 1860. RG 29. 1,438 rolls.

M661 Historical Information Relating to Military Posts and Other Installations, ca. 1700–1900. RG 94 and RG 407. 8 rolls.

M666 Letters Received by the Office of the Adjutant General (Main Series), 1871–1880. RG 94 and RG 407. 593 rolls.

M678 Compiled Service Records of Volunteer Soldiers Who Served During the War of 1812 in Organizations From the Territory of Mississippi. RG 94 and RG 407. 22 rolls.

M680 Records Relating to the Appointment of Federal Judges, Attorneys, and Marshals for the Territory and State of Utah, 1853–1901. RG 60. 14 rolls.

M681 Records Relating to the Appointment of Federal Judges, Attorneys, and Marshals for the Territory and State of Idaho, 1861–1899. RG 60. 9 rolls.

M685 Records Relating to Enrollment of Eastern Cherokees by Guion Miller, 1908–1910. RG 75. 12 rolls.

M687 Letters of Application and Recommendation During the Administrations of Martin Van Buren, William Henry Harrison, and John Tyler, 1837–1845. RG 59. 35 rolls.

M688 U.S. Military Academy Cadet Application Papers, 1805–1866. RG 94 and RG 407. 242 rolls.

M689 Letters Received by the Office of the Adjutant General (Main Series), 1881–1889. RG 94 and RG 407. 740 rolls.

M692 Compiled Service Records of Volunteer Union Soldiers Who Served in Organizations From the Territory of Utah. RG 94 and RG 407. 1 roll.

M693 Interior Department Appointment Papers: Idaho, 1862–1907. RG 48. 17 rolls.

M694 Index to Compiled Service Records of Volunteer Soldiers Who Served From 1784 to 1811. RG 94 and RG 407. 9 rolls.

M698 Index to General Correspondence of the Adjutant General's Office, 1890–1917. RG 94 and RG 407. 1,269 rolls.

M701 Letters Sent by the Department of Justice: Instructions to United States Attorneys and Marshals, 1867–1904. RG 60. 212 rolls.

M704 Sixth Census of the United States, 1840. 580 rolls.

M711 Registers of Letters Received, Office of the Adjutant General, 1812–1889. RG 94 and RG 407. 85 rolls.

M721 The Territorial Papers of the United States. 15 rolls.

M725 Indexes to Letters Received, Adjutant General's Office (Main Series), 1846, 1861–1889. RG 94 and RG 407. 9 rolls.

M732 Interior Department Appointment Papers: State of California, 1849–1907. RG 48. 29 rolls.

M742 Selected Series of Records Issued by the Commissioner of the Bureau of Refugees, Freedmen, and Abandoned Lands, 1865–1872. RG 105. 7 rolls.

M750 Interior Department Appointment Papers: Territory of New Mexico, 1850–1907. RG 48. 18 rolls.

M752 Registers and Letters Received by the Commissioner of the Bureau of Refugees, Freedmen, and Abandoned Lands, 1865–1872. RG 105. 74 rolls.

M754 Internal Revenue Assessment Lists for Alabama, 1865–1866. RG 58. 6 rolls.

M755 Internal Revenue Assessment Lists for Arkansas, 1865–1866. RG 58. 2 rolls.

M756 Internal Revenue Assessment Lists for California, 1862–1866. RG 58. 33 rolls.

M757 Internal Revenue Assessment Lists for the Territory of Colorado, 1862–1866. RG 58. 3 rolls.

M758 Internal Revenue Assessment Lists for Connecticut, 1862–1866. RG 58. 23 rolls.

M759 Internal Revenue Assessment Lists for Delaware, 1862–1866. RG 58. 8 rolls.

M760 Internal Revenue Assessment Lists for the District of Columbia, 1862–1866. RG 58. 8 rolls.

M761 Internal Revenue Assessment Lists for Florida, 1865–1866. RG 58. 1 roll.

M762 Internal Revenue Assessment Lists for Georgia, 1865–1866. RG 58. 8 rolls.

M763 Internal Revenue Assessment Lists for the Territory of Idaho, 1865–1866. RG 58. 1 roll.

M764 Internal Revenue Assessment Lists for Illinois, 1862–1866. RG 58. 63 rolls.

M765 Internal Revenue Assessment Lists for Indiana, 1862–1866. RG 58. 14 rolls.

M766 Internal Revenue Assessment Lists for Iowa, 1862–1866. RG 58. 16 rolls.

M767 Internal Revenue Assessment Lists for Kansas, 1862–1866. RG 58. 3 rolls.

M768 Internal Revenue Assessment Lists for Kentucky, 1862–1866. RG 58. 24 rolls.

M769 Internal Revenue Assessment Lists for Louisiana, 1863–1866. RG 58. 10 rolls.

M770 Internal Revenue Assessment Lists for Maine, 1862–1866. RG 58. 15 rolls.

M771 Internal Revenue Assessment Lists for Maryland, 1862–1866. RG 58. 21 rolls.

M773 Internal Revenue Assessment Lists for Michigan, 1862–1866. RG 58. 15 rolls.

M775 Internal Revenue Assessment Lists for Mississippi, 1865–1866. RG 58. 3 rolls.

M777 Internal Revenue Assessment Lists for Montana, 1864–1872. RG 58. 1 roll.

M779 Internal Revenue Assessment Lists for Nevada, 1862–1866. RG 58. 2 rolls.

M780 Internal Revenue Assessment Lists for New Hampshire, 1862–1866. RG 58. 10 rolls.

M781 Internal Revenue Assessment Lists for the Territory of New Mexico, 1862–1870, 1872–1874. RG 58. 1 roll.

M784 Internal Revenue Assessment Lists for North Carolina, 1864–1866. RG 58. 2 rolls.

M787 Internal Revenue Assessment Lists for Pennsylvania, 1862–1866. RG 58. 107 rolls.

M788 Internal Revenue Assessment Lists for Rhode Island, 1862–1866. RG 58. 10 rolls.

M789 Internal Revenue Assessment Lists for South Carolina, 1864–1866. RG 58. 2 rolls.

M791 Internal Revenue Assessment Lists for Texas, 1865–1866. RG 58. 2 rolls.

M792 Internal Revenue Assessment Lists for Vermont, 1862–1866. RG 58. 7 rolls.

M793 Internal Revenue Assessment Lists for Virginia, 1862–1866. RG 58. 6 rolls.

M795 Internal Revenue Assessment Lists for West Virginia, 1862–1866. RG 58. 4 rolls.

M798 Records of the Assistant Commissioner for the State of Georgia, Bureau of Refugees, Freedmen, and Abandoned Lands. RG 105. 36 rolls.

M799 Records of the Superintendent of Education for the State of Georgia, Bureau of Refugees, Freedmen, and Abandoned Lands, 1865–1870. RG 105. 28 rolls.

M803 Records of the Education Division of the Bureau of Refugees, Freedmen, and Abandoned Lands, 1865–1871. RG 105. 35 rolls.

M804 Revolutionary War Pension and Bounty-Land Warrant Application Files. RG 15. 2,670 rolls.

M805 Selected Records From Revolutionary War Pension and Bounty-Land Warrant Application Files. RG 15. 898 rolls.

M808 Interior Department Appointment Papers: Territory of Colorado, 1857–1907. RG 48. 13 rolls.

M809 Records of the Assistant Commissioner for the State of Alabama, Bureau of Refugees, Freedmen, and Abandoned Lands, 1865–1870. RG 105. 23 rolls.

M810 Records of the Superintendent of Education for the State of Alabama, Bureau of Refugees, Freedmen, and Abandoned Lands, 1865–1870. RG 105. 8 rolls.

M814 Interior Department Appointment Papers: Territory of Oregon, 1849–1907. RG 48. 10 rolls.

M815 Oregon and Washington Donation Land Files, 1851–1903. RG 49. 108 rolls.

M816 Registers of Signatures of Depositors in Branches of the Freedman's Savings and Trust Company, 1865–1874. RG 101. 27 rolls.

M817 Indexes to Deposit Ledgers in Branches of the Freedman's Savings and Trust Company, 1865–1874. RG 101. 5 rolls.

M818 Index to Compiled Service Records of Confederate Soldiers Who Served in Organizations Raised Directly by the Confederate Government and of Confederate General and Staff Officers and Non-Regimental Enlisted Men. RG 109. 26 rolls.

M821 Records of the Assistant Commissioner for the State of Texas, Bureau of Refugees, Freedmen, and Abandoned Lands, 1865–1869. RG 105. 32 rolls.

M822 Records of the Superintendent of Education for the State of Texas, Bureau of Refugees, Freedmen, and Abandoned Lands, 1865–1870. RG 105. 18 rolls.

M826 Records of the Assistant Commissioner for the State of Mississippi, Bureau of Refugees, Freedmen, and Abandoned Lands, 1865–1869. RG 105. 50 rolls.

M829 U.S. Revolutionary War Bounty Land Warrants Used in the U.S. Military District of Ohio and Related Papers (Acts of 1788, 1803, and 1806). RG 49. 16 rolls.

M830 Interior Department Appointment Papers: Wyoming, 1869–1907. RG 48. 6 rolls.

M841 Records of Appointment of Postmasters, 1832–Sept. 30, 1971. RG 28. 145 rolls.

M843 Records of the Assistant Commissioner for the State of North Carolina, Bureau of Refugees, Freedmen, and Abandoned Lands, 1865–1870. RG 105. 38 rolls.

List of Microfilm Publications Cited

M844 Records of the Superintendent of Education for the State of North Carolina, Bureau of Refugees, Freedmen, and Abandoned Lands, 1865–1870. RG 105. 16 rolls.

M845 Schedules of the Florida State Census of 1885. RG 29. 13 rolls.

M846 Schedules of the New Mexico Territory Census of 1885. RG 29. 6 rolls.

M847 Special Index to Numbered Records in the War Department Collection of Revolutionary War Records, 1775–1783. RG 93. 39 rolls.

M848 War of 1812 Military Bounty Land Warrants, 1815–1858. RG 49. 14 rolls.

M849 Interior Department Appointment Papers: Mississippi, 1849–1907. RG 48. 4 rolls.

M850 Veterans Administration Pension Payment Cards, 1907–1933. RG 15. 2,539 rolls.

M853 Numbered Record Books Concerning Military Operations and Service, Pay and Settlement of Accounts, and Supplies in the War Department Collection of Revolutionary War Records. RG 93. 41 rolls.

M859 Miscellaneous Numbered Records (The Manuscript File) in the War Department Collection of Revolutionary War Records, 1775–1790's. RG 93. 125 rolls.

M860 General Index to Compiled Military Service Records of Revolutionary War Soldiers. RG 93. 58 rolls.

M861 Compiled Records Showing Service of Military Units in Confederate Organizations. RG 109. 74 rolls.

M863 Compiled Service Records of Volunteer Soldiers Who Served During the Mexican War in Organizations From the State of Mississippi. RG 94. 9 rolls.

M869 Records of the Assistant Commissioner for the State of South Carolina, Bureau of Refugees, Freedmen, and Abandoned Lands, 1865–1870. RG 105. 44 rolls.

M871 General Index to Compiled Service Records of Volunteer Soldiers Who Served During the War With Spain. RG 94. 126 rolls.

M872 Index to Compiled Service Records of Volunteer Soldiers Who Served During the Philippine Insurrection. RG 94. 24 rolls.

M873 Letters of Application and Recommendation During the Administrations of James Polk, Zachary Taylor, and Millard Fillmore, 1845–1853. RG 59. 98 rolls.

M879 Index to Compiled Service Records of American Naval Personnel Who Served During the Revolutionary War. RG 93. 1 roll.

M880 Compiled Service Records of American Naval Personnel and Members of the Departments of the Quartermaster General and the Commissary General of Military Stores Who Served During the Revolutionary War. RG 93. 4 rolls.

M881 Compiled Service Records of Soldiers Who Served in the American Army During the Revolutionary War. RG 93. 1,097 rolls.

M904 War Department Collection of Post-Revolutionary War Manuscripts. RG 94. 4 rolls.

M905 Compiled Service Records of Volunteer Soldiers Who Served From 1784 to 1811. RG 94. 32 rolls.

M907 Index to Compiled Service Records of Volunteer Soldiers Who Served During the Cherokee Disturbances and Removal in Organizations From the State of Georgia. RG 94. 1 roll.

M908 Indexes to Compiled Service Records of Volunteer Soldiers Who Served During the Cherokee Disturbances and Removal in Organizations From the State of Tennessee and the Field and Staff of the Army of the Cherokee Nation. RG 94. 2 rolls.

M910 Virginia Half Pay and other Related Revolutionary War Pension Application Files. RG 15. 18 rolls.

M918 Register of Confederate Soldiers, Sailors, and Citizens Who Died in Federal Prisons and Military Hospitals in the North, 1861–1865. RG 92. 1 roll.

M920 Index to Compiled Service Records of Revolutionary War Soldiers Who Served With the American Army in Connecticut Military Organizations. RG 93. 25 rolls.

M929 Documents Relating to the Military and Naval Service of Blacks Awarded the Congressional Medal of Honor From the Civil War to the Spanish-American War. RG 94, 107, 153, 391, 393, 24, and 45. 4 rolls.

M940 Letters Received by the Department of Justice From the State of Louisiana, 1871–1884. RG 60. 6 rolls.

M947 Letters Received by the Department of Justice From South Carolina, 1871–1884. RG 60. 9 rolls.

M950 Interior Department Appointment Papers: North Carolina, 1849–1892. RG 48. 1 roll.

M967 Letters of Application and Recommendation During the Administrations of Franklin Pierce and James Buchanan, 1853–1861. RG 59. 50 rolls.

M968 Letters of Application and Recommendation During the Administration of Ulysses S. Grant, 1869–1877. RG 59. 69 rolls.

M970 Letters Received by the Department of Justice From Mississippi, 1871–1884. RG 60. 4 rolls.

M972 Computer-Processed Tabulations of Data From Seamen's Protective Certificate Applications to the Collector of Customs for the Port of Philadelphia, 1812–1815. RG 36. 1 roll.

M979 Records of the Assistant Commissioner for the State of Arkansas, Bureau of Refugees, Freedmen, and Abandoned Lands, 1865–1869. RG 105. 52 rolls.

M980 Records of the Superintendent of Education for the State of Arkansas, Bureau of Refugees, Freedmen, and Abandoned Lands, 1865–1871. RG 105. 5 rolls.

M987 Records of the U.S. Circuit Court for the Western District of Pennsylvania, 1801–1802, and Minutes and Habeas Corpus and Criminal Case Files of the U.S. District Court for the Eastern District of Pennsylvania, 1789–1843. RG 21. 3 rolls.

M991 U.S. Naval Academy Registers of Delinquencies, 1846–1850 and 1853–1882, and Academic and Conduct Records of Cadets, 1881–1908. RG 405. 45 rolls.

M999 Records of the Assistant Commissioner for the State of Tennessee, Bureau of Refugees, Freedmen, and Abandoned Lands, 1865–1869. RG 105. 34 rolls.

M1000 Records of the Superintendent of Education for the State of Tennessee, Bureau of Refugees, Freedmen, and Abandoned Lands, 1865–1870. RG 105. 9 rolls.

M1002 Selected Documents Relating to Blacks Nominated for Appointment to the U.S. Military Academy During the 19th Century, 1870–1887. RG 94, 107, and 153. 21 rolls.

M1003 Pardon Petitions and Related Papers Submitted in Response to President Andrew Johnson's Amnesty Proclamation of May 29, 1865 ("Amnesty Papers"). RG 94. 73 rolls.

M1015 Central Treasury Records of the Continental and Confederation Governments Relating to Military Affairs, 1775–1789. RG 39, 53, and 217. 7 rolls.

M1017 Compiled Service Records of Former Confederate Soldiers Who Served in the 1st Through 6th U.S. Volunteer Infantry Regiments, 1864–1866. RG 94. 65 rolls.

M1022 Interior Department Appointment Papers: New York, 1849–1906. RG 48. 5 rolls.

M1026 Records of the Superintendent of Education for the State of Louisiana, Bureau of Refugees, Freedmen, and Abandoned Lands, 1864–1869. RG 105. 12 rolls.

M1027 Records of the Assistant Commissioner for the State of Louisiana, Bureau of Refugees, Freedmen, and Abandoned Lands, 1865–1869. RG 105. 36 rolls.

M1028 Compiled Service Records of Volunteer Soldiers Who Served During the Mexican War in Organizations From the State of Pennsylvania. RG 94. 13 rolls.

M1033 Interior Department Appointment Papers: Nevada, 1860–1907. RG 48. 3 rolls.

M1048 Records of the Assistant Commissioner for the State of Virginia, Bureau of Refugees, Freedmen, and Abandoned Lands, 1865–1869. RG 105. 67 rolls.

M1049 The Territorial Papers of the United States: The Territory of Oregon, 1848–1859. 12 rolls.

M1050 The Territorial Papers of the United States: The Territory of Minnesota, 1849–1858. 11 rolls.

M1051 Index to Compiled Service Records of Revolutionary War Soldiers Who Served With the American Army in Georgia Military Organizations. RG 93. 1 roll.

M1053 Records of the Superintendent of Education for the State of Virginia, Bureau of Refugees, Freedmen, and Abandoned Lands, 1865–1870. RG 105. 20 rolls.

M1055 Records of the Assistant Commissioner for the District of Columbia, Bureau of Refugees, Freedmen, and Abandoned Lands, 1865–1872. RG 105. 21 rolls.

M1056 Records of the Superintendent of Education for the District of Columbia, Bureau of Refugees, Freedmen, and Abandoned Lands, 1865–1872. RG 105. 24 rolls.

M1058 Interior Department Appointment Papers: Missouri, 1849–1907. RG 48. 9 rolls.

M1062 Correspondence of the War Department Relating to Indian Affairs, Military Pensions, and Fortifications, 1791–1797. RG 107. 1 roll.

M1064 Letters Received by the Commission Branch of the Adjutant General's Office, 1863–1870. RG 94. 527 rolls.

M1086 Compiled Service Records of Volunteer Soldiers Who Served in Organizations From the State of Florida During the Florida Indian Wars, 1835–1858. RG 94. 63 rolls.

M1087 Compiled Service Records of Volunteer Soldiers Who Served in the Florida Infantry During the War With Spain. RG 94. 13 rolls.

M1090 "Memoir of Reconnaissances With Maps During the Florida Campaign," Apr. 1854–Feb. 1858. RG 393. 1 roll.

M1091 Subject File of the Confederate States Navy, 1861–1865. RG 45. 61 rolls.

List of Microfilm Publications Cited

M1104 Eastern Cherokee Applications of the U.S. Court of Claims, 1906–1909. RG 123. 348 rolls.

M1116 D.C. Building Permits, 1877–1949.

M1119 Interior Department Appointment Papers: Florida, 1849–1907. RG 49. 6 rolls.

M1125 Name and Subject Index to the Letters Received by the Appointment, Commission, and Personal Branch of the Adjutant General's Office, 1871–1894. RG 94. 4 rolls.

M1131 Record of Appointments of Postmasters, October 1789–1832. RG 28. 4 rolls.

T9 Tenth Census of the United States, 1880. RG 29. 1,454 rolls.

T132 Minnesota Census Schedules for 1870. RG 29. 13 rolls.

T275 Census of Creek Indians Taken by Parsons and Abbott in 1832. RG 75. 1 roll.

T288 General Index to Pension Files, 1861–1934. RG 15. 544 rolls.

T289 Organization Index to Pension Files of Veterans Who Served Between 1861 and 1900. RG 15. 765 rolls.

T316 Old War Index to Pension Files. 1815–1926. RG 15. 7 rolls.

T317 Index to Mexican War Pension Files, 1887–1926. RG 15. 14 rolls.

T318 Index to Indian Wars Pension Files, 1892–1926. RG 15. 12 rolls.

T496 Census Roll, 1835, of the Cherokee Indians East of the Mississippi and Index to the Roll. RG 75. 1 roll.

T498 Publications of the Bureau of the Census: 1790 Census, Printed Schedules. RG 29. 3 rolls.

T517 Index to Passengers of Vessels Arriving at Ports in Alabama, Florida, Georgia, and South Carolina, 1890–1924. RG 85. 26 rolls.

T518 Index to Passengers Arriving at Providence, R.I., June 18, 1911–Oct. 5, 1954. RG 85. 2 rolls.

T519 Index to Passenger Lists of Vessels Arriving at New York, June 16, 1897–June 30, 1902. RG 85. 115 rolls.

T520 Index (Soundex) to Passenger Lists of Vessels Arriving at Baltimore, 1897–1952. RG 85. 43 rolls.

T521 Index to Passenger Lists of Vessels Arriving at Boston, Jan. 1, 1902–June 30, 1906. RG 85. 11 rolls.

T522 Index to Passengers Arriving at New Bedford, July 1, 1902–Nov. 18, 1954. RG 85. 2 rolls.

T523 Index to Passengers Arriving at Gulfport, Aug. 27, 1904–Aug. 28, 1954, and at Pascagoula, July 15, 1903–May 21, 1935. RG 85. 1 roll.

T524 Index to Passengers Arriving at Portland, Maine, Jan. 29, 1893–Nov. 22, 1954. RG 85. 1 roll.

T526 Index (Soundex) to Passenger Lists of Vessels Arriving at Philadelphia, Jan. 1, 1883–June 28, 1948. RG 85. 60 rolls.

T527 Index to Passenger Lists of Vessels Arriving at New Orleans Before 1900. RG 85. 32 rolls.

T529 Final Rolls of Citizens and Freedmen of the Five Civilized Tribes in Indian Territory (as Approved by the Secretary of the Interior On or Before March 4, 1907, With Supplements Dated September 25, 1914). RG 48. 3 rolls.

T577 Index to Names of United States Marshals, 1789–1960. RG 60. 1 roll.

T612 Book Indexes, New York Passenger Lists, 1906–1942. RG 85. 807 rolls.

T617 Index to Passenger Lists of Vessels Arriving at Boston, July 1, 1906–Dec. 31, 1920. RG 85. 11 rolls.

T618 Index to Passenger Lists of Vessels Arriving at New Orleans, 1900–1952. RG 85. 22 rolls.

T621 Index (Soundex) to Passenger Lists of Vessels Arriving at New York, July 1, 1902–December 31, 1943. RG 85. 755 rolls.

T623 Twelfth Census of the United States, 1900. RG 29. 1,854 rolls.

T624 Thirteenth Census of the United States, 1910. RG 29. 1,784 rolls.

T655 Federal Mortality Census Schedules, 1850–80, and Related Indexes in the Custody of the Daughters of the American Revolution. 30 rolls.

T715 Passenger and Crew Lists of Vessels Arriving at New York, 1897–1942. RG 85. 6,674 rolls.

T718 Ledgers of Payments, 1818–1872, to United States Pensioners Under Acts of 1818 through 1858, From Records of The Office of the Third Auditor of the Treasury. RG 217. 23 rolls.

T734 Index (Soundex) to 1880 Federal Population Census Schedules: Alabama. RG 29. 74 rolls.

T735 Index (Soundex) to 1880 Federal Population Census Schedules: Arizona. RG 29. 2 rolls.

T739 Index (Soundex) to 1880 Federal Population Census Schedules: Connecticut. RG 29. 25 rolls.

T740 Index (Soundex) to 1880 Federal Population Census Schedules: Dakota Territory. RG 29. 6 rolls.

T741 Index (Soundex) to 1880 Federal Population Census Schedules: Delaware. RG 29. 9 rolls.

T742 Index (Soundex) to 1880 Federal Population Census Schedules: District of Columbia. RG 29. 9 rolls.

T743 Index (Soundex) to 1880 Federal Population Census Schedules: Florida. RG 29. 16 rolls.

T744 Index (Soundex) to 1880 Federal Population Census Schedules: Georgia. RG 29. 86 rolls.

T745 Index (Soundex) to 1880 Federal Population Census Schedules: Idaho Territory. RG 29. 2 rolls.

T746 Index (Soundex) to 1880 Federal Population Census Schedules: Illinois. RG 29. 143 rolls.

T747 Index (Soundex) to 1880 Federal Population Census Schedules: Indiana. RG 29. 98 rolls.

T748 Index (Soundex) to 1880 Federal Population Census Schedules: Iowa. RG 29. 78 rolls.

T749 Index (Soundex) to 1880 Federal Population Census Schedules: Kansas. RG 29. 51 rolls.

T750 Index (Soundex) to 1880 Federal Population Census Schedules: Kentucky. RG 29. 83 rolls.

T751 Index (Soundex) to 1880 Federal Population Census Schedules: Louisiana. RG 29. 55 rolls.

T752 Index (Soundex) to 1880 Federal Population Census Schedules: Maine. RG 29. 29 rolls.

T753 Index (Soundex) to 1880 Federal Population Census Schedules: Maryland. RG 29. 47 rolls.

T754 Index (Soundex) to 1880 Federal Population Census Schedules: Massachusetts. RG 29. 70 rolls.

T755 Index (Soundex) to 1880 Federal Population Census Schedules: Michigan. RG 29. 73 rolls.

T756 Index (Soundex) to 1880 Federal Population Census Schedules: Minnesota. RG 29. 37 rolls.

T757 Index (Soundex) to 1880 Federal Population Census Schedules: Mississippi. RG 29. 69 rolls.

T758 Index (Soundex) to 1880 Federal Population Census Schedules: Missouri. RG 29. 114 rolls.

T759 Index (Soundex) to 1880 Federal Population Census Schedules: Montana Territory. RG 29. 2 rolls.

T760 Index (Soundex) to 1880 Federal Population Census Schedules: Nebraska. RG 29. 22 rolls.

T761 Index (Soundex) to 1880 Federal Population Census Schedules: Nevada. RG 29. 3 rolls.

T762 Index (Soundex) to 1880 Federal Population Census Schedules: New Hampshire. RG 29. 13 rolls.

T763 Index (Soundex) to 1880 Federal Population Census Schedules: New Jersey. RG 29. 49 rolls.

T764 Index (Soundex) to 1880 Federal Population Census Schedules: New Mexico Territory. RG 29. 6 rolls.

T765 Index (Soundex) to 1880 Federal Population Census Schedules: New York. RG 29. 187 rolls.

T766 Index (Soundex) to 1880 Federal Population Census Schedules: North Carolina. RG 29. 79 rolls.

T767 Index (Soundex) to 1880 Federal Population Census Schedules: Ohio. RG 29. 143 rolls.

T768 Index (Soundex) to 1880 Federal Population Census Schedules: Oregon. RG 29. 8 rolls.

T769 Index (Soundex) to 1880 Federal Population Census Schedules: Pennsylvania. RG 29. 168 rolls.

T770 Index (Soundex) to 1880 Federal Population Census Schedules: Rhode Island. RG 29. 11 rolls.

T771 Index (Soundex) to 1880 Federal Population Census Schedules: Tennessee. RG 29. 56 rolls.

T772 Index (Soundex) to 1880 Federal Population Census Schedules: South Carolina. RG 29. 86 rolls.

T773 Index (Soundex) to 1880 Federal Population Census Schedules: Texas. RG 29. 77 rolls.

T774 Index (Soundex) to 1880 Federal Population Census Schedules: Utah Territory. RG 29. 7 rolls.

T775 Index (Soundex) to 1880 Federal Population Census Schedules: Vermont. RG 29. 15 rolls.

T776 Index (Soundex) to 1880 Federal Population Census Schedules: Virginia. RG 29. 82 rolls.

T777 Index (Soundex) to 1880 Federal Population Census Schedules: Washington Territory. RG 29. 4 rolls.

T778 Index (Soundex) to 1880 Federal Population Census Schedules: West Virginia. RG 29. 32 rolls.

T779 Index (Soundex) to 1880 Federal Population Census Schedules: Wisconsin. RG 29. 51 rolls.

T780 Index (Soundex) to 1880 Federal Population Census Schedules: Wyoming. RG 29. 1 roll.

T790 Book Indexes, Boston Passenger Lists, 1899–1940. RG 85. 107 rolls.

T791 Book Indexes, Philadelphia Passenger Lists, 1906–1926. RG 85. 23 rolls.

T792 Book Indexes, Providence Passenger Lists, 1911–1934. RG 85. 15 rolls.

T793 Book Indexes, Portland, Maine, Passenger Lists, 1907–1930. RG 85. 12 rolls.

T825 Publications of the Bureau of the Census, 1790–1916. RG 29. 42 rolls.

T840 Passenger Lists of Vessels Arriving at Philadelphia, 1883–1945. RG 85. 181 rolls.

T843 Passenger Lists of Vessels Arriving at Boston, 1891–1943. RG 85. 454 rolls.

T844 Passenger Lists of Vessels Arriving at Baltimore, 1891–1909. RG 85. 77 rolls.

List of Microfilm Publications Cited

T905 Crew Lists of Vessels Arriving at New Orleans, 1910–1945. RG 85. 189 rolls.

T938 Crew Lists of Vessels Arriving at Boston, 1917–1943. RG 85. 269 rolls.

T939 Crew Lists of Vessels Arriving at New Orleans, 1910–1945. RG 85. 311 rolls.

T941 Crew Lists of Vessels Arriving at Gloucester, 1918–1943. RG 85. 13 rolls.

T942 Crew Lists of Vessels Arriving at New Bedford, 1917–1943. RG 85. 2 rolls.

T944 Passenger Lists of Vessels Arriving at New Bedford, 1902–1942. RG 85. 8 rolls.

T956 Federal Nonpopulation Census Schedules in the Custody of the Pennsylvania State Library, 1850–1880. 24 rolls.

T985 Old Settler Cherokee Census Roll, 1895, and Index to Payment Roll, 1896. RG 75. 2 rolls.

T1019 Index to the 1810 Population Census Schedules for Virginia. RG 29. 35 rolls.

T1030 Index (Soundex) to 1900 Federal Population Census Schedules for Alabama. RG 29. 177 rolls.

T1031 Index (Soundex) to 1900 Federal Population Census Schedules for Alaska. RG 29. 15 rolls.

T1032 Index (Soundex) to 1900 Federal Population Census Schedules for Arizona. RG 29. 22 rolls.

T1033 Index (Soundex) to 1900 Federal Population Census Schedules for Arkansas. RG 29. 135 rolls.

T1034 Index (Soundex) to 1900 Federal Population Census Schedules for California. RG 29. 198 rolls.

T1035 Index (Soundex) to 1900 Federal Population Census Schedules for Colorado. RG 29. 69 rolls.

T1036 Index (Soundex) to 1900 Federal Population Census Schedules for Connecticut. RG 29. 107 rolls.

T1037 Index (Soundex) to 1900 Federal Population Census Schedules for Delaware. RG 29. 21 rolls.

T1038 Index (Soundex) to 1900 Federal Population Census Schedules for the District of Columbia. RG 29. 42 rolls.

T1039 Index (Soundex) to 1900 Federal Population Census Schedules for Florida. RG 29. 62 rolls.

T1040 Index (Soundex) to 1900 Federal Population Census Schedules for Georgia. RG 29. 214 rolls.

T1041 Index (Soundex) to 1900 Federal Population Census Schedules for Hawaii. RG 29. 30 rolls.

T1042 Index (Soundex) to 1900 Federal Population Census Schedules for Idaho. RG 29. 19 rolls.

T1043 Index (Soundex) to 1900 Federal Population Census Schedules for Illinois. RG 29. 475 rolls.

T1044 Index (Soundex) to 1900 Federal Population Census Schedules for Indiana. RG 29. 254 rolls.

T1045 Index (Soundex) to 1900 Federal Population Census Schedules for Iowa. RG 29. 212 rolls.

T1046 Index (Soundex) to 1900 Federal Population Census Schedules for Kansas. RG 29. 148 rolls.

T1047 Index (Soundex) to 1900 Federal Population Census Schedules for Kentucky. RG 29. 200 rolls.

T1048 Index (Soundex) to 1900 Federal Population Census Schedules for Louisiana. RG 29. 146 rolls.

T1049 Index (Soundex) to 1900 Federal Population Census Schedules for Maine. RG 29. 80 rolls.

T1050 Index (Soundex) to 1900 Federal Population Census Schedules for Maryland. RG 29. 127 rolls.

T1051 Index (Soundex) to 1900 Federal Population Census Schedules for Massachusetts. RG 29. 319 rolls.

T1052 Index (Soundex) to 1900 Federal Population Census Schedules for Michigan. RG 29. 257 rolls.

T1053 Index (Soundex) to 1900 Federal Population Census Schedules for Minnesota. RG 29. 180 rolls.

T1054 Index (Soundex) to 1900 Federal Population Census Schedules for Mississippi. RG 29. 156 rolls.

T1055 Index (Soundex) to 1900 Federal Population Census Schedules for Missouri. RG 29. 300 rolls.

T1056 Index (Soundex) to 1900 Federal Population Census Schedules for Montana. RG 29. 40 rolls.

T1057 Index (Soundex) to 1900 Federal Population Census Schedules for Nebraska. RG 29. 107 rolls.

T1058 Index (Soundex) to 1900 Federal Population Census Schedules for Nevada. RG 29. 7 rolls.

T1059 Index (Soundex) to 1900 Federal Population Census Schedules for New Hampshire. RG 29. 52 rolls.

T1060 Index (Soundex) to 1900 Federal Population Census Schedules for New Jersey. RG 29. 204 rolls.

T1061 Index (Soundex) to 1900 Federal Population Census Schedules for New Mexico. RG 29. 23 rolls.

T1062 Index (Soundex) to 1900 Federal Population Census Schedules for New York. RG 29. 768 rolls.

T1063 Index (Soundex) to 1900 Federal Population Census Schedules for North Carolina. RG 29. 168 rolls.

T1064 Index (Soundex) to 1900 Federal Population Census Schedules for North Dakota. RG 29. 36 rolls.

T1065 Index (Soundex) to 1900 Federal Population Census Schedules for Ohio. RG 29. 397 rolls.

T1066 Index (Soundex) to 1900 Federal Population Census Schedules for Oklahoma. RG 29. 42 rolls.

T1067 Index (Soundex) to 1900 Federal Population Census Schedules for Oregon. RG 29. 54 rolls.

T1068 Index (Soundex) to 1900 Federal Population Census Schedules for Pennsylvania. RG 29. 611 rolls.

T1069 Index (Soundex) to 1900 Federal Population Census Schedules for Rhode Island. RG 29. 49 rolls.

T1070 Index (Soundex) to 1900 Federal Population Census Schedules for South Carolina. RG 29. 124 rolls.

T1071 Index (Soundex) to 1900 Federal Population Census Schedules for South Dakota. RG 29. 44 rolls.

T1072 Index (Soundex) to 1900 Federal Population Census Schedules for Tennessee. RG 29. 188 rolls.

T1073 Index (Soundex) to 1900 Federal Population Census Schedules for Texas. RG 29. 286 rolls.

T1074 Index (Soundex) to 1900 Federal Population Census Schedules for Utah. RG 29. 29 rolls.

T1075 Index (Soundex) to 1900 Federal Population Census Schedules for Vermont. RG 29. 41 rolls.

T1076 Index (Soundex) to 1900 Federal Population Census Schedules for Virginia. RG 29. 174 rolls.

T1077 Index (Soundex) to 1900 Federal Population Census Schedules for Washington. RG 29. 69 rolls.

T1078 Index (Soundex) to 1900 Federal Population Census Schedules for West Virginia. RG 29. 93 rolls.

T1079 Index (Soundex) to 1900 Federal Population Census Schedules for Wisconsin. RG 29. 189 rolls.

T1080 Index (Soundex) to 1900 Federal Population Census Schedules for Wyoming. RG 29. 15 rolls.

T1081 Index (Soundex) to 1900 Federal Population Census Schedules for Military and Naval Personnel. RG 29. 32 rolls.

T1082 Index (Soundex) to 1900 Federal Population Census Schedules for Indian Territory. RG 29. 42 rolls.

T1083 Index (Soundex) to 1900 Federal Population Census Schedules for Institutions. RG 29. 8 rolls.

T1098 Index to Rendezvous Reports, Before and After the Civil War, 1846–1861 and 1805–1884. RG 24. 32 rolls.

T1099 Index to Rendezvous Reports, Civil War, 1861–1865. RG 24. 31 rolls.

T1100 Index to Rendezvous Reports, Naval Auxiliary Service, 1846–1884. RG 24. 1 roll.

T1101 Index to Rendezvous Reports, Armed Guard Personnel, 1846–1884. RG 24. 3 rolls.

T1128 Nonpopulation Census Schedules, 1860–1880, Nebraska. RG 29. 16 rolls.

A1130 Nonpopulation Census Schedules, 1850–1880, Kansas. RG 29. 48 rolls.

T1132 Nonpopulation Census Schedules, 1850–1880, Virginia. RG 29. 34 rolls.

T1133 Nonpopulation Census Schedules, 1850–1880, Illinois. RG 29. 64 rolls.

T1134 Nonpopulation Census Schedules, 1850–1880, Texas. RG 29. 59 rolls.

T1135 Nonpopulation Census Schedules, 1850–1880, Tennessee. RG 29. 39 rolls.

T1136 Nonpopulation Census Schedules, 1850–1880, Louisiana. RG 29. 15 rolls.

T1137 Nonpopulation Census Schedules, 1850–1880, Georgia. RG 29. 27 rolls.

A1151 Passenger Lists of Vessels Arriving at Portland, Maine, Nov. 29, 1893–Mar. 1943. RG 85. 35 rolls.

A1154 Nonpopulation Census Schedules, 1860–1880, Washington. RG 29. 8 rolls.

T1156 Nonpopulation Census Schedules, 1850–1880, Iowa. RG 29. 62 rolls.

T1157 Nonpopulation Census Schedules, 1850, Pennsylvania, Manufactures. RG 29. 9 rolls.

T1159 Nonpopulation Census Schedules, 1850–1880, Ohio, in the Custody of the State Library of Ohio. 104 rolls.

T1163 Nonpopulation Census Schedules, 1850, Michigan, Mortality, in the Custody of the State Library of Ohio. 1 roll.

T1164 Nonpopulation Census Schedules, 1850–1880, Michigan, in the Custody of the Michigan State Archives, Division of Michigan History, Department of State. 77 rolls.

A1188 Passenger Lists of Vessels Arriving at Providence, Rhode Island, 1911–1943. RG 85. 49 rolls.

T1204 Nonpopulation Census Schedules, 1850–1880, Massachusetts. RG 29. 40 rolls.

List of Microfilm Publications Cited

T1207 Private Land Grant Cases in the Circuit Court of the Northern District of California. 1852–1910. RG 21. 28 rolls.

T1208 Internal Revenue Assessment Lists for Arkansas, 1867–1874. RG 58. 4 rolls.

T1209 Internal Revenue Assessment Lists for Territory of Idaho, 1867–1874. RG 58. 1 roll.

T1210 Census Enumeration District Description Volumes for 1900. RG 29. 10 rolls.

T1214 Index to Private Land Grant Cases, U.S. District Court, Northern District of California, 1853–1903. RG 21. 1 roll.

T1215 Index to Private Land Grant Cases, U.S. District Court, Southern District of California. RG 21. 1 roll.

T1216 Index by County to Private Land Grant Cases, U.S. District Court, Northern and Southern Districts of California. RG 21. 1 roll.

T1224 Descriptions of Census Enumeration Districts, 1830–1890 and 1910–1950. RG 29. 146 rolls.

T1234 Township Plats of Selected States. RG 49. 65 rolls.

T1259 Index (Soundex) to the 1910 Federal Population Census Schedules for Alabama. RG 29. 140 rolls.

T1260 Index (Miracode) to the 1910 Federal Population Census Schedules for Arkansas. RG 29. 139 rolls.

T1261 Index (Miracode) to the 1910 Federal Population Census Schedules for California. RG 29. 272 rolls.

T1262 Index (Miracode) to the 1910 Federal Population Census Schedules for Florida. RG 29. 84 rolls.

T1263 Index (Soundex) to the 1910 Federal Population Census Schedules for Georgia. RG 29. 174 rolls.

T1264 Index (Miracode) to the 1910 Federal Population Census Schedules for Illinois. RG 29. 491 rolls.

T1265 Index (Miracode) to the 1910 Federal Population Census Schedules for Kansas. RG 29. 145 rolls.

T1266 Index (Miracode) to the 1910 Federal Population Census Schedules for Kentucky. RG 29. 194 rolls.

T1267 Index (Miracode and Soundex) to the 1910 Federal Population Census Schedules for Louisiana. RG 29. 132 rolls.

T1268 Index (Miracode) to the 1910 Federal Population Census Schedules for Michigan. RG 29. 253 rolls.

T1269 Index (Soundex) to the 1910 Federal Population Census Schedules for Mississippi. RG 29. 118 rolls.

T1270 Index (Miracode) to the 1910 Federal Population Census Schedules for Missouri. RG 29. 285 rolls.

T1271 Index (Miracode) to the 1910 Federal Population Census Schedules for North Carolina. RG 29. 178 rolls.

T1272 Index (Miracode) to the 1910 Federal Population Census Schedules for Ohio. RG 29. 418 rolls.

T1273 Index (Miracode) to the 1910 Federal Population Census Schedules for Oklahoma. RG 29. 143 rolls.

T1274 Index (Miracode) to the 1910 Federal Population Census Schedules for Pennsylvania. RG 29. 688 rolls.

T1275 Index (Soundex) to the 1910 Federal Population Census Schedules for South Carolina. RG 29. 93 rolls.

T1276 Index (Soundex) to the 1910 Federal Population Census Schedules for Tennessee. RG 29. 142 rolls.

T1277 Index (Soundex) to the 1910 Federal Population Census Schedules for Texas. RG 29. 262 rolls.

T1278 Index (Miracode) to the 1910 Federal Population Census Schedules for Virginia. RG 29. 183 rolls.

T1279 Index (Miracode) to the 1910 Federal Population Census Schedules for West Virginia. RG 29. 108 rolls.

Index

References are to sub-heading numbers except where specified otherwise. Sub-heading numbers consist of chapter number followed by the number of the sub-heading within the chapter.

A list of tables with page numbers appears in the forematter immediately after the Table of Contents.

A

B

C

D

E

F

G

H

I

J

K

L

M

N

O

P

Q

R

S

T

U

V

W

Y